A HISTORY OF ROME UNDER THE EMPERORS

A HISTORY OF ROME UNDER THE EMPERORS

Theodor Mommsen

Based on the lecture notes of Sebastian and Paul Hensel, 1882–6
German edition by Barbara and Alexander Demandt
English translation by Clare Krojzl
Edited, with the addition of a new chapter, by Thomas Wiedemann

London and New York

First published in 1992
by C. H. Beck'sche Verlagsbuchhandlung

This edition in English first published 1996
by Routledge
11 New Fetter Lane, London EC4P 4EE

Simultaneously published in the USA and Canada
by Routledge
29 West 35th Street, New York, NY 10001

Routledge is an International Thomson Publishing company

© 1992 C.H. Beck'sche Verlagsbuchhandlung, Munich
Translation © 1996 Routledge
Additional introduction © 1996 Thomas Wiedemann

This edition has been published with the help of Inter Nationes, Bonn

Typeset in Perpetua by Keystroke, Jacaranda Lodge, Wolverhampton
Printed and bound in Great Britain by Clays Ltd, St Ives PLC

British Library Cataloguing in Publication Data
A catalogue record for this book is available from the British Library

Library of Congress Cataloguing in Publication Data
Mommsen, Theodor, 1817–1903
[Römische Kaisergeschichte. English]
A history of Rome under the emperors / Theodor
Mommsen : [edited, with an introduction by Thomas
Wiedemann : English translation by Clare Krojzl].
Based on the lecture notes of Sebastian and Paul Hensel,
1882–86, edited by Barbara and Alexander Demandt.
München : C.H. Beck, c1992.
Includes bibliographical references and index.
1. Rome—History—Empire, 30 B.C.–476 A.D.
I. Wiedemann, Thomas E. J. II. Demandt, Barbara, 1938– .
III. Demandt, Alexander, 1937– . IV Title.
DG270.M6513 1996   95–41007
937–dc20   CIP

ISBN 0–415–10113–1

CONTENTS

CONTENTS

A history of Rome under the Emperors II
From Vespasian to Diocletian
Summer Semester 1883 [MH.II]

A history of Rome under the Emperors III
From Diocletian to Alaric
Winter Semester 1885/6 and Summer Semester 1886 [MH.III]

CONTENTS

MAPS

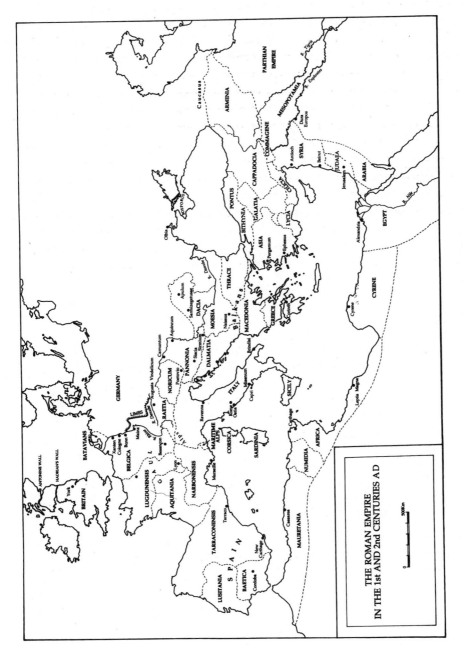

Map 1 The Roman Empire in the first and second centuries AD

INTRODUCTION

by Alexander Demandt

In 1902, only months before his death, Theodor Mommsen was awarded the Nobel Prize for Literature.[1] This was the first time the honour was ever bestowed on a German, as indeed it was the first, and so far only, time it has been awarded to a historian.[2] Furthermore, it was awarded for a historical work which at that point had already existed for almost fifty years and was in fact never completed. Mommsen's *History of Rome* remains a torso.

Mommsen recounts the genesis of the work, now in its sixteenth German edition, in a letter of 19 March 1877 to Gustav Freytag.[3] It states how Mommsen, having been dismissed from his professorial chair at Leipzig for his 'revolutionary' views, began work on it in 1849 at the suggestion of the publishers Karl Reimer and Salomon Hirzel,[4] who had been impressed by a lecture of his on the Gracchi. According to a letter by him to Wilhelm Henzen,[5] dated 1850, Mommsen accepted this proposal 'partly for my livelihood, and partly because the work greatly appeals to me'. The first three volumes (books 1–5), written in Leipzig and Zurich, were published between 1854 and 1856. These give an account of the history of Rome up to the victory of Caesar at Thapsus in Africa on 6 April 46 BC, i.e. up to the transition from the Republic to the principate. But the rest is missing.

1. WHY NO VOLUME IV?

An account of imperial history up to the collapse of the Empire in the period of the great migrations (books 6 and 7) was, however, envisaged. At any rate Mommsen still gave a promise to that effect in his Introduction to volume V, which he retained in all the reprints made during his lifetime. Educated society waited impatiently. When Jacob Burckhardt, looking forward to seeing how Cicero, whom Mommsen had attacked, would be defended, wrote to Wilhelm Henzen on 10 May 1857, he added: 'I would be even more keen, however, to read Mommsen's continuation, the age of the Emperors, and I suppose that we shall be kept waiting for this for some time to come.'[6] Mommsen raised public expectations further on several other occasions. Short of money, as he so often was, he sought in 1866 to have his lectures on the age of the emperors published in England and France.[7] On 12 July 1869 he complained to Degenkolb that he would not immediately be able to submit an account of the 'great age' of Diocletian and Constantine.[8] In 1874 he considered accepting a second offer of a Chair at Leipzig, partly in the hope that he would be able to complete his *History* there.[9] And on his sixtieth birthday in 1877 he distributed a hundred copies of a leaflet containing two essays[10] bearing the ironic title page 'A History of Rome by Theodor Mommsen: Volume Four'. Beneath was the motto to Goethe's *Epistles*: 'Gladly would I have continued writing, but it was left unfinished.'[11] The two essays were clearly intended either as contributions to or as first drafts for Volume IV, as were the articles on Caesar's military system,[12] and on the agricultural and monetary economies under the Roman emperors.

Following Mommsen's decision, at the end of 1883, to make another attempt at the *History of Rome*,[13] an understandable rumour circulated that he was working on volume IV. Contemporary correspondence reflects the suspense this evoked.[14] In February 1884 Dilthey[15] informed Count Yorck:

> Mommsen is indeed now writing the imperial history. But he is weary and quite travel-worn from treading the highroads of philology, epigraphy and party politics. And it is hard to imagine how anyone could write about the age of early Christianity without any religious feeling, or indeed without any spiritual yearning for the invisible Kingdom. I do not regard him as capable of writing an account even of the early history of the Germanic tribes.

Count Yorck's reply of the 3 March[16] reads: 'Mommsen really is writing on imperial history and is reading – critical studies of early Christianity!' There were many similar voices. 'I am in a position to disclose', wrote Theodor Storm to Gottfried Keller on 8 June 1884, 'that he is now writing the imperial history.'[17] On 12 October 1884 Storm wrote to his old friend Mommsen in person: 'So I look forward with pleasure to volume I of your imperial history, in which I will be taken along by you again after my own fashion.'[18]

There is nothing to suggest that the academic world was in error in this. On 4 February 1884 Mommsen sent Wilamowitz a draft outline which also included the internal history of the age of the emperors, arranged by dynasties.[19] In his reply of 11 February 1884, Wilamowitz enclosed suggested additions to book 6,[20] marking his comments on Achaea: 'M. History of Rome IV'.[21] At that juncture, therefore, Mommsen's intention was to complete volume IV, and it was only as work progressed that he decided to leave out imperial history for the time being, along with the description of Italy. The fact that he continued to refer to his history of the Roman 'provinces from Caesar to Diocletian' by the title of the series, as 'History of Rome volume V [book 8]', shows that despite this change of plan he still intended to complete volume IV, i.e. books 6 and 7. This is confirmed by his undated letter no. 176 to Wilamowitz.[22] Eduard Norden's[23] remark: 'After 1877 there are no traces of further work on volume IV' was no more than 'a family myth intended for public consumption'.[24] Mommsen never gave up his plan, and its fulfilment continued to be awaited. Even the speech made when he received the Nobel Prize[25] still expresses the hope that the *History of Rome* would see completion.

When Mommsen died on 1 November 1903 volume IV had still not been written. His *History of the Emperors* thus ranks alongside Kant's *System of Pure Philosophy*, Goethe's *Nausicaa* and Nietzsche's *The Will to Power* as one of the unwritten books of German literature.

Others tried to fill the breach. Gustav Friedrich Hertzberg's *Geschichte des römischen Kaiserreiches* of 1880 (based on Duruy), Hermann Schiller's *Geschichte der römischen Kaiserzeit* I/II of 1883 and Alfred von Domaszewski's *Geschichte der römischen Kaiser* of 1909 were all advertised as substitutes for Mommsen's work (in the last case by its publisher), but were not acknowledged as such by the reading public. Victor Gardthausen justified his work on *Augustus und seine Zeit* (1891–) on the grounds that Mommsen's account was missing. The age of the emperors has since been treated either within the context of a general history of Rome,[26] or in terms of particular perspectives[27] or periods.[28] There is still no original general narrative in German based on the primary sources.

The reasons for this are easier to understand nowadays than they were in Mommsen's day, when it was still feasible to control what has since become a vast specialist literature. Why, then, did Mommsen stop writing?

> This poses one of the best-known riddles ever to arise in the history of our discipline – a problem for which to this day solutions are proposed by those who know something about it and those who don't: why did Mommsen not write volume IV, the book intended to contain a history of the Roman emperors?[29]

On different occasions Mommsen himself identified particular factors that prevented him from continuing. They are of several different kinds. One of the objective factors lay in the source material. Narrative authors reported mostly about the Emperor and his court – matters which scarcely interested Mommsen, but which he would have been obliged to record. James Bryce, the historian of America,[30] wrote in 1919:

> As to Mommsen, I asked him in Berlin in 1898 why he did not continue his *History of Rome* down to Constantine or Theodosius; but he raised his

eyebrows and said 'What authorities are there beyond the Court tittle-tattle?' For his book on *The Provinces of the Roman Empire* he had at least materials in the inscriptions and in antiquities, and it is a very valuable book, though doubtless dry.[31]

The crucial epigraphical material was only gradually being collated and this is probably what is meant when Ferrero (1909) refers to another complaint by Mommsen about the nature of the sources on the age of the emperors. A letter to Otto Jahn of 1 May 1861 states:

> I can and will honour my obligations towards C.I.L.; for its sake I have, for the time being, and who knows whether for good, abandoned work on my *History*, so I suppose that people can trust me not to let this undertaking collapse irresponsibly . . . [32]

and in May 1883 Mommsen wrote to von Gossler, a government minister:

> The completion of my *History* has constantly weighed upon my mind and soul; I have interrupted work on it . . . having realized that in conjunction with what for me would be required to do it, I could not complete that undertaking as well as my work on the inscriptions.

He said the same to Schmidt-Ott.[33] The *Corpus Inscriptionum Latinarum*, his 'old original sin',[34] exerted a more powerful attraction on Mommsen than an account of the age of the emperors. One might question, as Wucher does,[35] whether it was in fact completely impossible to write the *History* without first doing the work on the epigraphical sources.

In addition to the problem of sources, the presentation of the material also posed difficulties. It is hard to find a coherent story line. Mommsen missed in the age of the emperors that sense of development characteristic of the history of the Republic: 'The institutions can be grasped to some degree, but the direction could not be seen even in antiquity, and we shall never guess it.'[36]

A somewhat jocular remark, passed on to us by the later President of Columbia University, Nicholas Murray Butler, brings us to the sphere of more subjective reasons. During a stay in Berlin in 1884/5, he overheard Mommsen say during a party at the home of Eduard Zeller:

> that the reason, why he had never continued his *Römische Geschichte* through the imperial period was, that he had never been able to make up his mind, as to what it was that brought about the collapse of the Roman Empire and the downfall of Roman civilization.[37]

Another factor, confirmed by Mommsen himself, was more serious: the ebbing of that emotional commitment without which he simply could not write history. In April 1882 he wrote from a villa at Naples to his daughter Marie, the wife of Wilamowitz:

> I too should like to move into such a villa – and soon, not merely as a prepa-
> ration for death, which I don't suppose needs any help from us, but to see
> if I can't find my way back to my young years, or rather younger years, since
> I was never all that young. I am obsessed with the idea, like a dream that
> refuses to go away, of moving here for six to eight months and trying to see
> if I can still write something that people would want to read; actually I
> don't believe I could – not that I feel enfeebled by age, but the sacred self-
> deception of youth is gone. I now know, alas, how little I know, and the
> divine arrogance has deserted me. The divine bloody-mindedness in which
> I would still be able to achieve something is a poor substitute.[38]

A letter to his son-in-law Wilamowitz, dated 2 December 1883, is couched in similar terms: 'What I lack is simply the lack of affectation or impudence of the young person who will have his say on everything and challenge everything, thereby eminently qualifying himself to be a historian.'[39] He wrote the same thing in different words before the reprint of the Italian translation appeared: 'Non ho più come da giovane, il coraggio dell'errare.'[40]

These remarks are rooted in Mommsen's notion of the nature and role of historiography as, in his own words, 'political education' in the 'service of national-liberal propaganda', which passes 'its last judgement on the dead *cum ira et studio*'.[41] The cool public response to volume V demonstrates that this was precisely what people wanted. Although the young Max Weber was most taken with it when he wrote 'He is still the same old [Mommsen]'[42] (i.e. the young Mommsen), volume V brought Mommsen no more than a *succès d'estime*, the recognition of respect.[43] Following publication of this volume, Mommsen nevertheless received 'countless inquiries after volume IV'. His reply was: 'I no longer have the passion to write an account of the death of Caesar.'[44] Mommsen feared that he would not be able to provide his readers what they expected of him. In 1894, however, he asserted that the public ('rabble') did not deserve any exertion on their behalf.[45]

In 1889 he wrote: 'I do not know whether any will or strength will remain after all this compulsory work for *RG* [*History of Rome*] IV; the public do not deserve any exertion on their behalf, and I prefer research to writing.'[46]

This brings us to a fourth group of factors. Time and again, Mommsen referred deprecatingly to the 'leaden dreariness' and 'empty desert' of the age of the emperors,[47] those 'centuries of a decaying culture', the 'stagnation of intellectual and the brutalization of moral life'.[48]

The sole dynamic element, Christianity, was so alien to him as a *homo minime ecclesiasticus*,[49] for all he was a pastor's son, that in his youth he preferred to be called Jens, rather than Theodor.[50] This marks a fifth self-professed factor. 'He has as good as confessed he would probably have completed his *History of Rome* if he had made Harnack's acquaintance sooner.'[51]

And it was indeed Harnack[52] who provoked Mommsen to his final judgement on the age of the emperors. At an education conference in Berlin in June 1900,[53] Harnack had recommended that more attention be paid to this period of history. For Harnack this was the age of early Christianity and the Church fathers. Mommsen said in reply:

> We have every reason to be grateful for the suggestion that we should pay more attention to the history of imperial Rome in teaching than has been the case hitherto. I too am in favour of this in general, but in specifics I believe that provisions and qualifications are called for. In general, the teaching of this field is in part impracticable and in part dangerous, since the tradition consists too much in court tittle-tattle or even worse things. In my view, teaching would specifically have to focus first on the Caesarian–Augustan period, which the Republican age leads into (and it has already been stressed that treatment of the latter would need to be substantially curtailed), and second on the age of Constantine. I regard what lies in between as unsuitable for fruitful treatment in schools.

The minutes later record:

> Dr Mommsen: In fact this matter can only be discussed in a more private forum. Mr Harnack would have my wholehearted support, were it possible to write a history of mankind under the Roman Emperors. What civilization as a whole achieved at that time – universal peace for one thing, and the generally fortunate circumstances of the population under the better emperors, notwithstanding any abuses – all this is something we still have to look up to today. The age in which a bathhouse stood next to every barracks – as Mr Harnack has pointed out – is yet to be achieved by us, as is much else that existed then. This is reality, not an ideal. But if the question is put: what was the best period of the age of the emperors as a whole, the ancient Romans themselves answer: the first ten years of Nero's rule.[54] Now, try representing, in a manner possible for a teacher and comprehensible to the children, that the first ten years of Nero's rule were the best period, and one of the most fortunate epochs in human history! Is this possible? Of course it would be, if every teacher could be equipped with the ability required to extract the kernel concealed inside the shell of

sordid court gossip. I have been studying this period ever since I have been able to think. I have not succeeded in extracting this kernel, and if I were a teacher I would refuse the task of teaching the history of the emperors in general. Much as I regret having to water down Mr Harnack's wine, I have to say I cannot accept this.

Objections to a treatment of the age of the emperors that could only be developed in a more 'private forum' presumably concern the scandals and sexual anecdotes reported by Suetonius, Martial, Juvenal and other authors – the degenerate court tittle-tattle that Mommsen maintained would have to be weeded out. Was this the true reason why Mommsen omitted to write an account of the age of the emperors?

'Questo quasi classico tema perchè il Mommsen non scrisse la storia dell' impero'[55] continues to vex scholars. Mommsen's own testimony is given various emphases and has been enriched by a variety of additional suppositions. One immediate line of approach is offered by the fire at Mommsen's home on 12 July 1880 (see pp. 22f.), but this view has not been taken very seriously. Other hypotheses are considered. Neumann,[56] Hirschfeld[57] and Hartmann[58] stressed the absence of inscriptions. Thus Fowler[59] and Eduard Norden[60] thought that 'volume IV was left unwritten because the time was not yet ripe for it.' Wilhelm Weber[61] was more definite: Mommsen 'gave up in face of the weight of problems', while Hermann Bengtson[62] was convinced that the picture Mommsen had elaborated of the principate in his Constitutional Law (Staatsrecht) 'if applied to a history of the Roman emperors, would inevitably have led to an untenable perception of the imperial system'.

Wilamowitz[63] emphasized that Mommsen had not in fact written his History of Rome of his own volition, but purely in response to external pressure. He claimed that Caesar was all that he felt deeply about; no artistically defensible continuation beyond the climax marked by Caesar's absolute rule was possible. Similarly, Eduard Meyer[64] writes: 'The decisive reason why he failed to continue the work and never wrote volume IV: no route leads from Caesar to Augustus.' This view elaborated by Ferrero as early as 1909, was endorsed by Albert Wucher,[65] Alfred von Klement,[66] Hans Ulrich Instinsky[67] and Zwi Yavetz.[68] Dieter Timpe[69] drew attention to the analogy between the Italy of 46 BC and Mommsen's own time, asserting 'that the ingenious character of the work also determined its internal boundaries, and made it difficult . . . to bridge the gap to the age of the emperors'. Lothar Wickert,[70] on the other hand, thinks that it was Mommsen's fear of a publishing flop that inhibited completion, suggesting as an objective reason for this the difficulty of combining the history of the emperors and the history of the Empire into a single whole.

Volume IV might have been relished by the connoisseur, and would, needless to say, have been impeccable in terms of scholarship; but set beside volume V, and detached from it in terms of subject-matter, the period would have struck the reader as a decline, or at least as stagnation at a level which seemed to have been successfully surpassed – the abandonment of true progress.[71]

Wickert offers Mommsen's ebbing emotional commitment as a subjective factor. Arnaldo Momigliano[72] suggested that Mommsen had already dealt with what for him was essential in the imperial period in his accounts of constitutional law and the provinces.

Other authors stressed the history of the scholarship of the discipline itself, the development of the historiography from a literary genre in the eighteenth and early nineteenth centuries to the empirical research of the late nineteenth and early twentieth centuries. With reference to Mommsen, this development has been greeted as a progressive step by Fueter[73] and Heuss,[74] and regretted as a retrograde one by Toynbee[75] and Collingwood.[76] In his lecture on Mommsen held at Berlin in 1982, Joachim Fest too expressed his support for the latter view. In broad terms, however, although such a shift of emphasis is discernible within historiography, it can offer no explanation for the question at issue here, since it leaves it open why Mommsen, unlike historians such as Burckhardt and Gregorovius, committed himself to turning history into a scholarly discipline.

Attempts at ideological or political explanations have also proved popular. In a letter to Wilamowitz of 1 December 1917, Adolf Erman repeats the view, allegedly propounded by Paul de Lagarde, that Mommsen ceased work because of his negative relationship to Christianity.[77] Grant[78] and Bammel[79] held similar views. Instinsky[80] pointed to the conflict between the universal imperialism of Rome and Mommsen's belief in nation-states. According to Srbik,[81] the age of the emperors was alien to Mommsen's 'liberal republican sentiment'. Similarly, Wucher[82] thought that Mommsen, as a liberal, was unable to relate to the imperial system. Clearly, 'the age of the emperors had no place in the heart of this republican.' This view was endorsed by Heinz Gollwitzer[83] and Karl Christ.[84] It can be challenged, however, not only on the strength of the relatively liberal character of the Roman Empire, which Mommsen[85] explicitly acknowledged, but also in view of Mommsen's support for the Hohenzollern monarchy, as repeatedly demonstrated in his addresses on the occasion of the Kaiser's birthday. As late as 1902 he was still defending the German imperial monarchy.[86]

Anglophone scholars believed that Mommsen suffered from the 'agonizing political neurosis' that the present era was witnessing late antiquity over again, and that he therefore wanted to spare his contemporaries this 'terrifying funeral epitaph', as Highet[87] and Lasky[88] phrased it. Mommsen did, indeed, frequently draw such parallels,[89] but if anything it might have offered a potential, indeed welcome, incentive to write a *History of Rome under the Emperors* from a National-Liberal point of view.

From a Marxist perspective, Mashkin asserts in his 'Foreword' to the Russian edition of Mommsen's volume V[90] that it was disenchantment with the Prussian German Empire that deterred Mommsen from writing on Rome under the Emperors. This view is repeated by Johannes Irmscher.[91] Similarly, Jürgen Kuczynski[92] maintains that Mommsen considered it beneath his dignity to write an account of imperial history, including the 'loathsome degeneration' of that system of exploitation. Instead he preferred to write about the 'oppressed peoples' of the progressive provinces. Kuczynski overlooks the fact that in Mommsen's view the advance of the provinces occurred not in spite of, but because of, Roman rule.

The diversity of opinion allows no definitive conclusion; it is not even possible to put forward a reliable order of preference among the factors mentioned that prevented Mommsen from writing volume IV. They may all have contributed to a greater or lesser extent. The emphases placed on them generally reveal more about the respective authors than about Mommsen himself. The fact that research intentions tend to change in the course of a lengthy scholarly career hardly requires any explanation in itself, and unfulfilled objectives can be found in the biographies of numerous historians; one need only look at the monumental projects of the young Ranke.[93]

Some of the assertions referred to above can be refuted. Two facts, for example, contradict Mommsen's alleged aversion to the age of the emperors. The first is Mommsen's stupendous research work, devoted overwhelmingly to the imperial period, including the *Corpus Inscriptionum*, the constitutional and criminal law, his editions of the law codes and the *Auctores Antiquissimi*. The second is Mommsen's teaching responsibilities at Berlin University.[94] The lecture time-tables show that for twenty semesters his classes – apart from reading classes – between 1861 and 1887 deal almost exclusively with the history of Rome under the Emperors (SS = Summer Semester; WS = Winter Semester):

1	SS 1863	History of the early Imperial Age
2	WS 1863/4	History of the early Imperial Age (see p. 20, lecture note 1)
3	SS 1866	History of Rome under the Emperors (see p. 20, lecture note 2)
4	WS 1868/9	History of Rome under the Emperors (see p. 20, lecture notes 3 and 4)
5	SS 1869	Constitution and History of Rome under Diocletian and his Successors

6	WS 1870/1	History of Rome under the Emperors from Augustus on (see p. 20, lecture note 5)
7	SS 1871	On the History and Political System of Rome under Diocletian and his Successors
8	WS 1872/3	History of Rome under the Emperors (see pp. 20f., lecture note 6)
9	WS 1974/5	History of Rome under the Emperors
10	SS 1875	On the Political System and History of Rome under Diocletian and his Successors
11	SS 1877	On the Political System and History of Rome After Diocletian
12	WS 1877/8	History of Rome under the Emperors (see p. 21, lecture note 7)
13	SS 1879	History of Rome from Diocletian on (possibly cancelled: see Mommsen to his wife, 28 April 1879, in Wickert IV 1980, p. 229)
14	WS 1882/3	History of Rome under the Emperors (see p. 21, lecture notes 8, 9 and 10)
15	SS 1883	History of Rome under the Emperors; continuation of lectures given in the previous semester (see p. 21, lecture notes 11, 12)
16	SS 1884	History and Constitution of Rome in the Fourth Century
17	WS 1884/5	History and Constitution of Rome in the Fourth Century
18	SS 1885	History and Constitution of Rome in the Fourth Century
19	WS 1885/6	History and Constitution of Rome in the Fourth Century (see p. 21, lecture note 13)
20	SS 1886	History and Constitution of Rome in the Fourth Century (this series of lectures took place, even though Mommsen had been excused from lecturing at his own request as of 20 August 1885: Wickert IV 1980, p. 230. See p. 21, lecture note 13)

Half of these lectures were devoted to late antiquity. Mommsen told both Sir William Ramsay and Mgr. Duchesne that if he could live his life over again he would devote it to late antiquity,[95] even though he saw nothing in it beyond overthrow, failure, decadence and protracted death-throes.[96] This reveals that his relationship with the history of the emperors was characterized less by dislike than by a kind of Tacitean love-hate that combined emotional aversion with intellectual attraction. The reverse applied to the Republic. 'I do not lecture on the history of the Roman Republic,' wrote Mommsen to Wattenbach[97] in 1864, and the Republic was indeed not one of the subjects he lectured on at the Friedrich

Wilhelm University. One might conclude from this that one of the reasons why Mommsen did not publish on the age of the emperors was in order to be able to continue lecturing on it. Mommsen's rhetorical achievement in the lecture room has been disputed by Dove,[98] although there are also positive voices (see below).

The question whether it would be desirable to have volume IV is as much discussed as why it is missing. On 15 October 1897 Treitschke wrote to his wife: 'What a pity that Mommsen has not committed himself to write about this age of powerful, and still almost entirely unknown, spiritual conflict.'[99] In 1891 a group of Mommsen's admirers from various faculties made a fervent plea to him 'that volume IV of the *History of Rome* might yet be added to your other contributions'. In 1899 the press reported Mommsen's intention to do just this, and Mommsen once again received begging letters on the subject.[100] C. Bardt wrote of volume IV as 'eagerly awaited';[101] Guglielmo Ferrero (1909) repeated the view of his teacher in Bologna 'that the world is united in its wish to see the final completion of this monumental work'. Giorgio Bolognini[102] spoke of a *deplorevole lacuna*. Karl Johannes Neumann[103] lamented that the 'showpieces' of the individual character-istics of emperors remained unwritten. George Peabody Gooch[104] held that the unparalleled merit of the *Constitutional Law* and of volume V on the provinces made it all the more regrettable that Mommsen had never added the crowning piece of his *History of Rome*:

> In Volume IV we should have had a wonderful portrait gallery of the Emperors, a masterful account of Roman law throughout the Empire, a masterly exposition of the place of Roman law in the imperial system, a brilliant picture of the growth and persecutions of Christianity.

Similarly, Hans Ulrich Instinsky[105] held that Mommsen, with his volume on the age of the emperors, would have 'infinitely surpassed all other existing literature on the subject, both in terms of material and as a literary achievement'. Most recently, A.G. Quattrini, in his 'Foreword' to the Italian edition of volume V of the *History of Rome* (dall'Oglio, Milan, no date) has said of the absence of volume IV: 'questa perdita è sensibilissima' ('This is a most serious loss').

This view stands in stark contrast to that of Count Yorck.[106] He wrote to Dilthey on 18 June 1884:

> Since that deplorable last open letter of his, Mommsen stands condemned as an impossible historian. Anything he writes now, aside from historical-philological groundwork, is in my opinion of no matter. He may shift a date here and there, or pinpoint his facts better than has been done before, but his judgements will always be bizarre – I'm tempted to say because of his

lack of honesty. In historical writing, however, a sound account depends on
a sound judgement.

Similar scepticism, albeit with a different emphasis, occurs in Wilamowitz, who
from 1882 to 1893 repeatedly urged his father-in-law to write the volume. On
2 December 1883, for example, he wrote:

> I also hope to be able to contribute a little to your repeated fresh resolu-
> tions, since they have to be constantly renewed, to carry on with the work.
> I should like to reawaken your desire. . . . Just as I used to read your *Republic*
> at night as a sixth former when I should already have switched the lights
> out, I would gladly have given a few of my own years for the *Emperors*. Surely
> you will believe that even now, with my grey hairs, I would happily do the
> same.[107]

Wilamowitz later changed his mind.[108] On Mommsen's eightieth birthday in 1897
he claims to have congratulated Mommsen for not having written the book,[109]
since all the essentials were already contained in either the *Constitutional Law* or
volume V. This renunciation marked a 'triumph of the true erudition of the
scholar . . . over the enticements of outward authorial success'.[110] Wilamowitz
reports in 1918 having once seen notes for the 1870 lectures on the age of the
emperors, describing Mommsen's account as so inadequate that it must seem
ill-advised to publish it. This view was also an element in Wilamowitz's advice
to the Prussian Academy in 1928 against purchasing another set of notes of
Mommsen's lectures on the age of the emperors, which had been offered by an
unnamed Italian. Wilamowitz held that publication of it would be 'embarrassing',
and would go against his sense of family duty.[111] The first of these texts seems to
have disappeared; the second was rediscovered in Göttingen in 1991 by Uwe
Walter (see p. 20, lecture notes 4 and 5).

Wilhelm Weber[112] believed that the imperial history would have become a
'foreign body' in the corpus of Mommsen's work, and that Mommsen had
admitted as much himself: 'he renounced it as a result of a wisdom that, by its
own greatness, recognized and set its own boundaries.' Weber held that
Mommsen immersed himself to such an extent in questions of detail that he 'was
no longer able to incorporate the overall picture of great events into his thinking
processes. He still lacked an overall view of the location and significance of the
age of the emperors in world history,' and therefore 'he gave up in face of the
weight of problems'.[113] Wucher expressed a similar view, holding that Mommsen
should invoke 'not only our understanding, our approval, but also be assured of
our gratitude' for refraining from publishing volume IV, asserting that this was a
mark of Mommsen's greatness. Wucher bases his judgement on a hypothetical

construction of how Mommsen's picture of the age of the emperors might have looked, declaring 'that volume IV would have been a pamphlet, all gloom and despondency'. [114] Alfred Heuss[115] voiced similar views: Mommsen '(fortunately) left unfilled the gap left by volume IV'. Heuss goes on to repeat Wickert's view that volume IV was in fact superfluous: some other authors might have fulfilled the task inadequately, none satisfactorily.[116]

2. THE HENSEL LECTURE NOTES

It is difficult to give a reliable answer, on the basis of volume V and Mommsen's numerous other statements about the emperors, to the question of what kind of picture of the age of the emperors would have emerged had Mommsen published books 6 and 7 in his volume IV. It is not even clear how the subject-matter would have been distributed between books 6 and 7. Wucher assumed a division into the principate and dominate.[117] In his preface to volume V, Mommsen himself envisaged that book 6 would include the 'struggle of the Republicans against the monarchy instituted by Caesar, and its final establishment'; and for book 7 the specific nature of monarchical rule, and the fluctuations of the monarchy, as well as the general circumstances of government caused by the personalities of individual rulers'. This is also the view of Karl Johannes Neumann.[118]

It would be helpful to have Mommsen's drafts for his lectures, but these are no longer extant. Fragments of writing on the age of the emperors found by Hirschfeld among Mommsen's estate[119] seem to have been lost (see below). Some lecture notes taken by students, on the other hand, have survived,[120] but they are so full of gaps and errors resulting from mishearing and misunderstanding that publication has been out of the question. They deal, moreover, solely with the early principate and not the late Empire.

Any account of the fourth century has hitherto been entirely missing, but this has been redressed by a stroke of luck.[121] In 1980, in Kistner's second-hand bookshop in Nuremberg, I chanced upon the sole complete transcript known to date of Mommsen's lecture course on the age of the emperors, including late antiquity.

Part I consists of three notebooks (perhaps out of an original four; see below) labelled: *History of the Roman Emperors W 1882/83 S. Prof. Mommsen*. On the bottom right-hand corner of the cover is written: 'Paul Hensel, Westend bei Berlin, Ahornallee 40'. They contain the history of Rome from Caesar's war in Africa, regarded by Mommsen as the 'beginning of the monarchy and the end of the Republic' [MH.I, 1] up to the Batavian revolt of AD 69/70, and consequently also the period from 46 to 30 BC, which Wilamowitz[122] maintained that Mommsen had never attempted to narrate.

Part II is bound, and bears the book stamp of Paul Hensel. The text, however, is in a different hand (that of Sebastian Hensel; see below) to that of Part I. On 367 pages it contains the period from Vespasian to Carus – AD 69 to 284. The title on the spine reads: *Mommsen, History of Rome under the Emperors Part II*. That this constituted the 1883 lecture course only emerges from the story of how the lecture notes came to be written (see below). Four cartoon drawings precede the text; it is also interrupted by an autobiographical insert containing a humorous account of a journey and a caricature in ink of Hensel on a trip from Berlin via Halle and Kyffhäuser to Frankenhausen. Hensel travels in a chamber-pot on wheels, drawn by a donkey.

Part III is likewise bound in book form. The title on the spine reads: *Mommsen, Diocletian to Honorius*. The inside cover again bears Paul Hensel's book stamp. The handwriting is the same as for Part II (i.e. that of Sebastian Hensel: see below), and it contains three cartoons. The first shows a photomontage of Paul Hensel wearing a laurel wreath. Underneath are two lines from a postcard which Mommsen wrote to Friedrich Leo in Rostock on 24 March 1886 (see below for text). The second cartoon, in watercolours, shows Mommsen from behind walking in a chestnut grove accompanied by the text:

> Thus far from the notebook of Ludo Hartmann, from whom I learned quite by chance that Mommsen was lecturing. From here onwards my own transcript. It was really nice, though, to go to the lectures in the bracing morning air through the delightful avenue of chestnuts behind the University, and to see the old man walking along with his notes under his arm. (MH.III, 31)

The third caricatures Paul Hensel as a member of a student fraternity: 'Thank God! The da-damned le-lectures are over, and now we can go to Hei-Hei-Heidelberg' (MH.III, 242).

An entry towards the end of the lecture notes (MH.III, 209), '23 July 86', reveals the year. The lecture schedule (for the summer semester of 1886) reports a course in 'History and Constitution of Fourth Century Rome, Mondays, Tuesdays, Thursdays and Fridays 8–9 *privatim*, 28 April to 15 August'. My original assumption that the beginning of the text corresponds with the beginning of the summer semester[123] was precipitate (see below).

It was no easy matter to reconstruct the genesis of these lecture notes. The first clue was in the name on the notebooks, Paul Hensel (1860–1930), who was later Professor of Philosophy at Erlangen. He was a student of Wilhelm Windelband and like him a neo-Kantian. The name Hensel leads us to a piece of Berlin family history. To understand it we must distinguish between three generations of Hensels: the philosopher Paul, his father Sebastian and Sebastian's father Wilhelm Hensel.

Sebastian Hensel was the only son of Wilhelm Hensel, the Prussian court painter,[124] and Fanny Mendelssohn-Bartholdy, the composer's sister. In the section of his *Rambles through the Mark Brandenburg* entitled 'Spreeland', Theodor Fontane describes Wilhelm Hensel's life. He had taken part in the wars against Napoleon; in the 1848 revolution he supported his patrons. His fame derives from pencil drawings of famous contemporaries, now housed in the copperplate engraving room of the State Museum of the *Preussischer Kulturbesitz* (Prussian Cultural Heritage) in Dahlem. Among those portrayed, apart from Goethe, Hegel, Humboldt, Schinkel, etc., were the great historians of the time, including Boeckh, Droysen and Ranke, but not Mommsen. There may have been political reasons for this: perhaps Mommsen was too liberal, after all. Wilhelm Hensel also drew his son Sebastian several times. These drawings were sold by the Hensel family in 1956, and it was at this time, according to verbal information provided by Cécile Lowenthal-Hensel, Paul's daughter, that transcripts of Mommsen's lecture notes also found their way to the second-hand bookshop in Nuremberg mentioned above, where they then lay dormant for a quarter of a century. One of the proprietors is related to the Hensel family by marriage.

Sebastian Hensel, whom we have to thank for Parts II and III, wrote an auto-biography which was published posthumously by his son in 1903. He was a farmer in East Prussia, but moved to Berlin in 1872 because his wife could not stand the climate. There, he took over management of the Kaiserhof Hotel, which burned down only days after opening. From 1880 to 1888 Sebastian was Director of the German Building Company. Embittered by the building scandals and large-scale corruption of the 1870s, Sebastian sought refuge in three 'oases': in the family history of the Mendelssohns, published in 1879 and reprinted many times; in painting; and with Mommsen. On this, he writes:

> And a third oasis were the lectures by Mommsen on the history of Rome under the emperors, which I attended for two winter semesters and one summer semester,[125] and which were a single, immense source of enjoy-ment. I had made Mommsen's acquaintance at the home of Delbrück,[126] and, as luck would have it, found favour with him through a witty remark. I was standing with Mrs Delbrück by a mantlepiece on which were placed many wineglasses, including a few fine cut-glass rummers [a large drinking glass, called *Römer* in German, hence a pun on 'Romans']. As he joined us, Mommsen knocked one of these wineglasses off with a careless movement of his arm. He apologized profusely, but I remarked: 'Professor, we owe you so many complete Romans, that we shan't begrudge you one broken one . . . '
>
> It had always seemed a pity to me that Mommsen had not written the history of Rome under the emperors; his history of Rome had ever been one of my favourite books. It was all the more fortunate, therefore, in the

winter semester of 1882/3, that he lectured on the history of the emperors, and moreover from eight till nine in the morning, enabling me to attend before I had to be at my office. All I had to do was get up rather early, but the pleasure of these classes was beyond comparison. My seat was right at the front by the lecture podium, enabling me to hear splendidly, and above all to have a close view of him and his expressive face. Standing up there, passing judgement on some great imperial transgressor or other, the impression he gave was sometimes demonic, and quite overpowering. Sometimes he would allow his temperament to carry him away, too, and he said more and went further than he had meant to. On one occasion, for example, talking himself into a frenzy about Constantine the Great, he plucked the poor man to pieces so thoroughly that not one hair remained on his head. Then he returned to the subject in the next lecture, covering the plucked scalp [sc. of Constantine] with a scanty wig of meagre praise. For all that, the judgements of Mommsen and Treitschke, however clouded with hatred and passion, are a thousand times more appealing to me than Ranke's frosty, colourless, so-called objectivity. . . .

One thing only struck me as a significant omission: throughout the entire course of lectures, Mommsen made not one single reference to Christianity.[127]

When volume V of his *History* appeared in print, however, I was disappointed: for anyone who had attended his lectures it gave a colourless impression. It was like holding a copperplate up to the painting from which it had been copied.[128]

Sebastian Hensel had five children; Paul was the third. He was frequently ill, was apprenticed as a bookdealer, but was then able to retake his school-leaving examination. Before enrolling on a philosophy course[129] he read history, and is listed on the roll of Berlin's Friedrich Wilhelm University from 1881 to 1883. A letter of 25 October 1882 from Paul to Mommsen's student[130] Christian Hülsen, the archaeologist, dates from this period:

What perhaps will interest you is the news that Mommsen is lecturing on the Roman emperors, and that Papa has managed to obtain permission to attend these lectures, so that father and son now sit side by side in the lecture hall, taking in the pearls of wisdom. To be honest, I am impressed: this is a course of four hours a week from eight to nine in the morning, and I doubt whether at father's age I would still have the flexibility to tear myself away from the arms of Morpheus at half past six every morning in order to attend lectures.

An unpublished letter from Sebastian Hensel to Mommsen[131] bears the same date:

> Westend Ahorn Allee 40
> 25 October '82
>
> Respected Professor,
> I enclose herewith the receipt from the University Registry quaestor, and humbly request that I might be assigned the best possible seat for your lectures. It would be most welcome if I could sit beside my son Paul.
> Most respectfully,
> Your devoted servant,
> S. Hensel

Following the lectures, Hensel presented Mommsen with a copy of the third edition of his *History of the Mendelssohn Family* (published in 1882; 1st edn 1879, 2nd edn 1880), with the following accompanying note:

> Berlin, 27 March '83
>
> Respected Professor,
> Permit me to lay this small token at your feet; it was my earnest wish to give you something of mine, in return for the many priceless things of yours that you have given me in the course of the semester. This too, in its way, is a small piece of history, and, albeit not so magnificent as the history you treated, on the whole more agreeable. I beg you to be so kind as to accept it.
>   Might I also take this occasion to ask you to reserve another place for me for the coming semester? I assume that you will again be lecturing from eight to nine. If (?) in the same lecture-room, I would prefer seat no. 5 or 6, or, should these already be allocated, 2–4.
>   Thanking you most warmly in advance, and looking forward to the fresh delights that await me,
> Your devoted servant,
> S. Hensel

Mommsen's lectures made a lasting impression on Paul Hensel. 'I draw on my memory of these lectures even today,' he would say again and again.[132] 'But even as a boy I [i.e. Paul] was interested in all things Roman, which is why it occurred to my father to give me the history of Caesar written by Emperor Napoleon III as a Christmas present. "Do you think this work is suitable for my son Paul?" he asked Mommsen. Back came the stunning reply: "How old is your Paul now? Sixteen? He's beyond that!"

This encounter must have taken place in 1876–7.

This story told to Glockner is confirmed by another reference to Paul's youth. In another letter to Hülsen, likewise from (Berlin-) Westend, dated 8 December 1882, he writes:

> Everything we expected of the lectures is certainly being provided by Mommsen as fully as possible. It is quite remarkable how, under his animating hand, all the *facta*, with which one is to some extent already familiar, are given shape and are transformed and come to life. It is like the recreation of a lost world, and in my entire student career I have never experienced anything so compelling as this course of lectures. My studies in Berlin will come to an end in the summer. I am planning to take up an appointment as a private tutor in Wiesbaden, and undertake and complete a major piece of work there in peace and quiet.

In a footnote, the editor of the letters, Paul Hensel's second wife Elisabeth, noted in 1947: 'An exact transcript of this course of lectures, i.e. the equivalent of volume IV of Mommsen's *History of Rome*, is in the possession of the editor.' It would seem that no scholar of antiquities read this passage, or these transcripts would have come to light sooner.[133]

This, then, clarifies the genesis of the lecture notes. When Paul was no longer living in Berlin (after 1 October 1885 he worked as a trainee at the library in Freiburg, passed his habilitation examination [postdoctoral qualification for teaching at German universities] in Strasburg under Windelband, and later taught philosophy at Erlangen),[134] his father completed the fair version of Parts II and III on behalf of his absent son. This is confirmed by the illustrations in Part II. The flyleaf shows a dolphin with the head of Paul Hensel and a tail-fin ending in a maple leaf, an allusion to the *Ahornallee*: Maple Avenue. Above in capital letters is: *In usum Delphini*. Beneath is a quotation in Latin handwriting: 'All Cato's writings were in the first instance intended for his son, and he wrote his history for the latter in his own hand in large, legible (?) letters. Mommsen, *History of Rome* [*RG*] vol. I, p. 869.'[135] The question mark was Sebastian Hensel's own and expresses his entirely unfounded reservations as to the legibility of his own handwriting.

The following illustration is a photomontage. The Goethe–Schiller Memorial in Weimar has acquired two new heads, those of Sebastian and Paul, with the blue, white and red sash and the cap of the Corps Westfalia [a student fraternity at Heidelberg University] in Heidelberg. In Stuttgart in 1851 Sebastian had accepted a challenge to a duel from a Polish fellow student, fulfilling this obligation as a Heidelberg Westfalian.[136] The inscription on the base is a free rendition of Schiller's *Don Carlos* (I 9): 'Arm in Arm mit dir, so fordr' ich mein Jahrhundert in die Schranken' ('Arm in arm with thee, I throw down the gauntlet to my century') in the most delightful 'pidgin' Latin: 'Arma in Armis cum tibi Saeculum meum in scrinia voco.' The third sheet, a watercolour, shows Sebastian standing in the presence of Mommsen as a Sphinx, taking down his words. On sheet four, likewise in watercolour, Sebastian dedicates his lecture notes to his son Paul, depicted as the Colossus of Memnon.

Prior to the 1885/6 winter semester, Hensel wrote to Mommsen again:

> Berlin, 9 September '85
>
> Respected Professor,
> My son tells me you will be lecturing on the history of the fourth-century emperors during the coming winter semester.
> If this is so, and the timetable is the same as previously, from eight to nine in the morning, I should very much like to be able to attend again.
> Would you be so kind as to arrange the necessary formalities for me, and allocate me a good seat?
> In happy anticipation of your most enjoyable classes,
> Your devoted
> S. Hensel
> Residence: Westend, Ahornallee 40

Evidently Mommsen did not reply immediately, so that Sebastian Hensel repeated his request on 2 November 1885, after the semester had already begun on 16 October:

> Respected Professor,
> Some considerable time ago I applied to you with a request for you to arrange for me permission to attend your course of lectures on the history of the fourth-century Roman emperors, and to be so kind as to allocate me a place at the front.
> Since I fear that my letter may have gone astray during your absence, I repeat my request, in the event that the lectures are held from eight to nine in the mornings. At any other time, greatly to my regret, it would not be possible for me to attend the course.
> Yours truly,
> S. Hensel
> Westend Ahorn Allee 40

It emerges from these letters that the text of Part III [MH.III], on late antiquity, began not with the summer semester of 1886, but already with the winter semester of 1885/6, and, like the anonymous Wickert text of 1882/3 ['AW'], comprises not one, but two semesters. This cannot be discerned either from the title on the lecture programme (see p. 10 above), or from the text of the lecture notes, which contain no sign of a break, but it is confirmed by two other indicators. First, the fact (which can be clearly seen from the letters and from the quoted remark about Ludo Moritz Hartmann [MH.III, 31]) that Hensel had missed the beginning of the lecture course. Second, the text of a postcard, cut up and pasted into Part III, sent by Mommsen after the end of the semester on 15 March, to Friedrich Leo in Rostock on 24 March 1886. In microscopically small handwriting, he writes: 'I suppose you are feeling better, and I am glad. Your father-in-law is attending my lectures with a zeal I wish I could find among younger people. Yours, M.' Leo's father-in-law was none other than Sebastian Hensel: Leo was married to his daughter Cécile. Urged by Mommsen, Leo had agreed to edit Venantius Fortunatus for the *Monumenta Germaniae Historica*. The evening before his marriage to Cécile Hensel, Paul's sister, Leo received a parcel of proofs with the request to send them back corrected by return of post. Doubtless Leo did not permit his marriage to keep him from philology.[137]

As far as is currently known, the following transcripts of Mommsen's lectures on the age of the emperors either existed or exist today:

1. WS 1863/4: Early imperial history; notes taken by Ettore De Ruggiero. Santo Mazzarino commented (1980, p. 167): 'ho trovato appunti, redatti in italiano, dal De Ruggiero, di lezioni del Mommsen "sugli imperadori romani" (piu' precisamente: sul principato da Tiberio a Traiano) tenute nel semestre 1863/4.' ('I have found De Ruggiero's notes, translated into Italian, of Mommsen's lectures on the Roman emperors (more precisely: on the principate from Tiberius to Trajan) held in the 1863/4 semester.') These notes, however, were not thought to be 'estremamente curati' (particularly accurate) (see Mazzarino 174, pp. 23ff.).

2. SS 1866: History of the Roman emperors. Anonymous lecture notes headed 'The Constitution of the Roman Empire from Aurelian to Constantine', dated 25 July 1866 to 1 August 1866, nineteen pages. In the possession of the Max Planck Gymnasium, Göttingen (=AG).

3. WS 1868/9: History of the Roman emperors, notes taken down by G. Hertlein, 270pp., from Caesar to Vespasian. In 1960 in the possession of Emlein, a secondary-school teacher in Heidelberg (Ehrenberg 1960/5, p. 616).

4. WS 1868/9: History of the Roman emperors, notes taken down by the law student Gustav Adolf Krauseneck. Endorsed by Wilamowitz in 1928 (Calder 1985; see above), 205pp. in the possession of the Ancient History Department of the University of Göttingen (=MK).

5. WS 1870/1: from Caesar up to at least Septimius Severus (Wilamowitz 1918/1972, pp. 30f. Wilamowitz refers to the year 1870, but according to the lecture list Mommsen did not lecture in summer 1870). Lost.

6. WS 1872/3: History of the Roman emperors, notes taken down by

L. Schemann (author of *Paul de Lagarde. Ein Lebens- und Erinnerungsbild*, 2nd edn 1920). From Caesar to Vespasian. Sections of this were published by Wickert (IV 1980, pp. 341–8). In the possession of Freiburg University Library. Schemann's daughter Bertha[138] commented:

> In Berlin the first 'great man' came into Ludwig Schemann's orbit: Theodor Mommsen. At that time, he was giving a course of lectures on his history of the Roman emperors. The student took notes with enthusiasm, and throughout his life he proudly kept his fair and accurately copied lecture notebook as a substitute for volume IV of the *History of Rome*, which, as the reader will be aware, was never published. He also kept his own doctoral thesis, corrected in Mommsen's own hand, on the Roman legions in the Second Punic War.

7. WS 1877/8: History of the Roman emperors, notes taken down by C. Berliner, 252pp. From Caesar to Vespasian. In the possession of Viktor Ehrenberg (Ehrenberg, 1960/5, p. 616, with excerpts, some containing bizarre mishearings).
8. WS 1882/3: History of the Roman emperors, notes taken down by O. Bremer, 60pp. Caesar to Vespasian. Part of the estate of L. Wickert (Ehrenberg 1960/5, p. 616).
9. WS 1882/3: History of the Roman emperors, notes taken down by Paul Hensel, three notebooks containing 64, 63 and 68pp. respectively. From Caesar to Vespasian. In the possession of Demandt (=MH.I; see above).
10. WS 1882/3: History of the Roman emperors, and (from p. 184 on) SS 1883, History of the Roman emperors, a continuation of lectures held the previous semester, anonymous, 343pp.; from Caesar to Diocletian; part of the estate of Wickert (=AW).
11. SS 1883 (29 April to 2 August): History of the Roman emperors; continuation of lectures held the previous semester; notes taken down by the archaeologist Erich Pernice (1864–1945) according to Ehrenberg 1960/5, p. 616; the name of the writer does not appear in this copy; Vespasian to Diocletian, 275pp. In the possession of the German Archeological Institute in Rome, shelfmark M 428 m Mag. (=MP).
12. SS 1883: History of the Roman emperors; continuation of lectures held in previous semester; notes taken down by Sebastian Hensel, 367pp.; from Vespasian to Diocletian. In the possession of Demandt (=MH.II; see above).
13. WS 1885/6 and SS 1886: History and constitution of Rome in the fourth century; notes taken down by Sebastian Hensel, 241pp.; from Diocletian to Alaric.[139] In the possession of Demandt (=MH.III; see above).

3. THE BERLIN ACADEMY FRAGMENT

The discovery of Hensel's lecture notes warrants the assumption that Mommsen's drafts for his lecture course might also have survived, but a search for these has proved fruitless. The archives of the Academy of Sciences in former East Berlin did not have them either, although it does house the manuscript for volume V of the *History of Rome*. When I examined it on 5 March 1991 to find material for my footnotes, I discovered a supplementary file marked 47/1, entitled 'A Further MS on the History of Rome'. This consists of eighty-nine pages which were later numbered, mostly folded sheets of exercise-book size, with broad margins partially filled with writing, recognizable as drafts by the numerous crossings-out and corrections. The edges, charred all around, prove that, like other Mommseniana in the Archive, the bundle is a survivor of the fire at Mommsen's house on 12 July 1880.

On the 18th of that month, Nietzsche wrote from Marienbad to Peter Gast (whose real name was Heinrich Köselitz):

Have you read about the fire at Mommsen's house? And that his excerpts were destroyed, possibly the mightiest preparatory research done by any scholar of our time? It is said he went back into the flames again and again, until finally physical force had to be used to restrain him, by then covered with burns. Undertakings such as that of Mommsen must be very rare, since a prodigious memory rarely coincides either with a corresponding incisiveness in evaluating, or with the ability to impose order on and organize such material – indeed, they generally tend to work against each another.

When I heard the story, it made my stomach turn, and even now I am physically pained to think of it. Is it sympathy? But what is Mommsen to me? I am not at all well disposed towards him.

Reports of the fire at the home of the 'esteemed fellow citizen' Mommsen at no. 6 Marchstrasse in the Berlin borough of Charlottenburg appeared on 12 July 1880 in the evening edition of the *Vossische Zeitung*, on 13 July in a supplement to the *National-Zeitung*, again in the morning and evening editions of the *Vossische Zeitung*, the *Neue Preussische Zeitung* and *Germania*, and on 14 July yet again in the morning edition of the *Vossische Zeitung*. According to these reports, Mommsen had been working on 12 July until two o'clock in the morning on the second floor of his home. A gas explosion caused a fire to break out that was noticed at three o'clock by workers at a porcelain factory. The voluntary Charlottenburg and gymnasts' fire brigades worked to douse the flames with manual extinguishers. Mommsen himself had to be restrained by the police from making further salvage attempts and was then carried away from the scene of the fire by those who were with him after sustaining burns to his left hand and face. A number of postdoctoral assistants searched through the charred remains that afternoon. According to the press, some 40,000 books, most of which had been stored on the landings, had been lost in the fire, including manuscripts from the Berlin and Vienna Libraries, the Palatine Library at Heidelberg and, it is said, even from the Vatican, as well as 'all Mommsen's manuscripts and *collectanea*', some 'on the history of Rome as constitutional science', and some 'more recent work still in the conceptual stage'. One of the unfortunate losses specified was an important manuscript of Jordanes.[140]

Neither the newspaper reports nor Mommsen himself referred to the loss of the *History of the Roman Emperors*. However, a tradition deriving from Alfred von Klement and Hermann Glockner does.[141] It refers to that 'part of the *History of Rome* that was intended to form volume IV, but was never published, since the half-finished manuscript was burned: the age of the "Roman Emperors"'. Since this tradition remains unsubstantiated, I have not listed it among the reasons why volume IV is missing.[142]

A preliminary examination of file no. 47/1,[143] which has been superbly restored by the State Archives in Dresden, shows that it contains (among other things) notes on the history of the Roman Republic, a framework for the history of the Roman constitution dated 'Zurich 1852', and a draft for the beginning of volume IV of the *History of Rome* for which Mommsen had allocated books 6 and 7 – as he writes in 1885 in the 'Introduction' to volume V, which comprises book 8, having included books 1 to 5 in the first three volumes. The text comprises three double sheets, twelve pages, of which two have not been used. It begins with the heading: 'Book Six: Consolidation of the Monarchy. Chapter One: Pompeian Rebellions and the Conspiracy of the Aristocracy'.

There follow four pages of text, intended as an introduction to the history of the emperors. This contains a general description of the era. There then follows a ten-page account of the unrest in Syria in 46 and 45 BC, and of Caesar's war with Pompey's sons in Spain up to the battle of Munda on 17 March 45 BC. Mommsen had ended his volume III (book 5) with the battle of Thapsus on 6 April 46 BC. This is where our account begins.

These pages presumably represent the material referred to by Hirschfeld (see note 119). They show that even before 1880 Mommsen had already made the attempt to write the history of the emperors. It is unlikely that he had committed to paper more than the extant ten pages, since the last two sides of the fourth sheet are blank. It cannot be ruled out, however, that other material was destroyed by the fire. We do not know when the text was written, but a reference to the Erfurt Union of March 1850 elsewhere, and the Swiss usage of referring to Pompey as a 'division commander' rather than a 'general', would suggest Mommsen's period of residence in Zurich.

23

4. MOMMSEN'S PICTURE OF THE AGE OF THE EMPERORS

Hensel's lecture notes enable both a more accurate understanding of Mommsen's view of the age of the emperors and its more precise location than hitherto within the history of the discipline.[144] On the one hand, they show the extent to which Mommsen shaped the pictures subsequently elaborated by his students Otto Seeck (1895–), Ludo Moritz Hartmann (1903/10; 1908/21), Alfred von Domaszewski (1909), Hermann Dessau (1924/30) and Ernst Kornemann (1930).[145] On the other hand, they also reveal the extent of Mommsen's indebtedness to Edward Gibbon.[146] In his introduction to volume V of the *History of Rome*, Mommsen expresses his hope for an account of the age of Diocletian as a 'separate narrative and in the context of a different world, an independent historical work with a precise understanding of detail, but written with the great spirit and wider sense of vision of Gibbon' (*History of Rome* [*RG*] V, p. 5). On 27 October 1883 Wilamowitz wrote to Mommsen: 'You will have no need of moonlight or devastation to spur you on to a new "history of the fall and decline [*sic*] of the Roman Empire": but even without sentimentality Rome would be the best location from which to dare to compete with Gibbon.'[147]

In his 1886 lectures [MH.III, 3], Mommsen declared Gibbon's *History* to be the 'most significant work ever written on Roman history'. Already thirty years earlier he had waved aside requests for volume IV by alluding to Gibbon.[148] In 1894 he was invited to London to mark the centenary of Gibbon's death. He declined.[149]

Despite his sympathy for Gibbon's enlightenment approach, Mommsen still evaluated the characters he described in his own terms; that was only to be expected. As in the *History of Rome*, prominent personalities are tersely characterized. Mommsen shows how the dissimilar pair, Caesar and Augustus, is mirrored in Diocletian and Constantine; on both occasions he opts against the illustrious heir, against Augustus and Constantine. He evaluates the tragic role of figures such as Caesar and Diocletian more highly [MH.III, 68] – tragic not merely because they both failed, but rather because they fell under the shadows of their heirs. In each case, Mommsen pleads for real reformers who were unjustly misunderstood. At the same time he finds words of acknowledgement for Augustus and Constantine.

Surprising is his negative assessment of Trajan, revoked in 1885 [*RG* V, pp. 397ff.], to whom he attributes a 'boundless lust for conquest' [MH.II, 295] and the pursuit of 'vainglory' [MH.II, 298], and of Hadrian, who is said to have possessed a 'repellent manner and a venomous, envious and malicious nature' [MH.II, 299], in contrast to his inordinately positive evaluation of Septimius Severus, which he did not repeat in 1885 (*RG* V, p. 172): the 'shrewd statesman'

[MH.II, 306] who was 'perhaps the most vigorous of all the emperors' [MH.II, 116]. In the summer 1883 lectures Mommsen particularly praised the British campaign as 'perhaps the most patriotic and sensible undertaking of the age of the emperors' [MH.II, 117], since Septimius Severus was seeking to achieve what Caesar had achieved for Gaul. This is hardly a reasonable appraisal, since the Romanization of Britain had few permanent results. In 1882 Mommsen described the conquest of Britain as 'detrimental' [MH.I, 72], and at the beginning of 1883 as 'of no benefit to the Empire' [MH.I, 175]. The evaluation of Septimius Severus is repeated in the Introduction to volume V of the *History of Rome*, where the reign of this ruler is described as the high point of the age of the emperors (*RG* V, pp. 4f.).

The anticipated avoidance of court gossip[150] proves an unfulfilled promise: although the domestic and private affairs of the imperial household are not reported quite as extensively as in the 1868/9 lectures [MK], adequate justice is done to them. 'We are obliged to concern ourselves with these domestic details: they were of considerable political importance' [MH.I, 98]. From Nero on, however, a narrative history of individual emperors is replaced by an account of the various 'theatres of war', similar to the geographical arrangement of volume V of the *History of Rome*.

As was to be expected, there is a repetition of the contradictory assessment of the principate as a whole, which is characterized as a 'republic with a monarch at its head' [MH.I, 32], 'a form of monarchy' [MH.I, 93], although not 'a straightforward monarchy' [MH.II, 331], but a 'constitutional monarchy' [MH.I, 119; II, 355] or a 'dyarchy' [MH.I, 49], even though the Senate was not on an equal footing with the Emperor [as is asserted at MH.I, 94], since the discretionary power of the Emperor even in terms of *imperium legitimum* 'was tantamount to autocracy' [MH.I, 37] and 'virtually unlimited' [MH.I, 42]. 'The principle behind the principate was a highly personal style of government' [MH.II, 350], and yet the princeps was nothing more than 'an administrative official . . . with a monopoly of power' [MH.II, 331; see *Collected Works* [*Ges. Schr.*] IV, p. 160]. How can these views be reconciled?

Similar incongruities emerge when Mommsen speaks of the 'democratic mission' of Caesar the monarch and his successors [MH.I, 39] and at the same time describes both the Republic and the principate as 'aristocracies' [MH.II, 1], or denounces the tedium and vacuousness of the age of the emperors, even stating that the 'age of politics' ended with Augustus [MH.I, 31], and nevertheless applauds the 'progress' [MH.II, 2] and peace (see below) made under the rule of the emperors. The aristocracy of this age strikes him as markedly superior to that of the Republican age, the 'change that occurred during the age of the emperors', Mommsen asserts with regard to urbanization, having been 'decidedly for the better' [MH.II, 1, 104]. And yet we also read: 'The monarchical order of the

25

principate was incompatible with an unforced love of the Fatherland' [MH.II, 99]. Mommsen's picture of history is dominated by political concerns: he is less interested in civilizing, cultural and religious aspects. There is no account of the *Pax Romana*. He describes only what he repeatedly calls the 'theatres of war'.

The importance which Mommsen attaches to fiscal questions is striking. He plagues his students to a hardly imaginable degree with monetary policy and taxation, currency parities and coinage issues in all their numerical detail. Court and civil administration, the army and building projects are all treated under the heading of 'Revenues and Expenditure', whose prominence is explicitly emphasized. The highly organized taxation system explains Mommsen's positive evaluation of late Roman bureaucracy, Diocletian's 'administrative and constitutional state' [MH.II, 354] – in contrast to Max Weber's negative assessment. The *Historia Augusta*, of which Mommsen (*Ges. Schr.* VII, pp. 303f.) wrote 'that these biographies represent the most worthless drivel we have from antiquity', are copiously cited as a source.

Among the manifest errors in the section on the principate, it is surprising that Mommsen promotes Augustus to the role of creator of the Roman fleet [MH.I, 63]; that he denies that chariot racing was held outside Rome [MH.I, 70]; denies the Messianic idea to the ancient Jews (AW.174 = MH.I, 231]; denies the existence of communal customs dues [MH.II, 94]; ignores the educational policy of the emperors [MH.II, 102]; associates the first reference to the Goths with Caracalla [MH.II, 272], and does not accept that the *limes* in Upper Germany– Raetia was a Roman military frontier [MH.II, 128] (he himself was to make a substantial contribution to its investigation only a short while later). His line of argument is characteristic: such a long frontier could not be defended and would consequently have been militarily nonsensical, and that could not be attributed to the Roman emperors. The erroneous evaluation of senatorial functions [MH.II, 355ff.] derives from Mommsen's dyarchy thesis.

In the section on the dominate, Mommsen is in error in ascribing a pro-Arian majority to the Council of Nicaea in 325 [MH.III, 144], in denying the ability of the Alamanni to conquer Roman cities [MH.III, 165], in associating the first reference to Paris with Julian [MH.III, 173f.], in dating the first tamed camels to the reign of Valentinian [MH.III, 201f.], in describing Valentinian as an Arian [MH.III, 203], and in believing the Ulfilas Bible to be the oldest of all translations of the Bible from the Greek [MH.III, 213]. A remark which Mommsen made twice, that eastern Rome collapsed as a result of the Persian Wars [MH.III, 151, 222], is obscure. In those passages where the lectures correspond to volume V of the *History of Rome*, it is worth considering which of the corrections to the latter are the result of advice given by Wilamowitz.

It would seem that the moment Mommsen started lecturing to students he regained the 'sacred hallucination of youth', the *corraggio dell'errare*.[151] His statement that there can be nothing more frivolous in the world than giving lectures',[152] confirms that in mature years Mommsen felt fewer scruples at the lectern than at his writing desk. Accordingly, the picture that emerges from our text is of a more ebullient, and as it were more youthful, Mommsen than in his published material of the same period. The restraint of volume V is not retained throughout the lectures. On the other hand, Mommsen here anticipates some of his later insights, such as that the basic meaning of the *consistorium* was architectural [MH.III, 49], that the establishment of the office of *magister militum praesentalis* was at the end of Constantine's reign and of regional ones was under Constantius II,[153] and the Roman background of Ulfila, generally regarded as a half-Goth [MH.III, 212]. In some particulars, even the most recent research still has something to learn from Mommsen's interpretation of public offices in late antiquity, a field where his juristic sensibility is superior to that of modern authors, for instance in his remarks on the origin of the separation of administrative and judicial functions.

A final noteworthy feature is Mommsen's observations on Christianity,[154] which he in no way overlooked as Sebastian Hensel (see above) claimed. Mommsen [MH.I, 232ff.] saw Judaism in terms of nationality and ritual and Christianity in terms of the idea and practice of humanity. The God of wrath had become a God of love. There are, however, some very critical comments: Christianity was 'a plebeian religion and so, too, therefore, was its style' [MH.III, 104]; the Christian faith was a 'charcoal-burners' faith', but one for 'counts and barons' too, and hence made its mark on history [MH.III, 109]. Mommsen deplores its effects on art and the state. The Church seemed to him to be a 'state within a state', its hierarchy a 'principle that threatened the state, subversive to the utmost degree', [MH.III, 107] and the bishops an 'alternative government', or even counter-government [MH.III, 142]. Mommsen did not use the term *Pfaffen-geschmeiss* (clerical scum) merely for astrologers and the priests of Isis under Tiberius. Polytheism and Christianity are dealt with in the same terms. But what Mommsen rejects is the enlightened 'indifference' of those such as Marcus Aurelius: 'Nothing can be accomplished by this' [MH.III, 63, 203]. In his view, religion should be exploited by politicians as a tool: what mattered was whether it was useful. For Mommsen, paganism had become ineffective. He therefore criticized Julian, whom he otherwise held in such high esteem: Julian had tried 'to set back the world clock' [MH.III, 58], and ought to have known that the old religion was a thing of the past [MH.III, 179]. Not surprisingly, Mommsen is hostile to the impending victory of the Church over the State: many of the 'finest people of the age' responded to both Christianity and Mithraism 'with the educated disdain of men of the world' [MH.III, 157]. This brings him back to the conflict between (in Hegelian terms) the higher law of history and individual character, which was crucial in his judgement.

Essentially, Mommsen's interest in late antiquity coincided with his interest in Roman history in general: it is linked to his own time on the one hand through historical descent and on the other through structural similarities. The former appears in the concluding remarks to volume II of his *History of Rome*, from which the conclusion to the lectures differs only in wording. Mommsen observed the history of the Goths, Vandals and Franks from the perspective of *Verschmelzung* (ethnic assimilation) [MH.III, 239]. Sebastian Hensel wrote in 1886: 'final lecture, 30th July: numerous faces never seen before appear, who will testify that they have conscientiously scived throughout the course'.

Despite his emphasis on continuity in the lives of nations, Mommsen realized that the Roman state and ancient civilization had run their course by the fifth century. The remark made by Mommsen above (p. 4), reported by Butler, that he had never understood the reason for the fall of the Empire, had naturally been intended ironically. Mommsen had made quite specific statements on this subject,[155] which he developed in the lectures.

Mommsen regarded the imperial age as an appendix to the Republic. In his view, the Romans had already dug their own grave in the second century BC, on the one hand with the ruin of the agrarian middle class, and on the other through Roman subjugation of foreign peoples, with whom, as he saw it, real assimilation was not feasible. 'The age of the Roman emperors shows us the Roman people up to the point of utmost senility, until it finally disintegrates: it was not the barbarians who overthrew Rome', as he put in in 1872/3.[156] At the beginning of the great migrations, when the legions were manned with Germanic soldiers, the Empire was faced on a wider scale with what befell Italy at the end of the Antonine era, when military service was abandoned to the provincials, particularly those of the Danube lands: 'when a country . . . renders itself defenceless and leaves its protection to others, it is bound to be subjugated' [MH.II, 268]. Without the army, the Empire is unable to sustain itself: 'The true reasons for Rome's subsequent misfortunes are to be sought in the decline of military discipline' [MH.II, 311].

The age of the emperors represented the 'total political, military, economic and moral bankruptcy of civilization at that time'.[157] Orientalization, barbarization, imperialism and pacifism – all this was an outrage to Mommsen, the liberal nationalist, and sufficient explanation for collapse. But his judgement is ambivalent. In 1868 he declared to his students [MK.110]: 'In both the military and administrative respects, the transition from Republic to monarchy can only be regarded as a step forward.'

On the one hand, therefore, the ethnic and tribal constitution of the late Roman world is one of his most important categories of judgement, speaking positively as he does of their national unity, their national interests and their national policy. On the other hand, Mommsen is more than sympathetic to the expansionist policy of Rome when he approves the 'service of civilization' or 'cultural historical mission' of Roman arms [MH.II, 204ff., 237], Augustus's attempt to reach the Elbe frontier, or the campaign of Septimius Severus in Scotland [MH.II, 117; compare RA, p. 106]. The pacific policy of the emperors is criticized as 'stagnation' [MH.I, 102, 129; II, 112, 115; cf. RA, p. 106]. What triggered the disintegration of the Empire in Mommsen's view was on the one hand its alleged financial ruination [MH.II, 105], and on the other 'the military monarchy in the inexorable momentum of its process of self-destruction', which 'reduced its subjects to the level of clones'.[158] It is precisely to peace that Mommsen ascribes the Empire's waning vitality:[159] 'Far from being military-minded, the age of the emperors was perhaps the most pacific and peace-loving era the world has ever seen across such a broad span of space and time' [MH.II, 63]. Similarly: 'Where the Republic was war, the Empire was peace' [MH.I, 135]. The policy of peace at any price was a flawed one for the state: on the whole, governments that take vigorous action tend to be the best' [MH.I, 191]. Mommsen commended a robust, courageous policy of expansion and occupation where the circumstances permitted it [MH.III, 94] – in contrast to a Trajan, who fought too much, or a Hadrian or Pius, who fought too little [MH.II, 299, 301].

Mommsen frequently sees parallels between later Roman history and that of his own time. He compares the disquieting extent of the great landholdings of the emperors to that of London landed property magnates [MH.II, 86]. On the other hand, it was the absence of national debt which, in his view, distinguished the fiscal policy of the principate from that of modern states [MH.II, 90]. Government supervision of towns seemed as beneficial to him as the demise of the Free Imperial Cities of Germany, 'with their short-sighted and narrow-minded parish-pump politics' [MH.II, 105]; the life of Romans in Gaul and Britain reminds him of that of the English in India [MH.II, 150], Rome's confrontations with Saharan nomads of those of the French Maréchal Bugeaud [MH.II, 203]. He also thought he recognized the petty rule-bound thinking of Constantius II in his own time [MH.III, 153]. His assessment of Napoleon [MH.II, 159] comes as a surprise. So, too, in the wake of the Charlottenburg defamation case brought against him by Bismarck in 1882, does his positive reference to the Chancellor [MH.III, 41], although his side-swipe at what he calls *Minister-Absolutismus*[160] is clearly a veiled comparison of Stilicho and Bismarck. A *tout comme chez nous* [MH.III, 136] can often be read between the lines. Wucher is correct in assuming that the 'intimate relationship between history and the present would undoubtedly also have been confirmed in the age of the Emperors'.[161]

Mommsen's hypothesis regarding a basic affinity between the Romans and the Germans, and of the essentially alien character of the Celts to both [MH.II, 169, 183f., 285], is contradicted by the Germanic–Celtic coalition against Rome during the Civilis rebellion. His analysis seems to have been determined by the power-politics of 1870/1, when Germany was hoping to win the sympathy of Italy in the war against France. Mommsen applies the same principle when he likens the arduous Romanization of the rural population in Gaul to the experiences of the French in Alsace, or of the Prussians in Pozen and Upper Silesia [MH.II, 160]. Prussia's German 'client-states' are used as a model for the barbarian chieftains allied to Rome [MH.II, 20].

There was no doubt in Mommsen's mind about the identity of the Germanic peoples with the modern Germans. Although he did distance himself from the adulation of the ancient Germans prevalent at that time right across the political spectrum, in contrast to such writers as Freytag, Dahn, Gregorovius, Engels and Treitschke, this simply reflected his ambivalent view of the Germans and their political ability. The rule of Augustus was the 'first occasion on which our own Fatherland stepped on to the stage of world history' [MH.I, 79]; Arminius witnessed the beginning of a German national sentiment: 'This was the first time one could speak of German concord and German discord' [MH.I, 133]. Mommsen saw the late formation of the Alamannic federation as an attempt to bring about German unity. 'This was, if I may say so, the first manifestation of the notion of German unity and, even in this extremely incomplete form, it was already enough to make an impact on world history' [MH.II, 141]. By the same token, however, the 'peculiar curse' of the Germans,[162] domestic discord, also first made its presence felt in the age of the emperors: 'as so often in history, . . . Germans fought and won against Germans' [MH.III, 155]. In his 1886 lectures he expounded what he had described in 1877[163] as the 'peculiar curse' of the German nation, the extreme contradictions in their political views that aroused in him 'blazing fury' and 'burning shame'. He set a 'peculiar blessing' against this 'peculiar curse', referring, in 1877, to such individuals as Frederick the Great.

5. EDITORIAL PRINCIPLES

On 15 December 1884 Julius Wellhausen wrote to Mommsen: 'The world may be less interested in Roman emperors than in Theodor Mommsen, and less in history than in your view of it.'[164] These words are even truer today, and are the primary reason for deciding to produce this edition. Even Wilamowitz[165] thought that the principal interest in publication of the lecture notes revolved around the insight they would provide into Mommsen's own 'historical development. . . . If publication is to take place, then so too must a meticulous examination and editing; and even the quotations will have to be checked'. This would require an 'expert and diplomatic individual'.

I do not suppose that this book will acquire a significance comparable with other posthumously published lecture notes – such as Hegel's *Philosophy of History* (1837) or *Philosophy of Law* (1983), Niebuhr's *History of Rome* (1844), Boeckh's *Encyclopaedia and Methodology of the Philological Sciences* (1877), Treitschke's *Politics* (1897), Burckhardt's *Observations on World History* (1905), Max Weber's *History of Economics* (1923), Kant's *Ethics* (1924) or Droysen's *Historik* (1937). These works were published and read largely for their contents, whereas Mommsen's lectures on the history of the emperors will probably only reach a readership interested in the history of the discipline. The book is intended to enrich our picture of Mommsen, regarded by A. J. Toynbee as the greatest historian of all time after Edward Gibbon.[166]

With all due respect to Elisabeth Hensel and Ludwig Schemann, it goes without saying that the lecture notes cannot claim to represent volume IV of the *History of Rome*, although they may, if we wish, be regarded as a substitute for it. The fact that in his will Mommsen prohibited the publication of his lecture notes[167] is as little binding on posterity as the last will of Jacob Burckhardt, requesting that his papers, including his *Observations on World History*, be pulped.[168] Fortunately for us, Augustus had already failed to respect Virgil's will: *iusserat haec rapidis aboleri carmina flammis*,[169] although Mommsen [MH.I, 112] was of the opinion that Virgil would have done well to burn his *Aeneid* himself.

The high quality of the Hensel lecture notes clearly emerges when the text is compared with available parallel texts, particularly comparing no.9 [MH.I] with no.10 [AW], and no.11 [MP] with no.12 [MH.II]. MH.I gives the impression of having been taken down by Paul Hensel in the lecture room, whereas the bound manuscripts MH.II and III are, as Sebastian Hensel points out, re-written down to the last detail [MH.III, 209]. In every section the handwriting is fair and legible, and proper names and citations in ancient languages for the most part correct. The editorial principle has been to alter the given wording as little as possible, while on the other hand creating a readable account. Since the text was not authorized by Mommsen, but partly taken down by others in the lecture room and partly re-written at a desk, the editors are free of any obligation to repeat it word for word. The aim has been to reconstruct what Mommsen actually said, rather than to edit what Hensel wrote. Should Hensel's text find sufficient interest, a textual scholar might like to edit the verbatim text with an *apparatus criticus* at some later date. Since our prime aim is to make the history of the emperors accessible to readers, we have sought a form that need not fear any *ex Elysio* criticism from Mommsen.

Work on the three parts proceeded differently, depending on the manner in which they were recorded. MH.I contains a number of misheard and misspelt words that garble the text, notably proper names and specialist terminology (e.g. *Cistophorus*, a type of coin, is written down as *Christophorus*), and which clearly did not originate with Mommsen. Similarly, the occurrence of abbreviations and key words, incomplete sentences, incorrect German word order, unnecessary changes of tense and numerous repetitions may be ascribed to pressure of time when taking lecture notes. A predeliction for words such as *freilich, allerdings, namentlich* and *auch* (of course, nevertheless, specifically and also), as well as the conspicuous frequency of *Es* ('It') as the opening word of a sentence, are equally unlikely to be authentic. In these cases, therefore, the text required selective but careful improvement. The length of sentences, punctuation and spelling have been standardized, the text divided into sections and given headings. Similarly a number of dates have been inserted, personal names given in full and modern equivalents given for ancient place names. Mommsen dates events 'From the Foundation of the City' (*ab urbe condita*, 753 BC), rather than BC/AD; in this edition all dates are given as BC or AD, as more familiar to the reader. Greek terms, sometimes given in Greek, sometimes in Latin script in the original, have been Latinized.

The anonymous Wickert manuscript [AW, see p. 21, no. 10], a parallel set of lecture notes, provided a welcome cross-reference; my thanks are due to the owner's generosity in letting me use it. This text contains fewer errors, and is superior in style, but considerably shorter. The textual comparison below should serve to illustrate this.

[AW. 37] The earlier judicial system recognized no appeals, only cassation. Augustus introduced appeals, but jury verdicts seem to have been excluded. Appeals could be made to the Emperor, or to consuls and the Senate. The death penalty was reintroduced, with power over life and death in the hands of the Emperor, the Senate or the consuls. Discretionary powers were likewise conferred on Augustus, such as during the rule of Sulla and the Triumvirate. Use of these discret. powers, however, seems to have been confined to matters in which the people were in agreement with the Emperor. Initially, each proconsul was allocated a specific area of jurisdiction; Augustus was given the proconsulate for the whole Empire.

[MH.I, 41f.] The former system had recognized only that a tribune of the plebs could set aside a previously pronounced sentence. An appeals procedure,[155] whereby a higher authority was empowered to replace an earlier sentence with another legally binding judgment, was completely unknown. The procedure of appeal to higher authorities – to consuls, the Senate, and ultimately the *princeps* himself – was instituted by Augustus and can be demonstrated for all categories of legal proceedings with the exception of jury courts. This was particularly important for criminal proceedings, which had been tightened up considerably with the reintroduction of the death penalty. Life- and death-decisions were in the hands of consuls, the Senate and the Emperor. No basis whatsoever for this can be discerned in the titular powers of the *princeps*. This undoubtedly also applies to the way in which other spheres of authority were exercised in practice, which we cannot go into here.

The transfer of power to the Emperor in the *lex regia* ends with the clause that he was empowered to do whatever he saw fit in the interests of the state. This discretionary power is virtually unlimited, like that of Sulla and the triumvirs, and it is possible to give specific instances of this. When, for example, in 27 BC, bribes were becoming all too conspicuous in the elections to magistracies, Augustus simply declared the elections void and appointed new magistrates on the strength of his own plenitude of powers. Nevertheless, this was an extreme, reluctantly and rarely used power. Effort was made to avoid using it, resorting to it only when the voice of the best elements in the population favoured extraordinary measures.

Despite this, one has to concede that the sum of legal powers united in the *princeps* bordered on totalitarianism. This category most particularly included the proconsular authority that extended across the entire Empire, which would have been quite unknown in the Republic in peacetime, and was not even achieved with the far-reaching powers of Pompey against the pirates.

Wickert's Anonymous [AW] evidently did more thinking and less writing. He also passes on numerous additional passages which I have inserted into the Hensel text. Most of them are so minor that explicit references to the source would have disfigured the printed text; only the most important have been indicated. The final quarter of the winter 1882/3 course is only available in the AW manuscript: there must originally have been a fourth notebook in addition to the three extant ones of Paul Hensel. Frequent agreement in wording between the two confirms the carefully preserved *ipsissima verba* of Mommsen.

Erich Pernice's [MP] lecture notes of the summer 1883 course, the History of Rome under the Emperors II, are scant. They have provided some extra passages, which are supplied in the Notes. Page numbering corresponds to the original text preserved in the German Archaeological Institute in Rome (see p. 21, no. 11). To complete the picture, some further material from Mommsen's 1866 lectures (Göttingen Anonymous) and 1868/9 (Mommsen–Krauseneck, lecture notes nos. 2 and 4: see p. 20) has been included in the notes. One longer passage [MH.II, 315–42] derives from Kurt Hensel, Sebastian's second son, later a mathematician at Marburg. Kurt stood in for his father when the latter was on a visit to his family in the Harz mountains.[170] The following letter, now in the East Berlin State Library, shows the nature of Kurt's later relationship with Mommsen:

Berlin W.
Kurfürstendamm 36
1 July 1901

Respected Professor,

Frau von Willamowitz [*sic*] has informed me that you would be interested in sitting for a photographer on Tuesday the 2nd inst., and that you would prefer me not to call for you. Would you please be so kind as to be at the premises of Noack the court photographer, 45 Unter den Linden, 3rd floor (the second building from the Friedrichstrasse direction) at ten o'clock on Tuesday? I shall be there half an hour earlier and make all the necessary arrangements to ensure the minimum inconvenience to yourself.

With humblest regards,

Your devoted,

D. Kurt Hensel

MH.II required fewer improvements, although even here it was necessary to correct some errors made by the person taking the notes. Wherever these are likely to derive from Mommsen himself, this has been indicated in the Notes. The Notes also occasionally refer to subsequent advances in research, but it would have overloaded this edition to bring Mommsen's account up to date in every detail. Not even Mommsen himself did this for the later editions of his *History of Rome*: he had the text of the second edition reprinted again and again, without changes. As far as possible the sources used by Mommsen have been traced and indicated in the Notes. This was not always an easy task, particularly with the inscriptions, over which Mommsen had greater command than any other ancient historian. Word-for-word quotations from Mommsen's memory have been supplemented with the correct original form where appropriate. Mommsen's prodigious knowledge of original sources enabled him largely to dispense with secondary ones. He cites Bergk, Bethmann Hollweg, Jacob Burckhardt, Albert Duncker, Gibbon, Henzen, Hertzberg, Hirschfeld, Hübner, Imhoof-Blumer, Kiepert, Marquardt, Missong, Nitzsch, Ranke, Richter, Seeck, Tillemont and Wilmanns. Since it has not always been possible to refer to the works used by Mommsen in the editions available to him, apparent anachronisms occur where later editions are used here.

The original pagination given for each of the three sections [MH.I, II and III, and AW] is intended to assist future editors in checking the editorial method. The title, RK (*History of the Roman Emperors*) was repeatedly used by Mommsen himself for his lectures (see pp. 9f.).

As already requested by Wilamowitz in 1928, the Hensel lecture notes will be donated to the State Library in Berlin. As regards Wickert's Anonymous (AW), the will of the present owner stipulates that after the death of his wife it should pass to his son, Dr Konrad Wickert, in Erlangen.

I am grateful to my wife for deciphering a text that is in parts scarcely legible, being written in a private shorthand, and for providing a preliminary typescript. Other help was provided by Geza Alföldy, Horst Blanck, Jochen Bleicken, Manfred Clauss, Werner Eck, Karin Fischer, Stefan Gläser, Werner Hermann, Sven Kellerhoff, Martin König, Hartmut Leppin, Cécile Lowenthal-Hensel, Burghard Nickel, Helena Oechsner, Annette Pohlke, Werner Portmann, Maria R. Alföldi, Sven Rugullis, Heinrich Schlange-Schöningen and Uwe Walter; the project was facilitated by financial support from the Fritz Thyssen Foundation. I should like to thank them all.

I am grateful to Frau Fanny Kistner-Hensel and to Frau Cécile Lowenthal-Hensel for their consent to publication.

Lindheim, Whitsun 1992
Alexander Demandt

MOMMSEN, ROME AND THE GERMAN *KAISERREICH*

by Thomas Wiedemann

The nature and extent of imperial power; the sources of its legitimacy and authority; and its relationship to the power exercised by local rulers and communities – in the years when Theodor Mommsen grew up these were not just academic questions about long-dead Roman emperors, but questions about what Germany was and what it was likely to become. The 'Holy Roman Empire' of Charlemagne, refounded by the Saxon Ottonian dynasty in the tenth century, had survived as the 'Holy Roman Empire of the German Nation' until 6 August 1806, when the Emperor Francis II resigned the imperial title (he had styled himself Emperor of Austria since 1804, when Napoleon had crowned himself Emperor of France). It had been replaced first by a federation under French control, the Rheinbund, and then in 1815, after Napoleon's overthrow, by a looser federation of thirty-nine territorial states.

From the beginning, the new German League was perceived as providing only an interim solution to the question of what sort of political framework Germany should have. During the short period of French hegemony, the rulers of some of the larger German states had adopted French administrative practices in order to impose uniformity on their territories. In many cases these states were artificial creations of the Napoleonic period (particularly of the *Reichsdeputationshauptschluss*, the statute of 1803 which abolished 112 ecclesiastical, civic and minor secular territories). Thus the population of Baden increased almost tenfold, of Württemberg almost ninefold and of Prussia more than fourfold. They had effectively become completely new states, incorporating formerly independent territories and imperial cities which had their own traditions and identities, and often different religious affiliations as well. The loyalty of the population to their new princes had to be earned through reforms such as the abolition of surviving feudal rights, the equal protection – and control – by the state of all religious denominations, and government by state officials who in theory would treat everyone equally before the law. Another requirement was for a new universal educational system, made doubly necessary by the need for conscription during the Napoleonic wars and, in the Catholic half of Germany, by the destruction of

36

the traditional Church-based educational system as a result of the secularization of Church property at the *Reichsdeputationshauptschluss*.

It was Prussia that led the way in transforming a collection of separate territories that happened to be ruled by one dynasty – the Hohenzollerns – into a unitary bureaucratic state. One of the most important elements in that transformation was the creation of a new educational system by Wilhelm von Humboldt (1767–1835), who chose to put the study of ancient Greece at the centre of the syllabus to be taught in the *Gymnasium*, the elite secondary school in which future officers and civil servants received their education. The enthusiasm for classical Greece which Humboldt showed had already been developing in the late eighteenth century; but by making it the focus of education in the new Prussian state, Humboldt invested it with the symbolic function of a standard of values which, precisely because it had no apparent relevance to the political problems of the early nineteenth century, could inspire equally Prussia's Protestant and Catholic subjects, aristocratic landowners and burghers, officers and industrialists. The very success of Greek studies in Prussia made it a symbol of pride in the new state, a pride which could be shared by social groups which otherwise had very different political and economic interests (as the nineteenth century progressed, other disciplines perceived as academic and therefore as above sectional interests came to play a similar role in Germany, particularly chemistry and medicine). But the emphasis on ancient Greece had another effect too. It drew attention away from Rome, and therefore weakened the symbolic value of 'Rome' as the source of legitimacy for the Holy Roman Empire, which Prussia was seeking to replace in the loyalties of its subjects. The downgrading of Rome also served the interests of the other new German states, whose claim to 'sovereignty' was based on the proposition that the Holy Roman Empire had not functioned as a proper state at all (at any rate since the end of the Thirty Years War in 1648), but as a tool of Habsburg dynastic interests which had actually interfered with the legitimate assertion of German rights by Prussia and her allies. Because of the academic authority of the Prussian university system created by Humboldt, this Prussian view of German history, perfected by the Berlin Professor of History Heinrich von Treitschke (1834–96), was generally accepted until recently. It was accompanied by an emphasis on the 'northern' origins of the Germans developed by romantic nationalists (and most notoriously reflected in the operas of Richard Wagner); both served the same function of denying the validity of Germany's past 'Roman' Empire as a basis for her future. It is no paradox that one of the memorials to the struggle against Napoleon's French Empire, some kilometres east of Regensburg, should have been called the 'Valhalla', but built in the form of the Athenian Acropolis.

Mommsen's interest in Rome rather than Greece was therefore exceptional (if not unique) amongst nineteenth-century German scholars of antiquity. The Greek world only interested him where it impinged on the Roman – with the

Greek-speaking communities of South Italy and Sicily, and more crucially with the Byzantine world up to the sixth-century, which interested Mommsen not so much because it was Greek, as because it continued to be Roman. The most important of the factors which explain why Mommsen was different was that he came from Schleswig-Holstein, whose dukes were also the kings of Denmark. He was born at Garding in Schleswig on 30 November 1817; soon after, his father Jens Mommsen (1783–1851) was appointed assistant pastor at Oldesloe, a spa in Holstein 45 kilometres north-east of Hamburg. His father apparently had a bad preaching voice (the son too was notoriously a bad lecturer), and there was no money to send the sons to school. Education at home meant that Theodor, like his brothers Tycho (1819–1900, later headmaster of a *Gymnasium* at Frankfurt) and August (1821–1913), became a voracious reader with an astonishing self-imposed capacity for work; but it also meant that the books he read were not the Greek texts studied in Humboldt's *Gymnasien* (which in any case did not reach Schleswig-Holstein until the middle of the century), but the Latin texts which throughout the seventeenth and eighteenth centuries had constituted the syllabus for the 'Humanities' throughout Europe – including amongst historical writers texts which were to find no place on nineteenth-century 'Classics' syllabuses, such as the *Epitome de Caesaribus*, Justin's *Epitome* of Pompeius Trogus and the *Historia Augusta*. For Mommsen, Late Antiquity was as much a part of Roman history as the early Republic eulogized by Livy. His first attempts at German poetry, too, were classically inspired epigrams, unaffected by the romanticism that had been fashionable for a generation.

Mommsen's fluency in Latin was reinforced by another effect of his upbringing in Schleswig-Holstein: Latin was no more artificial as a learned language than High German. His parents spoke dialect at home (cf. his references to the use of Low German on tombstones at MH.II, 176), and a sense of local tradition was strong in the family. As elsewhere in Scandinavia, this was an area where family names had only replaced patronymics in the eighteenth century (in the case of the Mommsens, the names had been alternately 'Momme' and 'Jens'): if the historian was usually called 'Jens' by his family, this was because it had been traditional in the family, and did not imply any rejection of the Christian symbolism of the name 'Theodor'. When Mommsen abandoned the Lutheran Christianity of his ancestors, it was because of his commitment to political radicalism, not out of any feeling that God had not given his father sufficient earthly reward for his loyalty. What Mommsen did inherit from his father was a deep suspicion of Catholicism, which he did not see as in any way connected with the Rome he admired or the Latin he wrote so fluently.

Mommsen was also a fluent reader of English. The political links with Britain via Hanover, and the commercial links via Hamburg, made English the medium through which liberal ideas influenced north-west Germany. Mommsen's mother,

Sophie Krumbhaar (1792–1855), came from Altona, a suburb of Hamburg although within the Duchy of Holstein. Between October 1834 and April 1838, Mommsen and his brother Tycho were sent for their only formal schooling to the *Gymnasium Christianeum* at Altona, founded by the Danish King Christian VI in 1738, and which after the incorporation of Kiel in the Danish realm in 1773 functioned as a feeder college for the university at Kiel. It was here that Mommsen was first confronted with literary romanticism, and systematically read both German and non-German writers such as Goethe and Heine, Shakespeare and Cervantes. Heine and the other writers of the 'Young Germany' movement drew his attention to the existence of a shared literary culture that united German-speakers far beyond the borders of Schleswig-Holstein, and to the association of that pan-German aspiration with a demand for political liberalism that could not be satisfied by the political institutions of the post-Napoleonic German League. These issues, both literary and political, were debated at meetings of the *Gymnasium*'s student society, in which the Mommsen brothers played a leading role. These were the years in which Mommsen became a radical liberal, veering towards atheism and republicanism. But the atmosphere of Altona steered him away from a romantic or racialist variety of nationalism: there is no evidence that he was interested in Nordic mythology (though he read the *Nibelungenlied*, with its resonances of the post-Roman world), and his reading of English historians made him see political freedom as a universal right rather than the product of a specifically Germanic tradition (he was particularly interested in *England and the English* by the liberal politician and diplomat Sir Henry Bulwer (1801–72), who had played an active role in securing the independence of both Greece and Belgium). In Hamburg and Altona, there were opportunities to meet foreigners, not just to read their books; Mommsen augmented his allowance by giving language lessons to English merchants (his star pupil was a Mr Pow). Nor, for the time being, did his growing identification with liberalism and German nationalism exclude a feeling of loyalty for his Danish sovereign. Mommsen was shocked by the irreverence with which Hamburg society received a false rumour of the death of King Frederick VI in 1836. The self-satisfied snobbery of Hamburg's elite alienated Mommsen from rather than attracted him to the idea of municipal self-government (cf. MH.II, 105).

That was to change during Mommsen's five years as a student at the University of Kiel, where he matriculated in May 1838. In the spring of 1843 he passed the State Examination allowing him to practise law with a dissertation on Roman guilds; the dissertation which he submitted for his doctoral examination in November was on another aspect of Roman administrative law, minor Roman officials. Given Mommsen's family background, the obvious career for him would have been as a clergyman; but his background had also given him enough experience of clerical poverty – he was to remain concerned about his own income throughout his life, and his unusual interest in the fiscal institutions of the Roman Empire ought to be seen in that context as well as in that of nineteenth-century economic theory in general – and in any case he had lost his faith in Lutheran Christianity. Of the other professions, teaching was not much more attractive, though after graduating from Kiel he found he had no alternative but to earn a living for a year teaching at his maternal aunts' girls' boarding school at Altona. Mommsen wanted something more political: he studied law, not (like his brothers Tycho and August) classical philology, and he will have expected to follow an administrative career as a civil servant in his native Schleswig-Holstein. Not that Mommsen was uninterested in classical philology: he formed a firm and lasting friendship at Kiel with the classicist Otto Jahn, a junior university teacher only four years older than he was. Not only did Jahn introduce him to the kinds of things that were happening in Prussian classical scholarship, but he also introduced him to the elite society of Kiel who frequented his father's house – the leaders of liberal politics in Holstein. Nevertheless, Mommsen still made it explicit in his doctoral dissertation that he saw himself as a lawyer, not a classicist, and that he associated Latin with the law, Greek with classical scholarship ('Res graecae philologorum sunt, latinae iurisconsultorum': p. 139).

But any hopes Mommsen had of an administrative career fell casualty to the unresolved consequences of the destruction of the Holy Roman Empire. Holstein had been part of that Empire, subject like every other imperial territory to the Diet at Regensburg. As Duke of Holstein, the King of Denmark had maintained a permanent legation at Regensburg, directed from a Chancellery at Copenhagen; and since imperial business constituted the major portion of Danish foreign policy, most aspects of Danish foreign policy came to be entrusted to this 'German Chancellery' staffed by German-speakers, many of them not from Holstein at all. Not only did German- and Danish-speakers live side by side in Copenhagen, they governed the constituent territories of the Danish monarchy side by side. This was a system that could not survive the fall of the Empire. To protect the unity of their domains against potential threats from the centrally administered states which were developing south of their borders, the Danish kings too sought to impose uniformity, a uniformity which naturally had to be based on the Danish language. In 1817, Danish was made a compulsory school subject in Schleswig-Holstein. In 1840, Danish replaced German as the administrative language of northern parts of Schleswig. This was justified in so far as most of the local population were Danish speakers; but it made it clear to both Danes and Germans that the principle of basing states on linguistic communities necessarily implied the separation of German- and Danish-speaking parts of Schleswig, and thus the destruction of Schleswig-Holstein as a single territorial entity which had been united under its own parliament for centuries. It also underlined the contradiction of nationalism as a political creed by bringing German and Danish liberals into

40

direct conflict: the Danish liberal movement supported the Copenhagen government so long as it excluded German-speakers (and dissolved the 'German
Chancellery'), while liberals in Holstein – and increasingly throughout Germany
– defended the 'Germanness' of the duchy. Symbolic for the German side was the
so-called 'Ripener Freiheitsbrief' of 1460, in which the estates of Schleswig and
Holstein had sworn to remain undivided forever ('dat se bliwen ewige tosamende
ungedelt'). In the context of the fifteenth century, their concern had actually been
that the duchy should not be partitioned between different heirs to the Danish
crown; but Holstein liberals (particularly the anglophile F. C. Dahlmann, one of
the seven Göttingen professors who were dismissed in 1838) reinterpreted it as
the charter of a unified Schleswig-Holstein state, distinct from Denmark.

The development of a unified Danish state, no matter how liberal its principles,
necessarily resulted in the exclusion of German-speakers, and undermined their
loyalty to even the most tenuous link with the Danish crown. German national
consciousness had been greatly strengthened by the hostility of the French
government of Thiers, which almost led to a European war in 1840 (cf. MH.II,
184). After 1840, German-speakers in Schleswig-Holstein increasingly saw their
future exclusively in terms of being part of a new German *Reich*. The crisis passed
the point of no return on 4 December 1846, when the Schleswig estates dissolved
themselves rather than carry out the policies of the government in Copenhagen.
By the time he completed his university studies, it was no longer possible
for Mommsen to think that he could both serve the King of Denmark and be a
German liberal.

So Mommsen was not given an appointment in the Danish administration of his
native duchy on graduation; instead, he won a Danish government scholarship to
study the antiquities of Italy, setting sail from Hamburg in September 1844. His
primary aim was to find and collate as many unpublished Latin inscriptions as
possible; this was a project that had been suggested to him by Otto Jahn, who had
put him in touch with the Berlin professor August Boeckh (1785–1867), who
had been producing a similar corpus of Greek inscriptions. Mommsen later said
that the most important result of his Italian sojourn had been that he had learnt
to be an epigrapher from the man who knew more about Roman inscriptions than
anyone else at the time, Count Bartolomeo Borghesi of San Marino (1781–1860).
When he returned from Italy in the spring of 1847 via Vienna, Leipzig and Berlin,
it was clear that his future was to be an academic Roman historian rather than a
lawyer or civil servant.

The Italian journey brought Mommsen a wealth of experiences that went far
beyond the merely scholarly. Paris in particular impressed him as the capital of a
world Empire, and became Mommsen's model for understanding Rome. In his
lectures forty years later, he still referred to what he had seen in the Père Lachaise
cemetary, or to the Algerian victory parade of Marshal Bugeaud (MH.II, 9f., 200,

203). He travelled by train for the first time (from Rouen to Paris); and one indelible experience was an attempt by a fanatical Irishman to convert him to Catholicism during the voyage from Marseille to Genoa (this experience is likely to have been a major factor in explaining Mommsen's prejudices not just against Irish Catholics, but also against the Celts in general and Druids in particular: cf. MH.II, 111f., 164–70, and the vivid description of the Celtic character in his *History of Rome*, bk. 2 ch. 4, I, 325f.).

During his absence the question of the future of Schleswig-Holstein had become a major plank of the German liberal movement. In 1848, revolutionary pressure forced the German states to summon a parliament to Frankfurt in order to re-establish a unified German Empire and decide on both its boundaries and its constitution. The refusal of both Habsburg and Hohenzollern to play the role of constitutional emperor was to lead to the collapse of the liberal movement in the following year; but in the spring of 1848, the Frankfurt parliament gave support and legitimacy to resistance to Denmark's decision to incorporate Schleswig. An armed uprising followed. Mommsen participated in the struggle in the best way he could, helping to edit the *Schleswig-holsteinische Zeitung*, the journal of the revolutionary provisional government in Kiel. But although Prussian troops occupied the duchies, and much of Jutland, in May 1848, Britain and Russia were not prepared to see Prussia control the Sound between the North Sea and the Baltic, and in August they forced Prussia to restore the duchies to Denmark. Like the liberal cause in Frankfurt, the German cause in Schleswig-Holstein seemed lost: the 'London protocol' of 8 May 1852 imposed the Danish law of succession on the duchies, thus giving their integration into Denmark the stamp of international approval. As a solution imposed by outsiders, this could only be temporary; and in 1863 the promulgation of a new unitary constitution for all Danish territories again provoked resistance among German speakers, this time leading to the combined intervention of Prussia and Austria in the war of 1864 and thus to the full integration of the duchies into Prussia after the Austro-Prussian War of 1866.

But Mommsen had already left Holstein long before that. In August 1848, he had been offered a post as supernumerary professor ('Extraordinarus') in Roman law at Leipzig; this at last guaranteed him a regular income, and he was obliged to accept (the offer had been engineered by his old friend Otto Jahn, who was now Professor of Classics there). During his time in Italy Mommsen had become clearer about the need for what was to become the greatest scholarly project of his life, a corpus of all surviving Latin inscriptions from every part of the Roman Empire – the *Corpus Inscriptionum Latinarum* (*CIL*). But such a project could only be undertaken under the auspices of a major research institution, and for Mommsen this meant the Prussian Academy of Sciences in Berlin, which had supported Boeckh. The Academy had already agreed to support a preliminary project of this sort by A.W. Zumpt, a Berlin *Gymnasium*-teacher; several years of sometimes bitter political infighting followed during which Zumpt resisted Mommsen's attempt to have the project taken away from him on the grounds that Mommsen was too junior and academically unproven. But Mommsen rapidly established his scholarly authority with a series of publications largely resulting from his studies in Italy: on southern Italic dialects (*Die Unteritalischen Dialekte*, 1850), Roman coinage (*Ueber das römische Münzwesen*, 1850), a fourth-century AD list of religious festivals (*Ueber den Chronographen von 354*, 1850), and in particular an edition of over 7,000 Latin inscriptions from southern Italy which secured his reputation as the world's leading expert on Latin epigraphy (*Inscriptiones Regni Neapolitani Latinae*, 1852).

What these apparently disparate themes had in common was that through comparative linguistics, numismatics and epigraphy, Mommsen was trying to create a body of material which had the status of archival evidence and which would serve as a control on the narratives of historical writers such as Livy and Appian. These narratives had already been subjected to scrutiny by earlier scholars, of whom the most significant was Georg Barthold Niebuhr (1776–1831; first a Danish, then a Prussian civil servant before becoming Professor of History at Bonn). But Niebuhr's method had been to apply the principles of 'Source Criticism' to unravel contradictions in the traditional account, and then to explain them by applying models developed in the light of his own experience, e.g. of conscription in a peasant society. Mommsen's work sought to establish entirely new categories of evidence for the use of the historian. Thus in bk. 1 ch. 2 (vol. I, p. 14) of his *History of Rome* he says that comparative philology can recover evidence about the social structure of prehistoric Italy 'as in an archive'. His words have reminded some scholars of the emphasis on the superiority of archival over narrative sources which is associated with the great historian Leopold von Ranke (1795–1886), who argued that the accounts of early modern history he himself had uncovered in archives at Venice and elsewhere between 1827 and 1837 were much more objective and reliable than those composed by contemporary historians. But in fact there is little evidence that Mommsen was influenced by Ranke: rather, Mommsen's interest in documents arose from another source, his wish as a Roman lawyer to base his judgements on documentary evidence. When Mommsen used the religious festivals of a later period as evidence for archaic Rome, he argued that they served as documents, 'eine Urkunde' (bk. 1 ch. 12 = vol. I, p. 161).

It was therefore much less surprising than it has seemed to some that at a time when he was producing these detailed scholarly studies, Mommsen should also have accepted a proposal from the Leipzig publishers Karl Reimer and Salomon Hirzel to write a two-volume Roman history aimed at a wide and non-specialist readership. Of course such a history represented a rival claim on Mommsen's time, but on the other hand collecting documentary evidence was more than an end in itself; it formed the basis for analysis and judgement. In any case Mommsen's *Corpus* project had not at this stage overcome the resistance of Zumpt, and as always Mommsen felt that he needed more money.

Reimer and Hirzel had heard Mommsen give a public lecture on agrarian reform in the period of the Gracchi. They realized that Mommsen would be able to produce a work that combined knowledge of the latest evidence recovered from antiquity with the ability to relate that evidence to the current concerns of a liberal German readership. They explicitly drew his attention to the liberal *History of England* written by T. B. Macaulay (1800–59), the first two volumes of which had just appeared in 1848. There can be no question that some of the themes Mommsen pursued in his *History of Rome* – and later - were inspired by Macaulay. Macaulay's programmatic statement that 'It will be my endeavour to relate the history of the people as well as the history of the government . . . to portray the manners of successive generations' (vol. I p. 3) could equally have been written by Mommsen. Mommsen's unremitting hostility to ancient slavery and its effect on Roman society can be traced back to Macaulay, whose father Zachary (1768–1838) had been a leading opponent of the slave-trade. It is less clear whether Macaulay also influenced key elements in Mommsen's interpretation of the Roman constitution, but he certainly expressed similar views: 'The Roman Emperors were Republican magistrates, named by the Senate. None of them pretended to rule by right of birth' (vol. I p. 70).

Mommsen had to pay the price for his active support of the liberal cause. In 1851 he was dismissed from his post at Leipzig for having helped to organize a rally of the liberal-constitutionalist 'Deutscher Verein' on 4 May 1849 which had been taken over by a more radical revolutionary group. In the following spring, he was appointed Professor of Roman Law by the liberal Swiss canton of Zurich; but he was not happy in Zurich, and as an outsider his experience of the closed merchant-aristocracy that ruled the city-state, liberal though their principles may have been, was no more positive than that of Hamburg earlier. He did his best to conform to Swiss national pride, with a volume on Switzerland under the Romans (*Die Schweiz in römischer Zeit*, 1853) and a corpus of all 350 Latin inscriptions found in Switzerland (*Inscriptiones Confoederationis Helveticae Latinae*, 1854). He also married Marie Reimer, the daughter of his Leipzig publisher, who was to bear him sixteen children.

The three volumes of the *History of Rome* were largely written during Mommsen's two years in Zurich. Volume I appeared in June 1854, volume II in December 1855 and volume III in the following spring. By then, the Mommsens had left Zurich. In 1854, he had been appointed to a Chair in Roman Law at Breslau in Prussia; in the same year he achieved his aim of being put in charge of editing all known Latin inscriptions by the Berlin Academy of Sciences, though arguments about funding continued for several years thereafter. In spring 1858 he was able to move to Berlin to devote himself to work on the *Corpus*.

The Academy was to be the centre of his activities for the rest of his life, though from 1861 he also held a professorship at the University of Berlin (invitations to Chairs elsewhere, including Strasburg – refounded as a German prestige university in 1871 – were declined because Mommsen needed to be at the centre of power). From 1873 to 1895, he was the Academy's Permanent Secretary. The full story of how Mommsen exercised his patronage as Secretary of the Academy remains to be told; but it is clear that he gave his support to a wide range of historical projects, including the *Monumenta Germaniae Historica*, a vast series of sources for medieval German history. He himself edited several volumes of late antique texts, including Jordanes and Cassiodorus, illustrating what was then known as the 'Age of Migrations' for the *MGH* series of the earliest authors, *Auctores Antiquissimi*. In the case of both *MGH* and *CIL*, the speed of production (and sometimes the use of inexperienced graduate assistants) resulted in mis-understandings and errors of transcription; unfortunately the authority enjoyed by both projects means that some of these errors remain unquestioned even today. Another project which Mommsen supported, or more precisely seized control of, as Secretary of the Academy was the study of the Roman *limes* in south-western Germany; by setting up a *Reichslimesforschungskommission* under Friedrich Schmidt-Ott (1860–1956) in 1892, Mommsen effectively took the study of the *limes* out of the hands of local South German archaeologists and transferred it to Berlin. He was also in a position to control appointments in ancient history at Prussian universities through the advice he gave the Prussian government councillor responsible for university appointments (Leiter der I. Unterrichtsabteilung), Friedrich Althoff (1839–1908). As other parts of Germany increasingly came under Prussian influence, Mommsen could arrange for his own pupils to be given university appointments throughout Germany, and even in German-speaking universities in all parts of the Austro-Hungarian Empire. Roman historians who disagreed with Mommsen, like Karl Julius Beloch (1854–1929), had to emigrate.

If Mommsen had no more reservations about the hegemony of Prussia over the Germany that emerged from the Franco-Prussian War of 1870 than he had over Roman hegemony over Italy, he was not so happy about its federal constitution. His analysis of the Roman constitution, the *Römisches Staatsrecht* which appeared between 1871 and 1888, reflects his strong belief in the undivided sovereignty which he saw instantiated in the Roman concept of *imperium*. The order he follows in the *Staatsrecht* is revealing: in volume I he describes the essential powers of Roman magistracy ('Wesen der Magistratur') in general, then in volume II he describes how that 'Wesen' manifested itself, or was exemplified, in particular magistracies. It is striking that the institutions which we would have expected a liberal like Mommsen to be particularly sympathetic to, the Senate and the popular assemblies, are dealt with much more cursorily, and that Mommsen denies them independent authority: their function is rather to assist the work of the magistrates by giving assent and legitimacy to their actions. The emphasis is on *imperium*, undivided sovereignty. His own political experiences in 1848 and since had persuaded Mommsen that sovereignty had to be indivisible, that institutions which might reflect conflicts of interest between social classes or geographical regions would result at best in inaction and at worst in disaster. The history of the Roman Republic showed what a state could achieve if its sovereignty was undivided, but exercised by a plurality of magistrates.

What then of Rome under the emperors? Mommsen did not see his liberal, constitutional ideal state as excluding rule by one man, as is shown by his admiration for Napoleon III as a new Caesar in the 1850s. Rather, the problem for Mommsen was that history was essentially an account of the development of constitutional law, but from Augustus on politics at Rome were rarely expressed in terms of arguments about constitutional issues. The Hensels' transcripts of Mommsen's lectures on the imperial period illustrate how important constitutional issues continued to be for Mommsen. Of course the question of the geographical limits of the German *Kaiserreich* had been solved in 1870/1, with the exclusion of Austria; but there were still unanswered questions about the relationship between the centre and the provinces. The political concerns of the Wilhelmine age are apparent in Mommsen's lectures, as one would expect from someone who was a member of the Prussian parliament from 1873 to 1879 and of the *Reichstag* from 1881 to 1884: they include the role of (the German) language as a way of assimilating (Polish-speaking) allophones into a newly unified state (MH.II, 3f. and 15), the introduction of a common currency in 1873 (MH.II, 21) and most strikingly the danger of an unsuitable monarch in a system of hereditary succession. Mommsen's private comments about Kaiser Wilhelm II show what he thought of him, and the Kaiser's support of colonial adventures, alienation of Britain and responsibility for the Great War was to confirm that Mommsen's anxieties were not exaggerated.

But these contemporary political issues could not provide Mommsen with a theme to enable him to integrate all the things he had to say about the Roman world under the emperors, as they had thirty years earlier for the history of the Republic. The imperial period simply did not contain enough 'constitutional history'. Very considerable sections of the Hensel transcripts consist of analyses of particular problems which are effectively separate digressions – on coinage, tax reforms, the inscriptions of Lyon, the *limes*. In one respect, these analyses illustrate how much new material had been brought to light in the previous thirty years, largely as a result of Mommsen's own research. But they also show how the sheer quantity of new material had led to a much greater level of specialization than was necessary in the mid-century. It has been pointed out that Mommsen's view of modern scholarship as highly co-ordinated team-work meant that his pupils were world experts in limited areas, but found it hard to synthesize. The same seems to have applied to Mommsen himself: in the thirty years since he had written volumes I–III of the *History of Rome*, he and his followers had produced so much detailed research that he was no longer in a position to produce a coherent account. After he had retired both from parliamentary politics and from some of his university duties in 1883, Mommsen had more time to return to the *History of Rome*. Volume V, on the Roman provinces, appeared in 1885, and here the emphasis on detailed research as opposed to an all-embracing story-line was not such a drawback; but the Hensel transcripts show how far Mommsen was from being able to combine (e.g.) domestic politics and the story of military activity in frontier regions. That the shortcomings of Mommsen's account of imperial history were recognized by Mommsen himself has been mentioned above; and Wilamowitz refused to have the text published posthumously, as unworthy of his father-in-law. Only in recent years has the fashion for 'deconstructing' narratives found this fragmentary nature of Mommsen's account of Rome under the emperors particularly interesting: the 1990s were an appropriate time for the *Kaisergeschichte* to be rediscovered.

My thanks are due to Sue Grice for preparing maps 1 and 3; to Professor Jürgen Malitz for providing me with technical facilities during my stay at Eichstätt as Otto von Freising Professor during the Winter Semester of 1994/5; to Almut Baier, Costas Mantas and Joachim Mathieu for their help with checking the Index; to the copy-editor, Nigel Hope; to Michael Pucci, for assisting with proof-reading; and to my wife Margaret Hunt for help with the English. This English version was prepared under the auspices of the Centre for the Study of the Reception of Classical Antiquity of the University of Bristol.

Thomas Wiedemann
August 1995

ABBREVIATIONS AND BIBLIOGRAPHY

This bibliography contains only works used repeatedly, and abbreviated in the Notes. Others appear *suo loco* only. Standard abbreviations are used for classical authors and texts: the reader may consult e.g. the *Oxford Classical Dictionary* for these.

AA: *Auctores Antiquissimi*.
AE: *L'Année Epigraphique*, 1928–.
AF: Berlin Academy Fragment of Mommsen for *History of Rome* IV.
AG: Göttingen Anonymous; see p. 20, lecture note 2.
ANRW: *Aufstieg und Niedergang der römischen Welt*, ed. Temporini, H. and Haase, W. 1972–.
a.u.c.: *ab urbe condita*.
AW: Wickert's Anonymous, quoted by MS pages; see p. 21, lecture note 10.
Bammel, E., 'Judentum, Christentum und Heidentum. Julius Wellhausens Briefe an Theodor Mommsen 1881–1902', *Zeitschrift für Kirchengeschichte* 80, 1969, pp. 221ff.
Bardt, C., *Theodor Mommsen*, 1903.
Bengtson, H., 'Theodor Mommsen', *Die Welt als Geschichte* 15, 1955, pp. 87ff.
—— *Grundriss der römischen Geschichte mit Quellenkunde, 1: Kaiserzeit bis 284 n. Chr.*, 1967.
BJ: *Bonner Jahrbücher* 1895–.
Bleicken, J., *Verfassungs– und Sozialgeschichte des römischen Kaiserreiches*, 1978.
BMC: British Museum Catalogue = *A Catalogue of Greek Coins in the British Museum*, 1873–.
Boehlich, W. (ed.), *Der Berliner Antisemitismusstreit*, 1965.
Bolognini, G., 'Teodoro Mommsen', *Archivio Storico Italiano*, V serie 33, 1904, pp. 253ff.
Bringmann, K., 'Zur Beurteilung der römischen Kaiserzeit in der deutschen Historiographie des 19. Jahrhunderts', in E. Gabba and K. Christ (eds), *L'impero Romano fra storia generale e storia locale*, 1991, pp. 57ff.
Burckhardt, J., *Die Zeit Constantins des Grossen*, 1853/80.
—— *Briefe an seinen Freund Friedrich von Preen 1864-1893*, 1922.
—— *Briefe III*, 1955.
Busche, J., 'Mommsens Darstellung der Kaiserzeit', *Frankfurter Allgemeine Zeitung*, 25 September 1982.
Butler, N. M., *Across the Busy Years: Recollections and Reflections* I, 1939.
Calder III, W. M. (ed.) 'U. von Wilamowitz, Selected Correspondence 1869-1931', *Antiqua* 23, 1983.
—— and Schlesier, R., 'Wilamowitz on Mommsen's "Kaisergeschichte"', *Quaderni di storia* 21, 1985, pp. 161ff.
CD: *De civitate Dei*, Augustine.
Chastagnol, A., *La Préfecture urbaine à Rome sous le Bas-Empires*, 1960.
Christ, K., *Von Gibbon zu Rostovtzeff. Leben und Werk führender Althistoriker der Neuzeit*, 1972.
—— 'Theodor Mommsen und die "Römische Geschichte"', in id. (ed.), *Theodor Mommsen. Römische*

Geschichte VIII, 1976, pp. 7ff.

—— *Krise und Untergang der römischen Republik*, 1979, 2nd ed. 1984.

—— *Römische Geschichte und deutsche Geschichtswissenschaft*, 1982.

—— '"... die schwere Ungerechtigkeit gegen Augustus". Augustus, Mommsen und Wilamowitz', in: *Tria Corda I* (Arnaldo Momigliano memorial edition), 1983, pp. 89ff.

—— *Geschichte der römischen Kaiserzeit*, 1988.

Chron. Min.: *Chronica Minora in Auctores Antiquissimi (AA)* of *Monumenta Germaniae Historica (MG)*: *Chron. Min.I*: *AA IX*, 1892; *Chron. Min.II*: *AA XI*, 1894; *Chron. Min.III*: *AA XIII*, 1898.

CIC: *Corpus Iuris Civilis*, ed. Krüger, P., Mommsen, T., Schoell, R., 1894–.

CIL: *Corpus Inscriptionum Latinarum*, 1863–.

Coarelli, F., *Guida archeologica di Roma*, 1974.

Collingwood, R.G., *The Idea of History*, 1946/67.

Croke, B., 'Mommsen and Byzantium', *Philologus* 129, 1985, pp. 274ff.

—— 'Mommsen and Gibbon', *Quaderni di storia*, 32, 1990, pp. 47ff.

—— 'Theodor Mommsen and the Later Roman Empire', *Chiron* 20, 1990, pp. 159ff.

CRR: H.A. Grueber, *Coins of the Roman Republic in the British Museum*, 1910.

C.Th.: *Codex Theodosianus*, ed. Krüger, P., Meyer, P. M., Mommsen, T., 1904–5.

Curtius, L., *Deutsche und antike Welt – Lebenserinnerungen*, 1950.

Demandt, A., 'Alte Geschichte an der Berliner Universität 1810-1960', in: *Berlin und die Antike, Aufsätze*, 1979, pp. 67ff.

—— 'Mommsens ungeschriebene Kaisergeschichte', *Jahrbuch der Berliner wissenschaftlichen Gesellschaft* 1983, pp. 147ff.

—— *Der Fall Roms. Die Auflösung des römischen Reiches im Urteil der Nachwelt*, 1984.

—— 'Die Hensel-Nachschriften zu Mommsens Kaiserzeit-Vorlesung', *Gymnasium* 93, 1986, pp. 497ff.

—— *Die Spätantike, Romische Geschichte von Dioletian bis Justinian (284–565)*. Handbuch der Altertumswissenschaft III.6. 1989.

—— 'Theodor Mommsen', in Briggs, W. W., and Calder, W. M. (eds), *Classical Scholarship: A Bibliographical Encyclopedia*, 1990, pp. 285ff.

—— 'Alte Geschichte in Berlin 1810-1960', in Hansen, R. and Ribbe, W. (eds), *Geschichtswissenschaft in Berlin im 19. und 20. Jahrhundert*, 1992, pp. 149ff.

Denecke, L. and Brandis, T., *Die Nachlässe in den Bibliotheken der Bundesrepublik Deutschland*, 2nd ed. 1981.

Dessau, H., *Geschichte der römischen Kaiserzeit*, I/II, 1924/30.

Dig.: Justinian's *Digest*, in *CIC*, vol. I.

Dilthey, W., *Briefwechsel zwischen Wilhelm Dilthey und dem Grafen Torck von Wartenburg 1877-1897*, 1923.

Dittenberger: see *OGIS*.

Domaszewski, A. von, *Geschichte der römischen Kaiser*, I/II, 1909.

Ehrenberg, V., 'Theodor Mommsens Kolleg über römische Kaisergeschichte', *Heidelberger Jahrbücher* 4, 1960, pp. 94ff.

—— *Polis und Imperium*, 1965.

Ferrero, G. 'Warum blieb Mommsens römische Geschichte ein Torso?' *Berliner Tagesblatt*, 30 October 1909, evening ed.

Fest, J., 'Theodor Mommsen. Zwei Wege zur Geschichte', *Frankfurter Allgemeine Zeitung*, 31 July 1982.

—— *Wege zur Geschichte. Über Theodor Mommsen, Jacob Burckhardt und Golo Mann*, 1992.

FGrH: Jacoby, F. (ed.), *Die Fragmente der griechischen Historiker*, 1923–.

FHG: *Fragmenta Historicorum Graecorum* ed. Müller, C., 1853–84.

FIRA: *Fontes Iuris Romani Antejustiniani*, Riccobono, S. et al. (eds), 1941–.

Fisher, H. A. L., *James Bryce* II, 1927.

Fowler, W. W., 'Theodor Mommsen: His Life and Work' (1909), in id., *Roman Essays and Interpretations*, 1920, pp. 250ff.

Fueter, E. *Geschichte der neueren Historiographie*, 1911.

Galsterer, H., 'Theodor Mommsen', in: M. Erbe (ed.), *Berliner Lebensbilder: Geisteswissenschaftler*, 1989, pp. 175ff.

Glockner H., *Paul Hensel, der Sokrates von Erlangen*, 1972.

Goldammer, P. (ed.), *Der Briefwechsel zwischen Theodor Storm und Gottfried Keller*, 2nd ed. 1967.

Gollwitzer, H., 'Der Cäsarismus Napoleons III. im Widerhall der öffentlichen Meinung Deutschlands', *Historische Zeitschrift* 173, 1952, pp. 23ff.

Gooch, G. P. , *History and Historians in the Nineteenth Century*, 1913/59.

Grant, M., 'Ein grosser deutscher Historiker. Zu Th. Mommsen's 50. Todestag', *Englische Rundschau* 6, 1954, pp. 84ff.

Harnack, A., *Geschichte der königlich-preussischen Akademie der Wissenschaften zu Berlin*, 1900; I Darstellung (quoted by page no.); II Urkunden und Aktenstücke (quoted by no.).

Hartmann, L. M., *Der Untergang der antiken Welt*, 1903/10.

—— *Theodor Mommsen: Eine biographische Skizze*, 1908.

—— and Kromayer, J., *Römische Geschichte*, 1903/21.

(Haym, R.), *Ausegewählter Briefwechsel Rudolf Hayms*, ed. Rosenberg, H., 1930.

HE: *Historia Ecclesiastica*.

Hensel, P., *Sein Leben in Briefen*, ed. Hensel, E., 1947.

Hensel, S., *Ein Lebensbild aus Deutschlands Lehrjahren* (1903), ed. Hensel, P. , 2nd ed. 1904.

(Hensel, W.), *Preussische Bildnisse des 19. Jahrhunderts. Zeichnungen von Wilhelm Hensel* (exhibition catalogue of West Berlin National Gallery), Berlin 1981.

Heuss, A., *Theodor Mommsen und das 19. Jahrhundert*, 1956.

—— 'Theodor Mommsen über sich selbst. Zur Testamentsklausel', in *Antike und Abendland* 6, 1957, pp. 105ff.

—— *Römische Geschichte*, 1960.

—— 'Das spätantike römische Reich kein "Zwangsstaat"?', *Geschichte in Wissenschaft und Unterricht*,1986, pp. 603ff.

HF: *Historia Francorum, Gregory of Tours*.

Highet, G., *The Classical Tradition: Greek and Roman Influences on Western Literature*, 1949/67.

Hiller von Gaertringen, F. and D.: see Schwartz.

Hirschfeld, O., *Die kaiserlichen Verwaltungsbeamten bis auf Diocletian*, 1876/1905.

—— 'Theodor Mommsens römische Kaisergeschichte' (1885), in id.: *Kleine Schriften*, 1913, pp. 926ff.

—— 'Gedächtnisrede auf Theodor Mommsen' (1904), in: id., *Kleine Schriften* 1913, pp. 931ff.

HLL: Herzog, R., and Schmidt, P. L., *Handbuch der lateinischen Literatur der Antike*, 1989–.

ILS: *Inscriptiones Latinas Selectae*, ed. Dessau, H., 1892–.

Imelmann, T., 'Mommsen über Gibbon', *Der Tag*, 12 November 1909, illustrated entertainment supplement, 266, p. 4.

Instinsky, H. U., 'Theodor Mommsen und die *Römische Geschichte*', *Studium Generale* 7, 1954, pp. 439ff.

Irmscher, J., 'Theodor Mommsen - Gelehrter und Demokrat', *Hestiasis* (S. Calderone memorial issue), 1990, pp. 221ff.

Jones, A. H. M., *The Later Roman Empire* I–IV, 1964.

JRS: *Journal of Roman Studies*.

Kiepert, H., *Atlas Antiquus*, many editions.

Klement, A. von, 'Nachwort zu: Th. Mommsen, *Römische Geschichte* IV', 1877/1927/1954, pp. 41ff.

Kolb, F., *Diocletian und die Erste Tetrarchie*, 1987.

Kornemann, E., *Doppelprincipat und Reichsteilung im Imperium Romanum*, 1930.

—— *Römische Geschichte*, 2 vols, 1938/9.

Kuczynski, J., 'Theodor Mommsen. Porträt eines Gesellschaftswissenschaftlers', in: id., *Studien zu einer Geschichte der Gesellschaftswissenschaften* IX, 1978.

Lasky, M. J., 'Warum schrieb Mommsen nicht weiter?', *Der Monat* 2, 1950, pp. 62ff.

loc. cit.: loco citato.

Leo F., *Ausgewählte Schriften* I, ed. E. Fraenkel, 1960.

Lowenthal-Hensel, C., 'Wilhelm Hensel und sein zeichnerisches Werk', *Jahrbuch Stiftung Preussischer Kulturbesitz* 23, 1986, pp. 57ff.

Lülfing, H. (ed), *Gelehrten- und Schriftsteller-Nachlässe in den Bibliotheken der DDR*, I–III, 1959–71.

mag.mil.: *magister militum*.

Malitz, J., 'Nachlese zum Briefwechsel Mommsen–Wilamowitz', *Quaderni di storia* 17, 1983, pp. 123ff.

—— 'Theodor Mommsen und Wilamowitz', in W. M. Calder III et al., *Wilamowitz nach 50 Jahren*, 1985, pp. 31ff.

Marquardt, J., *Römische Staatsverwaltung*, 2nd ed. 1881–.

Mashkin, N. A. (ed.), 'Foreword' to Mommsen, T., *Römische Geschichte* V, 1949 (in Russian).

Mazzarino, S., *Antico, tardoantico ed èra costantiana* I, 1974, II 1980.

Die Mendelssohns in Berlin. Eine Familie und ihre Stadt (exhibition catalogue of the State Library in Berlin), 1984.

Meyer, E., *Caesars Monarchie und das Prinzipat des Pompeius*, 3rd ed. 1922.

MGH: *Monumenta Germaniae Historica*.

MH: Mommsen–Hensel, see Introduction, pp. 13ff.

MK: Mommsen–Krauseneck, see p. 20, lecture note 4.

Michaelis, A., *Geschichte des Deutschen Archäologischen Instituts 1829–1879*, 1879.

Momigliano, A., *Contributo alla storia degli studi classici*, 1955.

Mommsen, T., *Abriss des römischen Staatsrechts*, 1893.

—— *Römisches Strafrecht*, 1899 (abbr. to *Strafrecht*).

—— *Gesammelte Schriften*, ed. Hirschfeld, O., 1950– (abbr. to *Ges. Schr.*).

—— *Geschichte des römischen Münzwesens*, 1860 (abbr. to *Münzwesen*).

—— *Reden und Aufsätze*, 1905 (abbr. to *RA*).

—— *Römische Forschungen* I 1864; II 1879 (abbr. to *RF*).

—— *Römische Geschichte* I 1854; II 1855; III 1856; V 1885 or later (same pagination; abbr. to *RG*).

—— *Römische Geschichte* IV, 1877/1927/1954.

—— *Römisches Staatsrecht*, 3rd edn 1887–8. (abbr. to *Staatsrecht*)

MP: Mommsen–Pernice, see p. 21, lecture note 11.

ND: *Notitia Dignitatum*, ed. Seeck, O., 1876.

Neumann, K. J., 'Theodor Mommsen', *Historische Zeitschrift* 92, 1904, pp. 193ff.

Nietzsche, F., *Friedrich Nietzsches Briefe an Peter Gast*, ed. Gast, P., 1908.

Norden, E., Prefatory note to Mommsen, T., *Das Weltreich der Caesaren*, 1933, in: id., *Kleine Schriften zum klassischen Altertum*, 1966, pp. 651ff.

OGIS: *Orientis Graeci Inscriptiones Selectae* I/II, ed. Dittenberger, W., 1903/5.

Oncken, H., *Aus Rankes Frühzeit*, 1922.

PL: Migne, *Patrologia Latina*.

PLRE: Jones, A. H. M., Martindale, J. R., and Morris, J. (eds), *Prosopography of the Later Roman Empire* I 1971, II 1980.

RAC: Klausel, T. (ed.), *Reallexikon für Antike und Christentum*, 1950–.

RE: *Pauly-Wissowa Real-Encyclopädie der classischen Altertumswissenschaft*, 1893–.

RF: *Römische Forschungen*; see Mommsen.

RG: *Römische Geschichte*; see Mommsen.

RIC: Mattingly, H. and Sydenham, E. A. (eds), *Roman Imperial Coinage*, 1923–.

Riccobono, S. (ed.), *Acta Divi Augusti*, 1945.

Rickert, H., 'Paul Hensel', *Kant-Studien* 35, 1930, pp. 183ff.

Rink, B. and Witte, R., 'Einundzwanzig wiederaufgefundene Briefe Mommsens an Jahn', *Philologus* 127, 1983, pp. 262ff.

Rodenwaldt, G., *Archäologisches Institut des Deutschen Reiches 1829–1929*, 1929.

Sartori, F., 'Mommsen storico e politico', *Paideia* 16, 1961, pp. 3ff.

—— 'Di Teodoro Mommsen', *Paideia* 18, 1963, pp. 81ff.

Schmidt, L., *Die Westgermanen* I, 1938.

—— *Die Ostgermanen*, 1941.

Schmidt-Ott, F., *Erlebtes und Erstrebtes 1860–1950*, 1952.

Schmitthenner, W. (ed.), 'Augustus', *Wege der Forschung* 123, 1969.

Schöne, R., *Erinnerungen an Theodor Mommsen zum 30. November 1917*, ed. Hermann Schöne, 1923.

Schwartz, E. (ed.), *Mommsen und Wilamowitz. Briefwechsel 1872–1903*, 1935.

Seeck, O., *Geschichte des Untergangs der antiken Welt*, I–IV, 1895–.

—— *Regesten der Kaiser und Päpste 311–476*, 1919.

SHA: Scriptores Historiae Augustae.

SQAW: Schriften und Quellen der Alten Welt, ed. German Academy of Sciences, East Berlin, 1956–.

Srbik, H., Ritter von, *Geist und Geschichte vom Deutschen Humanismus bis zur Gegenwart* II, 1951/64.

s.v.: *sub voce*.

Syme, R., *The Roman Revolution*, 1939/60.

Taeger, F., *Charisma* II, 1959.

Teitge, H. E. (ed), *Theodor Storms Briefwechsel mit Theodor Mommsen*, 1966.

Timpe, D., 'Theodor Mommsen. Zur 80. Wiederkehr der Verleihung des Nobelpreises', *Nordfriesland* 18, 1984, pp. 50ff.

Toynbee, A. J., *A Study of History* I, 1934/48.

Treitschke, H. von, *Briefe* III 2 (1871–1896), 1920.

Usener, H. and Wilamowitz-Möllendorf, U. von, *Ein Briefwechsel 1870–1905*, Leipzig and Berlin 1934.

VC: Vita Constantini, Eusebius.

Verhandlungen über Fragen des höheren Unterrichts, 1900, Halle 1901.

VS: Vitae Sophistarum, Eunapius.

Weber, W., *Theodor Mommsen. Zum Gedächtnis seines 25. Todestages*, Stuttgart 1929.

—— 'Theodor Mommsen', in *Die Grossen Deutschen. Neue Deutsche Biographie* V, 1937, pp. 326ff.

Wenskus, R., *Stammesbildung und Verfassung*, 1961.

Wickert, L., 'Theodor Mommsen. Lebendige Gegenwart', address given in honour of the 50th anniversary of Mommsen's death, 1 November 1953, Berlin (Colloquium) 1954.

—— *Beiträge zur Geschichte des Deutschen Archäologischen Instituts 1879–1929*, 1979.

—— *Theodor Mommsen. Eine Biographie* I 1959; II 1964; III 1969; IV 1980.

Wilamowitz, U. von, 'Theodor Mommsen. Warum hat er den vierten Band der *Römischen Geschichte* nicht geschrieben?', *Internationale Monatsschrift für Wissenschaft, Kunst und Technik* 12, 1918, pp. 205ff., and *Kleine Schriften* VI, 1972, pp. 29ff.

—— *Geschichte der Philologie*, 1927/59.

—— *Erinnerungen 1848–1914*, 1928.

Wolfram, H., *Geschichte der Goten*, 1980.

Wucher, A., 'Mommsen als Kritiker der deutschen Nation', *Saeculum* 2, 1951, pp. 256ff.

—— 'Mommsens unvollendete römische Geschichte', *Saeculum* 4, 1953, pp. 414ff.

—— *Theodor Mommsen. Geschichtsschreibung und Politik*, 1968.

Yavetz, Z., *Julius Caesar and his Public Image*, 1983.

Zahn-Harnack, A. von, 'Mommsen und Harnack', *Die Neue Zeitung* 6, no. 81, 5 April 1950, p. 2.

THE BERLIN ACADEMY
FRAGMENT

The text which follows is Mommsen's manuscript draft for volume IV of his *History of Rome*, now in the archives of the Academy of Sciences in former East Berlin (Mommsen Legacy 47/1). Words abbreviated by Mommsen have been printed in full. Asterisks ** frame Mommsen's own marginal notes. Dots . . . indicate illegible or destroyed/lost words. Pointed brackets < > contain the editors' reconstructions of words by Mommsen which are missing, generally as a result of burning. Notes and italic text in pointed brackets are the editors'. Parentheses ( ) are Mommsen's own. Sections of text crossed out by the author have been omitted. Minor errors of syntax arising out of later insertions or erasures have been corrected. Because of the way in which the folded sheets have been opened up, the archive's page numbering does not accord with the order in which Mommsen wrote; it is that sequence which has been reconstructed here.

<p. 6 right>

Book 6
Consolidation of the Monarchy

Chapter 1
Pompeian rebellions and Conspiracy of the Aristocracy

The edifice which had been under construction for half a millennium lay in ruins. The Republican constitution had been replaced by a monarchy, government by a closed circle of notable families with rule by one bold commander, the civic order by military organization, and Senate-appointed governors by the adjutants of the new monarch. A new era began, not merely in political regulations and principles, but also in men's attitudes, in social patterns, and in literature and language. Hitherto, the churning whirlpool of the capital's ruling clique had drawn all vigour and talent towards itself, whether to obtain entry to the circle of lords and masters by trickery or force, or to change or overthrow the existing form of government; but with the abolition of the parliamentary regime political life as such came to an end. Ambition no longer had any purpose, since the crown can be considered such only by a fool or genius, not by men of talent, * while to be the minister of a ruler is the aspiration of the political parvenu <?> or scheme-r, but never of the truly free <?> man.* People lowered their aims and aspirations; they no longer sought public activity, but peace; not power and honour, but a tranquil and <sated> enjoyment of life; not that which men leave after them, but solely the present.

There is little that makes the picture of that age bearable, occasionally even agreeable, to the observer <p. 7 left>. Rulers and ruled alike grew complacent. There seemed to be virtually nothing to be gained by expanding frontiers; on the contrary, a feeling that the Empire had already outgrown itself prevailed throughout the nation, and the inclination was rather towards gradual retrenchment. Just as the rulers laid aside their arms, so, too, men of talent laid down their slates and pens. The sober pursuit of scholarship and literature did not lack genius, even less education, so much as inspiration: and the most inspired literary work dating from this epoch is a debauched romance.[1] * The attempt to advance civilization was abandoned: and it stagnated on the level it had attained at the onset of the era.

Yet with each succeeding generation, the sense contemporaries had of being mere imitators of superior generations grew ever more immediate. Keen . . . was the endeavour – and this was <the least> agreeable, but by far the most lasting trend of this epoch – to exploit, <to commercial>ize and popularize the products of earlier scholarship and education. This was the age in which Graeco-Roman civilization, as it had evolved up to that point in Rome and Italy, became the property of the entire Roman Empire. But its <creat>ive energy was spent, and * people contented themselves with a tolerable existence.

Instead of being the obligation of a citizen, the administration of the affairs of state became simply a means of obtaining a livelihood. Bureaucracy, that mortal enemy of civil liberty, was gradually brought into play – until, beneath the branches of that poisonous tree which cast their shadows so widely, first the final stirrings of liberty, and finally the last vestiges of a comfortable and worthwhile life, expired in the lowest as in the highest circles. Military rule lapsed into despotism, and the world indeed became a vale of tears, a swift escape from which was an enviable lot, and where all that mattered was to escape into a dream-world until the moment of true salvation, to escape into a paradise beyond the clouds, bedecked with all the fantastic colours that are born of longing.

<p. 7 right> If, then, this new age began with Caesar, it was nevertheless quite impossible to make a rapid transition from the old to the new state of affairs. The gulf separating the two ages was too wide, the turmoil accompanying the crisis too tempestuous. A remarkable, though explicable, phenomenon is that the creativity of the former age was much more alive in the generation that ushered

the new age in, chiefly in the person of Caesar himself, than the rigidity and complacency of the new. This makes it all the easier to understand why, during the first phase of the new epoch, there were frequent attempts to return to the past, and why traditional groupings which had been eliminated for good by the founding of the monarchy nevertheless attempted to renew the war against it through conspiracies and rebellions. If such efforts came solely from the aristocracy, while democratic forces willingly and unconditionally submitted to the new leadership, this can be explained by the simple fact that democracy, as understood at Rome, was none other than an attempt to replace a parliamentary with a demagogical regime. Consequently the autocracy of the Roman Pericles fulfilled its aims entirely, in so far as it could be theoretically conceptualized and politically feasible at all <?>. The idea that the parliamentarianism of aristocratic coteries, as expressed in the Roman Senate, could be replaced with some other system of parliamentary rule, never occurred to Roman democrats. Nor could it, since the economic development of the country <p. 6 left> had destroyed the middle classes, reducing the choice to one between a regime of the upper classes and a regime of the proletariat, the latter being represented by the urban *plebs* and by the military. On the other hand the *nobili* of Rome, and to some extent the major banking circles who had been hard hit by Caesar's administrative reforms, had no intention of taking the outcome of Pharsalus and Thapsus lying down. Although their leaders, the Lentuli, Domitii, Marcelli and above all Cato, had fallen together in the civil war, or else had finally left the political arena, the bulk of the aristocracy, in particular the younger generation, had been spared through the clemency of the victor, and secretly nurtured hopes for a complete restoration.

Added to this turmoil was another ingredient for future civil crises. Where there are no political challengers to the development of a monarchical system, hereditary succession becomes inevitable. Ever since they had first been called to life by C. Gracchus, the architects of Roman demagogy had instinctively perpetuated themselves as potential monarchs through their emphasis on heredity, for which the story of the Gracchi and of Marius (even after the death of Caesar an imposter appeared claiming to be Marius' son * Liv. <epit.> 116)* showed sufficient proof; so that the death of Pompey by no means spelled the end of the Pompeian party. For <?> his sons Gnaeus and Sextus immediately and openly presented themselves as the heirs to his hopes and aspirations. Despite its victories over the constitutional party and over Pompey the Great, therefore, the new monarchy was forced to confront the dangers inherent in this fresh <?> campaign <on two fronts> – against the supporters of the old regime on the one hand, and <the personal supporters of the Pompeians> on the other.

<p. 8 right> Military insurrections marked the beginning. The sheer magnitude of the Empire, which required relatively meagre military forces to be spread

out over an area extending from the Atlantic Ocean to the Euphrates, made such insurrections generally difficult to avert; and the vast number of veteran soldiers and officers who had served under Pompey during his career of more than thirty years as a general and who supported him enthusiastically, as an officer as capable of leading a division as he was in his capacity as commander-in-chief, made attempts of this kind practically inevitable. This was exacerbated by the fact that Caesar, with his customary self-assurance <?>, had contented himself with disbanding the legions which had served under Pompey, whereas of the less battle-seasoned ones, two in nearer Spain and several of the Pharsalian legions in the East were kept in more or less the same formations.

And so the first attempted insurrections indeed broke out in connection with these legions, even before Caesar had occupied the last province still in the hands of the constitutional party after the Battle of Thapsus. * Dio 47,26.27; App. <civ.> 3,77;4,58; Liv. <epit.> 114; Jo. <i.e. Jos.ant.> 14,11; bJ <i.e. *bellum Judaicum*> 1,10; <Cic.> *pro Deiot*. 9,25 * When, in the first months of 708 <46 BC>, wildly exaggerated rumours about Caesar's predicament in Africa, dangerous as it indeed was, reached the East, Q. Caecilius Bassus, a former officer under Pompey then lying low <p. 9 left> in Tyre, exploited the situation. Producing a forged letter from Scipio, commander-in-chief in Africa, purporting to report the defeat and death of Caesar and the appointment of Bassus as legitimate governor of Syria on Scipio's behalf, he first took control of the city of Tyre, and was soon able to persuade most of the soldiers in the sole legion stationed in Syria to join him. * only 1 legion: <Cic.> *ad fam*. 12,11; 12; App. <*Civ.*> 3,77 (1 additional legion <?>) two Strab. 16,752; several? *b. Alex*. 66 *

Sextus Caesar, the governor of Syria appointed by Caesar, was a frivolous young individual with nothing to recommend him beyond the fact that his father was a cousin of Caesar. Unable to respond, he was slain by his own men. Even after learning of the victory at Thapsus, however, Bassus did not lose heart * Strab. 16,752 *. He cultivated a close relationship with the tribes of Mt Libanus and of the Syrian desert, with Ptolemy, the son of Mennaeus, ruler of Chalcis by Libanus, with the Arab sheikhs Iamblichus of Emesa, Alchaedamnus in the eastern desert and others, made an alliance with the Parthians, and then entrenched himself at Apamaea on the upper Orontes, where his oriental allies protected his rear * and where he could be reduced neither by force nor famine, given the incomparable location of the town on an exceptionally fertile, easily defensible peninsula of the Orontes. * He resolutely awaited attack, and when Caesar's new governor C. Antistius Vetus appeared, he took shelter in his stronghold and held out until Pacorus, son of the Parthian king, appeared, * <Cic.> *ad. Att*. 14,9 * and forced Caesar's commander to lift the siege with heavy losses (December 709 = 45 BC). Caesar felt compelled to send a strong force of three legions against him under C. Statius Murcus. But he, too, exerted himself in vain, and even after he had summoned his comrade in Pontus, Q. Marcius Crispus, to his assistance, Bassus's resistance to their combined force of six legions continued unabated.

<p. 9 right> The state of affairs in southern Spain was even more grave * <Cic.> ad fam. 12, 18,1 * where it was not just an obscure officer, who was not even of senatorial rank, but Pompey's two sons and the war-seasoned Labienus who had put themselves at the head of the insurrection. Here, too, it was not the military aristocracy who fomented the conspiracy, but a respectable provincial, the Cordoban T. Quinctius Scapula. * b. Hisp. 33; <Cic.ad> fam. 9,13; Dio 43, 29 (cf. Annius Scapula, b.Alex. 55) * Not without reason, the two legions and the township which had rebelled against Caesar in 706 (48 BC) feared that their punishment had merely been deferred; the Pompeian conspiracies among the army that had already led to a renewed, if only temporary, uprising in favour of the former general, had only been appeased, not suppressed. During the course of the year 707 (47 BC) the conspirators established contact with the government at Utica and demanded that one of their former generals, Afranius or Petraeus, be sent to Spain * Liv. <epit.> 113 *; since both declined, they chose Pompey's elder son instead.

Gnaeus Pompeius was then around 30 years old and had commanded the Egyptian squadron with distinction in the previous civil war; he was, incidentally, also an uncouth, ill-mannered man * <Cic.> ad.fam. 15,19 *, who attributed earlier defeats to his side's excessive forbearance and was now eager to seize the opportunity to exercise what he called 'energy' in the unfortunate province. In the meantime, however, he was delayed for some considerable time on the Balearic Islands, partly by the siege of Ebusus * <Cic.> ad. Att. 12,2 *, and partly by illness. Since, following the catastrophe of Thapsus (6 April 708 = 46 BC), Caesar had meanwhile sent the fleet from Sardinia to Spain under C. Didius (June 708) to put down the unrest there * Dio 43,28; b.Afr. fin.<98>*, the conspirators decided to strike without waiting for Pompey's arrival.

<p. 8 left> The two former Pompeian legions joined <?> them, but the equestrians T. Scapula and Q. Aponius assumed supreme command. Trebonius, Caesar's governor in nearer Spain, was forced to leave his province with the remaining troops * date. <= for the date, cf.}: bell.> Hisp.,1 *, and when shortly afterwards Cn. Pompeius landed near <sc New> Carthage in nearer Spain and laid siege to the city, Baetica * <Coins> Riccio, Pomp. 12,15[2] * greeted the new commander-in-chief already fully armed. Those who had escaped the African catastrophe made their way there: Labienus, Attius Varus, Pompey's second son Sextus, <and> Arabio, son of Massinissa the chieftain of Cirta * cf. Dio 43,26;[3]* Q. Fabius Maximus and Q. Pedius, sent to Spain with an army by Caesar to suppress the rebellion, found themselves fully occupied with the defence of nearer Spain, and had to abandon any offensive action. Equipment <i.e. for the Pompeians> was vigorously and remorselessly demanded voluntarily or by force,

and slaves fit for military service were first manumitted and then enlisted. Four legions – the two Varronian ones, one formed from the conspirators from the further province and one from the remnants of the African army * <bell.> Hisp. 7;34 * – were reliable and accustomed to arms, while another, levied from natives from the province or former slaves, was impressive in terms of numbers. * Some three thousand men of equestrian rank were numbered among the army of insurgents, some Roman, some provincial (<b.> Hisp. 31). A fleet was also raised, under the command of Varus.*

In the late autumn of 708 <46 BC> – the year of 445 days – Caesar felt compelled to travel to Spain in person to stem the ever-swelling tide. His arrival in camp at Obulco (Porcuna, between Cordoba and Jaen) * Strabo 3,160 * and a successful naval action against Pompeius' fleet by Didius at Carteia (in the Bay of Gibraltar) * <? outline map > 2,1,346 *, kept Pompeius to the inland areas of Baetica. Caesar marched directly on the capital of <p. 10 right> Baetica, Corduba, where Sextus Pompeius was commander-in-chief, forcing the enemy to raise their siege of Ulia (Montemayor, between Corboba and Antequera) when they had almost achieved their objective. But Pompey refused to give Caesar the battle he wanted. In order to force one, Caesar attacked the town of Ategua under the noses of the enemy army, taking it only after extremely stiff resistance (10 July 709 = 45 BC). The morale, especially of the provincials, declined; Pompeius' acts of terror – mass executions of Caesar's supporters in those towns threatened by him, and draconian penalties against those who deserted or switched sides * (he relied on the Lusitanian barbarians against the Romans and provincials) Val. Max. 9,2,4 * – encouraged rather than prevented this <i.e. desertion>. He <i.e. Pompeius> gradually lost territory through a slow retreat. He had already been pushed back from the Baetis Valley to the heights of the Sierra Nevada; when at last even Urso (Osuna) was threatened by the enemy, he decided to march out from Munda (Monda, 6 leagues from Malaga) and to offer battle before daybreak on the far side of the town on the assumption that Caesar would be less likely to venture an attack against him with his strong position on a hill defended in front by a marshy brook, since Caesar's army was no longer what it had once been now that he had already celebrated his triumph and had discharged most of the veterans from the war in Gaul. The cavalry and the light-armed troops (most of whom had been levied in Africa), in which Caesar was infinitely superior, were not much use on this terrain, while the legions were no match for the enemy, either in numbers or in combat experience. Caesar had little more than mostly untested legions * <bell.> Hisp. 28 *. In spite of all this, however, Caesar dared to cross the marshy brook and launch an attack on the hill from the plain below. It was a terrible battle * the core of the Pompeian legions had . . . * In all of the fifty-two battles, Caesar . . . <rest burnt>.

<p. 11 left> The small troop of volunteers from the tenth legion who were

positioned on the right flank finally gained the upper hand. The opponents withdrew troops from their right wing in order to support their reeling left, and Caesar's superior cavalry took advantage of this to attack the enemies' weakened right[4] flank. The general himself paid with <i.e. risked> his own life; seeing his soldiers falter, he sent his horse away * Frontin. 2,8,13 *, and, shouting to his men whether they wanted to hand their old general over to that boy * Plut.*Caes.* 56 *, he threw himself at the enemy spears on foot, followed by his officers.

* An attack on the Pompeian camp carried out by Caesar's light-armed African troops contributed to his victory: particularly because the soldiers, when they saw the reinforcements sent to the camp withdraw, assumed that a general flight had begun. Flor.<4, 2>, Dio <43,38>. *Il est un moment dans les combats, ou la plus petite manoeuvre décide; c'est la goutte d'eau, qui fait le trop-plein.* <'There is a moment in combat when the smallest manoeuvre can be decisive; it is the drop of water that causes the overflow.'> Napoleon 204 *

Victory was at last won, but with casualties compared to which the losses at Pharsalus and Thapsus had been slight; over a thousand men were dead; as with every victory won by Caesar, this one too was decisive; the core of officers and men, among them Labienus and Varus, had fallen on the battlefield, while the resistance which Munda, into which the remnants of the army had fled, Corduba, which was set ablaze by deserters when the city surrendered, * Hispalis, where the Caesarian garrison, which had already been let into the city, was then attacked again and cut down by a band of Lusitanians *, and some other cities still dared to put up, was hopeless and soon crushed. Scapula took his own life in Cordoba. The two brothers escaped, however – Gnaeus severely injured from the battlefield, and Sextus from Corduba. They wandered around Spain as fugitives, the elder first deprived of his fleet by the fleet commander Didius and then, when he continued his flight on land with a Lusitanian escort, caught up with by Didius' men and killed at Lauro (not far from Valencia). The Lusitanians nevertheless managed to avenge themselves on the fleet commander soon afterwards, appearing in force to burn his ships and cut him and his men down. The younger brother led the life of a vagrant bandit in the Pyrenees. * App. <*civ.*> 2,105 * <pp. 11 right and 10 left are blank>.

A HISTORY OF ROME UNDER THE EMPERORS I FROM AUGUSTUS TO VESPASIAN

Winter Semester 1882/3 [MH.I]

From Paul Hensel's lecture notes, supplemented from Wickert's
Anonymous [AW]

1

AUGUSTUS (44 BC–AD 14)

A) THE CONSOLIDATION OF THE MONARCHY

[MH.I, 1] Only under the Emperors did the Roman state attain its final form.[1] While the frontiers remained essentially the same, it was not only those who were legally Romans whose numbers increased during the imperial age, but also, to a small extent, those who belonged to the Roman nation. The work of Hellenization and Romanization, of internal consolidation, was a major achievement of the imperial period. It does not make for pleasant scrutiny, however. One is obliged with infinite effort to wrest the historical material from the tangle of court and gutter writers. The moments of illumination are rare, the rule of great and noble men. It was a cheerless, sombre age.[2]

Caesar's African War marks the beginning of the monarchical regime and the end of the Republic. From then on the Roman monarchy was an accomplished fact. Although the last general of the Republic had fallen on the field of Pharsalus,[3] the campaign was not truly over until the African War, with Caesar's victory at Thapsus.[4] No one now remained standing in the way of the new monarchy. The role of the Republican party shifted from aiming to preserve the status quo to that of an opposition. Admittedly, the embers of resistance did flare up again; Caesar was obliged to set out for Spain in person to put down a rebellion in support of Sextus Pompey, and, at the time of his murder, he was intending to set out for Syria against Quintus Caecilius Bassus, who defied Caesar's rule and had gained the advantage over Sextus Julius, the governor.[5]

The Republican party had gained victory as a result of the murder in the Forum.[6] They stabbed Caesar in the heart, but achieved nothing more. It was a horrific act precisely because it was so absurd and futile. [MH.I, 2] It is odd that Brutus should have acted like an executioner, carrying out the sentence on a condemned man because of an oath taken by the citizens of Rome half a millennium earlier.[7] And, like an executioner, he then went home. No one stopped to think what would happen afterwards. Marcus Aemilius Lepidus had served the dictator Caesar as Master of the Horse. He stood at the gates of Rome with a legion which he was about to lead to Spain. Some of the conspirators did indeed want to seize control of both the city and Caesar's supporters, but Marcus Brutus objected. Despite being urban praetor, he did not even think he had the authority to summon the Senate; this was the business of Antony, then second consul.

One would have thought that along with the tyrant, his enactments would also have been overthrown. The matter was considered, but when deliberations began the proposal was opposed for characteristic reasons: all present and designated magistrates would have had to resign. That was unpalatable. The Senate thus resolved to uphold Caesar's personal decisions.[8]

This circumstance shaped the history of Rome in the period immediately following. In the subsequent war, all offices were filled according to Caesar's instructions. Lepidus, an utterly inept man, was only a triumvir because he was Caesar's Master of the Horse, charged with leading the army to Spain. Other appointments were filled in like manner. This altogether insignificant factor proved decisive; the sole exception was the young Caesar,[9] who alone gained enduring influence.

[MH.I, 3] There was no question of any firm plan, as became clear from the general truce. The assassins and the friends of the victim agreed with regard to the funeral that they would not take any hostile steps against one another. The first to take advantage of this inaction was Antony, who showed immense shrewdness in momentous and difficult times. He did indeed acquiesce in this phoney truce, abolishing the dictatorship once and for all with a pretence of Republicanism.[10] This represented Caesar's activities as unconstitutional. Nevertheless, Antony deftly followed the footsteps of his lord and master Caesar in order to seize power for himself. Lepidus went off to his province with his legion.

The decisive factor once again was who held the governorship of northern Italy (Gallia Cisalpina), since no army could be stationed in Italy proper. Cisalpine Gaul was de iure a province, but de facto inhabited by citizens, like the rest of Italy. The governor was Decimus Brutus, who was in a position to control Italy. He had been appointed to this office by Caesar – firm proof of his trust. When he saw that matters had turned against him in Rome, Decimus Brutus went to the province to the army. He had to be removed, and Antony acted exactly as Caesar had done. The Senate rejected his request; it was not unfavourable to the Legitimists.[11] Antony had the province transferred to himself anyway, by means of a plebiscite.[12] This was tantamount to a declaration of war. Antony set off to take control of northern Italy, obtaining troops for the purpose from the inconsistent Senate. These were the legions Caesar had intended for the Parthian campaign, stationed in Macedonia. On the orders of the Senate they returned to Brundisium.

At this point a rival stepped into Antony's path – Caesar's son, whom the Dictator had adopted. [MH.I, 4] It was no insignificant man who sought to follow in Caesar's footsteps. Octavian had nothing but Caesar's name, and was, after all, only a nephew through his sister.[13] He nevertheless had a sense of the power which lay in this name, and resolved to adopt not only the name itself, but also the power and authority that went with it. He acted with firm resolve. First he sought influence over the military, showing an accurate perception of the real circumstances. He sought to win Antony's troops away from him, and since Antony for his part disdained to bribe them, two of the four legions sold themselves to Octavian.[14] The latter also levied substantial numbers of his father's veterans in Campania and Etruria, enabling him to raise a major fighting force. He nevertheless still sought to negotiate with Antony, to attack the Legitimists. This failed because of Antony, who had no desire to share power. The result was what Cicero reckoned as the ninth civil war.[15]

The Legitimists were the weaker party. Decimus Brutus withdrew to Mutina (Modena),[16] where he was besieged by Antony, but held out with perseverance. Three governors with military authority had been among Caesar's assassins: the governors of northern Italy, Illyricum and Syria. They had gone to their provinces and mobilized. In the East they were successful: Greece was in their hands. But not so in the West: Sextus Pompey had left Spain and was now in command of a fleet. The remainder of the West was occupied by Caesarians, but accepted the status quo in Rome. Lucius Munatius Plancus, Asinius Pollio and Marcus Lepidus, for example, had not shown which side they would support.

As we have seen, during September Antony came out against this [MH.I, 5] status quo in Italy. To be on the safe side the Senate, led by the consuls for the following year, Pansa[17] and Hirtius, had ordered military preparations in Rome. Cicero wanted no arrangement with Antony.[18] With his *Philippics*, he sought to force the Senate to abandon its more or less constitutional stance: given the course of events at Mutina, he was not entirely unjustified. A government that was still seeking to reach terms at this late juncture was *eo ipso* lost. Having burned all his bridges, Cicero had every reason to urge the Senate to act. Hirtius was dispatched to northern Italy for armed intervention.

Ultimately, however, the Senate had to decide. Swayed by Cassius's defeat of Dolabella, and in the expectation that an arrangement would be reached with Lepidus and Plancus, but above all in the hope of winning over Octavian by confirming his usurped command, the Senate sided with the Legitimists. Their hope was to bring Octavian under the authority of the consul Hirtius as a propraetor, and in this way to deprive him of his troops.

It was a remarkable struggle.[19] Hirtius and Pansa, Caesar's officers and Octavian fought against Caesar's successor, Antony, and broke the siege of Mutina after a hard-fought battle in which Hirtius and Pansa both fell. Decimus Brutus thus now commanded the senatorial troops within Mutina, and Octavian those outside the gates of the town. Marcus Brutus had been about to intervene in Italy from Macedonia. It was short-sighted of him to abandon this plan: Octavian's fateful command would not have been necessary. After the victory the Senate acted without leadership.

Antony had fought with immense skill, but had been too much at a disadvantage, confronted by four hostile armies including some seasoned troops. [MH.I, 6] It was the fault of his rivals that he escaped:[20] partly because of Brutus's military ineptitude, partly because of Octavian's unreliability. The blame lay at the door of the Senate, however, for having appointed the proconsul Decimus Brutus to command both armies after the death of the consuls – constitutionally a correct move, but diplomatically a monstrous blunder. Octavian was in no mood to relinquish command, and some of the consul's troops deserted to him. The men, however, were not inclined to pursue Antony with fervour; it is remarkable how the common soldier wanted to see unity among all Caesarians.

Then there was the incompetence of Decimus Brutus. His army was unreliable and starving; taking over command of the consular army was difficult, so that it was some days before he was able to march in pursuit. Antony's line of retreat lay through all of northern Italy to Lepidus, his sole refuge.[21] Had it not been for the blunders and ill will of the rival commanders, Antony might have been crushed, for all his military prowess. Thus he was able to reach Lepidus,[22] by whom he was well received.

The latter now became a crucial factor. If he rejected Antony now, the latter would be lost. However, Lepidus and Plancus had called on the Senate to preserve the peace. An odd proposal, but it showed that Lepidus and Plancus were not necessarily behind the government after all. Similarly, Antony was received by his friend Lepidus, after all. A detachment of Lepidus's troops may already have fought for the Legitimists at Mutina.

For the time being, Italy was free of troops. Decimus Brutus confronted Lepidus – as Octavian should also have done, but did not, leaving instead for Rome. [MH.I, 7] There a replacement had not been found to fill the consulate – a serious mistake. An interim senator managed affairs as Interrex for five days at a time. Why? Perhaps Cicero had his eye on the consulate and was only looking for a general to share it with him.

Octavian sent a detachment of his men to Rome as citizens to take part in the comitial elections.[23] The Senate wanted to fight fire with fire, but had no troops, apart from a Hispanic legion. Their attempt to hold the city against the Caesarians was a dismal failure, since the troops they had mobilized fraternized. The Assembly's choice fell on Caesar Octavianus, who became consul before he was 20 years old.[24]

The restoration policy was now abandoned. It was proposed, and agreed, that Caesar's assassins be punished.[25] This was a major step, allowing Octavian and Antony to join forces, the latter after all an opponent of Decimus Brutus, one of Caesar's murderers. It was only a matter of coming to an arrangement, if one had not already been reached. As with all ancient history, we are unfortunately not able to look behind the scenes, but there can be no doubt that shortly after Mutina a tacit understanding was reached between Octavian, Antony and Lepidus. Plancus and Pollio soon joined them. The contract was not signed until 13 November,[26] which marks the personal ratification of an agreement that was already in existence.

In Italy the Caesarians ruled unopposed. The triumvirate that was now formed[27] was a copy of Caesar's at Lucca. It is called the second triumvirate – constitutionally an incorrect term, since there had never been *tresviri reipublicae constituendae* in the Republic, but factually correct. What had previously been no more than a [MH.I, 8] personal arrangement now stepped brutally into the light of day in constitutional form.

One of the first laws proposed by Antony[28] had been the abolition of the dictatorship (see MH.I, 3). The letter of this law was observed, but in practice a tripartite triumvirate now exercised the dictatorship, lawfully exempted from being bound by the laws. Although it had a constitutional status, it was one that placed itself above all laws. Decisions taken by the triumvirs had the validity of popular resolutions. Just as the people was incapable of doing wrong, so too was the triumvirate. Each triumvir exercised unlimited powers without consultation with the other two. Triumvirate and dictatorship are identical.

At first, their powers were limited to five years – long enough to exterminate the opposition, and short enough to subvert the state. It is important to consider the army. The officers were politicians, some of the men old veterans. In all the wars of that time, the soldier represented the angel of peace, especially in the Perusian, or 'mother-in-law' war. At that time the junior officer (*centurio*) played quite a different role than in our army. The junior officers wanted all Caesarians to be united; they did not want war. Quite rightly, there was a widespread sense that the days of the Republic were now over. In the main, however, the men were motivated by plain self-interest. Even in the Republic the aim of soldiers had been to lead the life of an established citizen after completing their military service. The new rulers did this to an even greater extent. Antony pledged each man 100, Octavian 500 *denarii*.[29] These promises could not be kept, however, unless victory was achieved by an arrangement between the commanders. [MH.I, 9] The course of events in the East made such an arrangement imperative. In the meantime, the power of promises had induced part of Decimus Brutus's army to desert to Antony, and part to Octavian.

This provides the key to the apparently arbitrary ruthlessness of the proscriptions.[30] How did this come about, when Italy had been almost entirely subdued? They amounted to arbitrary ruthlessness. To some extent these atrocities were conjured up by the precedent of Sulla.[31] Practical considerations must also have swayed the rulers, however.[32] It would be wrong to lay all the blame at the door of Antony. Nonetheless, he did have the upper hand over the other two at the time. For all that, one ought not to whitewash one of the triumvirs at the expense of the other two. From the moral standpoint it is irrelevant. From the historical standpoint it only matters who was preponderant. In this respect, Antony was clearly in control.

This follows from the distribution of roles. The triumvirs had forty-three legions: Octavian and Antony twenty each, Lepidus three. This shows that Lepidus was no more than an accessory: he was overlooked even when it came to ceremonial honours. Lepidus was to become consul in 42 BC and garrison Italy; Octavian was given Africa and Sicily, Antony Gaul and Spain.[33] Sicily was actually under the control of Sextus Pompey; there were still Republicans in Africa too. Gaul and Spain, however, were entirely in the hands of the Caesarians, and this was what gave Antony his power – his provinces were secure against enemies. He had the edge over the other two triumvirs, and hence also control of the proscriptions. Nevertheless, Octavian managed to have his equal status recognized; he was intending to fight an independent war. For the time being Antony conducted the war in the East. Northern Italy, his province, still reckoned as part of Gaul, was initially under threat.

Only now did Octavian's greatness show itself. A repetition of Sulla's proscriptions was expected after his victory, [MH.I, 10] but this did not occur, at least not on a large scale. Octavian did not want to disgrace the new monarchy with slaughter. He viewed the protection of persons and property as the cornerstone of monarchical power.

Antony was not a wicked or cruel man. He was a good friend, but a petty, rather small-minded character, lacking Octavian's[34] nobility of soul. Octavian probably had a different approach. He sought a hereditary monarchy, and therefore the proscriptions could not have been welcome to him. He may have acquiesced because he had to. In August, when Octavian had himself elected consul, he had control of Italy while Antony was in Gaul. During this period, Octavian acted only against Caesar's assassins: this much he owed his father. Nevertheless, the legal forms were observed during proceedings against the murderers. Even Sextus Pompey was included in the investigation: a natural enemy of the Julian dynasty with whom no settlement could be reached. Nothing more was done beyond this. Cicero was left unharmed and there was no talk of proscriptions. Anyone who wanted to leave was allowed to do so, and many departed for the East.

In November, after the triumvirate was formed, seventeen respected men, including Cicero, were summarily executed.[35] The triumvirs' aim was to use a reign of terror to quash every last shred of opposition. First, however, they needed funds to pay off the soldiers and arm for the new war in the East. The treasury had been exhausted by payments made to the citizens in accordance with Caesar's last will. Marcus Brutus and Cassius[36] behaved similarly in the East; Rhodes was plundered by Cassius, Lycia by Marcus Brutus.[37] It was the property of the

proscribed that the triumvirs really wanted: those who were killed were not
[MH.I, 11] dangerous men – all of those had gone East. Respected persons were
proscribed, although personal enmity was frequently the motive, and their wealth
filled the coffers. Of course it proved so difficult to realize the value of their estates
that the objective was only partly achieved. The soldiers were paid off and the fleet
made ready. It was necessary to find even more resources to pledge to the troops,
however: their hardest battle was still to be fought. The triumvirs wanted to win
the loyalty of each individual, and to do so on a large scale. To this end, they used
taxation and confiscation. Fortunes of over 100,000 sesterces were taxed at an
annual rate of 10 per cent. Eighteen Italian towns were selected, quite at random,
for the distribution of their entire landed property estate to the soldiers.
Absolutely no principle of either revenge or political interest has been identified
for the selection of these towns. It was purely a fiscal policy, albeit an effective one.

First, it was necessary to deal with Sextus Pompey, the last offshoot of the house
of Pompey. He, however, had neither the talent nor the desire to be a pretender,
and proved content with the prospect of having his inherited property restored to
him. He left Spain and took ship to Italy – this was during the war of Mutina.
In Italy, Octavian had him proscribed, making either a landing in Italy or a return
to Spain equally impossible. He therefore went to Sicily.[38]

The war that now broke out was an exact replica of Caesar's war against
Pompey. Whereas in the former case, however, all had been clarity and strategy, in
the latter case confusion reigned. Marcus Brutus had been responsible for bungling
an opportunity to invade northern Italy. [MH.I, 12] Nor was there a confrontation
in the following year (42 BC): triumvirs and Republicans alike were preoccupied
with their finances. But why did Marcus Brutus abandon Greece and go to Asia?
Perhaps because the greater force of troops was on the side of the Caesarians –
a factor which the Republicans sought to offset by shifting the theatre of war
as far east as possible. Their two generals disagreed: Cassius probably wanted
to retreat to Syria, since the small fleet of the Caesarians and Syria's remoteness
from Rome made it impossible for them to land there with their forty-three
legions. An offensive was out of the question: it would have entailed giving too
great an advantage to the enemy. What was still feasible was a daring invasion of
southern Italy from Sicily. Both were conceivable, but the Legitimists chose the
disadvantages of both strategies, the offensive and the defensive.

Meanwhile, Antony had landed in Greece with eight legions.[39] Shortly thereafter Brutus and Cassius crossed the Hellespont and confronted Antony at
Philippi. Meanwhile Octavian had attempted to establish himself in Sicily. He
feared his opponents might land there, but gave up this plan after a defeat, the
landing in Macedonia having rendered it superfluous. It was crucial for Octavian
to be present at the moment of decision: he crossed over without difficulty,
despite his adversaries' control of the sea.

In spite of this panic, the armies were fairly equally matched. [MH.I, 13] The Republicans were superior in cavalry, commanding 20,000 to the 11,000 of the Caesarians. The Legitimists were generally at an advantage, but there were signs of discontent in their camps at Philippi. The exiles acted with all the more zest, their army being in general highly reliable. The Republic had put down particularly deep roots in the municipalities. Cassius was very popular, if only on account of the Parthian War. The Republicans had mastery of the sea, and hence more secure supply routes and provisions. The Caesarians were unable to transport all their fighting forces to the battlefield. A huge back-up force, the Martian legion, was destroyed at sea by the Legitimists under Domitius Calvinus in the autumn of 42.[40]

The Caesarians were dependent on the impoverished hinterland for supplies for the approaching winter. A postponement of the battle was in the interests of the Republicans.

The first battle was inconclusive:[41] Brutus defeated Octavian, and Antony defeated Cassius, each taking the enemy's camp. The day by no means ended in a rout. Both armies regrouped, but a chance event brought about the death of Cassius. Believing that his comrade Brutus had likewise been defeated, he took his own life. This was a bitter blow. The only genuine commander on the Republican side was now dead. What they should have done was to wait it out: the Caesarians could not force a fight. But Brutus was no strategist. The mainstay of the army was lost with Cassius's death. The men wanted to come to grips with the enemy and Brutus lacked the authority to hold them back. The decisive battle was triggered by a minor provocation. Antony was victorious, he extricated Octavian, and his triumph was complete. The enemy force did not disband immediately, providing Brutus with a respite which he used to commit suicide. [MH.I, 14] The decisive conflict in the late autumn of 42 BC lasted altogether from four to six weeks, and sealed the fate of Rome.[42] The fleet, however, continued to fight on against all hope.[43]

The true victor was Antony. Octavian had merely taken part and had twice been defeated. This was certainly reflected in the arrangements that followed the battle. The institution of the Praetorian Guard was established in Rome.[44] Although there had previously been a guard placed around the person of the general (*cohors praetoria*), this had never consisted of more than 500 men, some of them his personal friends. The Praetorian Guard, in contrast, consisted of 10,000 men[45] who had a privileged status. It was formed at that time. The Caesarians had crossed the Adriatic with nineteen legions, which had by then swelled to forty. Of these, they retained eleven, the remainder being disbanded. Among them were veterans who requested permission to continue military service, and these now became the first Praetorians. The province of Cisalpine Gaul was abolished and incorporated into Italy.[46]

First the soldiers' claims had to be honoured. They were now able to present their IOUs for redemption, and received 5,000 *denarii* – centurions five times that amount. The pledge to give them land was honoured: the enemy treasure chest had been seized. Since this was still not sufficient, however, the provinces and Italy had to foot the bill. Something would also have to be done about Sextus. Octavian took on this task, while Antony went to the East. To what end? No clear answer emerges. [MH.I, 15] Perhaps Antony, ever the imitative general, was copying the strategy of the great Caesar. Whereas Caesar had had to pursue Pompey east, however, this move was folly once Brutus and Cassius were dead.

The expropriation of land for the soldiers in Italy was a most disagreeable affair.[47] It entailed massive injustices to the towns without satisfying the soldiers entirely. It was also necessary to gain control of the sea from the land. Strategy was further complicated by the fact that Sextus might easily starve Italy with a sea blockade.[48] Lacking foresight, Antony avoided confronting this issue. Not wanting to burden himself with the odium, he transferred it to Octavian, whom he looked on as his lieutenant, which under the present circumstances he was.

Antony took six, Octavian five legions. For Antony they were superfluous: perhaps, analogously to Caesar, he was already thinking of his Parthian War. The Parthians had entered into an alliance with the Republicans,[49] which provided a pretext for war.

Antony tied Octavian's hands in all directions. In the West, Antony had retained Gaul, where a number of his best troops (Plancus etc.) were stationed. Octavian had obtained Spain, but this was insufficient to offset Gaul. Africa was likewise divided between Octavian and Antony. As a result of Octavian's demands, Italy acquired its Alpine frontier, rendering northern Italy free of military garrisons, and removing it from the direct influence of Gaul.[50] The previous status of Northern Italy now shifted to Gallia Narbonensis, where the troops nearest to Rome were now stationed. [MH.I, 16] Whether anything had been planned for the East is unclear, but it is evident that Antony, with his six legions there, was in control. To this was now added the situation in Gaul in the West. In that year (41 BC) Antony's brother was in office as consul in Rome[51] – a crucial post, despite the existence of the triumvirate.

Octavian did not set foot in Italy until the beginning of 41 BC, to assume military command and pay off the soldiers.[52] Unfortunately, all too many facts are missing, but confiscations did take place and were even extended to include other towns. Veterans also encroached on land neighbouring that assigned to them, for example at Cremona and Mantua. This had a devastating effect on the Italian middle classes. Significantly, the four great poets, Horace, Virgil, Tibullus and Propertius,[53] were all quite directly affected by these confiscations – a telling piece of evidence. Some communities even allowed themselves to be besieged when the veterans arrived. And still the veterans were not satisfied. A shortage of cash and working capital was an embarrassment, and here Antony left Octavian in the lurch. Without cash, the veterans were unable to maintain their farms. The war against Sextus Pompey was proving onerous: cutting off supply routes to Italy he sought to establish a foothold in Southern Italy. Octavian was later to call this war a Slave War,[54] which is not entirely inaccurate. Slaves fled to Sicily in great numbers, and, significantly, freedmen formed the vanguard of Sextus Pompey's fleets.[55]

[MH.I, 17] Political intrigues in Italy were a further factor. Lucius Antonius and Fulvia, Antony's power-hungry wife, looked after Antony's interests in Italy.[56] It was intolerable to this woman, who dominated her brother-in-law, to see Octavian in command in Italy. This was exacerbated by another factor: jealousy. In the autumn of 41 Antony met Cleopatra in Cilicia,[57] and soon fell under her spell – in this respect, too, he was Caesar's heir. Antony completely forgot about Italy and set off for Egypt without intervening in Italy with so much as a word. Fulvia, piqued by jealousy, was now determined to get him out of Egypt in any way she could.

As we have seen, soldiers and citizens alike were discontented.[58] Lucius Antonius proposed revoking the expropriations and paying off the soldiers in cash. His brother would pay them out of the wealth of Asia. This proposal was not well received by the men, however: it was too crude. The prospect of that money was too far off, and they were not willing to give up their property on the strength of it. But those who had been expropriated began to retaliate. Lucius had his resolutions ratified by the Assembly and troops levied for the defence of land-owners. Octavian put himself forward as Antony's representative. Delegates from the armies (junior officers) met at Gabii to examine the manifestoes and decided in favour of Octavian.[59]

Lucius refused to submit to this and war broke out, thus encapsulating a second civil war inside the first. Octavian was expelled from Rome for a time, and then the same happened to Lucius Antonius. Octavian laid siege to Lucius at Praeneste, then at Perusia. The decision lay with Antony's commanders in Gaul. Fulvia made threats, but the men were at a loss what to do. They never committed themselves. [MH.I, 18] Perusia fell in 40 BC.[60] Lucius Antonius was captured by Octavian. He and Fulvia were spared, since Octavian was, after all, representing the interests of Mark Antony.[61] It was the unfortunate towns who had to pay the price in horrendous massacres, although the soldiers were to some extent exasperated by their resistance. This greatly strengthened Octavian's position. He had surrounded himself with an able staff. Although courageous, he lacked strategic acumen as such, managing to train suitable men for this purpose, notably Quintus Salvidienus Rufus and Marcus Agrippa. Although the former was perhaps the more talented of the two, his loyalty later became suspect, and he was executed.[62]

Even now, Antony's generals in Gaul were still the stronger party. Octavian therefore set out for Gaul, where he met with a great stroke of fortune. When

Quintus Fufius Calenus, the general in command, died, his young son took his place, but lacked authority. Octavian managed to persuade him to place his troops under his command.[63] Some of the generals refused to recognize this arrangement, but Gaul was now effectively lost to Antony. Those legions which remained recalcitrant marched off for Brundisium under the loyal Antonian commanders Ventidius Bassus and Asinius Pollio.

Antony appeared to come to his senses. He received two adverse pieces of news, the first from the Parthian War. In 40 BC the Parthians had taken the offensive – something unprecedented. Moreover, this also to a certain extent marked a rekindling of the Republican War. Quintus Labienus, along with many Republicans, appeared on the Parthian side.[64] Initially they had great success: Syria and Asia were undefended and the Parthians [MH.I, 19] advanced rapidly. The second piece of news was that from Italy and Gaul. At first, Antony seemed inclined to take up arms against Octavian, despite conceding that his supporters had been in the wrong. But he could not leave his troops in Brundisium in the lurch. Circumstances were not entirely against him. Domitius Ahenobarbus placed himself under Antony's command with the Republican fleet;[65] he could scarcely do otherwise. Even Sextus Pompey offered Antony his cooperation; he proposed landing at Thurii. However, it was unpalatable for Antony, the Caesarian, to accept assistance from one who had protected Caesar's assassins. There was some skirmishing. Brundisium did not want to receive Antony.[66] The mood of the men, however, prompted immediate negotiations here too. This much is clear, although it is not specifically stated in the sources.[67] After all, Antony could not seriously hold Octavian's conduct against him. There was also the Parthian War to be considered: if war were now to break out in Italy, Quintus Labienus Parthicus[68] would have the advantage.

The peace of Brundisium had an entirely new character. Events had shifted in Octavian's favour. There had never been much collegial spirit between the two men: Antony had always been envious towards Octavian. At this juncture, a genuine moral basis for the relationship emerged. Particular credit for this goes to Maecenas, whose name occurs here for the first time.[69] Maecenas was Octavian's right-hand man —one of those men who were to become typical of the monarchy. Although his name is not listed in the Fasti, he was, nonetheless, a man of immense influence. Asinius Pollio, the famous historian,[70] negotiated on Antony's side. [MH.I, 20] Likewise an honourable character and convinced monarchist,[71] he was devoted to Antony, but his first loyalty was to Rome. The peace was negotiated by these two.

First, the spheres of influence were defined.[72] Octavian was to have the West, Antony the East, with the Adriatic as the border. Africa fell to the insignificant Lepidus. The task of subduing the slaves in Sicily fell to Octavian, the Parthians to Antony. To safeguard this arrangement, Octavia, Octavian's virtuous sister, who was very close to him, was married to Antony. The question of which woman was to acquire influence over Antony was crucial, and the plan succeeded to some extent. For the first time the brothers-in-law came to know and respect each other. The peace marked a definite change for the better, and was perceived as such.

A spectacular triumphal celebration was held in Rome in the autumn of 40 BC and was recorded in the *Fasti*.[73] Prior to this the celebration of a reconciliation between two citizens had been unknown, but in this case it was sanctioned by public feeling. *Magnus ab integro saeclorum nascitur ordo* was Virgil's[74] well-founded assessment.[75]

In the spring of 39 BC peace was concluded at Misenum with Sextus Pompey,[76] negotiated by Scribonia, Octavian's new wife and a relative of Sextus Pompey.[77] It was a mere caricature of peace, however. How could peace be maintained with an army of robbers? It was not possible to grant Sextus Pompey the homecoming from Sicily he longed for, but he was allowed 70½ million *denarii* in compensation for his father's legacy. He wanted to be received into the triumvirate as its third member in place of Lepidus. Judging by the actual state of affairs, he became a fourth triumvir. Styling himself 'Prefect of the Sea Coast', *praefectus orae maritimae*,[78] he retained Sardinia, Corsica and Sicily and was also to obtain Greece, but without an official position. [MH.I, 21] He was not formally recognized as an equal, but nor was he an inferior. This arrangement could not last. Still, public opinion supported peace in order to keep open the corn supply from Sicily. And so Octavian was obliged to make concessions for the time being. Antony, however, would not give up Greece. Sextus fell out with the freed slave Menas,[79] who saw himself as a victim of the peace and handed over to Octavian Sardinia and Corsica, together with their fleet. Both triumvirs thus broke the treaty. The peace had only been concluded in the first place as a spectacle for the benefit of the public, although Sextus Pompey had perhaps taken it seriously. He was a crude, uneducated man. He cared nothing really for politics, but now he took up arms once again.

Things seemed favourable in the East. Antony wanted to march against the Parthians immediately, but first celebrated his honeymoon,[80] and sent Ventidius Bassus on ahead of him. The latter made short shrift of the Parthians, expelling them from Roman territory and concluding the war, perhaps greatly against Antony's will.

In 38 BC Octavian's attempted landing in Sicily failed for want of equipment. His fleet was defeated at Cumae and Messana.[81] He realized the necessity of naval power. That year Ventidius Bassus again fought on his own in the East, defeating the Parthians a second time and thereby restoring peace. Antony, sojourning in Athens, recalled Bassus, but could not deprive him of his glory.[82] Labienus, *imperator Parthicus*, had fallen.[83]

A general calm prevailed in 37 BC. In Italy Agrippa was arming himself energetically, especially at sea, to advance on Sicily. The triumvirs met at Tarentum, seeking to reinforce their mutual understanding.[84] [MH.I, 22] Antony gave part of his fleet to Octavian to support him against Sextus Pompey; Octavian gave Antony elite troops for an offensive against the Parthians. They were on the most amicable possible terms.

Combat resumed again in 36 BC and proved fierce, despite the fact that even Lepidus had been called up in support. Agrippa commanded the fleet. Wherever Octavian appeared in person he failed. He suffered one serious defeat at Taormina.[85] Nevertheless, victory remained with the superior numbers of the attacking side, as indeed it could not do otherwise in the long term. The decisive battle was fought by Agrippa at Naulochos; the fleet was destroyed, so that the land army could no longer hold its ground. Sextus Pompey was thus eliminated.[86] This was a great coup for Octavian, who appeared to have rescued Italy from starvation. Another great stroke of luck ensued, similar to the death of Calenus (see MH.I, 18). Lepidus had also appeared and Sextus's troops capitulated to him. Lepidus, however, refused to deliver them to Octavian. At that point he had superior numbers in Sicily and now wanted to take a stand against Octavian. But he did not have control over his troops; they would not go into battle. They placed themselves under the command of Octavian, who had meanwhile, shrewdly, been making bold personal approaches to them.[87] There was no need to punish Lepidus; Octavian simply let him go free, and even allowed him to retain the office of Chief Pontiff into which he had insinuated himself.[88] This left him with the entire West under his control. A perfect duovirate had emerged, although it is never referred to as such.

In the Orient the Parthian War raged on.[89] Antony wanted to take the offensive in order to wipe out the disgrace of Crassus's defeat. The example of Caesar was also a factor here. The war did not go well, however. This year proved to be the turning point for Antony. He returned to Cleopatra.[90] Psychologically this is totally [MH.I, 23] incomprehensible. Octavia was more beautiful and younger than Cleopatra[91] and he seemed to be happily married to her. And yet the very first reunion with Cleopatra re-established their former relationship. This also reveals that Antony was not of the same mettle as Caesar,[92] but generally of inferior character. In judging this relationship, we have to remember that the Parthian War was utterly forgotten. Antony ought to have tried to confront the enemy at the earliest possible juncture. But instead of joining his army in the spring of 36 he delayed until the summer. He was relying especially on Artavasdes of Armenia, as that was the operational base of his army. The course of events is unclear: Antony accused him of treachery, Octavian denied this and regarded Antony's conduct towards Artavasdes as disgraceful. And indeed the Armenian does not seem to have done anything essentially wrong. Antony marched on Media through Armenia and invested Vera (Phraata, Phraaspa); during the siege two legions under Statianus were massacred to a man.[93] The siege failed and Antony was obliged to retreat. It was a superbly managed march, lasting twenty-seven days, under the noses of an enemy who outnumbered them. Even so, he returned to the Empire with only three-quarters of the army, thereby concluding the campaign with a defeat. Moreover, Antony had spread false reports of victory, and there was also his accusation against Artavasdes. Some 8,000 men had lost their lives in Armenia through sheer fatigue: had he been a traitor, Artavasdes could easily have wiped out the army, and yet he allowed it to retreat without harassment. This was to have consequences in the following year.

At this point we ask how Octavian saw things. It is generally assumed that he intended to make himself absolute monarch from the very outset. His opportunity to do so now appeared. We can only base our judgements on the facts, however, [MH.I, 24] and from these we are bound to deduce that he wished to rule jointly with Antony. Nevertheless, he had entered upon the inheritance of Lepidus by himself, and Antony, understandably, felt wronged.

On the other hand, Lepidus was too insignificant to jeopardize the entire supremacy over the West that Octavian had achieved; the latter had, furthermore, ceded Egypt to Antony as his conquest, even though it was not part of the Empire. We must be on our guard in general against viewing monarchy as the sole possible form of government. Octavian himself once entertained a plan for dividing East and West between his grandsons. A natural enough thought: the Empire was too vast for a single focus of authority.

Octavian was additionally involved in other tedious enterprises. In 35 BC he set about rendering the northern frontier of Italy secure – a laudable enterprise, since it was unrelated to his personal interests. He turned his attention to Dalmatia, where he secured the endangered land bridge to the East (see MH.I, 26).

Octavia did her best to break Antony's mood and reconcile him to Octavian. She informed Antony that she was on her way to him and dispatched to him large numbers of troops – 2,000 heavily armed cavalry – undoubtedly with her brother's knowledge.[94] Octavian probably wished to restore their former good relations. Antony, however, wrote back to Octavia telling her to remain in Italy. This could not have been foreseen, of course. First, Antony busied himself with renewing the offensive against Parthia. This was understandable enough. And yet he did not depart for the field until 34 BC. This brought him indelible shame. He marched into Armenia as an ally, as on the previous occasion.[95] When Artavasdes appeared he was arrested and charged, albeit [MH.I, 25] without success. But his country was taken away from him in this way. This was the success of the entire war.

Coins bearing the legend *Armenia devicta* show the portraits of Antony and Cleopatra. The legend *Cleopatrae reginae regum, filiorum regum* (Roman usage did not permit the insertion of the word *matri*)[96] may be translated: 'to Cleopatra, queen of kings, and her sons, who are also kings'. Antony was thus the consort of Cleopatra. A triumph was celebrated in Alexandria:[97] an outrageous course of action, transferring, as it did, all Roman pomp and circumstance to Egypt. He processed to the Capitol in Alexandria. Then the East was ceded to Cleopatra in the form of a paramount kingdom over Egypt and the other provinces, with Caesarion as co-ruler – utterly outrageous acts.[98] Caesarion was a 'true' son of Caesar, and hence also the real rival of Octavian. Antony's children by Cleopatra were also provided for: Ptolemy Philadelphus, Cleopatra Selene and Alexander Helios. This was tantamount to a complete partitioning of the Empire, and could not be accepted by Rome. It was the beginning of the end for Antony. The Senate declared war on Cleopatra[99] – the correct procedure, albeit only a matter of form.

Antony and Octavia were now formally divorced and his marriage to Cleopatra followed. Octavia was expelled from her husband's house in Rome.[100] The rift between the brothers-in-law thus now took on a constitutional significance. The *tresviri* had been appointed for five years (until 38 BC). They had not laid down their authority, and after the first term of five years had run out they had agreed at Tarentum on another five-year term, to run until 33 BC. This period had now expired, and the question of the future arose, although it was not of any major constitutional significance. There was thus talk of bringing the triumvirate to an end, although nothing is heard of the office-holders resigning. Antony described himself not as *triumvir iterum*, but simply as *triumvir* (although he styled himself *consul iterum*). The triumvirate was undoubtedly modelled on the dictatorship of Sulla, lasting until the dictator was of a mind to step down. [MH.I, 26] The ten years were, so to speak, a target that could be exceeded, rather than a term of office after which the official automatically retired into private life. The only option was whether or not to abdicate from the dictatorship voluntarily.

At this point, Appian's account unfortunately comes to an end.[101] Octavian was probably disinclined to be the one to end their tacit agreement, but Antony was resolved to sever relations and establish himself as absolute monarch.[102] This is particularly apparent from their respective attitudes towards external foes. Octavian was engaged in heavy fighting in Dalmatia,[103] but not preparing himself for civil war. He advanced as far as the river Sava. Antony was engaged in combat with the Parthians, but capitulated to the enemy before war broke out. He concluded peace and made an alliance with Artavasdes of Media, transferring to him a substantial piece of Armenia. In return, Artavasdes had to place his cavalry at the disposal of the Romans.[104]

The manner in which war was declared conformed entirely to Antony's nature. Here, too, he modelled his actions on those of Caesar. The two consuls in 32 BC, Gnaeus Domitius Ahenobarbus and Gaius Sosius, were loyal supporters of Antony.[105] They declared to the Senate that Antony was prepared to lay down his arms if Octavian did the same. They protested that Antony's authority had been infringed by the deposition of Lepidus. Assurances were given that it had been intended that the consuls would have Antony's donations ratified by the Senate. This is not impossible, since the acts had been publicly undertaken in Egypt. If that was Antony's wish, however, it was highly imprudent of him. All national sentiment in Rome weighed against it. In the event, the consuls did not dare see it through. It is impossible to ascertain whether they were ever intended to do so.

[MH.I, 27] The Senate was under the sway of Octavian, although a number of Senators set out for Ephesus with the two consuls.[106] Here a re-enactment took place of the flight of the people's tribunes to Caesar. Only arms could decide now; the initiative was seized by Antony, and in the crudest possible manner.

Both sides went on the offensive,[107] marching against each other towards Greece. Antony had the stronger force; he had been arming himself well in advance. His intention was to muster an army of up to thirty legions. He certainly had over 100,000 men, with prospects for reinforcements. Octavian was substantially weaker on land, although apparently he had the upper hand at sea. He commanded the Sicilian and African squadrons, as well as his own fleet, under the command of Agrippa. Antony had no able admiral – a further indication, incidentally, that he wanted a land war.[108] The decision was long in coming. In the spring of 32 BC war was declared. Antony was then stationed in Asia Minor. Had he so wished, he could easily have won decisive advantages and pressed on into Italy. This would have allowed him to face and defeat a totally unprepared Octavian. Instead, he made for Greece and set up his headquarters in Patrae. Soon, however, it became impossible to cross over; Agrippa occupied Corfu, enabling Octavian to lead his land army into Greece. He encamped opposite Antony.

It was not arms which decided the issue, however, but Cleopatra, who took the astonishing step of accompanying Antony to camp. She haunted him like a malevolent ghost, ruling him entirely and dictating the course of the war. Unable to fight Cleopatra, Antony's most loyal supporters, Plancus and Titius,[109] Ahenobarbus and Sosius,[110] left him in desperation. Tradition has it that she only had the battle of Actium fought at all in order to be defeated and retreat to Egypt. Her influence thus dominated even the battle. Unfortunately, accounts of Cleopatra are biased against her. [MH.I, 28] When battle was offered at sea, this was due to her influence, and against the advice of all his friends, but it is hardly acceptable to attribute some petulant treachery to her. As an Egyptian, she would obviously give preference to the fleet. There can be no doubt that she genuinely hoped to be victorious with her Egyptian fleet. If this was folly, however, the course of the battle itself is even more baffling. Octavian accepted battle without delay, and it turned in Agrippa's favour. This still did not mean defeat, however. Antony had no need of the fleet: he had every chance of success by relying on his loyal land forces. Understandably, Cleopatra made to retreat; what is incomprehensible, however, is that Antony immediately followed,[111] leaving the remainder of the fleet and his entire army behind. One might almost be forgiven for believing in sorcery. The battle was effectively lost without Octavian even having to win his victory. This is where Antony's story is really over.

There was no question of continuing the war. His land forces waited for him for seven days and then capitulated without giving battle. Octavian pursued Antony to Egypt. Antony defeated Octavian's vanguard at Alexandria, but this was his final victory. Most of his troops defected to Octavian. Cleopatra sued for peace in return for surrendering Antony. Antony committed suicide, but her plan misfired; she failed to captivate Octavian. Predicting that she would be carried off to Rome, she killed herself with her servants.[112]

It would be churlish to deny Antony a degree of compassion. In the first place, as an amiable, loyal and courageous follower of Caesar he had proved himself both as a politician and a soldier. He was made to serve, however, not to rule. A streak of coarseness and pettiness ran through his entire nature. He was a handsome man, but a Hercules, not an Apollo. Only half-educated, he would vaunt bogus snatches of knowledge, [MH.I, 29] enabling Cleopatra to ensnare him with similar empty show. Tradition holds that his speeches were a motley concoction, which entirely conforms to his nature. He combined Cato and Sallust with Asianist rhetoric. These traits dovetailed with his total lack of Roman national pride; no other Roman would have been capable of celebrating his triumphs on the capitol in Alexandria, or of distributing Roman land to foreigners.[113]

It was a huge stroke of fortune that the civil war concluded in this manner – one of those strokes of luck in which Rome abounded. Only the thoroughly common Canidius Crassus, who was able to ingratiate himself with Cleopatra, remained with Antony.[114] Had Antony been victorious, the victory would have fallen to Cleopatra and the Roman state destroyed.[115]

The reorganization of the state by Augustus is a difficult question, requiring the historian to fall silent and give way to the teacher of constitutional law. The matter of the constitution was curiously arranged: no definition fits the material, no material fits the title. We can forget about chronological order, since sometimes one, sometimes another function of the constitutional system was attended to. Augustus was born on 23 September 63 BC during the consulate of Cicero. He died on 19 August AD 14 at the age of 75, having held the reins of power for fifty-six years. Only in recent months have we learnt when he himself reckoned his reign to have begun: it was with his assumption of the consulship on 19 August 43 BC.[116]

This lengthy term of office was an immense stroke of fortune. A closer examination of his work suggests comparison with Caesar. He was certainly no match for Caesar, in brilliance, nature or birth. Augustus had his origins in the middle classes, the municipal notables of Velitrae, and was distantly related to the high-born Octavians. His father Octavius had advanced to the office of praetor, [MH.I, 30] but had otherwise occupied no curule office. Augustus was the grand-son of Julia, sister of the dictator and wife of Marcus Atius Balbus, and the son of their daughter Atia, who was married to the said Octavius.[117] This made Augustus Caesar's closest male relative. Caesar, therefore, had adopted him according to the Roman custom whereby a childless nobleman adopted his closest male kin. There is no evidence to suggest that Caesar looked upon him as the one who would bring his work to fruition.

Like his great-uncle, Augustus[118] was a handsome man[119] – slight, pale-skinned and blonde, well-proportioned, with sparkling eyes whose power he enjoyed savouring. Otherwise he was not particularly prepossessing. His health was poor; he suffered from nervous indisposition and chills and could abide neither heat nor cold. He wore four tunics and a thick toga and never went without a hat. There was altogether an air of the commoner about him. Unlike Caesar, female beauty left him largely cold[120] and personal vanity was quite alien to him. Frugal in his habits, he was moderate in both his eating and drinking. His pastimes were angling and dice. He loved children, was a good family man and wore clothing woven by his family. He instructed his grandchildren himself and had them with him at all times. He was thus a good-natured man, quite averse to anything that smacked of untamed genius.

It is difficult to make pronouncements about his morality. It may be pointed out that he was not free of a certain superstition. He was not religious in the ancient sense, any more than anyone else in his day was. What he did to restore the Church [sic] was purely political. Nevertheless, a belief in omina, auspicious and inauspicious days, was very marked in him. He paid heed to dreams. Bearing in mind the moral climate of the age, he cannot be accused of any significant wrongs. His marriage to Livia was a love-match and although it began with her abduction, [MH.I, 31] the very fact of the marriage makes it praiseworthy by the standards of the times. The politics of his household proved to be fateful for him. It is from him that the monarchy's shift towards the dynastic principle derives.

He was influential in the sphere of literature. An impeccably well-read dilettante, he knew his own limitations and never attempted to exceed them. He was consummately schooled in both Greek and Latin, although he avoided speaking, and even more so writing, in Greek. He knew that a foreign language always remains foreign and wisely placed a constraint upon himself. For the same reason he also opposed the Latin archaisms of Tiberius and neologisms of Maecenas. His common sense gravitated towards the happy medium; his model was Caesar, although he never attained the latter's grace and charm. His commentaries on the Dalmatian War were not widely disseminated, despite the weight of the name behind them. In conformity with the fashion of his day, he also attempted to write verse, but only very perfunctorily. He acted as patron even to talented writers who disliked him. His 'Statement of Accounts', the *Res gestae divi Augusti*,[121] which is still extant, shows that in his style he was particularly interested in accuracy of detail and clarity. Fully cognizant of the importance of the state, he sought to inaugurate a new age of art and literature, since the age of politics was, in his view, now over.

Caesar's talents as a general were denied to Augustus. Although courageous and a capable organizer, he was nevertheless personally unsuccessful. He thus resigned early from the army and delegated actual command to loyal generals. He accomplished far more as a statesman. Even here, however, he was no man of genius, merely possessing the skill of effecting a compromise between two things that in themselves [MH.I, 32] were impossible: between Caesarian monarchy and the old Republic. Out of this arose a third impossibility, a Republic with a monarch at its head, and yet it survived for 300 years. He always regarded himself as his father's son, the successor of the dictator. He therefore directed his efforts at transposing Caesar's unfeasible grand design into the realm of the humanly possible. Caesar's state had only been feasible with a genius at its head, only suitable for a single individual; its consolidation by Augustus was planned to last, and did so.[122]

The power he assumed, initially together with Antony and Lepidus, was that of establishing a constitution. All the old institutions had been called into question, enabling these rulers to rearrange everything anew at will, without any need for further authorization. The ending of the triumvirate's term of office was of no real importance; it expired only when the triumvirate itself abdicated, as Augustus wished it to after the Sicilian peace. But he continued in office, thus assuming the constituent power of both his colleagues after Antony's demise in his capacity as the last remaining *triumvir rei publicae constituendae*. On 13 January 27 BC he formally surrendered his power to the Senate.[123] It was the old triumviral authority he was returning to the Senate. The outward signal for this was the fact that the assembly once again elected magistrates in 28 BC. Three days later, on 16 January, the Senate bestowed the title 'Augustus' on Octavian.[124]

B) THE *PRINCEPS*

The new order[125] was the 'restored commonwealth' (*res publica restituta*), as Augustus styled it, a Republic with a monarch at its head.[126] At first the Republic rested on the sovereignty of the people, on the people's representatives. The order of the principate in fact had three fathers: Caesar, Augustus and Tiberius; Augustus built on Caesar's plan, Tiberius on that of Augustus. [MH.I, 33] However, a certain timidity, a fear of seeing things through to their final conclusions, was undeniably lodged in the character of Augustus. This was quite alien to Tiberius.

The Roman citizenry (*populus Romanus*) was still understood to mean those men who assembled on the Campus Martius in their electoral divisions. This was a sound arrangement for an agrarian community, but preposterous for an international state such as Rome. The assemblies too had grown into a futile machinery; by the time a matter reached their attention it was to all intents and purposes already dealt with (Nitzsch, my colleague in the field of research into Roman history, described the plebiscite in the same terms).[127]

The former sovereignty of the people was expressed in the first instance in jurisdiction. This was the first aspect to become obsolete. The people had never interfered in private lawsuits: but criminal trials were formally in the hands of the assembly.[128] This system had long been obsolete and had been replaced by the *quaestiones*, although this substitute was not empowered to impose life and death sentences, only financial penalties or banishment. The monarchy reintroduced the ultimate penalty via a dual system of jurisdiction consisting of the consuls and Senate on the one hand and the *princeps* on the other.[129] The *populus Romanus* was henceforth still formally regarded as the source of authority, but found its legal expression in the Senate and the *princeps* – an oligarchical and monarchical authority replacing the former Republican courts. These new elements had the same latitude as decisions of the assembly. Nor did they need to abide by existing law: they could both dispense from punishments and pass sentences for which there were no precedents.

Second, the sovereignty of the people resided in legislation. Initially nothing was done to undermine this *de iure*; *de facto*, however, it was substantially curbed. [MH.I, 34] Legislation did not carry the weight then that it does now. There was no budget – nowadays an annual legislative act and a focal point of interest; the state had no revenues from the taxation of citizens, only income from the provinces, which were treated as domains. The state thus lived on its income and was hence quite independent of legislative approval. The Senate could debate the issue, but this was not necessary for the *princeps*, and only ever occurred sporadically.

In the time of the Emperors the focal point of legislation lay with family law. Decisions about guardianship, inheritance, marriage and the freeing of slaves continued to be ratified by the people. It was difficult to organize opposition in the marketplace; an assembly with the power to vote only yes or no, without amendments or debate, had little choice but to ratify the bills put to it. The real opposition was, so to speak, a 'cabinet-opposition', residing in the Senate. These rights of the assembly were thus probably retained because of their innocuousness. *Leges agrariae* (bills for the redistribution of land) were no longer debated: proposals likely to prompt party infighting were prevented. Nevertheless, this recognition of the principle represented a most dangerous loophole in the Augustan constitution that was not dealt with until the time of Tiberius. From AD 19 onwards no more laws were passed by the assembly;[130] they were replaced by the *senatus consultum*, which effectively eliminated the Roman people as a component in the lawmaking process.

The sovereignty of the people was linked to elections. These remained spirited in the extreme and were the least assailable element, being the hub around which the life of the Roman citizen revolved. Elections to public offices were, after all, also elections to the Senate: the quaestor already had a [MH.I, 35] seat in the Senate for life. Augustus clearly wanted to do away with these elections, but never succeeded completely. He introduced imperial commendations to give the *princeps* more influence. The right of the *princeps* to appoint persons whose position was extraordinary was established.[131] This meant that the magistrate presiding over elections could only accept votes for persons who had been so recommended. One exception to this was the election of the consuls; the return to constitutional normality had, after all, been symbolized by the election of consuls. Although the use of commendation was extremely sparing, it was nevertheless *de iure* unlimited.

The first governmental act of Tiberius was to have magistrates elected in the senatorial *curia* and the results then announced on the Campus Martius.[132] This was the inevitable outcome of this development. It also gave his prerogative of commendation a clearer constitutional role. Thus some officials were appointed by the Emperor and some elected by the Senate.

Let us turn to the principate. How did it come about? What was its legal basis? These are difficult questions to answer.[133] It was partly based on popular election, and is entirely to be understood as the office of a magistrate, since the idea of hereditary succession never gained a foothold *de iure*.[134] No one ever thought to ratify what was already long established in practice. There was no legal continuity for the principate. If the Emperor died and had no co-ruler, the office remained vacant – after Aurelian for five months,[135] and after Claudius for four days.[136]

The principate was a composite of various institutions resting on disparate legal titles. Military (proconsular) and civil (tribunician) powers need to be distinguished. The military *imperium* was a magistracy,[137] and yet the *imperator* was never elected by the people, but proclaimed by the soldiers. [MH.I, 36] *Imperium* was acquired by a spontaneous seizure of power by the ruler on the strength of the will of the people, for the expression of which there was no existing institution. How did Augustus obtain his *imperium*? After all, he was already a general at the head of an army when he became proconsul. He seized power because he believed himself called to continue the work of Caesar, his right to do so resting on the fact that the soldiers recognized him as their *imperator*. Legally, therefore, a military rebellion[138] against the *imperator* was also admissible, although this was never in fact made explicit. A nomination by the Senate, such as is found in the ancient sources, did not amount to an appointment (the Senate lacked the power to do that), but only to an invitation to declare oneself *imperator*. And, significantly enough, acclamation was carried out by the army. Fourteen guardsmen[139] proclaimed Otho Emperor.[140]

The mystical streak in Augustus appears in the fact that he had himself proclaimed a god.[141] He needed the halo around his star. [MH.I, 37] There is thus a deeper meaning embedded in the claim to be *Divi Filius* (son of a god). Herein lies the riddle of Augustus' status. It should, nevertheless, be emphasized that his rank was that of a magistrate. Everything enacted by the *princeps* fell within the range of Republican offices. He is not above the law: the law is above him. If one contrasts the Empire of Augustus with that of Diocletian, the former is an *imperium legitimum* (*legibus circumscriptum*), whereas the latter is *princeps legibus solutus*.[142] Nothing could be more erroneous than to attribute the notions of the *Corpus Iuris* to the monarchy of Augustus and his successors. The *Corpus* was largely the creation of the third century, at the time of Caracalla. We do, however, have the *lex regia* (*de imperio Vespasiani*), in which the powers of the Emperor are set forth.[143] The Emperor was to be exempt from those laws which Emperors from Augustus onwards no longer had to abide by (such as the stipulation that the proconsul was not permitted to remain in Rome). It was only from specific laws that the Emperors were exempted. He was obliged to obey those from which he was not exempted. If he did not wish to do so, he had to obtain a dispensation. Augustus's will contravened his own laws on marriage.

Nevertheless, the new magistracy had such extensive powers that it was tantamount to autocracy. The obligations of annual rotation, collegiality and a specific sphere of competence, the most cohesive obligations of the Republican constitution, were set aside for Augustus.

With regard to annual rotation: constant changes of office-holders had made enduring influence impossible. This now ceased. Augustus did not initially hold the office of *imperium extraordinarium* for life, but had it prolonged from five to ten years, or prolonged it himself. The limit in the number of years was not abolished until the time of Tiberius. This was a major step, since this restriction had indicated that the powers invested in the office were extraordinary. Tiberius' proviso allowing for abdication was pure pretence. [MH.I, 38] In the time of Augustus, *imperator* became an element in his proper name; instead of 'Gaius Julius Caesar' he called himself 'Imperator Caesar',[144] thus making it a title for life.

With regard to collegiality: this was one of the chief cornerstones of the Republican constitution. There were always two authorities who could cooperate, but also keep each other in check. This also applied to the position of a *princeps* (*civium Romanorum*), the first of Roman citizens: he was *primus inter pares*, first among equals. This meant recognition of equality with the others, but at the same time the abolition of collegiality. An odd inconsistency was the establishment of two crown princes as *principes* (*iuventutis*), leaders of Roman youth.[145] The principle was there, but was not consistently applied. Augustus frequently set a colleague beside him – initially Antony, and later the most compliant Agrippa. He probably hoped to do the same with his two adoptive sons, and did so with

Tiberius. It did not occur to Tiberius to follow suit; he always kept the formal reins in his own hands.

With regard to a specific sphere of competence: all spheres of competence in the Republic were clearly defined. All magistrates, even subordinate ones, were autonomous within their own spheres of competence; they could, and indeed were obliged to, refrain from complying with orders from senior magistrates if these contravened the law. While the principate was also made up of a sum of individual special spheres, taken together these were tantamount to autocracy.[146] The Emperor was the personification of executive power, and yet he did not have the right to relocate the sacred city wall (*pomerium*). The same holds for extending the frontier of Italy. This right was not obtained by an Emperor until the time of Claudius.[147] Similarly, censorial powers did not lie within the scope of imperial power, needing a special grant, as in the case of Domitian.[148] Aside from these instances, however, the Emperor had wide powers. These consisted of two aspects: the proconsular *imperium* and tribunician authority. [MH.I, 39] These were quite unconnected. The Senate did not appoint the Emperor, since this would make it the supreme authority, which was impossible. The tribunate was not acquired through the *imperium*; this came about by way of popular resolution. The law [sc. *de imperio*] is based on a vote of the Assembly; it is a personal law applying to an *imperator* already in command, and transfers to him the tribunate and a number of other spheres of authority. The law was originally passed by the assembly; this procedure persisted for longer than the others. Even when the election of magistrates was transferred to the Senate under Tiberius, this legislative act continued to be the prerogative of the Assembly. This dual role forms the basis of the Augustan system, but was taken over from Caesar. It represents the democratic mission that the new leader of the people sought to fulfil. This association too is specifically Caesarian.

Now for *imperium*, technically proconsular authority.[149] Supreme military command had been passing more and more from consuls to proconsuls. This had occurred in the provinces, since no troops were stationed in Italy. Augustus left this as it was: he did not curb the military authority of the proconsuls, but they no longer had any troops. They all swore an oath of allegiance to the *imperator*. Although the Senate had legions in Africa, they could be recalled by the Emperor. He also held *imperium* over the proconsular (senatorial) provinces. The proconsuls could only command borrowed troops, as frequently occurred.

The power of a proconsul was restricted to his territorial province. The Emperor was exempt from this.[150] Even when troops were stationed in Italy, he was in command. The standing army was a legal institution. The Emperor also appointed its officers. This constituted the most significant aspect of his authority: the sword ruled. The more he realized this, however, the more heed he paid to emphasizing his civilian rank.

In terms of the legal foundation of the Emperor's civil authority, there is an apparent vacillation between the consulate and the tribunate. The former was not permanent. Until 23 BC Augustus had himself elected consul repeatedly, then resigned the office to reassume it only occasionally.[151] [MH.I, 40] Its very collegial nature made it incompatible with the new order, with the monarchical principle. It cannot be asserted that Augustus substituted the tribunate for the consulate. However, he did at all events introduce some changes in the office of the tribunate when he resigned the consulate, for example the way the years of his rule were enumerated. This was fitting, since a monarch who does not number the years of his rule is no monarch. Previously this was accomplished through the consulate. Nevertheless, the relative significance of the tribunate and consulate can easily be gauged from the fact that whereas Augustus still placed his title as consul before that of *tribunicia potestas* in his overall title, this changed under Tiberius, compelling the highest magistracy of the Republic to yield precedence to the *tribunicia potestas*. This change aptly expresses the relative significance of the two spheres of authority for the principate.[152]

Tribunician authority is of a preventive, rather than an executive nature. In modern terms, the tribune represents the official head of the opposition, on whom this legal term had been bestowed in order to pre-empt revolutionary tendencies. In this sense the office was now obsolete, since there was no longer any question of oppressive magisterial power. Its great significance for the *princeps* lay not so much in the office itself, as in the power invested in it. The tribune was empowered to summon the community and the Senate, make laws or initiate a *senatus consultum*, and the *princeps* could and would not give up these rights. Similarly, the authority to intervene in a crisis was a crucial right. The *ius intercessionis*, whereby the Emperor overrode other officials, found its expression herein.

Nonetheless, it is most rare to learn by what right any particular act of the Emperor occurred. This would not have been politic. The principate was, after all, intended to be perceived by the outsider as a seamless entity, not a conglomerate of [MH.I, 41] separate powers. The population at large was never supposed to ask from which right any particular act of the *princeps* derived. In this way, powers became associated with the tribunate that had never previously been attached to it. The tribunate is a purely municipal authority and yet the *lex regia* explicitly stated that decisions of war and peace were in the hands of the Emperor;[153] a principle, indeed, which was followed to the letter in practice. Foreign policy was not the concern of tribunes. At most the Senate was occasionally consulted on matters of foreign policy; otherwise this was entirely in the hands of the Emperor, in accordance with that special law.

Concerning his role within the judicial system,[154] it is not inconceivable that this was based on the powers of the tribunate; in any case it did not exceed such powers, and the reform of the judicial system should in fact be understood as an essentially innovative act. The former system had recognized only that a Tribune of the Plebs could set aside a previously pronounced sentence. An appeals procedure,[155] whereby a higher authority was empowered to replace an earlier sentence with another legally binding judgment, was completely unknown. The procedure of appeal to higher authorities – to consuls, the Senate, and ultimately the *princeps* himself – was instituted by Augustus and can be demonstrated for all categories of legal proceedings with the exception of jury courts. This was particularly important for criminal proceedings, which had been tightened up considerably with the reintroduction of the death penalty. Life-and-death decisions were in the hands of consuls, the Senate and the Emperor. No basis whatsoever for this can be discerned in the titular powers of the *princeps*. This undoubtedly also applies to the way in which other spheres of authority were exercised in practice, which we cannot go into here.

[MH.I, 42] The transfer of power to the Emperor in the *lex regia* ends with the clause that he was empowered to do whatever he saw fit in the interests of the state. This discretionary power is virtually unlimited,[156] like that of Sulla and the triumvirs, and it is possible to give specific instances of this. When, for example, in 27 BC, bribes were becoming all too conspicuous in the elections to magistracies, Augustus simply declared the elections void and appointed new magistrates on the strength of his own plenitude of powers.[157] Nevertheless, this was an extreme, reluctantly and rarely used power. Effort was made to avoid using it, resorting to it only when the voice of the best elements in the population favoured extraordinary measures.

Despite this, one has to concede that the sum of legal powers united in the *princeps* bordered on totalitarianism. This category most particularly included the proconsular authority that extended across the entire Empire, which would have been quite unknown in the Republic in peacetime, and was not even achieved with the far-reaching powers of Pompey against the pirates.[158]

It was characteristic of this imperial power that it had no name.[159] Initially, the title of proconsul would have been a title appropriate to this power. The Emperors, however, specifically avoided this title. It was not used until the time of Trajan, and even then only when he was in camp and not in the city.[160] Similarly, Lucius Verus adopted it when he was with the army, but not the Emperor Marcus, who remained in the city. When, in the third century, the Empire became more and more dependent [MH.I, 43] on the military, the most telling indication of this was the increased prevalence of the proconsular title. Similarly, the Emperor could not adopt the title of *tribunus plebis*, since he was not one. He possessed a superior power, that of *tribunicia potestas*.[161] Intercession against him by a colleague in the popular assembly was impossible, since he represented absolute power.

Formally, imperial power was concentrated in the principate; in substance, however, this was not at all the case. Augustus simply styled himself *princeps*, but in fact this was not a title.[162] It is highly significant that this term does not appear in the official *Fasti* (with the exception of Tiberius) and that over time it sank into complete obscurity. There was good reason for this, since if the term meant anything at all, it meant *princeps civium Romanorum* (the first of Roman citizens), and, in line with the increasing predominance of the military, it was bound to become less and less important as a purely civilian rank. The term thus conveys none of the awe-inspiring totality of power that was contained in the principate in reality. The term simply falls far short. No title describes Augustus's power.

In place of the title, therefore, came the alteration in his name:[163] instead of unity of power, unity of the person. The gentile name was dropped. Augustus was really called Gaius Julius Caesar, but from now on appeared only as C. Caesar. The same thing occurred with Marcus Vipsanius Agrippa, who, on becoming co-ruler, never appeared under his full name again, but simply as Marcus Agrippa. After all, he was his *collega*, if only *minor*. The ruler thus lacked that essential appurtenance of the citizen, the gentilician name. The new element was the *cognomen* 'Augustus', which was bestowed on Octavian three [MH.I, 44] days after he resigned his triumviral office.[164] It is a sacral designation, and implies recognition of the divinity of the person so named. This was how Augustus perceived it. His relationship to the sacral in general was an idiosyncratic one. In itself the rank of *princeps* is not sacral, of course, but the Roman mind was firmly convinced that public offices and priesthoods went hand in hand, and that the highest civil and sacral authorities should be united in one person. Here, too, Augustus followed the example of Caesar, who had already availed himself of the pontificate as the first rung on the ladder of power. Augustus could not deprive Lepidus of this office, however, since the office of Chief Pontiff became vacant only on his death. Not until after the death of Lepidus (12 BC), therefore, did Augustus have himself appointed *summus pontifex*,[165] having previously been a member of almost all priestly corporations. Every available sacral honour was united in his person, and it would be quite wrong to imagine that the title of *Divi filius* was forced upon him against his will, or that divine veneration of his person was practised throughout the entire Empire without either his knowledge or consent. Absurd as it may seem to us, it is not beyond the bounds of possibility that he himself took the notion that he was a god quite seriously as a fact. His fatalistic belief in his star would seem to suggest this.[166]

The name 'Augustus' is a personal name, but from Tiberius onwards it appeared only in conjunction with reigning [MH.I, 45] monarchs.[167] It represents a second, enhanced version of the title *imperator*, signifying the fusion of the sacred office with that of Emperor. The name was never borne by his co-ruler. It is, moreover, not exceptional for women to bear it:[168] 'Augustus' simply expresses the notion of 'by the grace of God'.

It has already been mentioned that the *tribunicia potestas* served to enumerate the ruler's regnal years. It was an odd course to pursue to use this office as the grounds for punishing high treason.[169] Inevitably, the ruler needed to distinguish offences against his person from those against other citizens. Such a position does not evolve overnight, however. This is where the sacrosanct status of the Tribunes of the People helped. For 500 years it had been the most heinous crime to injure a tribune and it is highly probably that this status, which is, after all, analogous to the privileged status of royal persons, led Augustus to assume the tribunician office.[170]

Regarding the outward signs of dignity,[171] military rank might easily have helped here. Augustus was entitled to wear the robes of an official, but there was nothing distinctive about these. Accordingly, he laid claim, as sole commander-in-chief, to the *paludamentum*, the general's cloak. Other officers had military authority, but were not commanders-in-chief. The *paludamentum*, however, was worn only in the provinces, never within the city. It was different with the laurel wreath. This was the privilege of the *triumphator* and was worn at festivals by other men who had had triumphs. Caesar had conferred on himself the right to wear it [MH.I, 46] at all times, and Augustus followed his example here, too. It became the distinctive attire of the Emperor and was later forbidden to private citizens.

As commander-in-chief, Augustus also wore a sword, which became a mark of the *princeps*, although not in Rome. The representation of the Emperor on coins likewise derives from his office as commander-in-chief. This was a significant innovation. Even in the later Republic generals such as Brutus and Cassius had claimed the right to mint coins and put their own heads on them. Coins of the *proconsul Africae* bear the heads of the *princeps* and the *proconsul*, who was also an *imperator*.[172] These date from the period when the Emperor recognized the equality between himself and the Senate. This has nothing to do with the right to mint coins as such: municipalities, the Senate, etc., continued minting at first.[173]

C) THE INSTITUTIONS OF GOVERNMENT

Unfortunately, we often labour under the misapprehension that the relationship between the *princeps* and the Senate corresponds to the interaction between our own constitutional bodies.[174] Unlike modern German provincial parliaments, the Senate was an administrative authority, not a representational one. Its position was weakened by the fact that the administration was divided into separate competences.

How was the Senate constituted? In general as it had been in the Republic. Augustus largely restored senatorial government along its former lines. How Caesar wished to deal with the Senate can no longer be ascertained; probably by reducing it to insignificance, by claiming for himself the right to appoint senators, thereby rapidly depleting the esteem [MH.I, 47] in which the Senate was held.

Augustus purged the Senate of undesirable elements.[175] First, truculent persons who had wasted their property had to be eliminated. He accomplished this quite ruthlessly by exercising the censorial powers vested in him – and not without some personal risk.

Augustus did not claim the right to appoint Senators. The Senate did not appoint the Emperor, nor the Emperor the Senator. The right to enter the Senate was acquired through holding the quaestorship, and thus rested with the assemblies. The appointment was for life – and formally became so with abolition of the censorship. [176] It is thus possible to speak here of popular election, though in fact candidates for the office of quaestor were always young noblemen. *De iure*, therefore, elections were held, but *de facto* the office of Senator was hereditary. It was most unusual for a man born into a senatorial family not to take his seat in the Senate. This hereditary tendency was reinforced by Augustus by bestowing the senator's title *clarissimus vir* on his wife (*clarissima femina*) and his child (*clarissimus puer*).

Electoral assemblies were now completely irrelevant and were soon transferred to the Senate by Tiberius (see above MH. I, 34). The Senate thus elected itself. Here, too, Tiberius was consistent in continuing the process. The Emperor could not remove a Senator from office, aside from stated exceptions. Generally speaking, he did not exercise his censorial prerogative. He exerted an influence on appointments through commendation (*commendatio*), but in practice this influence was restrained. It was quite unusual, for example, for an old man to hold the office of quaestor. [MH.I, 48] The Emperor could not bring an old man into the Senate without dispensing him from the lower offices; and that right of dispensation resided with the Senate. Thus Maecenas was not a member of the Senate (Tac. *Ann.* III, 30).

The Senate comprised a secure and self-assured aristocracy, then still in its full splendour and savouring its colossal wealth. These old Republican families did not face extinction until the reigns of Claudius and Nero. Under Augustus the Senate comprised 600 members, compared to 1,000 under Caesar.[177]

The Senate had the right to participate in government. However, its cumbersome manner of conducting business[178] and the large number of Senators rendered consultation impossible. The Emperor thus took counsel with a few advisers from the Senate. A debate *in pleno* was not feasible, only a roll-call. The Senate was generally presented with *faits accomplis*.

The Republican central government had been organized in such a fashion that people in the Italian motherland were oblivious of it.[179] Each municipality had its own system of jurisdiction, its own police force and even its own military administration. All small towns were effectively states that had been deprived of only a few prerogatives. During the imperial age the *princeps* was responsible for highways. A decree was still in effect, however, that in a case requiring supreme intervention, the Senate was the supreme authority – for example in the case of disputes between towns, the granting of privileges and so on. If there was a wish to form a corporation anywhere, permission to do so had to be granted by the Senate.

The main issue was the administration of the provinces: this was where the taxes came from. Italy paid precious little in the way of taxes, nor did it supply many recruits. Troops were stationed in the provinces. In 27 BC [MH.I, 49] the provinces were divided between the Emperor and the Senate.[180] Some were transferred to the Emperor for his lifetime, others to the Senate. The governors of senatorial provinces were appointed neither by the Senate, nor by the Emperor. Instead, they were allotted annually among the candidates, the former praetors and consuls.

It has already been mentioned that the Emperor assumed the military *imperium*. This is only partially true. This statement does not apply to the first constitutional settlement, since Augustus also intended to share military authority. The men were to be the Emperor's, but not their commanding officers. Originally, the senatorial provinces had been military. There were armies stationed on the Rhine, Danube and Euphrates, in Africa, Egypt and Spain. The Danube lands were at first governed by the Senate, as was Africa (Carthage). There, imperial legions were stationed under the command of proconsuls. In Spain the army in the north (Tarraconensis) was under the Emperor, while in Baetica, and the later Lusitania, it was under the Senate (the latter is disputed). The balance of military power weighed in favour of the Emperor, but the Senate was by no means impotent. But changes took place. Illyricum passed to the Emperor, as did Spain. Under Tiberius the Senate had soldiers only in Africa.

The dyarchy can also be seen in other respects. There were two central imperial treasuries, the *aerarium populi Romani* and the *fiscus* (chest) *Caesaris*.[181] The *aerarium* was an ancient institution and the destination of the traditional taxes, the revenues from the senatorial provinces. To this were now added the *fisci*, actually the private property of the Emperor, but no distinction was made between private property and the property of the crown. [MH.I, 50] There is good reason to assume that, although the *princeps* kept a portion of revenues for himself, his share of expenditure (the army etc.) was greater, and that the statement that Augustus spent millions of his own fortune is quite correct.

This income and the expenditure of the *aerarium populi Romani* both diminished, since the army, highways and grain (*annona*) were funded by the Emperor. By the end of Augustus's administration the *aerarium* was left only with the expenses for games and salaries for officials (*salarium*). This amounted to very little and left a considerable surplus, which was then mostly transferred to the Emperor by senatorial resolution. The Emperor was not empowered to make use of the treasury on his own authority. The most flagrant abuses in the administration of the *aerarium* were eliminated. Supervision was removed from the control of the quaestors and made the responsibility of a senatorial committee. Since this gave rise to even more outrageous abuses, it was then transferred to the praetors, who were men of greater maturity.

In addition a veterans' treasury was set up. Following a lengthy period of military service of twenty to twenty-five years the veteran was entitled to *praemia veteranorum* (veterans' gratuities). This was not unreasonable. The *aerarium militare* was created for this purpose. The very name indicates it to be part of the state treasury. Augustus, however, placed it under his own jurisdiction, rather than that of the Senate (*praetores aerarii*).[182] And this was the path along which the *aerarium* was to go: it came increasingly under the control of the Emperor.

The *fiscus Caesaris* was not a state treasury, but the private fortune of the Emperor, in the broadest possible sense. Taxes from the imperial provinces, as well as from some of the non-imperial, senatorial provinces, flowed into this [MH.I, 51] treasury, passing temporarily out of state ownership. It is necessary to recall here the generals of the Republic. Anything that could be construed as spoils was the property of a general, but he had an obligation to use it for the good of the state. How he did this was his own affair. The Emperor was supreme commander of the Republic. It is likely that the handing over of the provinces to the Emperor was perceived as a transferral of property rights in the land. The prevalent private-law notion was that all these provinces were *de facto* the possessions of the *populus Romanus*, and this principle was applied to the Emperor. This strikes us as odd, but Roman law was unfamiliar with the concept of a mortgage, for example, recognizing only *fiduciae* (pledged deposits). It was in consequence of such a *fiducia* that the Emperor assumed temporary control, for a period of ten years, of these lands and estates. Consequently the provinces became his possessions. In the case of Egypt this is clear in any case; there the Emperor was *eo ipso* successor to the Pharaohs, who were masters of the entire territory.[183]

Not only the income was transferred to the Emperor, however, but also the expenditure – chiefly the wages of the troops and later the *annona*. Both entailed increasing costs. It is not clear how tax revenues were distributed. What is clear is that everywhere, even in the senatorial provinces, the raising of taxes was supervised by the Emperor. This was a result of the scandalous corruption of the proconsuls,[184] who were replaced by *procuratores Augusti* (tax collectors). How further distribution was regulated, however, is not known.

The coinage is a crucial matter in passing judgement on the Roman Emperors.[185] Here, too, a constitutional development may be discerned. From 27 BC onwards both Emperor and Senate were equally entitled to mint coins, but only formally: the Emperor minted in massive quantities, the Senate on a more modest scale. [MH.I, 52] In 15 BC a change was introduced. Small coin was reintroduced, which the oligarchy had abandoned. The *denarius* was in wide use, the half-*denarius* much rarer and small change very rare. Augustus also rectified this serious abuse. There was now abundant minting of coins down to the *quadrans*. The Emperor minted gold and silver – copper was assigned to the Senate.[186] This stabilized the status quo. Although highly significant in formal terms, in substance it marked hardly any concession. It was the responsibility of the Senate to ensure that the required amount of copper coinage was struck and from then on this was done regularly. In the minting of gold and silver there was no intention of making a profit, and none was made; minting was not a source of income. Small change, in contrast, became token currency, and here substantial profits were made, which flowed into the *aerarium*.

The minting of copper coin contained an inherent danger. Any sum of money due could be paid in gold, silver or copper; this was formal Roman law. Had the Emperor been responsible for minting copper coin, this might have done harm. If not actually a strengthening of the Senate's position, the new arrangement was at least a curb on the Emperor's. And the prolonged stability of the currency, which was not undermined until the third century – through bimetallism – is due to this circumstance, making it one of the great achievements of the reign of Augustus.

As regards Republican magistracies, matters were left as they were. But the Emperor could not manage without numerous magistrates; auxiliary officials, however, such as the Republic had had, were something the *princeps* did not need. The fate of the office of quaestor teaches us this. This office acted as a check on the Republican general. The quaestor, although a paymaster under his orders, was nevertheless [MH.I, 53] subsequently answerable to the Senate. In this way, any illegal order issued by a general came to the light of day. This practice persisted in the senatorial provinces, but was irreconcilable with the office of *imperator* and was hence abolished immediately. The Emperor certainly had quaestors among his staff, but they did not accompany him to the provinces;[187] there, the sole authority was the Emperor's representative. The quaestors were employed with civil administration in Rome. The Emperor was under no obligation to be brought to account and could not do with any subordinate officials obliged to render such an account.

Most of the Emperor's officials were military officers. All legions were, after all, under his command; the commander appointed to each legion was a single *legatus legionis*, instead of the six [tribunes] with equal power. Legionary commanders also governed the provinces in which they were stationed. In addition, the raising of taxes called for many officials. The most tangible constraint on imperial power lay in appointments to official posts. The Emperor was bound to observe certain qualifications of rank when making his selection. He could employ only high-born people – 'gentlemen'. There was a marked admixture of oligarchy in this. This principle of the new regime persisted until the end of the century, and when it fell the monarchy fell with it. Indirect co-rule by senators and the equestrian class was a key factor: the 600 senators and 5,000 equestrians constituted a fixed body of men from whom Augustus was obliged to select his senior officials, and this was invariably adhered to.[188]

[MH.I, 54] It is difficult for us to comprehend this system; a single employee was not able to accomplish much within it. How was the auxiliary workforce organized?[189] Generally, the subalterns tend to disappear from our sight, the leader appearing as though he were on his own. And yet the workload of subaltern officials was much heavier then than it is today. They consisted of freedmen, or even slaves. There was thus no Minister of Finance – this office was in the hands of an excellent semi-freedman (the a *rationibus*). This ensured the most rigorous discipline. It can by no means be ruled out that these slaves were men of consequence. They frequently made appearances with much pomp and numerous subordinate slaves,[190] but they were neither citizens, nor were they answerable to citizens, only to their master.

This state of affairs should have led to the most absolute kind of monarchy – even to a 'dominate'. It was the position of the military which hindered this. Officers' posts were reserved for *cives Romani*, indeed equestrians and senators; *servi* and *liberti* were rigorously excluded. The army thus initially retained its exclusive, aristocratic character. This, too, had been different under Caesar: his Egyptian legions had been under the command of freedmen.

It became a principle that the post of *legatus legionis* required senatorial rank (a non-senatorial one was called *pro legato*). This was even more true of commanders senior to him – for governors in provinces where armies were stationed, such as Gaul. This practice was retained even after the division of the provinces. The highest provincial commands were linked to the highest-ranking class in the Senate (*consulares*), and command of a regiment to previous tenure of the office of praetor. This represented a serious constraint, narrowing the choice [MH.I, 55] to only a handful of men. It may be noted that the term of office for the consulate was later limited to six months, thereby doubling the choice from two to four candidates.[191] Augustus had at his disposal only fifty to sixty persons of consular rank. In comparison, he annually appointed only twenty praetors, where Caesar had appointed forty. This, too, was a not inconsiderable factor in the increasing role of the Senate.

The Senate was also treated with suspicion, however. Senators were excluded from certain posts. This applied in particular to all military posts in Italy and Egypt. Egypt was the Emperor's domain and no senator could go there without his permission. This is demonstrated by the accusation levelled at Germanicus.[192] Likewise Italy and the Alpine provinces, where no senator was permitted to carry the officer's sword.

Whereas the recruitment of non-Romans had once been exceptional, foreign peoples were now encouraged to join the cohorts in large numbers. But they were not commanded by senators. The post of *tribunus militum* was filled most often by equestrians, only rarely by senators.

The remaining administrative positions were filled not by ordinary citizens, but by members of the equestrian class.[193] An *eques Romanus equo publico* ('Roman cavalryman with a publicly provided horse') had to have a fortune of 400,000[194] sesterces, i.e. 100,000 *denarii*. He was also required to be of good birth. Freedmen could not occupy equestrian posts, nor could senators, a principle that was now rigorously enforced. The son of a senator was no longer an equestrian, but became *clarissimus puer*, although he still needed to be given this rank by the Emperor, and for this, in turn, he needed the qualifications mentioned. The equestrian class constituted a second aristocracy rivalling that of the senators. [MH.I, 56] The number of *equites* totalled some 5,000–6,000 – ten times that of senators. These figures are flexible. We are not told that there was a fixed maximum: the Emperor could create as many *equites* as he wished. This class provided the bulk of senior officers. The *eques* could not become a common soldier, otherwise he would have to relinquish his *equus*. Augustus adhered to this practice rigorously. The command of the Guard and of the fleet was likewise in the hands of *equites*. Military officers frequently supervised the raising of taxes by equestrian procurators – a task in which military assistance was frequently necessary. If a governor fell ill, the procurator stood in for him; this fact presupposed military authority. Later the *praefectus annonae* was also an *eques*.

The administrative duties of governors were not supposed to include any financial responsibilities. Augustus reimposed this rule, with stringent controls. The outrageous plundering of the provinces that had occurred during the Republic was no longer tolerated. In this respect the administration of justice became draconian. Payment of expenses ensured that no-one was left out of pocket as a result of holding office. Magistrates of senatorial rank remained in office for only one year and were hardly able to grow rich. The *equites*, however, were paid high salaries and often remained in office for years. They could, and did, grow rich and constituted a preparatory school for the Senate, which the upwardly mobile joined. The sharing of government by individual senators and *equites* is perhaps more significant than the formal co-rule of the Senate as a whole.

In the army,[195] the national identity was respected. Foreigners were strictly excluded from service in the legions, since Roman citizenship was a precondition. Military service was a general obligation of subjects.[196] Troops of Roman citizens – legions of 5,000–6,000 men – decidedly had precedence; units consisting of [MH.I, 57] non-citizens, at the most a thousand strong, had lower status.

Demobilization of the entire army – a return to normal peacetime conditions – had already been completely abandoned under the Republic. The war in Spain by itself made this impossible. What Augustus introduced was not a regular army, but regular service. There were probably no real professional soldiers before his time. There had been major armies, but no permanent service. There had been no obligation for it. During civil wars, armies had been levied with haste and speed, almost as if called up out of the ground. All this disappeared in the imperial age. It was a source of acute embarrassment to require supplementary troops. It was preferable to relocate legions from one province to another; conscription was no longer equal to the task.

Two periods may be distinguished in military administration: one from 27 BC on, the other from AD 6 on. The first arrangements came about under the pressure of civil war and the desire for peace. This gave rise to persistent defects in military organization. The twenty-year period of military service[197] did leave the bulk of the population unencumbered, but it also entailed the loss of seasoned, able-bodied reservists. The Empire now had a fine army of professional soldiers, but nothing in reserve.

The principle that only citizens could serve was abandoned next.[198] What had previously been granted to the Italians could now be demanded by all residents of the Empire. [MH.I, 58] At this juncture, therefore, the *cohortes* and *alae* (with some 500 men) were organized as *auxiliaria legionum* and attached to legions composed of citizens. Conditions of service were also intensified; this was already implied in the longer period of service. It was now all the more difficult for unseasoned men to join up. The cavalry, then in total disarray, was also reformed. Augustus once again regarded the legion as a mixed corps. Despite the small number of cavalry (120 per legion), this was still an improvement on the Numidian and Germanic mercenary cavalrymen found in the final period of the Republic. The *alae* thus now joined the auxiliaries as an assisting force. The precise ratio of citizens to non-citizens is unknown.

In 27 BC Augustus fixed the number of legions at eighteen. Since the troops were never at full strength this amounted to roughly 100,000 men. The number of auxiliaries has not been ascertained, but is assumed to have been roughly equal to that of the legions – if anything somewhat lower, to prevent a preponderance of non-citizens. This number, 200,000 men, was entirely inadequate for such a vast Empire, with its unruly neighbours and subject nations, especially in Spain. This was demonstrated in the German War. In AD 6 eight new legions were raised and this number of twenty-five legions[199] remained remarkably static until Diocletian.[200] Augustus may well have made skilful use, in that tense session of the Senate, of the alarm caused by the Dalmatian uprising in order to expedite army reorganization. It is, nonetheless, odd that a state such as the Roman Empire was unable to sustain a high military budget. This may partly be explained by the fact that Roman citizens were not taxed. [MH.I, 59] The fact remains, however, that it was largely financial considerations that impeded army reorganization.

In general Augustus adapted the *ordre de bataille* of Caesar. This was based on a defence of the frontiers and of critical inland locations by permanent garrisons. The army was thus made up of fortified garrisons: a glaring mistake. In order to defend one frontier, it was necessary at the same time to expose another flank. This was dictated by political considerations. Caesar had avoided this mistake by mustering a field army, in the first instance for the Parthian War. It is possible, although not at all probable, that this army was then intended to be disbanded. Augustus based his defences on the Euphrates, the Danube and the Rhine or Elbe.

This left a yawning gulf between Syria and the Danube: Asia Minor was undefended. Here, too, excessive thrift seems to have been a factor. Caesar had levied a Bithynian-Pontic army; Augustus disbanded it and sought a surrogate in client-states. Behind them the necessary military force was stationed in Syria; this was absolutely indispensable. Two substantial armies were quartered in the north and west of Spain. In 27 BC the Asturian-Cantabrian War broke out.[201] The senatorial province was well equipped for this – perhaps too well.

The province of Africa had to be defended against savage peoples. Similarly, Alexandria needed to be held in constant check by a large garrison.[202] It was also important to the Emperor to maintain a private army of sorts there, under a non-senatorial command. The distribution of legions changed, but in general the Rhine army had eight legions, the Danube army six and the Euphrates army four.[203] There was rivalry between these armies, [MH.I, 60] such as in AD 68/9, the Year of Four Emperors, when there was conflict among the armies over the office of *princeps*.

In Italy, we are struck by two dissimilarities between Caesar and Augustus. For political reasons Caesar had permitted a military command in Cisalpine Gaul (northern Italy), albeit only of one legion, which nevertheless covered the northern frontier. This legionary commander was master of Italy. This was completely abolished by Augustus. But how was the frontier to be defended? At first there was a foray into the Alps to subjugate the peoples on both sides. This was the Raetian-Vindelician War (15 BC).[204] Firm control was imposed on Bavaria, the Tyrol and eastern Switzerland. With only isolated exceptions, law and order was restored to unruly[205] Alpine valleys – a major achievement by Augustus. Northern Italy was secured.

It was not politically feasible to organize a substantial legion command in Bavaria. The procurator of Raetia obtained only auxiliary troops, who lacked the status of the legions. Noricum was presumably initially established as a client-state. Its kings did not even have auxiliary troops, only a territorial militia which there-fore posed no threat. The Wallis, which could have posed a threat to Italy, was placed under Tyrolean (Raetian) administration. In the Cottian Alps, with their capital Susa, a petty king ruled with the same status as a praetor. Savoy went to Gallia Narbonensis. There were no major commands there. The major commands began, in the one direction at Lake Constance facing the Germanic tribes, and, in the other, on the river Drava, facing the Illyrians.

Now to Italy proper. Caesar had played military ruler there with no troops and had paid for this folly with his life. This mistake was not [MH.I, 61] to be repeated. It was not feasible to bring legions to Rome, but the Guard[206] was formed, with its headquarters in the *praetorium* (*qui in praetorio militant*: 'those serving in the commander's headquarters'). This guard was formed after the battle of Philippi (42 BC). Previously, the 500-man guard had been insignificant; now, they were a force to be reckoned with.[207] Augustus created nine double cohorts (9,000 men, naturally without auxiliaries – as good as a legion).[208] The Guard was not conceived of as a discrete unit and was under the command of two fully equal Praetorian Prefects. This was done to pre-empt the formation of a close-knit regimental spirit and constitutes another contrast with Caesar. The former Philippensian guard had comprised long-serving soldiers. Augustus did away with this, recruiting young volunteers from the old Latin districts, which made them agreeable to the Latin population.

It emerges from this that the Praetorians were to all intents and purposes the garrison of Rome. *De iure* they were the Emperor's headquarters, and might accompany him if he left Rome, but in practice this did not occur. Augustus did not encumber himself with his full entourage on his frequent travels. Not until Domitian onwards did Emperors take the Praetorian guard with them on campaign. Augustus recruited only 1,000 men for service in the city of Rome. The others were stationed not in, but around Rome. It was only under Tiberius that they were installed in the *castra praetoria*, encamped in the capital.[209] Here, too, Augustus only began to do all that was necessary. The tenth, eleventh and twelfth cohorts were designated 'urban cohorts' (*cohortes urbanae*), bringing the Praetorian guard *de facto* up to 12,000 men. These remained in the city even in time of war.

[MH.I, 62] Besides the Praetorian guard, the fire brigade (*vigiles*) was also stationed in Rome. This was established later by Augustus – fire-fighting had fallen into serious disarray. Elsewhere, there were volunteer fire brigades with military status (*collegia fabrum sive centonariorum*). In the capital such municipal self-help appeared to be impossible. Augustus sought at first to entrust the command to magistrates, but this failed. Even a rigorously run fire brigade could achieve nothing under an annually rotating pair of commanders. In AD 6 Augustus established a fire-fighting corps of 8,000 men (seven cohorts).[210] These were divided into seven camps for the fourteen regions under the command of a *praefectus vigilum* of equestrian status, like the senior officers. That this was no mere administrative measure is suggested by the number of men and the year in which they were set up, since reorganization of the army itself followed immediately. The number of troops stationed in the capital was effectively doubled. The fire brigade always remained somewhat lower in rank to the military, so that *vigiles* could only be recruited from the lower orders – freedmen and humble citizens, but never slaves.

The chief of the *cohortes urbanae* was not a city official, but the Emperor; Augustus derived his authority for this from the earlier institution of the *praefectura urbis*, said to have existed as early as the time of Romulus.[211] In the absence of the Emperor as supreme magistrate, an urban prefect was appointed. This office did not become a permanent feature until the reign of Tiberius, in consequence of the Emperor's prolonged absence.

[MH.I, 63] One of Augustus's most beneficial acts was the raising of a fleet such as had not been seen since the Punic War.[212] It constituted a significant counterbalance against oligarchy. There was no need to fear an enemy at sea, but a naval police force was necessary. Small galleys were thus sufficient. Special fleets were created in all provinces where they were called for: on the Nile, Rhine and Danube. Although not a mighty force, they supported the land army. In addition, there were two major fleets for Italy, at Ravenna and Misenum.[213] Augustus also established these; they emerged from the war against Sextus Pompey. Here a unique arrangement came about. The Italian fleet was manned by slaves and freedmen, and hence regarded as belonging to the imperial household. This marks a singular breach of the principle of the citizen soldier.

Another exception comprised the mounted guard of Germanic troops, the elite bodyguard, also entrusted with guarding the ladies of the imperial household. These Germans probably enjoyed a higher status than the Praetorian guard – *de facto* soldiers, *de iure* slaves. The men selected were Germans from among peoples within the imperial frontiers. This provides another instance of Augustus not ignoring Caesarian precedents. Caesar had had a Spanish bodyguard. Italians were still suspect. Later the fleet was incorporated into the army and ceased to be an institution of the imperial household; likewise with the Germans (*equites singulares*). Both corps ceased to be constituted of slaves. But this did not occur until the time of Claudius.[214]

The fleets soon made a clean sweep at sea. Apart from a few periods in the third century,[215] the sea was completely free of pirates. [MH.I, 64] On the other hand, the fleet also served as a garrison for the defence of Italy – one fleet to the north, the other to the south. Both fleets had sub-headquarters in Rome, where there were the *castra Misenatium* and *Ravennatium*, which could be used to augment the garrison. Their strength may be estimated as equal to that of a legion. All told, the Italian garrison may have amounted to 40,000 men.

Reviewing these measures, we discover that the principle of keeping the capital free of troops was abandoned. *Cohortes urbanae* were also set up in other capitals, such as Lyon and Carthage. In Egypt, one legion was permanently stationed in Alexandria. The number of troops was very small, but the presence of municipal militias must also be taken into account. Every mayor had the authority of a *tribunus militum* in an emergency and it may be assumed that in unruly regions such as Spain it was exercised.[216]

In the military sphere too, the administrative reforms of Augustus were also hampered by political considerations. When an army has a Guard's regiment, this may be either detrimental or beneficial. In this case it was highly detrimental, since the Guard was given preferential treatment in every respect, particularly when it came to promotion. The legionary could claim the *praemia veteranorum* (veterans' gratuities) after completing his twenty years of service, whereas the guardsman needed to serve only sixteen years and could continue serving at the age of 36 as a reserve officer-in-waiting. In addition, a select corps of *evocati* was formed for the training of junior legionary officers. This was blatantly preferential treatment, and caused jealousy.

Whereas frontier legions were almost always engaged in combat, [MH.I, 65] the Praetorian guard was hardly ever confronted by an enemy. The guardsman was a peacetime, parade-ground soldier, rendering the guard the spawning-ground of revolutions. It would have been better to introduce rotation within the legions, but popular and Republican prejudice was too strong to permit this. It was a fatal mistake on the part of Augustus not to sweep this prejudice aside. His arrangements frequently bear the stamp of weakness.

In other respects, the state of affairs in Italy manifested numerous changes for the better. The state became a more efficiently functioning machine. Urban administration proper, and above all public works, had fallen into complete disarray. The cause was the disappearance of the office of censor, which now existed on paper only. The aediles and censors no longer did the work called for in a world capital. The principle of annual office-holding had not applied to the censorship. Public works were carried out on a shoestring and only ever planned for five-year periods. The office of censor had lapsed, however. Augustus's approach was twofold. The first duty of the censor was to carry out a census for conscription purposes, the second was to be responsible for public works. Augustus himself took on the former duty, which was politically maladroit of him. In the latter case he gave financial assistance out of his own pocket. The Forum of Augustus with its Temple of Mars is not his only work;[217] much more important was his restoration of public buildings. The still impressive prospect of Rome today was the work of the Emperors, particularly Vespasian, Trajan and Hadrian. Augustus restored eighty-two temples,[218] doing so without legal title. In addition to this activity there was his restoration of public-works authorities [MH.I, 66] and, furthermore, not only for Rome, but also for Italy, even though this was in fact outside his sphere.

Highways[219] were essential for control of the country: this had been one of the key ideas of the Republic. The country had been conquered by means of highways, and the Republic had never sought to foist the burden of highway-building on to the municipalities. The land on which highways ran was *solum publicum populi Romani* (public land of the Roman people). The consuls had supervised this work themselves (even today they are called *via consularis*). All this had fallen into lamentable disarray, and Augustus had to intervene. He took on the Flaminian Way himself; other leading figures restored other roads.[220] Besides this, a permanent authority was created to be in charge of maintenance. Augustus departed from the principle of centralization in this, since it was not feasible here. A number of specialist officials were appointed. Being a straightforward military operation, the building of highroads had a political aspect. Yet it was not really the concern of the *imperator*; he was encroaching here on the senatorial sphere of authority. This explains the form taken by the institution. The officials (*curatores*) were appointed by Augustus – all of them senators whom Augustus first had selected by the Senate. The six to eight great military roads each acquired special *curatores* from 20 BC onwards.

Somewhat later the aqueducts[221] were placed in the care of a five-man senatorial commission headed by a *curator aquarum*. Augustus likewise appointed specific officials for various public works (*curatores operum publicorum*). These were responsible not for constructing new stone buildings, but only for restoring existing ones. [MH.I, 67] Immediately after the death of Augustus, Tiberius added *curatores ripae et alvei* to regulate the Tiber.[222]

The task of supplying Rome was a difficult one.[223] Here, too, Augustus had to take on a task without being granted a budget. Expenditure on grain was a curse he could not avoid. It had been a fatal mistake on the part of the Republic to allow the *plebs* of the capital to grow accustomed to cheap corn. Grain was sold, or even given away, by the government at below the Italian cost price, which entailed the systematic ruin of Italian farmers. Augustus was fully mindful of the harm being done. He wanted to do away with the *frumentationes publicae* (public corn distribution), but this would only have resulted in the immediate appearance of a pretender. It often proves no simple matter to eradicate grave injustice. Some Italians took refuge in vegetable- and wine-growing, but many farms were abandoned. An efficient authority was needed to ensure grain supplies. The Republic had failed to provide this, thereby compounding its error. The career of Pompey had demonstrated that the office of *praefectus annonae* (prefect of the corn supply) paved the way to the throne.[224] The grain business thus had to be in the hands of the monarch himself: the alternative was political suicide.

In 22 BC Augustus took over the *cura annonae*, notwithstanding the municipal nature of the office.[225] Caesar had achieved nothing by raising the number of aediles from four to six. The young incumbents, who rotated annually, lacked even permanent funds and were dependent on the Senate for everything. This would have to change. Augustus assumed this office as ruler of Egypt, in a sense providing the money [MH.I, 68] out of his own pocket. He sought to obtain a representative as *curator annonae* chosen by lot from the Senate, but this failed. Remarkably, towards the end of his administration the *praefectus annonae* came to replace the *curatores annonae*.[226] He was an *eques* who had the Emperor's trust. The Senate no longer needed to concern itself. It is not known, however, when exactly this change occurred.

The *cura annonae* included responsibility for keeping the imperial granaries supplied. This eliminated the element of chance in supplying the capital. Distribution (*frumentationes publicae*) was not necessarily connected with this. It had been necessary to take over this abhorrent legacy from the ochlocracy. The transition did not occur without opposition, however. The Republic had disregarded need: each citizen was given something. Distribution had proceeded unchecked and the riff-raff concentrated in Rome. Caesar had largely eliminated this *sentina* (dregs) by dispatching them to colonize Carthage and Corinth, and had restricted the list of grain recipients to 150,000.[227] No longer was everyone in a position to feed himself at public expense. At first, Augustus let matters run their course. In 2 BC, however, he returned to Caesar's system, fixing the list at 200,000 persons.[228] This certainly provided for the poor, but was out of all proportion. It was only out of an exaggerated regard for political considerations that Augustus continued the *panes et circenses*.[229] This arrangement was part and parcel of the gifts of money at triumphs and in wills, also inherited from the Republic. For instance, Augustus distributed gifts in accordance with the will of Caesar.[230]

[MH.I, 69] The *congiaria* likewise fall into the category of money gifts. Already during the Republic, victorious soldiers had received donations of money, among other things. This, however, had been a gesture confined to the military class, defrayed out of spoils. It was Caesar who had extended this practice to all citizens, distributing 400 sesterces (approx. 100 Marks) per head among the populace of the capital.[231] This was to prove a fatal step. Once done, it could not be retracted. Augustus[232] elaborated this arrangement into a system, seeking to act in the interests of the new monarchy by making donations of money on the occasion of his own household festivals. The mob was thus given largesse (*congiarium*) when Gaius and Lucius Caesar put on the *toga virilis*. The donations were linked to the distribution of grain and bestowed on 200,000–300,000 people. Whereas *uterque ordo*[233] had previously only been excluded from this *de facto*, that exclusion now acquired the force of law. Augustus parted with the equivalent of some 120–150 million Marks in the course of his reign through these monetary donations alone. When one considers the constant monetary vice in which the *aerarium* was trapped under Augustus, one is bound to judge this a huge drain on the government, a drain that remained a constant burden to the Empire.

[MH.I, 70] The capital was also given preferential treatment with regard to public entertainment (*circenses*).[234] Specifically, this took three forms: stage plays, gladiatorial contests and *circenses* in the narrow sense (chariot races). The two former types were ubiquitous throughout the Roman Empire, albeit not as official institutions. The state and municipalities competed in this. In the early period under the Emperors stage plays were to the fore, even in the capital. It was not until Claudius that gladiatorial contests became part of the official festival calendar. Nevertheless, they had been frequent enough even before that, although requiring imperial permission.

The *circenses* were restricted to the capital alone.[235] Only Rome had a circus and 'jockeys'. Sports competitions had thus now taken the place of electoral campaigning, and it was in the interests of the Emperor to keep the people on this track. People must, after all, be at liberty to get excited about something. The green and blue clubs documented from the age of Constantine were already in existence under Augustus;[236] significantly, the term *factio* denoted these party factions of the racetrack. Why were there no jockeys in the municipalities? The answer is simple. Rome was furnished with a strong police force; the municipalities were not. That this is the reason becomes clear when we consider the degree of violence fomented by these contests at Pompeii.[237] The government [MH.I, 71] could not permit this in the municipalities, where such races could not be justified as a substitute for election fever, as in the capital. It was an unwanted privilege. This only began to change under Diocletian.

Jockeys enjoyed huge earnings. One earned 300,000, another even 6 million Marks. Augustus was shrewd enough, however, as in Republican times, to shift these exorbitant financial burdens from the public to the private purse. He loaded them on to the magistrates, from the rank of praetor upwards. This was plainly done with the intention of not making entry into the Senate (achieved by holding the office of aedile) too difficult. This was thus a tax paid by the cream of the aristocracy. As far as can be judged today, the amount paid out of the public purse towards covering the cost of games was minimal. It was forbidden for private citizens to maintain troops of gladiators in Rome.[238]

The population of Rome at this time was the worst imaginable. Rome was entirely devoid of industry: only a few types of large-scale trade flourished, employing few hands. Communal liberty was completely lacking: Rome was the least free municipality in the Empire. Then there was the disastrous peacetime garrison, which had nothing to do and succumbed to indolence and idleness, as did the great mass of those in receipt of petty state pensions, who continued to regard themselves as the sovereign people. The doors were closed to all laudable endeavour. The *plebs* had nothing but the passions of the circus and, if these were taken away, rioting. Revolution was not to be feared from this [MH.I, 72] quarter, however; the *plebs* were too enervated for that.

What, above all, made the principate so nefarious was its utter dreariness, emptiness and poverty of spirit.[239] That is the terrible thing about it. This brutalization was not caused by the monarchy, however, as Republican propaganda claims: on the contrary, the seeds had been sown more than adequately during the Republic. Gaius (Caligula), Commodus and others simply embodied the *plebs* on the throne. Even under the Republic there had never been a truly free intellectual life, not even in the time of Cicero. The Emperors, however, soon ushered in total intellectual senility, even in Pliny, to whom Cicero was congenial. From the capital, the corruption of language and of education spread to the provinces.

D) THE PROVINCES

Now for the administration of the provinces. Augustus had inherited a policy of conquest from his adoptive father. Caesar had intended to extend the frontiers of the Empire. This was intrinsic to his policies. The demise of liberty was to be gilded externally.

We know from the poetry written in the time of Augustus that the idea of expansion was of great significance. Augustus did not exactly seek to counter this, but rather to meet it with an appearance of success. His policy is understandable. The conquests made later in some cases proved detrimental, such as that of Britain,[240] and in some cases untenable, as with the land east of the Euphrates. But Augustus certainly wanted to win glory in Germany. [MH.I, 73] The policy of conquest derived from the political position of the *imperator*. The Republic still had deep roots in the hearts of the most hard-working municipalities – the battle-fields of Philippi and Pharsalus had demonstrated this much – and the sole means of redirecting these aspirations elsewhere lay in compensating for the loss of civic liberty through the glory of victories abroad.

In addition, the Roman monarch was essentially a general, a fact on which the greater part of his power rested. Residence in Rome, *socordia* (idleness), meant ruin for the *princeps*. Augustus understood this better than anyone, apart from Trajan and Hadrian. The Empire's centre of gravity was no longer in Rome, but in the provinces. Diocletian was thinking of this later when he established mobile capitals. Augustus trod in the footsteps of his father. Agrippa travelled everywhere with him. A good deal of history can be learned from his sojourns after 27 BC. Following his installation of the new order he immediately travelled to Gaul for a short time, then on to Spain for two years. In 24 BC he returned to Rome, where he remained for two years. In 22 he went to Sicily, and on to Syria, returning in 19 BC. From 16 to 13 BC he was in Gaul, and again in 10 and 8 BC. Agrippa also travelled, going to Spain in 20 BC, then spending a considerable time in Asia Minor and on the Black Sea. Tiberius was active in the Danube lands. These journeys in many cases involved direct military intervention, but the presence of the Emperor was essential for the organization of the provinces, for dividing them into cantons and tax assessment: this was his particular duty.

[MH.I, 74] By the nature of things, Sicily is part of Italy. This had not yet been grasped under the Republic. It was Caesar who had bestowed Latin rights on the island and thereby won the Greek island for Rome. Latin became the language of public business. Augustus took this a step further. The entire island was granted Roman citizenship.[241] Nevertheless, the Roman provincial constitution remained in force. Sicily had to be governed centrally, if only on account of piracy. However, this made little substantial difference: in practical terms, Sicily and Italy were united. In other respects the island was beyond help: it had been economically bled to death under the Republic. This is revealed in minor details. Not a single highway was built in Sicily. Only the coastal areas were colonized, and the towns there flourished – especially Catania and Panhormus (Palermo) – but agriculture had been ruined inland. The slave wars under Sextus Pompey may have been responsible for this.

Augustus likewise set to work in Spain, completely subjugating the peninsula. In the later years of the Republic the north and west had been under only very loose hegemony; there were no Roman settlements. In 26 and 25 BC the Asturians and Cantabrians put up some stiff resistance.[242] In 20 BC Agrippa completed the pacification; major colonies were established, such as Asturica Augusta (Astorga). The military colony of Legio Septima (Léon) grew from a garrison into a town. Arrangements of a civilian nature were more important. Augustan colonies appeared everywhere; these served the purpose of providing for veterans and were not connected with the general status of the province. It is curious, however, that towns obtained Roman or Latin rights without having Roman colonists. A sixth or eighth of the towns had these privileges. [MH.I, 75] This means that Romanization was imposed on towns from above by means of these rights and that Augustus planned the process of Romanization in these terms. And this plan was consistently carried out until the time of Vespasian, who Latinized the entire peninsula in this manner. At first, Spain was entirely in the hands of the Emperor; later, at the beginning of Tiberius's reign, the south-east (Baetica) was transferred to the Senate as a pacified province and very rapidly civilized. Lusitania remained imperial.

The name 'Africa' denotes the north coast excluding Egypt. Caesar had refounded Carthage as a colony, which rapidly flourished as a capital city. The king of West Africa, Juba of Numidia (Algeria), had been involved in the fall of Pompey. Only Mauretania (Morocco) retained its own ruler, because the latter had fought for Caesar. Nominally, Augustus re-established the kingdom under Juba II, son of Juba I, a relative of Augustus. Cleopatra, daughter of Antony, was his wife. Juba was Romanized and, as the antiquarian[243] of Fez, lived entirely in the intellectual world of a Roman. He ruled as a representative of the Roman people. Roman colonies were founded in his territory, in Mauretania and Numidia. We should not be surprised by a later shift in frontiers, therefore. In 25 BC a reorganization came about. The whole of West Africa was taken over by Rome. Morocco was assigned to Juba. In the east, however, Juba ceded Cirta (Constantine) to the governor. The reason for this lies in the organization of Cirta, where a major colony of Roman citizens had grown up. Even under Caesar, Cirta, governed by his supporter Publius Sittius,[244] had been half Roman, and there seems to have been a plan to incorporate the town into the circle of provinces. Juba was originally king of Numidia and from 25 BC king of Mauretania Tingitana. His territory extended as far as the Atlantic Ocean. [MH.I, 76] From this time onwards there is evidence of a considerable degree of intellectual and political development. This sudden change was introduced particularly with regard to Rome and the requirements of the *annona*. Agriculture was highly intensive. Even today the ruins of towns are to be found quite small distances apart. A garrison was also installed to defend the province. It was pushed forward in stages from *Tevessa* (Lambaesis) as the hinterland became Romanized. Cyrene remained relatively subordinate, as it lacked a hinterland capable of sustaining civilization.

Egypt was not regarded as a province in the strict sense of the term, but was bound to the Emperor in a personal union. Every *princeps* was their king (*basileus*) in the eyes of the Egyptians, and his representative was a viceroy (*basilikos*). The administration gradually extended beyond the frontiers of Egypt, to influence that of all imperial domains. Egypt represents a significant exception. In the foreign policy of Augustus, there were offensive wars on the upper Nile east of Syene. Gaius Petronius conquered the Nubians, advancing as far as Meroe (Khartoum).[245] These did not become permanent conquests, but peace was concluded, probably in the form of a commercial treaty.

Augustus pursued a similar policy in Arabia, but was not fortunate there. The Romans conquered little, ruling only parts of Petraea for a time. Augustus wanted to conquer Arabia Felix. Gaius Aelius Gallus marched as far as Aden to ensure control of the Red Sea. Operations were likewise conducted on the opposite coast, but the expedition foundered on natural obstacles.[246] [MH.I, 77] This campaign nevertheless reveals Augustus's objectives and was probably not entirely fruitless, since trade with India took an upward turn, with Roman coins passing to India in huge amounts. Trade with India now no longer passed through Syria, but through Egypt. Alexandria flourished rapidly; the imperial domain became the major emporium for trade with India.

In Asia, the status quo needed to be maintained. Here Augustus's policy of peace proved successful. An enormous army was quartered on the Euphrates, but Asia Minor was not covered. Client contingents served as a surrogate. The true hub of Roman hegemony was Galatia, with a population well practised in warfare. Their king, Amyntas, had been on Antony's side. In 25 BC he died and his kingdom was declared a Roman province, including the regions of eastern Phrygia, Lycaonia, Pisidia and Isauria.[247] Because of a shortage of soldiers, the new governor received no legions, but probably cohorts and alae. Here, the fighting capabilities of local manpower sufficed: the Galatians had been trained in the ways of Rome. In addition to them there were also the minor client-states of Cappadocia, Commagene (on the upper Euphrates) and Armenia. Augustus hoped to bring the latter important country under permanent Roman rule; this was the objective behind Roman policy regarding the Parthians. On the Black Sea coast the client kingdom of Polemon[248] was founded (the Crimea and eastern Pontus); this was the former kingdom of Mithridates. Hegemony over the Crimea, the Bosporan kingdom, was a firm bastion of Roman rule.

The Parthians were the sole neighbouring state with whom Rome dealt on an equal footing.[249] It was impossible to make it dependent. The Arsacid state never became a client-state of Rome. Augustus allowed this relationship to continue, pursuing a consistent policy of peace. [MH.I, 78] This was difficult, since Rome had suffered two severe defeats. The loss of the legionary eagles was an abiding humiliation.

Immediately after Actium, Augustus passed through Syria, but made a treaty with the Parthians and did not campaign against them. In 20 BC another action followed. He succeeded in persuading the Parthians to return the standards[250] and represented this as a major success. He had the eagles ceremonially brought back to the Capitol (hence the coins[251] bearing the inscription *signa restituta*). This was regarded as adequate revenge. Since the Parthian state was plagued by incessant dynastic disputes, it had good reason to keep on good terms with Rome. It thus ceded hegemony of Armenia. Tigranes was invested by Rome and all was accomplished by peaceful means. Tiberius marched into Armenia and installed him as the king. Augustus was completely satisfied.

Around the time of the birth of Christ, however, this relationship began to waver. In 6 BC Augustus deemed it necessary to undertake an expedition to reinstate the expelled Tigranes. Tiberius refused and as a consequence of this domestic discord the expedition failed to take place.[252] There was then a pause of several years to wait for a suitable man who was also an imperial prince. When Gaius Caesar was ready (by then 20 years old), he was made commander of the army in 1 BC.[253] At first, he carried out his task successfully. He installed Ariobarzanes. Gaius Caesar and the Great King conferred on an island in the Euphrates. The Parthians accommodated themselves. But nevertheless fighting ensued, because the Armenians objected to the king who had been forced upon them. Perhaps it was Augustus's wish that Gaius should prove his military worth. He laid siege to Artagira, was fatally wounded and died in AD 3. The expedition was nevertheless successful. The status quo ante was restored. Hardly had the Romans turned [MH.I, 79] their backs, however, before Ariobarzanes was expelled. The Parthians intervened and supporters of the two parties battled incessantly.[254] It was impossible to maintain hegemony of this kind merely through the influence of distant Rome. It was an abortive policy – abortive for lack of adequate military might to support it.

Of vital importance for the Empire was the theatre of war in Europe. The *imperium* was, after all, a European, and specifically an Italian Empire. In Africa and Asia, therefore, Augustus could afford to be completely on the defensive, despite his serious errors of judgement regarding Armenia. This did not apply to the Danube and Rhine lines, which were always mutually interdependent. For these two lines were now to be replaced by the Elbe line. This marks the first occasion on which our own Fatherland stepped on to the stage of world history. It was the crucial task of Augustus to secure and reinforce this frontier – in its way a very appropriate policy, and again a continuation of Caesar's grand design. In this respect also the Republic had fallen far short. Possession had, admittedly, been taken of the Mediterranean coasts at an early stage, but between Macedonia and northern Italy there yawned a huge gulf that had scarcely been subdued at all. As early as 35/4 BC, Augustus set about conquering Dalmatia.[255] He subdued the country slowly, moving out from Istria, first up the Kupa valley, then swinging back and inwards to Dalmatia. Although a Roman occupation force continued to be necessary for another century, Illyricum Superius remained under Roman rule.

Very little is known of the events in Gaul in 38/7 BC. Not only did Agrippa defeat the Aquitanians, which was part of the Spanish campaign, but [MH.I, 80] he also recrossed the Rhine and occasioned the founding of Cologne.[256] He removed the Ubians, who had acquiesced in Roman rule early on, to the left bank of the Rhine and gave them an *oppidum* to be their focus in the shape of the *ara* (*Augusti*), the 'Altar of Augustus'. This is how Ara Ubiorum came about. From then on Cologne[257] became the major Roman base. Its later name was Colonia Claudia Ara Agrippinensis, since the younger Agrippina was born there. This was a crucial step. The Romans established themselves securely on the Rhine, as Caesar's plan had probably envisaged. This seems to have exerted a consolidating effect for some considerable time; Augustus was probably for the time being content with the Sava and Rhine lines.

Little was done about the Lower Danube, although even here there is evidence of change. The Getic state of Dacia was organized, enabling a small people to become mighty as a result of theocratic-political reform. This was not without its dangers for the Romans: a unifed great nation was emerging. When Augustus marched against Antony, a Getic invasion of Italy was anticipated: they were in alliance with Antony. Marcus Licinius Crassus, grandson of the triumvir, dispatched an expedition against the Getans from Moesia, and celebrated a triumph over them in 29 BC.[258] The Sava frontier was established, the Rhine frontier consolidated. For twenty years there was nothing serious to report from Gaul; the war by Messalla against the Aquitanians in 27 BC was a prelude to the Spanish War.[259]

The pretext leading to the war against the Germans was the *clades Lolliana* of 16 BC.[260] The Germans crossed the Rhine and captured the eagle [MH.I, 81] of the fifth legion. Although a painful defeat, it was, however, no more than that. How did it come about that this chance event shaped Augustus's entire policy and led to an offensive? The real reason lies in the policy of Caesar. Agrippa's influence will have been minimal: in this, too, he proved subservient. The influence of Drusus will have been all the greater. He was believed to be the natural son of Augustus,[261] but in all probability this was idle talk. He was, however, born in Augustus's home and greatly loved by him, whereas Tiberius was always loathsome to him. Drusus was popular in every respect and liberal, like every crown prince.[262] He was expected to restore the Republic. It was probably Drusus who persuaded his father to go to war.

In 16/15 BC the Raetian-Vindelician War took place.[263] Bavaria was occupied, partly from northern Italy, partly from the Danube. The war was of no great military significance. The totally inexperienced, 23-year-old Drusus was in command, so it cannot have been a very perilous operation. It was a legates', not a generals' war; little is known about it. This makes it of all the greater political significance, however. The northern side of the Alps became Roman. From the Isarcol Drusus opened up the Brenner Pass by invading from Italy, while his brother Tiberius, four years his senior, cooperated from the direction of Lake Constance with markedly less brilliance. Raetia became a province, but without its own governor. Augusta Vindelicorum (Augsburg) was founded at the northern end of the Brenner route. This was a blessing for Italy and highly popular, but only the prelude.

From 16 to 13 BC Augustus was in Gaul.[264] This was a feature of the planned double-pronged project. [MH.I, 82] At this point there is a gap in the historical tradition concerning the establishment of Noricum (Styria and Upper Austria, including Vienna). This important province probably became a dependency of Rome at that time. It was always referred to as *regnum Noricum*, i.e. as a client kingdom, indicating the friendly transfer of supremacy to Rome by a king. Nevertheless, it could already be regarded as a Roman province.

In 13 BC the great war in Gaul and Noricum broke out. Augustus appointed Drusus and Agrippa as generals. Here, too, there was a combined strategy: Drusus was commander-in-chief in Gaul, Agrippa in the Alps.[265] Tiberius was passed over. The main battle was expected to take place on the Danube. In 12 BC Agrippa died quite unexpectedly;[266] Tiberius was now made commander of the Danube army.[267] This was a thankless task. In 11 BC Illyricum was transferred from the Senate to the Emperor,[268] thus drawing the province into the strategic plan. It is likely that a separate supreme command was established at that date at the mouth of the Danube; Moesia extended thus far from Belgrade. Lentulus waged a serious war on the Dacians in the wake of the one begun by Crassus.

Since the establishment of the province of Pannonia, Thrace and Macedonia had been peaceful provinces. Upper Illyricum was transformed into the province of

Dalmatia and swiftly grew into one of the most important ones (capital: Salona). These gains were important not so much in themselves as for the cover they provided [MH.I, 83] and for the pacification of the hinterland.

In 12 and 11 BC Tiberius waged the Pannonian War.[269] Although not of any great note in itself, it was important for its consequences. The line of the river Sava was crossed, and in its place the Drava line became the frontier of Roman hegemony. Poetovio (Pettau) in eastern Styria became the main camp. Although not a glorious war, it was nevertheless rich in solid successes. It made Dalmatia into a peaceful hinterland and mainstay of Roman culture. Soon it became possible to levy troops from the province. Hitherto the region north of Italy as far as the Danube had been known as Upper and Lower Illyricum. Upper Illyricum now became Dalmatia, and Lower Illyricum Pannonia. Noricum[270] was made into a military province, with Vienna or Carnuntum the farthest outpost. The line of frontier fortifications between Pettau and Vienna points, even at this stage, to operations directed at Bohemia.

Now to Drusus's Rhine campaigns. Drusus had departed for the Rhine before the death of Agrippa, invested with extraordinary proconsular powers. In 12 BC he launched an offensive on his own initiative with the aim of systematically occupying German territory. Three campaigns may be distinguished. The first was aimed at the North Sea coast. Drusus reached as far as the Zuydersee and concluded treaties with the Batavians and Friesians.[271] This provided cover for the northern frontier of Roman Gaul, which proved to be the sole enduring result of Drusus's conquests.

[MH.I, 84] The coastal peoples, lacking German national feeling, became particularly loyal subjects of Rome, from now on providing the imperial bodyguard. In return for exemption from tax they had an obligation to supply numerous recruits, which was by no means unpopular.[272] A battle fleet was built, and Drusus was the first to sail the North Sea with it. According to the two incomplete extant accounts,[273] he fought his way as far as the Bay of Jadebusen, extending the Roman frontier on this flank to the Elbe.[274]

Next came war along the river Lippe.[275] Military roads were built on both banks, and the fortress of Aliso at its source.[276] This indicates that the intention was to occupy the land permanently. The territories of the Cherusci and the Chatti were occupied and a major Rhine camp was set up at Xanten (Castra Vetera).

In the following years fixed quarters were also established further south at Mainz (Moguntiacum) and Bonn. Drusus occupied the line of the river Main and built the Taunus fortifications. In 9 BC war was resumed against the Marcomanni on the upper Main, who withdrew towards Bohemia.[277] Drusus pursued them as far as the Elbe, where he had a strange vision, fell from his horse and died.[278] Tiberius, who was generally burdened with the thankless task of taking up the operations of others, was consistent in carrying on in accordance with Drusus's plan.[279] The aim was to advance the military frontiers and turn Gaul and Dalmatia[280] [MH.I, 85] into pacified hinterland. The new line was to be the Weser or Elbe line. This was steadily worked at: year after year for six years expeditions were mounted which cannot be regarded as mere raiding. Without any major battles, Tiberius pressed ever closer to success. His campaigns of 8/7 BC made Germany *de facto* a subject province.

At this point the politics of the imperial household became a hindrance. There was dissension between Augustus and Tiberius. The latter left the army[281] and Augustus rightly complained that he had been betrayed by him (*se destitutum esse ab Tiberio dixit*).[282] From this point onwards offensive operations were completely abandoned. As was entirely consistent with the policy of Augustus's principate, such a major project could and should only have been undertaken by an imperial prince. The only man who qualified had refused the task, which could therefore not be attempted.

Despite this, there were a number of lesser projects over the next decade. Domitius Ahenobarbus moved across the Elbe from Pannonia. The Hermunduri were granted land in Bavaria.[283] Nevertheless, no serious projects were launched until after the deaths of Gaius and Lucius, when, following his adoption in AD 4,[284] Tiberius reappeared in the field. In AD 4 he crossed the Weser; the following year found him active on the Lippe, where he remained on campaign until December. He was most energetic in these campaigns. [MH.I, 86] The following year, AD 6, was to bring the final decision. This had to be won from the Marcomanni, who had established a mighty kingdom in Bohemia under Marobod.[285] It is possible, however, that its might was deliberately exaggerated for public consumption in order to justify a war against them. At all events it was a power not to be under-estimated, being in part (the infantry) organized along Roman lines. The main thrust was to be made from the Danube. Tiberius himself accompanied this army; the Rhine army under Gaius Sentius Saturninus was only of secondary importance.[286]

This calculation was discernibly based on a correct political assessment. As the frontiers were arranged at that time, the Rhine and the Danube formed the two arms of a right-angled triangle. This required a large number of troops and was in parts – for example along the Danube line – difficult to cover. A frontier along the hypoteneuse, represented approximately by the Elbe line, would have provided far greater security. And with a determined and consolidated attack on the region, this was not entirely unfeasible. Tiberius had already taken up positions five days' march beyond the Danube when all his plans were dashed by the Pannonian-Dalmatian revolt, which broke out in regions devoid of troops and only extremely superficially pacified.[287] These events, which forced Tiberius to turn back, were what spurred Augustus to undertake the reorganization of the army already mentioned.

[MH.I, 87] In itself, this war was not a major event in world history; it was rather an entirely normal reaction as had hitherto arisen in every nation that had not been completely subjugated. Nevertheless, the revolt was perceived as a terrible danger for Italy. As the leaders of the Dalmatians and the Breuci were both called Bato, the war became known as the *bellum Batonicum*.[288] Since the Romans had not yet engaged Marbod they were able to turn back towards the Danube. The entire southern and northern Danube region was in a state of revolt, in fact, but the major towns had not been taken by the Danubian Celts. In the Dalmatian mountains, in the angle between the Drava and the Sava, where the Breuci lived, this was something akin to a national insurrection. This was the decisive place. The conflict, about which nothing is known except that it was fairly hard fought, lasted four years from AD 6 to 9. The 20-year-old Germanicus, adoptive son of Tiberius, won his first laurels here. This subsequently proved to be of political significance.

Once this had been dealt with, it would have been possible to move against Bohemia with a fighting force that was now eight legions stronger. However, five days after news of the Pannonian victory reached Rome came news of the defeat of Varus in which three legions had been wiped out.[289] This was a major setback, but in itself only able to act as a delaying factor.

In principle the topographical question is not very important, nor is it very complex. The *saltus Teutoburgiensis* (Teutoburg Forest) is mentioned in only one source: Tacitus.[290] It was situated between the sources of the Lippe and the Ems; this suggests the Osning, parallel to the Weser, an area which could be described as a *saltus*. [MH.I, 88] The idea that the catastrophe occurred on Cheruscan territory is not plausible. The enemy commander was confused with the place. The assumption[291] that Varus was camped by the Weser is correct. It is not clear where, but the Romans had established themselves particularly securely on the Lippe. Aliso was situated in the vicinity of Paderborn. From there the road to the Weser passed through the Osning, which would suggest that the camp was located near Minden on the Weser. But what occurred was a trap. Varus was informed that a remote people had rebelled and that he should crush them. He broke camp with the bulk of the army – three legions – while two remained behind in camp at Minden on the Weser.[292] Very clearly he was lured off the great military road, but it is not clear where to. However, it cannot have been too far from the Osning, since the retreat did not take a long time and the catastrophe was in the Osning, in the vicinity of Osnabrück.[293]

We are well informed about the catastrophe: the course of events is identical with those in every war against the Germans. Drusus and Germanicus had similar difficulties, but overcame them more skilfully. Varus too might have averted the crushing defeat of his well-disciplined troops. At first they struck camp in regular fashion, then they became increasingly disorderly and finally the battlefield was reached. The cause of the catastrophe lies in personal factors. Varus commanded three legions, three *alae* and six cohorts – 20,000 men at normal troop strength. There were undoubtedly far fewer than this, however, since we hear of strong detachments[294] that presumably consisted of *alae*, rather than legions. The maximum number of men we can assume is thus 15,000.[295] One crucial factor was the distance from the military road and another the time of year – late autumn. It was difficult [MH.I, 89] to march on unmade tracks. Above all, however, the troops were demoralized. They were probably the recently recruited legions seventeen, eighteen and nineteen. These numbers subsequently disappeared and were not re-allocated. These three legions had been among those newly established. This makes sense. The old legions were on the Danube; the new ones had been deployed in the new Germany. Of course they will have included a large number of veteran soldiers and centurions. To compound all this, the officers failed to do their duty. Varus was married to an imperial princess,[296] which will have smoothed the path of his promotion. He was a peacetime general, not a true commander. Augustus gave voice to this feeling when he demanded the return of the legions.[297] In addition, it was disgraceful that a legate of Varus's should have mustered the cavalry and ridden off.[298] Both sections, foot and cavalry, were naturally annihilated.

What astonishes us, in the first instance, is the extent to which this catastrophe was perceived as a tragedy. It was, unquestionably, a bitter blow for a military nation, nor should it be denied that they had deserved it. All the same, it was not an enduring loss. What is remarkable is how three eagles and 15,000 men managed to alter the entire policy of the government. Such an about-turn did, however, take place.

The consequences of the victory were significant. Throughout Germany, the party advocating liberation gained the upper hand. Arminius sent Varus's head to Marobod[299] to induce the Suevi to joint action. This would have substantially aggravated the situation of the Romans. Furthermore, the Germans did not content themselves with looting the corpses of the fallen, but went on to Aliso, which was [MH.I, 90] not supplied with provisions and whose garrison troops had to fight their way out.[300] The two remaining legions that had remained behind at the Minden camp also managed to reach Castra Vetera on the Rhine safely under the command of Asprenas Nonius.[301] They were needed there, as the Germans in Gaul were proving equally restive. The right bank of the Rhine and the whole Lippe line were lost: a disquieting situation.

All the more energetically should this disgrace have been erased, however. The Pannonian War was over and troops were available. In fact, Tiberius moved towards the Rhine army and crossed the Rhine. He advanced and remained in Germany in AD 10 and 11.[302] Nevertheless, a total about-turn is discernible. Aliso was not restored.[303] One can observe a defensive posture in offensive form.

113

Germany had been relinquished. There remained only a sham Germany on the left bank of the Rhine, Germania Superior and Inferior. The reason for this about-turn lay in domestic policy.

Ranke[304] refers to Florus's account,[305] which relates how Varus was presiding over a court for the Germans when the Cherusci burst in through the doors. Ranke disputes the account of the departure of the army, but this is not a proper analysis. Although it is true that Florus lived earlier than Dio, we cannot overlook the reasons why a rhetorical compiler, such as the Spanish equestrian Florus was, should be given less credence than a statesman such as Dio.[306] Moreover, Florus does not concur with accounts by contemporaries, specifically that of Velleius,[307] or with the later but nevertheless reliable Tacitus,[308] who refers back to these events. Tacitus reports three different marching camps off the Roman military road; this would have been impossible if Varus had been attacked and massacred at the main camp. [MH.I, 91] Florus's account is a compilation of commonplace themes such as a dramatist might write. Florus also writes that the cavalry managed to save itself; and yet we learn from Velleius that they were massacred separately later. The catastrophe took place in AD 9.

The following year Tiberius marched to the Rhine frontier, secured it and made offensive forays (see MH.I, 90). In AD 12 he returned to Rome and celebrated a triumph *de Pannoniis Dalmatisque*, but not *de Germania*, as would undoubtedly have been done in later times.[309] It was, nevertheless, believed that this work had been completed. Policy towards Germany was totally transformed: Augustus contented himself with the former frontiers. This is demonstrated by the peace treaty between Tiberius and Marobod. Tiberius had been on the point of engaging Marobod when the catastrophe occurred; they were closing in on Bohemia on both sides. The peace treaty meant the abandonment of this plan – not only against Bohemia, but also the relinquishing of the Elbe line. What is difficult to grasp, however, is how this military state, so in need of *gloire*, could forgive and forget this loss of its eagles and not erase this defeat; or how Tiberius, who had set his heart on this operation against Germany and who felt it his duty, was able to come to terms with this retreat. There was no question of external pressure. Admittedly, there were military difficulties. Augustus had sent eighteen legions to Actium, then eight new ones had been established, and of these three had now been annihilated. At the time of his death there were only twenty-five legions,[310] i.e. two legions were restored, one remained unreplaced.

[MH.I, 92] The two new legions were numbered twenty-one and twenty-two. The former was made up of the *sentina*[311] of the city of Rome, otherwise never taken into service, and this was the legion sent to Germany. The latter, the *legio Deiotariania*, was made up of Galatian troops, or at any rate this is highly probable. They were new soldiers recently granted citizenship. This is an indication of how short of manpower Augustus was. This, too, is incomprehensible. After all, Italy,

Sicily, Narbonensis and many individual towns had Roman citizenship: How was it that a state such as this was unable to replace a corps of 20,000 men? The truth is that after the battle of Actium legionaries and Praetorians could only be persuaded to enlist, not conscripted. This was a fatal error and explains the colossal shortage of men. Particularly characteristic was the recourse to the *sentina*. On the other hand, the continuing unruliness of Gaul made it impossible to relinquish the Rhine frontier, and the territory between the Rhine and the Elbe would have required a great many troops. There were simply not enough men.

Other reasons undoubtedly also led Augustus to abandon his policy. He had, after all, been pushed into the great war against Germany by Tiberius and Drusus. The all-out offensive had never been his intention. After Varus's disaster he reverted to his former plan and forbade a continuation of the war.[312] At this stage Augustus was not a feeble old man being led by the hand by Tiberius; if anything, the latter was in a totally dependent position and was hardly entitled to express his own wishes.

In [MH.I, 93] military circles disapproval may have been stirring. This was to come to a head later with Germanicus. It is remarkable that Germanicus, instead of Tiberius, was then sent to the Rhine to assume this exceptionally high command over the two greatest armies.[313] This cannot have been for military reasons. It would almost seem that Augustus, through Germanicus, wanted to see the conquest of Germany through after all. This might be understandable in view of the strained relations between Augustus and Tiberius, but it is contradicted by the peace treaty with Marobod. At all events all long-term operations were abandoned. Augustus[314] contented himself with the Rhine frontier of the dictator Caesar, and Varus's disaster retained its momentous place in world history. It spared Germany the influence of Rome and showed, first and foremost, that a policy of conquest as such was not feasible under the principate, which was too weak to sustain one. No such attempt, moreover, was even seriously made after this major defeat. The conquest of Britain etc. were in fact minor details.

E) THE IMPERIAL FAMILY AND DOMESTIC POLITICS

Now to the internal relations within the imperial family. The prominence of the history of the imperial family constitutes a major element of the principate, while the latter was still new. It was undoubtedly a form of monarchy.

The creation of a rule of succession was imperative in order to ensure the durability of the principate. Here, Augustus went further than his father. Caesar, perhaps because of his idealistic, completely self-absorbed nature, had failed to do this. Of course, we cannot know what he would have done had he lived longer, but his rule invariably appeared to be a purely individual one.

This is not true of Augustus. He considered everything calmly and judiciously, seeking to create the right form for what was required. He found it, initially, in co-rule with Agrippa: in 28 and 27 BC they jointly occupied the offices of consul and censor.[315]

[MH.I, 94] The *princeps* could be appointed neither by the Senate, nor by the people. An appointment by the Senate would have nullified the principate, which was based on a relationship of parity between the *princeps* on the one hand and the Senate on the other. A vote of the People was even less suitable as an empowering, rather than merely ratificatory, instrument. The matter could thus only be handled by the *princeps* himself naming a successor, a selected crown prince, and this was the position of Agrippa.[316] At the same time, this also avoided the futile status normally held by an heir-in-waiting. Agrippa occupied an office that placed him above all other magistrates and immediately below the *princeps* himself. It was a secondary position, but only *vis-à-vis* the *princeps*. Like him, the co-regent had proconsular and tribunician authority: he was *collega impar*, an unequal colleague. It was this singular element, devised by Augustus, that subsequently formed the basis of the principate. Co-rule by the crown prince persisted throughout the whole of the second century. Adoption, on the other hand, remained a subordinate factor.

Astonishingly, however, this political idea was thwarted by the dynastic principle; this contradiction constantly comes to the surface in the Emperor's state of mind. In order to understand this, it will be necessary to pay some attention to the ladies at court: his sister Octavia, his wife Livia, and his daughter Julia. When the triumvirate had needed to be consolidated, Antony had married Octavia.[317] In this terrible age she had the noblest nature. At that time she was accorded an honorary status equal to that of Livia and retained it even after [MH.I, 95] Antony's fall. She was a patroness of scholarship and bequeathed the Roman people her library in her will.[318] She had children by both marriages, Marcus Claudius Marcellus from her first to Gaius Claudius Marcellus. A fine young man, he was Augustus's closest male heir and was expected to succeed him.[319] Besides Marcus she also had several daughters, including some by Antony, as well as bringing up the daughters of Cleopatra as if they were princesses.[320] In this way, an imperial court circle soon formed within which political marriages were made.

If ever a woman was cruelly maligned, then it was Livia.[321] The most monstrous tales were told about her.[322] This was not coincidental, however. Gossip served as a substitute for the participation in politics which was now denied to the Roman citizen. Only a handful of advisers knew what was really happening. Politics was an *arcanum imperii*, a secret of power. Indifference to politics led to malicious gossip. And this was especially directed at Livia, who was held responsible for all misfortunes and deaths in the imperial household. This escalated from century to century, until finally she was cast in the role of a professional poisoner, said to have been responsible for the deaths of Marcus Marcellus, Gaius and Lucius and even Augustus himself.[323] Marcellus tarried in Rome over the late summer and fell victim to the *perniciosa*.[324] Gaius died of wounds in Asia Minor and Lucius far from Rome in Massilia. One reason given for these alleged deeds of Livia is the succession of Tiberius. The motivation behind these insinuations was never made more specific. How could all this possibly have passed Augustus by unnoticed? Augustus died at the age of almost 77;[325] why should foul play be assumed here? What interest of Livia's would it have served?

Throughout the fifty-one years of her marriage Livia manifestly neither had nor sought political influence.[326] [MH.I, 96] Politics had had nothing to do with her marriage, which had been a love-match – in a somewhat unseemly form.[327] The 26-year-old Augustus had been hopelessly in love with Livia and had abducted her from her husband. This love had, moreover, endured. After the death of Augustus the now old lady said that she had preserved her happy marriage by keeping steadfastly within her circle of female acquaintances. She did, nonetheless, also develop a degree of leverage outside this which continued to be expressed in senatorial resolutions even after her death. She exercised the supreme woman's right of intervening on all sides to assist and support, especially financially. Aristocratic families were almost always in trouble over money. The *princeps* would step in to assist, and Livia helped with dowries. The Senate wanted to designate her *mater patriae* after her death, and yet in her latter years she had lived at loggerheads with Tiberius.[328] This is the role that history has attributed to her. Most issues, even family ones, were decided against the wishes of Livia, for example the repeated slights against Tiberius. It was precisely this compliance, however, which ensured her standing within the household.

Julia was the only child of Augustus, born in 39 BC to Scribonia.[329] Little needs to be said about her. Beautiful, clever and charming, she was the darling of literary society in the Ovidian *amores* set. This, however, was an abyss of the most abject immorality, and Julia embodied the dark side of court life.[330] Fate punished her enough for this. She was dear to her father's heart, even though he knew her weaknesses. Augustus had two difficult entities to rule – the *res publica* and his daughter. Nevertheless, his love for her did not impinge on his dynastic plans. It was not out of love for his daughter that he wanted to make her Empress of Rome, but rather his belief in the [MH.I, 97] *Iulium sidus*,[331] and the last in the line of this clan, the granddaughter[332] of the god, was Julia. Here is the selfsame notion of fate that we encounter in all its aspects in Augustus.

Augustus married Julia to Marcellus in 25 BC – as soon as possible, in other words. She was 14, he 20 years old. One can see how keen Augustus was on the marriage. It was a political event of the first order. His son-in-law was immediately given marked preferential treatment. He obtained a seat in the Senate without having first been a quaestor. It was envisaged that he would become an aedile at 23 and consul five years ahead of time. The status of aedile was specifically intended to give him the edge over Agrippa. Administration of the entire imperial treasury was entrusted to Augustus's son-in-law. Augustus was clearly breaking in Marcellus as his successor, and showed the young man preference over experienced colleagues. Agrippa sensed this, left Rome and went on strike.[333] He went to Lesbos into voluntary exile. Although this deeply wounded Augustus, it was a natural consequence of his conduct. At this point fate intervened. Already in 23 BC Marcellus died of a deadly fever while holding the aedileship.[334] This resolved the conflict. Agrippa returned home and resumed the running of affairs. The facts speak quite clearly here. Augustus acknowledged his mistake; he accorded Agrippa Marcellus's place and married Julia to him – certainly an extraordinary marriage. Augustus and Agrippa had been born in the same year and were twice the age of the 18-year-old Julia. They were also incompatible in other respects. Agrippa was an uncouth warrior, Julia refined and delicate. At first, however, the alliance seemed a happy one. Gaius was born in 20 BC, Lucius in 17 BC. Agrippa's relationship with Augustus was the most cordial imaginable. These were the years of the great reorganization. Augustus adopted Gaius and Lucius and the sons were taken into their grandfather's household.[335] This remarkable step [MH.I, 98] is difficult to explain. It is understandable that the Emperor saw his successors in the boys. But in all respects his son-in-law should have held pride of place. Adoption did not bring the grandsons any closer to their grandfather: it has to be explained by his belief in the *Iulium sidus* (see MH.I, 96–7). The dynasty was to be a Julian, not a Vipsanian one. Agrippa was of lowly origin.[336] This complication, so crucial in the event of succession to the throne, was abruptly removed by death. Agrippa died in 12 BC at the age of 51.[337]

In what position did this now leave the widow? We are obliged to concern ourselves with these domestic details: they were of considerable political importance. Even during her husband's lifetime Julia's conduct had not been blameless (see MH.I, 100). It was unthinkable that she should remain a widow; she needed the supervision of a husband, if only to avoid the worst. For a time there was some idea of marrying her to an equestrian who would not be able to make any claim on the succession. This did not occur. Tiberius Claudius Nero, Livia's son from her first marriage, was chosen. Some have seen the influence of the mother in this, preparing the way to the throne for her son. The opposite is the case. It was the most thankless role imaginable. Besides this, there was the unclear relationship towards the adoptive sons, the heirs-designate to the throne. The most Tiberius could claim was a guardianship status of sorts in the event of Augustus's untimely death and even this period could not last for long: Gaius, the elder, was 8 years old.

[MH.I, 99] This explains Tiberius's aversion. That it was no pleasant office may be discerned from the fact that Augustus omitted to choose his favourite stepson,

Drusus, to fill it. Both Drusus and Tiberius were, moreover, already married, both happily and blessed with children. Tiberius had Drusus the Younger by Agrippa's daughter. Since one marriage had to be annulled, it was that of Tiberius. The Emperor's will was done and the marriage to Julia took place in 11 BC.[338] Some compensation was to hand in tribunician authority and the higher political status generally that Tiberius immediately assumed, but with the proviso that it would be withdrawn later when the children had grown up.

A puzzling event occurred in 6 BC. Following the end of the war in Germany, Tiberius suddenly set off for Rhodes, against the will of Augustus and Livia alike (see MH.I, 85). He thus abandoned Augustus at a most critical juncture. He alone was able to command the Rhine army; he was the only great general. Augustus pleaded with him not to do it, but Tiberius went all the same. Two motives may be involved here. First, Gaius had just completed his fourteenth year and was being given preferential treatment à la Marcellus; he was made *princeps iuventutis*, i.e. crown prince. Some clash was bound to occur here soon, since five years later Gaius would be in a position to take the place of Tiberius. Second, there was probably marital discord. Julia simply could not stand Tiberius, nor he her. She would complain to Augustus about his sullen, coarse nature and denigrate him. The marriage remained childless.[339] The actual nature of the scandal, the pretext, is not known, nor is it of any importance. Things were happening which Tiberius could neither prevent nor complain about because of Augustus's love for his daughter. He thus took his decision in desperation – and he was desperate. Augustus never forgave him. But Tiberius was unable to tolerate his impossible position any longer; he went on hunger-strike for four days. So he was allowed to go.[340]

[MH.I, 100] In 2 BC the Senate was notified that the Emperor had exiled his daughter to the island of Pandateria (Ventotene) for indecent behaviour.[341] The outside world never learned any more than this, but in all probability the indictment was quite justified. It was no longer possible to connive at Julia's conduct. It was characteristic that not a word was mentioned to Livia. Augustus learned of the scandal by way of a police report; there were nightly revels involving public prostitution at the Forum.[342] The death sentence was passed on a large number of participants; others, such as Ovid, were exiled.[343] Political factors are also said to have been at work (*consilia parricidae*),[344] as is suggested by the involvement of Iullus Antonius, the son of the triumvir.[345] This is possible. It was the bitterest blow yet to strike Augustus. On hearing that a female slave, also involved, had taken her own life, he regretted that it had not been his daughter.[346] This indicates the public profile that he accorded to the relationship. How far must matters have been allowed to go for Augustus to disregard decorum!

These matters did nothing to change the political situation. It was one of Augustus's best sides that he had set an example for old-fashioned morality within the imperial household.[347] This, however, had been seriously put into question by his calamitous daughter. Some of the most respectable families were dragged into the affair. Tiberius continued to be out of favour. His tribunician authority was not renewed, his exile was now no longer voluntary;[348] despite the banishment of Julia he was not recalled to Rome.

A dark shadow also fell on the Emperor's two adoptive sons Gaius and Lucius. Some now ventured to doubt whether they really were the sons of Agrippa.[349] However, nothing was detracted from their honourablestatus: [MH.I, 101] both sons were, after all, now practically employed. In 1 BC Gaius was sent to the East to arrange matters there.[350] He had been designated for the consulship in AD 1. This, however, was more a promotion for appearance's sake. In the East his duties were concerned with matters of a more secondary and less vital nature. He was furnished with experienced mentors, such as Lollius.[351] Augustus saw his own early career as a model, but that had developed under pressure from external circumstances. It was these circumstances which had shaped Augustus's own character.

Augustus now appeared to have reached the culmination of his plans. He was on the point of recognizing the elder of the two young men as his co-regent. Tiberius was allowed home in AD 2, but under most irksome conditions,[352] since Augustus first consulted the prince Gaius for his opinion, and his stepfather was only permitted to return to Rome with his consent on condition that he expressly renounce any public position.

At this point the angel of peace intervened in the form of death. Both young men died within the space of eighteen months. Lucius, the younger, died first on the return journey from Spain in Massilia, Gaius in Cilicia, likewise on his way back to Italy.[353] Rome probably did not lose much in the case of Gaius, who was irascible, morose and violent.[354]

This now altered the entire political landscape. Augustus was obliged to rethink the succession. He vacillated for some time between three candidates. He still had one solitary grandson, Agrippa Postumus, born after the death of Agrippa, then aged fifteen. Besides him there was the slightly older Germanicus, the son of Drusus by Antonia, likewise a close relative. And, last, there was Tiberius. The dynastic interest favoured Agrippa, Augustus's personal preference was for Germanicus, who was 17, while his statesman's instinct favoured Tiberius. Augustus decided on all three simultaneously – a most extraordinary decision. [MH.I, 102] Augustus adopted Tiberius, who was now named Tiberius Julius Caesar, and also Agrippa, as Agrippa Julius. Tiberius was to adopt Germanicus, despite the fact that he already had a son, Drusus, who was thereby relegated to the status of second-born.[355] Augustus said he was adopting Tiberius *rei publicae causa*.[356] Indeed, he did not do so out of affection. Augustus was now 67 and needed to secure an able man to command on the Rhine. The good of the state, however, did not coincide with the adoption of Agrippa Postumus, so here we must assume that Augustus's own dynastic interest was the deciding factor.

It was only natural that Tiberius should submit to all this in his dependent position: he had no choice. At this point, another catastrophe occurred. All we know is that in AD 6 Agrippa Postumus was disinherited and disowned, his status as adoptive son revoked; he was exiled and treated as a prisoner of the state.[357] Livia may have had a hand in this, although there is no proof of that. Livia's antipathy towards Agrippa is completely understandable. On the other hand, it came hard to Augustus to disown him. Agrippa had a physically powerful, base, brutal and immoral nature and accused Augustus of underhand dealings. We can understand that Livia did nothing to stop Agrippa, rightly perceiving a danger to herself and the state, but she did not bring about the catastrophe. So only Tiberius remained. While these blows of fate were hard on Augustus, for Rome they represented yet another beneficent stroke of fortune. It was a blessing both for the development of the principate and for the well-being of the Empire that a man fit to rule succeeded [MH.I, 103] after the death of Augustus.

It remains for us to take stock. The Empire of Augustus always remained the ideal for later governments. The idea of conserving Greek culture in the East, while in the West allowing the various ethnic groups to merge within Latin nationality, had been Caesar's. The principate had been the idea of Augustus. The *urbs romana* in fact acquired a more passive role: it became a luxury institution sustained by the Empire as a whole. There was neither political life, nor communal government within it. The *plebs Romana* had become a great mass bent on the pursuit of pleasure: Rome was a *caput mortuum*, a dead head.

The situation in other cities was radically different. The degree of municipal liberty and development was generally high. Pompeii is an example of this. How vigorous was the life of its assembly! There was brisk campaigning and free elections.[358] The magistrates had a police force at their disposal; the military were only brought in occasionally against bandits. Latin culture was being increasingly transmitted to the provinces – to Sicily, for example, where the Latin language was introduced, to southern Gaul, and parts of Spain. Slowly but surely these populations were drawn into the sphere of Latin interests by means of Roman law and education. Latin was the language of public business in Roman colonies and in towns with Roman or Latin rights of citizenship. There was not a trace of this in the Greek-speaking regions. Although there were Latin-speaking enclaves here,[359] these were in a diminishing minority. The East remained the preserve of Greek culture.

The position of the aristocracy – the old families – was strengthened. No democratization of the state took place. The Julians were, and remained, patricians. [MH.I, 104] However, the old senatorial clan aristocracy was now joined by a new class of *equites Romani* who owed their status to the Emperor alone. These were not the business class of the Republic, but an upper class of officials who competed with the old society through their relationship to the Emperor. Besides these, an influential class of freed slaves also began to emerge.

It is fortunate that such a disproportionate amount has survived of Roman literature from this period. Nevertheless, it would be presumptuous to seek to paint a picture of the Roman state, which was at the same time a world, from this alone.

A primary concern was to rid the Mediterranean of pirates and Augustus accomplished this task thoroughly. Similarly, a great deal was achieved concerning the highways of Italy, which had become highly unsafe in the course of the long wars. Military posts were placed at critical points; otherwise municipal authorities were responsible for security. The posts were withdrawn later, when the danger had been eliminated. In southern Italy, however, Augustus built no highways. Here, as in Sicily, he had abandoned all hope of retrieving the interior (Apulia, Calabria) for civilization; the scale of the ravages had become too great. Trajan was to be the first to care for these regions again.

A great deal was likewise done in the provinces. The imperial postal system[360] dates from the time of Augustus. And yet it was not an innovation.[361] It was already familiar in the great states of the East,[362] [MH.I, 105] and it is one of the baffling aspects of the Republic that it allowed this crucial institution to disappear. Nevertheless, it should not be equated with our modern postal service. The ancient service was solely for the conveyance of dispatches and officials. Initially, Augustus instituted relays of couriers, then of carriages. This *cursus publicus* replaced the unserviceable Republican requisition system. However, this *vehiculatio* (obligation to provide transport) later became a heavy burden on the community and led to irregularities in services and transportation. In inhospitable regions *mansiones* were established as sleeping quarters for travellers.

There was little the government could do in the area of decayed morals. Here, Augustus sought to act through the example of his household, and not entirely in vain. Besides this, however, he also proceeded with legislation. His marriage laws served aristocratic interests,[363] since the aristocracy was developing a disinclination towards marriage, treating it as an irksome duty. Augustus hence acted more rigorously against celibacy and childlessness than against divorce. These measures were essentially restrictions of a pecuniary nature, especially with regard to the qualifications for being mentioned in a will, which affected the habit among old families of mentioning all one's friends in a will far more than it would in our own time. *Coelibes* and *orbi* (the celibate and the childless) were disqualified from receiving a legacy. The importance of these measures becomes evident from the staunch opposition they evoked, which was virtually unprecedented. The very name of the law, *de maritandis ordinibus*, denotes its purpose.[364] The *lex Papia Poppea*[365] followed later.

[MH.I, 106] Manumission was the most deplorable flaw of slavery. Since the freedman class was by nature impecunious, created at its masters' whim and frequently dependent on ill-gotten gains, its very existence was a terrible scourge, particularly in Rome, where freedmen were *de facto* possessed of citizenship rights, despite all legal constraints. It was impossible to grasp this flaw at its roots, i.e. by forbidding manumission, at least in so far as it was connected with citizenship rights. Augustus was, however, prepared to intervene against the most outrageous nuisance – mass emancipation by will and testament.[366] A maximum scale was introduced, based on property; morally dubious individuals who had been branded during their term of slavery, or convicted of serious offences, were excluded from emancipation, as were all children. A *iusta causa (probatio)* (proof of good reason) was demanded. It was impossible to deprive freedmen of their political rights, but they were excluded from the electoral tribes, i.e. the right to vote. Only in exceptional cases did Augustus permit them to take part in a vote. Unfortunately, this was shutting the stable door after the horse had bolted, since the electoral tribes no longer carried any political weight.

In keeping with his entire aristocratic propensity, Augustus's primary aim was to encourage the state cult. He was *pontifex maximus*[367] and a keen participant in all religious events. He initiated the *princeps*'s privilege of belonging to all high-ranking religious colleges. [MH.I, 107] Only the monarch could accumulate priestly offices. He likewise introduced a division among religious *collegia*. From this time onwards it is possible to discern a separation, analogous to the separation of modern orders into first- and second-class ones, a division of corporations into those for senators and those for equestrians. This process, in the main, can also be traced back to Augustus. It was obvious that religion was by then devoid of inner life, but this had already been the case even in the Republic. At all events Augustus did what he could. He revived all the ancient customs, for example the Secular Games.[368] Shrewdly, Augustus directed no formal bans against the introduction of new cults, but rather the contempt of the Roman nation. He regarded them as low and unRoman – and this approach was highly successful. Nevertheless, the state, in its present form, was obliged to adopt a negative attitude towards foreign cults. It was held to be base and unaristocratic to take part in foreign ceremonies. Augustus also cultivated the cult of the past, so to speak. The Forum of Augustus contained a gallery of statues of the outstanding men of the Republic.[369]

The Augustan age is regarded as the finest flower of literature and perhaps also of art. The reason for this is that its authors were the last links in a chain that came to an end with them. After Augustus, utter tedium reigned. Later no one was interested in literature. This was the last epoch of free Roman development. Since nothing more was written after this,[370] people had to have recourse to the literature of Augustus's day which, not entirely justifiably, thus came to dominate subsequent generations. The style and orthography of Latin were established for the future. These efforts issued from the school of Varro, with its archaizing tendencies.

[MH.I, 108] Augustus avoided all archaisms in both the spoken and written word.[371] He may even have supported this approach for reasons of statesmanship. Considerable work also went into antiquarian scholarship, although a great deal of this has been lost. Verrius Flaccus has survived through Festus, significantly in the form of a handbook for the circle of Roman research scholars.[372] One can see how much work was going on. This, too, is characteristic. Following the decease of the Republic its corpse was avidly subjected to the philological knife. We can see from this that the old times really were dead and gone. Scholarship largely took the form of compilations. Roman legends became popular.

From now on the highest achievements were denied to Roman literature, since the connection with political life was severed. During the imperial age politics lost its influence over the public, making its literature seem dull compared to that of the Republic. Poetry retreated from the marketplace from which it had drawn its vitality, and fell into ever greater decline.

The status of the poet in general was little changed. This had never been one of eminence: people of varying origins converged in the *collegium poetarum*, 'Poets' Club'. Significantly, the best poets hailed not from the senatorial ranks, nor from Rome, but from the wholesome middle classes of the municipalities. This is not contradicted by the fact that all talented poets were drawn to Rome. Nobles were mostly encountered only among orators: Asinius Pollio, Valerius Messala. This, too, is understandable: politics tended to drive nobles to the Forum. Nobles only dabbled in poetry, on the other hand.

Another unfavourable factor was the [MH.I, 109] relationship between poetry and the public. Major poetic achievements are unthinkable without constant and vigorous public criticism. Previously, something of this kind had existed in Rome – we think of Catullus, for example – but this all changed. The clique, and the claque which is inseparable from it, now took the place of the public. It is a harsh indictment of the age that it can properly be referred to as that of Maecenas. Maecenas, Asinius Pollio, Valerius Messala, etc. made literature, or, more accurately, had it made.[373] Literature was written and recited avidly everywhere, having been commissioned. These recitations, patronage and personal relations to some extent occupied the place of modern reviewing institutions, though without the public opinion that goes with it today. The worst of all this was that whoever was deemed a poet by this minute circle in Rome was also a poet for the *orbis terrarum*.

Even in the Republic, rhetoric had already become a parasitic plant. The spoken word became simultaneously the written word – pamphlets with which the public was inundated. This trend came to a sorry end under the principate, thereby also putting an end to the entire discipline of rhetoric. Although there were great orators under Augustus, such as Marcus Valerius Messala Corvinus[374] and Asinius Pollio,[375] they were, in fact, relics from the Republic. Pollio was fifteen years older than Augustus.

In historiography the situation was more favourable. The classic work by Pollio on the civil wars, extant in the form of Appian's extracts (fortunately accurate), dates from this period. The same is true of other works. In fact one cannot classify Pollio as part of Augustan historiography; although his work was written under Augustus, it is true to say that here too, it represents echoes of the Republic. This [MH.I, 110] is borne out by his even-handed apportioning of praise and blame.

The true historian of this age, however, is Livy. Recent research has adjusted his importance to its proper level. His work contains many misunderstandings and is completely devoid of pragmatism. We now know that Livy did not undertake a comprehensive study of sources and that the quality of his work falls far short of its quantity. He reproduces crudely without any historical perspective of his own, such as can be found in Polybius's great work. It is an exercise in rhetoric, and the secret of its success lies in the language. There was a gulf between him and earlier works similar to that between us and *Simplicius Simplicissimus*. Ancient chronicles could no longer be used, and were likewise the product of unskilled work. There was a need, however, for a national history. Here, Livy happily stepped in to fill the breach. Besides this, Livy's work also confronts us with an example of how a clique could assign success. Since there was no other work to compete with his, Livy's became the received account of the history of the Italian alliance. Nevertheless, superior works were not ousted by his. The need for a history of the world was met by Pompeius Trogus, which survives in extract form in Justin. One cannot deny his skill in weaving together disparate components, but here, again, there was a lack of any serious research.

There was a complete dearth of drama, although there were energetic efforts to produce tragedies. Ancient plays, such as those of Pacuvius, disappeared from both the stage and reading repertoires alike, and new ones were written. *Thyestes* by Varius and *Medea* by Ovid were greatly celebrated, but remained plays for reading, not performance. With comedy the situation was somewhat different. Since the stage is indispensable for comedy, the latter lapsed immediately, despite efforts on the part of Maecenas Melissus – significantly a freedman and trained librarian – to create a new genre, the *trabeata*.[376] Those who made their presence felt did so through public spectacles: all interest [MH.I, 111] was absorbed by pantomine and ballet – a terrible indictment of the new climate.

The realm of minor poetry was all the livelier for this. In addition the Latin epic also emerged, marking the high point of Roman poetry. How can this influence of Virgil be explained? His was no modest talent, as is clearly apparent from his *Georgics*, although this is in fact a didactic poem and thus not poetry at all. This

125

genre of poetic art was, however, generally fashionable at that time and, all in all, it is a quite magnificent poem, particularly those passages where the poet's enthusiasm for Augustus shines through full and clear. Written during the Sicilian War, the work breathes a sigh of relief after a time of horror.

[MH.I, 112] The princely status of Virgil in poetry, analogous to that of Cicero in prose, is quite a curious problem that is also of interest to the historian. It is a sorry task to compare Virgil, the modern epic poet, with Homer, and yet he did deliberately imitate the latter and this obliges us to persevere with the comparison. Virgil sought to fuse the *Iliad* with the *Odyssey*, as well as adding a somewhat vulgar erotic motif, the love of Aeneas and Dido, derived from the myth of Medea. The second half of the poem proceeds in similar vein. Here, the Hector of hearth and home is replaced by the jealous lover, Turnus. In Virgil's adaptation the other grand motifs from Republican myth are omitted and everything is reduced to the mediocre *niveau* of the age. Only when Virgil is celebrating the new Empire[377] does a warmer tone break through. The self-criticism expressed in his desire to burn the poem[378] was entirely justified. The success of the the work despite all this is due to a variety of causes. The first lies in politics. Written at the request of Augustus, it voices the syncretic trend of the age, the coalition between Romans and Greeks – since the Carthaginians[379] were treated altogether as Greeks, as in Homeric heroic poems. Equally welcome was Virgil's glorification of monarchy. In his own mind, Augustus was imitating the seven Roman kings.[380] The third, and perhaps most important, reason is Virgil's glorification of the Julian house through its ancestor Aeneas.

[MH.I, 113] An additional factor is his literary scholarship. Virgil was rightly called the *doctus poeta*. He studied a great deal, notably pontifical law (Amata is derived from the cult of Vesta).[381] Literary scholarship demanded that a poem could be provided with a commentary. The *Aeneid* became the eminent school textbook just as required, and continues to be used as such to this day.

Horace, somewhat younger than Virgil, and Tibullus and Propertius, rank infinitely higher on the literary scale than Virgil. The poetry of Horace pulses with full, vital life – notably, for example, the *Ars poetica* with its unconstrained, witty small talk, and the *Satires*. Less excellent are the *Odes* themselves, although these also contain some very fine poems, for example the *carmen saeculare*.[382] This combines Greek elegance with a full awareness of the greatness of the Roman state. There can be no question of genuine feelings of love in Horace: slavery destroyed it.[383] In this, Propertius is superior to him, and Tibullus even more so. In these two we find tenderness of feeling – the finest that the Romans ever achieved in their poetry.

It is remarkable how these talented poets died out so rapidly. At the same time as Agrippa etc. passed away, the poets also died. What followed was poetry of a different kind – that of the aging Augustus. Ovid appears, dubbed *ingeniosissimus* by the ancients.[384] He of all the poets had the lightest touch: his verse flows the best. It is nevertheless doubtful whether this makes him the best poet. All efforts to wrestle with language and metre were now over. The content is not very profound. Only his poetry dealing with prostitutes, the *Amores* and *Ars amandi*, are readable, and this is, after all, a very inferior genre.[385] The catastrophe of the poet's involvement with Julia typifies him (see MH.I, 100). [MH.I, 114] Otherwise, the poetry of Ovid is no more than rhyming.[386] He was capable of composing poetry fluently on anything and everything, but without the slightest poetic content. His most celebrated work, *Medea*, is lost to us. One is tempted to think that this ode[387] was the fruit of the fact that Ovid no longer lived within Republican traditions. The world was becoming emptier.

In the sphere of art the increasing prevalence of collections should be pointed out. The major libraries founded by Octavia and Augustus came into existence at this time, each with a Greek and a Latin section.[388] A similar trend towards a kind of museum manifested itself in the great temples of Augustus. In this the ancients were greater than ourselves: each work of art, displayed separately, has quite a different impact on its own than in a museum. Augustus worked tirelessly to collect such art treasures. Agrippa expounded on this in his speech *de tabulis signisque publicandis*.[389] Every work of art was to become the property of the state: a magnificent idea. This was never fully accomplished, of course, but the new public works projects were a step towards this ideal. Augustus himself proceeded in the same spirit, exhibiting his acquisitions to the public. Immense activity evolved in the sphere of architecture. But no outstandingly good artists are named, and this silence is eloquent enough. The watchword was collecting and exhibiting, not creating. Coins do nevertheless reveal great advances, especially in the portrait. The Forum of Augustus[390] was built for the purpose of exhibiting visual art and was embellished with portrait statues.[391]

Architecture came to the fore and rightly so. The patronage and promotion of this art depends primarily on the state. Magnificent buildings were built with which perhaps only those built under Trajan can be compared. First, utilities appeared, notably those established by Agrippa.[392] The old aqueducts, hitherto deplorably neglected, were restored and new ones built – not, as previously, privately for payment, but gratis. This was another aspect of bread and circuses. Besides these constructions there were the theatres of Balbus and Marcellus, a stone amphitheatre and buildings for public meetings. Similarly the fora, basilicas and public squares. Among the temples the Pantheon should be mentioned, a stunning work carried out by Agrippa.[393]

2

TIBERIUS (14–37)

[MH.I, 115] Posterity has erected a monument to Augustus the like of which has perhaps never been seen since. With Tiberius[394] matters were quite different. Under him the moral turpitude of the government came to the surface. It is worth the trouble to examine the deification of Augustus among all ranks, particularly the middle class. Much fuller information about the rule of Tiberius has come down through the *Annals* of Tacitus. However, Tacitus and his sources are partisan accounts of the first order. His political and personal animosities were fierce and spirited. His pen was frequently driven by hatred. The facts have passed on intact, however, so that one can often refute Tacitus from his own testimony. Nevertheless, there can be no question of using other sources to correct him.

What Tiberius achieved as both man and general in the first phase of his rule has been obscured by his period in Capraea (Capri); this alone was vividly recalled to shape the picture of the whole man. Tiberius was a member of the high-ranking aristocracy, the Claudii Nerones, albeit one of the less illustrious branches. He was undoubtedly every bit as noble as the Octavians and Julians. He possessed none of the traits peculiar to the Claudii.[395] He had lived in the imperial household since the age of 4. His father had died shortly after the annulment of his marriage to Livia. Tiberius had thus grown up as a ward of Augustus and was always regarded as an imperial prince and member of the *palatium*. He made an early début into public life.

His presence was massive and imposing: he had broad shoulders, and the back of his neck was covered with thick hair. His external appearance in itself revealed him to be a soldier. [MH.I, 116] Possessed of perfect health, from the age of 30 he never took a physician with him.[396] This stamina was to endure to the last. He was not a handsome man, however; with its large, brooding eyes, his countenance was unnerving and disagreeable (later, boils made it almost frightening). Tiberius went bald early in life, which was another reason why he avoided contact with people.

As regards his aptitudes, he was above all else a highly able officer. With his personal courage and talent he was virtually tailor-made for this profession.

128

Experienced in workaday military service and tirelessly punctilious, he paid attention to the baggage and weaponry of his soldiers and forbade his officers to take unnecessary baggage with them. He did not trouble himself with councils of war, availing himself of this institution, exceptionally, only after the Varus disaster, probably *exempli causa*.[397] Although not brilliant, he was able, and paid heed more to reality than to appearances. His aim was not to win battles, but to achieve the ultimate goal – pacification. In the wars he fought it was good policy to avoid battles.

Tiberius was better suited to the camp than the Forum. He spoke reluctantly and slowly. His conversation was poor, or at least not of a high standard.[398] He was not at all aggressive, rather morose. His arrival tended to banish humour, even in Augustus. He was not suited to court life. Women disliked him, and to rule Rome without the favour of women was impossible. This was partly his downfall. He was alleged to have indulged early on in his later vices, especially while at Rhodes. This is not authenticated, [MH.I, 117] however, so we must decidedly refute this assertion about his early life. His unnatural vices in the final decennia were loathsome and repulsive.[399] He was always a heavy drinker, which was in keeping with his soldier's disposition. Early on he was nicknamed Biberius Caldius Mero.[400] This habit too, made him ill-suited to the fine salon of Augustus.

As far as religion is concerned, Tiberius was both a non-believer and super-stitious at the same time. He lacked the belief of Augustus in his own divine nature, had no time for the ruler cult and was a staunch rationalist.[401] Alongside this, however, he was an avid devotee of astrology. This, too, has a ring of the camp about it. He cast his horoscope (*genitura*) and was wont to say: *omnia fato regi*, 'all is ruled by fate'. He also believed in portents and miracles, which was consistent with his brooding nature generally. His intervention as ruler against soothsayers, the so-called Chaldeans, was peculiar.[402]

By the standards of his day, Tiberius was well educated.[403] He was an admirer of Alexandrianism, venerating its semi-scholarly poetry, especially that of Euphorion.[404] He, too, prized scholarly study more than the creative beauty of poetry. When unprepared he spoke well; when he had pondered over his words he became so bogged down and pedantic that he was incomprehensible. He enjoyed conversing with scholars and wrestling over questions such as by what name Achilles had been called when wearing women's clothes. Tiberius also wrote himself, presenting his stepfather with a poem honouring the young Lucius Caesar. He certainly knew Greek, but did not like to speak it; in Latin he was a purist in the strictest sense of the term. He banned the use of foreign words in decrees, for example the word *monopolium*.

His position under Augustus has already been outlined. His exile in Rhodes embittered him. He was never able to conciliate Augustus. He had to wait a long time, although ultimately becoming his successor after all without any action on his part. Nevertheless, he was undoubtedly completely loyal as long as Augustus lived. [MH.I, 118] The heart of Augustus inclined not towards Tiberius, but towards Germanicus. Of course, this made Tiberius all the more bitter. Only months prior to the death of Augustus the same powers that were invested in the Emperor were conferred on him in all the provinces.[405]

The succession was an abrupt affair. Augustus died at Nola on a journey to Campania.[406] Tiberius was not present, or at least it seems so. Livia sent for him post-haste to come from northern Italy; whether he still found Augustus alive or not is not clear. It was now that the blunders in dynastic policy came home to roost. Augustus had initially placed Tiberius on an equal footing with Agrippa Postumus, who was later disowned. Now, however, Agrippa posed a terrible threat to the succession. There were plans to bring him out of exile to the army in order to head a revolt. Furthermore, such an appeal would not have remained without repercussions, as events subsequently revealed (see MH.I, 121).

How did Tiberius perceive his power? This is a much-disputed point. In some respects, he was eminently equipped for this autocratic form of government. He was an able officer and had been well schooled; he was in a much more fortunate position than his father had been on his accession. Nevertheless, he failed. Above all, he was now 56 and youth was no longer on his side. He had served a master for too long, and a domineering master at that. The golden days of his youth were too far behind him. There were other impediments, too. Tiberius was over-sensitive to the burdens of his station – he lacked the fresh [MH.I, 119] courage to take risks that is ultimately necessary in such a position and which we admire in Augustus and Caesar. 'Look before you leap,' the saying rightly goes, but it was the destiny of Tiberius only to look and never to leap. People did not know *quanta belua imperium esset*, he would complain.[407] For this reason Augustus was always Tiberius's ideal. But why? Tiberius was a superior officer and administrator. As a ruler, however, he lacked self-confidence, stepping timidly in the tracks of Augustus in both domestic and foreign policy.

This became apparent as soon as Tiberius came to power. The position of a second ruler is generally the more difficult. Strictly speaking, there was no change of government. Tiberius had, after all, latterly had equal status to Augustus, so there was no new accession as such. It was a matter of form rather than fact, since Tiberius immediately acted as Emperor by giving the watchword. It is not known whether the question of the accession was presented to the Assembly, but it was debated in the Senate. Nonetheless, this was no more than empty words. Nevertheless, Tiberius was someone who always wanted to rule in accordance with the constitution – the most constitutional monarch Rome ever had. Nothing was to be done without consultation with the Senate. So this question too [sc. the succession] was also presented to them for discussion. It was most probably a mistake. Tiberius probably wanted genuine involvement by the Senate in the government.[408] He was largely to blame for the fact that it failed to achieve the desired effect. It was an embarrassing situation for both parties, since the matter had already been decided. The attitude of Tiberius is clear from the way he immediately abolished the time limit on the principate.[409] Tiberius acknowledged all of this as Emperor. What is most remarkable is that Tiberius sought to shape the principate in as practical a manner as possible and to play down its ideal aspect. He did not reject the title of Augustus, and yet he felt uncomfortable with it, [MH.I, 120] probably on account of its sacral overtones. It did, after all, represent the manifestation of a god on earth. Tiberius resolutely and radically did away with divine veneration of the *princeps*.[410] He refused the title *pater patriae* that had been ceremonially accepted by Augustus. The oath of allegiance by officials was accepted not for Tiberius himself, but for the *acta* of Augustus. Tiberius did not want to be called *imperator*. Augustus, too, had wanted to be viewed as *princeps*, not *imperator*, and had therefore made *imperator* a personal name. Tiberius also put a stop to this practice. He called himself not 'Imperator Tiberius Nero', but simply 'Tiberius Caesar Augustus'.[411]

Immediately on Tiberius's accession the two most dreadful evils of military monarchy appeared, murder within the family and military unrest. It fell to Tiberius to atone for the reign of Augustus: this is how history retaliates. Tiberius was not directly responsible either for the death of Postumus or for events on the Rhine and Danube. Marcus Julius Agrippa Postumus had recently been in renewed contact with Augustus. Tiberius must have viewed him with concern and Livia undoubtedly shared these feelings entirely. Agrippa had to be eliminated for political and private reasons: with such a brutal nature it was impossible for him to coexist with Tiberius. Agrippa would have fallen an easy prey to any and every swindler.[412]

What the public was told was the following:[413] Augustus died in the absence of Tiberius. Directly thereafter the officer on duty on the island of Planasia received an order from Gaius Sallustius Crispus to execute Agrippa, which he did. Sallustius was only an equestrian without any official capacity, simply a friend of the Emperor. It is significant that [MH.I, 121] his authority was sufficient. When Tiberius learned of it, he threatened a criminal investigation before the Senate. This was formally correct. Crispus responded and pointed out to the Emperor the danger inherent in placing the matter before the Senate. Tiberius back-pedalled, thereby bringing the matter to an end. This much is clear, that the danger Agrippa posed to the government was not small. There were plans to abduct him to the Danube, as a rallying-point for rebellious soldiers. The emissaries were already on their way. The danger inherent in the affair became apparent through the false Agrippa Clemens, a slave whose claim to be Agrippa was believed and who had to be eliminated by Crispus.[414] Who ordered the murder? Certainly not Augustus. He had wanted Agrippa's imprisonment to be continued after his death and had a decree to this effect issued by the Senate. Crispus probably claimed that his order was on the instructions of Augustus, but Augustus would never have been capable of such a thing. It is conceivable that Tiberius issued the order, but highly unlikely: how could he then have entertained the idea of a trial before the Senate? Crispus in any case later fell from grace, presumably because of this incident. The order was probably issued by Livia before Tiberius arrived at Nola. It was a judicial murder *in optima forma*. It is possible that the murder had previously been agreed between Livia and Tiberius, but the real blame lies with Augustus. The only alternative lay between a crime and civil war, but it was Augustus who had created this alternative through his double adoption. What inner struggles Tiberius must have undergone we can only guess at. He found himself in a dreadful predicament; the general public laid the blame for the murder at his door.

[MH.I, 122] The second evil was military unrest.[415] In general, the soldiers accepted the accession without any demonstrations. This was not so on the Rhine and the Danube, where a curious movement arose simultaneously. It was not of a political nature, neither being aimed at a Republican revolution, nor deriving from any personal dislike of Tiberius, who was renowned for being a fine general. Not a single officer is known to have been involved in it: they were excluded. It was a breakdown in discipline, brought about by the ill-treatment the soldiers had received – entirely justified, moreover, since their treatment was quite beyond endurance.

The reason lay partly in the system. First, there was criticism of the length of military service. The soldier left service with his physical energies exhausted. This, however, had been the case even earlier. Second, there were complaints about the rigour of exercises. Training was focused entirely on hand-to-hand and single combat. The difference between new recruits and the *triarii* was immense.[416] There was no break in the period of military service. This lamentable state of affairs could scarcely be avoided, and was exacerbated by a shortage of both money and men. The length of military service was often even increased to over twenty years, since there was a shortage of money with which to pay the *praemium* (gratuity on discharge).

The *vexilla veteranorum*, veterans' standards, became the focus for the rebellion: an injustice had been done to them. Other reasons compounded this, for example the concentration of troops and their sense of being indispensable to the state. Nevertheless, *esprit de corps* had come to exceed tolerable levels.

The smaller[417] [MH.I, 123] units remained loyal, but the eight legions of the Rhine regarded themselves as the crack army of the Empire, and rightly so. This feeling was compounded by the resentment felt by the ordinary soldiers for the Guard. The latter had better conditions, higher pay and a shorter term of service. The Praetorians served for only sixteen years. This caused bitterness. All these grievances, however, had been precipitated by the vacillating approach of

Augustan military policy. Here, too, Tiberius reaped where he had not sown. It is significant that there had been no unrest during the lifetime of Augustus. The troops certainly did not hold back out of fear, since Tiberius was more to be feared. The men maintained their admirable loyalty towards Augustus, and the government should have acted to reinforce this feeling.

In the main, the soldiers' demands were modest. They sought parity between the front-line soldiers and the Guard, the demobilization of veterans, a rise in pay, disbursement of Augustus's legacy and a maximum period of service of sixteen years. This was equitable. [MH.I, 124] But the manner in which these demands were presented was unacceptable. Some individual centurions were killed, the fury of the men directed against both them and the *praefecti castrorum*, who were appointed from senior centurions. Curiously, the senior officers stood idly by.

The rebellion could only be suppressed by moral means. An envoy was sent to the Emperor from the Danube. The response of Tiberius is extraordinary, revealing his vacillating temperament. Had Tiberius the *imperator* made a personal appearance, the troops would have submitted. This much is clear from subsequent events. This is what Tiberius wished to do, and it was imperative that he should. He had to undertake the journey, even though it posed an immense danger. He did not do so, however, probably reflecting that the commander-in-chief cannot jeopardize his authority in such a manner.

Tiberius sent his own son Drusus with a young officer named Lucius Aelius Sejanus, son of the commander of the Guard, with whom he shared the command. It was a dangerous experiment. Drusus wanted to talk to the soldiers, but when he was unable to make any proposals, he was received with scorn. A second deputation was sent to Rome and with this the revolution petered out. The loyal party gained the upper hand over the disloyal, probably as a result of intervention by Sejanus. The men handed over the ringleaders and the affair was brought to a close.

[MH.I, 125] The unrest on the Rhine developed in similar fashion.[418] Here there was already an imperial prince on the scene, the heir-apparent, Germanicus. The demands were the same, but there were no soldier envoys. Germanicus approved the demands on the strength of ostensible imperial orders. These dispatches were false, however: Germanicus was acting with a forged mandate. Soon the soldiers grew suspicious. A delegation from Rome led by Munatius Plancus arrived with no concessions to offer. Once the soldiers realized this, the revolt grew more serious than before. Germanicus sent his wife and young son, Caligula, away from Cologne to Trier, which remained loyal. This filled the men with shame – that the granddaughter of Augustus was seeking refuge with Gauls instead of Romans. They themselves killed the chief ringleaders and begged Germanicus for forgiveness. It was the end of the revolt. This reveals the inferior character of the movement, which was no more than a revolt by an armed mob.

The result was deleterious, nonetheless. Tiberius did not revoke the concessions made by Germanicus, but limited them to a brief period of two years. All in all, however, the unrest among soldiers remains a sad reminder of the vacillation of Tiberius and the flawed nature of Augustan institutions. About one thing, however, we should be clear: there was no pretender. Had Agrippa still been alive, success would not have been impossible for him, if only temporarily. Indeed, there were even a few voices who called for Germanicus to take over the leadership; that would have been tantamount to suicide in every respect.

[MH.I, 126] The events on the Danube and the Rhine exposed for the first time the grave sickness that was to bring about the downfall of the state. They revealed that the soldier, the common soldier, was master of the house. If these movements ran out of steam before achieving their goals, this was only because officers were not yet involved. It was now clear, however, that under certain circumstances the soldier could seize the throne. The principate did not envisage any involvement of the will of the people, and if an audacious officer wanted to seize power, he could do so with the support of only a handful of bold men. The sole remedy was a proper relationship between the Emperor and the army. Augustus had known this and Tiberius was greatly remiss in not following his example in this. He could have had that relationship if he had made a personal appearance among his army. This will be seen later with other rulers: the Roman principate was impossible to sustain under a weak Emperor.

This soldiers' revolt was important for the development of policy with regard to Germany.[419] It was hardly over when Germanicus, at a quite inappropriate season not before the end of September AD 14, began a campaign. He took 12,000 legionaries and approximately 28,000 auxiliaries against the Marsians. On the return march he was surrounded as Varus's army had been. The Germans had learned a number of lessons and the expedition was a difficult one. All in all, the campaign cannot be described as successful. The roots of the campaign lay in the mutiny against Tiberius. Prior to this the Germans had shown themselves to be peaceable. It was not the Germans who attacked first. It was necessary to restore military discipline – this was the reason for the war. It did not stop at this, however: Germanicus had further plans.

The following [MH.I, 127] year, in AD 15, a major campaign was launched.[420] Germanicus wanted to revive the plans of his father. The entire Rhine army was mobilized against Germany. Upper and Lower Germany had eight legions, 80,000 men,[421] all of whom were united under the command of Germanicus as proconsul, who was also in authority over the whole of Gaul. The Lower German army was under Caecina. He marched into Germany from Casta Vetera (Xanten), while the Upper German army set out from Mainz. These were the two main bases. There was no German resistance to speak of. Evidently Germanicus was planning permanent conquests. We read only incidentally in Tacitus[422] of the building of fortresses. The castles between the Rhine and Aliso or the source of the Lippe were of a permanent character. The fortifications on the Taunus, abandoned by Drusus, were renewed. Previously, efforts seem to have been restricted to the Rhine valley, with Mainz as the main fortress. Later, the hill ranges opposite Mainz as far as Bingen were bridgeheads in the hands of the Romans. Securing the foreground was a major strategic measure, involving the Saalburg fort near Homburg.[423] Germanicus did not limit himself to this, however: he also interfered in the internal affairs of the Germans. Among the Cherusci the nationalist party under Hermann was fighting against the allies of the Romans under Segestes. Germanicus succeeded in capturing Thusnelda, wife of Arminius and daughter of Segestes.[424] Quite the old system, in other words: the exploitation of foreign discord. A great tumult followed, quite understandably. People must have sensed that Varus's plans were being revived.

[MH.I, 128] The Saxon tribes[425] now all closed ranks. After reconnaissance, Germanicus launched a combined attack on them by both land and sea in the summer of AD 15.[426] Caecina pressed on over land as far as the Ems, while Germanicus travelled by ship and had the cavalry advance on land. The two expeditions were intended to converge at the Ems, and at first the plan went well. There was cavalry combat, but with no decisive outcome. The Germans fought well and strategically, and a Roman victory could not be taken for granted. Since the year was already well advanced they had to turn back. This induced a repetition of the events of the Varus disaster. Germanicus managed to reach his ships without heavy casualties. The crews on the coast suffered as a result of the high tides, but not excessively. Caecina fared incomparably worse. It appears he was unable to find good roads for the return march and the old ones were not, of course, in good condition. The Germans set on the Romans eagerly with full force, outnumbering them massively. At first they only succeeded in severing the Romans' communications, placing them in great danger. But Inguiomer[427] attempted, far too rashly, to storm their camp, which provided the Romans with their opportunity. Caecina managed to fight his way back to the Rhine, where the army had been given up for lost. The Rhine bridge, which was already about to be demolished, was saved through the intervention of Agrippina.[428] The expedition may thus be regarded as a partial success.

The fighting of the following year of the war, AD 16, opened with the construction of forts, specifically the restoration of Aliso, controlling the Lippe valley.[429] Roads and entrenchments were repaired, and preparations made for occupation: the 'offensive defensive' approach was now abandoned. [MH.I, 129] Once again, a two-pronged expedition was launched, with a still greater fleet; we read of 1,000 ships. Once again the destination was the Weser. Essentially it was a repetition of the same events. On the Weser Arminius and his pro-Roman brother Flavus held a conference.[430] The Weser was crossed and a battle successfully

135

fought on the field of Idistaviso.[431] But for the Germans, such large-scale infantry engagements were an entirely unusual and dangerous innovation. Following a second great battle,[432] Germanicus considered it appropriate to raise a memorial to victory: the inscription declares the aspiration to make the Elbe the frontier of the Empire.[433] The return march through the country proceeded smoothly on the newly built roads. The fleet was less fortunate; it was battered in equinoctial storms and suffered terribly without even encountering an enemy.[434] This apart the campaign may be regarded as a complete success.[435]

Germanicus was, in truth, quite aware that his goal had not yet been achieved – that another campaign would be needed to make the conquest a fact. At this point he was relieved of his duties.[436] The command headquarters was disbanded and the two Germanies remained separate. This put paid to the offensive once and for all.

How do these campaigns accord with the policy of the Empire? They ran contrary to the directions of Augustus, and Tiberius had convinced himself that the Empire must refrain from them. It is understandable that Germanicus was of a different opinion, but he did not realize he was conducting a futile campaign. He was seeking to compel the government against its wishes into a conquest of Germany, as Caesar had succeeded in doing with Gaul. Where this had worked under the Republic, however, it was impossible in the principate. Rome did not have sufficient troops.

[MH.I, 132[437]] Germanicus acted improperly. Approving a plan to occupy Germany was a matter for the government, not a general. It was the prerogative of the government to decide whether it wanted to maintain existing conquests or not. However, this decision was rendered more difficult by Germanicus's rank. The position of senior officers under the principate was difficult enough in itself, and it was exacerbated by the proximity of Germanicus to the throne. He was commander-in-chief and heir-apparent at one and the same time.

This notwithstanding, we cannot overlook the mistake made by Tiberius. He should openly and unequivocally have forbidden Germanicus, who did not oppose him, from waging this war. Instead of this his vacillating nature led him to allow Germanicus to proceed with a war he had no wish for, just as he allowed everything else to slide. On the other hand, he could not simply have Germanicus removed; given the preceding events this would have given the impression of a conflict. It is strange, however, that Tiberius did not set off to visit the army himself. Perhaps it was not appropriate for him to confront the rebels, but he could easily have assumed supreme command himself at this point, thereby ensuring that all the glory would redound to his own credit.

Both parties were thus responsible for this outcome. Germanicus was relieved of his duties at the end of AD 16, probably on the pretext of the heavy casualties incurred during the naval retreat, which had, after all, been a severe setback.

Aside from certain regions along the Rhine, the situation was left to slide, with a return to a defensive posture. Germanicus was naturally fêted, the ostensible reason being the complex situation in the East. He was made consul for the following year, and was given [MH.I, 133] a triumph.[438] Relations do not seem to have cooled.

At this point our sources for events on the Rhine become extremely fragmentary. The Romans no longer wanted to go on to the offensive; Tiberius left the Germans to their own internal discord.[439] And events seemed to prove him right. This was the first time one could speak of German concord and German discord. Prior to this it is scarcely possible to distinguish between Celts and Germans; here, for the first time, we encounter a form of national consciousness. Conflicts with the Romans had consolidated the Germans in two areas. First, there was the kingdom of Marobod, about which we have spoken earlier and which had in the meantime been steadily becoming unified. We read of a detachment of Germans marching off to Raetia in connection with the assault by Germanicus.[440] In addition there had been a closing of ranks among the Saxon tribes as a result of engagements with Germanicus. The retreat of Germanicus particularly encouraged this process.

These two factors now came into conflict and set about destroying each other.[441] War now burst forth, born of the friction between the aristocratically ruled state in the north and the monarchy in the south. At first, the Saxons basked in their pre-eminent role in public opinion as the liberators of Germany. The Semnones and Lombards of central Germany declared their independence from Marobod and went over to the Saxons. [MH.I, 134] This led to civil wars and eventually to the destruction of both parties. The 'decisive battle' proved indecisive, but overall Marobod was defeated; he entered into negotiations with Rome. His state disintegrated. The Saxons seem not to have followed up their victory, but Marobod became unpopular. A Goth made a surprise attack on him with a small number of followers; Marobod fled and was sent by Tiberius to Ravenna, where he lived in exile for another eighteen years. His vanquisher, Catualda the Goth, soon followed Marobod's example[442] and out of these two bands a Suevic state developed in Moravia. It was under the protection of Rome.

Among the Saxons, total victory was followed by internal unrest over the leadership. Arminius is alleged to have aspired to the kingship. Naturally he immediately met with strong resistance from his kin and was murdered. This shattered any incipient German unity. When did this occur? According to Tacitus[443] it was in the year AD 19 and this is the date we should go by, not two years later. Arminius died at the age of 37 in the twelfth year of his pre-eminence, *potentia*. Some commentators have sought to date the latter from the Varus disaster, but incorrectly, since this dating presupposes his pre-eminence. Arminius may arguably be regarded as the liberator of Germany:[444] *canitur adhuc barbaras apud gentes*.[445] The monument in the Teutoburg Forest makes a joke of our historical knowledge of him. The Germans were not to make another independent appearance on the stage of Roman history until the Marcomannic Wars. The tribes fell apart and no longer posed a threat to the Roman Empire, which began to move its point of main military effort to the Danube. Germany was liberated more by *inopia stipendii* and *tironum*[446] than by the Cherusci.

[MH.I, 135] The situation in the East was not as important as that in Germany. The former was closely bound up with the dynastic history of the ruling family. The crucial question was that of Armenia. Augustus had paid more attention to appearances than to reality. Tiberius acted with greater vigour and rightly so. A Parthian ruler was incessantly fighting in Armenia, which was in a state of permanent anarchy. It was the duty of Rome to intervene in this country, once it had been recognized as a client-state. Augustus had been criminally remiss in this. Tiberius began with the integration of buffer states. Defence of the frontiers was in the hands of the weak client-states Commagene and Cappadocia. These were now ruthlessly transformed into provinces. Garrisons under independent command were not sent there, however, only auxiliaries.

The task of establishing these new provinces fell to Germanicus.[447] He set off in AD 18. The situation in Parthia proved expedient to the Romans for the execution of their plans. A dispute over the Parthian throne was raging between Artabanus and the rival pretender Vonones.[448] The latter fled to Roman soil in Cilicia, enabling Rome to use him to exert pressure on the Parthian government.

All in all the reign of Tiberius was an eminently peaceful one. Where the Republic was war, the Empire was peace, and this persisted throughout two centuries until the collapse of the Empire. Whether this peace was to the benefit of the Empire is debatable, but at all events the fundamental malady of the age, stagnation, was exacerbated by the attitude of Tiberius. [MH.I, 136] The fact that we read of a minor war in Africa[449] is owed to the fact that it was waged by senatorial generals and recorded in the senatorial minutes on which historians have drawn, but it was of no importance whatsoever.

The only state Rome needed to reckon with was Parthia, and the situation prevailing there was important for Rome.[450] In AD 18 Germanicus assumed the consulate with proconsular *imperium*; all armies and governors in the East were now placed under his authority and were bound to obey him. His primary task was to impose some order on the complex situation in the East. The policy of Augustus was no longer possible for Rome. To the north of Syria lay Commagene and Cappadocia, which were dependent on Rome under hereditary governors. The neighbouring kingdom of Armenia was *de iure* dependent, since every king was installed by Rome and could be deposed at any time. *De facto*, however, it was independent, if only because of its geographical location. The Parthians likewise staked a claim to Armenia: the country was a natural bone of contention.

At that time, total anarchy reigned. Gaius Caesar[451] had installed Ariobarzanes, then his son Artavasdes. The latter was murdered, leaving the throne vacant. Augustus installed Tigranes, who was related to the dynasty. He was unable to maintain his position and was soon eliminated, if, indeed, he ever ruled at all. Then Erato, a princess, bore the royal title for a time. A dual pretendership [MH.I, 137] ensued. The Parthians had persuaded Augustus to instal Vonones, youngest son of King Phraates. Vonones, however, had become a Roman and was highly unpopular. He was soon removed, and in his stead came a distant Arsacid, Artabanos (III). Vonones called on Rome to reinstate him. His wish was not met, however: he was interned in Syria for future eventualities.

Artabanus, king of Parthia, nominated his son Orodes as king of Armenia. The local Roman party, however, wanted Vonones, making the latter a double pretender. Rome could not tolerate this state of affairs. Germanicus settled matters swiftly and resolutely. First, he came to terms with Parthia. He recognized Artabanus on condition that the latter relinquish his claim to Armenia. For control of this kingdom Germanicus looked neither to Tigranes, nor to Vonones, instead installing Artaxias of the house of Polemon of Pontus, the king the Armenians themselves preferred.[452]

In place of their kings, Commagene and Cappadocia were given Roman governors.[453] All this was accomplished without arms. Germanicus wanted the Syrian army to occupy Commagene, but this did not happen as the governor of Syria was uncooperative. Matters were quite satisfactory as they were, however, and the situation remained settled for some considerable time. From now on the [MH.I, 138] Roman force occupying Commagene and Cappadocia exerted an effective counterbalance to Parthian influence on neighbouring Armenia, and this was the enduring component in the arrangement.

On the other hand, these matters also had personal implications. The conduct of Tiberius towards Germanicus cannot be described as other than considerate. By compensating him with the Parthian command for relieving him of his duties in Germany he was perhaps, if anything, carrying his beneficence too far. At the same time, however, Tiberius took certain precautionary steps which in the event turned out to be disastrous. The commander of the Syrian army wielded considerable influence in the East. In place of Creticus Silanus, Tiberius appointed Gnaeus Calpurnius Piso, a valiant soldier.[454] His personal relationship with Germanicus was strained, and their wives were sworn enemies. Nevertheless, he was particularly devoted to Tiberius. The latter had probably assigned him additional duties in the event of a Parthian war, because when Germanicus called for troops Piso did not provide them. It is not inconceivable that he did this out of recalcitrance, but this is not the point: one way or the other Piso was convinced that he should defy Germanicus.

For his part Germanicus failed to act with the necessary prudence. While nothing would be more absurd than to accuse him of a rebellion against his father, he did nonetheless [MH.I, 139] take questionable steps on the strength of his position. Being of an inquiring mind, he travelled to the wonderland of Egypt in AD 19.[455] This was natural enough, but unfortunately it involved a touch of treason: no senator was permitted to enter Egypt without authorization from the Emperor. The fact that he, as heir-apparent, failed to abide by this was reprehensible, to say the least. He, of all people, should have observed the formal courtesies to the letter. A sidelight to this high-handedness is shed by a peculiar coin.[456] Only one specimen of it exists, and it was minted in the East. It evokes the impression of Germanicus as ruler of the East. The obverse depicts him crowning Artaxias, the reverse shows the head of Germanicus. Tiberius is thus completely ignored. The government probably later suppressed the coin; at all events its minting was a highly questionable act. Germanicus might well have been accused of *res novae*. This led to discord between Germanicus and Piso. A conference took place that ended in serious confrontation. The journey to Egypt then followed, and on his return Germanicus found that all his orders had been overruled by Piso. He himself, of course, had also repeatedly interfered in the affairs of Syria. The confrontation escalated visibly.

In AD 19 Germanicus fell ill at Antioch, the capital of Syria, as he was on the point of leaving the province.[457] His wife and immediate entourage thought that he had been poisoned at the instigation of Piso. The truth is impossible to establish. At any rate Germanicus believed that he had been poisoned, and there were grounds for suspicion. What appears to have been a rigorously conducted investigation[458] was unable to prove anything against Piso. From a higher standpoint, however, there are grounds for suspicion against Piso and his wife Plancina. One is the relationship between Plancina and the professional poisoner Martina. [MH.I, 140] She subsequently died suddenly at Brundisium. On the island of Cos Piso gave thanks to the gods for the death of the heir-apparent. In Germanicus's bedroom, curse tablets were found that were traced back to Plancina. This did not bring about his death, however. The malefactor will also have used other, more effective means.

This is not to suggest that the existence of a crime has been proved. There is much to suggest the contrary, notably the character of Piso, a veteran officer with forty-six years of military service behind him who had grown old in honours. If a crime is to be presumed at all then female revenge springs to mind first. Germanicus believed his death was imminent. The heir to his authority was, in the first instance, Piso; he should have led the criminal investigation. It is therefore probable that Germanicus, while still on his death bed, wanted to have Piso expelled from the province. Characteristically, Tacitus[459] is vague on this point. Piso's overall conduct suggests that he was expelled on higher orders. Although Germanicus could not deprive Piso, who had been appointed by the Emperor, of his office, he could expel him; there are precedents from the Republic of a quaestor, for example, being expelled by a praetor. Clearly this would have had grave repercussions on his position *vis-à-vis* Tiberius.

An initial recovery of his health was not sustained and Germanicus died on 10 October AD 19.[460] *En route* to Rome, Piso had reached Cos when he heard the news and decided to turn back. Constitutionally he was entitled to do this. He had not lost his mandate, and according to the Roman constitution [MH.I, 141] he was bound only to fulfil orders issued by his mandator, and was released from this obligation on the latter's death. Piso's return to the East was a breach of decorum, but it was not treason. He thus landed without troops in Cilicia; his soldiers were still stationed in the province. He mobilized the Cilician territorial militia. Agrippina and the friends of Germanicus were in a desperate situation. It was decided to order Piso back: the senior officers favoured Germanicus. The two camps thus now reached the point of open confrontation. This curious conflict was acted out at Celenderis in Cilicia.[461] Piso was besieged and forced to capitulate, and now returned to Rome after all. This was unprecedented and could not be left without a conclusion before a court of law. Germanicus had asked to be avenged and Agrippina brought charges against Piso for murder by poisoning and for high treason, the latter with respect to the most recent events. Here we are purely concerned with the legal interpretation of the situation. In any event, however, the trial was a grievous calamity. The Emperor was a co-defendant, since he had generated the conflict between Germanicus and Piso. Naturally, the public drew further inferences. They looked upon Piso and Tiberius as the murderers of Germanicus. Never, probably, has so much love been showered on a man after his death as on Germanicus. The mourning over his loss was ubiquitous and most impressive. Abhorrence of Tiberius was expressed in love for Germanicus. His cheerful disposition, his renown and his literary status raised him to the level of general favourite. The suspicions [MH.I, 142] directed against Tiberius were both disgraceful and absurd. What matters, however, are appearances, not reality. Tiberius's concern that Piso's *liber mandatorum*[462] might be produced was understandable.

There were three possible ways of proceeding with the lawsuit: before a regular law-court, before one of the two extraordinary law-courts of the Senate or before that of the *princeps*. The plaintiffs wanted the hearing to take place before the Emperor. Tiberius refused, perhaps wrongly, since the trial was of an eminently political character and called for star-chamber justice. Tiberius's evasive action is understandable, however, since he was himself to some extent *in lite*.[463] The trial was thus held before the Senate, and for the most part fairly.[464] Murder was not proven, although the events in Cilicia were judged to be high treason, as indeed they were, even if Piso still regarded himself as being in office. Provincial governors could not be offered such an example. The judicial decision was undoubtedly influenced by mourning for Germanicus.

Piso called on the Emperor to intervene; this was flatly refused. It was expected that Piso would produce his imperial mandate. This did not happen. He took his own life.[465] However, even in this case the public assumed that Tiberius had killed him to prevent exposure. Once again, however, undoubtedly wrongly, as the circumstances of Piso's death demonstrate. The catastrophe thus came to an end with the death of the person [MH.I, 143] concerned. The third accessory, however, was the Emperor himself, and it was on him that the hatred of the people focused. He was held responsible for the death of Germanicus. Tiberius did not view the death of Germanicus as a misfortune – almost as if he had died at the right time. We can believe Tacitus in this.[466] Whether Germanicus had the makings of a tactful prince must be doubted, particularly if he should have ruled for decennia.

It remains to take another brief look at events in the East.[467] The existing order prevailed as long as Artaxias lived. Fresh complications erupted, however, when he died in AD 34 or 35. The Parthians sought to take possession of Armenia and Artabanus named his son Arsaces king. Despite his advanced age, Tiberius intervened with consummate adroitness, waging a war through pretenders. Phraates was being held at Rome; Tiberius sent him to Syria and, although he died soon thereafter, Tiridates, another prince, was immediately appointed. This gave Artabanus little room for manoeuvre. Lucius Vitellius was dispatched as governor, with the same sphere of command as Germanicus but without a Piso, since Vitellius was also made governor of Syria. The Iberians of the Caucasus were unleashed on Armenia. These were not actually a client-state; they lived in somewhat greater liberty. The Iberians invaded with the idea of making Mithridates, one of their princes, king. Tiberius had achieved his objective: Artabanus surrendered to the Romans and humbled himself before an image of the Emperor. [MH.I, 144] It was a triumph for Roman statesmanship. All had been enacted purely through diplomacy, without troops. This is a clear example of Tiberius's impressive mental vigour.

The rule of Tiberius ranks among the finest the Roman Empire ever had. Even Tacitus[468] acknowledges as much. In domestic policy, work was carried out consolidating the constitution. Elections once again became true elections by eliminating the popular assembly and transferring them to the Senate.[469] This, moreover, remained the cornerstone of the Senate's position, for in this way the senators effectively coopted themselves, since magistrates subsequently joined the Senate. The nobility naturally favoured themselves, thus well and truly realizing the aristocratic element as it had been envisaged by Augustus.

Nonetheless, the Senate could no longer boast any practical involvement in government.[470] Public interest in senatorial debates was sustained despite this. A bad Emperor invariably produces a still worse Senate. One of the crucial reasons for Tiberius's contempt for humanity may be found in the adulation of senators;[471]

this contributed in no small measure to the reign of terror during the final years of Tiberius. The mode of election excluded finer minds from the Senate, while the tedious rules of procedure, with the absence of sub-committees and suchlike, likewise contributed not inconsiderably to the powerlessness of the Senate. Senatorial government appeared to be by nature stillborn.

Otherwise the government of Tiberius was probably laudable. This is demonstrated by his arrangements for the succession. He preferred his nephew and adoptive son Germanicus to his true son Drusus, not allowing the latter to celebrate a triumph over the Germans until AD 20, after the death of Germanicus.[472] At that point Drusus was openly named as successor. Although relations between father and son were not exactly good, Tiberius arranged in AD 22 [MH.I, 145] for Drusus to share in tribunician authority, apparently for life.[473] This gave him the highest authority after that of the *princeps*.

The rule of Tiberius was aimed at regulating the state by means of a strict monitoring of officials and stringent policing. Viewed from this standpoint, personal intervention by the *princeps* in the judicature was something positive. By presiding over the courts in the Senate and in the Forum, by participating in debates and summoning litigants before his own court, he supported the praetor in the execution of his office and averted some miscarriages of justice. The senators were thereby given the Emperor's support. There were vigorous interventions against prostitution and adultery, stringent policing of religious affairs and severe penalties were imposed for soothsaying and Isis worship.[474]

The Emperor's circumspection was most evident in the selection of magistrates. The primary criterion was good birth, but noble magistrates were not permitted to plunder willy-nilly; they were carefully controlled.[475] Never were complaints from provincials so carefully investigated as they were in the time of Tiberius,[476] or so few. Provinces that had suffered greatly, such as Achaea, were transferred for a time from the senatorial to the imperial administrative sphere.[477] Naturally, even with the best will in the world, a senatorial official in office for only one year could not exercise effective administration. On the other hand, Tiberius replaced his own officials as infrequently as he possibly could, leaving even the most high-ranking governors in their posts for years at a time.[478]

[MH.I, 146] With regard to the military sphere, Tiberius saw to the security of highways and the suppression of robbery in Italy, where brigandage had been on the rampage in the aftermath of civil war. In this respect Tiberius ensured a century of peace. Either he, or perhaps Sejanus, concentrated the Guard from the vicinity of Rome into the city itself and built the Praetorian camp for them.[479] A garrison of 30,000 men was none too many for a city of a million inhabitants of such dubious character. Unfortunately this move also strengthened the Guard's dominance over the Emperor himself.

The urban *plebs* were kept under control; during no other reign were there so few donations to the common people of the capital. This did nothing to increase Tiberius's popularity, of course. When all is said and done, though, it was only drinking-money, and these measures rank among the best features of Tiberius. He likewise stopped the donations to soldiers, which were, if anything, still worse. He will, on the other hand, have made sure that the soldier punctually obtained what was due to him; thanks to his invariably well-filled treasury he was in a position to do this. He was able to ride 'stock market crises'. He boosted the public economy through interest-free loans – a most rare occurrence during the badly controlled fiscal regimes of the Emperors. He allocated huge funds to Asia Minor to relieve towns devastated by earthquakes.[480] He also saw to it that financiers invested a proportion of their fortunes in real estate and restricted their usury somewhat more than these gentlemen were accustomed to do.[481] [MH.I, 148[482]] All this, and in particular the regulation of financial administration, were ideals of the Roman principate which Tiberius knew how to transform into reality. No wonder later rulers saw in him a model they could not live up to.

This shining light must, nevertheless, be offset by a dark shadow. This was connected with the affairs surrounding his family and confidants. Let us examine trial procedure, particularly for treason.[483] How did the *crimina maiestatis* (accusations of treason) come about? In this case institutions were more at fault than individuals. Criminal procedure was a legacy of the Republic and took the form of civil action. Each action required a denunciation by a plaintiff from among the citizenry. This was a great defect. The office of plaintiff was embarrassing and perilous, an act of personal insult against the accused's entire kin. On the other hand, the state needed to ensure that a sufficient number of plaintiffs came forward, necessitating the principle of personal advantage, the *praemia accusatoria* (accusers' rewards), which allocated part of the fine or fortune of the condemned to the plaintiff.[484] This institution was a long-standing one which was not eradicated by the Emperors – nor could they eradicate it, despite its blatant defects.

The Emperors, indeed, enhanced this system. It was comparatively tolerable in the case of pecuniary penalties and offences (corruption and peculation), but the more it was applied to political offences, the more intolerable it became. The practice of political crime became totally different. The Republic had had the highly elastic element of the *laesa maiestas populi Romani* offence,[485] on which [MH.I, 149] all social law is based [*sic*]. Use of this charge had been sparing in the Republic; it was made only in the event of treason or cowardice. The *populus Romanus*, after all, was not capable of personal injury. Moreover, proceedings invariably took place before a jury, which constituted a substantial limitation, as did the *de facto* abolition of the death penalty.[486]

All this now changed. The element of the offence was expanded – *iniuriae* (personal damage) had already been included by Augustus. Cassius Severus, who made himself an immense nuisance to the public with his lampoons, was charged not with *iniuriae*, but with *laesa maiestas*, and convicted: he was sent into exile.[487] This was the first, in itself wholesome, step on a slippery downward path. Furthermore, confiscation of property and the death penalty were introduced – not entirely without justification, since *laesa maiestas* was a grave offence. A court of senators was instituted, that is a court made up of ex-magistrates, rather than private individuals.

Now we can envisage the litigation process. However vague the latter might be, the death sentence could be passed and the plaintiff could anticipate substantial gains from the accusation he had lodged. This is how the institution of professional accusers[488] came about. Indictments were invariably directed at wealthy people, and if informers did not wish to lodge an accusation they could blackmail them. This institution developed swiftly under Tiberius; under him the seed of abuse sprouted.

[MH.I, 150] The trial of Marcus Drusus Libo[489] does not fit into this category. It concerns a person whose culpability is not in doubt. He was related to the ruling house and had the insane idea of becoming Emperor himself. Tiberius so utterly despised this immature, childish, ambitious customer that he completely failed to respond. Two years after his accession, and apparently against the Emperor's wishes, the plot was denounced by an informer. The senators had no alternative but to find him guilty[490] and Tiberius allowed justice to take its course. It would have been wise to prevent this lawsuit, as indeed Tiberius was asked to do. He did not do so, however, and Libo killed himself. Tiberius declared that he had wanted to pardon him. The most terrible aspect of all is that this conviction was recorded in the calendar, something which happened without Tiberius's consent. Later Tiberius often intervened against abuses of the *maiestas* law, but it should be added that in general he allowed justice to take its course – *exercendas esse leges*, he is reputed to have said.[491] We shall be returning later to this fearful proliferation of judicial murder.

A key factor in the latter part of Tiberius's reign was his relationship towards Sejanus, his confidant. Here we encounter indirect rule for the first time, although the principate is supposedly entirely based on the person of the *princeps*. Lucius Aelius Sejanus was an equestrian of humble origins. His father, Strabo, had been Praetorian commander under Augustus,[492] but had had no political influence. His son was appointed to command alongside him by Tiberius. Sejanus was born in 7 BC. He passed his first test during the suppression of the soldiers' revolt in AD 14 on the Danube, where he acted as Drusus's right-hand man. He [MH.I, 151] showed himself eminently capable during this incident.[493] Thus, equipped with shrewdness and loyalty, he took first place among the advisers to Tiberius. His father became governor of Egypt, leaving him as sole commander of the Praetorian guard. No *adlatus* (associate) was given him. In this, to his own detriment, Tiberius departed from ancient custom. Sejanus was from now on *socius laborum* (sharer of my labours) in all matters, as the Emperor used to describe him in the Senate. He appointed all officers and administrative officials in the Guard. This was not, in fact, within his competence. He combined the position formerly occupied by Maecenas and Sallustius[494] with that of captain of the Guard. As early as AD 21, Tiberius wrought an alliance between the two families through the betrothal of Claudius's son to a daughter of Sejanus.[495] This was regarded as the beginning of the *nimia spes* (excessive hopes) of Sejanus, and rightly so. It was in any case a *mésalliance*, and the favour prompted Sejanus to aspire to even greater heights. To render the Emperor's confidence complete, there was also the cave incident. During a journey outside Rome, Sejanus physically shielded the Emperor from a roof fall.[496] Sejanus cannot be accused of disloyalty. He aspired to power, even to succeed Tiberius, but not to eliminate him. Sejanus was a man of extraordinary ability, immense talent and rare loyalty.[497]

He did, nonetheless, incur severe guilt with respect to the death of Drusus, the Emperor's son. At first his death was assumed to be the result of dissipation, but this was not correct. Drusus was a man of crude and irascible, but good-humoured [MH.I, 152] disposition. Tiberius had subordinated him to Germanicus, with whom Drusus was nevertheless on good terms. There was nothing false about him. His relationship with Sejanus was openly strained: Drusus is reputed to have struck him. It is understandable that Sejanus was none too fond of him: Drusus could become king at any moment [*sic*]. It emerged, however, that Sejanus had induced Drusus's wife to murder him.[498] [MH.I, 153] For seven years Tiberius had no idea who was responsible for the death of his son. Then the crime[499] came to light. It would seem we are standing on firmer ground here than usual. Someone who knew the secret informed on Drusus and his slaves confessed to it. Livilla,[500] wife of Drusus, was severely punished, so the matter seems certain. The motive was to enable Livilla to marry Sejanus. Sejanus must have been possessed of veritable demonic powers, especially over women. What could he offer Livilla apart from his person and the prospect of resuming at his side the same position she already had? Tiberius had initially believed that Drusus had died of dissipation. Sejanus asked the Emperor for Livilla's hand, patently in order to move closer to the position of heir-apparent, as Tiberius had himself once done. Tiberius refused, although without any cooling of his relationship with Sejanus.[501]

Next in line to the throne were now the sons of Germanicus, who were still adolescents. The elder, Nero, born in AD 7, was 16, Drusus only a year younger. Tiberius presented them to the Senate in AD 23;[502] however, he did not give them any official positions: they were still too young for that. Sejanus had moved not one jot closer to the throne.

At court women played the main role: Livia, the dowager Empress, now Julia Augusta,[503] Livilla, Tiberius's daughter-in-law, and Agrippina, wife of Germanicus. Disastrously strained relations developed between mother and son, and not only through the fault of the son. Livia's conduct towards her son was entirely different from that towards her husband. She [MH.I, 154] made demands on Tiberius that she would never have made on Augustus. We cannot deduce an actual involvement in affairs of state from the title Augusta. According to Roman thinking, such involvement was impossible, but the title did, nonetheless, confer a mark of imperial respect. Livia had her own court, where there was constant carping at Tiberius. Breaches of etiquette only served to strain relations still further.

Tiberius never neglected the outward deference due to his mother. If anything, the converse could be asserted of Livia. She frequently reproached him severely, claiming, for example, that she had helped him to the throne. This was not untrue, but she had no right to make an issue of it. She gave him confidential letters from Augustus to read in which Tiberius was severely criticized for his recalcitrant nature.[504] She thereby made him increasingly unable to live in society, contributing not inconsiderably to his self-imposed exile on Capri.

It is quite conceivable that Agrippina suspected a crime in the death of Germanicus. Her bearing towards Tiberius was insufferable; she laid claim to an independent household on account of her two sons, regarded herself as guardian of the future ruler and sought influence in affairs of state, which Tiberius flatly refused. Worse than this were the malevolent aspersions she cast on Tiberius himself, implying that he wanted to poison her. She refused fruit handed to her by Tiberius at a public feast.[505] In this she exceeded legitimate mourning for the death of her husband, creating an intolerable relationship. Tiberius could not put up with this; it drove him [MH.I, 155] out of the home that had become hell for him.

Tiberius was totally unpopular with the public, too.[506] The Senate obeyed him, but seethed with secret hatred. Satirical verses about him circulated incessantly, although the author could never be pinned down.[507] Tiberius will also have grown weary of the constant need to negotiate with an uncooperative Senate. It is unlikely, however, that he planned never to return to Rome. In AD 26 he left, in the first instance for Campania.[508]

The consequence of this was that the government slipped out of his hands and shifted from Piso, the urban prefect, to Sejanus, the Praetorian Prefect. These circumstances cannot be compared with modern ones. In Rome the Emperor had to intervene personally. He was first and foremost commander-in-chief, and could not allow himself to be represented by delegated officers. No official term exists for the respective authorities these two men now assumed. It was, of course, in their interests that Tiberius remained out of Rome.

First of all, Sejanus worked towards toppling Agrippina and her children. In 27 Agrippina and her sons were assigned secret minders. The most bizarre rumours circulated, prompting Tiberius to permit this. Agrippina was allegedly planning to travel to the German army on the Rhine.[509] Livia, as long as she was still alive, hindered open conflict. In 29 she died at the age of 86.[510] Disaster immediately swept over the house of Germanicus. The Emperor openly complained to the Senate about Agrippina's presumptuousness and Nero's frivolousness, although these were hardly [MH.I, 156] capital offences. The Senate and public alike were at a loss. The public response was one of extreme vigour: crowds gathered outside the *curia*. The Senate equivocated. Tiberius responded with still more vigour and when the Senate finally understood the Emperor's real wishes, it resolved to exile Agrippina and Nero.

Drusus was soon dealt with in like manner, held under strict house arrest in the palace.[511] This brought Sejanus considerably closer to his goal. Tiberius was now obliged to make a decision about the succession to the throne and probably had Sejanus in mind. In 31 he assumed the consulate with Sejanus.[512] By Roman standards this was incredible, since Sejanus was a mere equestrian and not even a senator. A breach of this class distinction ran quite contrary to the tradition of Augustus. At the same time Sejanus retained command of the Guard. He was brought into the family of the Emperor and betrothed not to Livilla herself, but to her daughter[513] – who may even have been his own. He was additionally invested with proconsular powers. All he now lacked, therefore, to set him on an equal footing with Tiberius was tribunician authority.

At this moment the terrible catastrophe occurred. Why? There was talk of a conspiracy led by Sejanus.[514] But why should there have been? What could induce him to do such a thing, now he was at the peak of his power? He may well have captivated a large number of people who looked more to him than to [MH.I, 157] the Emperor, but this was natural and inevitable in his position. He was the rising sun.

The widespread belief that there was a conspiracy[515] has no real foundation. It is difficult to see what he could have been seeking to achieve. All he needed now was to wait for tribunician authority, and this would come from the Emperor. Nothing of this kind emerged during the investigation. However, a fragment of a speech survives in a stone inscription referring to someone prosecuted for his association with Sejanus which mentions *improbae comitiae* [*sic*] *in Aventino*.[516] This would indicate some kind of democratic movement, but remains a riddle. Flavius Josephus[517] reports that Sejanus was overthrown as a result of a letter from Antonia warning Tiberius about him. But what was to be done? Sejanus could not simply be dismissed like a normal official. He was effectively co-regent and had to all intents and purposes ousted Tiberius from his rule. Tiberius was probably alarmed by his own handiwork – the position of the man he himself had made.

It is plain that Sejanus had never felt entirely secure. He, after all, knew Tiberius better than anyone. With his taciturn nature, one could never know where one stood. Despite all the honours showered on Sejanus, moreover, indications that different arrangements were being planned for the succession had been mounting up. Gaius, the third son of Germanicus,[518] had been brought to court and married. This suggests that he was seen as an alternative to Sejanus. Dispatches from the Emperor to the Senate were becoming increasingly cryptic; the senators did not know what he wanted. Sometimes Sejanus was not mentioned at all, sometimes he was praised effusively. Perhaps Sejanus was planning opposition to Tiberius in view of these circumstances, but he never got that far: he remained undecided to the last.

[MH.I, 158] Then came a messenger from the Emperor on Capri, Gnaeus Sertorius Macro, a senior Guards officer.[519] He brought one message for the Senate and one for Sejanus. The latter was convinced that he had achieved his objective, and anticipated being invested with tribunician powers and thus becoming true co-regent. The procedure used against him bears all the hallmarks of a conspiracy. It is characteristic of the way the system of imperial confidants functioned that here, too, Tiberius failed to make a personal appearance, which would have been the proper thing to do. Macro had a twofold order: to take control of the Guard and to make contact with the *vigiles*. Here the *vigiles* were played off against the other troops. The Praetorian camp and the *curia* were surrounded. Macro presented himself to the Praetorians as their new commander and was immediately accepted, which would not have been possible if Sejanus had been planning a conspiracy. This set the seal on the fate of Sejanus. An interminable dispatch was read out in the *curia*. Macro had made contact with the consul Aemilius Regulus, who was party to the Emperor's plan and was pleased to carry it out. The *curia* and the people were happy to acquiesce, since Sejanus was widely hated. He was arrested in the *curia* without putting up any resistance.

A frightful war of litigation ensued. Sejanus, of course, was executed in prison, but even his divorced wife Apicata and his children, still minors, had to die.[520] Apicata, indeed, denounced Sejanus's poisoning of his son Drusus to the Emperor and named the accomplices. This brought on a new wave of bitterness in the Emperor: no mercy could be expected now. A terrible judicial bloodbath swept [MH.I, 159] over the Roman aristocracy, the recurrence of which so thinned its ranks that it came to be destroyed. Friendship with Sejanus was in itself sufficient for a capital indictment without further grounds. Countless numbers were condemned and their whole families with them. Persecution took on the repulsive character of fiscality: informers joined in in order to grab the *praemia accusatorum*. The Emperor was not without blame: the utter vagueness of the grounds for indictment made all this possible. Some of the convictions were made at Rome, some before the Emperor on Capri. If anything, the court at Rome was even more merciless.

It was generally believed that Drusus, the son of Germanicus, would be released from gaol and the family of Germanicus rehabilitated. Tiberius had, indeed, issued a contingency order to pit Drusus against Sejanus. This had not been necessary: and in 33 Drusus and Agrippina were killed.[521] The following year a mass sentence was passed on the accused. The Emperor was growing weary of trials and wanted to have done with it all. This was one of the frightful consequences of the continual acrimony and distrust people displayed towards him.

In other respects the policies of the Emperor remained unchanged, even in his latter years. These coincided with the end of the Parthian War and massive support to the tune of 100 million sesterces for the Aventine, which had been devastated by fire in 36.[522] On 16 March 37 Tiberius died in his bed, probably of natural causes.[523] He was an unhappy man whom fate had dealt the heaviest blows precisely with respect to his best intentions. Wherever he placed his trust, he was surrounded by subterfuge and treachery. [MH.I, 160] He had grown up under Augustus; although not attached to him by ties of affection he had the utmost admiration for him politically. Augustus had dealt lovelessly with Tiberius, only grudgingly bestowing his position on him *rei publicae causa* (for the public good) after a series of setbacks. The relationship between Tiberius and his mother, Livia, was similar; his latter years were made bitter by this conflict. His relationship with his first wife, Vipsania Agrippina, had been one of genuine affection – a trace of sentimentality is unmistakable.[524] He was obliged to dissolve this happy union for reasons of state, in order to marry Julia, who was totally incompatible with him. This was the severest trial for him, a domestic hell from which he fled to Rhodes. His luck was no better with his sons – his true son, Drusus, and his adoptive son, Germanicus. He found few friends. His relationship with Sejanus, however, was at first positively ideal. He believed he had found a loyal aide in him. That Sejanus met with such a dreadful end was their common fault. In the company of Sejanus people took the liberty of making vulgar quips about the Emperor, calling him a bald dwarf. Then came the setbacks in foreign policy, which were not his doing. His adolescent dream of expanding the Empire by means of military success did not come to fruition. If anyone could have the sense of having ruled well it was Tiberius, and yet he was rewarded for it with bitter hatred. No wonder his misanthropy was so overwhelming. He had much in common with Frederick the Great.[525]

As far as literature is concerned, what survives is inferior. Interest shifted: it was a gloomy time. The songbirds fall silent when a thunderstorm rages in the skies. There is the poetry of Ovid in his old age, but otherwise literary production was insignificant. Velleius Paterculus was certainly a brilliant man; Valerius Maximus is quite inferior: both are distinguished by the pitiful adulation and the most execrable servility that were characteristic of the whole period. The leaden fear in which the world was steeped meets us on all sides. The rhetorical work of the elder Seneca [MH.I, 161] is characteristic of this. His florilegium of famous lawyers' speeches is a particularly disagreeable work – devoid of real charm or any vestige of juristic insight, it strikes florid poses about nothing, about emptiness. 'Sand without lime' was how the Emperor Gaius (Caligula) described the dismal indifference of that time.[526]

3

GAIUS CALIGULA (37–41)

It is with some vexation that we turn to the third Julian Emperor.[527] Tiberius and Augustus were men of importance, distinguished personalities of the kind with whom the historian is constantly having to occupy himself. This Emperor, however, was a boy not yet of age – pure, unadulterated mediocrity, half-crazed and half-witted. There is no other Emperor about whom so many anecdotes are told, but they do not help us to gain a sounder assessment.

Even after the fall of Sejanus Tiberius generally remained outside Rome. Although[528] in the vicinity once, he turned back and died at Misenum.[529] Remarkably enough, Sejanus's place was taken by Macro, likewise commander of the Guard without a colleague.[530] All matters passed through his hands, and yet he was invariably close to the Emperor. In Rome there was absolutely no ruler. The time was approaching to make arrangements for the succession, as Tiberius had invariably done in the better years of his reign. Now, he did not do so. It has been pointed out that his will instituted both his grandsons, Gaius (born in 12) and Tiberius (born in 19) as equal heirs; however, this is not to be construed as an arrangement for the succession. The will was a purely private act and had nothing to do with the political succession.[531] For this reason, too, historians maintain that *de tradenda re publica dubitavit*.[532] He simply failed to get round to it. [MH.I, 162] On his very deathbed he pulled the ring from his finger to hand it over to a successor, thought about it at length and then put it back on his own finger.[533] Decision-making had never come easily to him. He may also have foreseen that the succession of his eldest grandson was beyond doubt. This nevertheless marks one of the gravest mistakes of which he has been accused. He knew the young man, who was now 25. If Tiberius had done his duty, he would, like Augustus, *rei publicae causa* (for the public good) have placed a truly able man at his side. Tiberius did not do so, leaving the question open. Formally speaking, a restoration of the Republic ought now to have ensued, the Senate to have assumed government, and the extraordinary office of principate to have been abolished.

The question as to the form of government was not raised, however, nor was there any doubt as to the person of the ruler. The Senate did not assert itself.

The family of Germanicus was extremely popular and people had persuaded themselves that the son of Germanicus would bring good fortune. Everything favoured him over his 18-year-old cousin. This corresponded to the interests of the senior officers. Macro had cultivated the acquaintance of Gaius and won him over. The commander of the Guard was thus prepared to support Gaius with the consent of the people. So the accession passed smoothly. Gaius could have had himself declared Emperor immediately after the death of Tiberius on 16 March 37 in Campania.[534] He did not do so. On 18 March the Senate declared Gaius *imperator*. There was general rejoicing, [MH.I, 163] but even in this there lurked a disagreeable element. Ruling and being ruled are serious matters; here all appeared from the bright side. People were delighted with the new ruler, because they had rid themselves of the heavy burden of the old one. This was a genuine and justified sentiment. At first the Emperor appeared willing to concede everything to everyone. The people would have been only too pleased to blacken the memory of the dead Emperor. Gaius did not permit this, although the deification which he proposed was not voted by the Senate. Gaius overruled Tiberius's will, and not unreasonably, since a division of the huge fortune of the imperial household in accordance with private law was not practicable. The new Emperor appropriated it in its entirety, foolishly adopting his cousin in return. This was a most imprudent step.

Funeral rites were solemnly performed for the ashes of his mother and brothers.[535] Gaius invited Claudius, the later Emperor, and his sisters to court. The aged Antonia (Minor) received the same honours as Livia; there was a huge family feast. The Emperor's sisters were fêted everywhere in an almost too extravagant manner.[536] They were included in the oath of allegiance to the Emperor. In the case of Drusilla this had a repulsive, sensual reason. Gaius is reputed in an act of madness to have named his sister as his successor. When she subsequently died as a result of a premature delivery she was, incredibly, even deified.

No Emperor so fully recognized the rights of the Senate as Gaius. He declared it to have full co-regent status. Appeals from the senatorial provinces from now on went only to the Senate. Nor were the people forgotten: there was a proposal to reinstate the electoral assemblies that Tiberius had abolished.[537] However, this was not implemented even during his own reign. Political clubs [MH.I, 164] were once again permitted in Rome and taxes reduced in Italy. The *ducentesima auctionum*[538] was scrapped. Fiscal administration likewise became public again to a certain degree. Augustus had published audits of the fiscal situation, Tiberius had stopped this and Gaius reinstated it, although there were no debates on fiscal issues.

The same approach was applied outside Italy. Tiberius had, wherever possible, set aside the client-states in the Orient and introduced provincial constitutions. Gaius restored their rights to kings as hereditary rulers in Judaea, Commagene, Pontus and Cilicia,[539] even reimbursing the revenues raised by Tiberius.[540] In this way, public finance was soon out of control. Not even the rich treasury of Tiberius could have withstood such onslaughts. Within scarcely nine months Gaius was in dire financial straits, the treasury exhausted.

This was what induced the abrupt change. Showering the people with favours was now replaced by its antithesis. The new philanthropic ruler revealed his true colours; the honeymoon was over. It would be unworthy of history to venture yet another salvage attempt in the teeth of such superlative baseness and unbridled perfidy, and yet one must at least offer some explanation.

This man had grown up schooled in vice and horror. His family had been sacrificed by his grandfather Tiberius. For years on end he had lived under the threat of Tiberius and Sejanus, escaping only through the accident of Sejanus's fall. He lived in constant fear of death. He would have needed nerves of steel to withstand all this, but he did not possess them. His was the contemptible nature of a servant; he received the news of the execution of his family without altering the expression on his face. All this was compounded by his [MH.I, 165] loathsome schooling in vice through Tiberius on Capri, where Gaius committed adultery with the wife of Macro at the latter's wish. This, indeed, was what first paved his way to the throne.[541] It is Tiberius, rather than this wretched boy himself, who bore the guilt for his regime. His portly physique was soon atrophied with excess; he was frequently ill. Gaius was the first physically repulsive figure to appear in the mighty iron-constitutioned line of the Julians and Claudians.

His sense of ancestral pride was extraordinary. He was ashamed of his grandfather, Agrippa, and fabricated a tale that Augustus had sired his mother in an incestuous relationship with Julia.[542] This already reveals his total worthlessness. He hated all that was illustrious, all that was Republican, and sought to blacken its memory. He took away their torques from the ancient family of the Torquati.[543] He wanted to ban Livy, Virgil, even Homer,[544] partly for reasons of literary taste, partly out of professional jealousy, so that they would not put him in the shade. His reign abounded in madcap, fantastic plans. The attempt to erect a bridge from Puteoli to Baiae swallowed up vast sums, and very nearly induced a famine in Rome by making use of the grain fleet.[545] This is sufficient to characterize the man, and the recorded political changes were connected. The very first accession had already been accompanied by the murder of a potential pretender. Accordingly, immediately upon his accession to the throne, Gaius had his nephew and adoptive son Tiberius killed for quite infantile motives.[546] This left Gaius as the sole, and final, Julian. He dealt with Macro and his wife in identical fashion – they were immediately put to death.[547]

There then followed the first genuine conspiracy. Remarkably, at the forefront of this stood his two surviving sisters, in the background Marcus Aemilius Lepidus, a relation of the imperial house, and Gnaeus Lentulus Gaeticulus, a former consul and one of the most prominent and brilliant men of Rome. [MH.I,

166] The conspiracy was discovered, the sisters sent into exile and the others killed. This marked the end of the Aemilii Lepidi.[548]

The large number of victims, however, is explained by the desperate shortage of funds. Gaius introduced new, frequently nonsensical taxes, for example a 5 per cent deposit for every civil trial.[549] When this produced results too slowly proscriptions were enforced. The need for money was urgent, leading to the conviction of wealthy persons for *maiestas*.[550] When it emerged, too late, that a proscribed man was poor, Gaius said: 'He could have stayed alive, he was unjustly killed.'[551] The history of the later Julians is synonymous with the demise of the ancient Roman aristocracy. Italy was soon financially depleted, so in 39 Gaius undertook an expedition to Gaul. He also planned an expedition to Egypt.

In so far as it is possible to speak of foreign policy in the case of such a ruler, his interventions were random. Cappadocia was restored as a kingdom,[552] only to be recovered later by Vespasian. Of greater importance was a trend in the opposite direction. In Mauretania[553] Ptolemy, son of Juba II, was on the throne. His state included all the land from Constantine (Bone) as far as the ocean. This, the most important of the client-states, was rapidly Romanized; Caesarea (Cherchel in Algeria) particularly flourished. Ptolemy fell victim to Gaius, who had him executed in 40 in order to seize his wealth. The country became a province, although it was not administratively established as such until the reign of Claudius.

A significant measure was carried out in the easterly neighbouring part of Africa in AD 37. Military rule had been very unevenly distributed by Augustus. [MH.I, 167] He had, in fact, left the Senate only one military command, in Africa where a single legion was stationed. Tiberius had already been displeased with this: there was friction. Gaius divided the province into two districts of which one, Numidia, the military district, was removed from senatorial governorship and transferred into the control of an imperial legate.[554] From that time on the Senate had no more troops.

The expedition to Gaul (see MH.I, 166) was a comedy. Gaius was indeed a child of the camp, as his nickname 'Caligula' (*enfant de troupe*), hardly used in antiquity, indicates.[555] This popularity probably contributed to his success among the soldiers. No Emperor, however, so avoided militarism in his title. He was *imperator*, but never referred to himself as such. The pretext for the march on Gaul was retribution for the revolt against Tiberius thirty years earlier. Gaius wanted to win the favour of the Rhine legions. He was further interested in supplementing his bodyguard using prisoners from Germany – they were cheaper than bought slaves – and above all with plundering the wealthy in Gaul. This was a complete success. Besides this, the Emperor wanted to conquer Britain. This was a Roman whim of sorts and boiled down to collecting seashells.[556] Nonetheless, the expedition continued to be an element of government policy. Claudius later brought it to fruition. These events fall within the reign of Gaius, but one cannot assert that they were his 'deeds'.

All in all, the public proved to be every bit as pathetically servile to him as they had been to Tiberius; the obedience of the governors in particular continued to be remarkable. Gaius met his end as a result of a palace conspiracy.[557] A handful of junior Guards officers carried it out, bringing about the downfall of the imperial household. [MH.I, 168] The conspirators were Cassius Chaerea and Sabinus, two Guards tribunes piqued by personal insult because of the Emperor's bad jokes. As Gaius was coming out of the imperial court theatre they stabbed him in a portico and shortly afterwards his wife and 2-year-old daughter. It was like a horror story. Gaius died on 24 January 41, only 29 years old. He had hardly reigned four years. It has been asked whether the assassins were the tools of more senior senators. This is unlikely, since the assassination was purely the result of resentment against the Emperor among his staff. This may be deduced from the utter confusion that subsequently set in. There was no ready plan.

4

CLAUDIUS (41–54)[558]

The Julian dynasty died out with the Emperor Gaius. It was a bitter mockery on the part of history to bring this illustrious house to an end with such a worthless person. When Tiberius died there had still been two men waiting in the wings to succeed; now there was no one. Understandably, Gaius had made no provision for the succession. Nor, however, did the conspirators have any plan in this regard. This is suggested by the declaration of Valerius Asiaticus in the Senate: he regretted that he had known nothing of the conspiracy.[559] The political establishment, assembled at the court theatre, initially took the news to be some ruse by the Emperor. A silence fell over them, and then they dispersed. The German bodyguard avenged the murder by slaying some innocent senators near the body of the Emperor.[560] Cassius Chaerea and Cornelius Sabinus were not senators, only equestrians; perhaps they were counting on pro-Republican sentiment. They placed themselves at the disposal of the consuls Gnaeus Sentius Saturninus and Pomponius Secundus. This was the proper thing to do. The entire Senate decided [MH.I, 169] in principle for a restoration of the Republic. The officers involved in the conspiracy were favourably received and likened to Brutus and Cassius, and *libertas* proclaimed as the watchword for the guardsmen. There was sporadic talk, however, of the Senate electing an Emperor. At first the Senate was in control of the situation.[561] The Praetorian guard was utterly demoralized; there was a lack of leadership. No one thought of the Praetorian Prefects. Instinct told the soldiers that if the Republic were restored the Praetorian guard would be abolished. This was instantly clear to everyone. It is striking that not one soldier was in league with the assassins. Storming the palace, the Guard at least managed to discover a prince of sorts for the succession.[562]

The stepsons of Augustus were also part of his family. Through the adoption of Tiberius, the Claudians had become Julians; this line had died out, but Tiberius Claudius Germanicus was still alive. His father was Drusus, son of Livia's first husband; Germanicus was his elder brother. Initially he was called Tiberius Claudius Nero,[563] thus bearing the family's gentile name. Claudius was mildly deranged, an insignificant, apolitical person who had had to wait until the reign of Gaius even to be made consul.[564] Stricken with terror by the Emperor's death, he hid in a corner and was discovered by the Praetorians. The Guard was convinced that the principate must be maintained and improvised a succession, since no well-known figure was available. It was not an able soldier they sought, but someone who could meet the dynastic interest. The plan was most probably hatched by a handful of junior officers. Claudius was taken back to camp.

In the city itself the opposite party, the Senate, was in control. The wife and daughter of the Emperor were murdered by Cassius Chaerea that very evening of 24 January 41,[565] significantly with the consent [MH.I, 170] of the Senate. Any other troops in the city, probably four cohorts, fell in with the Senate. Following the model of the Sejanus catastrophe, the plan was to play off against the Guard the urban cohort under the urban prefect, the *vigiles*, the marines and the imperial gladiators. Within a few short hours the Republic was restored. The Senate exhorted Claudius to join them; he replied that he was being forcibly detained.[566]

The turnabout occurred swiftly. It is not possible to say through whom. Josephus[567] asserts that it was the Jewish prince Agrippa who had persuaded Claudius to accept the offer to rule. It was at all events clear that Claudius was chosen to rule, rather than chose to rule. Suffice it to say that the Guard and Claudius came to terms: each soldier was to be paid 15,000–20,000 sesterces, i.e. approximately 5,000 Marks. Quite a tidy sum, therefore. The Guard struck a favourable deal – all the more so since it became standard practice. For an instant, catastrophe loomed as the old power struggle seemed to resurface. Nevertheless, it did not. The troops dispersed: first the *vigiles* and the marines, then the urban cohorts, who went to join the Praetorians. The mood of the masses likewise turned against the Republic. This is not to be wondered at. The *plebs* could want for nothing better than the continuation of the principate; remunerated idleness, bread and circuses were very much to their liking.

Soon, therefore, the Senate found itself alone. It was no longer prepared, as in the days of Caesar, to betake itself overseas and fight its battles there. They no longer had the power to fight a Philippi in the streets of Rome. They capitulated to Claudius and sent him a message that the Senate was ready to proclaim him Emperor as soon as he appeared in the *curia*. It is doubtful whether this was sincere. Claudius replied that it sufficed that the troops had proclaimed him as such. [MH.I, 171] The Senate yielded, betook itself to the camp and paid homage to the Emperor. Thus the ancient Republican aristocracy was defeated not by the army, but by the Guard, who had successfully defended their own interests.

The following years witnessed the so-called Dalmatian revolt, in which Camillus Scribonianus rebelled with two legions.[568] Born into the ancient aristocracy, he had Marcus Annius,[569] leader of the senatorial party, at his side. The Republican character of this revolt is explicitly mentioned. Scribonianus sought to restore *libertas*, although to all intents and purposes he was indistinguishable from a pretender. He commanded the troops nearest to Italy – this was dangerous. However, this movement likewise disintegrated. It proved impossible to tear the legionary standards out of the ground, and the men abandoned their officers. The whole army, not only the Guard, seems to have favoured monarchy. The rebellion is still remarkable, however. The seventh and eleventh legions were later called *Claudiae piae fideles*. This was the first instance of troops stationed outside Rome concerning themselves with the election of an Emperor, which makes the episode noteworthy. Monarchy prevailed over oligarchy. It must be conceded to the Emperor that the catastrophe claimed few victims. Chaerea and Sabinus were, of course, condemned to death.[570] This was inevitable. Claudius went no further. If he had wanted to proceed by means of legal prosecutions, he might well have done so.

Claudius's regime is of little general interest. As a person he is the easiest of all Roman rulers to ridicule: it is hardly even possible to deal with him seriously. [MH.I, 172] Generally speaking he followed Tiberius's example[571] in avoiding the name *imperator*. It is significant that Claudius called himself *Caesar*.[572] Originally, this was a clan name of the Julians, and Claudius probably adopted it at this time to support his right to the succession. Officially, he regarded himself as a Julian. Other rulers followed his example, so that gradually the name *Caesar*, like *Augustus*, became a title.

Claudius was a man of extremely odd appearance and this is how tradition has captured him. The *Apocolocyntosis* of Seneca, tutor to his son, is largely responsible for this. Claudius was essentially a handsome and imposing man, albeit with a tendency to corpulence.[573] He had quite a stately appearance when seated. His impressive features were his head, his well-made neck and his attractive hair. He walked badly; his legs carried him poorly and his gait was laboured. Whenever he lost his temper he lost control of his body completely. His head would wobble and he would foam at the mouth. He was not deranged, but not quite all there, as his mother was wont to say. She would mock him with the phrase 'simple as my son Claudius'.[574] It was Antonia, therefore, who began to belittle him, and the public followed her example. The private correspondence of Augustus and Livia provides strange accounts of him. He was reputedly unable to speak, and yet superb at recitation, often absent-minded and yet showed signs of great talent. He alone was not adopted into the family by Augustus, who kept him out of politics and gave him only a priesthood. Similarly, under Tiberius he failed to achieve a consulate, being invested only with consular honours.[575] He did not appear in public. Claudius lived among women until well advanced in years. This changed with Gaius. He turned the family's political relationships upside down, just as he did everything else. Claudius was made a consul (see MH. I, 169). In his leisure time [MH.I, 173] he devoted himself to the pleasures of the table and of love. Few Emperors pursued luxury so avidly.

In his spare time, Claudius was a scholar[576] – the only one ever to sit on the throne of Rome. Perhaps prompted by Livy, he threw himself into the study of history, writing a history of the Etruscans and one of the Carthaginians. It was thoroughly unRoman to be interested in foreign nations. This proclivity also emerges in his speech on the civic rights of the Gauls, with its argumentation based on Etruscan history,[577] and likewise in his speech on the civic rights of the inhabitants of Val di Non near Trent.[578] He continued his writing even as a ruler. He organized the soothsayers into an official college of sixty *haruspices*. He attempted to reform the alphabet by adding three new letters; as censor he published an edict recommending the public to imitate him in using them. His distinction between U and V was most reasonable, but the adoption of the Greek letter Psi, on the other hand, most unreasonable.[579]

It is not clear if he was an unambitious man. Frequent mockery shaped a man with no will of his own. In this respect he was wholly unsuited to the office of *princeps*. Complaints about him are directed more against the system than against him as a person. As the *bête noire* of the family, bullied and derided on all sides, particularly by Tiberius, and constantly in the charge of women, he naturally grew up totally unsoldierly, undignified and cowardly. Cowardice was the curse of his reign. It is an irony on the part of history that this should be the case with the first Emperor chosen by soldiers. It was, nonetheless, a bloody irony. His conviction that everyone was after him, the imperative to secure his position, led him to commit dire atrocities. Had he been able to find a secure retreat somewhere he would gladly have abdicated.

The hallmark of his reign was that he himself did not reign: others reigned under him. Anything laudable that occurred under him derives not from him, [MH.I, 174] but from those who surrounded him. These were not statesmen, but court attendants and women who anxiously kept any statesman away from him. This probably related to his own anxiety: he saw a swindler in any man of excellence.

From among the impenetrable throng of freedmen around the Emperor the *a litteris* (correspondence secretary), Narcissus, was the most outstanding.[580] As luck would have it he was a highly talented man. Although there is no explicit tradition to this effect, it would seem that Narcissus ran the state. We encounter him everywhere – in both domestic and foreign policy, in family politics and public works policy. It was Narcissus who overcame the problems of the British expedition, he who brought about the demise of Messalina and who opposed Agrippina. It would be wrong to suggest that he did not abuse his influence, and yet caution is necessary here: his fortune[581] may have been made in an entirely honest manner. Narcissus protected the Emperor from his wives and at the last, prior to his death under Nero, burned his entire correspondence to avert a wave of persecution.[582] He undoubtedly knew how to exploit the better nature of the Emperor to his own ends. At his side were Callistus, who as *a libellis* examined petitions, and Pallas, the treasurer (*a rationibus*), who later, together with Agrippina, brought about the downfall of Narcissus. All these were freedmen.

No other ruler after Augustus made such frequent use of the title *imperator*.[583] Mostly this was prompted by only minor battles, but it is characteristic of Claudius that no-one had such liberal recourse to military honours as he did. He wanted to celebrate a triumph after every rumpus.

Armenia[584] had been making itself increasingly independent; the dismal former circumstances had reasserted themselves. Claudius intervened in Parthian affairs only through diplomacy and pretenders. Preparations for the war which Corbulo later fought were already under way, but Claudius had no desire to wage it. On the Rhine[585] there were [MH.I, 175] innumerable reasons for vigorous intervention, particularly in Lower Germany. German pirates, Chauci, Saxons and Friesians, were plundering the northern edge of Gaul, and Domitius Corbulo wanted to undertake an expedition across the Rhine. Claudius forbade him to do so and Corbulo reluctantly obeyed. It is plain how powerful Augustan principles were in the cabinet. The establishment of the province of Mauretania[586] in Africa was a major event and yet we have no means of studying it in any detail. The Romanization so avidly pursued later was begun at this time.

In one respect only was the Augustan tradition abandoned. Although of no benefit to the Empire,[587] it remains a significant step to this day. This was the expedition to Britain.[588] Although the extant accounts are relatively detailed,[589] they fail to take account of the true circumstances, particularly the geographical facts. The following is certain: the expedition was launched by the government without any external prompting; it was almost a problem to find a pretext. In 43 the expedition set off under Aulus Plautius, commander of Lower Germany. The soldiers were not keen on participating in the endeavour and were recalcitrant. They took to ship after Narcissus had put in a personal appearance. The country was subjugated without major resistance, quite unlike the course of events among other Celtic peoples. Mass uprisings by a confederation of tribes did not occur until later. The Romans landed on the Isle of Wight, crossed the Thames and established a foothold in Camulodunum (Colchester),[590] capital of the Trinobantes,[591] to the north of London. Once the expedition had proved a success Claudius joined the army and returned home a victor. He had been on the island for only sixteen days. This is documented by lead ingots dating from 49 found at Bristol,[592] where there was mining activity. In Wales the Romans encountered serious opposition, particularly from the Silures. Later, too, there was a strong military presence here. Further to the north, Norfolk and Suffolk were occupied. The whole of central England passed into Roman hands. There was still no attempt to take on the mighty Brigantes. [MH.I, 176] The general uprising led by the Trinobantian prince Caratacus, the Vercingetorix of the Britons, was a failure. In AD 50 Colchester became a military colony.[593]

The expedition was celebrated extravagantly,[594] although there had been little to it from the military viewpoint. But why was the expedition launched in the first place? Britain had been nominally a province for a century, since the time of Caesar – a province *in partibus*[595] that had never paid tribute but had never been given up by Rome either. Claudius felt that the government had an obligation to implement this legal claim. In doing so, however, he deviated from the rule applied by Augustus following the Varus disaster. The thought might have occurred that Britain, which was of no military value, was bound to remain a dubious gain. Augustus had, indeed, left it alone. It cannot be asserted that Claudius did not look for reasons of any kind. There was, after all, no thought of giving Britain up later, which would certainly have been done if the campaign had been utter foolishness.

The reason is most probably to be found in the national and religious links between the Gauls and the Britons. There could be no hope of subjugating Gaul unless the fire of the Druid cult could be extinguished. Tiberius had tolerated the Druid cult in the case of the Gauls,[596] Claudius banned it completely;[597] there is a connection here. This was exacerbated by the economic situation. Even at this late juncture Roman conquests were still instigated by merchants. This was especially the case with Britain. We are not told that London needed to be conquered; that entrepôt was probably already in the hands [MH.I, 177] of Italian merchants. Hence the military colony was located not in London, but to the north. Of crucial importance were the tin and lead mines, which formed the basis of commerce.[598] The primary aim of the government was to bring these mines into its possession. In both cases where the boundaries set by Augustus were crossed, in Dacia and Britain, mines were probably the deciding factor. In Dacia the enticement was gold. To this extent, therefore, the conquest of Britain was by no means a shot in the dark. Wales, Scotland and Ireland were excluded.

This conquest for trade policy purposes had military repercussions. Significant fighting forces had to remain there. Three legions[599] were required – a very strong garrison. It became necessary to increase the number of legions from a total of twenty-three to twenty-five. It was an isolated military position; the British occupation force remained an insular garrison army and was not used on the mainland. Britain was Romanized with great intensity; the ground for this, too, had to some extent already been prepared.

Turning to internal events, we see that even as ruler Claudius remained something of a Republican. He embellished the state with antiquarian-Republican relics. Claudius regularly spoke as a leader invested with tribunician authority, dropping the title *imperator* as often as possible.[600] This was the only period in which the Senate genuinely displayed a degree of independence. Admittedly, this was partly because of the deficiency of the court.

[MH.I, 178] Among the attempts to retrieve Republican customs was the revival of comitial legislation.[601] Nothing was done to change the elections, which remained the prerogative of the Senate, but there was an attempt to include the people in lawmaking again. Of course this was in vain: the measure remained no more than a whim of the Emperor. To some degree in contradiction of this was the establishment of *senatusconsulta* in the sphere of private law.[602] This seems to have originated with Claudius, who combined earlier instances into an organic whole to create an institution. Claudius regulated the *fidei commissa* (legal trusts), which had hitherto had a decidedly vague legal status.[603] He also passed laws benefiting aged slaves[604] and set public works in order;[605] he took action regarding the devastated sites in towns where houses were demolished without new ones being built in their place. From the private law perspective the reign of Claudius was beneficial.

Changes to the treasury made by Augustus had not worked out well. He had placed this under praetors, who were thus now officials aged 30 instead of 25, but all of whom remained in office for only one year. This had been a mistake. Claudius handed the office back to the quaestors.[606] This was an antiquarian act, but a beneficial one. The administrators were not chosen by lot, but selected from among the twenty quaestors. The Emperor decided on the suitable persons, who remained in office for three years. Clearly, however, he thereby acquired greater and greater control. It brought him indirect control of the senatorial treasury, too.

Claudius's censorship was extraordinary, an antiquarian fad. The censorship had lapsed with the onset of the principate after having already fallen into disarray even by the end of the Republic. Augustus adopted the census, but not the censorship. Claudius chose a colleague, Lucius Vitellius, a trusted, highly obsequious man.[607] The new censorship followed entirely in the footsteps of the old. There were vigorous controls on claims to citizenship, [MH.I, 179] especially against claims by peregrines.[608] Significant measures were undertaken for the Gauls. Citizenship had already been granted to a substantial proportion of them earlier, but in a limited form lacking the *ius honorum*: they were not permitted to hold office. Claudius abolished this,[609] a measure that was to prove significant for the Romanization of the West, which was the principal task of the principate. The other side of the coin was that Italian citizenship was increasingly being replaced by an international citizenship, obliterating national character.

The Republic had had no legal provision for creating patricians. There was no way of making a noble family. An aristocracy by appointment began under Caesar. Nevertheless, the Emperor had hitherto not had the right to name patricians. Tiberius never created a single patrician, but Claudius did.[610] He did so as censor, not as Emperor. Soon, however, the censorship was annexed to the principate, so that this right too fell to the *princeps*.

No magistrate was permitted to move the city walls; this could only be done under certain conditions by a decree of the People. Claudius did so, again expanding imperial authority – not, however, by usurpation, but by a transfer of authority from the people.[611] He likewise passed laws legitimating the college of the *haruspices* (soothsayers who inspected entrails),[612] the worship of Isis,[613] popular with high and low alike, and the banning of Druids. The latter was also of political significance.[614] With these measures Claudius brought to completion the legislation of the Republic. East and West became increasingly equal.

Claudius applied himself to the administration of justice,[615] laudably and energetically as no other Emperor. [MH.I, 180] He threw himself into jurisdiction with genuine passion, probably to some extent out of a sense of duty. One satirist[616] has it that he even administered justice during the court recess in July and August. Occasionally his judgments were distinctly odd, but in general he acted wisely and with good will. He dropped all cases pertaining to treasonable offences, which were in any case impossible to pursue. The list of victims cited by Seneca's *Apocolocyntosis* is horrendous in length. These were due to imperial advisers who played on his anxiety and extracted death sentences out of him by rousing his suspicions. He was almost invariably a tool in the hands of others.

The most brilliant aspect of Claudius's reign was his public works.[617] From no other reign can so much that was illustrious be reported. Augustus had created luxury buildings; Tiberius nothing at all. Under Claudius, utility buildings were constructed as a matter of course, but on the most magnificent scale, absorbing colossal sums. Given the dearth of funds under Gaius, this permits us to assume an orderly management of finances. Claudius found the treasury empty and Rome on the verge of starvation. He brought all this back under control. There was no evidence of any shortage of funds, and he even managed an intensive programme of public works. The fact that a few freedmen feathered their own nests in the process was a minor abuse compared with the budget of the Empire, although the moral damage cannot be denied. Claudius had the *Aqua Claudia* and the *Anio Vetus* built,[618] both of which benefited the population greatly and were in use for a long time. Of more importance was his vigorous tackling of harbour construction – always an embarrassment for the state. It is, after all, dreadful that throughout all these years nothing was done for Ostia; Puteoli always remained the major harbour. This circuitous route across Campania was particularly irksome for the grain supply, and as a result Rome was in constant jeopardy. Caesar [MH.I, 181] and Augustus had considered expanding Ostia, but did no more than consider. By constructing large moles, Claudius created a large harbour for Rome, thereby to some extent dealing with this evil.[619] In addition, Claudius had an outflow dug to drain the Fucine lake[620] as part of a long-planned drainage system. The plan was not to drain the lake completely, but to reclaim a large area for tillage. Narcissus supervised this project for eleven years, until it succeeded, or rather did not – the obverse side of the coin did not fail to turn up here either. Scholars are now convinced that the work was slipshod: the supports collapsed because they had been badly installed. This corresponds exactly to the Claudian principle: grandiose in conception, but shoddy in detail. The same applied to the harbour construction work, which likewise remained inadequate.

Let us turn now to the history of the household and court – the worst aspect of Claudius's reign. His benevolence is unmistakable. At home he was ever the distinguished Roman and preserved a degree of middle-class simplicity. He married his children to the high aristocracy. There were no marriages within the family. He refused the title *Augusta* for his wife[621] and sought to blur the distinction between himself and the nobility.

Nevertheless, under Claudius servants and women ruled. At the time of his accession the Emperor was married to Valeria Messalina, by whom he had a daughter, Octavia. Shortly after his accession, probably in 42, Tiberius Claudius was born, and soon thereafter named Britannicus. Messalina was one of the most beautiful and voluptuous women of Rome. The sensuality of the Emperor increased from year to year, and with it the influence of the Empress. [MH.I, 182] Messalina nonetheless had one negative trait that was not fully appreciated until the advent of Agrippina: she did not concern herself with politics.

It is difficult to sketch a portrait of this woman, because there was so little that was distinctive about her. As great-granddaughter of Octavia, the sister of Augustus, she ranked among the highest nobility of Rome. This in itself was sufficient to provide her with political status, and this, again, was characteristic of the age. But Messalina was not merely unprincipled, she was also utterly heartless and brainless. Her depravity and whorelike vulgarity were bywords. She was without ambition: carnality and greed were the two sole motors of her being. As long as she was left alone to pursue her private affairs she was content. This recommended her to the servant regime mentioned earlier: her wantonness was restricted to the imperial household. Claudius was of a benign disposition and took no active part in any of the many misdeeds; the same would seem to be true of the ministers who dominated him at that time. All the atrocities of the early Claudian period had their roots in petty female interests and the intrigues of Messalina.

This was the case, for example, right at the beginning when Julia Livilla, the youngest daughter of Germanicus, was deported and executed in exile.[622] This was an act of jealousy, since Julia had attempted to start a liaison with Claudius – unsuccessfully, unlike her sister later, who succeeded. Seneca was involved in this catastrophe and sent into exile.[623] Their trials were nominally for adultery and fornication. Equally characteristic was the case brought against Poppaea Sabina. Claudius was not enough for Messalina: she started liaisons with all and sundry. One such liaison was with Mnester, who resisted her for a considerable time, only giving way on the orders of Claudius himself.[624] Messalina, [MH.I, 183] however, was jealous of Mnester's relationship with Poppaea, and he was charged with adultery. Valerius Asiaticus was also involved in this sentence – ostensibly for adultery, but in fact because he owned the villa and gardens of Lucullus, which Messalina coveted. Asiaticus defended himself brilliantly and Claudius was on the point of acquitting him, but an unfortunate phrase in Vitellius's speech in his defence proved disastrous for him.[625] Similarly, at the very beginning of Claudius's reign, Appius Silanus was ensnared by Messalina for resisting an illicit liaison with her.[626] Two identical dreams which Narcissus and Messalina claimed to have had sealed his fate. Silanus was killed and Claudius publicly thanked Narcissus in the Senate for his solicitude. There was a pact of mutual collusion between Messalina and Narcissus as long as they did not intrude upon each other.

The status of the servants was quite unprecedented. Narcissus (*ab epistulis*: correspondence), Polybius (*a studiis*: literary secretary), Callistus (*a libellis*: petitions) and Pallas (*a rationibus*: accounts) ran the state, sharing all appointments between them.[627] They were the true rulers of the state. Illustrative of this is a letter from Seneca to Polybius – ostensibly a letter of condolence, but in reality a petition. No bones were made about the fact that Polybius was among the most influential men in the state. He was very much the all-powerful minister on whose desk lay the petitions of the world. This is declaimed upon by Seneca, the foremost writer of the Roman world. Polybius came by his position through his erudition. He translated Homer into Latin and Virgil into Greek, and must, therefore, have had perfect mastery of both languages. The letter of condolence stresses this. This is remarkable, since he was, after all, a former slave. The [MH.I, 184] educational system was partly dependent at that time on such able slaves. The literary education of slaves was particularly well provided for in the imperial household. It was this very fact, however, which led to the contamination of education: it was no longer the 'liberal arts' it had once been.

This notwithstanding, the reign did not proceed badly, aside from the moral aspect. It foundered on the wantonness of Messalina. She entered into a liaison with Gaius Silius, consul-designate, who seems to have encouraged it to further his ambition. The details are pointless and repugnant. Perhaps Claudius unwittingly consented to a form of divorce. Silius wanted to adopt Britannicus, but first and foremost to seize power for himself. In the Senate he opposed the charge against Poppaea. Then he 'married' Messalina,[628] thereby openly placing the Emperor at risk.

This was a political act threatening Messalina's pact with the freedmen. Their survival was at stake; Claudius had to continue to reign. Besides, Messalina had previously eliminated Polybius, and that had already rocked the relationship. Callistus, Pallas and Narcissus conferred. The courage of the two former failed them, but Narcissus set about saving himself and the Emperor. He succeeded.

Claudius had been sent to Ostia while Messalina and Silius celebrated their nuptials. Narcissus made haste to join him there and wrested a death sentence from him. Messalina's attempts to influence Claudius were not entirely in vain, but Narcissus knew how to make him stand firm. It is highly indicative that command of the Guard was transferred to Narcissus for the day of the execution, as the real prefect was not trusted. This was, indeed, an unprecedented move: freedmen [MH.I, 185] were not even permitted to serve in the Guard.[629] Silius and Messalina were executed and the Emperor's rule saved. The freedmen were fully aware, however, that the sensually minded Emperor could not remain without a wife. They had not only to remove Messalina, but also to replace her. Narcissus was in favour of restoring Aelia Paetina, Claudius's first wife. This would have led to tranquil relations. Callistus recommended Lollia Paulina – rich and beautiful. Pallas supported the idea of Julia Agrippina, the Emperor's niece and last surviving daughter of Germanicus. She had already exerted considerable influence for some time. Beautiful, charming and 33, she knew how to sweep her co-paramours aside. This marriage between kin was in fact impossible under Roman law, but that was easily changed. Before the Senate, Vitellius proposed that the regulation be changed. This was done, and the marriage took place.[630]

This brought a perilous intrigue in its wake. The fate of Drusus and Germanicus was repeated. The morals of Agrippina were little better than those of Messalina, and she was madly ambitious. Her innate desire was to bring the dynasty of Germanicus to the throne. All his children looked on themselves as rightful heirs. Born in 14, her first husband had been Lucius Domitius Ahenobarbus. She was married in AD 28; in 37 Nero was born, then called Gnaeus Domitius Ahenobarbus. It was this son she wanted to set on the throne. Agrippina had him betrothed to Octavia, the second daughter of Claudius by Messalina. This led to the downfall of Lucius Junius Silanus,[631] to whom Octavia was already betrothed. From the outset Agrippina was not satisfied with her status in the household. She wanted to share in government. She was immediately given the title *Augusta* (see MH.I, 181 and n. 621). Although not much can be deduced from this, it was nevertheless a name inseparably associated once and for all with supreme authority. Agrippina coveted *consortium imperii* (partnership in government), [MH.I, 186] but she did not attain it. She is reputed to have demanded that the Guard take an oath of allegiance to her: this demand was not met. She did, for all that, jostle her way into government in a manner that was irreconcilable with the nature of the Roman principate. Since the chronology is uncertain here, it is not quite certain what Claudius was responsible for and what Nero was responsible for. For the first time the portrait of the Empress appeared on coins.[632] She was furnished with her own court and received envoys, and even attended senatorial proceedings from behind a curtain. Hence the deadly enmity between Narcissus and herself.

167

Narcissus was ousted from his position. Pallas, however, colluded with her plans. This put paid to harmonious court rule. Agrippina held the advantage from the very outset, but was not able to bring about the downfall of Narcissus. She attempted to do so by bringing charges of embezzlement relating to the Fucine lake project,[633] but in vain. Otherwise, Agrippina had her own way in everything. First, she betrothed Nero to Octavia. Nero's adoption followed on 25 February 50;[634] for this she obtained the support of the Senate, apart from a handful of opponents. Vitellius was among her supporters. While the adoption was a natural act, it was glaringly irreconcilable with the betrothal. Illegality was circumvented by having Octavia transferred out of Claudius's paternal power.[635]

Had Augustus's principle been adhered to, the natural thing to do, given the tender age of Britannicus, would have been to name a mature man as successor. In the event, however, a 13-year-old boy replaced a 9-year-old. Nero was immediately invested with all the honours that could possibly be showered on an imperial prince. He was received into all priestly colleges; this prerogative reserved for members of the imperial family was granted to him. Britannicus was passed over; he obtained nothing of this kind. In 51 Nero became co-regent at the age of 14 and was given the *toga virilis* and proconsular powers, which were not legally associated with any age. [MH.I, 187] The consulate was promised him for his twentieth year.[636]

Before anything else, Agrippina brought the Guard under her control. Afranius Burrus was made Prefect of the Guard without a colleague, in place of the previous Prefects, who had been devoted to Messalina.[637] This secured the succession of Nero as far as possible. Beside Burrus, but without any official position, Agrippina appointed Lucius Annaeus Seneca, the so-called philosopher and among the most celebrated writers of his time. The graceful form of his works makes diverting reading even today, even though they are devoid of content. He had been driven into exile by Messalina; Agrippina summoned him home, thereby ensuring his devotion to her.[638] He was Nero's tutor. The fundamental tone of Seneca's works was Republican, like those of Tacitus, even though his life did not quite correspond to these principles. Perhaps his appointment as tutor was intended to win over for Nero the Republican opposition in the Senate.

The Guard was purged. Any officers who were not pro-Nero were dismissed. Narcissus and the Senate were unable to prevent this, although the Senate did put up some sporadic resistance. Following his marriage to Octavia in 53 Nero was also outwardly qualified to succeed to the throne, and it is probable that Agrippina was behind the death of the Emperor in 54. There are specific allusions to murder by poisoning here, but all date from as late as the time of Trajan.[639] We are compelled to leave the matter open. At all events it was a favourable moment for a crime. Narcissus was absent from court; he had gone to Sinuessa to take the waters, leaving the Emperor bereft of his natural protector. Agrippina lived in constant fear of meeting the same fate as Messalina, and Narcissus had every reason to treat her in the same way. [MH.I, 188] Even more indicative are the circumstances relating to the two princes. Nero had been appointed heir-apparent, while Britannicus still wore the child's toga. On the other hand, Agrippina could at this point still expect to rule in the name of her son, whereas this could no longer be certain when he was older. Agrippina was a person to whom one could ascribe such a deed.

5

NERO (54–68)[640]

The accession passed without incident. Burrus presented Nero to the Guard and won them over with generous donations, and the Senate followed suit. There was no resistance in the provinces either. However, the smoother an accession, the worse the reign generally turns out to be. This now proved to be the case.

There is some doubt as to where Nero obtained his name. After his adoption he was known as Tiberius Claudius Nero Caesar; up to that point he had probably been called Gnaeus Domitius, but there is doubt as to whether it was the cognomen of his father that was added, or that of the eldest son of Germanicus Nero. The latter is probable. Nero described his ascendancy in a quite extraordinary manner, calling himself not the son of Agrippina, but the grandson of Germanicus, great-grandson of Tiberius and great-great-grandson of Augustus.[641] His use of the name of Augustus is indicative, since he was related to him only on his mother's side. The corollary to this was the execution of Junius Silanus, brother of Octavia's first betrothed. At that time he was proconsul of Asia, an entirely innocent man. The sole reason for this act was that Silanus was also a great-great-grandson, *abnepos divi Augusti*, and thus of equal standing with Nero. Agrippina thus eliminated someone with a title equal to that of Nero. Narcissus was obviously also murdered at the same time; that was to be taken for granted.[642]

The memory of Claudius was upheld by Nero. To the many follies of Claudius was added his last, posthumous, one – his elevation to the realm of the gods. He was made a colleague of the deified Augustus. The eulogy to Claudius was penned by Seneca, the great stylist.[643] [MH.I, 189] At the same time, however, he also wrote the *Apocolocyntosis*, a highly amusing satire on the consecration of Claudius. This in itself speaks volumes.

Initially the style of rule changed not at all: Agrippina happily ruled beside Nero, who had no interest in politics, either then or subsequently. Soon, however, the dowager Empress began to encounter opposition from among her own protégés – Burrus and Seneca, the Emperor's advisers. The real mainspring behind this was undoubtedly Lucius Annaeus Seneca, the most outstanding scholar of his age and for some time the most powerful man in Rome. His most remarkable work is a letter of condolence to Marcia dating from the first months of Caligula's reign; at that time there were hopes for a restoration of the Republic. Seneca was no strong character, but Rome was never better ruled than it was under him; Trajan recognized this. The first five years of Nero's reign were the golden age of Rome.[644]

Burrus[645] was Agrippina's right-hand man – an able soldier, but of a subservient disposition. Seneca himself held no official position. The Roman state machinery under the *princeps* had no place for an influential man. Seneca was the Emperor's friend. The apathy of the Emperor towards all affairs of state suited him eminently. Nero was glad to be relieved of this onerous business. He was a total blank as far as affairs of state were concerned and, although a capable wrestler, totally unfamiliar with the handling of weapons. He wanted nothing more than a *carte blanche* for vice, which was initially pursued in spheres of lesser importance.

Seneca counted on this. Agrippina expected of Nero dignity and breeding, a commitment to his station in life and tactful handling of Octavia, through whom he had ascended to the throne. This led to acrimony against his mother from her utterly heartless and superficial son. [MH.I, 190] Seneca as tutor was more accommodating than Nero's mother. She could not and would not face this fact. Nero fell in love with Acte, a lowly freedwoman, and a friend of Seneca gave up his house as a trysting place.[646] Do what she might to prevent it, Seneca paved the way for Agrippina's downfall by encouraging Nero's amour. The road was not a pretty one, but it was beneficial for the state. The two allies now made a clean sweep of the remaining freedmen; Pallas had to go, albeit with a certificate of good behaviour,[647] leaving Burrus and Seneca to assume a moderate control of government.

This is borne out by the charge brought against Agrippina for the attempted murder of her son. Nero wanted to have her summarily executed, but Burrus prevented this and her accusers were punished. There was thus a concern to preserve decorum.[648] They were not entirely able to hold Nero back from foul deeds, but anything of that kind which did occur has to be laid at the door of the Emperor himself. The first was the murder of Britannicus. He collapsed at the dinner table; his body was immediately cremated and there was no inquest. It was evidently murder by poisoning.[649] The reason is plain. It was the old motto of the principate: the pre-emptive elimination of potential pretenders. Agrippina was reputedly involved in that she had threatened to place Britannicus on the throne. This is not credible: perhaps the story was simply concocted for Nero's benefit in order to prompt him to the deed. The ministers were not involved; this was a personal idea on the part of the Emperor.

From the perspective of the government, the reign was more positive. The administration under Nero was the one in which there was the most vigorous warfare. In general a policy of peace was in full ascendancy; one can see the

[MH.I, 191] robust intervention of the ministers here. The policy of peace at any price was a flawed one for the state: on the whole, governments which take vigorous action tend to be the best. The action here derived, furthermore, not from the generals, but from the ministers.

In the East the Roman government was determined to do nothing. There had been no combat here since the campaign of Antony. Seneca represented this as a blot on Rome's escutcheon, which indeed it was. Crassus[650] and Antony had yet to be avenged, and under Claudius the situation in Armenia had been totally unsatisfactory. The Roman pretender who had been expelled and then reinstated against the will of the Parthian party was in dire straits. He capitulated and Tiridates, brother of the Parthian king Vologaeses, now ruled Armenia.

Gnaeus Domitius Corbulo, the ablest general, was immediately appointed to command the army.[651] This meant that the challenge of war was being taken up. Corbulo departed in 54. The following years passed peacefully. Corbulo concluded a treaty with the Parthians. Plagued by unrest, they made concessions. Tiridates remained, but wanted to be invested with his crown by Rome. The real reason for Corbulo's procrastination was that the Syrian army had become lax and was not fit for combat.[652] War did not break out until 58.[653] We do not know why. Perhaps there were fresh claims from the Parthians, perhaps Corbulo was carrying out a plan laid previously. This testifies to the continuity of government. Corbulo was in command for ten years. The plan was to reorganize the men, then strike and thereby impose Roman control thoroughly. Corbulo's demand was within modest limits. He did not challenge the position of any individual, simply calling for the recognition of Roman suzerainty. Tiridates had probably refused this.

[MH.I, 192] The chronology of the Corbulo story is uncertain because of Pliny's account[654] of an astronomical phenomenon that has been associated with an eclipse of the sun at Artaxata. At all events, Corbulo marched into Armenia in 58, wintered there and continued the advance in 59. He captured Artaxata and remained there for the following winter. In 60 he pressed on to Tigranocerta, conquered this city as well and thereby set the seal on total victory.[655] At this point the government wanted to eliminate Tiridates and instal a Cappadocian by the name of Tigranes who was dependent on Rome. This accorded with the wishes of Corbulo, since it would lead to war with the Parthians themselves, who had not been directly involved in the first war. There had not even been a declaration of war.

The war proceeded without military successes and was concluded in a manner scarcely designed to bring honour to the Romans. Corbulo dropped Tigranes and recognized Tiridates under Roman authority, thereby returning to the terms of the treaty of 55. Corbulo was manifestly at odds with his government here, since the latter wanted to drive the Parthians out of Armenia completely. The government did not ratify the treaty and restricted Corbulo's command. He retained Syria, but

Lucius Caesennius Paetus[656] was sent to Cappadocia. The plan was for him to march on Armenia, perhaps to establish a Roman province there.

The feared Parthian invasion of Syria failed to occur. In Armenia, on the other hand, there was heavy fighting. In the autumn of 61 Paetus marched in and camped for the winter; in 62 he confronted the Parthians and suffered an ignominious defeat. The Roman legions were spread over a wide area and poorly led. They were besieged and the general was compelled to capitulate. Although he saved the lives of his men, this was only on the condition that he immediately retreat from Armenia.[657] It is incredible that Vologaeses let it go at that. He did so on the certain assurance and on the freely given commitment that the Romans would never set foot in Armenia again. [MH.I, 193] Corbulo was unable to avert this crushing débâcle: he arrived too late. Paetus had not held out as long as he could have. Corbulo's enemies accused him of marching too slowly;[658] unreasonably, for Corbulo had not received the news in Syria in time. The upshot was that the dual command was restored to Corbulo.

The Parthians sent envoys to Rome requesting recognition of Tiridates, who had been invested by Rome. The government was not in favour: it would have been tantamount to a ratification of their defeat. Corbulo thus received the two provinces, with the intention of vigorously resuming combat. He entered Armenia. There were a few clashes, but no serious fighting. What now occurred was precisely the conclusion that had previously been rejected; once again the general proved more conciliatory than the government. Tiridates was forced to humiliate himself and make a personal appearance in Rome. Under constitutional law it made no difference whether the declaration was made orally or in writing. First, Tiridates went to Vologaeses and obtained permission to travel. At this point the government relented. This is strange; perhaps they had been intimidated by the fiasco of Paetus. Although this had by now been to some extent erased, the Parthian prince remained on the throne. A shift in circumstances in Rome may have exerted some influence here. Burrus and Seneca had been eliminated, and the young Emperor was now ruling himself. Thus in 66 Tiridates came to Rome. The chance for a show of pageantry will undoubtedly have helped Nero to make up his mind.[659]

This campaign was not a very illustrious one for Rome; the goal the Romans had set for themselves was not at all commensurate with this result. Nevertheless, the conquest of Armenia had been a brilliant military undertaking. All that had really been achieved was that discipline had been restored to the Asian legions. Corbulo wielded tremendous authority for a long time, despite not being a member of the imperial household,[660] which indicates the considerable confidence he was held in by the government, which otherwise viewed all the major commanders under the Emperor with suspicion.

[MH.I, 194] Corbulo was probably right in his assessment. Armenia could only be retained in the long term by establishing a major general command in

Cappadocia. Vespasian subsequently did just this with two legions, and thereby secured Armenia. In setting Corbulo beside celebrated Republican generals, however, the judgement of Roman authors[661] will have been clouded by their hatred of Nero, to whom Corbulo later fell victim.[662]

There was likewise fighting in the far north-west, again bringing little glory to Rome. Peace had long prevailed in Britain. In 61 the Romans launched a fresh offensive.[663] On the one hand, the plan was to eradicate the Druidic cult, and on the other hand to tackle discontent among the subjugated population, who were being oppressed by Roman merchants. Suetonius Paullinus, a distinguished officer, was in command. He landed on Mona (Anglesey) to root out this lair of the Druidic cult. From this citadel, its tentacles stretched to England and Gaul. Paullinus managed to occupy the island, despite fierce opposition, but while he was fighting there a general uprising broke out in Britain itself. The entire territory rose up as one man. The notorious taxation system of Roman officials, and even more so the merchant class, had exasperated the Britons. Paullinus was not a circumspect man. In earlier times the Romans had always created fixed military bases for such eventualities. At this date, however, Camulodunum (Colchester) was without walls and had only a small garrison. The whole island was lost. The veterans under Petilius Cerealis were massacred in Camulodunum and a legion marching to assist them completely annihilated. Paullinus retreated, but was able to muster his troops and resume combat. There followed [MH.I, 195] a general massacre – not only of soldiers, but of all foreigners, men and women alike: over 70,000 Romans were killed, as in the time of Mithridates.[664] In Rome the abandonment of the province was considered,[665] and doubts were expressed as to whether possessing it was worth the price that had to be paid.

Paullinus, however, restored the position. Managing to muster half his troops, he gave battle with two legions in the vicinity of Colchester. Had the Britons taken evasive action the outcome might well have been different. As it was, the depleted troops of the Romans were victorious and routed the entire rebellion. Queen Boudicca, one of the leaders of the insurrection, took her own life.[666] The island was retained, but Roman culture was severely impaired. It is understandable that Paullinus's exercise of his office was criticized; he was recalled, despite full recognition of his valour. Nevertheless, the island was retained, which might not have happened if the battle had been lost.

Little was happening on the Rhine; indeed, it became possible to withdraw troops from there and send them to Britain. The Germans were quite docile, a fact which must be related to internal events of which we know nothing. On all sides, therefore, we can observe vigorous offensives and sustained attempts at expansion.

As far as the management of finances[667] is concerned, the situation in the first phase of Nero's rule must have been highly favourable. There is evidence of particular improvements, large-scale projects of benefit to the populace and proposals of a utopian nature, such as the abolition of customs duties. At all events there were draconian measures against tax farmers (*publicani*). In AD 57, 40 million sesterces were transferred from the imperial to the state treasury; as late as 62 Nero was still able to pay 60 million to the state. A similar practice had been current under Augustus, but it is remarkable that these subsidies amounted to such huge sums. By 64, however, the situation had reversed: Nero received 10 million from the state treasury.

[MH.I, 196] Coinage was the pride of the Roman state. No other state has been able to sustain such a continuity of fine coins. The carat-value of gold and silver coins was not reduced until AD 62, the year Burrus died and was replaced by Tigellinus. The experiment with bimetallism ended with the disappearance of good silver. Forty-five gold coins instead of 40 were now minted out of every pound of gold, and 95 silver coins instead of 80 out of every pound of silver.[668] Here, too, there was thus a turn for the worse. Nero's futile extravagances were undoubtedly a contributory factor, but others included the British rebellion and Paetus's Armenian expedition, both of which cost enormous sums.

Let us turn now to the person of the ruler himself. We have already mentioned his elimination of Britannicus. The second catastrophe of this kind was the elimination of Agrippina (see MH.I, 197f.). She is a mass of riddles. When we consider Nero's personality, we need above all to be on our guard against the sympathy of bad poets for their colleagues. Nero showed no trace of brilliance whatever. There was not even any evidence of energy in his external appearance. There was nothing original about him; he was all triviality. With dull blue eyes and blonde hair, he was disfigured by corpulence. Anything to do with politics was of no interest to him. His proclivities were all in the direction of artistic dilettantism. He dabbled in anything and everything, with no particular interest and no particular gift. He had not concerned himself with philosophy: his mother had kept him away from that. Nero was the first Roman Emperor who had his speeches written for him: all the others, without exception, wrote their own. The sole activity that interested him was his obsession with excelling as an actor and singer. Even in this, however, he proved utterly inept.

One of his striking features was his antipathy towards Romanness. He liked to pose as an artist and a Greek, a predilection he carried over into politics: he restored [MH.I, 197] freedom to the Achaeans,[669] even though they did not know what to do with it. His personality was bereft of a single redeeming feature. He was arguably the most contemptible Emperor ever to sit on the throne of Rome, and that really is saying something. He was a cowardly adolescent who was conscious of his power. In his phantasmal mentality he sought the total destruction of the entire globe.

In the early years of his reign he would go on nocturnal rampages through the streets at night, beating up passers-by. Then he took to being accompanied by his Guard,[670] and so it went on. Then there was his lewdness. He constantly voiced admiration for Caligula, because he himself found it difficult to outdo him in extravagance. Then, there was his repulsively superstitious nature, which was hideously connected to his passion for acting. Following his act of matricide he became convinced he was being pursued by Furies, like Orestes. Long had he reigned, he was wont to say, before knowing all the things an Emperor might do (*quid principi licuit*).[671] As the last of the Claudians, he regarded himself as having the right to annihilate the entire globe – a bizarre mutation of the principle of legitimacy.[672]

His attitude towards serious politics has already been indicated. Only a complete blank can be ascribed to him. The draconian police system under him was the work of his ministers; the business of government was repugnant to him. While able to admire spectacles such as that put on by Tiridates, he had no appreciation for large-scale endeavours, particularly of a military kind. He was the first *imperator* who did not feel it at all necessary to be at the head of his troops. And yet there was more combat under him than under any other Emperor. At the end of his reign he wanted to stage a parody of Alexander's campaign;[673] the world was spared it. He utterly loathed the Roman aristocracy, seeking to eradicate the Senate entirely and rule with freedmen and equestrians only. His was a cowardly, unmilitary nature.

His second heinous crime was the matricide[674] of 59, about which we know the exact details, although not the chain of events that led to it. Agrippina's influence had been broken long before that. This was enough for the ministers; they did not want to go further. Poppaea Sabina, who had taken the place of Acte, is named as an accessory to the plan. The imperial ministers had to tolerate this, although there was inherent danger in her desire to become not only the Emperor's mistress, [MH.I, 198] but also his wife. Agrippina is reputed to have hindered this, but this is not likely. The divorce from Octavia took place not in 59, but in 62, after the downfall of Burrus.[675] From the political standpoint, therefore, the murder was a completely pointless act and arose out of the acrimony the Emperor nurtured against his mother. The plan was carried out without Seneca and Burrus, indeed in spite of them. Anicetus, commander of the fleet at Misenum, was willing to kill her by means of an unseaworthy ship, but this failed.[676] At this Nero accused Agrippina's messenger of the attempted murder of himself. He threw off his final mask, summoned the ministers and asked what could be done. The failed murder was more perilous than the one actually carried out. Nero wanted Burrus to have her executed, but he refused to carry out the plan. This is praiseworthy, after all, but Burrus and Seneca both allowed the inevitable to occur and remain tainted by the stain. Anicetus carried out the deed with his own men.[677]

The overall situation did not change until 62. Generally speaking, the first eight years of Nero's reign were marked by judicious and wise government. Evidently this was the work of Burrus; his death set the ball rolling. This is understandable: he was sole commander of the Guard and Nero was too cowardly to eliminate him as Tiberius had eliminated Sejanus. There are stories that Nero killed Burrus by poisoning him,[678] but the evidence is so slight that it is not credible.

Certainly, however, the death of Burrus brought a total reshuffle in its wake. Seneca immediately relinquished his position and retired to private life; he had been sustained by Burrus. Burrus himself was replaced by Sofonius Tigellinus and Faenius Rufus; the latter became the real driving force behind Nero's regime. Nero now legally divorced Octavia; [MH.I, 199] on 9 July 62 she was executed in exile on the island of Pandateria without any charge being laid.[679] Twelve days after the divorce Nero married Poppaea.[680] She became *Augusta*.[681] This fulfilled all her ambitions: she neither had nor sought particular influence over affairs of state.[682]

A change in the administration of criminal law is highly indicative. Up to that point *maiestas* charges had creditably fallen into abeyance in favour of slander and libel suits. This now changed: after 62 the *lex maiestatis* was applied once more. A senator who had recited a satirical poem was brought to court. Thrasea Paetus, not a man of outstanding rank, became the leader of the political and literary opposition. He had written a *Life of Brutus*. His defence prevented a death sentence and the Emperor, still in the early stages of his power, let it go at that.[683]

Terrible calamities followed. In 64 there was a great fire in Rome that lasted for six days.[684] This partly helps to explain the later cash shortage of Nero's government. It is not certain who was responsible for the fire. Nero himself was generally pinpointed as the culprit: that rumour started immediately after the fire. Even later commentators, such as the conscientious Pliny,[685] adhere to this. Nevertheless, it is unlikely. In a matter of fire-raising it is particularly important to be on one's guard against popular rumour. It is true that some people deliberately spread the fire and prevented efforts to put it out – such things invariably occur during such calamities – but it was not proved that they were imperial emissaries. However possible it may be that Nero declaimed on the theme of the burning of Troy, this does not mean that he caused the fire of Rome. It would be difficult to reconcile with the fact that he was absent from Rome when the fire broke out: had he wanted to see the fire he would have remained. The idea that he wanted to make room for a building site[686] is simply too lunatic. We can give little credit to this thesis, therefore.

[MH.I, 200] The persecution of the Christians[687] is connected with this event. In order to quell suspicions against himself Nero cast aspersions on the Christians, of whom there were considerable numbers living in Rome. Thus far this is plausible enough. No one believed that the fire had broken out by accident and anti-Jewish feeling was immense, particularly since the great Judaean War was looming.[688] Tacitus asserts that some Christians had confessed to the deed; if such confessions existed at all, they must have been obtained under torture.

Nevertheless, a mad wave of persecution against Christians ensued, for which Nero incurred a profound hatred that persisted for millennia. This was no religious persecution, however, but the persecution of a number of fire-raisers. In the Empire as a whole no religious persecution took place.[689]

This leaves the persecution of Roman nobles. The pretender question was not involved here: Nero had eliminated all his rivals. Under Burrus the sole *abnepos*[690]*Augusti*, Rubellius Plautus, had simply been instructed to leave Rome.[691] Cornelius Sulla, Claudius's son-in-law, was likewise banished from Rome.[692] However, this was no longer enough: Nero wanted to eliminate people who could succeed him on the throne. In 65 both men were executed.[693] This was followed by anti-conspiratorial measures. It is not possible to give details of what the trials were about. It is unlikely that Nero wanted to make a clean sweep of the Senate.

We do, however, have very precise information about the Piso affair of 65.[694] We are in general greatly at the mercy of chance gaps in the historical record. In this case we are better off. This was a genuine attempt to eliminate Nero. Gaius Piso was popular among his peers, wealthy, noble and ambitious. The conspiracy was widespread, largely in senatorial circles, had been planned for years with an incredible degree of ineptitude and, from an intuitive perspective, it is entirely [MH.I, 201] proper and obvious that the conspiracy should have come to light. Gaius Piso, Annaeus Lucanus (Lucan, the nephew of Seneca, a poet and poetic rival of Nero) and others were killed; Faenius Rufus, Prefect of the Guard, presided over the hearings, which lasted over a considerable time period. There is no question as to their guilt, but the ranks of the aristocracy were thinned dreadfully. Even Seneca, reputedly innocent, was drawn into the affair. It is highly unlikely that he wanted to become Emperor: his inside knowledge of affairs was far too thorough for that. Now, however, Nero was out for all men of excellence. Perhaps Seneca's fortune tempted him. Seneca had already wanted to hand this over to the state earlier, but his offer had not been accepted. In this way the pupil entered on the inheritance of his tutor. In consequence of a gap in Tacitus's account, nothing is known about a second conspiracy.

Next followed the catastrophe of Thrasea Paetus.[695] The cause is not known. He had no connection with Piso: the 'Cato' of that period did not participate in such affairs. He was a leader of the very tame senatorial opposition, and exasperated the government by his passivity and refusal of higher offices. His literary opposition was a tacit protest against the government through admiration of the Republic. The entire circle was destroyed. Many of his comrades, such as Barea Soranus, were also executed. The downfall of Corbulo came in 67.[696] We are told that Corbulo was summoned by Nero when the latter was making a triumphal tour of Greece. Corbulo was committed for trial – tantamount to a death sentence – and committed suicide. Here too the charges against him have not come down to us. All in all, this was the method of Tarquinius Superbus,[697] to make a *tabula rasa* of the aristocracy. This was the decisive battle against the old Republican families, and it was waged victoriously. Under Vespasian entirely new names came to the fore. Tigellinus was Nero's tool. [MH.I, 202] The acquiescence of the army and the people in all this was appalling.

The end came from quite a different quarter. The demise of the Claudian house was not brought about by an upsurge of Roman national sentiment, but rather by chance. The impetus came from Gaul. It was in the nature of things that when Latin nationality expanded, Gaul offered the most suitable terrain. The south, around Narbo, had long been Latinized. In Provence every town enjoyed full Roman civic rights and this gradually spread to the north as well. Caesar himself had made the region from Lyon as far as the Rhine and both seas into a northern province, placing it under a single command. The capital was Lyon, with its Altar of Augustus as a Gallic national shrine.[698] There the Gallic provincial assembly of sixty-four *civitates*[699] met, where the Celtic spirit survived and was exploited in the service of Romanization. The priests of Augustus took the place of the Druids. Latin was the official language. Lugdunum was granted Roman civic rights and completely organized as a Roman colony. *Civitates*, or districts – not towns – were created; this was the ancient Celtic tribal concept and ran contrary to the Roman municipal constitution. In addition, Roman civic rights were granted to many individual citizens, but not to the whole country, and the *ius honorum* (the right to hold magistracies at Rome) was denied to these citizens. Claudius had been the first to challenge this in AD 48 when he abolished the restriction for the Aedui (see MH.I, 179). Even this limited form of civic rights, however, was successful in suppressing the national vernacular.[700] Roman and Greek education permeated the culture from above. Bibracte (Augustodunum, Autun) became a university. Finally, as in all provinces, for example Lycia, material prosperity increased rapidly right across the board. Little information on this survives; only rarely does a spotlight fall on these conditions. Prior to the principate, the war of all against all had prevailed; now came widespread harmony under abler officials.

[MH.I, 203] It is not possible to judge all the effects of the principate simply by the conditions prevailing in the capital. Side by side with the atrocities in Rome there was peaceful growth in the provinces. Although the indebtedness of provinces is mentioned and exploitation by Roman merchants did not cease, things did improve. Gaul was one of the wealthiest provinces, as Gaius's expedition attests (see MH.I, 167). State schools were established, and a few centuries later Gaul was in the vanguard of Roman culture. Despite all this, a feeling of independence persisted. People spoke Roman but were not Roman – something akin to the relationship between the Americans and the English. We must recall the Gallic uprising of AD 21 under Tiberius[701] in order to picture this. *Resumenda libertas* was the rallying cry of the Treveri.[702] The attempt soon foundered when confronted by the Roman army of the Rhine. But it is the sole example there is during the principate.

This was now repeated in a different form. There was a minor rebellion in Gaul, of no significance from the military viewpoint. Gaius Julius Vindex was governor of Aquitania at that time.[703] He had been born into a notable Gallic tribe which had enjoyed Roman civic rights, perhaps in full form, since the time of Caesar. Members of this family soon rose to senior official positions. His father had already sat in the Roman Senate. As often happened, the son was now governor of the province in which he had been born. (Similarly, a Batavian always commanded the Roman cohorts among the Batavians). Vindex wrote Nero a letter withdrawing his allegiance and unfurled the flag of the Republic. Personally he was courageous, respected, wealthy and ideally accomplished, but, as is often the case with such temperaments, did not always have a sound estimation of his own strength. It was to Roman, not Gallic, liberty that he appealed: the *senatus populusque Romanus* was to be restored. Thereafter, however, Gaul was to take its place as a federated state within a Republican association of states. Moreover, this was not unrealizable, [MH.I, 204] since the Republic had, after all, been no more than an alliance of states. This occurred in the spring of 68.

Nero took the matter lightly. Out of superstitious considerations he wanted to travel to Gaul himself, but he did not believe that it would come to fighting. He occupied himself with the composition of epinician poetry. He was not altogether wrong. However, apart from the southern towns, Gaul proper stood by Vindex: the Allobroges and Aedui joined him. Nevertheless, he encountered resistance among the Rhine legions: the standing army was only guaranteed under the principate. This was compounded by military pride. Moreover, Lyon isolated itself completely, forcing Vindex to lay siege to the town. To the east the Germanic element was also stirring, among the people of Trier, for example.[704]

Vindex's rallying-cry was also directed to Roman governors – he did not think in nationalistic Gallic terms. He thus called on both nations. The support of Vienne prevented that of Lyon: an ancient feud raged between these two towns. Financial motives contributed to the fact that the two Germanies did not participate. The garrisons brought a great deal of money into the country and Roman culture was highly intensive, leading people to remain loyal to the *imperium*. Even here, however, sympathy for the Celtic cause was not entirely lacking. It is likely that Julius Civilis, leader of the later Batavian uprising, already sympathized with Vindex at this time. Civilis was taken prisoner and sent to Rome.[705] Nevertheless, Vindex was still able to muster 100,000 men; this points to the existence of territorial armies over and above the imperial army, which was, after all, incredibly small for the size of the Empire. So this numerous if not always able territorial militia assembled at Lyon.

Vindex was resolutely rebuffed by his colleagues, for example Fonteius Capito, governor of Lower Germany, who reported what was happening to Rome and imprisoned a number of suspects. Lucius Verginius Rufus in Upper Germany was of like mind and mobilized and marched on Vindex. [MH.I, 205] Servius Sulpicus Galba, governor of Spain, did not denounce him to Rome, but neither did he join Vindex. He was an able veteran general. His relations with Nero were strained, but what prevented him from taking a firm stand was his general inability to take decisions. In keeping with his wavering disposition he adopted an attitude of wait-and-see.

Rufus laid siege to the rebels in Vesontio (Besançon). Vindex wanted to relieve the rebels, but his cause seemed lost. At this point, events took an odd turn. Vindex and Rufus conferred and concluded an agreement, which can only have been that Rufus to some extent aligned himself with Vindex's plans. He could have annihilated his adversary and yet he opened the town to him. His decision may have been affected by the situation in Spain.

Seeing that his vacillation had finished him with Nero anyway, Galba revoked his allegiance, placing himself at the disposal of the Senate. This was a similar plan to that of Vindex. At all events it was clear that Nero was finished. Rufus probably knew of this, and considering how scandalous Nero's reign had been, it is quite understandable that he chose such a similar course when faced with the likelihood of civil war.

However, this was not to the liking of soldiers of the rank of centurion down-wards. Seeing the Celts march past, they unexpectedly attacked without waiting for the word of command. The army of Vindex was overcome by the army of Rufus. Vindex took his own life. The soldiers were equally aware that Nero was finished. They acted as the Spanish army had done and declared Rufus Emperor. The latter declined, however; like Galba, he placed himself at the disposal of the Senate and the people of Rome. The troops in Britain did not intervene, but the legions on the Danube, Lower Rhine and in Africa joined them. The [MH.I, 206] eastern legions were not available because of the Judaean War.

Nero had not responded to Vindex, but seeing the troops secede one after another, the Emperor realized that he was lost. At first he sought, in his infantile cowardly fashion, to save his own pitiful life. He wanted to become governor of Egypt, or flee to the Parthians, etc.[706] He had a firm grip on the Guard, but there was nothing they could do against the provincial legions, nor did they want to go down with the sinking ship. They let the Emperor fall. Tigellinus resigned and his colleague Nymphidius Sabinus called on the Guard to revoke their oath of allegiance. They did so, and the question now was to find a new Emperor. All the generals had refused the title of *imperator*. Nero was finished, but what was to happen next? Perhaps Sabinus himself had aspirations to the purple. Although he was the son of a slave, his father was reputedly the Emperor Gaius. However, this was not relevant. An Emperor was needed who was to the liking of the legions, and hence eyes fell on Galba, doubtless on account of his age and infirmity. He was a compliant man and Sabinus hoped to do as he liked with him. Under pressure from the Guard the Senate declared Nero deposed and outlawed. The cowardly tyrant crawled into a hideaway in the vicinity of Rome. Not until his discovery was inevitable did he kill himself on 9 June 68 with the words: 'Oh, what an artist perishes with me.'[707] Thus departed the last descendant of Augustus. The Julian–Claudian house went with him.

6

THE YEAR OF FOUR
EMPERORS (68–69)

Servius Sulpicius Galba met with general approbation. His rise to power marked the advent of a new lineage completely unrelated to the founder of the Empires. Hopes for the Republic had been dashed by the resistance of the Praetorian guard. Rufus declared his allegiance to his former colleague. The only place where there was fighting was Africa, where Lucius Clodius Macer ruled for a few months as a Republican governor. He was soon removed. [MH.I, 207] Galba's regime stood on unsure foundations, however. Before he had even appeared in Rome Sabinus was demanding 7,500 *denarii* per guardsman, had eliminated Tigellinus and laid claim to sole command of the Guard for his lifetime. This was tantamount to a claim to mastery of Rome in hidden form. Opposed by the tribune Honoratus, however, Sabinus was already a corpse before Galba had even set foot in the city.[707]

Having come to power very much against his will, Galba immediately fell under the sway of his advisers Icelus and Laco,[708] who governed most unwisely. Galba launched his reign with extreme frugality, imposing strict order on the Guard and not paying out the gifts they demanded. His very entry into Rome was associated with bloodshed. A legion of marines raised by Nero vehemently demanded recognition of its privileged status. Galba ordered them to be massacred, thereby arousing great displeasure among the citizenry. Furthermore, he displayed rash imprudence by dismissing his Spanish troops. Although he was acting in accordance with the strict letter of the law, this left him defenceless. In Gaul he proceeded equal imprudently by acting as the avenger of Vindex. This grievously angered Rufus's troops, who were looked on with the utmost suspicion by Galba. They considered themselves to be superior to the small Spanish army and took offence at the election to the principate of this legate of the single Spanish legion, while their own general had been passed over. The new Emperor did not trust Capito and Rufus, the commanders on the Rhine. This was not natural. Capito was executed for disloyalty, for having been hostile towards Vindex. Rufus was honourably removed from office. This was resented by the German troops, particularly since the generals were replaced by notoriously undistinguished men. Aulus Vitellius obtained Lower Germany, Hordeonius Flaccus Upper Germany.[709]

[MH.I, 208] Galba's performance was equally imprudent in other respects. He gave his protection to towns which had been in revolt against Rome. Government by freedmen was reinstated[710] and irritated the Senate. Even sound measures created confusion. In order to fill the depleted treasury, Galba demanded the return of gifts made by Nero,[711] which led to countless bankrupcies. Exiles were recalled, but the restitution of their property brought about further financial dislocation. Galba was far too weak to see these well-intentioned reform plans through. It was thus only a few months before the troops revolted simultaneously in the capital and provinces. Again, the senior officers were scarcely involved in these rebellions. It was the *soldatesca* of professional soldiers who brought matters to a head.[712]

According to Roman custom the new oath of allegiance was to be taken on New Year's Day 69.[713] The two Mainz legions refused, tore down Galba's portraits and revoked their allegiance, but elected no new Emperor. They were peeved about the candidate of the Spanish army – the choice was left to the capital. Nevertheless, there was no question of restoring the Republic; the Praetorians were called on to elect a new Emperor. In the meantime the legions placed themselves at the disposal of the Senate and People.[714] There was probably widespread awareness that appointment of an Emperor would provoke the rivalry of the other legions. Heed was therefore still paid to the central position of the Praetorian guard and the Senate.

The news soon reached Cologne, where Aulus Vitellius was encamped with his staff. [MH.I, 209] Here, there was a desire to join the rebellion, but no submission to the *Senatus populusque Romanus*. On the contrary, a particular candidate was demanded, and the decision was for Vitellius. A poor choice: Vitellius was the son of one of the Emperor Claudius's minions and had been stationed there because of his very incompetence. Although not a bad man, in fact good-natured, he was of a base, crude nature and above all a great gourmandizer. Vitellius had no desire to become Emperor, but in such cases rank is crucial; he placed himself at the state's disposal and allowed himself to be made Emperor.[715]

The appointment of this Emperor had to be made effective and this required a campaign against Italy. This signalled a change in the military system. Its target was the Guard and their privileged status. The German army was to step into their place. Both major armies on the Rhine were to send a strong detachment to Italy. The two able legates, Fabius Valens and Alienus Caecina, assumed command of 70,000 men.[716] Many of the militias of eastern Gaul volunteered to join the campaign.

All this occurred on 3 January 69 in Cologne.[717] In the days that followed the entire army declared for Vitellius. On 8 January the news arrived in Rome. Galba, conscious of being enfeebled by old age, adopted a younger man, but was unfortunate in his choice. Lucius Calpurnius Piso, from one of the most illustrious noble lineages, was upright and competent, but had no military background, no connection with the army.[718] As a counterweapon Galba relied on the troops on the Danube, where news that the German troops[719] had chosen an Emperor had caused resentment.

Events did not develop that far, however, for another menacing coup was being hatched in Galba's immediate circle. His entourage had from the outset included one Marcus Salvius Otho, who had made his fortune at Nero's court as the husband of Poppaea Sabina [MH.I, 210] and as one of Nero's fellow-revellers. Recently, he had defected to the court of the victor.[720] He had cherished hopes of being adopted, especially since he was superior to Piso in rank and popular among the Guard. His hopes dashed, Otho resolved to topple the Emperor – and succeeded. One fine day, fourteen contemptible guardsmen proclaimed him Emperor. There was rioting in the streets; the remaining guardsmen declared for Otho, more out of hatred for Galba and his stinginess than out of love for Otho. Galba had sent his Spanish troops home and, since there were no other forces in Rome, there was hardly any fighting. Galba and his protégé Piso were killed in the public market-place and Otho's theft of the crown was complete. This was on 15 January 69. The Senate took note of the incident; this was the sum total of its lamentable role. The senators recognized the new Emperor without a murmur.[721]

This left outstanding the confrontation between Vitellius and Otho. Perhaps the Guard were aware what a threat Vitellius posed to them. They could not save themselves now by declaring for Vitellius. The Rhine army was threatening the privileges of the Guard, hence their support of Otho. Both events were soldier-revolutions: all the details point to this. The system of buying leave had become a means whereby junior officers could practise blackmail: the pay of those purchasing leave went into their pockets. This had led to serious grievances. Buying leave had ruined the soldier class and was also detrimental to public security. Now, in Rome and on the Rhine, a new arrangement was introduced whereby double wages were paid for the soldier granted leave – for him, on the one hand, and for the leave-granting junior officer on the other, so that the state coffers had to bear the expense. All this was the consequence of having soldier-Emperors. All those who had been involved in the trial of Capito[722] were executed, as were a number of junior officers.[723]

The troops of the entire West followed the Rhine army without further ado, as did Raetia, Noricum, [MH.I, 211] Britain and, after some vacillation, Spain. Not so in the East. The troops on the Danube, in Illyricum and in the East declared for Otho. This points to the crucial status of Rome: the decision in the capital and its recognition by the Senate were looked upon as a legitimate election. *Esprit de corps* also played a role in the Illyrian and oriental armies.

Numerous negotiations took place between Otho and Vitellius.[724] Both would gladly have stepped down, but were coerced into combat by their armies. The battle was not exactly swift in coming, however. Neither of the two sides was precipitate. Valens and Caecina marched across the Alps into Italy in the spring of 69, encountering no resistance. The Rhine frontier was left to its own devices; the core of the army had departed. In March the German troops appeared on the river Po. Had those in Rome been eager to make a move – and there were able generals there – it would have been easy to confront them at the Alps. The legions from Poetovio (Pettau in Styria) could have made an appearance within a matter of days without leaving the frontier in any danger. Orders were issued to this effect, but the troops arrived too late, despite encountering no obstacles. They occupied the plain east of the river Po. Simultaneously, the Guard and a legion of marines mobilized and marched to the river Po under Vestricius Spurinna. On 15 March[725] Otho left the city: he wanted to observe the battle, not take part in it. Vitellius, who remained on the far side of the Alps, conducted himself with similar lack of involvement.

Initially neither of the two armies was up to full strength. Caecina had crossed the Great St Bernard by himself; Valens had not yet arrived. Caecina occupied Cremona and the Guard held Piacenza. There was fighting; overall the Othonians were victorious.[726] When reinforcements turned up for Otho under Annius Gallus, establishing themselves at Betriacum to the north of the Po, Caecina held them completely in check. At this point, however, Valens arrived. This left the Othonians significantly outnumbered and obliged to await reinforcements. All they had at their disposal was one of the Illyrian legions, and, furthermore, a large detachment [MH.I, 212] had remained south of the Po with Otho. As long as they could wait it out, they were relatively secure. Valens and Caecina could not advance on Rome. The generals on the Othonian side were excellent – if only they had been made use of. But the perversity of their high command ruined everything. Otho, together with a substantial proportion of the Guard, ignominiously failed to join in the battle. And despite all this he was driven to a decision with the boldness of a desperate gambler risking all on a final throw. Instead of seasoned officers he deployed his brother, Salvius Titianus, a totally useless man. The soldiers sensed this incompetent leadership and were disgruntled.

The battle took place on the road between Betriacum and Cremona. At first all went well; the troops threw themselves into the fray with gusto. This all changed when Valens attacked, thereby giving his side the advantage in numbers. This notwithstanding, the Othonians still hoped to take Cremona. It was a fierce battle. A newly recruited legion of Otho's took the eagle of the *legio XXI Rapax*. In the end the Othonians succumbed and the battle was lost. It was not a rout, but it turned into one. The troops in the camp capitulated. When he realized this, Otho gave up, much to the dismay of the Guard. They remained loyal to him and wanted to resume battle by joining forces with the Illyrians. There was no need to give up the fight yet, but Otho had grown weary of life. After burning his papers he took his own life at Brixellum (Brescello) on 15 April, thus leaving his supporters in the lurch.[727] Otho's demise has been much admired, but this is a disgrace for the historian. Anyone who sets himself up as a pretender and then kills himself is an out-and-out coward by any standards. He betrayed not only the Guard, but all Italy.

[MH.I, 213] The consequences of this victory for Italy now became apparent. There seems to have been a premonition about what would happen; this would explain the loyalty of the pro-Othonians. The Illyrians were sent back to their garrisons. The loyal fourteenth legion was sent not to Illyria, but to its former fixed quarters in Britain. Together with its auxiliaries, this legion is an important one for the historian. It included eight auxiliary cohorts of Batavians who were in constant contact with citizen soldiers. The Batavians were very fine warriors; exempt from taxes, they were given priority during conscription and formed the core of the British army. The victory of Paullinus (see MH.I, 195) was largely owed to them. Nero had had them brought to Italy in order to use them against the East. When Nero was toppled the legions were for him, the Batavians against him, and these two parties sworn enemies. The fourteenth legion was sent to Illyricum, the auxiliaries to Germany;[728] at Betriacum they fought on opposite sides. Now there was an attempt to restore the former comradeship of arms in spite of the resentment. On the march to Britain there was even a fresh outbreak of fighting in Turin. This was to prove important later. Vitellius prevailed without difficulty and was recognized by the Senate on 19 April 69.

His very title is noteworthy: he called himself *imperator*, but refused the title *Caesar* and only later accepted that of *Augustus*.[729] Conversely, however, he bore the appellation *Germanicus*, which was his way of indicating that the German army had been victorious over Italy.[730] The break with the past was clear and his actions confirmed this. Here too some useful things were accomplished. Vitellius was not a bad man; he showed mercy where he could. He was concerned to suppress the system of government by servants. For the first time the offices of imperial secretary and treasurer were filled with *equites*.[731] This was probably done under pressure from the military leadership, since these *equites* were officers. The Emperor also took steps to penalize equestrians who threw their reputation away as actors. He used police powers to bring about various improvements and curb unbridled superstition, etc. Now there was [MH.I, 214] rule by a military, not by a servant, regime. Vitellius was probably innocent of all this. An incorrigible gourmand, all his efforts were directed to his table,[732] although he did look to his own safety as well. Cornelius Dolabella was executed[733] for no other offence than being related to Galba.[734] Vitellius had his own son of 6 years immediately designated *Augustus*.[735]

Key military measures were taken. Chief among these was the vengeance directed against the soldiers, particularly centurions. Salvius Titianus, the brother of Otho, was left untouched, as were senior officers, but many centurions were killed – in fact without cause: one could hardly count their obedience as a crime. In fact, this was really about regimental rivalry: the soldiers of the Rhine had fought against those of the Danube, who were now subjected to their vengeance. Naturally, this aroused terrible resentment among the Illyrians. As a conquered country, Italy was now systematically plundered, notably when Vitellius followed later with fresh troops. Cremona and other towns in northern and southern Italy were abandoned to the soldiers ruthlessly and without cause, since the government no longer had an enemy.[736] The eastern army in Syria likewise accepted Vitellius.

Then came the entry into Rome.[737] This was intended to terrorize the city population. Only a concerted effort prevented the Emperor from donning a uniform, but the troops certainly did so. Their real quarry was the Guard, for Otho had been their Emperor. Even the institution itself had to pay the penalty. The entire corps was disbanded and all soldiers, including those in the urban cohorts, were dismissed.[738] A new garrison was created out of the legions: twenty cohorts, sixteen of them Praetorian cohorts and four urban cohorts of 1,000 men each. There is no way of knowing to what extent this was innovative. [MH.I, 215] Previously there had only been twelve Praetorian cohorts; the number of urban cohorts is uncertain. Together, this adds up to approximately 20,000 men, and the number was probably not a substantial increase. What was new was the mode of selection. Hitherto, soldiers of the Guard and the front line had been kept strictly separate, even in nationality. No one ever entered the Guard from the front-line troops. The Guard was entirely Italian, whereas the legions, apart from centurions, consisted largely of provincials. The Rhine legions hailed from southern Gaul.[739] Even those who had been born in Italy were provincialized by their protracted periods of service. The result was a clash of nationalities in full measure. This is an organic idea and undoubtedly justified. Although our view of Vitellius's reign is unfavourable, we cannot allow ourselves to forget that all these things were the fruit of the Augustan system. What Augustus had sown was now being reaped. However ephemeral this structure instigated by Vitellius may seem, time and again, whenever the military leadership prevailed, the Guard was revived – by Severus, by Constantine[740] – since it simply was not feasible to do without a Guard. Abler people than Vitellius must have been at work here.

Extraordinarily, therefore, there ensued a complete disbanding of the victorious army. Those in control of the army must have been convinced that they would be able to build up an army organization in complete peace. The dismissal of 20,000 men (see MH.I, 214–15) already shattered legionary cohesion. Many who were not in the Guard asked to be discharged and this could not be refused them. Clearly no combat was expected in the immediate future.

The house of Caesar had met its end [MH.I, 216] and the question now arose whether the Caesarian Empire was not going the same way. Co-rule by the Senate was on the agenda – not so much its ancient rights, which were of no consequence, but rather the custom, according to the constitution, of filling the posts of senior officers and magistrates with senators, i.e. the Italian aristocracy. The promotion of equestrians has already been noted. Vitellius conferred on himself the title of *consul perpetuus*[741] – not, we may be sure, out of any respect for the office, but rather to ensure that he would have no colleagues around him, as was to occur later, in the third century.[742] The dignity of a consul entitled him to the highest offices. If, therefore, the Emperor was *consul perpetuus*, then the institution of consuls was earmarked for the scrapheap, as, indeed, later occurred under Diocletian.[743]

The rebellion of Vitellius led to rivalry between the regiments. The legions of the East were jealous – not of the person of Vitellius, but at the idea of the seven Rhine legions enjoying the fruits of victory. There was talk of the German legions changing places with the eastern legions and wanting to take over the latter's sumptuous garrison quarters. Although this was just camp rumour, it was indicative of the prevailing mood. The Illyrians had tried to proclaim Verginius Rufus Emperor in Otho's place. He had only escaped them by secret flight.[744] The Illyrians were beaten; the thirteenth legion had to carry out the ignominious task of building an amphitheatre.[745]

In the East it was different. An army had been concentrated for the war against Judaea and Flavius Vespasianus[746] was put in command.[747] Licinius Mucianus was his neighbour in Syria, and Tiberius Julius Alexander in Egypt. Their consultations brought about the downfall of Vitellius. Never was a movement carried out with less fuss. These officers cannot be accused of being driven by ambition; their concern was to preserve the order of Augustus, to put up a candidate against an invading enemy. They needed a leader, an Augustus, and what initially mattered was military rank. [MH.I, 217] Licinius Mucianus was selected as Augustus by the council of officers,[748] but he refused the crown and recommended Vespasian instead. Some of the reasons for this are beyond the scope of our vision, others were of a personal nature. Although the son of a senator, Vespasian came from a municipal family in Sabine country and was not particularly distinguished.[749] His brother, Flavius Sabinus, who had governed in Moesia for some length of time, was at the time urban prefect,[750] a man of both means and understanding. Vespasian had fought well under Nero in Britain and Judaea. His association with the Illyrian army particularly recommended him. The *legio III Gallica* had fought under Vespasian earlier and was now stationed on the Danube. They had an affectionate reverence for Vespasian,[751] which was of immense importance at this juncture. The mistake made by the Rhine army in ignoring other armies was now avoided and an agreement was reached.

Furthermore, Vespasian had two sons; one, Titus, commanded a legion and was highly popular. Mucianus had no children.[752] This was a crucial factor: the crown prince could be chosen along with the Augustus. Mucianus's refusal left Vespasian as the only other viable choice, since the governors of Egypt were *equites*. On 1 July 69 Vespasian was first proclaimed Emperor,[753] significantly in Alexandria, by the Egyptian army. This had apparently been prearranged. The remarkable thing was that they waited three months after Vitellius's entry into Rome to reach this decision. This shows that it was not the person, but the politics of Vitellius that they were not prepared to tolerate.

Initially, Vespasian was Emperor of the East. The Judaean and Syrian armies supported the *pronunciamento*. Another remarkable factor here is the extent of their sense of patriotism. The front line against the Jews was not denuded of troops; they could not even spare the generals. Only a few units, therefore, were earmarked to march west: the sixth legion and 13,000 auxiliary troops set off,[754] a total of 20,000 men. This [MH.I, 218] is surprising, since the Rhine army alone consisted of seven legions. Perhaps the expedition was initially intended not for Italy, but for the Danube, where it was assumed that the legions there would join them. Vespasian took no part at all in the military action. He himself set off for Egypt,[755] where he had been fully acknowledged. He certainly had no need to travel there to halt the grain fleets. The aim was to keep the future Emperor out of the necessary intrigues. Mucianus stood in for him in the concert of generals, thereby taking on himself the odium of the affair. The whole business hardly appears like a coup; it was more reminiscent of a foreign war. The fourteenth British legion was approached, not without success. There were also attempts to negotiate with the Batavians under Julius Civilis on the Rhine.

Asia Minor and Greece sided with Vespasian; the Illyrians too joined him as soon as they were asked. In Italy the price was now being paid for the disarray among the troops. Events took a similar course to that under Otho. It would undoubtedly have been feasible to confront the rebellion on the Danube, but Italy was undefended and Mucianus's outposts crossed the Alpine passes. The adversary was not encountered in significant numbers until the river Po. Mucianus still lagged far behind. Only his vanguard under Antonius Primus had reached Italy.[756] The latter had made quite a mark on history and was an able soldier, but he had an ugly past and had made his name *per nefas*.[757] Primus was confronted by eight Vitellian legions. The Guard was not with them, but these were veteran, able soldiers, albeit with an admixture of new recruits. With moderately sound leadership the war could have been brought to a halt here at least, had treachery not crept in.

[MH.I, 219] Mucianus prohibited Primus's army from proceeding any further. He and Vespasian had no desire to bring the confrontation to such a swift end. The sub-commanders were not to proceed beyond Aquileia. This we can understand: Vitellius had already mobilized all the forces he could, while the Flavians could obtain reinforcements from Syria at any moment and intended to wait until the following year. Aside from the Guard, Vitellius had eight legions[758] – a substantially superior fighting force. Nevertheless, the official commanders were not those whose voice was heard. Antonius Primus was the soul of the offensive. Through a military revolution of sorts he compelled the official commanders, the elderly and unbeloved legates of Pannonia and Moesia, to transfer the supreme command to him. The highly popular Primus took their place. On his perilous advance he was counting on the defection of the opposition, and not without reason. Vitellius's officers did not remain loyal. Similar motives were probably at work here to those which had led to the election of Vespasian. Lucilius Bassus, commander of the fleet at Ravenna, was the first to defect and place himself under the command of Vespasian.[759] The movement spread from the commander outwards, although there may also have been a national factor at work, too. Illyrians and Greeks served in the fleet and they wanted nothing to do with the *exercitus Germanicus* (Rhine army). This was the beginning of the end: the fleet now threatened the rear of the enemy on the river Po.

Another success soon followed. Leadership of the eight legions lay with Caecina and Valens. The latter was absent and Caecina now also abandoned Vitellius for reasons unknown, perhaps out of rivalry with Valens.[760] He is reputed already to have opened negotiations in Rome with Flavius Sabinus, the brother of Vespasian, who had quietly remained in office[761] – this is typical of Vitellius's good-naturedness. Anyway, Caecina defected and harangued the officers, and the portrait of Vitellius was torn off the standards.[762] The troops, however, refused to accept this and remained loyal to Vitellius; Caecina was taken prisoner by his own men and replaced by Fabius Fabullus.[763] Since both sides were now commanded by officers chosen by their men; confrontation was inevitable. This situation was reflected in strategic operations. Valens was still absent. Six legions of Vitellian's were stationed at Mantua, two in Cremona. The army now evaded combat in order to regroup, and crossed back over the Po. Antonius Primus took over their abandoned position and advanced on Cremona, where combat occurred on 24 October 69, once again at Betriacum on the Postumian Way. It was a fierce battle; both sides fought bravely. The Flavians gained victory through their superiority of numbers and their five legions forced Vitellius's two back on Cremona.[764] In the meantime, however, the Vitellian forces from Mantua had hastened to Cremona on a march of 30 miles (6 German miles). [MH.I, 220] There, in the moonlight, the battle raged on despite their fatigue from the march. By dawn victory seemed to be within the grasp of the Flavians. Theirs was the superior leadership; that of Vitellius's army was too disorganized. The Vitellians withdrew to their encampment, which, incredibly, was immediately stormed, followed by the town of Cremona itself. The town was plundered and razed to the ground.[765]

Victory was total: a single, once-and-for-all event, a full-scale battle. This brought the cause of Vitellius to an end, both militarily and politically. Caecina

191

was released from his chains and sent to Antonius Primus.[766] The defeated, but still sizeable army capitulated: they had the Po at their backs and no possible line of retreat. The skirmishes that followed were born of pure desperation.

Attention was next turned to the Guard, stationed at Narno (Narnia in Umbria). They totalled fourteen cohorts, but were an increasingly inferior force, totalling only 20,000–25,000 together with the marines. They capitulated to Antonius Primus.[767] Likewise in southern Italy, where Vitellius's brother was stationed. The Misenum fleet at Terracina also capitulated.[768] The Emperor realized that all was lost. He was very willing to lay down his office and asked only that his life be spared, as he had spared those of his opponents. Vitellius laid down his office in the marketplace and transferred authority to Caecilius Simplex, the consul.[769] Understandably, Flavius Sabinus agreed.

Here again, however, they had failed to take the soldiers into account. The Praetorians in the city, 3,000 men, compelled the Emperor to play out his role and return to the palace. This led to street-fighting. The Praetorians vented their anger on Flavius Sabinus, who took refuge on the Capitol. Vitellius would gladly have protected him, but was unable to do so. Sabinus and Domitian, Vespasian's second son, were besieged on the Capitol. They tried to seek sanctuary in the temple, but were taken prisoner and the Capitol was reduced to ashes.[770] The besieged men may have set it ablaze themselves. Sabinus was slain in the Forum.[771] The burning of the Capitol made a strong impression, particularly in Gaul.[772] Primus might, perhaps, have been able to prevent this; perhaps he thought Rome would fall into his hands of its own accord. Now, he pressed on; sporadic skirmishes and street-fighting ensued, although this cannot have been particularly hazardous. Vitellius fled for his life, but was slain on 20 December 69: the blood of Sabinus called for revenge.[773] This effectively established the reign of Vespasian.

All that remains now is to examine the catastrophe of the Rhine legions and the war against Judaea. The bulk of the German troops had finished up in Italy, but a considerable corps, notably the Batavians, had remained behind in their fixed quarters. Command of all Germany was still in the hands of the aged and gout-ridden Hordeonius Flaccus. Vitellius had not dismissed him, nor had he even filled his own place; he was completely innocuous. Then the troops were given their marching orders to Italy. Flaccus remained loyal at first.

[AW, 164 = MH.I, 221][774] The insurrection of the Germans in Gaul under Civilis[775] was curiously linked to the Gallic insurrection of Vindex. On the previous occasion, i.e. under Vindex, Germanized Gauls had not participated in the revolt. Now the situation was reversed: the revolt was led by Germanized Gauls – the Sequani, Nemeti, Treveri, Lingones and Batavi. Claudius Civilis, a most valiant and nationalist-minded soldier, might well [MH.I, 222] be compared to Arminius. The Batavians were true Germans.[776] Veleda,[777] the soothsayer in Germany proper, was in contact with Civilis. The Romans had respected the special status of the Batavians among the provincials. Batavians who had been conscripted served mainly in the imperial bodyguard.

In the autumn of 69 Civilis agreed to the plans of the Flavians and recognized Vespasian on his island in the Rhine. The governor of Gaul, Hordeonius Flaccus, on the other hand, adopted an ambivalent position towards Vespasian's uprising. Despite this, the Vitellians obtained no support from Gaul. The Canninefati, a small tribe, were the first to take up arms. Civilis wanted to be sent to deal with them. When forbidden to do so he seceded openly. The cohorts of the Tungrians and the Rhine fleet defected to their fellow-tribesmen. (The Tungrians were already a Gallic people.) Many reinforcements arrived from the Germans to the east of the Rhine. Hordeonius now sent the troops from Castra Vetera (Xanten) against the island, but the Gallic auxiliaries defected and the legions were obliged to return to Xanten. At this, Civilis besieged Vetera and obtained reinforcements from the Batavians associated with the fourteenth legion. Civilis's emissaries called on them – there were 8,000 battle-seasoned troops – to abandon their march to Italy and join Civilis instead. They did, indeed, turn back from Mainz, having made unprecedented demands of Flaccus. Flaccus ordered the legate at Bonn to halt the enemy with his single [MH.I, 223] legion. This did not succeed, since Flaccus himself failed to advance to assist him. The Romans in Vetera were particularly short of food supplies, but still managed to fend off the onslaughts against the town.

Hearing news of the Flavian victory on the river Po, Flaccus recognized Vespasian, even if the *exercitus Germanicus* only grudgingly did so. Civilis pressed on with his fight all the same, although now deprived of a pretext, having previously apparently raised the flag of insurrection in Vespasian's name. The fifth and fifteenth legions were besieged in Vetera along with four other legions. The legate in Mainz, Dillius Vocula, now assumed command and finally broke the siege of Vetera after numerous vicissitudes, forcing Civilis back to his island. The liberated fifth and fifteenth legions, proud of their success, tore down Vespasian's standard at Mainz and declared their continuing loyalty to Vitellius. A substantial proportion of the army was persuaded to join the insurgents, and Hordeonius Flaccus was slain for having betrayed Vitellius. And yet the cause of Vitellius was now manifestly lost, and news came of his final catastrophe. This left the two insurgent legions isolated. Those loyal to Vespasian marched to Mainz under Dillius Vocula.

At this point the revolt of the Gauls erupted. In the wake of the burning of the Capitol there was a firm belief that the demise of Roman hegemony was imminent. Julius Classicus, [MH.I, 224] Julius Tutor and Julius Sabinus, who traced his descendants back the to dictator Caesar, seceded from Rome in order to found an independent Roman–Celtic Empire of a federated kind. In the meantime Civilis had made a fresh onslaught on Vetera. Vocula attempted to break the siege of Vetera, but the Gallic auxiliaries seceded and – an event without parallel – the

Roman legions took an oath of allegiance to the *imperium Galliarum* (Empire of the Gallic provinces). The fourth and twenty-second legions were the first to revoke their allegiance to the Roman Empire. Now Vetera capitulated as well and the occupying force was likewise compelled to take an oath of allegiance to the *imperium Galliarum*. They were massacred, nonetheless.[778] The first and sixteenth legions similarly took the oath of allegiance and Mainz fell.[779] Vindonissa (Windisch) was the sole point on the Rhine where the Romans still held out.[780]

There is no parallel to the catastrophe brought on the Romans by the Gauls and Germans in the period of the better Emperors. Its chief cause lies in the desperation of the Vitellian Rhine army. The western and southern states of Gaul refused to take part in establishing the *imperium Galliarum*. A futile assembly was held in the territory of the Remi.[781] Incessant discord among the Gauls prevented the *imperium Galliarum* from becoming a reality. A cooler view of matters was taken in western and central Gaul. Nevertheless, once Vespasian's rule was secure, the twenty-first legion arrived from Vindonissa, the second from Italy, the time-honoured fourteenth from Britain and two more from Spain.[782] Numerous auxiliary units came from Noricum and Raetia. At their head were [MH.I, 225] Annius Gallus and the rash, but still outstanding Petilius Cerialis, who in fact had supreme command over all seven legions.

It was soon clear that the Gauls could not rely on the troops who had gone over to them: they returned to the Romans and swore allegiance to them. The people of Cologne, too, murdered their German occupiers and joined the Romans. Imprudently, Cerialis did not wait for the troops who had not yet arrived to join them. Only with great effort and heavy casualties did he manage to fight off an attack by Civilis at Trier. He did not give the city over to the soldiers as they demanded.[783] Civilis was defeated by Cerialis at Castra Vetera.[784] Nevertheless, the core of the revolt consisted of Germans from east of the Rhine. Civilis made a surprise attack on Cerialis, and at any rate captured the generals' ship.[785] Cerialis, however, forced the Batavians ever further back, even taking the Batavian island and finally forcing the Batavians to the eastern bank of the Rhine. At this point he shrewdly opened negotiations with the Batavians and other Germans. Once Civilis realized that nothing more was to be gained, capitulation followed. Mercy was shown to the Batavians, who were restored to their former status *vis-à-vis* the Romans. Of the six insurgent legions at least five were cashiered with dishonour. Only the twenty-second was spared, [MH.I, 226] perhaps in honour of the legate Dillius Vocula, who had remained loyal. We know of two legions which replaced those that had been disbanded.

The war in Judaea[786] left no particular mark on Roman history. Its history was written by the insurgent leader Josephus,[787] who later went over to the Flavians.[788] In the time of Augustus Judaea was ruled by a hereditary governor,

Herod, known as Herod the Great. In AD 6 his son Archelaus was deposed and the kingdom broken up into a number of smaller states. The capital, Caesarea Maritima, was taken under direct Roman administration, ruled by the governor of Syria. A Roman cohort was stationed at Jerusalem. On the other hand, the descendants of Herod retained the right to appoint the High Priest.

The cause of the rebellion is generally attributed to the malevolent personalities of the individual governors. Antonius Felix, governor from 54 to 60, was a very bad fellow, while Gessius Florus, governor after 64, seems to have been little better. But there were other causes. *Polykoiranie* (multiple rule) was worse than when the land had been a province, and tax oppression greater than if the country had been a direct dependency. Co-rule by procurators and proconsuls was equally deleterious. The procurator of Judaea seems to have been subordinate to the proconsul. The chief cause, however, was the ethnic separateness of the Jews. Such futile rebellions were extremely rare in the imperial age. Nationalist [MH.I, 227] sentiment among the Jews was totally steeped in their religion, in a manner unknown in any other territory. When the High Priest was called on to sacrifice for the Emperor and did so, a movement swept through the entire country that bordered on revolution.

King Agrippa probably realized that the rebellion was futile. Ananias, the High Priest, was leader of the moderate party, who were aware that it would do no good. Nevertheless, all the politically inexperienced groups in Judaea – writers, women and young men – supported the rebellion. There were very large Jewish communities outside Judaea which sustained the country with substantial donations of money and moral support. Another factor was the uncivilized condition of the country. Jerusalem was one capital, the spiritual one; the other, administrative capital was Caesarea, founded by Herod. An advanced culture prevailed in these cities. However, the rural population were primitive and easily roused to fanaticism. Only one cohort of 1,000 men was camped at Jerusalem, despite its very large urban population. In response to oppressive taxation, so-called robber bands formed, known as *sicarii*, 'dagger-men', such as are now to be found in Ireland. The belief was that these *sicarii* had been formed by the Romans in order to eliminate the national leaders.

The pretext for the rebellion was trivial. In Caesarea the Greek population pre-dominated. A Greek merchant there refused the Jews access to the synagogue.[789] Many Greeks were slain. The government intervened. In Jerusalem Roman soldiers were insulted. A submissive Jewish delegation appeared before the governor, but the Roman soldiers mocked them and many Jews were killed. This happened on 16 May 66.[790] King Agrippa arrived and the city capitulated. Soon, however, a fresh rebellion broke out. The insurgents took the city and the Roman troops were forced to withdraw. Records of debts were burned and the retreating troops killed. At this point the Zealots' rebellion turned against the moderates. [MH.I, 228] Ananias was murdered. The response to this was persecution of Jews in the Diaspora; 20,000 Jews were reputed to have died in Caesarea. Cestius Gallus, governor of Syria, marched in with 20,000–30,000 men. At first he was successful. Encamped before Jerusalem, Gallus suddenly withdrew, perhaps bribed with Jewish money. He suffered greatly on the return march.[791]

In 67 Titus Flavius Vespasianus appeared as governor of Syria.[792] His military career in Britain had hardly been brilliant, but quite respectable. He was not of noble birth. Vespasian had three legions totalling 40,000 men, including auxiliaries; he advanced slowly, but surely. By now, however, the entire nation was resolved on a war of independence. The Idumaeans, Galileans and *sicarii* formed a united front against the Romans. Vespasian subdued the various towns; Josephus was taken prisoner at Jotapata.[793] In 67 Vespasian occupied Galilee, in 68 Jericho, with the aim of advancing on Jerusalem. At this point the downfall of Nero intervened, resulting in a pause of a year and a half in this theatre of war.

An offensive was not to be expected from the Jews. So they could be left to their own devices; securing the areas that had been won back was all that was required. When war was resumed, however, it was with an army double the size. Vespasian's son Titus marched on Jerusalem in the spring of 70.[794] In the meantime the Jews had been decimating one another. Notables had been severely persecuted and oppressed by the Zealots, led by Eleazar ben Simon and John of Giscala from Galilee. The Zealots had possession of the Temple in Jerusalem and its associated buildings. The moderates [MH.I, 229] sent for the Idumaean *sicarii*, led by Simon bar Giora. Eleazar was later murdered. John of Giscala and Simon bar Giora led the defence. They had 24,000 men[795] and the population is said to have numbered 600,000 persons. The Jews did not even make use of the interval in order to lay in sufficient supplies or to evacuate non-combatants from Jerusalem. All the same, the city was defended with great vigour. The siege was horrendous. The besieging army consisted of six legions – 60,000 men, including auxiliaries. The suburbs were stormed within a relatively short time. During one sortie, however, the Romans' siege equipment was burned, leading Titus to trans-form the siege into a blockade. At intervals he had 6,000 deserters executed.[796] Food supplies were growing desperately short in the city. The Antonia fortress fell into the hands of the Romans. Finally, the Temple was set ablaze during the storming of the city. There has been controversy as to whether or not Titus ordered this,[797] but the question is of no major importance. At all events it had been decided to destroy the main ethnic focus of the Jews, the Jewish religion, even though Titus wanted to spare the Temple on account of its architectural merits. By September 70, after a five-month siege, the Romans were masters of the city. They had suffered rather heavy casualties.

The war cannot, in fact, be viewed as a major military success, although a triumph was celebrated in Rome.[798] King Agrippa retained his [MH.I, 230] position, since he had remained loyal to the Romans. The country, however, was transformed from a procuratorial into a praetorian province. One legion, the tenth, were quartered there. In accordance with Republican practice, the communal institutions of Jerusalem were dissolved; it was not even replaced by a Roman colony. However, the total destruction of the Jewish nation which was intended did not occur. The annual Temple tax was from now on paid to Rome as the *fiscus Judaicus*.[799]

The general atmosphere is reflected in the Apocalypse of St John, written in 69, during the war.[800] It refers to the siege of Jerusalem, and the seven Caesars pertain to that time. The number 666 is reputed to mean Nero. The text draws on the legend that Nero was not dead.[801] The sixth Emperor is Vespasian; Galba, Otho and Vitellius were not counted. The conquest of Jerusalem is already a fact in the Apocalypse. The 200 million horsemen refer to the Parthian horsemen advancing to destroy the West. For the historian, this book represents the protest of the Orient against the destruction of Jerusalem, the cry of vengeance by Jews against the destroyers. This means it was written after the [MH.I, 231] destruction. The Apocalypse also reveals the attitude of Jews towards Christians. The primary group is that of Jewish Christians and only then come the proselytes. At that time Christianity was still a Jewish sect. The Jews appear as the true Christians, the proselytes are more in the background.

The other group of Christians was that of Paul. This cannot be called a Jewish sect. Ancient Judaism was unfamiliar with the notion of a Messiah, because it had no need of one.[802] The state of Judaea was proud of its special status, protected by the God of wrath who watched over its laws and exclusivity. Then, however, rule by foreign powers appeared, one after another, giving rise to the Messianic idea. Whereas the Sadducees held fast to the old ways, the Pharisees worked towards developing the idea of a Redeemer.[803] The Book of Daniel, now known to be a fake,[804] is the finest monument to the idea of a Redeemer. The Lord of heaven will send the Messiah, who will liberate the nation from foreign rule and defeat the Romans, as he did Pharaoh. This was why the Pharisees adhered so staunchly to outward ceremony – only in this way could one hope for the Messiah. One such Messiah [MH.I, 232] is Christ, here initially a Jewish figure. Only His second coming, however, will bring redemption and the new world. There is nothing new in this. What is new is the inner humanization of this idea. The God of wrath became a God of love. At the same time, this also harbours a universalist tendency. The rigid observance of ritual fell into abeyance; ritual signified a religious police state.

Further progress was made by the apostle Paul. He brought the foundations of Christ to fruition in a deeper, more complete way. Whereas Christ and his

197

disciples had been Jews, Paul, although himself a Jew, was part of the Diaspora. Born in Tarsus[805] and educated in the Greek tradition, he had quite different horizons. And yet he, too, anticipated the return of the Messiah Christ and wanted to prepare his contemporaries for this event. The entire movement is Messianic, but the powerful and significant thing about it is its abandonment of both the dominance of ritual and its restriction to the Jewish nation. Herein lay the conflict between Jewish Christians and the followers of Paul. There could no longer be a chosen nation, at the most chosen individuals. This represented a transformation of the entire perspective of the new movement. Whereas sumptuous oriental imagery is the hallmark of the Apocalypse, the hallmark of the First Letter to the Corinthians is occidental logic.

Judaism and Christianity were both equally opposed to the Roman state. Judaism, however, implied continual opposition. Christianity, too, implied a rejection of Rome, but of a kind that abandoned the temporal world. The hope of Christians was for a kingdom of heaven; the righteous awaited heaven upon earth. Everything earthly was viewed with indifference, hence the renunciation of wealth and concern for the poor and destitute. Whereas the Jews rebelled against authority and did not want to pay taxes, Paul taught to render unto Caesar that which was Caesar's,[806] since all authority came from God.[807] In this way a deep division arose between Jews and Christians. The Jews adhered ever more assiduously to ritual, the followers of Paul discarded ever more of the old tradition. Jewish Christians were gradually absorbed into both parties. Paul did not live to see the destruction of Jerusalem: he probably died during the [MH.I, 233] reign of Nero. After the abandonment of Judaism in favour of humanitarianism there were ever-increasing efforts to win over pagans. Paul himself thus travelled widely, to win proselytes. Paul's teaching endured; the destruction of Jerusalem enhanced it, for Judaism could now no longer progress. It was limited to preserving what it already had. The more aggressive developments were now left to the Christians.

The age of Claudius and Nero left a not inconsiderable literary legacy. Compared to the Augustan age, however, a lamentable retrogression is unmistakable here, as in all other spheres. There was no historiography to speak of, although the situation was marginally better in specialist literature. Philology proper began with the Syrian Marcus Valerius Probus, who first introduced rigorous textual criticism under Alexandrian influence. There was no dearth of poets; with a handful of exceptions, however, there is not a tolerable work among them. Tragedy, beloved by Nero, was represented by Seneca, but these tragedies are devoid of all innovation; they are ancient Greek themes written in finely crafted verse, but with no feeling. *Octavia* is somewhat superior to the others, but this was not written by Seneca at all. It appeared only after Nero's death and even then was only intended for recitation. There was no comedy to speak of; laughter was lost on Nero's contemporaries. The higher genres of poetry were cultivated – tragic and epic poetry, as well as the novel and satire. A remarkable feature of Seneca is the way that his Greek ideas had much in common with Christianity. He thus exerted an influence on early Christian theology.[808]

The real mark of this age is its tedium. [MH.I, 234] Here the palm goes to Lucan, whose writing was tendentious and utilitarian. Had his work been completed it would have been entitled *The Punishment of the Dictator Caesar*. Yet mixed in with this there is a servile fawning. Even the ancients said of Lucan: 'He is a historian, not a poet.'[809] Only the second part of this statement is correct. He is dreadfully dull.

The satirist Persius was a young man, evidently still wet behind the ears! He had not yet fully digested Stoic theory. His powerlessness conceals itself behind ponderousness and gloom. He was detached from practical life and was a novice in Stoic theory. This poet thus clearly reflects how the ancient Roman world was drawing to a close.

Titus Petronius, known as 'Arbiter', was something of a *maître de plaisir* at the imperial court. He bore the title *arbiter elegantiarum*,[810] since people consulted him when they wanted to know what was elegant. He had the nature of an Alcibiades. He failed to use his immense gifts: he was the most gifted of all Roman poets. Unfortunately, only fragments of a lengthy novel – part poetry, part prose – have survived. It places some poems in the mouth of the absurd poet Eumolpius. Hardly anywhere [MH.I, 235] does sound common sense find such powerful expression in a Roman as it does in Petronius in those passages where he speaks of the perverted upbringing of the young. 'Trimalchio's Banquet' is a hilarious section. He could be placed on a par with Cervantes. He deals with everyday folk life; the characters emerge through their language. At the same time the novel is a prodigy of immorality; in that respect too it cannot find an equal.[811]

7

VESPASIAN (69–79)[812]

A process of rejuvenation took place under Vespasian. Such processes were to occur later: under Diocletian (or Constantine) and under Justinian.[813] When Nero fell Vespasian was in Egypt. Licinius Mucianus, left with the dirty work, was his representative. He had to eliminate the pretenders, the sons of Vitellius and of Piso.[814] These were appalling acts of bloodshed, since neither was remotely guilty of anything. Domitian was not fully trusted; even at that time it was rumoured that he wished to eliminate his father Vespasian and his brother Titus.[815] By the time Vespasian arrived in Rome his rule was fully established.[816] An epoch of almost unbroken peace followed. The Emperor closed the temple of Janus after the fall of Jerusalem.[817] The title *imperator* was placed before the Emperor's name, as in the time of Augustus.[818] It was Vespasian's wish in general to restore the rule of Augustus. He associated his [MH. I, 236] rule with the consulship, having the office bestowed upon himself annually.[819] It was the consuls who gave the years their names. He did not begrudge the Roman nobility the distinction of having the year named after them. The consular dignity remained.

His was a thoroughly reforming reign, above all in the military sphere. The Guard was restored to its former status, raised from Italian volunteers. Its numbers were probably also reduced. Vespasian was acutely aware that it was not numbers that mattered, but strengthening the garrison in the capital. There was potential danger in the post of commander of the Guard. Initially Vespasian appointed his relatives to the post. Licinius Clemens was the first commander of the Guard; the office then passed to his own son Titus, who was his co-regent.[820]

Augustus had left twenty-five legions; after the conquest of Britain there were twenty-seven. One legion was added under Nero, two under Galba. Vespasian created three new legions, but cashiered five, leaving a total of twenty-eight. Only under Trajan was the number of legions probably raised to thirty. Vespasian, the military Emperor, was motivated largely by considerations of economy in this. He restored military discipline.[821] The soldiers obtained neither gold nor honours from him when they proclaimed him Emperor. Vespasian's achievement lies less in his innovations [MH.I, 237] than in his maintenance and execution of existing institutions.

Vespasian estimated the war damage of the preceding years at 40,000 million sesterces,[822] that is, 10 million Francs, although this figure is open to doubt. In any case the public treasury was empty and the state bankrupt. The public treasury, which was invariably in deficit, was probably dependent on subsidies from the imperial domains. Within the brief span of a decennium Vespasian managed to set the financial situation to rights. Little is known of the details. He is reputed to have sold fullers the urine from public lavatories that they needed for their fulling trade.[823] He was unjustly accused of parsimony. Vespasian reinstated the *quadragesima* (probably that of the Gallic provinces) abolished by Galba.[824] The main thing was that he laid down more rigorous norms for provincial tribute. The Colosseum was built mainly by Vespasian,[825] so there must have been a surplus in the state's finances. *Male partis optime usus est*, used to be said of him.[826] The first part is false, the second part correct. The famous *Forum Pacis* was also built by him[827] and he renovated the Capitol.[828] However, he also alleviated destitution outside Rome; like Augustus, he assisted impoverished noble families out of state funds.

Now to the administration in general. The administration of justice had become a shambles. In order to settle long-standing litigation he passed [MH.I, 238] extra-ordinary measures; he introduced police procedures[829] for dealing with numerous abuses, for example quasi-marriages between free women and slaves. Debts incurred by sons still in their fathers' *potestas* were declared void.[830] He sought to do away with the more sinister doings of philosophers and astrologers (casters of horoscopes).[831] Above all he appointed publicly funded professors (rhetors),[832] in order to attract the finest minds to the capital.

The true watchword of the Augustan regime had been communal liberty – a recompense for forfeited political liberty. However, this had led to abuses, particularly in small Greek communities. As a result, Augustus had sought to restrict this communal liberty, for example in Lycia and on Rhodes and Samos. Beside the proconsul in Achaea we also later find an imperial legate who oversaw the municipal liberty of individual towns.[833] This can probably be traced back to Vespasian. The modest beginnings of this restriction were also to be found in Italy. An imperial *curator operis* was thus appointed to head public works in the munici-palities. In Italy, however, this process advanced very gradually.

Commagene, which was ruled by kings, was incorporated and organized as a province.[834] The military situation in the Orient in general was greatly improved and the imperial frontier against the Parthians secured. Vologaeses, king of the Parthians, was on good terms with Vespasian. At the very outset he had offered Vespasian 40,000 cavalry against [MH.I, 239] the Vitellians, although he had naturally refused.[835] Cappadocia was transformed from a procuratorial into a proconsular province.[836]

Relations between Vespasian and the Senate were the same as they had been under Augustus. It was by no means a constitutional regime in our understanding of the term. The Senate only participated in government at all to the extent that Vespasian chose his senior officials from the body of senators. His was a very moderate reign. There were none of the bloodbaths seen under previous Emperors, with the sole exception of Helvidius Priscus, who was executed for his opposing political views.[837] One of the most remarkable passages in Tacitus[838] is a digression on the decline of luxurious feasting under Vespasian. The ancient Roman nobility had already been virtually wiped out by Gaius, Claudius and Nero. Vespasian inherited a Senate in ruins; the ancient senatorial equestrian families had almost vanished. In 74 the Emperor assumed the office of censor together with his son Titus. In 75 a *lustrum* was celebrated.[839] It was one of the most extraordinary censorships ever to take place and the last ever in the Roman Empire. Men whose mismanagement of their finances or immoral life-style precluded them from membership of either of the orders participating in government[840] [MH.I, 240] were ruthlessly expelled from the Senate. Vespasian replaced them with the municipal nobility from whom he also traced his own descent. Senatorial families could no longer boast colossal wealth.[841]

Vespasian's court life may be described as exemplary. He was neither niggardly, nor was there immense extravagance any longer; peace reigned in the imperial household. Like Nero, Vespasian, too, found his imitators. To discern the difference between the two, it is necessary to examine the *Columbaria*, the urn chambers of the Emperor's servants. These began under Augustus and Tiberius and extend to the time of Nero. These magnificent structures last only up to that time. Their end was probably linked to the *parsimonia* (frugality) introduced by the Flavians.

Lastly, something about Vespasian's personality. Roman government fared best when led by second-rate men. This was the case with Augustus and with Vespasian. His father had been first a banker, then a customs collector. Vespasian was born in the Sabine town of Reate.[842] His eldest brother, Flavius Sabinus, it will be recalled, died during Vitellius's overthrow (see MH.I, 220). Vespasian had originally had little ambition, but his mother prepared him for a career in public life. His earlier life had not been particularly virtuous from the moral viewpoint. [MH.I, 241] He venerated previous Emperors. Under Nero he fell into disgrace for falling asleep while the Emperor was reciting.[843] There was something common about Vespasian, although he was not an uneducated man (he spoke fluent Greek and wrote an account of the Judaean War).[844] The constancy with which he attended to the business of government was remarkable. 'An Emperor must die on his feet' is a saying illustrative of the man. He disliked imperial pomp and lacked the aristocratic streak of the Julians. His was a practical, able nature which knew how to reorganize a state which had declined.

A HISTORY OF ROME UNDER THE EMPERORS II FROM VESPASIAN TO DIOCLETIAN

Summer Semester 1883 [MH.II]

From the fair copy of lecture notes by Sebastian Hensel, supplemented from Wickert's Anonymous (AW.184ff.)

1

GENERAL INTRODUCTION

[MH.II, 1] The beginning of the story of the Emperors may equally well be regarded as the final story of the Roman Republic, in so far as it is not a series of biographies of individual rulers. Just as the history of Athens is unthinkable without Pericles, so the history of the Roman Republic is unthinkable without Caesar and Augustus; without them it is decapitated. The history of the Caesars of the Julio-Claudian house is the history of the final phase of the rule of the Roman nobility. The attempt to replace it with a democracy must be considered to have failed; one aristocracy was merely replaced by another, albeit a superior one, by and large. We shall be seeing in what an awful manner the last of the Julio-Claudian rulers swept away the ancient noble families who had once ruled. The aristocratic Julio-Claudians themselves ultimately fell with them.

Aristocracy died out with the accession of the Flavians. Vespasian, from Reate, was himself not aristocratic by nature. The history of foreign affairs lapsed entirely; noteworthy events in the usual sense of the term [MH.II, 2] hardly occurred at all until the time of Diocletian and Constantine. Nothing of note occurred, no great wars were fought; individual kings [*sic*] came and went, raised up by military rebellions, and for the most part also destroyed by them. In general, however, the world was stable and conservative until the centre of gravity was shifted from Rome to the Bosporus. Throughout the work of centuries the vision of Caesar, Augustus and Tiberius, the three great, creative Emperors, was put into practice with some consistency, although often at a dilatory pace. Consequently, our account can no longer proceed chronologically. What I am offering here might more properly be termed 'Observations on the Roman Imperial State'. However, even major events such as the Marcomannic Wars and the age of Septimius Severus can be dealt with better with this kind of presentation.

Our sources are poor in worthwhile information, although, as is unfortunately so often the case, more copious in biographical anecdotes and metropolitan sensations. It is often no more than city gossip. Writers, particularly the *Scriptores*

Historiae Augustae,[1] were chroniclers of the urban *plebs*, well versed in narrating about the *panem et circenses*,[2] the *commoda* of the common people. Rome, however, this *caput mortuum*, had no history of its own in the imperial age. Progress was everywhere in evidence – in the provinces and [MH.II, 3] on the frontiers alike – but not in Rome. Literature, too, flourished in Gaul, Asia Minor and Africa, but not in the capital. Nonetheless, it is not proper for a workman to complain about his tools.

2

DOMESTIC POLITICS I

A) PEOPLES AND LANGUAGES

Let us first examine the various national groupings and the Latin and Greek languages.[3] Language is a crucial vehicle for national integration: the spread of Latin signifies Romanization. Greek identity stood on an equal footing with Roman identity. It has been asserted with certainty that the Roman world was bilingual and founded on the equal recognition of the two languages. This needs to be taken with a grain of salt; some qualification is necessary if we are not to have a false understanding. The two languages were not equal.

The western half of this Empire, which had been gradually pieced together, was part Roman, part – in the Roman sense – barbarian. Not that there was a dearth of other advanced cultures. The Punic civilization was highly advanced, in many respects perhaps higher than the Roman, but it was not viewed by Romans as of equal standing; with a handful of exceptions it was despised.

The East was predominantly Greek-speaking. Hellenism was readily acknowledledged as an advanced culture worthy of emulation. However, the manner in which the two languages were treated from Caesar onwards was very different. Latin expanded, [MH.II, 4] but Greek did not. There was significant colonization activity in the East, notably in major ports: Corinth, Berytus, Smyrna and Sinope were all Latinized by Caesar. Augustus continued along the same lines, although the chief motivation behind this was that of making provision for veterans. In this way, Patrae, Alexandria in Troas and Nauplia, *inter alia*, became Latin-speaking enclaves within Greek-speaking territory. The official language was solely and exclusively Latin. In private, everyone was free to speak whichever language he was comfortable with, but officially Latin had to be spoken. These colonies thus effected an expansion of the Latin element.

Even much later progress continued along these lines, if somewhat less enthusiastically. In the eastern frontier regions it was mainly Osrhoene[4] in Arabia, Tyre and Hemesa which became Roman, Latin-speaking colonies at the beginning of the third century. An intelligent analysis of these important circumstances would be highly desirable, but has so far not been forthcoming. In addition to these towns there was the quite extraordinary use of Latin and Greek side by side, e.g. at Ephesus. Antioch had multilingual coins long before colonization: the name of the Emperor was in Latin, that of the governor and everything else in Greek. Caesarea in Cappadocia had similar coins. [MH.II, 5] There was nothing of this kind in Egypt. Just as the status of Egypt was to a certain extent merely that of a country in personal union with the Roman Empire, so in Alexandria, as in all Egypt, Latin was entirely excluded. Greek was the sole permitted language there. Egypt was the true seat and bastion of pure Hellenism. A number of other factors that we shall be examining here likewise worked towards an expansion of Latin.

Roman citizenship was frequently granted to individual Greeks, notably respected municipals. Although largely a personal favour, this was by no means devoid of substance. It is more than just an anecdote about a crotchety Emperor when we are told that Claudius[5] revoked the citizenship bestowed on a respected Lycian who had to conduct litigation in Rome, but had no command of Latin. *Noblesse oblige*: one was not a Roman citizen for nothing; one was also obliged to be able to express oneself in the language of the Roman citizen. The granting of citizenship to men of standing was thus a prelude to national integration.

Equally important for Romanization was the Roman military. The legions obviously consisted exclusively of Roman citizens. Even in the auxiliaries, however, the commanding officers and the entire *esprit* were Roman and Latin. With twenty-five years of service behind them, [MH.II, 6] the auxiliaries were disseminators of the Roman way of thinking and the Latin language. Nonetheless, the recruitment process made far less use of the eastern peoples than of the western; there were many more Spaniards and Gauls than Syrians etc. in the auxilia, and wherever they were stationed they formed Latin-speaking enclaves, for example on the Euphrates. Probably hardly any epitaph for a Roman soldier dating from the best period was written in Greek alone; mostly they are in two languages, with Latin first.

Even in the days of the Republic the government had dealt with Greeks mainly in Greek, although demanding that the latter speak and write in Latin if they wished any issue or lawsuit to be dealt with. Decrees were always promulgated in Greek and sentence passed in Greek. As late as the fourth century the Emperor administered justice in Greek in the East. The Emperor's chancery was bilingual, with two departments: a Latin secretary and a Greek secretary.[6] This had its limits, however: all universal legal pronouncements were made in Latin. As late as under Theodosius II in the fifth century a minister named Cyrus was removed from office in Egypt[7] for having written a general legal regulation in Greek – or at least this act was a decisive factor in his removal from office. Latin was thus compulsory for an official career; no Greek who lacked perfect mastery of Latin could become an official, even [MH.II, 7] long after the seat of government had been removed to Constantinople. Western culture greatly predominated in officialdom and the army alike; Appian and Cassius Dio had been obliged to learn Latin as officials. There was a major school of Roman law at Beirut from the third century on, and here, in Syria, tutors and students alike were Greek. Writers on jurisprudence wrote in Latin, although their scholia[8] were often in Greek. Among jurists at that time the relationship of Greek to Latin was comparable to that today among modern jurists between Latin and German. Papinian the Phoenician and Ulpian of Tyre both wrote in Latin, even though Greek was their mother tongue. This is likewise noticeable in literary scholarship. Byzantine grammarians of the third to fifth centuries have become of crucial importance to us today. Whatever was recommended in Byzantium survived and was preserved; the rest perished.

Caesar's idea – global in scale, like all his ideas – was to Romanize the entire Empire from the Atlantic Ocean to the Euphrates. This idea was never abandoned; it was maintained throughout the entire imperial age. Caesar's ideas were far more of a legacy to posterity than those of Napoleon, for example. But they flagged in the implementation. Augustus was already more hesitant in its execution than Caesar had been, and his successors were even more so. Persistent as it was, the idea ground to a halt in the execution, which compels us to regard it as a [MH.II, 8] failure. As so often in history, the possible was achieved by wanting the impossible.

Since, in view of what we have said, we have to deny the equal status of Hellenism in the Roman Empire, what position did it hold? It had not been Caesar's intention to eradicate it; he had far too much insight for that and was far too steeped in the high, ideal values of Hellenism. The idea was to perpetuate Greek as a common legacy for all educated people, to make it the language of a superior culture, much as French is today in the Slavonic world, in so far as it has not been eroded by their Slav chauvinism, or as Latin was in the early Middle Ages for Germans, French and Italians. Hellenism had to perish in order to survive forever.

The Roman literature of the earlier, Republican age was already steeped in Hellenism; people wrote in Greek before they wrote in Latin. There was a shift under Augustus: writers such as Horace and Virgil, Varro and Livy set Latin on an equal footing with Greek. There was a similar relationship as in the last [i.e. eighteenth] century between German and French both before and after our great classic authors. Lessing, Goethe and Schiller exerted an influence on German literature comparable to that of the Augustan writers on Roman literature. After Augustus no Roman author of note wrote in Greek any longer,[9] just as after those German authors it would have been unthinkable for anyone to write in French as Frederick the Great had done. [MH.II, 9] We must, of course, allow for minor exceptions, such as occasional epigrams, which still appear in the *Greek Anthology*.[10]

The extent to which the boot was on the other foot is demonstrated by Latin literature written by native Greeks – unheard of in the Republican period, this was not rare in the age that followed. This is shown by Ammianus and Claudian, the most outstanding talents of their time. The true seat of Greek writing was Alexandria, and was fostered by the magnificent library there. Remarkably and characteristically, it never occurred to the Emperors to have it removed to Rome. Besides Alexandria, however, particularly in the Augustan age, stood Rome itself. As early as Caesar's time the geographer Posidonius wrote in Rome; Strabo the geographer completed his great work there too at an advanced age during the first years of Tiberius's reign. Timagenes the historian lived in Rome, as did Dionysius of Halicarnassus. The foremost Greek literary authorities wrote in Rome.

In contrast, let us examine the position of Hellenism in the West. To what extent did Greek hold its own there as a vernacular language? There is a widespread view that in Rome, or at least in Ostia, Greek was a second vernacular beside Latin. This is quite erroneous. There were, of course, foreigners and immigrant Greeks there on a large scale, just as there are foreigners and immigrant Germans in London today and as there were – at least before the war [1870/1] – in Paris.[11] This incorrect impression is largely [MH.II, 10] created by Paul's Epistle to the Romans, written in Greek. Of course Paul, who came from Tarsus, wrote in Greek, for the simple reason that he was unable to write in Latin. Greek cannot be regarded as in current use among the lower orders of Rome. This is documented by the inscriptions. A clear view of these is greatly hindered by the preferred method of classifying them by language. Although some of the ancient Christian ones, edited by de Rossi,[12] are in Greek, they are for the most part lost in the crowd: of the first 200 up to AD 367, there are only eight, i.e. a ratio of 1:24. A similar ratio might be found in Paris with German graveyard epitaphs in relation to French ones.

As far as the inscriptions in the Jewish catacombs in the Vigna Rondanini in Rome are concerned, not one is in Hebrew, which does not appear until much later, in the sixth century. Two-thirds are in Greek, a third in Latin,[13] and the Latin inscriptions also include some Greek words written in Latin script, particularly the stereotype closing formula ('Rest in peace'). Since Paul's Epistle to the Romans was essentially aimed at this community, this explains how Paul could assume that his Greek would be understood by his readers. Jews and Greeks had no organization, *collegia*, etc. in Rome; the former attended solely to their religious affairs. Epitaphs, including those of Roman nobles, [MH.II, 11] were generally in Latin, apart from some elegant epigrams.

As far as the rest of Italy is concerned, the principate inherited a substantial legacy from Greek culture. Since language was largely determined by legal status, Greek national identity received its death blow in the aftermath of the Social War and the granting of citizenship associated with it. A distinction needs to be made

210

in Italy between Greeks in Apulia, Tarentum, Rhegium and Naples. As coins show, in the latter days of the Republic Apulia was still an entirely Greek region, somewhat like Sicily. Hellenism was suppressed there in the imperial age. From then onwards Latin was spoken and written for official purposes. There are a number of inscriptions purporting to be in Latin, but containing Greek turns of phrase and grammatical howlers.[14] Horace derides the bilingual Canusians;[15] his remark is not intended as praise – 'learned in either language'[16] actually implies inadequacy, which makes the remark a reproof.

Tarentum, Rhegium and Naples were the three cities exempted from taxation; when citizenship was granted to them they preserved their right to remain Greeks, despite their status as *cives Romani*. They are portrayed by Strabo[17] as Greeks not only in fact, but also in law.

Of these cities, Tarentum soon became so depopulated that it [MH.II, 12] almost ceased to exist; under Nero veterans moved there to obliterate its Hellenistic character more and more. There are only a few meagre inscriptions. Naples, in contrast, was still a purely Greek city as late as AD 81. Here both decrees and dates were in Greek. An inscription by the Emperor Titus concerning games celebrated while he was a magistrate there is in both languages, but the Greek comes first.[18] As late as the first century there were still archontic and demarchic inscriptions (*arxas tessaron andron – quattuorvir*) in Rhegium and Naples. By the second century, however, Latin had precedence in Rhegium.

The circumstances pertaining to Naples were entirely unique: it was to a certain degree protected and maintained as a special seat of the Muses.[19] Greek games modelled on the Olympic games were instituted by Augustus[20] and, just as Olympus had been the pinnacle and focus of Greek Hellenism, so Naples became the pinnacle and centre of Italian Hellenism. There was a Greek university with state support, but all this activity was restricted solely to the literary sphere, since the commercial and economic focus of Campania at that time was not Naples, but Puteoli and Baiae, which were ports and trade emporia. The rise of Naples and the decline of other cities date from a later period. The upshot was that southern Italy was Latinized with [MH.II, 13] the sole exception of Naples, where the atmosphere was intended to remain Greek.

Necessary and explicable as this course adopted by the government was, it had a deleterious, sombre aspect: the total decline of southern Italy in the imperial age was substantially aggravated by this cultural upheaval. Such a process cannot occur without having repercussions on the organism of the state – it attacks its very life force.

Let us examine the remaining seats of Hellenism in the Roman Empire, Sicily and Massilia, the latter the most distant outpost of Hellenism in the Occident! A substantial process of change occurred in Sicily from the latter days of the Republic until the imperial age. Up to the time of Cicero Sicily was still largely

Greek, at least in so far as the island was not completely ravaged by the terrible slave wars. Caesar and the first Emperors Latinized the island; they granted its municipalities first Latin, then full Roman civic rights, as is unequivocally and expressly stated by Diodorus.[21] This is borne out by the inscriptions, and any attempt to refute this fact is foolhardy. Panormus (Palermo) and Taormina (Tauromenion), for example, were first Latinized by Augustus;[22] nowhere was Latinization imposed by force so resolutely as it was on Sicily. This went hand in hand with steady devastation, assuming there was still anything left to devastate after the terrible war of Sextus Pompey. The *Coloniae civium Romanorum* founded by Augustus were officially permitted to speak Latin [MH.II, 14] only; side by side with these there were also *municipia civium Romanorum*, for example the Lipari Islands[23] and Haluntiun,[24] where Greek was still written, but only sporadically and in early imperial period. The alliance of the islands with its natural mainland of Italy, geographically both predestined and justified, became reality in the imperial age, but no landscape was more grievously devastated than this island; so generously provided with wealth by nature, it has never recovered.

Massilia is the most extraordinary and unique municipality in the Mediterranean basin. Varro[25] still called it trilingual. Founded by Greeks from Asia Minor, it had always been firmly allied with the Romans and, by virtue of its geographical location, naturally enjoyed close ties with the Celts, hence its trilinguality. As late as the war between Caesar and Pompey the city still wielded significant power. The principate, however, found Massilia broken; Caesar had brought this about.[26] In the Republican age Massilia was the foremost political power in southern France; it possessed a territory extending from Fréjus (Forum Iulii), Nîmes (Nemausus) and Arles (Arelatum) far along the coast and deep inland. The people of Massilia were adherents of the constitutional party and avid Pompeians, and no city paid more dearly for its defeat. It lost its territory; Arelatum and Forum Iulii and other colonies were founded on it. The Greek character of the city in itself remained untouched; the Romans planned to proceed here much as in Naples, [MH.II, 15] since the principate continued to subscribe to the idea that true culture was not feasible without Hellenism. Gaul had here, so to speak, its own Greek university. Tacitus[27] still depicts Massilia as a city of provincial simplicity and Greek charm, a seat of the Muses and a den of iniquity. Gaul hence became a new seat of culture. The constitution of Massilia was similar to that of Naples; the city had Roman civic rights and was permitted the option of using Greek. Magistrates, for example, could call themselves *archon*. Its territory still remained impressive; Nice, for example, was one of its possessions.[28] Nonetheless, exceptions such as Naples and Massilia merely prove the rule of thoroughgoing Latinization of the West.

So what was the relationship between Latin and Greek and other languages of the vast Roman Empire? This matter will be taken up in detail elsewhere; here we can only touch on it in broad terms. The fact of the all-pervasive triumph of the Latin dialect is then unprecedented and completely new phenomenon in the history of the world. However, all great nations overcome and outgrow earlier tribal characteristics: this is how they become great nations. This is a historical necessity, although often not very pleasant in specific cases; much that we find likeable is lost in the process. The fact remains, however, that the consistency and scale on which this [MH.II, 16] occurred in the case of Latin makes this absorption unprecedented. Hellenism allowed ancient Doric and other dialects to survive into much later centuries. The *koine* was never fully implemented as Latin was with regard to Oscan and Etruscan. The Hellenism of Alexander's successors in the conquered eastern territories of Syria and Egypt was imposed in much the same way, but the perceived need to obliterate the alternatives first manifested itself in the Roman Empire. Nowadays this process is ubiquitous and the struggle of languages for survival is a trait shared by all great modern civilized countries.

First of all, let us examine Italy. The later Republic was still multilingual.[29] The Sabellians spoke their Oscan dialect, and the Umbrians, Etruscans and Celts all spoke their own dialect or language. This was still very clear as late as the time of the Gracchi, for here the linguistic disparities were still greater than in Greece, where Thebans, Athenians and others spoke a far more similar language among themselves than was the case with the various Italian tribes. It was the Social War that first destroyed nationalities and languages. The coins of the insurgents are in Sabellian script;[30] had they been victorious, their language would also have prevailed. As events transpired, however, we can find no inscriptions other than in Latin after Sulla.[31]

We no longer know how long these vernaculars survived in private communication and, given the manner in which our knowledge has been handed down, we shall probably never know. In those days no heed was paid to such things, as it is among the English, who know [MH.II, 17] the very date on which the last Cornish-speaking woman died.[32] All we know for certain is that, with one solitary exception, no post-Republican grave inscriptions are extant from southern Italy in the Samnite language. Strabo assures us that in his day, at the beginning of Tiberius's reign, a separate Samnite ethnic identity was already dead.[33] By the time Pompeii was destroyed, it was Roman. Numerous Oscan inscriptions can be found there beneath the plaster on the walls. The later ones, written on the surface of the stucco, are in Latin. Varro,[34] who was somewhat older than Cicero, still knew Samnite-speakers and some scholars perhaps still knew this dead language even later. The process of depopulation already repeatedly referred to was greatly accelerated by the destruction of the vernacular.

This was the state of affairs in the south and on the west coast. In ancient Calabria we can still find an abundance of Messapian inscriptions,[35] although it is uncertain whether these date from the late Republican or early imperial period. In such a remote corner of the world the local-national element naturally survived longer than in Campania. After all, private communication continued undisturbed, and the influence of the government was slight: the government had little cause to intervene here.

A detailed, reliable analysis of Etruscan still remains to be written. We have innumerable inscriptions,[36] to which we are unable to ascribe a precise date. Although the custom of writing funerary epitaphs dates from an earlier time in this region than in those discussed so far, it is, nonetheless, probable that Etruscan inscriptions were still being written in the imperial age. [MH.II, 18] Archaic inscriptions are rare. The resistance to Latinization manifested by Etruscan was more tenacious than in the case of Sabellian; the latter is also more similar to Latin than Etruscan, which facilitated the transition from one dialect to the other.

Northern Italy was largely conquered, colonized territory, so that here, as in Picenum, the ancient national identity had been exterminated: we find only Latin inscriptions. This region was heavily Romanized. Mediolanum, Verona and Brixia were originally Celtic localities, later thoroughly Latin. Here, too, the Social War was decisive: these localities were granted, or rather condemned to, Latin rights. Umbrian, Raetic and Celtic died out. Very sporadically, around Verona for example, the worship of Raetic deities survived into the imperial age. This region was not organized along urban lines; outlying peoples were allowed to retain their cantonal system. Surrounding districts were 'attributed' to certain cities. The *civitates* of Eugone were thus assigned to Brixia, as the Carni were to Trieste. All these *civitates attributae* had Latin status; only the towns to which they were assigned had Roman rights.

Having examined conditions in Italy in some detail, we shall now turn to some general features of the provinces. The first proposition is that the use of Latin was permitted everywhere. Every citizen was permitted to speak Latin in the imperial age. This had not always been the case. [MH.II, 19] The Republic had adopted an exclusive and intransigent attitude towards this trend. Cumae, for example, had had to petition for the privilege, which it was granted as an exception.[37] It is not possible to pinpoint the exact date in the imperial period when this policy changed, but it was in the natural course of events that it should, and since it was *a priori* necessary, it did so. Roman magistrates whose terms of office alternated annually could hardly be expected to be familiar with the local vernacular, apart from Greek, if they happened to be posted to Syria, Egypt or a Celtic region. Administration would have been rendered impossible; communication in Latin between urban and provincial authorities had to be permitted and the provincials had to negotiate in Latin.

Present scholarship on the imperial age reveals not a trace of consideration towards those peoples and tribes who were regarded as 'barbarian' in the Roman sense of the term, i.e. non-Latins and non-Greeks.[38] However, in the later

Byzantine Empire we find the appointment, within the department of the Master of the Offices, of *interpretes diversarum linguarum*;[39] these, however, were probably responsible for communicating with peoples who were not ruled by the Romans – Slavs, Turks, Armenians, Persians and others – with whom the Byzantine Empire often had to deal.

It may be asserted that in the West the government marginalized whatever could be marginalized. The best source of information on this is what is really the sole surviving archival material, [MH.II, 20] aside from inscriptions, namely coins.[40] The remnants left to us by historians and chroniclers, particularly for the West, are a sorry affair; we possess far richer sources for the later periods of the Byzantine Empire and its institutions.

Regarding coins, we have numerous issues from Spain dating from the Republican era,[41] bearing indigenous, Punic and Celtiberian inscriptions. During the imperial age there were probably only Latin legends in the West, which is really most extraordinary, in view of the extensive practice of local self-government that was ubiquitously tolerated by the Empire. Africa is even more striking in this regard. There are many civic coins dating from the Republican age[42] with legends in Punic script, but only one exceptional example from the era of the principate, which is most odd. These are coins from Tingis (Tangier),[43] a city in the most distant and remote corner of Mauretania, which are bilingual and, furthermore, date from the early days of the reign of Augustus. They were minted while Agrippa was still alive. The right to mint coins was exercised by provincials with the proconsul's permission.[44]

The client monarchies, the kingdoms of Mauretania, Cappadocia and the Cimmerian Bosporus, minted quite profusely, but using Latin legends. This was quite natural: these countries were in fact elements in the government of the Empire, but with lifelong, hereditary administrative positions, similar to the Prussia's German client-states today.[45] Mauretanian coins likewise bore Latin inscriptions, probably by command of the Roman [MH.II, 21] government. Juba, king of Mauretania, a notable author, wrote in Greek, not in the vernacular of his country.[46] There are coins bearing the portrait of Cleopatra Selene, the daughter of Cleopatra of Egypt and of Antony.[47] These coins refer to her as *basilissa* in Greek characters, but Juba's name is in Latin. The *sufetes undecim principes* (eleven leading magistrates) in Africa likewise used Latin for coins and official documents. The rigour with which Latin was imposed on coin legends should not be wondered at. This money was struck according to the standard of the Roman *denarius*; the currency was interchangeable with the Roman in the wider exchange and therefore had, of necessity, to bear a legible marking, as do the modern coins of the German Empire.[48]

Gallic coins[49] manifest a rapid decline in the use of the Greek alphabet from the time of Caesar to the early part of Augustus's reign. Prior to this the Celts used

Celtic words when writing, but wrote them in Greek letters.[50] This practice ceased from the time of Caesar onwards. These coins, particularly those from northern Gaul, frequently bear the most barbaric stuff, written in unbelievable Latin, but at least it was supposed to be Latin. As has already been mentioned, coins and inscriptions are our sole surviving material. But it is highly probable that Latin was also obligatory for municipal accounts and the minutes of meetings, in short for any activity supervised by Roman officials, particularly in the West. In the East, although we find no trace of barbaric idioms in inscriptions and on coins from the era of the principate, matters were different. The beginning [MH.II, 22] of the principate, in contrast to the Republic, made a less marked difference there than in the West, in as much as other idioms had already given way to the dominant Greek.

Quite unmistakably, in this sphere the onset of the principate marked an immense watershed; nowhere is a departure from the traditions of the Republic more discernible than here. And this is natural: an urban government is narrow-minded, whereas a state has broader horizons; the city rejects foreign elements, whereas the state assimilates them. The sole applicable analogy from a later era is perhaps the Republic of Venice, which never contemplated the national integration of its eastern possessions. For Caesar and the principate the *arcanum imperii*, the secret of politics, was assimilation. Explicitly or implicitly, this course guided government policy for centuries.

B) MONETARY AND FISCAL MATTERS

Let us turn to administration – first and foremost to fiscal policy, the foundation of all administration, the sinews of political events.[51] Before examining the political events, the sinews must be considered. We begin with that branch of fiscal policy about which we happen to be best informed and which can hence be dealt with in the kind of detail that would not be possible otherwise: coinage. Coins provide a highly readable, lucid history. If one wishes to know how a state is situated, one need only look at its coins; herein are reflected [MH.II, 23] its fortune and misfortune, its decline and its revival. This is still the case today: all countries – France, England, Italy, Germany, Russia – can be assessed more or less by their coinage.

Throughout the entire Roman Empire the standard of reckoning was based on the silver *denarius*, equivalent to 4 sesterces. Its implementation can undoubtedly be traced back to Augustus.[52] From his time onwards it was obligatory; only coins struck according to the *denarius*-standard were authorized. Typical of this fact is an extant inscription[53] stating that a certain sum of money has been paid in Rhodian drachmas; in the inscription the sum is expressly converted into *denarii*,

216

with 10 Rhodian drachmas equivalent to 16 *denarii*. Conversions are invariably into *denarii*; all other types of coin, even when they were legal tender, such as in the Rhodian example, were converted into *denarii*. A certain discrepancy was at work here, however, in so far as at Rome itself the coin used for reckoning was the *sestertius*, not the *denarius*. There it was customary to say that an item cost 400 sesterces, not 100 *denarii*. In the East, however, the *denarius* was readily accepted, replacing the customary reckoning in drachmas prevalent there up to that time.

There was one highly characteristic exception to this, which only confirms what has already been asserted about the status of that country: Egypt, where reckoning in talents prevailed. The talent was the large and the Egyptian drachma the [MH.II, 24] small unit of reckoning or coin.

The uniformity of coinage examined here marked a huge step towards uniformity and similar steps probably ensued in the sphere of weights and measures, too. At least once a year there was an official standardization of the pound into which all weights had to be converted for purposes of administration.

The Roman system of coinage was in fact a blend of monometallism and bimetallism. Originally it had probably been based on the latter, but the natural force of mercantile logic led to a *de facto* predominance of monometallism, in this case the gold standard. One might even call it cryptobimetallism. For large-scale commercial transactions, gold was the sole currency; silver was the normal standard, and copper was used for small change.

Let us examine the right to mint coins as it was organized under the principate. The Republic had not been familiar with gold in the form of minted coin,[54] but even here the rule was that large-scale commerce preferably, or even exclusively, used gold for its transactions. Logically, the Republic did not permit the minting of gold anywhere. Caesar was the creator of a gold currency; he reserved the right for the central government, with the sole exception of the Bosporan state, now the Crimea.[55] Bosporus Taurica did strike gold coins, as was probably necessitated by its trade links [MH.II, 25] with the peoples of the north. Nevertheless, these Taurian coins were up to a point Roman. They naturally had the same coin standard and always displayed the portrait of the Roman Emperor beside that of their own ruler.

What is most remarkable is that, even far beyond the frontiers of the Roman Empire, Rome *de facto* had the exclusive right to mint gold: even the Parthians, the only rivals of Rome who were any match for her, refrained from minting gold until into the third century. The Persians did not begin minting coins until AD 226 with the fall of the Arsacids and the succession of the Sasanids, who brought with them a national Persian religion and in general a national reaction against the Panhellenism that had held sway hitherto.[56] Unlike the Roman coins of that time, moreover, Sasanid coins were of high quality and full weight. Up until the time of Justinian, according to the testimony of Procopius, only coins bearing the portrait of the Roman Emperor were accepted in the commercial world.[57] Rome monopolized the minting of gold – indeed, even in the Middle Ages gold coins were still referred to as 'Byzantines'. When the Frankish states began to develop in the sixth century, however, this monopoly of gold ceased.[58] What modern-day bimetallists long for so ardently – the setting of gold and silver equivalents for the whole world by common agreement – was *de facto* a reality in the ancient world.

Silver was also treated differently in the East and the West. The East was inundated with masses of old silver money that could not be taken out of circulation, since it could only have been recalled for [MH.II, 26] reminting at enormous expense. Hence the old Rhodian silver system, for example, was left as it was.

An examination of the silver and copper currency has to restrict itself to general historical features: three to four regions, largely in the East, need to be distinguished. In fact only three, since the fourth, Macedonia, was one of the most run-down provinces in the Empire and minted very little in general; it was in a complete state of economic collapse.

The first of these regions comprises western Asia Minor, with Ephesus, Nicomedia, Bithynia, Pontus, Lycia and Pamphylia. This part of the world had a local coinage dating from the time of the Attalids of Pergamon, on the ruins of whose state Roman hegemony had been built. *Cistophori* were their large silver coin, silver drachmas their small coin. These were retained, continued to be struck and were accepted as payment by the state treasury, but at an unfavourable rate against Roman currency. There was thus a clear tendency to relegate the *Cistophorus* to the sphere of minor commerce. Of course imperial silver was in use side by side with it for large-scale commerce, and certainly also for some kinds of local commercial activity.

The second coinage region comprised Syria and Cappadocia. Local coin was minted here even more profusely than in the first region, viz. the tetradrachmas of Antioch and the drachmas of Caesarea.

The third currency region was Egypt, where quite unique circumstances obtained. Under the Ptolemaic kings Alexandria had had a two-tier system of coinage – an abundance of well-struck gold and silver, as well as token money similar to our paper money. The latter was retained during the principate, but local gold and silver minting was halted completely and only imperial gold authorized. [MH.II, 27] The government naturally made substantial gains out of this. Modern scholarship is no longer able to ascertain the extent of this token money economy, which used Alexandrian tetradrachmas. However, it is probable that the old Ptolemaic token currency was withdrawn from circulation at the outset and replaced with a new one. In that case the initial gains must have been enormous. All these coins circulated within a limited territory only.

The West was treated quite differently. From the time of the Emperors, the minting of silver by provincials was completely forbidden there and only imperial money authorized. The Republic had issued numerous minting rights, for example in Spain; at that time a great deal of *argentum Oscense*[59] was in circulation. This all ended with the principate. As has already been mentioned in another connection, Mauretania constituted an exception, but after Gaius made it into a Roman province in AD 40 this naturally ceased and from that time onwards, aside from very small coin, there was only one type of gold or silver coinage throughout the entire West: that of the state.

In this sphere, therefore, we can observe the same relationships as we saw in the question of language, if anything writ even larger: the different treatment of East and West. In the East, where the Romans were dealing with ancient, educated, civilized countries, they shrewdly allowed a freer rein, preserving what already existed; in the West, in Africa, Spain and Gaul, on the other hand, a strict and ruthless process of centralization was implemented.

Let us take another look at small coin. Imperial small coin was the brainchild of Augustus.[60] The Republic had [MH.II, 28] actually ceased minting such coin; from the last century of the Republic we have only the *denarius* and half-*denarius*, sesterces and asses were entirely absent. The smallest coin then minted was worth half a Mark. One of the ugliest aspects of this aristocratic regime was that it was so indifferent to the interests of petty trade that it did not deem it necessary to provide the currency required. We may well imagine what extraordinary conditions would obtain in the German Empire today if there were no coins under the value of half a Mark. The coins of the municipalities were of some, albeit very scant, assistance, but there was none at all in Italy itself, where a *colonia* or *municipium civium Romanorum* did not have minting rights. The sole and inexplicable exception to this is Paestum, which minted quite a considerable amount. In Gaul, Spain and Africa, however, coins were minted, which helped to alleviate the direst shortage of small change in these regions.

Augustus set this situation to rights: roughly in the middle of his reign, when the Emperor's *tribunicia potestas* came into force,[61] he implemented a desperately needed reform of the coinage system, in a superb and exemplary manner. In the Republican era minting rights had been the prerogative of the government and its generals; the Senate and the Emperor initially issued coins side by side. Augustus now laid claim to the right of the *princeps*, not *qua* general, but *qua* Emperor, to mint all gold and silver coin, and bestowed on the Senate the right to mint copper coin.[62] There has perhaps never been small coin superior to that which followed this decree; it bears the stamp of distinction and soundness. It is made of excellent, high-quality material, a [MH.II, 29] well-struck brass alloy pertaining to all coins from the *sestertius* down to the *quadrans*. Changed conditions had rendered the minting of smaller denominations undesirable. The earlier *uncia* was discontinued. All these small coins bear the marking SC (*Senatus Consulto*). However, this is not a numismatic marking, but a public guarantee of these coins for the benefit of commerce. This SC small coin is also found at Antioch, the most important centre of the eastern coinage area. It was, of course, legal tender throughout the Empire, not just in Syria.

Besides this, under the first Emperors there was also an abundance of municipal small coinage. Self-government, and the minting rights that went with it, accrued to a large number of municipalities. It was probably no longer a question of the possession of formal sovereignty, but of special authorization by the proconsul, who, before granting permission, naturally secured the consent of the government. This permission was probably never denied in the early days of Augustus, but there was a contrasting shift in administrative approach in the latter part of his reign. In Gaul, the most important western province, a stop was first put to municipal minting rights, some time around 10 BC. An imperial small-coinage mint was established at Lyon as a replacement. Analogous African municipal mints mostly survived the reign of Tiberius. The Spanish mints were closed under Gaius and from then on the issuing of silver and gold coin was an imperial prerogative in the West.

[MH.II, 30] As matters stood in practice this was the only right course of action, since in principle there was no longer any difference between silver and copper: silver coin was *de facto* also small change. It can hardly be asserted that the municipalities were deprived of anything of value through the revoking of their minting rights. Given the restricted circulation of this coin (which was all that municipal small coin had), it was not to their advantage, in fact it was merely a form of lending among local inhabitants, similar to the promissory notes of Italian cooperative banks in modern times, which were quite absurd from the national economic standpoint.

In the East, the situation was naturally of a different complexion. In the locations mentioned earlier there was silver minting and hence also copper minting. This did not disappear there for centuries, until the second half of the third century; in Constantine's state, regenerated after a period of deep decay, all the coinage of the Empire was imperial, without exception.

There remains a final word to be said on the nature of minting. Caesar's coinage system was based on bimetallism, i.e. on the setting of a standard correlation between gold and silver by law. In the preceding period this had probably been 1:10. Caesar established a ratio of 1:12 and based his coin issues on this, whereby 1 gold *denarius aureus* was equivalent to 25 silver *denarii*, or 100 sesterces, or 400 asses. This realistic ratio seems, indeed, to have persisted for a considerable period without substantial or lasting fluctuations. [MH.II, 31] The kind of disruption experienced in the [sc. late] Middle Ages following the discovery of America, or, in more recent times, following the opening up first of Australian and Californian gold deposits and then the silver mines of America, did not occur, despite the fact that then, too, gold deposits were discovered in Dalmatia[63] and unleashed a rush similar to the Californian one. It soon petered out, however, and made no lasting impact on the standard correlations of precious metals. Nevertheless, we can find significant alterations in the minting of coins which permit us to draw conclusions about the character of successive governments.

The correlation of 1:12 persisted from the time of Caesar and Augustus up to that of Nero.[64] From Nero until Trajan it was 1:10.3 and from Trajan to Septimius Severus 1:9.3. This had less to do with a change in metal standards than with a curtailment of minting activity: the government made a profit on silver. Assuming a standard correlation of 1:12, a high profit could be achieved by minting only 9 *denarii* to the aureus instead of 10. What evolved, therefore, was a concealed, but nonetheless definite, monometallism in which silver coin gradually became a larger form of small change that no longer corresponded to its true value. A similar correlation obtained as nowadays in the German Empire between the Taler and Mark coins on the one hand and gold coinage on the other. In ancient imperial Rome bimetallism resulted in out-and-out bankruptcy, despite the fact that if ever there was a fertile ground for bimetallism then Rome provided it. [MH.II, 32] If it ever had a chance of being implemented anywhere, it was there and at that time. Such favourable conditions never arose again – first, there were no rival gold-producers in the entire world and, second, Rome presided over a vast territory encompassing the entire civilized world and ruled by a single government. And yet even here bimetallism brought about bankruptcy, albeit in an embarrassed, concealed form. This notwithstanding, it is unmistakable that the relative prosperity enjoyed in the Empire by and large partly found its expression in, and partly derived from, the superb coins provided to the nation by the Emperor.

There were, however, changes in the carat-value of gold coinage. Caesar minted gold at 40 pieces to the pound and this persisted until the time of Claudius. Under Nero, to be precise after the fall of Seneca and Burrus in AD 62, the carat-value of gold coins was substantially debased, with 45 coins minted to the pound. Later, Vespasian had to combat a serious cash shortage for which not he but his pre-decessors were responsible. Titus's reign was too short to bring about decisive reforms. Domitian, however, in other respects so ill-famed, but whose provincial administration was entirely praiseworthy, minted superior coins of high carat-value. The two great military Emperors, Trajan and Severus, again debased the coinage —Trajan the gold, Severus the silver. The fresh laurel leaves added by these Emperors to the wilted wreath of Roman military fame cost money, [MH.II, 33] after all. Following a brief improvement under Hadrian and numerous fluctuations under the later Emperors, a rapid and unstoppable process of decline set in from the third century, from Caracalla onwards. As a result of a palpable lack of gold reserves, gold coins were minted in increasingly debased form and the entire system of gold coinage was utterly ruined.

221

As regards silver coinage, its minting likewise deteriorated under Nero[65] analogously to that of gold. At first 84 were minted to every pound of silver and then 96. The natural consequence of this was that the old coins of full weight disappeared from circulation, whereas the lighter ones remained in circulation until much later periods, similar to the light-weight *denarii* which Mark Antony had had struck during the fiscal shortages of the civil war.[66] In silver there was no reduction in standard after Nero, but a fresh evil erupted: the increasing alloying of silver with base metals. It was the privilege of the mint in good times to use pure unalloyed metals for gold and silver coin. From Vitellius onwards this debasing of the material by alloying was palpable and from his time onwards each of the military Emperors was more culpable than the last in this respect. In the course of time a fifth of the mass became copper, a quarter under Marcus. From the time of Severus onwards one can scarcely speak of alloying, rather of a cessation of silver minting. When new, the pieces still looked like silver, but the silver content now varied from as little as 10 to 20 per cent. This negligible admixture of silver made these coins virtually baser and of less value than real copper coins. Since they purported to be silver coin their format was small and the quantity of metal obtained was worth less than in the case of copper coin. This ultimately placed [MH.II, 34] copper coins at a premium.

Hand in hand with this debasement of the coinage went the embezzlement of precious metals on a large scale by the mint staff. Since the alloy ratios fluctuated and were not fixed, one can imagine the free rein they had for fraud. Officials might claim for 10 per cent silver in manufacture and use only 2 per cent, thus making a huge profit at the public expense. Aurelian attempted to bring this abuse under control, unleashing perhaps the most extraordinary civil war there has ever been in the history of the world: a rebellion by the staff of the mint in which 7,000 people are said to have been killed in Rome alone.[67]

Coin hoards invariably illustrate the situation of coinage. There is naturally a preference for burying the best that is available, hence gold first, then silver. In good times copper rarely finds its way into the ground, and only then sporadically and more by chance. For the third century, however, there is always a preponderance of copper in hoard finds; in one hoard, for example, 30,000 copper coins were found and only 6 gold pieces – these were simply unobtainable. From the third century onwards copper coins retained a relatively superior standard because, as we have seen, the Senate, which minted them, did not keep pace with the Emperor in the debasement of the coinage. Material and minting quality alike thus adhered to time-honoured traditions until the time of Heliogabalus (218–22). From then on, however, the rot set in even here and superior alloys and quality minting disappeared.

[MH.II, 35] From the third century coinage was in an unparalleled state of disarray.[68] Crucially, however, despite some fluctuations, minting was largely of good quality. Gold coins were very rare and quite unequal. From this time on we know nothing at all about the coin standard; it apparently ceased to exist. Gold coin *de facto* disappeared from circulation and was only used for transactions in ingot form, i.e. it now existed only for large-scale banking transactions. Up to the third century there had been only one sort of gold money, the *denarius aureus*. From the time of Valerian we can also find smaller gold coins, particularly the *trientes aurei*.

The earlier problem caused, despite fluctuations in standard, by the parallel existence of gold and silver coin can probably largely be resolved by reflecting that up to the third century both gold and silver were accepted by government coffers as payment. This to some extent maintained an equilibrium. Naturally the public preferred to pay in the sort of coin that was most advantageous to it, which led to an amassing of silver and copper in state coffers and a gradual phasing out of gold. If metal money were at a premium in our society in relation to paper, then naturally all payments into state coffers would be made in paper money, which they would be obliged to accept.

In order to alleviate this state of affairs, the government ordered the payment of taxes in gold from the third century onwards. Those smaller gold coins were probably minted in order to facilitate [MH.II, 36] the payment in gold of taxes in smaller sums. At the same time the soldiers' donatives and other treasury expenses were ordered to be paid in gold. Or, at least, it was expressly stated whether payment was to be made in gold or silver. We have, for example, a remarkable letter[69] dating from the time of the Emperor Gordian (AD 242). A notable from Gaul had won the favour of the governor of Gaul by successfully contesting a complaint to be brought against him; in return he was appointed a military tribune and received an annual income of 25,000 sesterces in gold. In the case of New Year's gifts, it was specifically stated how much was to be disbursed in gold, how much in silver and how much in copper.[70] The procedure was much more rigorous in the case of payments to the state. This naturally dealt the death blow to the old, high-carat, quality coins; they disappeared from circulation completely. Typical is the expression *follis* (sack) which began to become customary in the third century.[71] Copper was brought into the service of large-scale commerce by filling great sacks with it; notwithstanding its inconvenience, payment was accepted in sacks of 1,000 *denarii*, which were kept in circulation, similar to the rolls of coins issued by banks.

This flood of valueless small change persisted throughout the third century. No one seriously intervened to deal with it. The greatest achievement of the Diocletianic–Constantinian reform was its serious and successful attempt to address this scourge. Aurelian did not lay an axe to the [MH.II, 37] root of the evil, he merely took action against fraud.

It is Missong in Vienna[72] whom we have to thank for the most recent detailed research into this situation. Constantine was hitherto regarded as the sole reformer, but it is now clear that the main credit should go to Diocletian. There was regular minting from 290 onwards. Sixty pieces of gold were struck to the pound, and 96 to the pound in silver. The coins bear the Greek letter Xi as a mark of value [=60]. In the confusion following Diocletian's abdication another period of fluctuations set in, but from Constantine onwards reform continued. Throughout the entire Byzantine period 72 pieces were struck to the pound, so that Roman gold dominated the world market into much later times.

One important measure made this last even longer, and to a certain extent made coining irrelevant: gold was henceforth accepted by the state purse not according to face value, but according to weight, making a pound ingot as good as 72 pieces. This also had a substantial effect on private commerce. In consequence of this measure the state had no interest in stinting on gold content and minting debased coins, since from now on it made no profit thereby.

Little in the way of silver coin was struck in the Constantinian and later periods. By this time it was of secondary interest, since international commerce now focused exclusively on gold. Token money had not been completely eradicated, and the sacks of copper also persisted, but people liable for tax had to pay in gold. In private commerce the manner of payment would be stipulated. The differential rate remained, but now gold was also [MH.II, 38] available. Of all the innovations of the era of Diocletian and Constantine this restoration of an orderly system of coinage was the most palpable and perhaps most important, since it most affected the weal and woe of millions.

This question has been dealt with in some detail because it is more important than what people commonly call history. We now turn to public finance – first and foremost the manner in which taxes were imposed.[73] Here, too, we shall go back to the period of the first Emperors, which we have already examined.

In the early imperial period tax legislation represented a remarkable curb on the principate. The Emperor did not have the right to impose taxes. Augustus introduced a novelty in the shape of a right of confiscation of sorts imposed on testaments, known as the *caduca*, whereby unmarried and childless persons (*caelibes et orbi*) did not have equal rights of inheritance with married men and heads of families; their portions went partly to the *aerarium populi Romani*.[74] The state must have acquired substantial sums in this manner. It is highly characteristic that this fresh burden on the public arose as a result of the *Lex Julia* and the *Lex Papia Poppea*, i.e. decisions of the People, so that the machinery of the assembly was brought into motion again to pass them.[75] The law met with vigorous opposition.[76]

Much the same occurred in AD 6 and 7 in connection with the differential inheritance tax brought about by the *aerarium militare*, which imposed a 5 per cent land tax on Roman citizens, but not on non-citizens.[77] [MH.II, 39] Since this was opposed by the public and the Senate alike, Augustus threatened to reimpose the *tributum*, the earlier land tax. In fact, the Roman citizen was not exempt from taxes as such; the law provided for the levying of rates on land; to a certain extent this had the character of enforced loans at irregular intervals;[78] in better times these might be paid back. Augustus eventually managed to push the inheritance tax law through, but did not dare propose this measure before the Senate and the assemblies. Instead, in this one isolated case he resorted to the *acta Caesaris*, as Antony had once done, declaring that a provision to this effect had been found among the papers of Caesar[79] and thus had the force of law. Not even Augustus, therefore, claimed for himself a general right of determination.

There was no authority empowered to impose taxes in Rome at all. This is also confirmed *a posteriori*: hardly any new taxes came about: the 2.5 per cent tax (*quadragesima litium*) imposed by Gaius[80] on lawsuits was only a provisional measure, while the famous urine duty of Vespasian[81] is something quite different. He was taxing the right of fullers to draw off urine from public lavatories, which were already public property.[82]

The situation was different in the case of provincial tribute; it might be added, however, before we go on to examine this, that Caracalla, the most fiscally minded of all the Emperors, manipulated inheritance tax, which as we have seen applied only to the *cives Romani*, but he did not manipulate provincial tribute. In order to increase the [MH.II, 40] revenue from inheritance tax, for example, he granted Roman civic rights to wealthy people *en masse* and also raised the tax rate from 5 to 10 per cent.[83] These manipulations were ill-suited to the overall character of the Roman tax system. The hallmark of the period from Augustus to Diocletian was that there was no change in rates of taxation – a stability unparalleled in any other period of history, in complete contrast to the reforms of Diocletian and Constantine, which introduced variable scales of taxation.

Equally unparalleled, and connected with the permanence in taxation levels, was the permanent establishment of an army, as already touched on earlier, which during the first centuries from Augustus onwards scarcely grew on a scale to keep pace with the size of the population. It increased from twenty-five to a mere thirty-three legions. The fundamental tenet of the Roman tax system was that neither the Emperor nor the Senate were empowered to impose new taxes, that this power did not, in fact, exist at all in the Roman Empire.

Provincial taxes[84] were dealt with differently. We know, for example, that after his accession Galba increased the tribute[85] of those municipalities which had supported the opposing party – a spiteful, if not illegal, measure within the Emperor's sphere of competence. Vespasian inherited a bankrupt Empire and abolished this measure, restoring the old order. Indeed, he went further: it is probably beyond doubt that from as early as Augustus up to the time of his reign —quite apart from the more exorbitant extravagances perpetrated by the bad

Emperors – the state [MH.II, 41] had suffered from chronic deficits and that regular revenues were never sufficient to cover regular expenditure.[86] In this respect Vespasian restored order, perhaps his most beneficial act for the good of the state; he restored the balance of payments, albeit by a marked increase in, sometimes even a doubling, of provincial taxes, as Suetonius[87] reports. Here, too, political retribution against supporters of the opposing party may have been a factor, but by and large the measure arose from the prudent objective of thoroughly reordering finances.

Land tax was constantly increased. This involved provincials and provincial land which, under a strict interpretation of ancient Roman statutes, was the property of the Roman state.[88] These increases were thus a purely administrative measure; the Assembly was not consulted. They were probably put into effect by the Senate in the senatorial provinces and by the Emperor in the imperial ones. As we know, the richest provinces, which were at the same time the most important ones – Gaul, Egypt and Syria – were under imperial control. Land tax was the main source of revenue, but not the only one.

Overall, we unfortunately have only a very faint idea of the tax situation in the Roman Empire: it was probably heterogeneous rather than uniform. This heterogeneity stems from the period before these territories were incorporated into the Empire; they had developed over the course of time and their systems were interfered with as little as possible. These are the crucial aspects, about which [MH.II, 42] we unfortunately know so little – for, after all, what do we know about a state if we know nothing about its system of revenues! Its outgoings[89] were obvious; we can reconstruct with some accuracy how they were distributed among the army, public building and other major works of the state.

Essentially, therefore, it was the provinces which had to bear the brunt of Roman state expenditure. Their taxation was based on the *tributum*, which was a *tributum soli*, a land tax, on the one hand, and a *tributum capitis*, a personal tax, on the other. Roman land, i.e. all of Italy and all non-Italian municipalities with Italian rights, was exempt from land tax;[90] only provincial land was taxed. Roman citizenship applied to the person and did not exempt the land; if, therefore, a Roman citizen owned landed property in the provinces he was liable for tax on it. It was, and remained, *ager stipendiarius*, regardless of who owned it. The *coloniae civium Romanorum*, on the other hand, were to enjoy the same liberties as Italy. If, therefore, a municipality was granted Roman civic rights, its *ager* thereby became exempt from taxation. Later, when the granting of civic rights extended to the provinces, it was exceptional for Italian rights to include tax exemption, for this would have done away with too many sources of revenue.

The pandects provide us with two interesting cases, one affirming, the other negating this. A dispute arose with regard to Caesarea in Palestine as to whether or not release from the *tributum capitis* also entailed release from the *tributum soli*.

In this case the answer was in the affirmative. When, on the other hand, Caracalla made [MH.II, 43] the city of Antioch a *colonia*, this was done *salvis tributis*, i.e. Antioch continued to be liable for taxation.[91] All this was quite in keeping with this, the most fiscally minded of all the Emperors. Later, Diocletian changed all this; he established a completely different tax system, of which we shall be hearing more later.

It is not clear whether land tax was thought of as a tax or as an annual rent. The Republic distinguished between *ager vectigalis*, which the state owned and drew rent from, and *ager tributarius*, which the state taxed, but did not own. This distinction receded more and more during the imperial period, but did not disappear entirely. The ancient notion, whereby the state claimed a right of ownership on all the land of its subjects, was frightful and gave way during the imperial age to a more humane notion. Hence the distinction between *ager vectigalis* and *ager tributarius* likewise became unimportant. As we have seen, however, it was not allowed to lapse entirely – nor could it be allowed to do so, for the institution of military colonies continued to exist. Since *ager privatus civis Romani* (the private estate of a Roman citizen) was guaranteed, the state had to have the use of provincial land for the purposes of military colonization. Although by the time of the Emperors compensation was given in such cases, this fell far short of the full value of the land. As late as under Gaius the ownership rights of the provincials was not recognized and only very meagre compensation was assessed. Use of this land was regarded not as expropriation, but as the exercise of sovereignty. Nonetheless, in the course of time the *fundus vectigalis* diminished and the *fundus tributarius* increased.

[MH.II, 44] Let us now examine the levying of taxes.[92] The land was surveyed and valued and the tax assessed accordingly.[93] This may have been implemented according to the Egyptian model, where a similar system had been perfected from the most ancient times. Thus there was a fixed revenue for each *iugerum*. It is unfortunately impossible to give specific figures, most important and interesting though this would be, as we possess too few data on these matters. It appears that revenues may have been paid either in kind or as a money payment, either one-fifth or one-seventh of total returns, or a fixed sum of money. These two forms of revenue existed side by side, so that, for example, a monetary revenue will probably have been imposed on vineyards, whereas payment in kind was frequently demanded from arable landholdings. It will be seen that the tax was neither negligible nor exorbitant. The sum was fixed once and for all when the province was established. Augustus had this done for the entire Empire, for example by Drusus and Germanicus in Gaul, and whenever new provinces were added they were surveyed and valued. The well-known, albeit incorrectly dated[94] but essentially correct, reference in St Luke's Gospel fits into this picture: when Palestine was incorporated into the Roman Empire, a census was carried out, i.e.

it was surveyed and valued with a view to incorporating it into the Roman tax system.

This census, unalterable and carried out once and for all, made the tax burden light, in a certain sense, over the long term. Naturally, a potential new buyer would take account of such a well-known and unalterable tax in his calculations; it represented no more than a confiscation of the [MH.II, 45] property of the first owner at the time the tax was introduced. In Britain, for example, the land tax could even be paid off. Minor changes did, of course, occur. If, for example, the manner of cultivation of a landholding changed – if arable land became a vineyard, or pasture was turned into arable land – then the tax also changed. By and large, however, it was unalterable; it is well known, for example, that Tiberius, on being presented by an over-enthusiastic provincial governor with a larger annual sum than should have been levied, was displeased and uttered that well known saying of the master to his shepherd, that he should shear the sheep, not flay them.[95]

Land tax, therefore, was a fixed annual rent drawn by the state. In later times the land register was revised every fifteen years. This measure can be traced back to Hadrian,[96] but in his reign it was intended to exert a substantial effect on the auditing of the tax coffers, thereby definitively putting an end to illicit tax demands. Diocletian then had this revision developed into a tax scale; he had tax assessments revised and, where possible, increased every fifteen years.[97] If, prior to his time, we frequently encounter officials concerned with taking the census, this was probably essentially related to the drawing up of conscription lists, not to taxation. It should not be forgotten that up to the time of Diocletian the hallmark of financial administration was its fixed character, its permanence, whereas the principle of Diocletian's reform was its unfixed character, its potential for revision. Diocletian ordered valuations and demanded an annually fluctuating percentual tax rate from every [MH.II, 46] appraised unit of 1,000, at the discretion and according to the needs of the government. This may be regarded as a step forward in the art of taxation, but at all events it represents a major about-turn in policy.

Besides these land taxes, probably as a supplementary rate by way of taxing non-landowners, i.e. the taxation of movable assets, there was a personal tax, a *tributum capitis*. This tax is, indeed, to be construed as such and not as a poll-tax as the name might suggest, i.e. it was not levied per capita at a flat rate, regardless of the capacity to pay. Rather, as Appian[98] documents for Syria and Cilicia, it will have been a percentual capital tax, affecting chiefly merchants and towns. There was no tax on buildings in towns as a complement to the rural land tax.

At the present time it is beyond the scope of our knowledge to answer the question as to how the assessment of capital in the cities was carried out. There will, however, have been a labour tax for persons who had no liquid taxable assets, and this will have been more akin to a poll-tax. Unfortunately, however, our insight into this is very vague and unclear. The term *tributum* generally encompasses both land and personal tax, from which the Roman citizen was exempt, provided he owned no taxable provincial landed property. [MH.II, 47] He never paid *tributum capitis*.

Diocletian[99] overturned this entire system and declared all subjects, without exception, liable for tax. Up to his time there had been a substitute of sorts for the direct taxation of Roman citizens, in the 5 per cent estate duty introduced by Augustus as a *privilegium odiosum* and the 1 per cent auction tax (4 per cent in the case of slave auctions). This had not applied in the provinces and must have brought in quite considerable sums. We shall be returning to this in more detail later. Here, by way of summing up, it remains only to emphasize that up to the time of Diocletian land tax was not levied everywhere, but only on provincial land, and was fixed, whereas Diocletian made this tax universal and liable to fluctuate. Up to his reign the land-tax system had had a great deal in common with the hereditary tenancies of major landowners nowadays, although we must be on our guard against interpreting the concept of 'fixed taxes' as strictly as in the case of such hereditary tenancies. The state, nonetheless, retained a claim on the right of ownership, so that tax increases were not ruled out as such. Indeed, particularly in the third century, when they were frequent, these did occur, and were inevitable in that age of coin debasement, since the returns from taxes paid in steadily devaluing coin would otherwise have become negligible.

We are not able to state precisely how, where and when these increases occurred. [MH.II, 48] Our data on this are too scant. At all events these increases, when they did occur, were perceived as an injustice and were not infrequently used as a means of retaliation against political enemies. As has already been mentioned, Diocletian abolished the distinction between Italy and the provinces, had landed property assessed entirely in cash and imposed a 1, 2 or 3 per cent tax on it, as required. Here, therefore, we have the tax scale in its clearest form, as in our own time. We possess detailed information about this procedure in the case of Gaul under Julian.[100] In essence, it was our modern-day tax system and it cannot be denied that it was much more rational and represented a step forward from the point of view of the state. The state now had more room for manoeuvre and was, in particular, able to meet military expenditure as required without being condemned to absolute inaction by a shortage of funds, as had so often been the case previously.

As has already been stated, the *vectigal* (rent paid on state-owned land) also concealed a capital tax; where there was no capital, it was a head tax. In Syria and Asia, for example, a 1 per cent property tax was paid in the towns, but there were a number of other sources of revenue in addition to this. The inheritance tax that we have already mentioned was levied as *vicesima*, i.e. at 5 per cent. Smaller inherited sums, as well as the immediate next of kin, that is the son inheriting from the father, were exempt. The tax applied both to the substantial intestate legacies of collateral relatives and to distant testamentary heirs and must have brought in not inconsiderable sums.

[MH.II, 49] Nowadays customs duties rank first among taxes on commerce. In antiquity this and the entire system of indirect taxation[101] was still relatively undeveloped; the cumbersome nature of the machinery and the indolence of officials prevented it. In most cases, therefore, the leasing of customs collecting was resorted to, which proved ruinous both for the taxpayer and the state. This type of taxation was thus less practised, although not neglected entirely. The Roman Empire did not constitute a homogeneous customs zone; it would have brought in little anyway, since trade with peoples living beyond its frontiers was in most cases undeveloped. The Empire consisted of individual customs zones which had developed historically and in which some frontier customs duties and some interterritorial duties were levied, both for imports and exports.[102] In Strabo[103] we find an interesting discussion of whether it would be expedient to make Britain a province; the answer was that it would be disadvantageous in terms of taxation policy and financial interests, on account of the forfeited import and export duties. The four Gallic provinces with Raetia and *Noricum* constituted such a customs zone. All imports and exports here paid the so-called *quadragesima Galliarum*, i.e. 2½ per cent. In other provinces a *quinquagesima*, i.e. 2 per cent, was levied. Overall, therefore, this was a very moderate duty.

Often duty was not the same for all goods and a different percentage was levied; in the case of luxury goods this could amount to 12 per cent or more. The paradigm and model for this was naturally [MH.II, 50] provided by Egypt, which likewise constituted a separate customs zone. Pliny reports that in Egypt the annual customs revenue for pearls alone, which must, of course have been taxed at a high rate, amounted to 100 million sesterces, i.e. 20 million Marks.[104] One can see from this example that quite considerable sums flowed into the coffers from these duties.

It is not known whether this customs duty system was implemented universally. We possess a remarkable bilingual inscription from Palmyra[105] about the customs duties there. It would seem that they were supervised by the imperial government, but that customs duty was levied for the benefit of a number of cities. A special rate in Africa is known, whereby duty was not calculated according to value, but a remarkably low fixed rate was levied, for example 1½ *denarii* for a horse and 1 *denarius* for an ox.[106] Generally speaking, until the time of Diocletian the imperial revenue from customs duties was low. In his reign these, too, were greatly increased; from then on the average rate seems to have been an *octava*, i.e. 12½ per cent, which certainly contrasts markedly with the *quadragesima* and the *quinquagesima*.

An excise tax is mentioned here and there, for example one for Rome under

Gaius, but does not seem to have been a general arrangement, since trade within customs zones was in general probably exempt from state taxes. It is likely, on the other hand, that the municipalities availed themselves of this source of tax, just as the *octroi* continues today [MH.II, 51] to be the main source of income, for example, of Paris.[107] The auctions taxed at 1 per cent by Augustus for the benefit of the *aerarium militare* and the sale of slaves, which he taxed at 4 per cent, have already been mentioned.

In addition to these there were a few other revenues which we should touch on. First the domains of the Emperor.[108] It should be remembered that, strictly speaking, they do not fall into this category, since they were the property of a private citizen. Although the *populus Romanus* and the Emperor were parallel legal entities, the property of the Emperor and that of the Roman people remained separate. In the days of the Republic the property of the *populus Romanus* had been quite substantial – a tenth share of the grain produced and a fifth of the wine brought in major revenues from the *ager publicus*. By this time, however, this revenue had largely disappeared; there were probably still *viae publicae populi Romani* (roads belonging to the Roman people), but not much that brought in earnings. The imperial domains, on the other hand, were significant and constantly expanding and, since the *de facto* separation of state and imperial revenues had never been rigid despite the legal distinction between the two, they must be mentioned here and enumerated among the revenues accruing to the state by direct or indirect means. *Vectigal* and imperial domains rank first among these.

Gifts likewise played a by no means inconsiderable role in the budget at that time,[109] though not as important as that of the imperial estates. These took two forms. The origins of the *aurum coronarium*[110] derive from the Republican era. By that time it was already the custom for municipalities which had been [MH.II, 52] saved from their enemies to present a victorious general with a gold wreath, which in later times had to weigh a certain number of pounds.[111] In the time of Augustus this custom was then extended, so that all cities of the Empire had to donate such wreaths to the *imperator*, i.e. the Emperor, after a major victory. This later developed into a quite regular source of revenue[112] and by the third century had become liable to serious malpractice and a very burdensome tax.

Another already ancient and very widespread custom was the donation of greater or smaller sums to highly esteemed persons in wills. It became practically the fashion under Augustus for every loyal citizen to leave something to the Emperor. The sum of these Augustan legacies amounted to 1,400 million sesterces, i.e. 300 million Marks.[113] Later, under the pressure of mounting imperial tyranny, the income of Emperors from these semi-voluntary bequests increased even more significantly and was even to some extent fixed by law: freedmen were obliged to bequeath something to their *patronus*. Anyone aware of the hordes of imperial freedmen who existed and of the size of the fortunes they were able to amass, rightly or wrongly, will be able to form some idea of the sums that flowed into the Emperor's coffers in this way. Nero decreed that when a *primipilus* had achieved the highest possible civil rank and died without bequeathing anything to the Emperor, [MH.II, 53] his will was to be rendered void as that of an ungrateful man. Under Nero this still attracted attention as an irregularity, but later it became a standard element of imperial revenue.

The New Year's gifts will have been more of an expenditure than an income. Although Augustus regularly received a small donation, he himself donated four times as much in return.

War booty[114] was negligible in the imperial age compared to that of the Republic. The conquest of Gaul and Egypt had enriched the state; the conquests of the imperial age, in contrast, brought little profit and indeed not infrequently resulted in losses, as has already been stated earlier in connection with Britain. The acquisition of Dacia, on the other hand, meant the acquisition of important gold mines for the state. In general, however, wars incurred increased expenditure and in general the rule of the Emperors was peaceful.

Initially there was not much in the way of fines.[115] Then came the *caduca*;[116] fines for being unmarried and childless also flowed into the imperial coffers.[117] With the growth of Christianity and its different, more favourable outlook on celibacy, the fine for celibacy disappeared.[118] An ancient principle of Roman law was that capital punishment entailed the confiscation of the condemned person's fortune.[119] This was fiscally exploited by the Emperors from Tiberius onwards, which had not been done under the Republic, whatever its other iniquities had been. Tendentious actions for treasonable defamation [MH.II, 54] were unknown until the imperial age, particularly under Tiberius and Nero. In fact the goods of the condemned flowed into the coffers of the *populus Romanus*, but gradually the *fiscus Caesaris* came to replace the *aerarium populi*. We are unable to say what the state received in terms of actual sums; it is impossible to give specific figures as these are so vague, and it is equally impossible to either prove or refute them, so what is the point of giving them?

There were no monopolies in the legal sense.[120] The Emperor did, admittedly, annex the cinnabar mines in Spain[121] and, since there was practically no competitor, thereby effectively acquired the monopoly for cinnabar. There was no preclusion of competition by law, however.[122] Likewise with gold and silver mines: the state did, indeed, seek to gain possession of these, but not as a royal prerogative. It was not until later that institutions other than the state were forbidden to sell certain goods.[123]

Let us turn to the outgoings of the Empire. By far the greater proportion of these related to the military, the field of activity of the *imperator*.[124] We have quite an apt analogy for this in the modern imperial budget of the German Empire, where military activity likewise accounts for the lion's share of expenditure. The generally prevailing view that all military expenditure in the Roman Empire was the responsibility of the state is incorrect. The very fact that no military units at all were stationed in the senatorial provinces [MH.II, 55] refutes this. Even in the imperial provinces, however, the imperial army was evidently insufficient. We ought rather, therefore, to assume from the outset (and as we know more, this is confirmed in an increasing number of cases) that part of the burden for defence rested on the shoulders of the municipalities. Towns had to maintain their walls and to raise their own militias. This was chiefly the case, of course, in the case of frontier territories where no military were stationed, or of municipalities exposed to attack for some other reason. The Helvetians, for example, maintained a fort with its own garrison as security against invasion by Germanic tribes.[125] The town of Amida, now Diyarbakir, in the Roman province of Syria, looked after its own defence against the Parthians.[126] And these were municipalities located in provinces occupied by large numbers of troops; how much more will this obligation for self-help have devolved on other towns? We know, for example, that Baetica in southern Spain had to defend itself against Lusitanian bandits from the Sierra Morena: the surviving municipal charter stipulates that its mayors were granted the rights of a military tribune when mobilizing the urban militia.[127] The same will have applied to the Near East, which was no more peaceful or secure for persons and property then than it is today. Although other causes were also involved, the decline of the municipalities was brought about in no small measure by this evidence of poverty, which the great military state admitted by being unable to provide fully for the security of its citizens. Of course Italy itself lived in complete peace until well into the third century, and military expenditure by the municipalities [MH.II, 56] was something quite unknown there; this is why we hear so little about it from literary texts.

C) THE ARMY

The numerical strength of the army was highly stable. Augustus fixed it at twenty-five legions; there were twenty-five to twenty-six of them until the time of Trajan, who increased their number to thirty.[128] This persisted until Severus, who created three new legions; indicative enough of their purpose is the fact that they were named the First, Second and Third 'Parthian'. Considering the growth of the Empire after Augustus – with the additional conquests of England, Dacia and the territories east of the Euphrates, that is the three great frontier bulwarks of the North Sea, the Danube and the Euphrates – it may well be assumed that the thirty-three legions under Severus were less adequate than the twenty-five had been under Augustus.

Assuming a legion to comprise 5,300 men (6,000 is at all events too high) and bearing in mind that, given what was, after all, in general the lax economy of the Empire, normal levels were not always maintained, thirty legions would not amount to many more than 150,000 legionaries. This represented the personal military service imposed on the *civis Romanus* in lieu of taxes. These troops were supplied for the most part by Italy in the early imperial age under Augustus and Tiberius; later, with the rapidly growing spread of citizenship in the West, Sicily was added first, but played no major role in recruitment, since it was depopulated, destitute and ravaged as a result of the crisis. Next came Narbonensian Gaul; Vespasian bestowed Latin rights[129] on all Spain, which was soon granted full Roman rights. This extension of Roman citizenship [MH.II, 57] to the entire civilized West, inclusive of Africa with Carthage and Utica, since the time of Caesar, opened up all these regions to legionary conscription, which brought about a steady decrease in Italians in the legions. Inscriptions from the Rhine are instructive about the legionaries' places of birth. Later the Danube provinces became additional regions supplying legionaries. The Pannonians were coarse, but good soldier material and were heavily represented in the legions, particularly after the Marcomannic War. Although municipalities here lacked Roman citizenship, a pragmatic approach was later taken: the Emperor Marcus awarded citizenship to those individuals who joined up. The East was far less involved in military service than the West, but provided most of the taxation revenue. Egypt, for example, provided virtually no troops apart from some for the fleet, but how it was taxed!

Aside from legionaries there were other contingents – the *alae et cohortes* established by Augustus for non-legionaries.[130] In principle every inhabitant of the Empire was liable for military service, but in practice we find diverse nationalities represented here and in particular a preponderance of Germans. The Batavians, for example, were exempt from taxes, but subject to heavy recruitment demands.[131] We do not know the exact figures relating to the numerical strength of these troops, which is a distressing gap in our knowledge. Some of them were attached to the legions as so-called auxiliaries and then placed under the legate in command of the legion. We must, therefore, estimate a legion in practical terms [MH.II, 58] not at 5,000, but at 8,000–10,000 men, inclusive of auxiliary troops. There were also, however, detachments consisting solely of *alae et cohortes*. The sole relatively reliable reference to the strength of troops that we possess is in Tacitus,[132] who states that this part of the army was not much fewer in number than the legions. This is probably true. In better times, at least, auxiliary troops will no longer have been taken into service as Roman citizens. This brings us to a total strength of both types of troops of roughly 300,000 men.

To these were added the Italian troops: the Guard with its appendages the *cohortes urbanae* (urban guard) and the *vigiles* (fire brigade).[133] The Praetorians had nine to ten cohorts of 1,000 men each; the *cohortes urbanae* approximately half that number, although we now know that these were not only stationed in Rome, but also separately in Lyon and Carthage. The vigiles comprised seven cohorts of 1,200 men each.

We lack any information whatsoever about the fleet.[134] It was stationed in two centres, one to the east, one to the west, at Ravenna and Misenum.[135] If surviving monuments are any indication, the latter was a considerably stronger force. Individual detachments were stationed in Sardinia, Ostia, southern Gaul and elsewhere. We know nothing about the numbers involved. Large numbers of troops [MH.II, 59] were not left in one place in the later imperial age; double camps for two legions disappeared and one legion at most was left in one place. All told, we might allow for 20,000 men in the fleet. This produces a figure of 50,000–60,000 men for Rome and Italy together, and a total figure for the state armed forces of 350,000–400,000 men – a very small number in relation to the enormous size of the Empire and its huge military expenditure. Hence we also observe the regular phenomenon of wars being started with insufficient forces. Those troops that happened to be stationed nearest were obliged to make the first thrust until succour arrived from a distance; it was only the superlative technical training and discipline of the legionaries that regularly brought eventual victory.

Examining military affairs from the fiscal point of view, the principal item was soldiers' pay. Caesar had fixed this at 225 *denarii*, the equivalent of 200 Marks – a sum that was probably appropriate in its day and was retained unaltered until Domitian. The latter increased it to 300 *denarii* (260 Marks).[136] This led to a considerable shortage of funds and the *aerarium* fell into disarray. There were no further increases after this. The debasement of coins did not affect soldiers, since their pay was disbursed in gold. These calculations are superficial, nonetheless, since soldiers' pay was [MH.II, 60] not uniform: there were distinctions between different types of troops. The Praetorians[137] received higher pay than the legionaries, the *alae et cohortes*, and particularly the fleet, lower pay. Assuming that the above effective numbers are correct, this gives an annual budget of 100–130 million Marks for troops' pay. By modern standards this is a modest sum, but it was not the sole item of expenditure; it was augmented by many others for which we are no longer able to ascertain the figures – in the first instance supplies, and then weapons.

Responsibility for provisioning soldiers, which had devolved on to the individual in the Republican era and had to be defrayed by him, was assumed by the state in the imperial age. The state provided everything: grain, arms and all equipment, so that the pay received by the soldier could be saved and accumulated. The imperial age thus witnessed the growth of military savings banks on a large scale.[138] Military buildings, war machines, buildings and equipment needed for the fleets were likewise all drains on state expenditure. However, these did not amount to quite as much as one might *a priori* assume, since the system of military craftsmen[139] in Rome was developed to a degree that we can scarcely imagine. Every corps had its own shoemakers, tailors, swordsmiths, etc., so that these needs of the army were met largely within the army itself. More than this, indeed, other government works – roads etc. – were built by soldiers. Nevertheless, many supplies will have been required. The costs in the event of war cannot be estimated.

[MH.II, 61] So far we have spoken only of regular outgoings, but there were also very substantial irregular ones, chiefly gifts.[140] Although called 'gifts', these became so much part of the system that they had to be given. In general, ideas about their scale are grossly overestimated. Their origin lies with Caesar, who bequeathed a gift to the soldiers in his will, as he also did to the citizens. This was distributed by Augustus,[141] who also bequeathed a gift to the soldiers. Originally, therefore, the Emperor made gifts to soldiers not as one ascending to the throne, but as the executor of his predecessor's will. According to Tacitus, the legacies bequeathed by Augustus and distributed by Tiberius[142] amounted to 12 million *denarii*, or 10 million Marks. The Praetorians certainly obtained most of this, then the legionaries; it is doubtful whether the remainder received anything.

The first Emperor who effectively bought his rulership was Claudius, by giving every Praetorian 3,000 Marks, 3,570 *denarii*, and the others less.[143] In stark and characteristic contrast to this was the gift by Vespasian, which totalled 25 *denarii*,[144] i.e. roughly 20 Marks per man – no more than a tip. Marcus, who succeeded lawfully to the throne of his adoptive father and therefore had no reason to make extraordinary donations to the soldiers, again gave every Praetorian 5,000 *denarii* and another 3,000 during his co-rule with his brother Lucius, so that every Praetorian obtained 8,000 *denarii* during his reign.[145] We possess information only about the [MH.II, 62] gifts made to the Praetorians: the other troops will probably have received less, but at least something. This entailed substantial outgoings for the state treasury.

Concerning old-age pensions for the military under the principate, it should be pointed out that this was a vital necessity. Given a period of service for the legionary of twenty years,[146] soldiers leaving the service had to be provided for. It should not be forgotten that with respect to length of service the principate made considerably higher demands than the Republic had done. In the Republic twenty years had been the maximum that could be expected of an individual under extreme circumstances and was never demanded for any length of time – this would have been a glaring *contradictio in adiecto* for an army of citizen-soldiers.

It has often been asserted that the Emperors neglected the common good of the state out of an exaggerated concern for the soldiers. This is not, in fact the case,[147] since the principate resorted to lengthening the period of service as a contingency measure in order to reduce to a minimum the number of conscripts. This provides a drastic illustration of the boundless desire for peace and hatred of war and everything connected with it that motivated the population after the century of civil war that had preceded the principate. In the second century the period of service for legionaries was increased to twenty-five years,[148] and to twenty-eight years for marines, who had always been relatively worse off and whose period of service had hitherto already been twenty-six years.[149] The Guard, who were generally privileged and pampered, had a shorter period of service. Furthermore, these terms of service of legionaries and marines were not [MH.II, 63] even strictly adhered to, at least under Augustus and Tiberius: men frequently had to serve longer in practice,[150] until the legal prolongation of the period of service just referred to. From this time onwards complaints about unlawful extensions ceased. This was probably done less out of humanity and respect for the law than in the interests of the military administration itself, which had no further use for the men. Anyone lucky enough to survive the twenty-five years – and there were relatively few of them – was simply no longer fit for service. He was close to 50 years old, since recruitment as a *tiro* took place at the age of 20, and had to be provided for as an invalid, either from injury or exertion. Since their number was not very great and was probably also restricted to Roman citizens, the burden for the state was a tolerable one. The provision for veterans introduced by Augustus, however, was by no means a sign that the soldiery dominated the principate, as it has often been interpreted. It was a vitally necessary measure; a totally exhausted man, completely alienated from civilian life by a lengthy period of service, had to receive provision for his old age. Far from being military-minded, the age of the Emperors was probably the most pacific and peace-loving era the world has ever seen across such a broad span of space and time.

[MH.II, 64] Compensation for veterans did not always consist of land.[151] What, after all, would the majority of these ageing men, unaccustomed to work in the fields, have been able to do with it? They were not the stuff of which farmers, *coloni*, could be made. Allocations of land did occur, but these were the exception. Nero settled discharged Guard troops in Puteoli and Tarentum,[152] but they were stronger and younger. We know from inscriptions[153] that Vespasian planted colonies in this way at Reate in Samnium, which was thoroughly depopulated, and that Trajan did the same in Pannonia.[154] These constitute isolated cases, however, and probably involved hand-picked men, chiefly those who had savings, the capitalists among the demobilized. There was no more mass colonization as there had been after the civil wars.

The old-age provision as such consisted of a sum of money,[155] which in the early period amounted to 3,000 *denarii* for the ordinary soldier (2,500 Marks). Caracalla raised this to 5,000 *denarii* (or 4,350 Marks). This is not a large sum, even if it was augmented by savings during the period of service (see MH.II, 60). Junior officers (centurions and *primipili*), however, received substantially more and were regarded as well-to-do in the municipalities to which they retired.

In the third century an institution whose beginnings date back much earlier began to become widespread: hereditary service.[156] Originally recruits had been obtained my means of a levy (*dilectus*); since this, however, posed difficulties, which increased as time went on, it soon became necessary to resort to other [MH.II, 65] means. Soldiers were supposed to be unmarried and for the most part were so in the early period. Given the lengthy period of service, however, and the fact that soldiers lived completely cut off from the outside world in permanent camps, this proviso was virtually impossible to maintain. Many soldiers thus had quasi-marriages, which were illegitimate under law – the women in question were called *focariae*, 'hearth women'[157] – but had to be tolerated. Indeed, they were not unwelcome for the government, since the children of soldiers born from these marriages were given preferential treatment in recruitment. However, these camp children did not belong to any particular community; they grew up with the army and were not citizens in the eyes of the law, i.e. they did not inherit the *tribus* of their fathers. They were ascribed to the *tribus Pollia* and provided superb fighting material.

This became widespread from the second century onwards. Through allocations of land, Severus Alexander did for these common-law soldier families[158] something akin to what existed until recently on the military frontier in Austria: we find frontier camps, with soldier-farmers, and hereditary military service obligatory for the son, the *miles castellanus*.[159] As the state organism floundered, it sought, in fact, to make everything hereditary and compulsory and restored a caste system in all spheres, thereby ultimately reverting to the same social institutions that had obtained at the outset. All the same, it saved the *aerarium* money, since the costs incurred by these soldiers were nominal. This institution, which will also have to be examined in another context, is mentioned because of its relevance to the financial system.

D) ADMINISTRATION

There was not actually much else in the way of regular [MH.II, 66] expenditure[160] for the state. The imperial household was included in this, however, since the coffers of the Empire and of the Emperor were practically one. Here, we are obliged to put aside modern conceptions according to which the private expenditure of the ruler is strictly separate from state expenditure. All the Emperor's expenditure figured as state expenditure. *Aerarium* and *fiscus*, however, were not one and the same. The *fiscus* was not identical with the imperial privy purse; military expenditure, for example, devolved on the *fiscus*.

We are inclined to make too much of the personal expenditure of the Emperors. Considering the vast expanse of the state which contributed, and bearing in mind that this was the sole state requiring such a royal household in the whole of this vast

238

territory,[161] one comes to the conclusion that the burden was none too heavy, given the number of shoulders bearing it. Like every other prominent person, the Emperor lived in Rome, in villas at Baiae, etc. But the household was in general moderate. Recent discoveries of inscriptions at Carthage[162] reveal the existence of imperial servants in the province of Africa; these, however, served the administration of the imperial domain, not of the household. This changed in the Byzantine age, when in addition to Rome there were also imperial residences in Milan, Ravenna, Trier, Nicomedia, Antioch, etc. Outgoings varied, of course, with individual rulers. The greater part of the currency debasement, for example, may be attributed to personal wastefulness during the reign of Nero, an Emperor as extravagant in building as in everything else. Generally speaking, [MH.II, 67] however, the personal expenditure of Emperors was not too high, even by modern standards.

Civil servants' salaries were unknown in the Republic, at least in its better days. Magistrates and officers alike served for the honour of office. This ceased with the principate, to some extent even earlier, from the time when proconsuls sought, at least by circuitous routes, to ensure that they were not out of pocket as a result of holding office. Under the Emperors, in contrast, the Empire regularly paid all officials; admittedly senatorial office-holders only, in that they were paid a *salarium*, reimbursement for expenses, but in practice this amounted to the same thing by a different name. Slaves were an exception – the vast majority of them were not remunerated for performing menial official duties. Freed slaves were probably treated the same as freemen. The military tribune was also paid. Officers' salaries seem not to have been very lucrative, whereas financial officials, tax collectors and administrative officials received enormous salaries, clearly in accordance with the essentially correct principle of 'Lead us not into temptation'. Such vast sums passed through their hands that they had to be made well-off in order to avoid misappropriation. Procurators, in particular, remained in office for a considerable time, compared to the military tribunes and other holders of senior military office, indeed often permanently, and these offices provided the basis for making fresh fortunes. The route to success in Rome was the ladder from junior office (*militia equestris*) to procurator.[163] The son of such a parvenu was then a senator, on equal standing with high-ranking families.

Although official salaries constituted a major item of state expenditure, there was, as has already been mentioned, [MH.II, 68] extensive use of slaves; complaints that officials were eating away the state did not arise until after Diocletian. The introduction of an orderly, remunerated officialdom did at least put a stop to corruption – apart from in the very highest places, where at all events vast fortunes were made with ill-gotten gains; one need only think of Pallas.[164]

Other expenditure pertained not to the state in general, but to Italy and Rome.

The notion of the provinces as *vectigalia populi Romani* had not yet died out. This held good chiefly with regard to the cost of building highways. Major Roman roads[165] were first and foremost military roads, and just as today the railway network has an eminently strategic function, so in Rome the redeployment and transfer of troops were only made possible by the road network. It would, therefore, have been both reasonable and cost-effective if the responsibility for imperial roads had been assumed by the imperial treasury. In fact, however, this was only partially accomplished. From the wealth of material, alas still awaiting an able editor,[166] the following may be mentioned.

Augustus took on responsibility for the Italian roads,[167] at least from the river Po as far as Naples. Trajan – when an Emperor excels in the military sphere his names often appear on milestones —took the south of Italy into his care. He installed *curatores viarum* for all Italy, assumed state control of the roads and devolved the costs on the state treasury. Only the new local roads [MH.II, 69] were built from the contributions of the local residents. Outside Italy, however, the burden of road construction was borne by the municipalities, with at best imperial subsidies where these fell short. To the north of the Po the only imperial road was the *Julia Augusti* built by Augustus from Rimini to Narbonne. Verona, Padua, etc. had to maintain the major roads in their territories from their own means —probably because these cities were powerful. Lombardy was an indestructible region then, as it is still today.

The only imperial road in Africa was the great road from Carthage through the Medjerda.[168] In many cases the reasons are not yet clear why one particular road or another was made imperial; military considerations will probably have been the main criterion. Frequently, old memories from Republican days will also have played a role as in the case of the *Julia Augusta* already referred to, which probably owes its origins to the fact that there was a state road along the same route in the Republican era. In the case of the great African road from Carthage through the Medjerda to Tebessa,[169] both military and administrative reasons were crucial; this was a communication between the main legionary camp and the military and political centre. Under Vespasian and his sons a state road project was launched in Cappadocia, motivated by the organization of Cappadocia under Vespasian and the establishment of a number of legionary garrisons there. It is remarkable that in this context the distinction between senatorial and imperial provinces disappeared entirely; Africa and Gallia Narbonensis were senatorial provinces.

[MH.II, 70] This system of imperial roads administered by the state did not survive the second century; the Emperor built no more roads in the third century. The creeping bankruptcy in all branches of state affairs spread to this sphere too. The state no longer defrayed the costs of provincial roads, instead transferring the burden on to the municipalities and thereby accelerating their downfall.

Augustus had created the institution of the imperial post, a system of personal transportation by means of courier horses and carriages,[170] but this was in fact an encumbrance on the municipalities, which were obliged to offer horses and carriages for compulsory labour. This *vehiculatio* (transport provision) was perceived as particularly onerous on account of its erratic nature: this was not a regular service in permanent operation, such as we are inclined to envisage nowadays. Rather, as is still the case in Turkey today, passes for the imperial post were issued as required, entitling the holder to demand transportation within the borders of each municipality. A document of Claudius is still extant relating to the abolition of this burden,[171] as well as coins of Nerva referring to its abolition in Italy.[172] In both cases, however, abolition was never implemented, and the crushing burden for the municipalities continued.[173]

Whereas the measures examined hitherto pertained more or less to the whole Empire, others were restricted solely to Italy or Rome, for example the Emperor's public works. In themselves, public works were a municipal burden, but in Italy they were greatly encouraged by the Emperor. [MH.II, 71] In Venafrum Augustus built an aqueduct.[174] Trajan built superb and lasting harbour facilities on both the Italian coasts, at Ostia and Ancona. In the latter the arch is still standing that was built to celebrate this work of Trajan's.[175]

The Emperors also undertook the erection of particular temple buildings. Vespasian restored many derelict temples in small rural towns. We hardly ever hear of an Emperor intervening in this way in the provinces. In Rome itself public works devolved entirely on the imperial treasury; this was in consequence of Augustus having revived the office of censor. This shows clearly the special status of Rome: all water facilities, of such crucial importance to Rome, the Tiber facilities and all utilities, were imperial.[176]

Other expenditure included alms and games, which constituted a substantial drain on the state treasury, particularly the *annona*.[177] The *annona*, or corn supply, fell into two quite separate categories: first, a number of inhabitants of Rome obtained an 'annual' quantity of grain *gratis* – a remnant of the general civic benefaction of the Republic,[178] which had developed into a kind of poor relief. Caesar had excluded the two higher orders *ipso facto*,[179] and restricted distribution to the *plebs urbana*, and this only at a specific number of locations.[180] Some element of personal favouritism and unfairness must have been involved, but the fundamental idea was to provide assistance not only to the completely destitute, but also to poorer families [MH.II, 72] with many children. Augustus brought the number of those entitled to this support to a norm of 200,000.[181] We are no longer able to say what percentage of the population this figure represented. Since only citizens qualified, however, and *peregrini* and slaves were excluded, it must have been quite a substantial percentage. This number was not increased during the imperial age, despite the addition of certain other categories, such as soldiers, who, as has already been mentioned, received free supplies. Trajan appears to have instituted some kind of care for orphans: children and minors were included in the relevant lists.[182] An estimate of approximately 50 million Marks for the burden to the state of this part of the *annona* ought not to be too wide of the mark. Nevertheless, to reach an accurate assessment of the entire scope of state food supplies, it is necessary to bear in mind its second aspect: supplying the capital with cheap grain for all.

This matter was fairly easily accomplished. The bulk of the *vectigalia* was paid in kind, which served in the first instance to fill the granaries of the capital. This did not constitute a direct monopolization of the grain trade in the capital, since the measure was not motivated primarily by fiscal reasoning. On the contrary, the grain was sold at a loss in order to keep the good common folk sweet-tempered. It did become a monopoly in practice, however, precisely because of the give-away price at which the corn was sold and with which, of course, no one else could compete. To all intents and purposes, therefore, the corn trade was [MH.II, 73] in government hands. For the latter this did, at least, have the advantage of enabling it to convert the vast quantities of grain it amassed into cash, albeit at rock-bottom prices. It is impossible to state with anything even approaching accuracy what costs were incurred by maintaining these artificially low prices. At all events the practice did result in full granaries and preserved Rome from starvation – an incalculable advantage in those days of inadequate communication and underdeveloped commerce, but equally, however, a substantial factor in government fiscal policy, given the crucial imperative to preserve a good atmosphere in the capital.

The games[183] were of no great moment for the state treasury, but were very important for maintaining a good atmosphere among the urban population. Rarely were games organized at state expense; they were more of a tax on the ambitions of the wealthy. The office of praetor, in itself of no substance, was a precondition and prelude for higher office, for *honores et sacerdotia*, magistracies and priesthoods, and the organization of games was its main responsibility.[184] The passionately adored circus games were a privilege of the capital. Provincial towns also had gladiatorial contests and stage plays. The right to hold chariot races, however, was reserved for Rome.[185]

The Emperor was probably also involved in the holding of games, but was under no obligation; when he did so, which occurred chiefly after some military success, it was naturally done with the maximum of pomp and circumstance.[186]

[MH.II, 74] There were also distributions of money to the *plebs urbana*, which might more properly be regarded as a supplement to the *annona*, since they were provided explicitly to the favoured *plebs urbana quae frumentum publicum accipit*.[187] Many surviving coins attest to the importance attributed to these *congiaria*, since nothing is more frequently indicated on them than the sums of donations given by the Emperor.[188] There is another very remarkable document,[189] which in addition to all the other odd information it contains – such as how a great ship ran aground at Ostia and the sighting of a wolverine in Rome – also provides detailed information about the donations of each of the Emperors.[190] It emerges from this document that these donations had greatly increased, from average totals of 2 million Marks in the first century to 6 million Marks already by the second century – and this is a squandered sum, an expenditure made out of weakness and an unjustified privileging of the idle *plebs* of the capital. Given a tolerably well-ordered administration, however, the state could put up with this burden quite well.[191]

No such arrangements are to be found for the other towns in Italy. The municipalities provided their own *annona* without state support. There are signs, however, that the Empire extended its provision to Italian municipalities in the latter stages of its development; Nerva[192] and Trajan (see MH.II, 72), for example, expanded the child-support programmes (*res alimentaria*) throughout Italy and donated huge sums in the form of capital, which were converted in perpetuity into real estate, the interest being used for the benefit of minors. Trajan, for [MH.II, 75] example, donated 1 million sesterces to the town of Velleia, an insignificant place near Parma; the interest (50,000 sesterces or 10,000 Marks)[193] was intended to benefit minors. Grants were allocated to 245 boys and 34 girls in the case of legitimate children and a number of others for illegitimate *spurii* and *spuriae*. The income was paid to the parents.[194] A number of towns were provided with institutions of this kind. The plan had been devised by Nerva. It came to a standstill under Marcus after the shortages incurred through the Marcommanic War. It is worth noting that the main patrons of this kind of establishment were the Empresses, who were best suited to this kind of charitable supportive work and were its natural promoters.

It is difficult to say how these measures, which called for substantial sums, were implemented financially. The idea in Italy must have been gradually to provide most municipalities with such institutions; outside Italy, on the other hand, we can find no trace of them, although there was no lack of private charitable establishments in Africa, for example. In this respect, too, therefore, although the omnipotence of Rome was broken in the course of the principate, Italy nonetheless remained the dominant, privileged land up to the time of Diocletian and Constantine, when this preferential treatment and special status came to an end.

[MH.II, 76] Let us turn to fiscal administration. The institution of the state treasury, the *aerarium populi Romani*, dated from the Republican era.[195] Its administration was the responsibility of the Senate, not of magistrates. The imperial age inherited this institution. In addition to this there was also an imperial treasury, the *patrimonium principis*, which in the second century became generally known by

243

the term *fiscus*.[196] *Fiscus* actually means 'money chest' and in the early imperial age there were various individual imperial *fisci*, e.g. the *fiscus Asiaticus* etc. Later *fiscus* became a technical term, the 'chests' were centralized and people referred to it simply as the *fiscus Caesaris*.

Under Augustus the *aerarium populi Romani* was divided into two parts, the *aerarium publicum* and the *aerarium militare*;[197] as has already been repeatedly mentioned, the latter was based on the *vicesima populi Romani*,[198] inheritance tax, and on the *caduca*.[199] These were treasuries of the Roman people, not of the Emperor. This, however, was no more than an administrative distinction: quaestors, praetors and municipal magistrates administered the *aerarium publicum*, whereas the Emperor alone administered the *aerarium militare*, since he alone could command and dismiss soldiers. This, indeed, was the best aspect of the arrangement: that the Emperor administered it and the Senate had practically no say in it. If, then, the legal expert classifies the *aerarium militare* as a state treasury from the strictly legal point of view, the historian may with equal justification classify it as a treasury belonging to the Emperor. [MH.II, 77] Strictly speaking, therefore, this leaves us with a threefold division of the treasury into a double state treasury and an imperial treasury or *fiscus*.

The *aerarium populi Romani*, although formally the chief public treasury, had been materially the least significant since before the beginning of the principate, and its significance continued to wane. By rights the *vectigalia* from the provinces should have flowed into this treasury, but only those from the senatorial provinces were in fact paid into it. As far as customs duties (*portaria*) are concerned, although we are not clear about this, they were probably paid into this treasury too, and likewise the ancient manumission tax of 5 per cent of the value of the freed slave. Similarly, fines and confiscated monies also belonged to this treasury. The *caduca* flowed into the *aerarium populi Romani*, according to the *lex Julia*, and this persisted until after Antoninus Pius. In contrast, Julian asserted in the third century: *hodie fisco vindicantur*,[200] a statement which in all probability goes back to Caracalla. The *bona damnatorum* (property of condemned persons) were also intended by law to flow into the *aerarium populi Romani* and were probably diverted elsewhere not as a result of a general decree, but by means of numerous individual encroachments (we know, for example, that the huge fortune of Sejanus was subsequently reclaimed for the *fiscus* by Tiberius after first being transferred to the *aerarium populi Romani*). It gradually became common practice for these *bona damnatorum* to be absorbed into the *fiscus*, rather than being used for the benefit of the state treasury.

[MH.II, 78] Thus the *aerarium populi Romani* was eroded on all sides. It was probably also encumbered with the obligation of paying a portion of its revenues to the Emperor. This is known to have been the case with Asian and African revenues, for example, which were both from senatorial provinces. Probably all payments in kind were claimed by the Emperor when he took over the *annona* for Rome.

The subordinate levels of financial administration were intrinsically imperial. According to both tradition and law, from the Republican era onwards the praetor, consul, proconsul, or whoever was in authority over a province, was responsible for collecting taxes. Under the principate this became a separate responsibility and was assigned to imperial officials who were the senior financial officials in the province. In the early period the senatorial official probably retained a certain right of adjudication and a casting vote in the event of disputes. As a rule, however, the imperial financial official was an equestrian, not a member of the Senate. He was a personal adviser of the Emperor, and in the absence of the proconsul (the senatorial official) the procurator (the imperial tax official) stepped in for him as a natural substitute.

Customs duties[201] were raised essentially by being farmed out, but control of these was likewise [MH.II, 79] in the hands of the *princeps*. In this way, a substantial imperial staff of non-senatorial officials grew up who had a similar status to that of government commissaries in private railway companies today. The authority of the principate increased constantly.

Ultimate administrative control of the *aerarium populi Romani* was in the hands of the Senate, which authorized its expenditure. Even the Emperor Marcus still had subsidies decreed to him by the Senate. Originally praetors, later quaestors, were in charge, and had to present accounts when handing over the office to their successor, i.e. to the Senate. These controllers of the treasury were elected by the Senate, and frequently by lot. The Emperors had no influence over this until the time of Claudius, who claimed the right of the *princeps* to appoint quaestors and also changed the hitherto yearly term of office into a *triennium*. It was Nero who first transferred the municipal administration of Rome to the *praefecti aerarii Saturni*,[202] thereby also transferring authority over the central state treasury to the Emperor. The idea of being someone's representative is implicit in the very official title of *praefectus*, and representative of who else if not the Emperor? The Emperor could only appoint former praetors, men of senatorial background, to this office and when extraordinary payments were required, he was obliged to procure a resolution to this effect from the Senate.

It emerges from all that has been said so far that the *aerarium* and *fiscus* were tantamount to one and the same thing: both were *de facto* imperial treasuries. The definitive realization of this [MH.II, 80] was probably carried out under Vespasian, and was entirely consistent with his centralized style of government.

Let us turn now to the *aerarium populi Romani militare*, the imperial military treasury. We already know the latter's financial sources: inheritance tax and auction duties, further augmented by grants from other treasuries. It would seem from a passage in Dio that the Emperor had an obligation to make a yearly contribution. Dio asserts this of Augustus,[203] but it is uncertain in the case of later Emperors. Tacitus mentions that after Cappadocia was declared a province it became possible to reduce auction duty substantially;[204] the *fiscus* was thus able to increase its contribution as a result of this new source of income and hence reduce the level of other contributions.

Right from the foundation of this treasury (AD 6), its administration was in the hands of the *praefecti aerarii militaris*. As we have already seen, whenever the Emperor intervened vicariously, he was obliged to make use of senators. Here, where he acted independently, senators were excluded. We can see from this, therefore, that what Vespasian did for the *aerarium populi Romani* had already been done for the *aerarium militare* by Augustus, i.e. it had been brought fully within the Emperor's power.

Ultimately, the *fiscus* was effectively the private property of the Emperor and yet here, too, we may in a sense speak of a state treasury. The most ancient term [MH.II, 81] for this bundle of estates was the *patrimonium* (inherited estate) or *res familiaris* (family property).[205] It included everything that belonged to the Emperor, as well as other items. In both theory and practice, therefore, it marked the most significant innovation of the principate when, while maintaining the ownership rights of the *populus Romanus* with respect to estates in the senatorial provinces, these became the private property of the Emperor in the imperial provinces. This was explicitly stated by Gaius.[206] Implicit in this statement is the notion that the *fiscus* is not private property in the same sense that other property is private: it was *res fiscalis*, not *res privata*. Ancient Roman law stipulated that state property was not liable to prescription;[207] this stipulation likewise pertained to the Emperor with respect to his landed possessions, whereas the property of private owners was liable to prescription. This is analogous to the customary practice in Rome whereby when an owner left his land for any length of time he would make a fiduciary transfer of his property to a friend, on the understanding that it would be given back to him when he returned. The *res fiscalis*, too, should be understood in the same way: when the *princeps*, who in any case initially only assumed the principate for a limited period, wished to renounce his monarchical rank, his property would also return into the ownership of the state. Imperial property, therefore, [MH.II, 82] and its administration were something substantially different from the property of a private citizen.

This likewise emerges from the order of succession. It is important to note what occurred after the death of Tiberius. In keeping with this character, Tiberius had made no statement about the succession; he wrote his will like any ordinary private citizen and bequeathed his property equally to his two grandsons. The Senate, however, declared this will void and transferred the entire inheritance to Gaius, the successor to the principate,[208] with the idea that if not according to law, then in practice the successor must inherit everything, even if this necessitated such a violent act as the setting aside of an Emperor's will by the Senate. From then on it was taken for granted that the successor to the throne was at one and the same time the sole inheritor of his predecessor's property. In other words, what was in name the Emperor's private property was in fact the property of the state and fell to the successor by legal necessity. It could thus also happen that some Emperors gave away their private property on their accession to the throne: Pertinax, for example, transferred his to his daughter,[209] while others disposed of theirs in favour of someone else. It is thus impossible to speak of the separate property of the Emperor.

In his most excellent and instructive book on the imperial administrative officials up to Diocletian (1877), Otto Hirschfeld states that the *fiscus* inherently [MH.II, 83] lacked central direction. How was this possible? How could such a vast, complex and highly proliferated estate not be centrally controlled? This control could, of course, reside in the person of the Emperor himself, as supreme administrator, and initially this was the case. Although a central official was missing, therefore, central control was not. If Augustus left among the papers for his successor specifications concerning the treasury's cash balance and outstanding debts, we can be sure that he kept himself informed of such matters. This, of course, required subordinate officials, and if their names are no longer preserved and we know no details about them personally, this is probably because they were from the lower orders – freedmen, or even slaves – just as the names of personal servants are not known either.[210]

And yet there is some truth in the claim that the *fiscus*, compared to the *aerarium*, lacked central control; the entire organization of the two treasuries was different. The *fiscus* had no auditors or treasury. All payments to the *aerarium* were made to Rome via the chief contractors; the assets of the *aerarium* consisted of cash in the state treasury. The Emperor's management of the *fiscus* was more like that of a major landowner possessing brickworks, mines, manufacturing concerns of various kinds, farms, vineyards, etc., who delegates or divides up his financial affairs into innumerable smaller [MH.II, 84] accounts. In earlier, better times, at least, that essentially barbaric way of bringing together income from different sources was not yet in evidence. Greater centralization did, nonetheless, begin to creep in, particularly under weaker governments – first under Claudius, when we also begin to encounter the auditor, the *a rationibus principis*. These were men who had not been manumitted, low-born servants, who soon began to play at being ministers of finance; Pallas[211] was the first and most important of them (see MH.I, 183). They shaped future developments. Later these matters were entrusted to men of the middle classes, who by that time bore the title *procurator a rationibus*. In the fourth century greater importance accrued to this office and the official was known as *comes sacrarum largitionum*[212] and *procurator summarum rationum*.[213]

There was thus an audit office for balancing all individual transactions, but with no centralization of funds. The central authority for this, however, remained the Emperor himself.

Imperial administration was a system of direct control which never had any truck with the ruinous indirect system of farming out through 'publicans' – ruinous for all concerned, not only for the publican himself. When, therefore, the *aerarium*, as has been outlined above, gradually became insignificant and was absorbed, the *societates*, the great tax-farming companies, disappeared of their own accord once the basis of their activity had disappeared, without ever actually being abolished by a specific decree.

[MH.II, 85] Each of the *fiscus*'s centres of income or expenditure had a separate accounting office. Every army, every separate unit, had one of these – this is known for certain in the case of the army in Africa and the fleet at Misenum. We learn this from the tomb inscriptions of servants, since these office administrators were from the lower orders. Within the palace, the court, kitchen and cellar of the Emperor, as well as the training of children, were all likewise organized separately, as has been shown by Hirschfeld.[214]

The chief source of revenue was the administration of the imperial domains,[215] which were in the custody of provincial procurators. The rapid concentration of domains in the hands of the Emperor, who ultimately[216] became the greatest landowner in the Empire, is a characteristic feature of decline. It was different in the beginning. Egypt had probably always been considered part of the private property of the Emperor[217] and in a certain sense this is true, since all Egyptian revenues, including fines, flowed into the Emperor's coffers. Legally, however, land in Egypt was no more the property of the Emperor than than it was in other imperial provinces, such as Syria. It was administered by an authority left over from the Ptolemaic era which hence bore the Greek name *idios logos*.[218] The idea that Egyptian soil was the private property of the Emperor was a legal fiction. Since its artificial creation by Alexander, Alexandria seems to have been an exceptional case, in that its citizens were not [MH.II, 86] freeholders, but long-term tenants, rather as the land and property in London today – to the detriment of urban development – for the most part belongs to wealthy property owners. In Alexandria, therefore, the Emperor was the true, not merely the fictitious owner of the land.

In the early imperial age the landholdings of the Emperor, in Italy for example, were still relatively trifling; Tacitus expressly states of Tiberius: *rari Caesaris agri*.[219] This all changed with the confiscations,[220] which gradually transferred major, mostly lucrative, landholdings into the ownership of the Emperor. This was, indeed, frequently the purpose behind initiating the confiscations in the first place. All brickworks, in particular, gradually passed into imperial ownership, as is revealed by brick stamps.[221] These were augmented by the delightful villas at Baiae,[222] the Italian mines and the great pasture lands in Apulia. A remarkable document[223] survives from the time of the Emperor Marcus. Imperial tenant herdsmen, migrating from the winter pastures in Apulia to the summer pastures in mountainous Samnium, had a dispute with the towns through whose territory they had to drive the herds. The authorities intervened energetically to protect the *conductores*.

In Africa there was a still greater concentration of landholdings in the hands of the Emperor, chiefly in Africa proper, i.e. the vicinity of Carthage, with less [MH.II, 87] in Numidia and none at all in Mauretania.[224] From Nero onwards Carthage became the promised land of the imperial domains. These major conglomerations of estates probably date back to the Punic Wars; following the conquest of Carthage during the Republic, the aristocracy appropriated these estates, which were then inherited by the Emperors during the imperial age. Pliny[225] reports that the entire *latifundia* of Carthage were in the hands of six landowners until Nero executed them; all their estates were then absorbed into those of the Emperor. Virtually all of Africa gradually became imperial property. The central bureau was the *tabularium* in Carthage, the local audit office, whose organization has lately become known to us in detail. A document survives from the time of Commodus, a complaint lodged by the *coloni* against the major imperial tenants.[226] Here in Africa we find the clearest evidence for the increase of *latifundia*: the fact that they withdrew from municipal organization. Although organized as towns, they were recognized as groups of estates, and were administered by procurators, not magistrates.

Further growth of imperial domain possessions came to a standstill in the better times following the year of the four Emperors. However, after Septimius Severus had defeated Clodius Albinus, i.e. the rebellion of Gaul against Illyricum – since this is what the great war between Italy and the East, Gaul and Illyricum, may well be called – mass confiscations took place once again, this time in Gaul and Germany in particular.[227] [MH.II, 88] These new domain possessions were called *res privata principis* (the Emperor's private estates): the name was new, but the aim was old. From this time onwards a distinction was made only between the *patrimonium Caesaris*, old estates, and the *res privata Caesaris*, new estates.[228] Later, in Constantinople, the office of a second finance minister, in fact a minister of imperial domains, the *comes rerum privatarum*,[229] evolved out of this fact.

One of the negative manifestations of the administration of these domains was the way it gradually removed itself from common law. Tacitus still notes that in the early days of Tiberius's reign litigation between the Emperor as a landowner and another private landowner was recognized by the courts as if between two private citizens.[230] It is known for certain of Claudius,[231] and can probably be traced back to the latter days of Tiberius, that the Emperor, as landowner, later refused to allow the courts to dictate to him on matters of litigation and contrived exemption from common jurisdiction for his administrators. This personal jurisdiction represents a substantial encroachment on private law and is a symptom of the transformation of the monarchy into despotism, a fatal development.[232] Often, indeed, procurators were furnished with a military force. The African procurator, for example, received one cohort, which was the cause of the complaint lodged by the *coloni* mentioned above.

[MH.II, 89] One negative and characteristic feature of the Roman fiscal system was the total absence of a national debt.[233] By this we do not mean the frequently occurring situation whereby the state for a greater or shorter length of time is unable to pay salaries and wages – a different form of national debt. I mean it in the sense commonly understood today, but which was unknown in antiquity. Not that this ploy had not already been invented: the municipalities made not infrequent use of this expedient,[234] and there were municipal loans even in the Republican era. The question is, why did the state not resort to this expedient? The answer becomes clear from an examination of those cases in which loans did occur in antiquity – chiefly, that is, in the case of dependent municipalities, not (or at least only very rarely) in the case of independent ones; for the Italian municipalities, at least, this was almost invariably the case. The reason is clear, therefore: if someone wants to borrow, there must be someone available to force repayment if the contingency arises. In the case of the Italian municipalities this was difficult, if not impossible; even under the Emperors they retained a certain degree of independence and there was no regular court where complaints against them could be lodged. It was certainly permitted to lodge a complaint with the Senate, but this could hardly be expected to result in much success. It was, in any case, impossible to go to law with the state [MH.II, 90], nor could it be forced to make restitution of debts. Whilst it is true that most modern states also groan under the burden of debts frivolously contracted for no good reason, it cannot be denied that where the potential for national debt exists for the purpose of realizing major projects, subsequent generations are the beneficiaries, often the chief beneficiaries, of them, so that those generations may also be permitted to share in costs which it would be difficult or impossible for the present generation to cover. All this, nevertheless, presupposes orderly conditions and a high degree of confidence in public integrity. Even today, barbaric, disordered and unstable states have little or no credit. The principate never matured to such a level.

Let us take one final look at the fiscal situation of the municipalities. The picture would be incomplete if this aspect of financial management in the imperial age were to be overlooked. Unfortunately, it is difficult to describe, as the record of it consists of countless inscriptions, a subject which modern research has neglected. It would be a highly commendable, feasible and fruitful undertaking to make a thorough study of this topic.[235]

[MH.II, 91] Urban life was the most glorious aspect of the principate; it was here that the flower of the Empire truly blossomed. We can gain a vivid idea of this from looking at Pompeii, a small rural town with few resources, albeit located in the most richly endowed region on earth. Ten years before the final catastrophe that buried and preserved Pompeii, the town already went through something similar. It rebuilt itself out of its own resources, made an exemplary rapid recovery and restored its public buildings. Graffiti, of which we can still read a relatively large number, indicate quite a high standard of education: even slaves could write well and correctly. They document a lively interest in civic affairs. The election of municipal magistrates prompted involvement even from women and slaves, if only as supporters; the municipal life of this city had a healthy pulse.[236] And what we find here was equally the case in all towns in Italy, Africa, Spain and Gaul. Neither before nor since has Africa ever flourished to this extent, and all this is chiefly the work of the principate. By encouraging municipal ambition, by granting municipal self-government and a remarkable degree of room for manoeuvre in all communal affairs – municipal elections were abolished in Rome only – the principate, greatly to its credit, achieved in the second and third centuries a full flowering of municipal life and administration.

[MH,II, p. 92] What did the municipal budget consist of, and where did its revenues come from? The analogy between the state and municipal budgets is striking, *mutatis mutandis*. Both are based on the same essential idea: an almost complete absence of taxation. Municipalities could no more impose regular cash demands on their fellow citizens than the state could in practice make use of the *tributum civium Romanorum*,[237] although the latter still existed in law. As in the case of the state, the main source of revenue was their own assets. When cities were established they seem to have carefully received a landed property base, and for the most part they owned real estate that produced income. When colonies were founded, that portion of land not already assigned to citizens, particularly pasture and forest land, was frequently reserved as communal property. However, it was not then used by all citizens of the municipality, but leased out, with the rent from leasing, or *vectigal*, forming the municipality's revenue. If a municipality was wealthy and possessed superfluous capital assets, it probably purchased additional landed property. This is documented by a most instructive exchange of letters between Pliny and Trajan about a case in Bithynia, to which we shall return later. The town of Nicomedia called in its debts and used them to purchase landed property.[238] Another source of income consisted of gifts by local, patriotic, well-to-do citizens, [MH.II, 93] and this local patriotism, which often looks ridiculous and absurd in inscriptions, took on a delightful and praiseworthy aspect in these gifts, which often took the form of bequests.

Not infrequently the municipalities also owned land outside their territory: Naples, for example, owned significant estates on Crete for centuries.[239] Atella, a town in Campania, had possessions in Gaul.[240] Usually, however, such estates were located in the city's own territory. The range of different sources is illustrated, at least in one special case, by the accounts of a Pompeian banker's dealings with the city of Pompeii: it was his task to collect and pay in the municipal revenues.[241]

In addition there was the interest ledger of debts, the *calendarium*; this listed the capital assets of towns which had been loaned out and for which interest was payable on the calends of each month.[242] These revenues played a crucial role in municipal budgets. In the correspondence of Pliny just referred to we read of such a case: the town had left money idle, because those in need of money preferred to borrow privately, since the formalities of dealing with a municipality were inevitably more cumbersome. The town is thus uncertain what to do with its money. In order to achieve the rate of interest customary in the province, Pliny suggests a compulsory distribution of money to individual [MH.II, 94] members of the Senate. Trajan is more just and humane and rejects this suggestion as incompatible with the justice of his age. He offers the agreeable advice that the municipality content itself with a somewhat lower rate of interest.[243] In inscriptions we frequently encounter three to four special *calendariae*, each with its own particular administration. In the first century the Emperors left the towns to run their own finances. As tends to happen all too easily, however, corruption, embezzlement and all manner of underhand dealings soon arose, so that restrictions were put into force from Vespasian and Trajan onwards; the Emperors appointed inspectors of the *calendariae*.

We can see, therefore, that ground rent and interest on capital were the chief sources of revenue for the municipalities. It is not possible to prove that urban customs duties were imposed and, this being the case, it is unlikely that they were, since otherwise they could not have remained unknown to us.[244] It was also very sensible that urban territories could not be made into districts with their own customs barriers; aside from the major state frontiers referred to earlier, trade was free throughout the entire Empire. Nonetheless, a few inscriptions have been cited in support of the argument that municipalities imposed road tolls, but they have probably been misinterpreted. [MH.II, 95] One of these, from Africa, states that a road has been built using road-toll money, *vectigal rotarium*.[245] However, this was most probably an allowance from the Emperor, who had allocated this imperial tax for the improvement of roads in the municipality. The other instance concerns a case in southern Italy, where Roman highroads and their maintenance were dependent on the proceeds from estates; these had become diverted from their original purpose and the Emperor restored the original relationship.

Procedure was similar in the case of taxes on imported and exported goods, *portoria*, which comprised not only port taxes, but all customs duties of this kind, regardless of whether they were collected on land or sea routes. A resolution of the People dating from the time of Cicero states that a *civitas libera* was to be granted the right to collect such *portoria*.[246] Although the *civitates liberae* may not have had quite such a free hand under the principate, there were, nonetheless, exceptions – Athens, for example, which enjoyed a special status generally out of regard for its former greatness, may have had this right as an immune city; this was undoubtedly not generally the case, however. Trade within the Empire was free in principle.

Under certain circumstances towns were permitted to impose a personal tax on their inhabitants. Chief among such taxes were the *operae*, the compulsory labour and the closely related provision of transport. These were proper day-labour services and undoubtedly of ancient origin. [MH.II, 96] They did not, of course, have to be performed by everyone in person, but could be redeemed in cash. There are precise extant accounts of this from Spain,[247] where every male inhabitant in the municipalities, whether citizen or resident, freeman or slave, had an obligation to serve five days annually between the ages of 14 to 60; likewise every owner of a *iugum*[248] (this originally meant a yoke of oxen for tillage, but later came to apply to anyone who owned a team of horses) had an obligation to provide three yoke days annually. Public works in particular were constructed in this manner.

The municipality furthermore had the right to demand personal service from every citizen according to his capacity; he was reimbursed for actual expenses, but not for personal toil or the loss of his time. These services included the journeys of messengers to the Emperor's court or to the governor of the province.[249] They were a very frequent occurrence, for the purposes of personal business or for ceremonial reasons. They constituted an onerous burden for more well-off members of the municipality, since such legations could not be avoided. The imperial court or governor would issue a certificate proving that the journey had taken place, on the basis of which the cost of the journey would be reimbursed with a *legativum* (envoy's expenses).

Equally, people had to be willing to conduct litigation for the municipality, to take on the offices of chief of police and [MH.II, 97] harbour master, and to discharge the duties of a militia officer for the security of the city's territory. We know of one such case from Switzerland.[250] The state obligations incumbent on the municipality also had to be fulfilled: the collection of imperial taxes within the territory, the postal service (*vehiculatio*) and the equipping of the *cursus vehicularis* with carriages and horses by those who owned teams. The direct burden on the municipalities from the *munera mixta* and *munera patrimonii* eventually became so crushing that it completely ruined them.[251] It proved an extremely irksome requirement for tax collectors, the *decemprimi*, from the third century onwards, when they were liable for arrest in case of a tax deficit and obliged to make up the difference themselves in corn or money.[252] In theory there was a distinction between *munera* and *honores*, i.e. municipal obligations and municipal magistracies,

253

but in fact every *honor* was a *munus*. The municipality was able to compel a person to assume an office and frequently did so: in this way *honor* receded and *munus* came to the fore. The desire to hold office and the pleasure in doing so, the readiness to assume office as an honour, disappeared, leaving only the obligation to take it on as a duty.

The outgoings of an ancient municipality were much simpler than they are now. Their principal duty was the maintenance of the *sacra*. The latter were not endowed, so that the upkeep of temples [MH.II, 98] and rituals devolved on the municipal purse. Since, however, no salaries had to be paid, apart from those to subordinate officials, the equivalent of modern sacristans, and since the material costs, aside from the buildings themselves, were not particularly significant, this burden was not an onerous one. We know from Spanish inscriptions[253] that the supply of the required *fana*, i.e. the required equipment, was a municipal matter. The *stips*, i.e. the small gifts laid by temple visitors in the *thesauri*, analogous to modern alms boxes and collection bags, were undoubtedly of some importance. The amounts that flowed into the temple coffers in this way and thereby alleviated the municipal purse were certainly not trifling. Temple regulations were in force in Ascoli (Asculum in Picenum) whereby anyone who wanted to put up a *clupeus* (plaque) had to pay 2,000 sesterces.[254] Although, understandably, such things do not often appear in inscriptions, they were nevertheless practised.

As regards public works, we have already stated to what extent these were the responsibility of the Empire; what remained was a matter for the municipality. Great disparities prevailed with regard to road building. Italian municipalities had nothing to do with main highways, but were supposed to service local and urban roads, as well as all other public works, wherever imperial generosity did not intervene. The state treasury assumed [MH.II, 99] none of this burden. We are obliged, nonetheless, to praise a unique Roman institution for its immense importance: municipal patriotism, which was far greater then than it is nowadays, not only in Germany, but even in Italy, where it is still of far more importance than in other modern countries. The reason is not difficult to identify: a man must have something to call his own. Patriotism for the state did not, and could not, exist. The monarchical order of the principate was incompatible with an unforced love of the Fatherland. The municipality, the city, took its place as the object of all those aspirations which could find no expression with respect to the state. Although no more than a surrogate, it was, after all, better than nothing, and bore much welcome fruit. This local patriotism was fully in keeping with municipal conditions, with aristocratic government by individual families, and was amplified and publicized so that it could be confirmed in every possible manner. For example, the *nominis inscriptio*, the right to name oneself as the builder in an inscription on a public work which one had built with one's own money, *sua pecunia*, easy and trivial as it in fact is, was highly effective and an innovation of the imperial age, unknown [MH.II, 100] in the Republic. New public works thus almost invariably owed their existence to private initiatives and cost the municipal purse nothing, while maintenance costs were of no great consequence.

Every municipality on a small scale had the same need for public entertainments and provision for its members, the *panem et circenses*,[255] as Rome had on a large scale, except that outside Rome these have to be referred to as *panem et ludos*,[256] and had to be paid for out of municipal funds. Strictly speaking, the games were religious acts and consequently non-Roman municipalities received subsidies to organize them, albeit only nominal ones. Inscriptions bearing Spanish municipal charters, for example, specify that this contribution totalled 250–500 Marks.[257] Essentially it was those magistrates responsible for organizing games who contributed and covered the invariably very substantial deficit out of their own pockets.[258] To this extent the games constituted a tax on magistrates, i.e. the wealthy from whose circles they were exclusively recruited. A further tax came to be associated with this: magistrates were frequently burdened with some other task instead of the games, for example erecting a building *pro ludis*. This is borne out by numerous inscriptions.[259]

While this represents a form of indirect taxation on magistrates, there was, by the same token, no lack of direct taxation, in the form of [MH.II, 101] so-called entry fees. These did not exist at first, but later became considerable. They applied to anyone who assumed either municipal or priestly office, in Rome and the provinces alike. Indeed, for those wealthy people who were excluded from public office on account of their origins or for some other reason there were even special organizations enabling them to be taxed, for example the *Collegium Augustale*. Although this tax is not mentioned by writers, it occurs very frequently in inscriptions.[260] Well-to-do freedmen in particular belonged to it, and membership had the same significance for them as the decurionate had for freeborn men. Although it was an empty honour, it cost money; an *Augustalis gratuite factus* was a great exception.[261] The provision of games certainly also devolved on the *Augustales*.

What was done by the Emperor in Rome for the *annona* devolved on a smaller scale on municipal magistrates in provincial towns, but it was less a matter of *frumentationes*, the free distribution of grain to the poor, than of ensuring continuous, cheap supplies to the market. The municipal aediles probably bore direct responsibility for this task, which placed a heavy burden on municipal coffers. Official provision was primarily of grain, [MH.II, 102] as well as oil and other general items. These were obligations of a vague and yet most onerous kind, of dubious value to the national economy, even though to some extent they created a substitute for what we call poor relief, since the notion of municipal social obligation was unknown in antiquity.

Public education was not yet known in the Republic.[262] But in this sphere, as in others, the imperial age was both retrograde and progressive. Education became the concern of the towns, not an imperial concern, not a matter for the Emperor.[263]

Public primary education, however, was never provided under the principate, but always remained a private affair and did not fare too badly. Reading, writing and arithmetic were relatively widespread skills. It cannot be denied that slavery facilitated their spread; wealthy people had a vested interest in having their slaves learn something, since the slave thereby increased in value.[264] We thus find slaves being taught in every noble household. In many regions today the educational picture is a far sorrier sight than it was in antiquity.

Secondary education was provided largely by the municipalities, and in many places there was a [MH.II, 103] university of sorts, as there still are today in medium-sized Italian towns, where grammar, rhetoric and philosophy were taught, and indeed in both Latin and Greek. There was rivalry among municipalities as to the merits of their establishments, which often led to the appointment of well-paid tutors, who thus did well out of this rivalry. The much-vaunted 'Gallic rhetoric' refers to this sphere of municipal achievement. Such establishments also existed in Rome.

Salaries for magistrates, on the other hand, were unknown in antiquity. A respectable man performing liturgies was not paid for them, and the municipal system claimed these liturgies free of charge. This does not of course apply to subordinate offices: scribes, readers and court ushers were paid.

All in all, therefore, we can observe reasonably healthy, acceptable conditions. Ordinary duties were subsidized and extraordinary ones imposed on the spirit of private sacrifice, which flourished and did not avoid the claims made on it. *Ambitus*, ambition for public office, was first taxed in practice, then in law – a tax on the wealthy. Some seeds of decay were there, admittedly, notably in the *annona* and the *ludi*, but municipal life was in general hale and hearty.

In the early days especially, self-government had a completely free hand. A supervisory right on the part of the state, i.e. the proconsul, existed very early on in the case of [MH.II, 104] subject municipalities, but otherwise complete room for manoeuvre by the municipalities was the sacred principle of the principate. Although there was undoubtedly a certain degree of reluctance to grant self-government, it would, nevertheless, be unjust to refrain from giving credit for altruistic motives. The task of the provincial governor was limited to inspection and correction and even the most liberal form of self-government is quite compatible with a supervisory right on the part of the state and remains unaffected by it.

The change that occurred during the age of the Emperors was decidedly for the better and consisted not so much of a restriction of self-government, as of bringing under control those cities which had previously been immune – Athens, Massilia and all Italian municipalities (where there was no supervisory proconsul as in the provinces). In Achaea the post of proconsul had in fact been no more than a sinecure up to this change, since there were virtually no subject municipalities to supervise. The governor had no say concerning Roman colonies, such as Apamea in Bithynia (see MH.I, 104–5).

Vespasian was the first Emperor to restrict communal self-government. An inscription is extant in which a supervisor of public works (*curator*) is appointed for Nola.[265] Similarly, there is a passage in the correspondence already referred to between Pliny and Trajan in which Pliny complains about the municipality of Apamea, which, although submitting its accounts for inspection [MH.II, 105] to Pliny as he toured his province, nevertheless did so only under protest, claiming that it was under no obligation to submit to such an inspection. Trajan approves this act, asserting that if the town had not submitted them voluntarily, it would have been forced to do so.[266] In the second century *correctores*, *logistai* in Greek, were appointed for the free cities, *ad corrigendum statum liberarum civitatum*.[267] There was a concerted effort to improve these, in Achaea and Syria first of all; in Italy there was some embarrassment about it, but gradually even here certain aspects of municipal government were taken under higher supervision. This prepared the ground for parity of status between Italy and the provinces. It is characteristic that these *curatores* preferably came from other towns and were often senators, who were outside the circle of the municipality's office-holders and its coteries. On the whole, this measure was as sensible and beneficial as the abrogation of the status of the Free Imperial Cities, with their short-sighted and narrow-minded parish-pump politics, ultimately proved to be for the German Empire.

It seemed necessary to me to deal first with this overall view of the financial affairs of the Empire and of the municipalities in their mutual relationship, since the history of decline and fall in the financial sphere, the history of economic ruin and bankruptcy, ultimately proved to be the chief cause of the political ruin of the principate.[268]

3

WARS IN THE WEST

[MH.II, 106] If our expectations are modest, we could claim to be constructing a history of Gaul, Britain, etc. on the basis of the material available to us. These are the provinces which make up the Empire, and which develop an independent existence as it decays. From now on it is this, rather than court history and the biographies of Emperors which go with it, which will be our chief focus of attention.

A) BRITAIN[269]

We have already seen how Claudius revived Caesar's plans for Britain, dispatched four legions across the Channel and established a permanent garrison in the southern part of the island. Camulodunum, modern Colchester, and Londinium, now London, were the focal points of the occupation at that time. Nero continued the work of Claudius, furthermore with a measure of constancy characteristic of the far-sighted and consistent provincial government in the early part of his reign. We have already discussed the energetic and successful crushing by Suetonius Paullinus of a major uprising of the conquered tribes.

The work of Nero's time was continued by Vespasian, who inherited a garrison of four legions and a number of minor detachments (*vexillationes*). Inevitably, provincial history is closely associated with the history of regiments and legionary quarters.[270] These formed the focal points of Roman civilization, and Romanization emanated largely from them. The history of the legions is thus in most respects more important [MH.II, 107] than that of the Emperors. The legions stationed in Britain were the second *Augusta*, the ninth 'Spanish', the twentieth *Valeria* and the fourteenth *Gemina*. It appears that in addition to these there were also powerful auxiliary units under separate commanders, particularly suitable for use on their own. They had to defend themselves there against semi-civilized peoples. Tacitus[271] states that in the great battle on the Mons Graupius 8,000 infantry took part, besides 3,000 cavalry, which permits us to conclude that in total there were probably more auxiliaries than legionary troops stationed in Britain, since these numbers alone correspond to three legions.

Vespasian reduced the number of legions by one: the fourteenth *Gemina*, which had distinguished itself in the battle against Boudicca[272] and probably earned its nickname *Martia Victrix* there, had been transferred to Italy in the latter part of Nero's reign. It then fought against Vespasian and was later used against Civilis. It was then sent back not to Britain, but to permanent quarters in Pannonia. Although *de facto* not in Britain from Nero onwards until Domitian[273] sent it to Pannonia, it was, nonetheless, part of the British garrison and only temporarily relocated. From Vespasian onwards until the lattermost period, the British occupation force consisted of three legions, the second, ninth and twentieth. The ninth was completely annihilated in combat [MH.II, 108] against the northern border peoples[274] and replaced by the sixth *Victrix*. No section of the legions remained so stationary and undisturbed by the internal political strife that rocked the Empire as these British legions, which were shielded by their very separate, insular location. Tacitus[275] expressly states that they did not participate in the wars relating to the year of the four Emperors. They had better things to do.

Vespasian continued the policy of occupying Britain and we can observe this make slow, but sure progress. The life of Agricola, written by Tacitus after the death of Domitian,[276] provides us with an extremely valuable source for this period. Nevertheless, it can only be used with caution, for it is a biography, written from a false, one-sided point of view; it puts us in the same position as Sallust's account of the Jugurthine War. Had we similarly detailed accounts of other periods of British history, the relative importance of the events portrayed by Tacitus would probably appear in quite a different light.

Vespasian was well-informed about conditions in Britain; he had served and fought there himself as a legionary legate.[277] As Emperor he sent three outstanding men in succession to command the army there: Petilius Cerialis from 71 to 74, the writer Julius Frontinus from 75 to 78, and Julius Agricola from 78 to 85 – he had already served as a legate there.[278] The chronology of this period has not been precisely established, but [MH.II, 109] the minor discrepancies are irrelevant for the historian here.

Cerialis was frivolous and rakish, but able and invaluable in a crisis. He turned his attention to the north and fought largely against the Brigantes, who lived between the Humber and the Tyne. Here he established the permanent quarters of the ninth, 'Spanish' legion, and later of the *Sexta Victrix*, in the vicinity of modern York, Eburacum.

His successor Frontinus turned his attention to the West, against the Silures in modern Wales, and established the camp at Isca-Caerleon (a corruption of *castra legionis*) and that at Deva-Chester (from *castra*). The importance that evidently accrued to these camps is clear from the fact that their names live on in the

259

modern place names. The latter two camps were intended to hold the restless inhabitants of Wales in check, just as the one at York was intended to restrain the north. The south-east was already in an advanced stage of subjugation and no longer needed to be secured in this way.

Agricola first subjugated the peoples of north Wales and the island of Mona, modern Anglesey,[279] then he turned his attention to the north, where he achieved significant successes. As a preliminary measure he undertook what one might call a geographical-military reconnaissance expedition into the northernmost part of the island, probably with the aim of forming a clear notion of the extent and military importance of its northern territories. Agricola occupied the strategically important line between [MH.II, 110] the Clyde and the Firth of Forth, approximately between Carlisle and Newcastle.[280] Later an even narrower neck of land was found between Glasgow and Edinburgh, and this was fortified. These successes roused the indigenous peoples, prompting them to a concerted attempt to throw off the yoke. The conspiracy had a religious character, involving the Celtic cult of the Druids and its priests. There was fierce fighting. The rebellious Caledonians' total force is estimated at 80,000, undoubtedly an exaggerated figure. Agricola confronted them with at most 20,000 men, but the victory was his and that of the tested superiority of the Roman soldiers.

Soon thereafter Agricola was recalled. Tacitus[281] cites the Emperor Domitian's distrust and jealousy of his generals as the reason for this. Although it is possible that such motives played a part, we must also consider what Tacitus maliciously fails to tell us. The reason behind these events is no longer known, but the fact remains that Agricola's recall was accompanied by a complete reversal of policy with regard to the whole of Britain. Hitherto the principate had adhered to a consistent and methodical plan to conquer Britain; as the successor of two generals, who had served for longer periods than normal, Agricola remained the longest in office perhaps because he was the ablest of them. He had retained his post without interruption under [MH.II, 111] three Emperors, and had achieved very significant successes in both the west and the north – successes that had been the result of a well-thought-out strategy requiring substantial material support and at all events only practicable with the closest possible agreement from the government at home. Agricola had still greater plans: he was the mastermind behind the British fleet, a superb tool for maintaining Roman hegemony on the island and capable of linking up with Gaul on the one hand, and subjugating that part of Britain that was still free on the other.

The battle of Mons Graupius points to Agricola's continuing plans.[282] It is not known where exactly this battle was fought. The Grampians are thought to derive their name from a corruption of that name by a change of the letter 'u' into 'm'. At all events the site of the battle probably lay beyond the Roman fortifications, in that part of Britain which was still unsubjugated. Agricola likewise envisaged a conquest of Ireland. Tacitus[283] relates that Agricola often spoke to him about this; in his opinion the conquest could be managed easily with a single legion. He regarded this conquest as necessary since the nationalist opposition of the Celts, which surfaced time and again in both Gaul and Britain in the form of serious rebellions, could only be broken once [MH.II, 112] and for all by defeating the Irish druids, since this nationalist opposition was essentially also a religious one.

All these plans came to a halt when Agricola was recalled. His successor is unknown, but was in any case undistinguished. The entire policy was changed; the conquest and expansion of Roman territory ceased. The gradual retreat from ambitious goals which is so typical of the late imperial period is clearly expressed in this change.

It is debatable whether the conquest of Britain was wise in any case. Once it had become an objective, it would certainly have been better to carry it through in its entirety and completely subjugate both the main island and Ireland. The reason why this aim was abandoned ranks among the *arcana imperii*. The severity of the Pannonian Wars may in the interim have been a factor in putting off these plans of conquest. But why did an Emperor such as Trajan not take them up again? After all he had pushed the frontiers of the Empire far forward on the Danube and the Euphrates. Did these conquests leave him no time or means to spare? We are confronted with a riddle, but the fact of a complete reversal in policy is indisputable, and clearly far transcends some petty fit of personal jealousy against Agricola on the part of Domitian.

After this brief period, illuminated by Tacitus's life of Agricola, British history fades once again into deep obscurity. We know nothing at all about the period of Trajan's reign, but [MH.II, 113] it is clear that Roman arms made no progress.

A severe catastrophe must have occurred under the following regime. We read of a great uprising of the Britons. Fronto,[284] under the Emperor Marcus, speaks of the huge number of soldiers who fell in Britain during Hadrian's rule. What is more – and this speaks more eloquently than any written account – the ninth legion, stationed at Eburacum, disappeared entirely and was not renewed. Some catastrophe must have occurred similar to that of Varus in the Teutoburg Forest. It was Roman custom not to re-establish under the same name a legion annihilated in this way. This was the case with the legions wiped out in the Teutoburg Forest and so also with the ninth legion, which was exposed to attacks from the Picts and Scots. But we have no details about this catastrophe, which occurred some time around 120.[285] By contrast, a great victory over the Britons was won in 143 by Lollius Urbicus under Antoninus Pius.[286]

What we know about the great fortifications of the Romans in northern Britain is of greater importance. The two walls, which for the most part still stand today, deserve our close interest. The first was built under Hadrian.[287] It extended from Carlisle to Newcastle, that is approximately along the present English–Scottish border, and consisted of a 6-metre-high stone rampart, 2 to 3 metres thick, for a total length of 80 Roman miles (16 German miles).[288] To the north, that is, facing the enemy side, it was constructed of squared stones, and had 320 towers and 17 forts. It was a most magnificent structure. Under Pius, this was followed to the north [MH.II, 114] by a second rampart[289] between Glasgow and Edinburgh, which was not so massive, had no squared stones and was only half the length. These structures evidently stood in a causal relationship with the military events associated with the destruction of the camp at York and of the ninth legion.

These great fortifications have frequently been interpreted as the frontier of Roman territory; this is certainly as false as to read into the construction of the great German fortifications on the Rhine, at Wesel and Ehrenbreitstein near Koblenz, etc., the intention of relinquishing that part of Germany lying on the left bank of the Rhine.[290] The southern ramp was by no means abandoned when Pius built the one further north; Pius demonstrably also had work carried out on the former structure. In fact they constituted a double *enceinte*. Lollius Urbicus, who had won the great victory over the Britons in 143,[291] certainly did not want to abandon the area beyond the wall; he wanted to control it.[292] A document dating from the fourth century indicates roads extending as far as Pius's rampart.[293] And if the *Itinerarium* dating from the beginning of the fifth century[294] lists the posts along Hadrian's Wall, then this wall was indeed a line of defence, but not the frontier of the Empire.

Nevertheless, it cannot be denied that these structures were a symptom of the fact that Roman defence was no longer, as in better, mightier days, being conducted offensively, but was now to be conducted defensively. The Romans no longer wanted to secure themselves by striking at hostile neighbours along their frontiers to render them harmless, [MH.II, 115] but with ramparts, ditches, and strong points. The permanence of the legionary camps was integral to this approach. The three camps mentioned earlier had existed at least since Agricola, perhaps even longer, and they remained unchanged as long as Roman rule persisted; they were never relocated. It is surprising that a small country like Wales needed two camps to hold it in check for several centuries. One might have thought that once it had been subjugated, it would have been appropriate for the permanent quarters to be relocated to the north. Nothing of the kind occurred, which means either that Wales was not permanently and completely subjugated, or that idle stagnation seized the leadership of the British army. The fact that troops were never led north of York seriously or for any length of time indicates that no progress was made. And if there was no progress, then there was regression. The *classis Britannica*, the British fleet, was never allotted a significant role either, however suited it was to one. Agricola's plans slumbered and were never reawakened. Matters were in a sorry state under Marcus Aurelius, with the menace of incessant forays by the northern peoples. Under Commodus, the governor Ulpius Marcellus won great victories.[295] But these victories signify and confirm that there were wars. The frontier territory was not pacified, as a consequence of which the north [MH.II, 116] shows only scant traces of Roman culture.

The history of Britain during the reign of Septimius Severus is unusually peculiar. This was the sole occasion[296] on which Britannia, i.e. the legions there, played a part in politics generally. As at the time of the Year of Four Emperors following the demise of the Julio-Claudian house, the great military territories once again vied for supremacy in the catastrophe which followed the death of Commodus. In 193 the eastern legions proclaimed Pescennius Niger, the Pannonian legions[297] Septimius Severus, and the Praetorians Didius Julianus. The German legions were very depleted, which explains why their candidate came to be Clodius Albinus, commander of the powerful and intact British legions. The German commanders had only two legions each, but Albinus had three.[298] After his victories over the other pretenders, Severus overcame Albinus in a battle near Lyon.[299] An immediate consequence of this victory was that Severus divided the British province into Upper and Lower Britain, so as not to leave such immense power in the hands of one man. This designation has nothing to do with geographical altitude or lowness: the southern province, closest to Rome, was called 'superior', the more distant, northern one 'inferior'. The garrison of Britannia Superior consisted of two legions, at Isca and Deva in Wales, that of Inferior of one legion at Eburacum.

When he had concluded his great eastern wars, Severus, by now advanced in years, plagued with gout and scarcely able to mount a horse, turned his attention to Britain. No specific events prompted him, perhaps the most vigorous of all the Emperors, to this enterprise. [MH.II, 117] There had certainly been some fighting, but not exactly of an unusual nature; arms were silent as all along the northern frontier. Severus wished to make up for lost time regarding what ought to have been done long before: he, too, built a wall, 32 Roman miles long. The alternative version, that it was 132 miles long, is untenable; there was no place for such a construction on the British northern border. No traces of it remain, so we know nothing about it from epigraphical sources, and it is uncertain where and what it was. However, Severus undoubtedly set an on-going operation in motion and his construction is certainly not identical with that of Hadrian,[300] but was probably a modification, a shortening, of the Antonine Wall between Glasgow and Stirling. It was no more a frontier than the other ramparts had been. Severus intended to subjugate the entire island and carry his arms as far as the northern sea.[301] A peace was concluded with the Britons and they surrendered some territory.[302] The return to an offensive policy had proved successful.

Soon thereafter a second insurrection occurred. Severus moved forward again, but death caught up with him in 211 in Eburacum (York) and his plans died with him.[303] This had been perhaps the most patriotic and sensible undertaking of the age of Emperors.[304]

His sons Caracalla and Geta [MH.II, 118] immediately abandoned their father's plans, partly out of fraternal discord, partly out of indolence, and concluded a fresh treaty with the rebels which rendered void the surrender of territory.[305] The third century marks a gap in our knowledge; no wars were waged, or at least certainly no major ones. This may be deduced, *inter alia*, from the imperial titles: Severus called himself Britannicus,[306] as did Caracalla,[307] but subsequent Emperors did not.

During the Diocletianic era the inhabitants of the North Sea coast, the Saxons and the Franks, began to make those raids which were later to play such an important role as the so-called raids of the 'Northmen.'[308] Diocletian created a new division of the British fleet, the Channel fleet, which had not existed before – a sensible measure. Its first general, Carausius, fell out with Maximian, who wanted to dismiss him and have him tried. Soon thereafter, in 287, Carausius, a man of lowly origin and not a Roman but a Menapian, unilaterally established a quasi-state.[309]

His secession differed from the other British rebellions, which had originated with the subjugated indigenous population. It was an aspect of domestic Roman politics with a most remarkable outcome. Maximian made an unsuccessful attempted to crush it, but instead a peace was concluded in which the Emperors Diocletian and Maximian formally recognized him as an equal, [MH.II, 119] thus allowing him *de iure* the independence he already enjoyed *de facto*. Carausius met his death at the hands of an assassin in 294. His successor, Allectus, was incompetent and the commander in Gaul, the Caesar Constantius, brought his rule to an end. He sailed over to Britain with an army, and literally burnt his ships behind him in order to demonstrate to his men that they must either be victorious or die, and once again brought the island under Roman rule, where it remained for another century. The Empire was weak and, as the example of Carausius shows, the Britons could long have freed themselves had they wanted to, but it is quite clear that they did not.

At the beginning of the fifth century, when under Honorius the entire West was in conflict in the aftermath of the execution of Stilicho, the Britons requested help from Honorius, while their governor Constantine was being attacked by the Spaniard Gerontius[310] and they themselves were being inundated by Saxons, Picts and Scots. Honorius declared himself unable to help them and said they must help themselves as best they could. In effect, therefore, they were voluntarily abandoned by the Emperor.[311]

The ending of Roman rule in Britain, although in fact beyond the scope of the period we are describing, has been included here because it shows clearly the deep roots that Roman rule had put down in this province, despite its late date of conquest and its remote [MH.II, 120] position beyond the seas. As is often the case in frontier provinces, the Roman Britons displayed an intensity in their sense of belonging to the Empire which tends to be absent in provinces closer to the centre, and which almost increases in direct proportion to their remoteness.

Not much is known about the state of Roman civilization and culture in Britain. Britain was not a colonized territory, like Dacia; few emigrants from Italy went there. There was, however, one very important exception to this: Britain had a very large garrison – at least 30,000 men. The veterans, who were either Roman citizens by birth, or Romanized by their lengthy period of service, were granted Roman citizenship on discharge and for the most part remained in Britain. The effects of this steady immigration of robust men should not be underestimated.

Above all, however, Britain became Romanized through the gradual adoption of Roman customs by its inhabitants. The life of Agricola is highly instructive in this regard.[312] Here Tacitus relates how Agricola eradicated taxation abuses. It emerges from this that tax collection was, on the one hand, a universally implemented and strictly controlled burden, and on the other that it was a heavily oppressive one. And yet [MH.II, 121] Britain was not a net source of profit. Appian[313] states this to explain why the Romans did not hasten to conquer the entire island. Bearing in mind its large garrison, the statement that Britain brought in little revenue over and above what was required to cover its own costs is quite credible. But it by no means follows that Britain was not efficiently, even oppressively, taxed. Tacitus also states that Agricola[314] realized that the country could not be ruled by force of arms alone, and worked towards introducing the conquered population to urban life, which was foreign to their inherited customs; as indeed the municipal constitution, the *municipium* in general, was the magic formula used by the Romans to retain the foreign peoples under their rule. Tacitus asserts that whereas the Britons had previously railed against the Latin language, they were now eager for it. Roman dress, the toga, previously abhorred, was likewise now sought after. Tacitus mentions all this in the context of a laudation, but it clearly had a factual basis and is confirmed by everything else we know. Evidently we are dealing not merely with a personal aspiration on the part of Agricola, but with a well-deliberated government policy, of which Agricola was simply a proficient representative.

[MH.II, 122] This government policy was crowned with great success, even if the Romanization of Britain cannot be compared with that of Gaul. Higher seats of learning in Gaul were often attended by the sons of British families. The inscriptions of Britain have been collated,[315] those of Gaul not yet, so these sources cannot as yet be compared. We do, however, already know, for instance, that the British inscriptions are nowhere near as numerous as the German ones. Compared to 400–500 military inscriptions from Mainz there are all of 29 from Eburacum (York)! In order to make the comparison fair, however, it is necessary to bear in mind that the garrison in Mainz was normally concentrated there, whereas substantial detachments were sent away from Eburacum. If, on the other hand, we compare Eburacum with Argentoratum (Strasburg), the difference is much smaller.

Whereas, therefore, the culture of Britain is not to be compared with that of the most cultivated parts of Germany and Gaul, such as Narbonensis, it was, none-theless, on an equal footing with that of (for instance) Normandy. We should picture Britain as rich and flourishing, with great landed estates, many monuments and a degree of luxury. Commerce was highly developed and the *vectigalia* provided rich sources of taxation. There were numerous mines in operation, customs duties were remunerative and agriculture flourished. [MH.II, 123] The Pictish and Caledonian raids themselves ensured that patriotism and loyalty to the Empire were maintained and kept alive. Some idea of the high degree of development in agriculture and trade may be derived from the fact that in the fourth century the Rhine camps in Germany were extensively provisioned from Britain.[316]

B) THE RHINE FRONTIER[317]

If, as in the case of Britain, we want to discuss the military situation first of all, effectively the skeleton of the province, then it should first be pointed out that a clear picture is hampered by frequent relocations and changes in the garrisons. An accurate, comprehensive history of military conditions under the principate is yet to be written,[318] and its main problem is that it would have to cover all the provinces of the Empire, since the various legions belonged sometimes to one province, sometimes to another.

The Gaulish–German legions on the Rhine had formed the core of the army since the time of Caesar. However, after the catastrophe of Varus under Augustus the impulse to expand was abandoned here too; it was now deemed sufficient to fend off attacks from the Germans, and to this end a well-thought-out system of defence was put in place. Eight legions, a third of the entire army, were stationed on the Rhine; this river was the hub of Roman defence strategy, at any rate in the sense that the Romans were always at pains, at least along the upper course, to retain control of both banks and [MH.II, 124] thereby to be able to enter enemy territory without hindrance.

The army was divided into two halves, the *exercitus superior* and *exercitus inferior* respectively. The garrison of Upper Germany originally consisted of four legions and gradually decreased, first to three, then to two. In Vespasian's time the eighth *Augusta* was stationed in Alsace at Argentoratum (Strasburg), where Ptolemy[319] still locates it in Pius's time. Argentoratum was probably the headquarters of this legion, although detachments were posted throughout Baden. The twenty-second *Primigenia* was encamped at Mainz, where it had been for centuries. (A brief transfer to Lower Germany is a problem.) The first *Adiutrix* was stationed at Baden-Baden under Trajan and later occupied quarters at Vindonissa in Switzerland. The twenty-first *Rapax* was cashiered under Domitian and later replaced by the eleventh *Claudia*. The first *Adiutrix* and the eleventh *Claudia* later went to Pannonia, while the eighth *Augusta* remained in Upper Germany, and when the eleventh went to Pannonia the twenty-second returned from Lower Germany. These relocations were probably a result of the Marcomannic Wars under Marcus, when the eighth and twenty-second legions alone constituted the garrison of Upper Germany. Whereas, therefore, Vespasian inherited four legions in Upper Germany, Trajan left three and Marcus two.

[MH.II, 125] During the Flavian period the twenty-second *Primigenia* was stationed in Lower Germany until Domitian; it was then moved to Upper Germany and replaced by the first *Minervia*, a new legion probably established by Domitian as successor to the *Rapax*, but which had a different permanent base. The first *Minervia* remained in Lower Germany. As we have seen, the sixth *Victrix* was sent to Britain by Hadrian and was replaced by the tenth *Gemina*. Trajan transferred it to Pannonia, relocating the thirtieth *Ulpia* to Lower Germany instead. Vespasian thus reduced the number from four to three and Hadrian from three to two. The net result was that in the period from Vespasian to Hadrian the garrison of Germany was reduced from eight to four legions, with headquarters at Vetera (near Xanten), Bonn,[320] Mainz and Strasburg. In the case of Strasburg there is some uncertainty; although Ptolemy[321] still mentions it, it does not really fit into the defence system as a whole, and it is not beyond the bounds of possibility that the eighth *Augusta* was likewise re-located to Mainz, although this too – the stationing of two legions in one camp – was an anomaly in the later imperial age.[322] We can see that the Roman system of defence and fortification was based on much the same premises [MH.II, 126] as modern strategy, and that the importance of Mainz was as clearly recognized by the Romans, as has been depicted by our own great strategist[323] in his marvellous introduction to the account on the war of 1870/1 published by the General Staff.[324]

As regards the boundaries[325] of these two provinces, which were treated quite differently, there have been some rather foolish arguments about this, if you allow me to say so. Ptolemy's account[326] is unintelligible: he names the Obrincas as the boundary river – a name that occurs nowhere else and bears no resemblance to any modern river name. His further account is muddled: for example, he includes Mainz in the lower province, which is undoubtedly wrong.

It seems to me that the matter is reasonably beyond doubt: all we have to do is look at the tile-stamps. No tiles of Lower German legions have been found beyond Bonn. The seals of the Upper German legions extend far beyond the rivers Nahe and Lahn as far as Antunnacum (Andernach). Everything found there pertains to the eighth and twenty-second (i.e. Upper German) legions. We must thus seek the boundary near Neuwied, and there is nothing to stop us from taking the river Wied to be Ptolemy's Obrincas. It could quite as easily be this as any other.[327]

As we have already seen, the overthrow of Vitellius led to the uprising of the Batavians and of Julius Civilis [MH.II, 127], which was put down. Unfortunately the conclusion of Tacitus's *Histories* containing the end of this war is missing. Complete calm will have reigned on the Rhine under Vespasian. What we read about the capture of Veleda[328] is not proof of a fresh war. This renowned priestess was probably taken prisoner already during the Batavian War, and Suetonius's silence concerning any further wars demonstrates that there can have been none. The campaign of conquest during this reign was directed at Britain; moreover, the first reduction in the size of the German army dates from Vespasian, which allows us to assume that there was peace.

Nothing of any importance occurred in Germany under Titus either, so far as we know. Under Domitian, however, there was once again a substantial reduction of the garrison, albeit following one serious war and in association with a completely new form of frontier defence and regulation. This war, which ended in AD 84, was waged against the Chatti, who inhabited the region to the east and north opposite Mainz towards the river Werra, that is approximately the modern territory of both parts of Hessen; at any rate only the Chatti are mentioned. To the south of the territory of the Chatti, in modern Baden, there was a gap in the inhabited territory. Once the Helvetians had inhabited the region as far north as the river Main,[329] but they had later abandoned these northern regions of Baden and Württemberg. Since then there had been a vacuum – a thinly populated, or even completely unpopulated, cleared wasteland that suited Rome admirably [MH.II, 128] as a defensible forefield against the territories beyond.[330]

The war against the Chatti was waged mainly from Upper Germany. Extant accounts of it by Frontinus relate that a triumph was celebrated.[331] Frontinus is, admittedly, a *laudator* (he writes in praise of the Emperor); nevertheless, these successes, apart from the vivid manner in which they are depicted, may not have been trivial ones. Border fortifications were raised *in finibus Cubiorum* – but who were the Cubii?[332] The fortifications are reputed to have extended for 120,000 paces, i.e. 120 Roman miles, or 30 geographical miles.[333] A huge amount has been written about this *limes*. However, a *limes* is by no means a frontier wall, as is so often asserted.[334] This would be called a *vallum*. A *limes* is a boundary, in the sense of a division. Velleius[335] says that Tiberius *aperit limites*: these were roads through the forests. The notion of fortification is by no means necessarily implicit in the term, although such roads must, of course, have been fortified, or at any rate defended;[336] this, however, can be done in any number of other ways. In short, a *limes* is not a *vallum*. This *limes* should rather be envisaged as a road of that length; but where should it be sought? Hübner's work[337] on this subject is a compilation of all the specialist studies made by local archaeologists. Although it already departs substantially from ghost-like notions of fortification,[338] too much of it still survives. The idea of a [MH.II, 129] continuous line of defence extending from the Danube to the Rhine, like the one in Scotland, is certainly wrong. First, the terrain is unsuitable; Scotland had the natural conditions for such a line from one strait across to the other, but this was not feasible between Regensburg and Frankfurt. Second, even if it had been possible to construct such a line, how was it to be defended? The army's strength had been reduced! One need only compare the fighting force assigned to the defence of the British fortifications and the impossibility of doing it in Germany instantly becomes clear.[339]

There were no such fortifications in Lower Germany; in Upper Germany and Raetia there were some, but likewise they were not homogeneous or continuous. We need to distinguish a pair of lines here: the Taunus fortifications around Wiesbaden, and those in Baden. In his *Germania* (ch. 29), written in the first months of Trajan's reign, Tacitus describes Baden as part of the Empire. His *Annals* contain references to earthworks at Aquae Mattiacae (Wiesbaden) under Claudius,[340] which were not, however, maintained for long. It is stated in the *Histories* (IV, 37) that the Mattiacii launched an attack at the time of Civilis's rebellion. Pliny[341] speaks of the *aquae Mattiacae* as being in 'Germania', by which he always means free Germany, not the part subjugated by the Romans. The *aquae Mattiacae* are the warm springs near Wiesbaden. [MH.II, 130] Under Vespasian, therefore, these lands were evidently still free; *extra veteres terminos imperii Romani*, as Tacitus puts it in his *Germania*.[342] These lands were, therefore, undoubtedly subjugated under Domitian, as a result of the war against the Chatti. Tacitus refrains from mentioning the name as a result of the abhorrence with which he treats Domitian generally. This acquisition was attractive to the Romans, first on account of the warm springs, to which they attached importance (not just here, but also at Baden-Baden), and second for its strategic importance as forefield of the crucial city of Mainz. Although Castel already belonged to the Romans, Wiesbaden represented a useful extension into the territory beyond. The line of fortifications constructed there is easy to idendify: the Saalburg on the far side of the Taunus near Homburg and a number of other forts were all part of it.

While this was the result of the war against the Chatti, the passage in Frontinus[343] refers to the *limes* extending 120 miles. Since there was no room for such a length in Hessen, the quotation must refer to the 'Agri Decumates'.

In the passage already referred to,[344] Tacitus writes that 'frontiers had been established and garrisons moved forward'; they appear as part of the province. But again, he fails to state by whom they had been incorporated; here again, therefore, we have reason to assume that it was Domitian. Had it been anyone [MH.II, 131] else, Tacitus would have named him.

But what does 'Agri Decumates' mean? First and foremost, the term itself poses problems: it is a most unusual formation. *Primates*, which does occur, has quite a different meaning. Furthermore, the word is encountered only in Tacitus; we interpret it to mean 'titheland', i.e. arable land from which a tenth of the yield was paid as tax. This would constitute a most exceptionally light tax; the customary rate was a fifth or a seventh. This low tax would, in fact, be understandable, since these lands were very exposed and the danger that they would be ravaged was very great. It is therefore conceivable that the government leased the arable land to those prepared to shoulder the risk in return for a low rent. The fact that there was no ethnic designation for the land and instead a designation in terms of taxation was chosen resulted from the devastated character of the countryside, which was void of inhabitants, apart from *levissimi quique Gallorum*. However, this unusual term may equally well have arisen as a result of scribal error.[345]

Although no hero, Domitian was a most sensible administrator, and the modification and securing of the German frontier was essentially an administrative act. The *limes* was no *vallum*. The Romans distinguished between *limes* and *ripa*; they spoke of *milites riparienses* and *milites limitenses*. [MH.II, 132] The *limes* thus constituted a boundary, whose skilful selection contributed something towards its defensive capability. We are no longer able to ascertain how much of the limes was established by Domitian and how much by his successors up to Marcus. Inscriptions are rare and do not date far back – it is not like England, where a great deal of the history of the Wall can be deduced from inscriptions. Nothing can be deduced from the constructions themselves. For us Germans, however, these works are of such extraordinary interest that a somewhat closer examination seems appropriate. Frontinus's 120 miles (see MH.II, 128) correspond quite well to the fortifications of the Agri Decumates, in so far as it is appropriate to say 'correspond', given such enormous uncertainty. We do not know where they began or ended. Kiepert's map offers a reliable outline of all the extant fortifications.

The *limes* begins at Regensburg.[346] Below this point the Danube provided adequate cover, whereas above it could not be used for protection. From Regensburg the *limes* goes west, with various angles and bends, as far as Aalen[347] – presumably this section was not Domitian's work – where it meets the Gallic *limes*[348] at an acute angle. The line cannot have run like this originally: it completely disregards the terrain. In the *limes Raeticus*, we are dealing with two separate constructions. Originally the boundary rampart probably started at Günzburg on the Danube. Günzburg and Lautlingen were important sites in Roman times.[349] From the lower Main [MH.II, 133] as far as Homburg, there exist a number of lines.

The military character of the construction consisted not of a *vallum*, but freestanding forts. Frontinus expressly states this. Certainly forts were incorporated into the *vallum* in Britain, but here it is different. In Britain the focus was the Wall

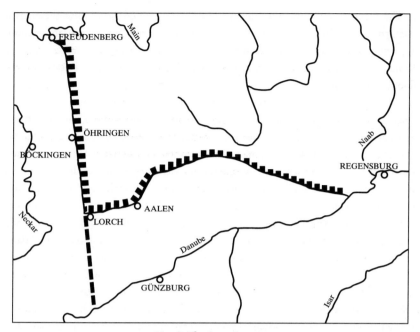

Map 2 The *limes Raeticus*

itself, from which the forts projected; but, as Duncker,[350] one of the best experts on the Main-line fortifications, states, in Germany the focus was the forts, although this does not exclude the possibility of their being linked. But wherever (for example) it was possible to make use of a river, there was no such link – as between Miltenberg and Hanau-am-Main. There we can still trace a series of forts. From Lorch, on the other hand, the embankment extends for 50 miles up hill and down dale in a straight line to the north as far as Freudenberg-am-Main. A completely straight embankment constructed for defence purposes would have excited the scorn of the military; it cannot possibly have been built for such a purpose. So we have to think of some other function. Such an embankment would have been superb as a line of march and as a line of communication for fire signals. Such a line of signals can be of immense importance in the event of an enemy breakthrough. Elsewhere, under different conditions, the construction was different. Nothing could be more erroneous, however, than to ascribe to this *limes* some unified military project, as it certainly existed and was consistently put into effect in the case of the British construction. Perhaps there was an embankment on the Taunus, but the Main offered an adequate river boundary; then there probably came a series of forts according to the requirements of particular locations. This construction was not, after all, built at a single [MH.II, 134] stroke. Oehringen was called 'Vicus Aurelius' and was thus built by Marcus Aurelius. Benningen can be traced back to Pius, from whose time we have some inscriptions.[351]

271

The Neckar valley and the Odenwald became part of the Empire through the construction of this road, as did the region around Rottenburg in southern Württemberg. Rottweil was called 'Arae Flaviae'[352] and is the earliest trace of Roman settlement to be found in this area. The main credit for this is probably due to Domitian.

Trajan's work focused more on Upper Germany; nevertheless, there is hardly another Emperor about whom we know so little. Some traces suggest that he was similarly active in Lower Germany as Domitian had been in Upper Germany. Probably, however, he acquired the appellation *Germanicus*[353] through the wars with the Danubian Germans, since he seems not to have fought any wars in Lower Germany. On the other hand the extension of the frontier from the sea beyond the territory of the Batavians, who had long been part of the Empire, can be traced back to him. The Roman Rhine frontier was located at the mouth of the Old Rhine and thus far further north than now. The region between the Waal and the Old Rhine belonged to the Batavians. According to Tacitus, the Friesians and the Canninefati[354] [MH.II, 135] were still free Germans, but soon thereafter we find *cohortes* and *alae* constituted from them. With one sole exception,[355] however, it was a resolute Roman principle to recruit Roman troops only from Roman territory. The Canninefati from the Leiden region must, according to the inscriptions, already have been subjugated at the time of Trajan.[356] Bearing in mind the date of Tacitus's reference, this means that they must have been incorporated into the Empire in the first years of his reign. They were located between the Rhine and the Zuiderzee and were certainly part of the great Friesian tribal grouping. It was there that Trajan[357] learned of the death of Nerva and was informed at the same time of his election as Emperor, or rather of his sole rule. Otherwise we have only the brief note in Eutropius:[358] *urbes trans Rhenum in Germania reparavit*. This suggests a continuation of the work of Domitian. Rottenburg[359] and Heidelberg[360] bore the title *Ulpia*. Trajan must, therefore, have contributed to the further spread of cultivation in this wasteland. Baden-Baden was called 'Aquae Aureliae',[361] which refers to a later Emperor, but Trajan and detachments from two of his legions are named in the inscriptions there. Municipal rights were not granted to the place until later; in [MH.II, 136] Trajan's time it was only a *vicus*. Legion garrisons were only reluctantly granted urban rights, as the two statuses were not particularly compatible. Ammianus speaks of a *castellum* built in the Agri Decumates.[362] Sidonius[363] states that Cologne was a terror to the Sugambri. This suggests that Trajan resided there in person, and it was from there that he held the Germans in check.

The following period was one of profound peace. Hadrian attended to military organization, but is expressly described as *pacis amator*,[364] although he made sure that his soldiers exercised hard. An extant reference to him,[365] that he appointed a king for the Germans, is very vague and probably does not refer to this area, but rather to the Danube Germans, since the Rhine Germans had no kings. Pius's activities in Germany are likewise rather obscure. *Germanos contudit*, 'he crushed the Germans', asserts his biographer.[366] Incidentally, he had done work on the fortifications. Similarly, we know little about the German activities of Marcus – a conspicuous gap. The Chatti are mentioned for the last time when Marcus's general, Aufidius Victorinus, defeated them at Mainz and seems to have annihilated them.[367] A re-drawing of the line of the boundary rampart, the *limes Raeticus*, probably took place under him. It was most fortunate that the Rhine Germans remained peaceful, since the Danube lands were consumed by the turmoil of war.

[MH.II, 137] Nor do we read of any military complications under Septimius Severus. This silence on the part of writers is undoubtedly no coincidence, but demonstrates that the second century, from the reign of Nerva up to the end of Severus's reign, was a period of complete peace and uninterrupted cultural development for the territories along the Rhine.

There is one area in which we encounter a particularly remarkable phenomenon of the Gallic world. The *leuga* (league) [the Gallic unit of road measurement], equivalent to 1½ miles,[368] does not appear on earlier milestones, where all distances are given in miles (*millia passuum*). Under Severus, however, milestone distances in Gaul were calculated in leagues. Whence derives this quite unique and uncustomary appearance of national particularity? In the face of such a problem, we start to make guesses and hypotheses: could it be connected with the uprising of Clodius Albinus, who for some time was recognized as Severus's co-regent? It is not inconceivable that this, to some extent 'nationalist', uprising, attempted officially to restore an institution which in practice had survived all along. The public will have always calculated in leagues; such notions are extraordinarily fixed and cannot easily be banned out of existence. So it is not inconceivabe that the government retained this convention after the uprising had been suppressed.

[MH.II, 138] The Raetian *limes*,[369] it should be borne in mind, was both newer than the German line of forts and shortened it. Extant inscriptions show that it already existed under Pius; we have some dating from 148. This would be compatible with the assumption that Domitian initiated it and Trajan or Hadrian constructed the final shortening. The region as a whole, the last to become part of the Empire (around Eichstätt and Nördlingen) and only in Roman hands for around a hundred years, was remarkably devoid of towns; while a wealth of cities can be shown to have developed in the Agri Decumates, military facilities can indeed be found here, but no towns or municipal constitution.

The third century marked the period of collapse. Whereas from the time of Domitian to Severus Germany remained undisturbed, in the third century this changed. This was the period which contained the seeds of the great migrations[370] and is of exceptional interest to us Germans in particular. Unfortunately, our surviving accounts are poor, unreliable and inadequate, leaving so much to guess-work concerning the political issues that it is precarious to speak about them at all. This is exacerbated by the fact that most of the accounts in our possession are narrated from the Roman standpoint; it would, perhaps, be better to see them illuminated from the German standpoint, although we could hardly expect even this to reveal anything satisfactory.

In 213 Caracalla led one more expedition, of an offensive nature, into Germany. A few years [MH.II, 139] ago a fragment of records of the proceedings of a priestly *collegium* was discovered in which the blessing of the gods was invoked on an expedition by the Emperor *per limitem Raetiae ad hostes extirpandos*.[371] The war was waged on the Main, which was reached directly from the *limes Raeticus*. The Alamanni fought well, especially on horseback. This time victory went to the Romans, although it is not clear whether it was won by arms alone, or by gold as well. Caracalla is reputed to have operated a great deal through bribery.[372] Roman supremacy was maintained once again, and was effective as far as the Germans settled along the Elbe.

The chief distinguishing feature of this war is the appearance of new names. This is the first occasion on which the Alamanni are mentioned, shortly to be followed by the Franks. The ancient tribal names, familiar from the earlier struggles of the Romans in these parts, now disappear. This profound change in circumstances lies in the fact that from now on we are dealing with tribal confederations. What are the Alamanni? Asinius Quadratus, a Greek historian who wrote under Philip the Arab,[373] probably experienced this début of the Alamanni at first hand, and calls them a 'gathered, mixed people'. This is exactly how one might describe a tribal confederation. German language experts nowadays unanimously agree that 'Alamanni' means 'the common, all-mannish', which is exactly what Quadratus says. We know less about the peoples who constituted this Alamannic union than we do in the case of the Franks. Perhaps it included the Chatti, although others dispute this.[374] [MH.II, 140] Given the geographical location they must have been peoples who faced the Agri Decumates. Their union was the new element with which the Romans now had to reckon, and which in the long term they were not able to deal with. The fall of the Roman Empire was brought about neither by the mere degeneration of the Roman element nor by the personal incompetence of the Emperors.

The emergence of the name 'Alamanni' can only be explained in terms of a union of previously separate tribes. They were not ruled by a single ruler. The *reguli* mentioned by our sources[375] were local kings; an overall ruler does not appear until the Frankish period.[376] What Gregory[377] says about the Franks will also have applied to the Alamanni – that they consisted of a number of cantons organized according to lineage, and with one noble family at their head. The head of this family was the local king, the *regulus*. In other words, a purely aristocratic system. This was traditional; what was new was their alliance, the cooperation of separate regions. For what reason did they join forces? This question has been much discussed, but to little avail. Overpopulation may have been a contributory factor; likewise the pressure of tribes inhabiting regions further to the east, and now in migration. It was certainly not the case that the Germans were suddenly possessed by an urge for planned conquest instead of their earlier raiding and plundering campaigns. It is totally ahistorical for a national character [MH.II, 141] to experience a sudden change of this sort of its own accord. Obviously, however, successes gradually led campaigns for booty to develop into campaigns of colonization. Originally, however, these were campaigns for booty and plunder *par excellence*; only later was the territory overrun, which they would otherwise usually quit every year or every few years, retained as a permanent possession. Once Arminius's vision crystallized, something of this kind would emerge.[378] Once the Alamannic union had been formed and proved successful, the Frankish union soon followed. This was, if I may say so, the first manifestation of the notion of German unity and, even in this extremely incomplete form, it was already enough to make an impact on world history and to force it on to a new course.

In the aftermath of Caracalla's victory bitter wars ensued under Alexander Severus and Maximinus in 234. The Germans seized the offensive. Alexander himself was killed during these wars in Germany[379] and his successor Maximinus had to fight on for years. At last victory favoured the Romans once more.[380] The final counter-attack against the German offensive took place on the far side of the *limes*.

A few years of peace followed. The collapse of the Empire finally came under Valerian and Gallienus, favoured by the diversion which the Persian War in the East created for Rome's western enemies. The garrisons [MH.II, 142] on the Rhine had to be depleted, and it was no longer possible to stem the tide of Germans. Individual details are lost and we can only deduce events from their results. Gallienus styled himself *Germanicus maximus quintum*[381] – this was mere court flattery, intended to cloak the unlimited defeat. We know that Spain was overrun by the Franks under Valerian, who held Tarraco, the capital, in their possession for no less than twelve years, and advanced across the Mediterranean to Africa.[382]

Peace in Italy came to an end at the same time. The Germans – in this case Alamanni – advanced as far as Ravenna.[383] In the reign of Gallienus they launched a second raid and ravaged Gaul. A remarkable inscription documenting the requirements of this period is still extant, necessarily cloaked in flattery. Above one of the city gates of Verona we read that from 3 April until 4 December 265 Gallienus had a new wall built about Verona Nova Gallieniana.[384] The truth is that for centuries it had not occurred to anyone to fortify an Italian city; everywhere the ancient walls lay in ruins, since they were simply no longer necessary. But clearly, if Tarraco and Ravenna were no longer safe, it was time to think of protecting cities once again. This being the case, how must matters have stood in small towns, or out in the countryside? [MH.II, 143] An inscription from Grenoble dating to 269 provides an insight into this. In this peaceful territory, the Provincia Narbonensis, a great army was mustered from the most diverse detachments – unfortunately its component parts are not named – under the authority of the commanding officer of the local Roman fire brigades![385] And this was for protection against barbarians: so far had things come!

We can take it for granted that the Rhine frontier[386] had been lost first, and it becomes clear what the honorary title assumed by Gallienus actually meant. One document, however confusing and muddled in its particular details, is clear in its essentials: at the conclusion of the *Laterculus Veronensis*, the Veronese provincial register,[387] it is stated that the Romans had been in possession of a territory of 80 leagues, i.e. 120 German miles, on the far side of the Rhine beyond the *castellum Montiacesenam*, and that this was occupied by the Germans in the time of Gallienus. '*Montiacesenam*' evidently stands for '*Mogontiacense*',[388] but the Romans never possessed so much territory there. Other references in this list are also incorrect, for example the one to Belgica Prima, since the division of Belgica into a 'Prima' and a 'Secunda' did not occur until the time of Diocletian.[389] But the main point which emerges, however, is that in the time of Gallienus the trans-rhenan possessions had to be relinquished.

[MH.II, 144] But the point had almost been reached where Gaul was lost. The era of the so-called thirty tyrants is a most unfortunate label.[390] This was purely and simply a period of dissolution. For a considerable period, Britain, Gaul and Spain sought to go their own way under Marcus Cassianius Postumus.[391] Who this man originally was and what office he occupied is unknown. He was not *Transrhenani limitis dux* (Duke of the Frontier beyond the Rhine), as he is styled in one obviously forged letter of Valerian's:[392] no such office ever existed. Duces were not created until the end of the third century and at that time it was impossible to appoint anyone as *duces transrhenani limitis*, since no *limes transrhenanus* existed any longer; it had been irrevocably wrested from the Romans. Postumus was probably governor of one of the two Germanies. After his father Valerianus had met his end in 260 in the military complexities of the East,[393] Gallienus departed for the Danube lands, leaving his under-age son Saloninus behind at Cologne in the care of Silvanus and Postumus.[394] The motives underlying subsequent events are unknown to us. According to some accounts Postumus felt slighted in comparison with Silvanus and was jealous of him. But the crucial factor will have been that Gaul had been left to its own devices; the mother country was no longer [MH.II, 145] able to provide protection. What was to be repeated later during the demise of the western Empire[395] now made its first appearance: the time of Gallienus is oddly prophetic of the period of the great migrations. It is striking that while the Franks were invading, pillaging and plundering in Spain and the Alamanni Italy, Gaul was left unaided. This was enough to bring the senior officers together to eliminate Silvanus and proclaim Postumus as Emperor not only of Gaul, but of all the West.

The following example graphically reveals the weakness of our sources: writers know and name Postumus solely as ruler of Gaul. However, inscriptions[396] show that he also ruled over Britain and Spain, which helps us to understand the expression that it was *exercitus consentientes*, a consensus of the armies, which brought Postumus to the throne. That was the unanimous wish of the German, British and Spanish legions. Postumus called himself *restitutor Galliarum*,[397] and with every justification. If the Franks quit Spain after years of occupation, and Gaul of necessity remained united, this was his doing. The *ingens virtus ac moderatio* for which one reliable writer[398] praises him, is revealed in the immense feat of saving the West once more. It is remarkable that, when the West did collapse definitively [MH.II, 146] and irrevocably, it was once again Gaul that kept up the struggle for some years more.[399]

What forms did this Empire of Postumus take? Written sources know nothing about this; they were mere local chroniclers whose vision and interest did not extend beyond the horizons of their cities. Once again coins and inscriptions must come to our aid.[400] According to these sources this Empire appears as a discrete entity, unconnected to the rest of the Empire. The minting of coins was a separate, Gallic affair. But Postumus also made no attempt to extend his rule, although he styled himself *Pius Felix Augustus*[401] after the manner of the Roman Emperors, and could with little effort have annexed at least northern Italy had he so wished. We are left with the impression that he wanted to establish a Gallic Empire. His rule lasted for a fairly long time.[402] A great deal of road construction was evidently carried out. One specifically Gallic feature is that his coins frequently display local deities; it is as though the Gallic Hercules was the heir of the *Iuppiter Optimus Maximus* of Roman coins. His residence was at Cologne: this very fact, as well as the title *Germanicus Maximus Quintum* on his coins, permits us to deduce that there were continuous and successful wars against the Germans. The coins show high-quality workmanship; the gold coins especially reveal finer artistic execution than coins of the city of Rome from the same period. It almost seems as if Gaul [MH.II, 147] became a haven for artists and scholars obliged to flee from depopulated, devastated Italy. Postumus died fighting for a fine and just cause, the attempt to protect the great cities from the plundering mania of discharged soldiers. Rome neither marched against him nor recognized him, although a rival Emperor, Laelianus, was proclaimed within Gaul itself. He was overcome by the troops of Postumus, who aimed to plunder Mainz, where the battle had taken place. Postumus refused to allow them to do this and, in making his stand for civic liberty, met a glorious death in the ensuing tumult.[403] His Empire did not meet its end with him; various pretenders – Victorinus, Tetricus and others – perpetuated it for a time, but its demise came from a different quarter.

Gallienus was assassinated in 268; there followed the brief reign of Claudius, who probably wished to reconquer Gaul; the Grenoble inscription mentioned above was erected in his honour. No serious fighting took place, since events on the Danube were too pressing and occupied all of his strength. He died in 270.

He was followed by Lucius Domitius Aurelianus, one of the most outstanding and forceful of all the Emperors. He and Postumus between them kept the great migrations at bay for two centuries.[404] [MH.II, 148] Fortune was not with Aurelian in the first years of his reign: he had to contend with incessant raids by the Alamanni. Indeed, in 271 the Romans suffered an exceptionally severe defeat at Placentia.[405] A clear symptom of the fear this engendered was the construction of a wall around the capital, carried out in 271 in the direct aftermath of this defeat.[406] It is a colossal construction, three miles long, but exploitative in the worst sense of the word, built using hastily robbed materials under the force of urgent necessity.[407] One can already sense in advance the siege of Rome in the fifth century.

At this point there was a turn in the Empire's fortunes. Aurelian achieved great successes against the Juthungi, one of the tribal components of the Alamanni. Probably the ancestors of the Swabians (Suevians), they resided in modern Bavaria and plagued Augsburg with frequent plundering forays. We still possess a very interesting fragment of Dexippos containing some of the speeches and episodes of this war.[408] We learn from this that the Romans had already reached the point of paying the Germans tribute, i.e. buying freedom from attack by means of annual payments. In this fragment, which despite its rhetorical tenor provides valuable and authentic information, the Juthungian envoys deal with the Romans on a completely equal footing. Despite their defeat near the sources of the Danube, they demanded [MH.II, 149] continued payment of tribute. They pointed out to the Romans the immense fighting force their people were able to muster – 40,000 cavalry and 80,000 foot soldiers – entirely out of indigenous tribal folk with no outsiders. Although these figures cannot be taken as quite accurate and some degree of rhetorical exaggeration is involved, what astonishes us is the startling ratio of cavalry to infantry, which may well be correct and characterizes these Germans as a significant cavalry force: *Alamanni mirifice ex equis pugnantes.*[409] Bearing in mind that these numbers relate to a sort of home guard, this figure may not even be exaggerated. The upshot of these negotiations was that the Alamanni were routed on the upper Danube. Nonetheless, there is no doubt whatever that the trans-rhenan and trans-danubian territories were definitively relinquished and remained so. All that could be hoped and striven for now was to maintain the river border and safeguard Vindelicia and the cities such as Augsburg.

A respite ensued. In 274 the separate regime in Gaul came to an end. The true political cause of this is to be sought in the consolidation of Italy and the East. This removed the reason for separation in the minds of the Gallic Romans, who had, after all, not seceded willingly from the Empire, but had set themselves up 'in answer to need, not their own desire'.[410] [MH.II, 150] Gaul was not really reconquered. Admittedly Aurelian went there, but Tetricus, Emperor of this western military state, hastened to submit himself in order to shake off his dependence on his army; he became Aurelian's governor in Italy.[411] His willingness to submit is most remarkable: we see the same circumstances as in Britain. In order to understand these we need to bear in mind that in both countries Romans were still in fact living 'abroad' and sought a natural connection with Rome whenever they found themselves there. These were conditions similar to those under which the English live, for example, in India and would, when necessary, lead to similar consequences.

This, then, resolved the great catastrophe of the independence of the West. In 275 Aurelian was overthrown by a military conspiracy;[412] immediately after his death the Germans flooded across Gaul yet again. The historical tradition for this period is extremely scant; we frequently only learn of Roman defeats at all through accounts of subsequent victories for Roman arms. During the brief reign of Aurelian's successor, the Emperor Tacitus, some sixty Gallic *civitates* fell into German hands.[413] The only possible way of interpreting this is that the Germans crossed the entire line of the Rhine and swept far across the land.

Tacitus's successor Probus conducted a serious [MH.II, 151] campaign against the Germans in 279. For once we encounter intelligible geographical names in the accounts. The Germans were driven out of the Neckar region back across the Alba. The Alba is the Swabian Alb.[414] This cannot be taken to mean that the entire territory beyond the Rhine was reconquered. Inscriptions from this region date only up to the time of Gallienus and, although coins of later Emperors are not entirely absent – as a result of continuing lively commercial links – they are present in such greatly reduced numbers that the facts speak clearly for themselves. We are thus obliged to assume that Probus did carry out a victorious campaign in these parts, but did not occupy them permanently. This is borne out by the reference that *Contra urbes Romanas in solo barbarico castella condidit*.[415] *Contra* is used of a camp opposite a city located on a river; this means, therefore, that he established bridgeheads, fortified points, on the German side of the Rhine and the Danube. The Danube and Rhine, linked by a *limes* on Lake Constance, now constituted the border, not the old *limes*.

The pressure of the Alamanni is a true piece of the great migration, characterized by the ensuing advance of hitherto unknown peoples. All we can observe are the vanguards of their columns springing into action; what was taking place behind this curtain, [MH.II, 152] actually the true motor behind events, is now lost without trace.

It is no coincidence that all was quiet in the Rhine regions in the mid-imperial period. Tacitus speaks only of the 'peaceful Hermunduri'.[416] These lands were truly peaceful and Roman civilization advanced under the protection of armed Roman rule. This scene suddenly changed under Gallienus. We witness the appearance of the Alamanni and of a number of other, previously unmentioned, entirely new peoples. The attack was launched with greater force than ever before; so we have to infer that there were irresistible masses pushing them forward from behind. The force of the attack was particularly directed against Italy. All these factors permit us to conclude the presence of fresh elements which had not yet come into contact with the plunderers. The Huns were the tribe that was now pressing forward.[417] The consequence of this movement was the loss of all territory on the far side of the Danube and Rhine. But the movement also came to a halt at these rivers. It was here that this wave of peoples accumulated, not to cross over the Rhine for another century, at least not permanently. The enemy also made raids across this river from time to time, but until the beginning of the fifth century the attacks on modern-day Switzerland and Alsace were successfully warded off. Only then did this frontier too collapse.

[MH.II, 153] Like the Alamanni, the Franks were undoubtedly also a confederation of tribes rather than a homogeneous people.[418] The origin of the name is unclear. We cannot ascertain whether it derives from some national trait or whether, as reported by John Lydus[419] (a Byzantine from the time of Justinian), they were originally called Sugambri and renamed after their leader (*hegemon*).[420] The substance itself is clear, however: Arminius's vision became reality with the formation of a strong union, similar to that of the Alamanni. Although the individual sections of the confederation were called *partes*, it should not be construed as a mere alliance, but was rather like the Latin League, which had virtually the cohesion of a homogeneous state and defied the assaults of Hannibal. The component parts of the Frankish federation are more easily identifiable than those of the Alamannic union. In a word, they were the peoples who had fought at the catastrophe of Varus.

They first appear on the old Roman map of post routes, the Peutinger Table: *Chamavi qui et Franci*.[421] Other component tribes are named by Gregory of Tours,[422] or rather by Sulpicius Alexander, whom he excerpted; thus the Bructeri, Ampsivari and the Chatti. The latter, however, are doubtful. Ammianus[423] names the Chattuari. Generally speaking, they were the peoples on the right bank of the lower Rhine. The Cherusci are not named. As was generally the case with one or other of these smaller tribes, they had probably been wiped out in the course of time. It should be noted that in later times [MH.II, 154] the terms Sugambri and Franks were used interchangably, especially by poets who cultivated classical vocabulary.[424] The conclusion apparently to be drawn from this, that the Sugambri numbered among the Franks, is uncertain; this is a poetic reference and a poetic name. It is more likely that the Sugambri, like the Ubii, were assimilated not by the Franks, but by the Romans. It should not be forgotten that they had already been relocated to the left bank of the Rhine in the time of Caesar.[425]

The Franks[426] are first named under Postumus, who had *auxilia Francica*, and during whose reign they carried out their campaign against Tarraco.[427] Their presence is fully authenticated under Probus.[428] Aurelian had no time to make the most of his victories. Probus completed them and drove the Franks out of the Empire. We possess no further details, however. Their original regions of habitation were in the vicinity of the Lippe as far as the sea and in particular the Dutch coast. We have already had cause to refer to them as pirates who ranged as far as the Mediterranean. Conditions in northern France are less certain and more fluid. Here the Franks took part only in internal wars. Carausius acquired his position of admiral in combat against Franks and Saxons,[429] but his opponents maintained [MH.II, 155] that he was in league with the Franks in northern France.[430] When Maximian then made an attempt to suppress the insurgents the entire Scheldt region was in Frankish hands and Maximian made no headway either against them or against Carausius.

Constantine did manage to defeat them, but not to drive them out. One panegyric asserts that he *ipsos in Romanas transtulit nationes*.[431] Translating from panegyrical into everyday parlance, this probably means that he had to countenance leaving them in the conquered territories and to be content with their formal submission. From then on the Franks inhabited these lands; the main tribe, the Salian Franks, can certainly be located in Toxandria (Tongeren and Maastricht), according to Ammianus's testimony.[432] This thus makes them the first German people to settle permanently in Roman territory. Julian also fought against them,[433] but made little headway and, indeed, had to look on while they expanded further. This may have been called 'transferral to new territories', but we should assume that here too Rome conducted itself with great passivity during this 'transferral'.

When mixed kingdoms developed later and [MH.II, 156] the vigour of German nationality became fused with Roman civilization, the Franks naturally played a leading role. Their presence in northern France can probably be traced as far back as the time of Postumus and Carausius, if not even earlier. It appears as if they had been settled in those parts for centuries and had made themselves at home in the place where they were later to play such a significant role in world history. The wars of the Franks against the Romans proved to have repercussions for the future that were out of proportion with their relative lack of ferocity. The Alamanni and the Franks were two peoples who show that the overall picture of the fourth and fifth centuries had already crystallized long before it actually appeared.

There are two other peoples we should also mention, at least in a few words: the Saxons and the Burgundians. The Saxons were similarly a federation of peoples.[434]

Ptolemy[435] already mentions the *Saxones* as a small tribe in Holstein. According to Eutropius,[436] they make their début in history alongside the Franks as enemies of the Romans in the time of Carausius. We may hope that this information given by Eutropius is derived from his sources and [MH.II, 157] not from the point of view of his own time. At the time the Saxons were not yet frontier neighbours of Rome, but were making their presence unpleasantly felt at sea. The Chauci[437] in Hanover formed the core of the Saxons; 'Quadi' are named in one corrupt passage,[438] but this has been amended to 'Cauchi'[439] without any real substantiation. This kind of thing should not be done.[440] The Saxons doubtless encompassed all those people living to the north of the Elbe.[441]

The Burgundians were a people living on the Vistula with an ancient name that goes back to the second century. In the Alamannic Wars they appear immediately to the rear of the Alamanni, pressing forward towards the upper Main region. I mention this here in support of my earlier statement that the Alamanni were being pushed forward. If the Burgundians pressed forward from the Vistula towards the Main, this should be taken as a clear symptom of the vast waves of migrating peoples disrupting Germany at that time.

This concludes the history of Germany,[442] if such a modest term is permissible for such a [MH.II, 158] scant outline.

C) GAUL

To give an account of the culture of the Gallic lands is a task both magnificent and appealing, but unspeakably difficult. But we can at least characterize the gaps that yet remain to be filled.

Gaul[443] is not a single entity, but falls into three to four different regions. The first was Aquitaine, from the Pyrenees to the Garonne. Although little is known of its cultural development, it is at any rate clear that this area has more in common with Spain than Gaul. The tribal population is Iberian, not Celtic. The same peaceful development occurred here as in Spain. The second region is the Provincia, or Provincia Narbonensis, which really had nothing at all to do with Gaul, since reference is invariably made to the 'Tres Galliae' and, separately, to the 'Provincia'. Third, there is Lugdunensis, the region between the Loire and the Seine, the heartland of modern France and Celtic territory proper.[444] Fourth, there are the Germanic borderlands, which should be taken to include not merely Germania Inferior and Germania Superior, but also most of Gallia Belgica. Difficulties are posed here by the impossibility of drawing either clear geographical boundaries or precise cultural ones.

[MH.II, 159] We should be on our guard against one fallacy from the outset:

in order to understand Roman Gaul, we must put modern France completely out of our minds. We must forget the last three hundred years and go back to a time before Rousseau, Diderot and Voltaire, before the French Revolution and before Napoleon, whose impact on the military sphere has, indeed, been erased, but whose administrative impact can never vanish. We must go back to Louis XIV or earlier to find, at last, a France similar[445] to the one we shall be dealing with here.

Aquitaine seems to have been Romanized intensively. An examination of this process is instructive for an understanding of the development of Gaul, showing how much less capable of resistance the Iberian nation is than the Celtic. The countryside is devoid of cities. Burdigala (Bordeaux) was the only city of any size, and was Celtic. Otherwise we encounter only small rural towns; a striking feature are the quaint deities with peculiar names which frequently appear in the inscriptions and were venerated here.[446] There is an abundance of inscriptions; the culture is very similar to that in Tarraconensis and Baetica.

The Provincia Narbonensis came under Roman rule[447] as early as the Republic and could already boast a very ancient culture by the era of which we are speaking. [MH.II, 160] Narbo Martius (Narbonne) was the oldest colony. Still more important than this rival Roman foundation was Massilia (Marseille), a very ancient Greek colony,[448] which had possessed virtually the whole of the province's territory. It was Massilia which was primarily responsible for the expulsion of the original Celtic character from the area, with the result that southern France came to assume quite a different form from northern France. Already under the very earliest Emperors the Provincia was regarded as fully Romanized. Other factors were involved besides the impact of Massilia itself, principally direct colonization by Caesar and Augustus. Nowhere else were there so many native Italian immigrants, who were, moreover, important not merely for their numbers, but also for their intelligence, wealth and mercantile acumen. Roman speech and custom prevailed completely. Strabo[449] already says of the Cavari, the inhabitants of the lower Rhône, that both urban and rural residents alike were fully Romanized; and rural people are invariably the most unyielding to such influences, as the French have discovered in Alsace and the Germans are discovering in Posnan and Upper Silesia. Pliny[450] calls all of Provence more a piece of Italy than a province, and that was indeed the case as regards the coastal territory.

We have already referred to Caesar's plan to add Gallia Transalpina to the [MH.II, 161] main body of Italy alongside Gallia Cisalpina and this plan was carried out. A state that was essentially a Mediterranean state, a state whose focal points were Naples, Rome and Genoa, could not do without Massilia. Even today the remnants of Roman antiquities, the Pont du Gard, the Maison Carrée at Nîmes, the land richly strewn with ruins, still strike us as a piece of Italy. The language is all part of this. France used really to be a country with two languages, the Langue d'oc and the Langue d'oui,[451] and even today, despite centralization, the Provençal element continues to flourish.

Clearly, all this is true only with reservations: even the Provincia, after all, was also ancient Celtic territory and the Celtic character was never completely eradicated. But the political boundaries did not coincide with the cultural ones. The major municipalities of Tolosa and Vienna in the north-eastern and north-western part of the Provincia reveal more of the Celtic element, e.g. in the inscriptions. Tolosa blended the Iberian with the Celtic character. Vienna had been an ancient Allobrogic community and in its way occupied an intermediary position *vis-à-vis* the 'Tres Galliae'. Vienna was never fully Romanized. It possessed a vast territory extending from the Rhône to Lake Geneva. [MH.II, 162] Whereas one town pressed against another in the province, the Vienna region was sparsely urbanized. Whereas Roman citizenship was universal in the province, Vienna, although a very early colony (it was called Colonia Julia), was probably not granted Roman citizenship until the time of Gaius, judging by a speech of Claudius.[452] Augustus granted Vienna Latin rights only.

From the literary standpoint the province was entirely within the Roman sphere of influence. Martial,[453] the fashionable poet of the capital, states that what was acclaimed in Rome was also read in Tolosa and Vienna. It was thus the direct, and fulfilled, intention of the government to make the Mediterranean littoral part of Italy. This is borne out by the inscriptions: it was no paltry achievement that this land was so thoroughly Romanized that even the common man erected a tomb-stone in Latin, as we so frequently find. Even in its very name this land was detached from Gaul: when speaking of 'Gaul', no one ever means the 'provincia'. This was referred to as the 'Provincia Narbonensis' or simply 'Provincia'. And this was the most flourishing part; it was undisturbed by the nationalist and religious movements that raged through the rest of the territory and it is devoid of all traces of Druidism. There were indeed [MH.II, 163] local deities, but there was nothing alien about these – nothing that could not also be found in Italy; wherever one looked one might think oneself in Italy.

Town and country need to be dealt with separately in the Tres Galliae. The two Germaniae were not part of them, but we will leave that aside for the moment to deal with the Tres Galliae in the ethnic sense. This is Celtic territory between the Loire, Seine, Garonne and Scheldt, the provinces of Lugdunensis and Belgica – the greatest portion of Caesar's conquests. The collection of inscriptions which could help shape a view of the culture of these lands is so far totally lacking. Monuments, too, survive only in very small numbers. Bearing in mind that we are dealing here with cities such as Augustodunum (Autun), Lutetia (Paris), Durocortorum (Reims) and Vesontium (Besançon) and that this was the territory of the Aedui, Arverni and Sequani, one is astonished by this paucity, by the tiny number of monuments. The inscriptions from Paris have now been compiled and published,[454] and it is a meagre yield. These localities were not poor and needy; the reason for this striking phenomenon is silent resistance, the rejection of Roman civilization.

[MH.II, 164] There is also mention of a seat of learning, a university of sorts, at Augustodunum; in all probability this was where the nationalist opposition was centred. During the Gallic rebellion under Tiberius, Sacrovir, their leader, seized this seat of learning with the aim of holding hostage the young Gauls who studied there to guarantee the allegiance of their parents.[455] Druidic religion and Druidic learning were taught there. The Druidic priesthood was thoroughly rooted in scholarship and their schools took it as seriously as our modern schools of theology do today. Youths were expected to learn 20,000 verses by heart[456] and to study a great deal generally. Rome had as fierce a struggle against this nationalist priesthood as England has today against the Irish Catholic priesthood.[457] Augustus banned the Druidic cult, at least for Roman citizens.[458] He dared not go further than this, as he was not as yet able to oppose this nationalist cult as such. When Roman writers assert that it was aberrations like human sacrifice etc. that they were combating, this is undoubtedly to some extent true; but what was really loathed and feared was [MH.II, 165] their nationalist basis. Pliny[459] asserts that Tiberius eradicated Druidism. Nevertheless, the same is later again said about Claudius.[460] Such things are not so easily eradicated; they cannot be abolished by decree. As late as the reign of Vespasian, Tacitus[461] has to report an uprising that led to the rebellion of Civilis: the Druids had preached that the burning of the Capitol signified not only the demise of Roman world domination, but that the Celts would become the heirs to Rome. So very much alive was the Celtic idea, therefore – however often it had been 'eradicated' and 'done away with'– that it did not shrink from laying claim to world domination. The theme is found again in later sources in the form of an anecdote: a Gallic priestess prophesied the fall of Rome in the Gallic tongue to Alexander Severus.[462] When Diocletian was stationed with the army at Tongeren and settling accounts with his landlady and disputing the bill, the latter prophesied that he would be proclaimed Emperor.[463] Diocletian retorted that if he really became Emperor one day then he would pay the bill, but that for the time being he felt no compulsion to do so.

Bearing in mind what we have reported about Britain, the [MH.II, 166] conquest of the island of Mona (Anglesey) and Agricola's plans for Ireland[464] – the promised land of Druidic activity – Druidism almost appears to have been an insuperable obstacle for Roman rule. Inscriptions and monuments also suggest cultural conditions which had not yet accommodated themselves at all to Roman conceptions: the altar to the four gods in Paris with the deity Cernunnos,[465] with its priestly garb, horns, purse and other strange appurtenances, is conspicuously alien to Roman images of deities.

Celts served in the Roman army, since from the time of Augustus onwards not only Roman citizens but all subjects were liable for military service – Roman citizens in the legions, subjects in the *cohortes* and *alae*. Citizen troops as such were no longer conscripted in Italy alone, but also in the remainder of the Empire and an outstandingly large number in Narbonensis. In contrast, there is virtually a complete absence here of *cohortes* and *alae*, with the sole exception [MH.II, 167] of the Voconti. There is evidence of an *ala Vocontiorum*,[466] but no *ala* of Tectosages or Allobroges, etc. This is explained by the fact that the Voconti, as is also demonstrable in other respects, maintained their separate identity for longer; the *ala Vocontiorum* is documented as late as the second century. This does not, however, force us to conclude that the Voconti were deprived of citizenship rights for all this time. All that is certain is that they did not yet have them when this *ala* was established, i.e. at the beginning of the imperial age; the *ala*'s name was thus retained merely as a mark of its origin, just us nowadays regiments frequently bear names whose explanations must be sought in the period in which they were established. Nor was it only Voconti who served in this *ala*. One tombstone thus mentions a Treverian by name, who served in the cavalry division.[467]

The military conditions prevailing in the Tres Galliae contrasted starkly with those in Narbonensis. Here there was no military service in a citizens' army, but a superb auxiliary militia was set up. One aspect which as far as I know has not yet been looked at is the very different manner in which Belgica and Lugdunensis were treated in this respect compared to Aquitania. A close [MH.II, 168] examination of the list of military units will reveal that although there were cohorts of Aquitanians, actually four, and cohorts of Gauls, actually eight, these had provincial designations only, and not those of individual *civitates*, with one sole exception: in Aquitaine there was a cohort of Bituriges.[468] The Bituriges constituted the northernmost canton of Aquitania and were Celts, while the remaining Iberian Aquitanians served together in the Aquitanian cohorts. In other words national identity was taken into account, and the Celtic Bituriges were left to themselves. Commanding officers were, naturally, Latin everywhere. There were, in contrast, no *cohortes Belgarum*. The sole *cohors I Belgarum*[469] that occurred was a British formation.[470] In Belgica each individual *civitas* had its cohort, from the Sequani in the far south to the Batavians in the far north, and what is more in completely irrational ratio to their population. There were, for example, at least six cohorts of Nervii, almost as many as for the whole of Lugdunensis, and eight cohorts of Batavians. It has already been pointed out that these peoples were almost completely exempt from taxes, but bore an exceptional burden of conscription.[471] In total, Belgica was three to four times as well represented in the army as the other Celtic provinces. This was connected with the overall political [MH.II, 169] system of Augustus. The Romans preferred the Germanic element to the Celtic, since it seemed to them more homogeneous and perhaps of greater military use. They had a thoroughly negative attitude towards the Celtic element.

Recruiting policy corresponds to the political treatment of the Celts in terms of municipal organization, where there is a similar distinction between municipalities enjoying citizenship rights and those with subject status. This corresponds to regions of Celtic and non-Celtic nationality. The Tres Galliae are missing from the list of provinces in which Augustus had settled colonists. This demonstrates that Roman citizenship was not granted to municipalities in these regions in his time, aside from Lyon, whereas in Narbonensis they almost all either already had these rights or received them. However, these rights were frequently granted to notable persons, even here. Later Emperors often departed from this policy of Augustus; Claudius, for example, granted citizenship rights[472] to the Colonia Agrippina (Cologne) in Ubian territory, as well as to several others in Belgica. Under later Emperors, however, the granting of citizenship to towns was always rare, whereas personal citizenship, already employed in the Republic as a powerful incentive, was granted more frequently, to the individual and to his heirs.

But here too, on the basis of the oft-quoted speech of Claudius[473] and of some passages in Tacitus, we can identify a most [MH.II, 170] peculiar restriction on the personal citizenship that had been granted. All these places in fact obtained citizenship only nominally, merely the *vocabulum civitatis*, as Tacitus[474] puts it. They did not obtain the *ius honorum*, i.e. the right to administer Roman magistracies and hence the opportunity to obtain a seat in the Senate. What they had, therefore, approximated to what the Republic called *civitas sine suffragio*. Since there were in any case no longer any real people's assemblies under the principate, the citizenship awarded to the Gauls was politically worthless, albeit valuable in the event of criminal trials and in some other cases. To all political, and practical, intents and purposes, this is another instance of the denial of the Celtic character. This makes a most interesting contrast to Narbonensis. Spain and Pannonia experienced no such restrictions when awarded citizenship. When we put this in conjunction with what has already been reported about the Druidic cult, membership of which was forbidden for Roman citizens, it represents a fresh indication of the apprehension with which Rome regarded this national-religious, Celtic Druidism.

The essence of Claudius's speech, however, was to make it clear to the Senate that this manner of dealing with the Celts [MH.II, 171] entailed an injustice. These distinctions became more blurred in subsequent times and Celts are not uncommonly encountered in the Senate.

As far as municipal organization was concerned, there was no departure from the ancient principle whereby the Roman state existed as a total entity, subordinate to which each individual province consisted of a greater or smaller number of autonomous municipalities. However, understanding of the term 'municipality' in the Celtic lands differed fundamentally from that in Italy. The Romans, albeit out of aversion, left to the Celts their ancient *civitates*, as they had existed prior to the conquest. Among the Celts the *civitas* was not based on the town, as everywhere in

Italy, but was simply a canton. The local concentration and centralization of people within city walls was absent. In Rome, the wall did not signify a territorial boundary, whereas in the Celtic lands the town existed simply as a fact, not as a legal entity. I have already given a detailed account of this in *Hermes*, vol. XVI,[475] where anyone interested can find further details. In Rome, all magistrates were under an obligation to live together within the city; a senator had to be domiciled in Rome. The same applied to local office-holders in Roman municipalities (*coloniae*). This was different in the [MH.II, 172] Celtic *civitas*. Anyone, wherever he might live, even near the territorial borders, could become a *decurio*. Wherever Roman civic organization applied, the locality was a village with no political existence; wherever, however, cantonal organization applied, the city differed from all other localities in size only and had no more political existence than all the rest.

Of all Gallic cantons, that of Helvetii is the best-known;[476] Roman culture penetrated there the soonest, but its cantonal organization survived. The main centre of Aventicum (Avenches) on Lake Neuchâtel[477] was very important. Its citizens were not *cives Aventicenses*, but *cives Helvetici*.[478] Aventicum, however, had its own local administration. Lousonna (Lausanne) on Lake Geneva was scarcely less important and it too boasted its own particular institutions and *curatores*. The cantons represented themselves as comprehensive communities. Although in Italy, in the region of Verona for example, places other than the city can be identified, they lacked any special institutions. This was particularly important in the sphere of public works: in Roman municipalities public works could only be carried out under the auspices of the authorities in the capital, with the result that such works were almost invariably erected in capital cities. In the cantons there was greater decentralization. Aventicum, Lousonna and each individual locality erected its own buildings. Obviously, however, a town could never make as much of a name for itself under these circumstances [MH.II, 173] as the Roman municipalities.

By the same token, the administration of justice was a key vehicle for centralization in Roman municipalities. The notion that justice may be administered solely within the city is a cornerstone of Roman law – hence the importance of city walls for delineating the locality. In the *civitates* (cantons) magistrates will probably have been peripatetic and administered justice everywhere.

This profound distinction was never completely eradicated, nor was the principle ever shaken. We shall see that Caracalla, for example, granted Roman citizenship to all subjects of the Empire.[479] Much thought has gone into the significance of this measure; but it was probably fiscal in nature and did not replace Latin, peregrine, or citizenship status as such. Its aim was to be able to demand inheritance tax from everyone, hateful privilege of the Roman citizen. The granting of personal citizenship to a number of individuals had no effect on legal categories. Thus, although Gallia Lugdunensis was thereby effectively incorporated into the Roman state, the profound distinction, far from being erased by this, was if anything accentuated. Although the Roman Emperors undoubtedly also aspired to the Romanization of this part of the Empire, that aspiration was not nearly so ardent as in the case of Spain or Pannonia.

[MH.II, 174] What has already been said about the calculation of distances in leagues needs to be understood in the same terms: although the *leuga*[480] did not appear in the Tres Galliae until the time of Severus, it can scarcely have been introduced by him. Perhaps Augustus allowed the Tres Galliae to use the *leuga* for the local roads, and the practice was then extended to imperial roads under Severus. It is worth noting that besides Lyon only Noviodunum (Nyon) on Lake Geneva, the sole Roman colony founded by Caesar in those parts (Colonia Iulia Equestris), still reckoned in *milliae* in the third century, which it must legally have done as a Roman colony.[481]

The language of the Celts outlived Roman rule; this fact is completely incomprehensible, but we have the very best authorities for it. Some have quibbled with the testimony of St Jerome,[482] who claims that the Galatians of Asia Minor spoke the language of Trier, but I fail to see the strength of the counter-arguments. In any case, it is not possible to refute a passage in the *Digest*[483] citing Ulpian, who lived in the third century, who states that *fideicommissa*, unlike legacies,[484] could be made in every other language spoken in the Roman Empire, for example *in lingua Punica vel Gallicana*, whereas legacies had to be [MH.II, 175] written in Latin.[485] This makes it absolutely clear that Punic and Gallic were still current languages in his time. This is less remarkable in the light of the fact that Celtic is still spoken in Brittany today. Admittedly there is some doubt as to whether it is a remnant of the original, indigenous idiom, or whether it was reintroduced through return migration from Britain. We may assume that there was continuity from the Roman era; return migration has not been proved and is most uncertain.[486] We do know, however, that even in Caesar's time these parts were the least affected by the Roman conquest and on the other hand enjoyed constant and lively contact with the British Isles – that bastion of Celtic Druidism. In the light of this, the persistence of the Celtic idiom becomes quite explicable. And this persistence is a fact. Of course, the Celtic idiom must have survived among decidedly subordinate social strata and contexts. Although we have no direct evidence, aside from Strabo,[487] about how Latin spread, this was in the nature of things: business transactions were undoubtedly conducted in Latin and all *civitates* must have kept their records and accounts in Latin. Although we [MH.II, 176] cannot prove this *a posteriori* it is obvious *a priori*. Supervision by and accountability to Roman officials would otherwise have been impossible. This has already been discussed in another connection.[488]

Monument inscriptions in Celtic are rare; all Celtic inscriptions written in Greek script[489] probably fall into the pre-principate era. This would suggest that the currency of Celtic was of a purely private character. Naturally there was no linguistic coercion: it was not forbidden to place a Celtic gravestone or to make an oblation to a Celtic deity in Celtic. It simply was not done, any more than anyone today, in those parts of Germany where Low German is spoken conversationally by high and low alike, would inscribe a gravestone in Low German.

This extraordinary scarcity of Celtic private inscriptions in Latin script is all the more striking when compared to the abundance of private inscriptions[490] in Pannonia or on the Ebro, where they can be found even in the remotest valleys; in Lugdunensis, on the other hand, [MH.II, 177] they are rare and couched in a barbaric Latin. The absence of full-blooded Latin inscriptions is far more significant than the presence of Celtic ones. Celtic, therefore, was customary in private use, and this was in turn contingent upon and fostered by relations with Celtic Britain, although these contacts were officially suppressed.

How, then, did it come about that a Romance language evolved in this very region after the collapse of the Roman Empire? This is a most interesting question on which the following may shed some light: it was the official use of Latin that was the crucial deciding factor, and because of this common medium of Latin, Germanic invasions welded immigrant Romans and immigrant Celts together, to form a single ethnic mix. The Franks spoke[491] Latin in Gaul for the same reason that the Vandals did the same, and were obliged to do so, in Africa and the Goths in Italy. The higher and more developed levels of state and municipal officialdom, and above all the influence of Christianity, which was inextricably linked with Latin in the West, were cogent forces. The West knew [MH.II, 178] holy scripture only as Latin texts and the representatives of the Church had a linguistic and governmental mission in addition to their religious one. One need only recall that for a long time the last refuge of Roman Christian culture was Ireland, whence converts once again issued forth. For this reason the Celtic idiom could never again reign supreme; politically it was long dead. No political resurgence of Celtic culture took place again after the protest of the Civilis rebellion; from then onwards it was suppressed. And it should not be forgotten that the Franks were not Gauls, but Germans.

The status of the capital of Gallia Lugdunensis, Lugdunum, modern Lyon, was a most extraordinary one.[492] In his book *Lyon in der Römerzeit* (*Lyon in the Roman Era*), Vienna, 1878,[493] Otto Hirschfeld has provided us with a most elegant account of the most recent investigation there has been into a question of this kind. Lugdunum was founded by Munatius Plancus in 43 BC during the great civil war. By its very nature, the city stood in the starkest contrast to the regions whose capital it was intended to be, and we shall see that everything we have said about Celtic towns and their organization does not apply to Lyon. It had an extraordinarily favourable position; on the confluence of the Rhône and the Saône and with a commanding position of the entire river basin, it had the [MH.II, 179] prerequisites for prosperity. The city was raised on the site of an ancient Celtic settlement. It was an incomparable location for trade and military purposes. The city really belonged more to Narbonensis than to Lugdunensis; it was ancient Allobrogan territory and it was thoroughly characteristic of Roman policy towards the province to locate its capital virtually on its border and right next to Narbonensis. From the very outset Lugdunum was not a *civitas*, but a *colonia*, in fact the only one in the Tres Galliae. It was not a capital in the way that Tolosa was, for example; it was inhabited largely by immigrant Italians. Even Tacitus[494] still distinguishes it in this respect from other Gallic cities, calling Vienne a *civitas externa*, but Lyon a *civitas Romana*. The granting of citizenship to immigrants and to natives was not one and the same thing.

However, Lyon was not merely the capital of Lugdunensis; as Paris is for modern France, or Rome for ancient Italy, Lyon was the hub of the road network for all Gaul, including Narbonensis. As in some other respects to be touched on later, this would appear to have been in direct [MH.II, 180] and deliberate imitation of Rome. The city had a powerful administrative character: the entire *census* of Gaul was carried out from here. By chance the epitaph of an imperial slave employed as an official in Lyon during Tiberius's reign has survived; he died on tour, and the servants who accompanied him erected the monument to him, adding their names to the inscription. The entourage comprised three physicians, a secretary, a treasurer, a business agent, two attendants in charge of silver, two manservants and two footmen.[495] This gives us some idea of the size of the official staff residing in the city. In addition, there were also the imperial procurator's office and the imperial legate and his staff. The military hub was at Mainz, the administrative hub at Lyon. However, Lyon had a garrison – another parallel with Rome. One of the urban cohorts was stationed there. There was also a mint. Another remarkable feature is the complete absence of a municipal administration. Among the enormous number of inscriptions we find ones referring to members of the municipal council and to the priesthoods, but never to a mayor or municipal official as such; this is another analogy [MH.II, 181] to Rome. The same situation is be found in Milan, Ravenna (the main base of the fleet) and some other large cities. All this is quite explicable: the larger the city, the more dangerous was free municipal administration. Lyon, the great administrative capital, Ravenna, the base of the naval command, and Rome, capital of the Empire, were thus restricted as much as possible with regard to their municipal administration.

On the other hand, Lyon was the seat of the regional assembly[496] for the Tres Galliae and its *sacra* (religious ceremonies), or to put it more accurately perhaps, of the *sacra* which were the occasional sessions of something like a regional assembly. The origins of the division of Gaul into the Tres Galliae ('Three Gauls') are not entirely clear: it may have evolved by chance. Caesar had already wanted to divide the old and the new possessions in Gaul administratively. We do not know, however, when the division into the 'Three Gauls' occurred. It probably did not yet exist when Augustus was implementing his reorganizations from 15 to 12 BC.

Here, as everywhere, the *sacra* were connected to the cult of the Emperor. A great altar was erected for the veneration of Augustus and all sixty-four *civitates* had to participate in its ceremonies. It is unclear whether the German municipalities were included: to the best of my knowledge they were not. Among the Ubii, at least, there was a [MH.II, 182] separate altar to Augustus[497] and the ceremonies of Lugdunum probably existed for the Gallic *civitates* alone. It thus constituted a communal focus to which was attached a common regional assembly of a kind. Complaints against officials and expressions of thanks for legates were among the items on the agenda about which we know.

By its very nature, therefore, Lyon is a major city in contrast to all other towns in Gaul that are known to us. It was also a focus for the wine trade and the younger Pliny[498] is pleased, as has already been mentioned of Martial earlier in connection with other towns, that his small publications have found a market among the booksellers of Lyon. All in all, Lyon is a facsimile of Rome.

Belgica cannot be measured with the same yardstick as Lugdunensis; there the national component was totally different. Numerous Germans inhabited the region from Alsace to Cologne. The Triboci, Nemeti, Vangiones and Ubii – the latter transferred to the left bank of the Rhine by Agrippa – contrasted sharply with the Celtic character. Nonetheless, the bulk of the population was still of Celtic stock, although the strong admixture of ethnic Germans made [MH.II, 183] the overall ambience semi-German, or at least significantly modified it. The Batavians, Frisians, Nervii and Treveri were Germans. Consequently – and in this respect the national uprising of Vindex is uncommonly instructive – there were also two parties in Belgica, a Celtic national party and one that carried the banner of allegiance to Rome. The greater part of Belgica was hostile to the movement of Vindex. The separation of Belgica and Lugdunensis probably had its roots in the high percentage of ethnic Germans, which would also explain the differences in their military treatment. Conscription was far heavier in Belgica than in Lugdunensis: the eastern parts of Belgica were, after all, far less Romanized than Lugdunensis; the centre of the Roman ethnic presence lay in Narbonensis and the Rhine region. Naturally the camps established along the line of the river Rhine were important vehicles of Romanization, but another factor was the greater congeniality of these two nations and the irreconcilable antipathy between the Celtic and Roman national spirit. The Germans and half-Germans did not adopt such a hostile attitude towards the Romans as did the Celts.[499]

This antipathy was nationalist on a variety of levels. It was keenly felt in the later imperial age and [MH.II, 184] treated accordingly. As a result of the closer familiarity with the land and its people imparted to the Romans through Caesar,[500] the failure to distinguish between Gauls and Germans came to an end. Neither Italians nor orientals, let alone Celts, were ever accepted to serve in the imperial bodyguard[501] (not to be confused with the Praetorian guard), which kept special watch in the palace over the person of the Emperor. At first, Spaniards were recruited into it, but later exclusively Germans: Frisians, Batavians and whatever they were all called. The antipathy towards the Celts thus appears clearly here.

Quite in keeping with this, it was necessary to station free German guards on the Rhine as a frontier garrison against free Germany: *ut arcerent, non ut custodirentur*.[502] They inspired confidence with their reliability. This, too, was a 'watch on the Rhine',[503] but one directed eastwards and carried out by Germans against Germans.

Besides these the bulk of the population consisted of Celts, as we have seen. Viewed overall, however, there is a contrast with the Celtic heartland of Lugdunensis, and we would not be far wrong to describe the Vindex uprising in a sense as a war waged by Lugdunensis against Belgica. It was the latter province [MH.II, 185] which was the true seat of Romanization. The high level of conscription in Belgica also was a contributing factor: all Batavians, Nervii and Sugumbri entered the army as foreigners and left it as Romans after their twenty years of service.

At the centre of urban development stood Mogontiacum (Mainz). Even today the inscriptions[504] and public works still tower above all other finds in these territories in both number and importance. In many respects Moguntiacum constitutes a counterpart to Lyon; just as the latter was the hub of civil administration, so Moguntiacum was the hub of military administration for the entire West. It was the residence of the legate of Upper Germany: it formed the hub of the military road network; the major supply depots were located there and the Rhine fleet which played a key role in defence of the frontier was stationed there.[505] Just as in Lyon, the civil administration had a low profile, indeed here even more so. Whereas there we registered the absence of urban magistrates as such, but still the presence of decurions and *seviri*, even these are absent in Mainz. Not until the third century, later than in Argentoratum (Strasburg) and Castra Vetera (Birten near Xanten), did [MH.II, 186] civic municipal conditions begin to evolve in Moguntiacum.[506]

We know a great deal about Colonia (Cologne) and its development and importance. This city grew out of a settlement of Germanic Ubii. Under Augustus these had been hostile frontier neighbours on the right bank of the Rhine and during his reign Agrippa transferred and settled them on the left bank of the Rhine,[507] where they formed a powerful buffer against the free Germans. They were also provided with a focal point, an altar to the Emperor, the *ara* of the Ubii.[508] There is doubt as to whether this shrine was intended for the Ubii alone, or whether it was intended to serve as a general focal point for the Rhenish Germans. During the wars of Germanicus, Cologne (*ara Ubiorum*), together with Mainz, played the leading role.

The younger Agrippina was born there;[509] it became a colony under Claudius[510] and henceforth bore the name 'Colonia Claudia Ara Agrippina' in honour of his wife – a remarkable name that encompasses its entire history *in nuce*; the *ara* was not dropped. From this point onward Cologne ceased to be the military hub; the legion [MH.II, 187] was probably transferred to Bonn.[511] The population of Cologne consisted of Germans, not of Italian settlers. Next to Mainz, Cologne evinces the highest number of inscriptions[512] and the most intensively Roman lifestyle.

In many respects the history of Trier[513] poses a problem that is still awaiting a solution. It was known as 'Colonia Augusta Trevirorum', but this city can hardly have been a colony of Augustus. The Tres Galliae are completely absent from the roll of colonies established by Augustus, and it would have been a most remarkable anomaly if he had made an exception with such a far-flung location. Nevertheless, Trier must have become a colony relatively soon after Augustus, since Tacitus[514] calls it a 'colonia' in the year of four Emperors; at any rate before AD 68, therefore. Whether it was given the title by Gaius (Caligula) before Claudius is unclear, but we do know that the colony was established by means of a decree. Colonists were not sent there. In the *Annals* Tacitus still speaks of the inhabitants of Trier as *externae fidei homines*, in contrast to others.[515] We may infer from this that the character of Trier long remained that of a foreign land, as is also attested [MH.II, 188] by the paucity of inscriptions from the early centuries. Romanization made slow headway here, despite the early grant of colonial status. Later, of course, Trier was to become a major seat of Roman civilization, hence the abundance of relics of public buildings and sites. As you will know, there is still a dispute about whether the Porta Nigra is a work of the Augustan or a later age.[516] We do know for certain that in the fourth century, when Rome had ceased to be the capital, Trier become one of the main residences of the Emperors. Zosimus[517] states unequivocally that it was the greatest city north of the Alps. There are still major remains of the baths dating from the later imperial age. Its location was, indeed, eminently suitable for such an imperial residence – directly behind the military frontier, and thus close at hand and yet protected.

Reliable information about the culture of this territory is provided by Ausonius in his *Mosella*, his finest poem, written in Trier in 371, in which he depicts the life and fashions of the fourth century. This was during the period in the reign of Valentinian, one of the few effective Emperors of this period, following the successful repulse of hostile [MH.II, 189] Germans across the Neckar. These descriptions convey a vivid impression of the prosperity of the country. Sumptuous villa-estates, *praetoria*, extended in an unbroken line along both banks of the

Moselle, with magnificent colonnades, summer-houses and bath-houses in lush, cultivated gardens. Surviving ruins with their mosaics and murals, etc. provide an eloquent commentary on the poem. This must have been a highly favoured part of the world. Indeed, the culture is distinctive and unique. We possess an excellent account of the Neumagen finds by Hettner in volume 36 of the *Rheinisches Museum*.[518] It was the site of a villa between Trier and Bonn. There are significant remains of grave monuments in the old palace there. In the village cemetery – which is precisely what this was – only sculptured monuments are to be found, providing a unique artistic treatment of art-historical significance. The monument at Igel is the best-known; similar ones also occur in the Luxemburg region, but not outside Belgica. The genre-like treatment of the figures is noteworthy: [MH.II, 190] elsewhere tombs of the period are characterized by hackneyed mythological elements like sarcophagi with Phaeton or Amazons. Not so in Belgica: these tombs are brimming with life and real, live human beings, recorded by the artists with immediacy as they go about their business. The monument in Igel is probably to a baker – the tomb of an army supplier. It displays all the routine tasks associated with the subject. Other scenes from daily life are to be found in Neumagen: the obligatory deliveries to an estate owner by his tenants – grain, a cow and hens. Money transactions are depicted on the monument of a banker or tax collector; another tomb shows reliefs of Moselle ships laden with wine barrels – this was the funerary monument of a wine merchant. Although not first-rate works of art, these monuments are true to life, fresh and unconventional. People are depicted in their indigenous, Gallic costume: the coat with a hole in it for putting the head through, with a hood (*sagum*), and shoes and stockings. They do not wear the toga; as it had disappeared in real life, so it no longer appears in pictorial representations. The faces have a manifestly [MH.II, 191] portrait-like quality, depicting characteristic features. Funerary monuments of this kind are to be found there in such quantities that they may be regarded as a speciality of the province and, as has already been mentioned, they occur nowhere else.

D) SPAIN

Spain[519] stands in sharp contrast to Gaul. Roman culture was two centuries older there, leaving aside Narbonensis. Consequently Spain played no part in the great upheavals of the Empire. Although it appeared to do so during the downfall of Nero, this is merely appearance. It was pure coincidence that Galba happened to be in command in Spain following the demise of Vindex and continued to work for the cause there. Similarly, Spain was also swept along by the uprising of Postumus, but it had no history of its own.

Let us again examine the military situation first: Spain was no frontier land bordered by barbarians, i.e. non-Romans. Its subjugation was not brought to completion until Augustus,[520] who advanced to the ocean coast. Prior to this the Cantabrians and Asturians had been Roman in name, but not in reality. Augustus took on the arduous Cantabrian War of his [MH.II, 192] own volition, in pursuit of his political principle of making the Occident fully subject to Rome and bringing this to a conclusion where it still fell short. After Augustus there were no more serious revolutions in this once so rebellious land. Suppression contributed to this, but even more so the extraordinarily intensive programme of colonization. Caesarea Augusta (Zaragoza) and Emerita (Merida) were veteran colonies. Pacification proceeded with such speed that the garrison of three legions deployed there under Augustus could soon be reduced to one. The first Emperors initially left three legions there; we may conclude from this that leaders of the state did not yet entirely believe that Spain had been pacified. Lusitania had no garrison; the legions were concentrated in Hispania Citerior, i.e. the north-western region – two in Asturia, one in the Pyrenees. The conquest of Britain was also a factor; one legion was withdrawn from Spain in consequence. Which Spanish legion was relocated has not been fully established; probably the *Quarta Macedonica* was withdrawn.

Vespasian [MH.II, 193] probably undertook a further, temporary reduction. The withdrawal of the sixth *Victrix*, and the tenth *Gemina* is said to have been occasioned by the rebellion of Civilis;[521] they did not return and left in the country only the seventh *Gemina*, which was stationed there for centuries.[522]

The true cause of this troop reduction was probably the situation in the East. There was no problem about such a removal of troops, since by that time Spain was an essentially pacified province. If anything in the manner of unrest did occur, it was not initiated by the Spanish, but caused by Moorish invasions from Africa. The silence of our written sources, however, proves nothing, and it is still striking that even one legion was left in Spain. It lives on to this day in the name of a city: modern Léon in Asturia was the permanent base of the *Legio Septima Gemina* and the fact that it remained there leads us to conclude that the government continued to consider this mountain people worthy of monitoring by an armed force. This was the sole non-frontier province which retained a standing garrison.

[MH.II, 194] The administration of Spain was divided into a nearer and a further i.e. a northern and a southern, part. The former comprised the lands as far as the Ebro, the latter Lusitania (Portugal) and Andalusia. Later these became three when the southern province was redivided into Baetica and Lusitania. The latter came under imperial administration, but without a garrison: a *provincia inermis*. We do not know when this occurred, but it was probably under Tiberius, which is remarkable, since it would therefore have been Tiberius who divided the great senatorial province and deprived the Senate of part of it. Later the northern province was also redivided into Asturia and Gallaecia, which were under new legionary legates and separated from Tarraconensis. From then on Tarraconensis was also a *provincia inermis*.

Spain was ethnically largely Iberian. Celtic immigration undoubtedly occurred in pre-Roman times. This is borne out by the name Celt-Iberian[523] and a number of name endings of towns in *-dunum* and *-briga*, as Kiepert[524] points out. Bearing in mind that the areas to the north of the Pyrenees, notably Aquitaine, contained a largely Iberian [MH.II, 195] population, this immigration of Celts into the land south of the Pyrenees is quite astounding. But it cannot be doubted. The manner in which it occurred is suggested by analogy with other events in this period of the great Celtic inundation. Wherever Celts were to be found they never eradicated the original population, but settled in among it, for example in Pannonia or northern Italy. It will have been like this in Spain, too. In any case some town names ending in *-briga* still occur in the Roman era, for example Juliobriga or Flaviobriga, so that the significance of the Celtic element may have been overestimated. This name ending probably no longer has any significance in ethnic terms, any more than when we today call a place 'Castell'.[525] The Iberian element probably always dominated in Spain.

This was augmented in the south by Punic immigration. Gades, Carthago Nova – the latter founded by Hannibal[526] – retained their Punic character throughout centuries of the Roman era. This is attested by the coins, for example.[527] Nevertheless, Punic influence did not extend beyond Baetica. In the rest of Spain [MH.II, 196] the Carthaginians did rule for a time, but never gained a firm foothold, never 'Punified' the country.

The Romans in Spain entirely followed in the footsteps of the Carthaginians. There was an intensive programme of Roman immigration, as in the case of Narbonensis. This was augmented by the influence of the legions stationed there, where the towns are known to have been founded by the children of the soldiers. The exploitation of the mines was always important. Next to Italy, southern Spain was incorporated into the Roman state first and most firmly. Strabo,[528] the sole ancient writer to pursue the crucial issue of ethnicity, calls the inhabitants of Baetica and southern Tarraconensis *togati*. The original state of barbarism had already been eradicated in the pre-Roman era, so the Romans no longer needed to eradicate it. By Tiberius's time the whole of Spain was to all intents and purposes Roman. The wine and oil trades were flourishing. As in the case of Narbonensis, we see in Spain another piece of Italy. This was a proper consequence of the Roman vision of Mediterranean supremacy and applies first and foremost to the Mediterranean [MH.II, 197] parts of the country, much more than to the Atlantic coast.

Pliny describes the constitutional situation at length.[529] Vespasian granted the entire country Latin rights, tantamount to semi-citizenship status. We do not know when and if the next step to full citizenship was taken; however, Latin rights were as a rule only a transitional stage. The major cities of the south were probably granted *civitas Romana* (full citizenship) early on. By the end of the first century, however, education, custom and law were all Roman.

A study of the names on soldiers' tombstones is important for understanding the circumstances of military conscription.[530] In the legions there we encounter names from Baetica and Tarraconensis, just as there are names from Narbonensis to be found in the Rhine legions. The *alae et cohortes* were frequently named after places, although we can also find cohorts 'of Spaniards', which may perhaps simply be an abbreviation. References to the names of tribal communities occur largely from the less Romanized north and west: Cantabrians, Asturians or Lusitanians. The net result here too is that the entire country —albeit in varying forms and degrees – adhered firmly and loyally to Rome.

Lastly, Spain occupies a [MH.II, 198] distinctive and outstanding place in the history of literature. As we have seen, Gaul was hardly fruitful at all in the literary sphere, nurturing itself instead on the intellectual fare offered by the capital. Spain was decidedly fruitful, which is a clear indication of how old Roman civilization there was. Cicero[531] already speaks of the 'poets of Cordoba', albeit ironically, and needles generals who allow themselves to be adulated by them. In the first century of the Emperors, however, this situation was completely reversed, and from the reign of Tiberius onward Spanish writers took over the leading role in literature: the elder Annaeus Seneca was a native of Cordoba, the capital of Baetica. It was there that he made his name; then he moved to Rome, where he generated a great and impressive output. He was the first Professor of Eloquence. His son was Seneca the philosopher, whose key role under Nero is well known.[532] The grandson of the elder Seneca, Marcus Annaeus Lucanus,[533] was also an impressive poet. None of them sought to hide their Cordoban origins.

The geographer Pomponius Mela hailed from a small place near Gades.[534] Columella, the agricultural writer, came from Gades. [MH.II, 199] They were joined in the Flavian period by Valerius Martialis of Bilbilis (Calatayud) in the upper Ebro valley in Tarraconensis. He too first made his name in his native country, then lived in Rome for thirty years, returning to end his life at home. In the sixty-first epigram of book 1 he names a number of famous authors of his day – almost all of them Spanish. Lastly, the most outstanding author is Marcus Fabius Quintilianus, a Celtiberian from Calagurris in the Ebro province.[535] His father had already gone to Rome and he followed at a young age, then returned home, but was summoned back to Rome by Galba,[536] where he lived as a teacher and tutor to imperial princes.

There was nothing provincial or foreign about any of these men; they are highly diverse, but did we not know the contrary we would take them for Italians. There is no finer master of style than Quintilian, who was the leading literary critic of his day. What we have said, however, was true only of Mediterranean Spain; we learn nothing comparable about the region of the *alae et cohortes*, of the legionary bases. This confirms what we said above. [MH.II, 200] From the time of Tiberius onwards Mediterranean Spain assumed the literary leadership in Rome that had been held by Venusia and Mantua[537] in the Augustan age. Rome herself always only consumed, she never produced. Rome's position *vis-à-vis* the provinces was rather like Paris's today, where all talented people gravitate in pursuit of success and recognition.

This completes what needs to be said about Spain. It is not history in the true sense; it represents a complete fusion with Rome, like that of Lombardy. Spain was also the first province to provide Rome with an Emperor: Trajan,[538] of the house of Ulpian, and Hadrian[539] were natives of Italica (Seville).

E) AFRICA

Africa[540] had a position similar to that of Spain. Here again, we cannot speak of history proper on the grand scale. Although there is a provincial development which might even be called rich, and with it a domestic history of a sort, it has no external history. We learn little of wars and battles.

The principate was arguably more beneficial and creative here in Africa than in any other region. Nevertheless, many aspects of its events are shrouded in obscurity. [MH.II, 201] There is doubt as to how much of its flourishing agriculture and municipal constitutions go back to the pre-Roman, Punic era. Africa is, nonetheless, substantially a Roman creation and of imperial, not Republican, Rome. We are already familiar with the extraordinary treatment of Africa by the Republic. The destruction of Carthage and the eradication of all its political vestiges had been an *idée fixe* of the Republic and yet there was no positive justification for this negative aspiration. Once this rival in trade, power and civilization had been overthrown the country was largely left to its indigenous Numidian princes, of the dynasty of Massinissa. What Rome retained was negligible, but it was the most fertile part of a fertile land. Hadrumetum and Utica were major cities, but their earlier, Punic character remained intact. No military garrison was deployed in Africa; only when the urgent necessity arose, such as during the Jugurthine War, were troops sent over to Africa temporarily, in marked contrast to the way in which Spain was dealt with. The indigenous [MH.II, 202] Numidian princes were obliged to create a military cordon to defend the country.

The Romanization of Africa too can be traced back to Caesar, as can all fundamental ideas of the principate. It did not arise out of the coincidence that King Juba was a supporter of Pompey: Caesar saw that the situation was untenable, made his decision and began to incorporate the country into the Empire, without regard for such personal considerations. In the aftermath of the battle of Thapsus in 46 BC he expanded Roman territory far to the west. How far he wanted to proceed with this is not known, but it was probably his intention to incorporate all of Mauretania. Augustus retreated from this aim: here, as so often, he adopted the ideas of Caesar, but also limited them. He so to speak re-established Numidia, by returning to Juba's son of the same name his paternal inheritance in restricted form, and dividing the country at the river Ampsaga into the province of Africa and the kingdom of Mauretania.[541] The province consisted of the former proconsular province of Africa and Numidia. The remainder was the legacy that came to Juba, who was also bound to the Roman, and specifically dynastic, interest through his marriage to the daughter of Antony and Cleopatra (also called Cleopatra),[542] who was treated by Augustus [MH.II, 203] half as royal princess and half as step-niece.[543] Juba became a major mediator of occidental culture, and his kingdom became the model of a client state with a measure of independence.

This did not last for long, however. In AD 40 the Emperor Gaius incorporated the kingdom and divided Mauretania into two parts, the western half of which approximately corresponded to modern Morocco. The other half, with its capital Caesarea (Cherchel), was called Mauretania Caesariensis.[544] From then on the entire northern coast of Africa became Roman and remained so.

It is difficult to trace the boundary between Africa and barbarian territory; just as today, it was partly demarcated by nature. Where the desert and the nomadic tribes begin, where agriculture ceases because of lack of water, where the palms trailed off into shifting dunes, there was the border, and the Romans had the same problem that the French have today in protecting agriculture and the sedentary population from nomadic tribes. They accomplished this through a system very similar to that of Marshal Bugeaud,[545] except that they carried it out on a larger scale and with greater intensity.

[MH.II, 204] Our present state of knowledge, alas, prevents us from tracing the nature of their organization in detail, but it would be of great interest to know how Roman arms were in practice employed here in the service of civilization. All we have are vague outlines: Mauretania Tingitana (Tangier; approximately equivalent to modern Morocco) was not an integral part of the rest, but formed an adjunct to Spain. It had a moderate-sized territory, and little is known of it, since the territory has not been opened up even today. Once the ruins there have been thoroughly studied it will probably emerge that the Atlantic coast will reveal far more of Roman civilization than we think. No significant numbers of troops were stationed in Tingitana. There was an unoccupied zone between Tingitana and Caesariensis. The region to the east, where a tract of land extended between Tripolis and Egypt, was similarly unoccupied, apart from the valuable oasis of Cyrene. Similar conditions still obtain today. There was little in the way of culture beyond Oran. [MH.II, 205] Troops, forts and garrisons all ended here: the land was defended by cavalry divisions. Inland there were few vestiges of culture: the Roman government abandoned this as worthless.

The most recent finds inland to the west of Carthage have revealed important data about the base of the sole legion in Africa, the *Legio Tertia Augusta*, which was, of course, supplemented by *alae et cohortes*. From Augustus on, this legion was stationed south of Carthage at Theveste (Tebessa) for the defence of Carthage – as a barrier against nomadic desert tribes. The war against Tacfarinas described by Tacitus[546] was still fought from Theveste. Later, however, the legion was moved to Lambaesis, which has a similar location in relation to Cirta as Theveste has to Carthage. This was probably done in order to defend the newly acquired territory, equivalent to modern Algeria. From a recently discovered inscription of Hadrian,[547] in which he addresses troops stationed at Lambaesis and praises the competence they showed in two changes of camp 'within his memory', it may be deduced that prior to their relocation to Lambaesis there was [MH.II, 206] an intermediate stationing in Timugadi (Timgad). Timugadi was a colony of Trajan and was probably founded when the troops were withdrawn, not when they were first stationed there. Hadrian then continued their redeployment further west, to Lambaesis. Connected with this is the fact that first-century inscriptions are very few and far between, but increase sharply from the time of Trajan onwards; this confirms that this period witnessed an increase of civilization. The troops thus undoubtedly had a civilizing mission. There was no real *limes* here, such as in Germany, nor was it necessary. One concentrated central point with a network of roads on which to conduct raids was sufficient, as it still is today. Wars as such did not occur, but there was probably constant fighting with the Numidians and inhabitants of the Atlas Mountains. The oases and the land, in so far as it was capable of sustaining culture, were both in Roman hands.

Agriculture in Africa flourished. African grain, together with that of Egypt, provided not only for Rome, [MH.II, 207] but also for all Italy, where farming was declining more and more in the imperial period as a result of luxury. In the way of major cities it had Carthage and Cirta, the capital of Mauretania, which still had a unique constitution, dating from the time of the Numidian kings, that was later retained. Tingis was less outstanding. The most remarkable feature is the great number of flourishing small rural towns, village upon village, nowadays ruined site upon ruined site, all pressed close to one another, and we can find astonishingly luxurious buildings in the most obscure spots. There must have been an uncommon degree of prosperity; vast villa precincts, mosaics and other valuable remains give us a sense of this private wealth. A far more advanced culture prevailed then than today. This land suffered little in the way of hostile attacks. The military cordon provided a defence against southern neighbours, and attacks such as those which had to be faced by the frontier lands on the Rhine, Danube and Euphrates could not occur here. Think of all that had to be done and all that had to be destroyed before the Franks and Vandals could make their way to Africa! As late as the third and fourth centuries, when other parts [MH.II, 208] of the Empire were already rapidly declining, Africa was flourishing; the country was too rich for the government to be able to ruin it.

A characteristic feature was the absence, or rather meagreness, of the military presence. The entire occupation force totalled a mere 12,000 men – 15,000 at most. The level of conscription was also extraordinarily low. Admittedly the one and only legion did recruit from the province itself, but that meant little. The *alae* and *cohortes* were insignificant; there were no *cohortes* of *Afres*[548] as such. There were certainly Africans in the legions elsewhere in the Empire, but undoubtedly in small numbers and by preference from regions still only half-subjugated – as in Spain, where the bulk of recruitment was also carried out in the north and west, not from the Mediterranean coast. Highly prized cavalry troops were raised from Gaetulians, Mauri and Numidians. The true African was left to work the plough.

The modern notion of the military is to exploit all usable human material for military service. This did not occur in Rome; if it had, very different [MH.II, 209] armies could have been raised. Vast territories were left free of conscription, as we have already seen in the case of Lugdunensis. In Africa this was done on a still larger scale, albeit for quite different reasons – perhaps the population was not suitable material for military service. At all events people were needed for farming and were left to do this work.

The situation with regard to education and national identity was similar to that in Spain. The original inhabitants, the Libyans, were not wiped out; their descendants, the Berbers and Kabyles, still live today relatively unchanged in the same regions. Not infrequently inscriptions are found written in the Phoenician alphabet and in the vernacular;[549] the cultural elements of the Phoenician era were retained. As late as the fourth century Augustine[550] spoke to an audience that was not quite up to understanding Latin, but spoke Punic. This is of great importance for provincial literature and for early Christian history.

There is far more abundant evidence of the persistence of Punic as a living language than in the case of Celtic. When the sister of Septimius Severus arrived [MH.II, 210] at Rome she was sent home again because her command of Latin was so poor that she was an embarrassment at court.[551] Inscriptions in Punic also document the survival of the language. Whether this was simply the survival of a spoken language or of a living literary language is a different matter, however.[552]

When Caesar wanted to include Africa in the Empire, it was probably his intention to give it a Punic character, or rather to leave its Punic form intact. It would have been an idea worthy of one such as Caesar not to deprive the adjoining countries of their national culture, but to leave them undisturbed in it and not try to force them into the Roman mould. Similarly, on coins from the restored city of Carthage, we find magistrates called 'sufetes'. How Punic organization fitted into the Roman organism in terms of constitutional law is unknown.[553] The cult of the Dea Caelestis of Carthage was widespread, and together with her other ancient Punic deities she found a place among the highly privileged gods of the imperial age. Their temples were reduced to ashes when Carthage was destroyed; they [MH.II, 211] were rebuilt and we possess abundant evidence that the ancient Punic religion survived all over Africa. The veneration of Pluto, which scarcely existed in Italy but was widespread in Africa, is an aspect of this. Augustine[554] still rails against the veneration of the ancient Punic gods. It is nevertheless clear that this lacked the nationalist ethnic base of the Celtic cult of the Druids in Hibernia (Ireland) which proved such a thorn in the side of the Romans in Gaul. In Africa the Romans could look on the matter without apprehension. Access to the Roman Olympus was not difficult to achieve, and the Romans absorbed both foreign people into their state and foreign gods into their heaven without great difficulty – what difference did one god more or less make? Besides this, we can also see that the three Capitoline deities, Jupiter, Juno and Minerva, did not lack veneration in Africa: on the contrary, they were almost more revered there than in Italy. The Mithras cult, on the other hand, was less well-received in Africa.[555] The survival of Punic culture is thus well attested, but it was not a cultural driving force. From the second century onwards the Roman municipal constitution became widely customary [MH.II, 212] in Africa and hence also Latin as the language of business, as we have already seen.

Literature did not avail itself of Punic at all; all extant literary development is in Latin and the role of Africa in literature was indeed an outstanding one, and deserves to be dealt with in some detail. Up to the time of Trajan the role of Africa was a negative one, in keeping with the establishment of the southern military frontier, which there alone led to the lively development of Roman life. From the mid-second century onwards, however, Africa assumed the leading role in Roman literature, just as Spain had done in the first century. While other provinces were growing barren, the virgin soil of Africa was still yielding rich intellectual harvests.

The writing of Marcus Cornelius Fronto spanned the greater part of the second century. Born in Cirta[556] during the reign of Trajan, he wrote in the time of Pius and died at a great age some time around 175. He was still young when he arrived in Rome: like the Spanish writers mentioned earlier, his talent and early career were provincial, but he experienced fame in Rome. His was no great mind; he is well known to us from his numerous surviving letters, which reveal his [MH.II, 213] individual personality. There has hardly ever been a writer more devoid of content; in this he outstripped even the younger Pliny. He nevertheless remained the leading rhetorical and literary genius of his time, again like the younger Pliny. A rigorous purist, he applied himself to archaic, pre-Ciceronian Latin and shunned all vulgarims. This, his attempt to stem the tide of the modern age, also marks him out as provincial. He played a significant role as a tutor to princes – Marcus and Lucius were his pupils – and was celebrated as successor to Cicero, as a shining example of eloquence. He stood for the most rigorous classicism.

His contemporary, rival and diametrical opposite was Apuleius. He was just as devoid of content, but wrote some brilliant pieces in the vulgar vernacular that Fronto opposed. The specialities of Apuleius were the novel, the virtuoso speech and the philosophical treatise – the whole gamut of fashionable literature – all in the most up-to-date colloquial Latin. He was also the opposite of Fronto in that, born in Carthage,[557] he did none of his major work in Italy, instead spending his life as a teacher [MH.II, 214] of rhetoric and headmaster in small African towns and ending it as a professor at the university of Carthage. Our knowledge about this university, which undoubtedly exerted considerable influence, is unfortunately very incomplete.

Aulus Sulpicius Apollinaris, Gellius's teacher, was likewise a teacher in Carthage. He represented the critical philological trend. We can see from this that it is incorrect to speak of 'African Latin' as a language with its own particular characteristics. Both the classicist and the colloquial tendencies found their most fertile expression in African authors, but they were universal, worldwide trends, not specifically African ones.

Africa came to assume a remarkable and unique position in Christian literature. It was here that Christian books arrived first on their way from East to West; acquaintance was mediated through the Greek Old Testament, the Septuagint translation of the Bible. The first Christian writings in the West were likewise then still written in Greek; Irenaeus wrote in Greek. Latin Christian literature began with translations of the Bible. It is nowadays widely believed that the earlier Latin translations of the Bible before Jerome's [MH.II, 215] were made on African soil. In an absolute sense, this is decidedly erroneous.[558] Scholars have been misled by the assumption that vulgar Latin was identical with African Latin and have, indeed, been reduced to such a blinkered, naive frame of mind by it that it has even been asserted of Petronius, the most outstanding Italian there ever was, that his vulgarisms were of African origin. Petronius wrote vulgar Latin because it was spoken all over Italy and especially in the local Neapolitan vernacular. Likewise, everything else that is asserted about African Latin is also mere myth.

In one respect only can the African origin of a colloquial usage be demonstrated: in the formation of names ending in -osus, which originally implied the idea of cleanliness and served only as a name-ending for differentiation of cognomina, e.g. Primosus, Juliosus, without any additional meaning. This usage demonstrably arose in Mauretania Caesariensis, whence it spread elsewhere.[559] Nonetheless, there is an enormous gap between such minutiae and a provincial Latin dialect. It is a fact that even Cicero did not write exactly as he spoke. There is even a discernible disparity between his letters and his other writings. [MH.II, 216] This disparity grew in the course of time, as colloquial language became further and further removed from the written form.

The penetration of literature by Vulgar Latin can largely be traced back to translations of the Bible, which were obviously anonymous. We have Augustine's statement about their origin: even he no longer knew who their authors were. The primary motive for these translations lay in the poor knowledge of Greek among the lower social classes. There were a considerable number of these translations, of which Augustine names his *Itala* as the best. Some scholars have sought to correct his text and substitute *alia*, but this is certainly wrong. Although Greek was widely understood throughout the Roman world and a translation of the Bible was not so urgently needed, there were, even in Italy, sufficient rural and other humble folk to necessitate such a translation. It is, nonetheless, correct that if he labels one particular translation 'Italian', there must have been other, non-Italian ones, of which the majority will have been African. Although there are certain variants among the quotations known to us today, these look more like later corrections [MH.II, 217] than different original versions. Several separate translations of the Bible are not known of, however. Augustine will have been better informed than we are. He is probably right, which means that the other translations of the Bible have since been lost, but did exist in the second century and were widely current in Africa. Knowledge of Greek was negligible in Africa compared to Italy and Provence, where Greek universities flourished, such as those of Naples and Marseille. The number of Greek inscriptions from Africa is likewise tiny.[560] Africa was a Latin country, which also made it a favourable region for the dissemination of Latin translations of the Bible.[561]

Third-century Christian literature is exclusively African; at least we know of nothing of any other origin, with one sole exception: probably the earliest Christian piece, the beautiful dialogue of Minucius Felix, originated in Italy. Its author was an Italian lawyer; one of the chief protagonists in the dialogue is Caelius Felix[562] from Cirta. The piece is utterly Ciceronian, in the finest Italian spirit.

From then onwards, however, everything that has come down to us is African, [MH.II, 218] like Tertullian of Carthage. He was the most brilliant, and yet also the most formless and themeless, author imaginable. His *Apologia* was written around 198, during the reign of Septimius Severus. Tertullian is the oldest Church author known to us today.[563] He was later joined by Cyprian, Bishop of Carthage, who was not his equal in talent, and Arnobius. All these authors paid homage to vulgarism. Lactantius was the representative of classicism, a native African summoned to Nicomedia by the government.[564]

305

This literature was, indeed, something new and found its most fertile soil in recently Romanized Africa. Characteristically, it availed itself for the most part of the colloquial language. This includes Augustine, the greatest Christian genius of all and another native African,[565] who taught widely in Africa itself, although he also worked as a professor in Rome and Milan.

4

WARS ON THE DANUBE[566]

We come next to an examination of the Danube lands, which may generically be labelled 'Illyricum'. Viewed from the outside, these are the most important territories – which does not mean that the main centres of intellectual culture were located here, but that it was here that the beginning of the end, the catastrophe that befell the Roman Empire, [MH.II, 219] was prepared, and from here that it was carried out.

A) THE GARRISON

The main focus of military might, formerly located on the Rhine, shifted to the Danube. Up to the time of Vespasian the banks of the Rhine had had a garrison twice as strong as that of the Danube. Both the numbers and the prestige of the Danube armies grew with the defeat of the Rhine army on the accession of Vespasian and their associated numerical and moral diminution. Augustus had stationed six legions in the Danube lands – two in Moesia, two in Pannonia and two in Dalmatia. The latter, however, were not really involved in frontier defence and were no more than a memento of the Dalmatian Wars. Raetia and Noricum, the middle and upper Danube frontiers, were free of troops from about upstream of Vienna. The reason for this was political, not military: their proximity to Italy. The idea was to keep major military commands at a distance; a major military camp at Augsburg or Innsbruck could have exerted quite different pressures on Italy than one at Mainz or Bonn.

Probably already under Vespasian the number of Danube legions rose from four to nine, and in addition the two Dalmatian legions were moved up to this frontier without jeopardizing the peace that prevailed in the mountain valleys there. [MH.II, 220] After the acquisition of Dacia, Trajan raised yet another legion and Marcus another two, so that from AD 70 until around the time of Marcus the strength of the Danube army increased from four to twelve legions.

Two factors contributed to this: first, domestic political considerations. By its very nature, the rise to power of the Flavians was a defeat for the Rhine army at the hands of the united legions of the Orient, Illyria and Italy. In the aftermath of this defeat and the quelling of the rebellion of Civilis that immediately followed it, the Rhine army was cut back and relegated to a secondary role in the military sphere. A second factor, however, was the necessity of defending the Danube frontier.

From now on the Danube legions shaped the destiny of the world, both domestically and externally. After the defeat of Italy by the African Septimius Severus, the Danube army succeeded where the Rhine army had failed; from then on the Danube army chose the Emperor. The Danube legions, recruited from Illyricum, and therefore the Illyrians, ruled the world. The armies of the Rhine and Euphrates assumed flanking positions, with the real centre of power in Illyricum. In future, too, the destiny of the world, of eastern and western Rome alike [MH.II, 221] was decided here. The Goths were advancing from the lower Danube. The subjugation of Gaul was just a flanking movement: after the decisive battle between Alaric and Stilicho, the Suevi and the Alani invaded the Empire from the Danube.

The question of the national identity of these communities is difficult and more complex than in the case of Gaul and Africa. In some places we are dealing with ethnic groups which have since disappeared, a fragmented indigenous population variously mingled with Germanic hordes. The western border, the *Vallis Poenina* – the name has persisted unchanged to this day – was in fact much closer to Gaul. It is a thoroughly Celtic land, and only Augustus's political preference for minor governorships in the vicinity of Italy had separated it from Gaul, of which it ought more sensibly to have been part, and made it part of Raetia instead. Towns such as Sedunum and Eburodunum[567] were patently Celtic, as was their cantonal constitution. The separation of Raetia and Vindelicia from Gaul was equally artificial. These lands were Gallic too; Kempten and Augsburg were Celtic and only external considerations severed these ties.

Raetia and Vindelicia constituted a double province. Vindelicia (Bavaria) was a Gallic land at that time. The Raetians, who inhabited the Tirol, eastern Switzerland [MH.II, 222] and the mountain regions of northern Italy, are a riddle. They were neither Celts nor Germans. It is possible that they were Illyrians, but more probable that they were Etruscans.[568] It is not beyond the bounds of possibility, however, that they embraced various indigenous populations. Nonetheless, the similarities they bear to the Etruscans are quite substantial: we can find significant traces of Etruscan culture and inscriptions.[569] However, it is no longer possible to ascertain whether they were themselves Etruscans, or whether they were another tribe whose culture was merely adopted from the Etruscans. Nor is this of any importance. What is interesting is that *sacra Raetica* (Raetic ceremonies) were still performed around Verona in the time of the Emperors.[570] This people lived completely remote from and inaccessible to Roman culture, and must have been a distinctive tribe that was difficult to assimilate. The fact that Latin is still spoken there today[571] may be explained by the fact that these remote, inaccessible valleys became the final bastion and refuge of Roman culture when the Germans overran the lowlands, bringing from the sixth century onwards the appearance of Latinity into those very lands that were least hospitable to it. The Raetian component is of minimal importance to history in general.

[MH.II, 223] Noricum, the modern provinces of Styria and Carinthia, differs greatly from Raetia, since it became thoroughly Romanized at an early date. According to the account of Velleius,[572] there were important and thoroughly Roman towns in existence there in the time of Claudius. Claudia Celeia (Cilli) and Virunum (near Klagenfurt) were early towns. We are not really sure as to the manner in which Noricum was acquired by Rome. Strikingly, Regnum Noricum was the name given to this territory in a period when there are certainly no longer any kings. A *redactio in formam provinciae* probably never occurred there at all; the country was probably still governed for a time by indigenous kings, who were later replaced by procurators. Claudius's foundations simply formalized a state of affairs that had long existed *de facto*. Noricum was probably acquired through commercial channels, rather than as a conquest by arms. Aquileia, a Roman town of very early date, and the mines of Styria were crucial factors. The Guard, membership of which, as we have seen, was restricted to Italians, likewise soon accepted Noricans and Tauriscans, as well as Italians. Although originally Celts, they were Romanized very early on.

The Illyrians proper, or more correctly Pannonians, [MH.II, 224] as Tacitus calls them,[573] had a language which was different from Celtic.[574] They represent a people apart, neither Germanic nor Celtic but indigenous. Istria, Dalmatia and Pannonia were all Illyrian, and the rebellion in the reign of Augustus was a decidedly nationalist uprising. The Pannonians possessed Dalmatia and both Upper and Lower Pannonia, interspersed with other tribes, such as the Boii and others. They must have disappeared from the region known as the 'Boian desert'[575] – a multifarious population. The modern Albanians are probably the last remnant of this not very widespread people.

The Thracian tribes lived to the right and left of the lower Danube in both parts of Moesia, in Dacia (later to be conquered by Trajan) and as far as the Black Sea towards Constantinople. They were interspersed with Celtic and Germanic groups, such as the Bastarnae.[576] We do not find such homogeneous ethnic groups as in the West.

In addition there were the Germans, who occupied a unique position. They did not originally belong to this region; they were immigrants and the occasion for their arrival is known to us. Around 9 BC Marobod, leader of the Marcomanni, withdrew eastwards from his homelands to the west [MH.II, 225] in order to evade

Roman influence. He settled in modern Bohemia, which originally belonged to the Celtic Boii, hence the name Bohemia.[577] As we have seen, the catastrophe that Germany anticipated on the Rhine under Augustus failed to occur; the German federation was not smashed, nor was Marobod threatened. Evidently the Romans no longer dared to undertake any drastic action after the defeat of Varus in AD 9. We have seen that this event prompted a radical and enduring shift in Roman policy. Marobod consolidated his position. Nonetheless, what Augustus's arms had failed to accomplish was accomplished by the policy of Tiberius, who either kindled or exploited dissension among the Germans. Catualda the Goth took up arms against Marobod – this is the first ever mention of the Goths.[578] The expelled princes submitted, Marobod was interned in Ravenna and Catualda too was captured. The personal aspects are somewhat obscure, but in any case of little import; the point is that these German tribes formed a buffer against the Romans' frontier neighbours, like the Ubii on the Rhine. We are not precisely informed as to what happened to Marobod's kingdom. At all events his men were peaceful and showed allegiance to Rome up to the time of Domitian. Another kingdom, the state of the Quadi, [MH.II, 226] was created by the Romans themselves under Vannius from German refugees in modern Moravia.[579] These two states provided protection for Noricum on the other side of the Danube. This was an extraordinary achievement on the part of Tiberius.

A profound calm then reigned until the end of the first century. Under Domitian, however, the entire Danube line was suddenly threatened in the regions of the Marcomanni, Quadi and Dacians.[580] This looks forward to what was later to occur under Trajan and Marcus, but first we should cast a glance at the overall development of these territories up to that point.

The situation on the Rhine was largely stable; the fortresses had remained the same for centuries; the limits of Romanization were also relatively constant. This was not so in the Danube lands: Augustus[581] claimed to have made the Danube a frontier, but what is a frontier? Whilst it is true that Augustus did not tolerate any independent peoples between the Danube and Roman territory proper, the Danube in the time of Augustus was far from a frontier in the sense that the Rhine was. What took place up to the time of Pius was that the frontier was pushed forward, and civilization with it.

[MH.II, 227] The history of this movement and development is enigmatic: the sources are too meagre. Epigraphy is of great assistance here and the history of the legions throws light on some aspects. One thoroughly acceptable source, at least for the roughest of outlines, is the study of city names. Julian, Claudian and Flavian colonies provide a substantial amount of provincial history. The first conclusion is a negative one: there were no Julian colonies, with the exception of Emona (Ljubljana);[582] this means that this part of Pannonia was already being Romanized by that time.

Subsequently the Claudian colonies form a quite distinct chapter. They include all the territory of Noricum.[583] Iuvavum (Salzburg), Celeia Claudia (Cilly), Virunum, Teurnia and Aguntum were old Claudian municipalities and colonies. Only one community on the outermost frontier, Seckau,[584] was founded under Vespasian. Savaria (Stein am Anger) in the Boian desert was founded by Claudius.

We have little information about fighting in the time of Vespasian. However, although our sources for this period are scant, we may at least deduce a state of peace and the absence of major military events from this silence. [MH.II, 228] In contrast, this period was all the more eventful in terms of civilizing, administrative and military changes. The period from Vespasian to Domitian (i.e. under the Flavian Emperors; more than this cannot be deduced from the bare names of towns, but probably already under Vespasian) witnessed the founding of the cities on the Sava: Siscia, Sirmium and Scarbantia (Sopron). Further afield than these we encounter only Aelian or Aurelian city-foundations.

These municipal phenomena were matched by military ones: the course and character of the Rhine generally made it a good basis for defence. In contrast, the Danube, particularly on account of the great abrupt angle it makes as its course suddenly turns southwards, is not suited for defence. Augustus's strategists therefore selected the lower course of the Danube, the Sava and Drava, as their military frontier. Under Augustus, the major focal point, the 'Mainz' of the Danube line, was Poetovio (Pettau) in southern Styria. Carnuntum (Petronell near Schwechat, just outside Vienna) formed the base for the offensive against the north.[585] It was here that Tiberius, preparing for his expedition against Marobod in Bohemia, mustered his army. Carnuntum was not yet a fortress at that time. Velleius[586] states that Carnuntum was part of Noricum, but later as a fortress it [MH.II, 229] belonged to Pannonia. Until recently it had been my belief – an idea which greatly recommends itself *a priori* – that Carnuntum followed Pettau as a troop garrison, but this is incorrect. Hirschfeld[587] has demonstrated the contrary. There was already a legionary fortress there in 73, and we possess even earlier military inscriptions from there. The urban layout of Savaria likewise speaks against the theory; it would have predated the fortress. The two fortresses in fact exclude each other. Vienna and Pettau can only have existed as fortresses at the same time for a transitional period of short duration.

Trajan shifted the frontier eastwards. Pettau was abandoned, the Danube bank garrisoned, Brigetium (Komorn) established, and from then on the line from Brigetium to Carnuntum, i.e. from Komorn to Vienna, became the Noricum line of defence in Pannonia. Domitian[588] fought two wars against the Dacians and against the Suevi and the Sarmatians. These Suevi are the Danube Suevi, consisting of Marcomanni and Quadi. The Sarmatians were not yet frontier neighbours; we should envisage them located in the Vistula region, or perhaps even further afield; they had concluded an alliance with the Suevi.

B) THE DACIAN WAR

A legion was wiped out by the Sarmatians under Domitian.[589] This Suevian-Sarmatian War was itself only a consequence of the Dacian War. The Dacians[590] resided on the far side of the Danube [MH.II, 230] and shifts in population must have occurred among them in this period, leading to a consolidation of their kingdom, similar to the Ariovistus episode in the time of Caesar. A theocratic monarchy arose among the Dacians which, nevertheless, like that of Ariovistus, soon collapsed and probably only came about at all on account of a single outstanding personality. In the case of the Dacians this personality was King Decebalus, who was associated with a priest-god.[591] Decebalus amassed great power and behaved aggressively towards the Romans, crossing the lower Danube and overrunning Moesia. The governor, Oppius Sabinus, himself fell in the action.[592] The Dacian horde departed as swiftly as it had arrived.

Domitian deemed it necessary to avenge this outrage and marched to Moesia at the head of the Guard. The bodyguard under Cornelius Fuscus crossed the Danube and advanced into Dacia, only to suffer yet another crushing defeat and witness the death of its general. Finally Antonius Julianus achieved a great victory at Tapae which is mentioned by Tacitus [MH.II, 231] in his *Histories*.[593] The Dacians sued for peace and Domitian celebrated a triumph.[594] It was presented to the capital as if the Dacians had been crushed. In truth this served only to camouflage an ignominious defeat for the Romans, the circumstances of which became clear when Trajan assumed power. Domitian had had to submit not only to providing Decebalus with Roman artisans of various kinds, but also to paying tribute.[595] Although the Romans were in fact very frequently defeated at the beginning of their campaigns, it had never happened before that a campaign was brought to an end under such ignominious circumstances. The Dacian War was followed by the Suevian-Sarmatian War, since these peoples, it appeared, kept common cause with the Dacians (see MH.II, 229), making it a far-reaching, nationalist movement. The course of this war too was ill-fated.

Roman prestige needed to be restored and, fortunately for the state, a man of Trajan's calibre now came to power who was fully capable of doing so. He inherited the still unconcluded Suevian War, which had continued through Nerva's reign. Apart from the East, Trajan was most occupied with imposing some order on Illyrian affairs. He immediately abolished the [MH.II, 232] Drava line and shifted the line of defence forward to the upper Danube. The division of Moesia has probably to be traced back earlier to Domitian. At the very outset Trajan divided Pannonia into Upper and Lower Pannonia, the former larger and to the west, the latter smaller and to the east. The legion of Lower Pannonia was not relocated to Aquincum (Budapest) immediately, but first to Acumincum where the

Tisza flows into the Danube and where it could communicate with Viminacium in Moesia. Later, it was relocated to Budapest, and the lines of communication were with Komorn and Vienna. This probably did not occur until the time of Pius, however. Under Trajan, during the Dacian War, the southern fortress of Acumincum was more suitable than the northern one.

Trajan immediately set about imposing order in Illyria. According to an inscription from Orsova he regulated the roads there in AD 100.[596] Directly thereafter in 101 the Dacian War began,[597] with the aim of nullifying the ignominious tribute to Decebalus. It was an offensive war from Moesia. After a number of bloody encounters Decebalus was forced to sue for peace in 102. This war must have been fought before the plan to seize Dacia came to fruition; [MH.II, 233] otherwise it would not have been so swiftly ended.

In 105[598] the Second Dacian War broke out, ostensibly because Decebalus failed to abide by the peace agreement and attacked the Jazyges, but more probably because Trajan still deemed Decebalus and the Dacians too powerful to be accommodated within a client-state relationship and therefore resolved not merely to humiliate, but also to subjugate and destroy them. This was an individual, unforced decision by Trajan. He may have been enticed by the familiarity with this rich country gained during the first war, by the gold mines[599] for which Rome was everywhere so greedy. It was at all events a fight to the finish; the Dacians knew this and fought to save their skins, but were annihilated. Decebalus fell[600] and the Roman victory was complete.

The details of the Dacian War are largely unknown to us, but we still have a history of it in stone in the form of Trajan's Column in Rome.[601] It depicts the storming of Dacian village huts and scenes from battles. This was no dangerous war with an uncertain outcome. Although hard-fought, the end was a foregone conclusion; it was the desperate struggle of a barbarian nation against a civilized great power. Its repercussions were extraordinary. First, it brought about the downfall of a renowned nation: the Getae, Dacians and Thracians here lost [MH.II, 234] the last bastion of their people. Surrounded on all sides by enemies – Scythians, Sarmatians, Jazyges and Germans – they now had no refuge. It is clear, even from the pitifully scant extant accounts, that this was a desperate war of destruction and that the land was turned into a desert. But on the other hand, we also learn that a tremendous wave of fresh migration into this region took place, as is borne out by the monuments. This new wave of settlement was not of the same density everywhere; vast stretches of Wallachia are quite devoid of Roman remains.

Whereas elsewhere traces have survived of the original population, in the form of indigenous names in Illyria, Dalmatia and also in Istria, there is nothing of this kind in Dacia – no proper names, not a trace. The nation ceased to exist. In Thrace this process was to last somewhat longer, but then the original population disappeared there, too, and a new people made its appearance.[602] This was the only creation of this kind shaped by Roman arms. Rome did, of course Romanize everywhere, but nowhere else did it bring about such a complete metamorphosis. The immigrants into this wasteland, this vacuum, came for the most part from Galatia, Commagene and Asia Minor generally, as is still attested by many inscriptions and traces of the veneration of the deities of Asia Minor, including [MH.II, 235] the name of the capital, Metropolis, an epithet that occurs nowhere else in the whole of the Empire and is reminiscent of Asia Minor.[603] It was essentially a civilian wave of migration that suddenly streamed into this devastated land, attracted both by its fertility and by the mining industry. The latter especially attracted Pirustae, tribesmen from the border between Dalmatia and Epirus, where the mines had by then been exhausted, just as the populousness of Chemnitz and Kremnitz today are due to similar causes. Alburnum was founded by them at this time. The Dacian forts and the capital were in the vicinity of the mines.

The Roman element remained weak, but the immigrants spoke Latin, not Greek, and formed the easternmost Latin outpost. This linguistic region corresponds to Romania, Wallachia and Transylvania. The foundation of these states demonstrates that the powerful sun of Rome still shone brightly even while setting. This was the last offshoot from a great trunk, and it remained Roman for a mere century; and yet how firm and indestructible are its traces! The Romanians have retained their language to this very day.[604]

[MH.II, 236] The country's borderlines are curious. Located entirely on the far side of the Danube, it is largely devoid of natural boundaries, so that the country is dependent on strategic ones, or none at all. Transylvania, on the other hand, is naturally well defended. To the north its frontier is formed by the course of the river Samosul, and a *vallum* was established where this river curves too far north. The remains of this, although paltry, can be traced and are quite unmistakable near ancient Porolissum. The southern border, of course, was formed by the Danube. The civilizing process progressed with greater intensity in the north than in the south, even though it was nearer to earlier Roman possessions. The forts, mines and arable land were all in the north. The eastern frontier is uncertain, but it is clear, at least, that the Prut region was not part of the province; the left bank of the Danube estuary was barbarian.

Few points along the Black Sea coast were in Roman hands, although the southern coast was Roman. The Romans never directly extended their rule to the northern coast; although seen as part of the Mediterranean the Black Sea did, in fact, fall into their sphere of influence. As we have seen, however, they had had the major ports in their possession since the time of Nero, for example [MH.II, 237] modern Akerman (Odessa) at the mouth of the Dniester, the Greek port of Tyras. The Romans were, after all, still conscious of their cultural-historical mission: to preserve what had been established by Greek merchants. Inscriptions in Olbia[605] testify to the fact that the Greeks resident there, threatened by Scythians, Galatians and Bastarnae, were afforded protection by Rome, even though this protection was not always sufficient. Olbia, which was not treated as part of the Roman Empire, lies between the estuaries of the Dnestr and Dnieper. Pius likewise sent the Olbiopolitans protection against their foes.[606]

As we saw earlier, the Crimea, ancient Bosporus Taurica, was ruled by a Thracian dynasty; it was a client-state of sorts, under Roman protection. The unusual situation with regard to the coins of this state has already been discussed. It was permitted to mint gold, which made it formally sovereign.[607] It was the Roman side which rejected full incorporation; the state was regarded as a buffer. The garrisons on the coast were formed of detachments from the Moesian legions and the country as a whole was always considered part of Lower Moesia. It had no connection with Dacia, which had a thoroughly continental character. The two were divided by the Prut valley. Pausanias[608] speaks of a raid made by [MH.II, 238] Costoboci, a Sarmatian-Scythian tribe on the Black Sea, deep into Greece. This means that the northern coast was so little Romanized that not even the security of the Black Sea was absolute. It was here that the *facies Hippocratica*[609] of the Empire first revealed itself. The river Siretul (Hierasus) was held to be the frontier of Dacia, but God knows whether it really was. The frontier was probably never defended; it simply did not matter to anyone.

To the north the country extended to the border with Germania; milestones of Trajan can be found on the road from Napoca (in Dacia) as far as Potaissa (Kluj).[610] In the west the situation was even more extraordinary. One might expect the Tisza valley from the great bend in the Danube as far as Kluj to form a natural part of Roman territory. Such a rounding out would have been even more natural than that created by the Agri Decumates on the Rhine. Uniting Dacia and Pannonia would have shortened the military frontier, but it did not occur. Perhaps the inhospitable nature of the region and the constant danger of flooding were deterrents, but the key motives were probably political. The region was inhabited by a [MH.II, 239] Scythian-Sarmatian tribe, the Jazyges, who very early on had been driven to these parts from their tribal lands further to the north, hence their appellation Metanastai. Pliny[611] was already familiar with them in this location. They may have been supported by the Romans in their conflicts with the Dacian peoples to whom these parts had once belonged. At all events the Romans looked upon them as a buffer. Nonetheless, the Romans failed to hand back to them the tracts of land they demanded after the Second Dacian War and which had allegedly been seized by Decebalus. Assuming, therefore, that the Jazyges constituted a sort of Roman military client-state, this explains the curious frontier. Furthermore, there are no traces of Roman colonization anywhere here. In fact, therefore, Dacia was a country isolated on all sides, apart from the south, where the Danube formed its border with the Empire. Later Emperors did nothing to change this.

The capital city was the same as in the era of the country's independence. It bore the proud name of 'Colonia Ulpia Traiana Augusta Sarmizegetusa'.[612] Trajan called it Metropolis and it was a wealthy, rapidly flourishing city, boasting an abundance of monuments and organized [MH.II, 240] from the start as a true citizens' metropolis. In addition, there were military fortresses: the first was formerly located in the Olt region[613] and was later relocated to Apulum (Alba Julia), which was a more convenient position from which to cover the capital and at the same time defend the mines. Troops were not deployed on any of the frontiers. Trajan formed the garrison from one legion and Severus deployed a second to the north at Potaissa along the course of the Marisus (a river in Dacia).[614] The region was rapidly civilized – it was an attractive region, amenable to culture.

The period under Hadrian and Pius was a peaceful one. The legionary camp in Pannonia was relocated, as we have seen, from the lower Danube to Buda and Pest (Aquincum and Contraaquincum). Even if Dacia was not connected to the Danube, the acquisition of Dacia undoubtedly lay behind this relocation, since those regions that could not be controlled from the Moesian fortresses at the confluence of the Tisza could be controlled from Aquincum. Osiek (Mursa) was another town established by Hadrian. The line from Vienna to Komorn and Budapest created at that time unmistakably took Dacia into account.

C) THE MARCOMANNIC WAR

[MH.II, 241] In 161 Marcus Aurelius came to power. He, and the Empire with him, paid a heavy price for the twenty-four years of peace that had elapsed prior to his succession. Pius had allowed matters to slide as far as was possible. In fact those years ought not to have been years of peace; war had already broken out and had only been suppressed with great difficulty: the Romans had stuck their heads in the sand and temporized. Then what came to be known as the Marcomannic War broke out.[615] Although apt, the name is inaccurate; the war was named thus *a posteriori* because the Marcomanni had a part in it, albeit a significant one. More precisely, however, this was a war waged by the Roman Empire along the entire line of the Danube from its source to its estuary against the barbarians living on the far side of it – a vast theatre of war. The war was more significant and rich in repercussions than perhaps any other. It was in fact here that the die was cast – from then on the Roman Empire was in decline. Although the Empire was already old after Trajan, it was still not decrepit. But this war marked the beginning of the end.

The domestic situation was in numerous respects crucial in shaping the foreign political one. As far as the *dramatis personae* were concerned, Pius died on 7 March 161,[616] having named as his successor his eldest adopted son, Marcus Aurelius. The latter's peculiar disposition, characterized partly by lack of interest and partly by lack of [MH.II, 242] energy and ambition, led him to adopt his brother Lucius as his co-Emperor.[617] This was a terrible mistake. The principate was based to the utmost degree on the unity of the supreme institutions of authority, far more unequivocally even than modern monarchies, which are ruled by ministers, on whom a considerable amount of power devolves; see, for example, the administration of Frederick of Prussia. This dual regime coincided with the grave events of an outbreak of war, thereby wreaking double havoc.[618]

Marcus was a man of great moral nobility and outstanding talent; we are familiar with his *Speculations*.[619] He enjoyed good relations both with his tutor, Fronto, and with his brother, which was to have such negative consequences. Marcus was upright, talented and not undistinguished, but he was not the one thing which an Emperor ought above all to have been in that era: a soldier; and he knew it. It was principally for this reason, apart from his fraternal affection and selflessness, that he appointed Lucius as his colleague, a brilliant *bon-vivant* whom he considered to be an equally brilliant general.

The succession coincided with the [MH.II, 243] onset of the Parthian War, which had long been looming on the horizon.[620] Marcus sent Lucius to Asia, but the latter's complete military incompetence soon came to light. He acquitted himself poorly and the relatively fortunate conclusion of the war is attributable to anyone but the supreme commander himself. It was not this notoriously inept man, but his able junior officers who salvaged the Roman cause (see MH.II, 302).

Marcus felt it necessary to set out for the Danube, taking Lucius with him, but since he could no longer trust Lucius, he assumed the supreme command himself.[621] The presence of the Guard, and above all a unified personal command, were essential in this war, which extended from Raetia to Dacia. The organizational structure in operation for normal times should not be forgotten: every province had its own commander, who was fully equal to his counterpart in the neighbouring province and was neither empowered to issue orders to him nor obliged to take orders from him. Each took the initiative, or not, as he deemed fit. Only the Emperor himself was empowered to intervene to improve matters.

Marcus acquitted himself better [MH.II, 244] than one might expect. The required supervision was more of a moral than a military character, and it was more important to avoid friction than to issue positive orders. When Lucius died in 169 the dual command[622] went with him. The tasks which now devolved on Marcus called for application, a keen assessment of people, authority and something nowadays provided by a general staff: overall direction. Marcus was equal to these tasks and it was not his fault that the end result was inadequate.

An exacerbating factor, however, was that the war followed immediately on the severe Armenian-Parthian War, as a result of which the treasury was empty. This financial crisis[623] is incomprehensible; Marcus was obliged to spend two successive months in Rome holding auctions and selling off the family jewels in order to refill the empty state coffers to some extent.[624] The calamitous state of the coinage in this period has already been discussed in another connection (see MH.II, 32ff.). As if all this were not enough, matters were further compounded by the plague,[625] and by the famine and depopulation that came in its wake. The plague broke out during the war in the East and was a consequence of it; the epidemic was spread by the army and raged [MH.II, 245] throughout Marcus's reign. Italy and the Danube forts were horribly ravaged for a period of fifteen to twenty years, at the very same time as the bitterest of warfare. Galen's accounts provide us with quite precise information about this epidemic. The capital and the forts were the worst affected.

Accounts of the war are extraordinarily sparse. Nevertheless, it should not be impossible to piece together a relatively accurate picture on the basis of the extant material, particularly the various fragments and accounts which go back to Dio – Xiphilinus's excerpts are poor, those by Peter the Patrician are better – combined with coins and inscriptions, so important for reconstructing a chronology, which yield dry, but usable results. We shall at least make an attempt here.

All accounts agree that the war was protracted.[626] There was probably already sporadic fighting during the reign of Pius and certainly during the eastern war, but this was unplanned and lacked any common initiative. Every governor made war on his own initiative, thus making the presence of the Emperor there much more necessary than that of the Guard.

It was hordes from the north who were advancing and began the attacks, not simply the frontier neighbours of Rome, who were being pushed out of the way. This was the prelude [MH.II, 246] to the great migrations. This pressure from behind can be confirmed from our sources;[627] we have a valuable account of this first phase of the war from the Byzantine Peter the Patrician, whose account derives from Dio.[628] Peter relates how the Lombards crossed the Danube. The true homeland of the Lombards is to be sought in the Elbe lands, which makes their sudden appearance so far from their homeland striking. A total of some 6,000 men are reputed to have been slain by the cavalry prefect Macrinius Vindex. The Marcomanni king is named among the envoys sent to sue for peace. This was thus a combined attack by frontier neighbours together with the peoples living in the hinterland, who swept them along with them. This was the occasion (168) of Marcus's fifth imperial acclamation.[629]

The next attack was launched with even greater force and drew in all the provinces along the Danube. The enemy crossed the Julian Alps and descended into the plains of Italy; some 100,000 prisoners from Upper Italy are reputed to have fallen into the hands of the Marcomanni, Quadi and Jazyges. Opitergium (Oderzo) in Venetia was [MH.II, 247] reduced to ashes and siege laid to Aquileia, the largest and wealthiest city in those lands.[630] These events revealed to the Italian public for the first time, and very profoundly, the true nature of what was occurring: the heir to world dominion was beating on their gates.

The years 169 and 170 must have witnessed a series of catastrophes: since there is a complete absence of imperial acclamations, we must assume that no victories were won. A number of senior officers met their deaths, which naturally leads us to conclude that military losses were heavy. Two Guard commanders met their deaths: Furius Victorinus and Macrinius Vindex.[631] Once the Emperor had appeared on the scene, the Prefect of the Guard was, naturally, his *alter ego* in the theatre of war. The governor of Dacia, Marcus Claudius Fronto, fell after a series of successful encounters with the Jazyges; his tomb survives.[632] In his appreciative fashion, Marcus had monuments erected in Rome in honour of the fallen officers that soon filled Trajan's Forum. The death of Furius Victorinus came in 168, since we know that Verus was still alive at that time and he died [MH.II, 248] in January 169 in camp near Altinum.[633] The other defeats of the Guard probably also occurred in this period.

Seeking to rid himself of the lesser evil, Marcus initially plied the Quadi with sweet words. The Quadi were more dependent on Rome than the Marcomanni and the Jazyges. Pius had already sent them a king – coins bear the inscription 'A King granted to the Quadi'.[634] It would appear that the princeps wielded something akin to a right of confirmation,[635] which was not the case with the other peoples mentioned. Peace was thus now concluded with the Quadi. This was the severest phase of the Marcomannic War, when Roman arrogance was forced to do obeisance to a semi-dependent people. One of the conditions for peace was the return of deserters and prisoners, of whom some 13,000 are reputed to have been handed over by the Quadi.[636] However, it was maintained afterwards that they had only released the useless, aged and sick and retained men capable of bearing arms, which points to an enormous number of deserters. The principal condition for peace, however, was that the Marcomanni and Jazyges should be denied Quadian territory; a glance at the map reveals the importance of this condition. [MH.II, 249] The territory of the Quadi was the link which connected the other warring nations, for unrest was also brewing in Dacia. The Dacians themselves had been wiped out and no longer posed a threat, but the Asdingi[637] and Sarmatians of the lower Danube were trying to force their way into the country; here, too, there was heavy fighting as far as the Black Sea. Only a nebulous outline of events is accessible to us; for the time being the invasion appears to have been fended off in this sector, certainly not least as a consequence of the division between the theatres of war on the Tisza and in Bohemia by the territory of the Quadi.

Events on the middle and upper Danube are even less well known. Pannonia was undoubtedly the hub of the war, since the headquarters were at Carnuntum near Vienna, although there was also fighting in Noricum and Raetia. Specific facts illustrate this: for example, we learn that Pertinax[638] reconquered these provinces, which means that they must previously have been lost. Then there are the most peculiar changes in the layout of fortifications and the relocation of troops. Up to the time of Marcus there were no [MH.II, 250] major camps located upstream from Vienna. The garrison had consisted of substantial cohorts, not of legions. Conditions had, after all, been peaceful. Now, two new legions were formed whose names were also significant: the *Secunda* and *Tertia Italica*. They were quartered in the permanent camps at Lauriacum (Enns) and Castra Regina (Regensburg).

This was the approximate situation in the first agonizing and ill-fated years of this major war. Marcus deserves the utmost credit for staying the course in the task confronting him, which was by no means congenial to him; he fulfilled his duty tirelessly, courageously and steadfastly. His personal presence in the theatre of war was of crucial importance and it was not least because of it that matters eventually took a turn for the better.[639]

The first success was achieved in 171, although our sole piece of concrete evidence is an imperial acclamation of that year.[640] Although this victory did not yet lead to peace, it did enable Rome to break with its false friends, the Quadi, and to treat them openly as foes. Mention has already been made of the distasteful peace that Rome had been compelled to [MH.II, 251] conclude with them. The Quadi had expelled the king installed by Marcus and chosen a new one, Ariogaesus, without the sanction of Rome.[641] This became the pretext for breaking with them. Combat was fierce and not really conclusive. A major victory over them was won in 174 and became the occasion for the seventh imperial acclamation.[642] The army had been in great peril as a result of a shortage of water[643] and virtually cut off. This victory saved the army, but still the war dragged on; we learn of numerous attempts to make peace, of treaties which were immediately broken; the course of events is pretty unclear. This much is clear, however, that after some personal vacillation the resolve ripened in Marcus's mind to make a clean sweep on the far side of the Danube. His ultimate aim, according to his biographer,[644] was to create two new provinces from the lands of the Jazyges and Marcomanni, Sarmatia and Marcomannia, i.e. Bohemia and Moravia. Although the account contains numerous incongruities and we have no more than *disiecta membra*,[645] this will have been the core of the plan. The Jazyges offered to become subjects, but meanwhile the belligerent party among them gained the upper hand, deposed [MH.II, 252] the king, disavowed him and took him prisoner. Combat was resumed with such ferocity that for a time they were the principal enemies of Rome.

The return of prisoners was invariably a central point in the various negotiations. Over and above this, Rome also demanded that the Germans remove themselves from the Danube and be settled 16 Roman miles[646] from the river on the far side of a broad strip of wasteland which was not to be tilled. The Emperor also demanded the provision of a cavalry force of 8,000 men, of whom 5,500 were sent to Britain[647] – cavalry were characteristic of the Jazyges, a true equestrian people who made war from their small, tough horses.

Then events took a new turn, favouring better treatment of the Jazyges. The true principal enemy of Rome was, after all, the Germans, and Marcus seems to have succeeded in making the Jazyges their sworn enemies. In peacetime, the Jazyges insisted on continuing their war of extermination with the Germans, thereby giving rise to a tacit alliance between themselves and the Romans. The Jazyges were now only required to give up their islands in the Danube and to maintain no ships on it. Since they were separated from related tribes [MH.II, 253] for example the Roxolani, by Dacia, they were permitted in return to travel through this province, provided they abided by certain security measures: notifying the governor and being accompanied by an escort provided by him. Marcus clearly intended to use the Sarmatians as allies against the Marcomanni and the Quadi, against whom war was now being waged all the more fiercely. Here, too, there is sporadic evidence of negotiations similar to those with the Jazyges and involving similar conditions (a frontier strip, settlement away from the river). One interesting stipulation was that trade be permitted only on certain days and under military supervision.[648] Trade with the northern barbarian peoples was clearly very lucrative for the Romans, nor could it be otherwise, given the different cultural levels of these two parties, so that the Romans were evidently reluctant to see this trade completely curtailed.

War must have been resumed, however, a war which the Romans were resolved to pursue until the foe had been destroyed. Marcus had a series of forts built on the far side of the Danube and a 20,000-strong Roman occupation force was stationed in garrison forts facing each of the two main enemies. Agriculture was totally destroyed – this was a war of desperation as the Dacian War had been, and it turned decidedly in favour of the Romans, forcing [MH.II, 254] the Quadi to prepare to quit the region to join the Semnones on the Elbe. This draws our attention to the Lombards, who had pushed forward from the same region and begun the war that was now drawing to a close. The Romans did not permit them to leave, however: Marcus barred their way, intending that they meet the same fate as the Dacians, and they were routed. Marcus upheld this aim when a rebellion broke out among the Syrian legions in 175. Avidius Cassius, the highly competent local governor, was proclaimed Emperor.[649] Since this represented an urgent danger, Marcus abandoned the war on the Danube with his plans on the brink of fruition, hastily restoring tolerable relations with his foes, and thereby changed the course of world history.

As his success showed, it had not been necessary for the Emperor to travel east. The rebellion was swiftly crushed before he even appeared on the scene. Nonetheless, the danger to the succession led him to name his still under-age son Commodus as his successor, a most unfortunate choice. This, and the failure to destroy the Marcomanni and Quadi, which had almost been achieved, were the consequences of the Syrian uprising. [MH.II, 255] Marcus celebrated a triumph in

Rome on 23 December[650] 176. Although the triumph was richly deserved, he did not regard it as a definitive end, nor his task as accomplished. War was resumed in 178. There could be no lack of reasons as long as they were sought, which they were. The Marcomanni had certainly not abided by all the conditions of the peace; nor, however, had they taken the offensive.[651] It was Marcus who wanted to continue the war, for it is a matter of indifference whether one chooses to call it the Second Marcomannic War or a continuation of the First. The Romans were firmly resolved on complete subjugation.

The course of the Second Marcomannic War is even less well known than that of the First, where we at least have some detail, albeit confused. In 180 a major victory was won by Tarrutenius Paternus, as a consequence of which we have the tenth imperial acclamation.[652] But then Marcus suddenly died at the age of 58 in Vindobona (Vienna) on 17 March 180.[653] Marcus is one of the most tragic figures in history. With unparalleled self-sacrifice he dedicated his entire life to the simple [MH.II, 256] fulfilment of his duty, and yet he accomplished little that he set out to do and much that he did not wish to. He and his successor are vivid examples of the importance of individual personality.

Commodus was 19, scarcely capable of ruling, when he came to power in 180. His nature was unspeakably bad: subservient, cowardly, simple-minded and averse to all political activity, the exact opposite of his father, for whom the fulfilment of every duty was a pleasure. The son found every duty irksome; his sole aim was to bring the war to an end as swiftly as possible. In fact the goal was already within grasp; it was simply a matter of plucking the fruit of victory, but this foolish young man lacked patience and his sole thought was to return to the capital. There were men, however, who were not happy to stand idly by and let this happen. A council of war was held; Commodus wanted to conclude the war at any price, but Claudius Pompeianus, the leading general under Marcus and brother-in-law to Commodus, was opposed to this outrageous surrender and the deliberate abandoning of well-thought-out and tenaciously executed plans.[654] This provides a graphic example of how damaging [MH.II, 257] hereditary succession could prove to the principate. Family affection and sentiment were misplaced: world history might have taken a different course if Marcus had chosen not the useless Commodus, but the capable Claudius Pompeianus as his successor.

Initially the ideas put forward by the council of war were successful; the war was continued, although only for a few months, after which Commodus concluded peace after all. The conditions achieved provide clear evidence of the progress that had been made and of how little remained for the complete accomplishment of the goal, how close the Romans were to total subjugation. The Marcomanni were charged with returning their prisoners, paying tribute and providing troops; this in fact covered all the essential Roman requirements. Even subject provinces provided little more than troops for military service and the payment of taxes. Unfortunately, these conditions existed on paper only: the tribute was remitted and the troops were not provided. Worst of all, however, all the forts built by Marcus on the far bank of the Danube were abandoned and the [MH.II, 258] 40,000 strong garrison small-mindedly withdrawn, thus effectively leaving the country to its own devices. The Marcomanni and Quadi had to promise not to molest the Jazyges, the Vandals (a major German tribe in Silesia) and the Buri (on the northern border of Dacia).

Overall, the war was not entirely without results: from now on the Marcomanni and Quadi were no longer a threat; they were erased from history. (In this respect the work of Marcus had been a success.) The flood of Germanic tribes which followed swept them away, and there were no more wars on the middle Danube. To the pressure of the barbaric peoples behind them was added the severity of the attack they had had to suffer from the Romans. This stream of Germans from the Oder and Vistula regions later shifted to a more south-easterly direction, and we find the great Gothic migration moving towards the Crimea. They no longer exert pressure on the Danube: the dress rehearsal for the great migrations had reached its conclusion here, where a period of fifty to seventy years of peace now ensued. This should, nevertheless, be understood with reservations. Accounts of smaller-scale migrations have not come down to us, but they will have taken place. It is mentioned in passing,[655] for example, that under Commodus there was fighting with the northern neighbours of Dacia; [MH.II, 259] similarly Albinus and Niger, the two candidates for the throne in 193, both won their first laurels in Dacia.

Although some successes were achieved, one detrimental consequence of the Marcommanic Wars which outweighed any number of successes was the barbarization and provincialization of Roman troops.[656] Up to the time of Marcus the extent of conscription carried out among the Illyrians had been light. It had generally only involved levying troops into *alae* and *cohortes* for deployment in the provinces: thus there were eight such detachments of Raetians, a very considerable number, besides Pannonians and Dacians, but few Noricans. Noricum had been awarded citizenship very early on, so that these troops could be incorporated into the legions. There were not many *cohortes* and *alae* of the tribes, one exception being the Breuci in Pannonia.[657] Nevertheless, conscription was much lighter than, for example, among the Rhine Germans, or in Belgica. If, however, by the third century the army had become Illyrian and could rightly be so described, then it was the exigencies of the Marcommanic Wars that were to blame. The *auxilia* had always played a secondary role, with the legions setting the tone. From now on, however, the latter were barbarized and provincialized. As we have seen, [MH.II, 260] there had already been a great deal of recruitment from the provinces. If we find Roman citizens from Narbonensis or Baetica in the army, this corresponds to the outstanding role in literature which we see Quintilian and Seneca assuming. However, it is quite a different matter when the system reaches the point of not commissioning provincials who are already Romanized, but instead levying any number of barbarians and bestowing citizenship on them *ad hoc*. Although they were then legally citizens, in fact they were not. And Marcus Aurelius did this on a large scale, by force of circumstance.[658]

This profound transformation is not expressed in so many words in the annals of the period; it has to be read between the lines, from isolated, sporadic hints. However, it is also self-evident *a priori* from the given state of affairs: after a century of peace, this was again a time of serious warfare, major epidemics and famine, and manpower was needed. We need only recall that Marcus was the first Emperor in seventy years to increase the size of the army by two legions. The situation was exacerbated by kidnapping by the enemy and the depletion of the population by defection and desertion. Even under such [MH.II, 261] circumstances, however, it is still amazing that the huge Roman state was unable to raise recruits for an army of only thirty-two legions from among its own citizens. Our amazement is, nonetheless, mitigated by a consideration of the prevailing social conditions. What, after all, is the citizen body? The higher social orders are automatically excluded, since they were not required to join the legions at all. In this regard it is remarkable that whereas previously junior officers were selected from among the private soldiers, from this time onwards anyone who joined up and had a modicum of education was immediately given the rank of centurion, so that the private ranks were increasingly filled from the very lowest and poorest-educated social orders.

Another aggravating factor was that the institution of marriage was in sharp decline and the birth-rate falling, particularly in the capital; the *vernacula multitudo*[659] was useless. Fictive, juristic descent by adopted freedmen still to some degree had the appearance of filling the gaps among the citizenry; freedmen, however, were themselves not permitted to perform legionary service, only their children. It may well have been the case, therefore, that the recruiting officer was obliged to reject as unsuitable and degenerate a great deal of the material at his disposal. Here, too, Marcus [MH.II, 262] did no more than his duty by thinking only of the needs of the moment: he looked for soldiers where they were to be found, and if they were non-citizens, he simply made them citizens.

We can find traces of these events in virtually all the contemporary authors; Dio states that Marcus bestowed citizenship on a great many.[660] Victor[661] likewise reports in his life of Marcus that he readily bestowed citizenship *en bloc*. This only makes sense in connection with the exigencies of recruitment. The *Life* says that[662] *latrones Dalmatiae atque Dardaniae milites fecit*. This will be a reference to the two new legions he established. There are indications that these were recruited principally from the lands to the north of Greece. Other regions had suffered too much from war, whereas here a relative state of peace prevailed. The *Life* immediately goes on to say that he *emit et Germanorum auxilia contra Germanos*.[663] This is evidently a reference to the auxiliaries. Dio[664] confirms this. So levies from the ranks of defeated enemies were not frowned upon. It should not be forgotten, however, that the old titles of units in terms of ethnic origin were by then no more than names and that, for example, the [MH.II, 263] *cohors Thracum* had for a long time no longer consisted of Thracians and that foreigners could quite easily be incorporated into *alae* and *cohortes*. If, then, even prisoners and deserters were accepted, how far fewer scruples will have been involved in accepting any usable subject!

The inscriptions tell the same story. Twenty years after Marcus these men were all called Marci Aurelii.[665] They were clearly either those who had been granted citizenship for this reason by him, or their immediate descendants. The erstwhile Roman citizen was by now no more than a hollow name in the army; understandably, therefore, the legion was called *barbarica* in the third century, in contrast with the Praetorian cohort, which still paid somewhat greater heed to ethnic origin.

The only remarkable aspect of all this is that it had to be Marcus of all people who inaugurated this transformation. It was a bitter and profoundly tragic irony of fate that this Emperor, who, along with the best of his age, prized general education and was steeped in humanity – a philosopher-king, as he is sometimes styled and not entirely unjustifiably, who wrote his *Meditations* in the midst of the army camps of Carnuntum and Vindobona[666] – [MH.II, 264] barbarized the army and robbed it of its national character. It was tragic, but it was an urgent and unavoidable duty which Marcus never flinched from fulfilling.

The army acquired not only a provincial, but also a specifically Illyrian character. Although it naturally also contained orientals and Rhinelanders, the greater bulk of it hailed from the Danube lands, especially to the north of the Greek peninsula and in particular many Thracians. The latter, as has already been observed, had suffered least from the fighting. Septimius Severus then also appointed many Thracians to the Praetorian guard. Furthermore, the Illyrian army was by far the mightiest: the Rhine Germans were broken and feeble in this period, and for this reason the war did not spread that far, petering out in Raetia. This enabled the Romans, as we have seen in that context, to reduce the army on the banks of the Rhine and to increase the Illyrian army to twelve legions. Here, too, in the mightiest army, *esprit de corps* was also most keenly felt.

But conscription became more and more of a local affair. Augustus had envisaged the precise opposite of this, that the place of conscription should not coincide with the place where a soldier was stationed. There had been [MH.II, 265] a preference for deploying legions in regions outside their own tribal lands. This was an undeniably irksome practice and later the opposite was preferred. It found its application in different ways, in Africa first, where it was most desirable, given its isolated situation, but increasingly everywhere else as well. As a consequence, Illyrian units were increasingly constituted of Illyrians. Additionally, the Illyrians were superb military material; their descendants, the Albanians, have frequently demonstrated in the history of the Turkish Empire that they are not to be underestimated as soldiers, and continue to do so to this day. The army could thus be regarded as Illyrian in a dual sense, and this trend became increasingly marked as time went on. An interesting detail in this regard is that Severus, when he recruited provincials into the Guard, raised a special shrine at Rome for local Thracian deities.[667] It evidently suited him for the closed, provincial character of the unit to be preserved in this respect too.

It would be pertinent at this point to say something about the colonate,[668] the later manifestation of which was virtually identical with serfdom and which, perhaps – although it is a [MH.II, 266] big perhaps – evolved from the serfdom practised by the Germans. We do at any rate know that Marcus settled 3,000 Naristi on the far bank of the Danube.[669] There is no doubt that this occurred repeatedly and that very probably these settlers for the most part brought their indigenous customs and institutions with them. In later times recruitment was based on the colonate, i.e. on the farming proletariat. Earlier sources are unfamiliar with this. The *colonus* (tenant farmer), is not personally unfree – as a slave he would have been unable to discharge military service – but he was bound to the soil as a dependent bondsman, one who 'belongs to' the land. In fact, however, this is a *contradictio in adiecto* quite alien to the exact concepts of Roman law and hence probably a foreign import, probably connected with the army from the beginning.

One final aspect that needs to be mentioned here is the hereditary nature of service in the forts, where soldiers worked the fields, were married[670] and owned land, on the basis of which their children had an obligation to do military service. Like the colonate, these *milites castellani* probably also date back to the Marcomannic [MH.II, 267] Wars. These measures enormously accelerated the provincialization of the army. Once the legions ceased to represent the entire nation, the Empire was ruled by the territory which had the strongest army.

An account of the dominance of the Illyrian legions forms part of the general history of the state and its cities. We need only make a few references here: the period from the death of Pertinax up to the uncontested sole rule of Severus witnessed a virtually blow-by-blow repetition of the catastrophe that had occurred in the Year of the Four Emperors.[671] Just as a war between army groups had broken out then after the end of the Julian dynasty, so also there was a war when the Antonine house died out.[672] The armies vied for control of the throne. Italy, whose feeble pretension was represented only by the Guard, proclaimed[673]

Julianus, the Orient Pescennius Niger, the Rhine Clodius Albinus and Illyricum Septimius Severus. This time the Danube and Rhine joined forces against the Orient, resulting in a victory for Severus and hence for the Danube army. This victory was exploited in the same [MH.II, 268] way as on the previous occasion: the Guard was dismissed, a bodyguard of Thracians was formed and the *legio Secunda Parthica* established in Albano near Rome, where it remained. This was the first time a legion was stationed in Italy. However, whereas on that previous occasion Vitellius, the victor in the first battle, was later defeated by Vespasian, this time the outcome of the first battlefield decision was final. This established the rule of the sword[674] in Italy. What happened was no more than was necessary: when a country like Italy at that time renders itself defenceless and leaves its protection to others, it is bound to be subjugated.

The dynasty of Severus endured for a generation and raised Illyricum more and more into the ascendancy. It was not quite true that the Emperors had to be of Illyrian birth – Severus himself was an African.[675] The first true barbarian on the imperial throne was Maximinus, a Thracian,[676] from 235.

The events that followed the death of Gordian in 245[677] are highly instructive. Philip, commander of the Guard, had had him assassinated and himself declared [MH.II, 269] Emperor.[678] This aroused the indignation of the Illyrian army, which declared Marinus Pacatianus Emperor. However, the latter was soon defeated and Philip sent Trajanus Decius to Illyria to bring the troops back under his sway. Decius went very reluctantly, even asking to be spared this task, but was forced to go. The Illyrian troops thereupon promptly declared him Emperor, leaving him with a choice between most unwilling acceptance or immediate murder.[679] In this way he succeeded to the throne. It is quite plain from this that the Illyrian troops were little, if at all, interested in the person who was to become Emperor. Anyone suited them so long as he had the favour of Illyricum. The second half of the third century saw rule exclusively by Illyrian Emperors: Claudius Gothicus, Aurelian, Probus, Diocletian and Constantine were all Illyrians. This race now played the principal role.[680]

On closer examination a decline in the general level of education is unmistakable. Barbarization and brutalization spread from the common soldier upwards to the officer corps, and ultimately to the very highest rank. Comparing the Emperors of the third century with those of the second, or even [MH.II, 270] the first, we find that highly educated men from the best society increasingly gave way to men of lowly origin who were at best capable junior officers.[681] Severus, however, did not fall into this category,[682] since his upbringing and education still belongs to an earlier era: he was a highly educated man, a writer and outstanding jurist. His descendants were not in the same category. Caracalla may have been coarse, but the 'dregs' of the aristocracy are often similar to those of the mob. Caracalla was a base nature born to the purple. Maximinus, however, was the first of these junior officer figures: all that is said in his favour is that he was of massive build, a superb runner and swordsman.

The historian Victor,[683] himself an intelligent and educated man, has a remarkable passage about Diocletian and his co-regents: 'They are all Illyrians', he states, 'with little learning, but with an understanding of the minds of farmers and soldiers, and hence useful to the state.' This is a remarkable statement; the Emperor's shortcomings are recognized, but only mentioned in order to highlight a positive quality, and, what is more, a positive quality, for which there had been no understanding whatsoever in previous centuries.

[MH.II, 271] We can observe from the official register[684] how from the second half of the third century senators were ousted from key positions, which were then, particularly from the time of Gallienus[685] onwards, occupied by chief centurions. The rigid and unbridgeable distinction which had previously obtained between the common soldier and the officer, the sacred principle of education – Italian education, to be precise – now ceased. Now that men who wore the *clavus*[686] had become unqualified for the posts they had previously monopolized, the common soldier ruled. Nevertheless, this military reorganization did introduce sundry elements of vigour into the previously lax system.

The wider repercussions of these charges were realized in the Diocletianic and Constantinian periods. The step from using internal to using foreign barbarians was a short and easy one to take, and this ultimately led to situations like that under Stilicho, when the foreign mercenary was in control. Wherever we look in the third century, every book, inscription or building attests to the huge gulf between the age of Pius and that after Gordian. Latin itself – even spelling – is in decline.[687] The legislation pertaining to the discharge of soldiers[688] gives us a yardstick. Up to the time of Severus we find no grammatical errors [MH.II, 272] in these legal documents, but after Severus they are couched in more and more corrupt Latin. Coins, sculptures, everything bears the same stamp and the ultimate reason[689] for this profound decline was the Marcomannic War with its repercussions, first for the army, then for the nation. It should be reiterated here how profoundly tragic it was that it had to be Marcus who conjured up this end to the world.

D) THE GOTHIC WARS

Peace reigned on the Danube during the reign of Severus, and there were no outstanding events in Caracalla's reign either. One noteworthy fact, however, is that the name of the Goths was first heard at this time,[690] at the same time as that of the Alamanni. The name was first intoned as part of a malevolent quip by a senator: when the excessive adulation of the Senate accorded Caracalla the honour of a triumph, one senator inquired during the debate on the issue whether they did not wish to bestow on Caracalla the appellation *Geticus maximus*.[691] This was an allusion to the murder of Caracalla's brother Geta, for which Caracalla was held responsible. It must, however, have been prompted by combat with the Goths, mistakenly called Getae. The Goths had undoubtedly played some role behind the scenes previously, [MH.II, 273] but this marked their debut on the stage of world history. In this period we encounter them on the Black Sea, where the Getae also resided. 'Getae' was the Greek word for Dacians and the confusion of the two names was an easy mistake to make. The Getae were Thracians, the Goths Germans, and apart from the coincidental similarity in their names they had nothing whatever in common; but this identity of tribal names has caused a great deal of havoc in historical accounts.

The supremacy of Rome on the middle Danube was unshaken. Caracalla had the king of the Quadi[692] executed and fomented war between the Marcomanni and the Quadi. The Empire remained untouched by this. This peace lasted until 238, the year of the great revolution in Africa.[693] Maximinus fought against the two Gordians, then against the senatorial Emperors Pupienus Maximus and Caelius Balbinus, until, after they had all been eliminated, the son and grandson of the two elder Gordians, Caesar Gordianus, finally ascended the throne at the age of 13.[694] This year also marked the beginning of the Scythian War, i.e. the war against the Goths. The vagueness of the name is unfortunate. It is well known that, unlike the Romans, the Greeks rejected all non-classical names, and therefore referred to all lands to the north of the Black Sea as 'Scythia', gathering under the generic name 'Scythians' everyone that the Romans had any dealings with in those parts. The chief people among them, however, were the Goths. We are somewhat better informed about these events [MH.II, 274] than we are about others in the same period on account of the Athenian Dexippus,[695] who had himself been involved in fending off an attack by the Goths[696] on Athens at the beginning of 238 and wrote a history of these campaigns in 267.

Prior to the onset of hostilities there must have been an accord between the Romans and the Goths; at that time they were probably not immediate neighbours. The Goths were principally a seafaring people, even more so than the Franks in the West. The price now had to be paid for the lack of a Roman fleet. Augustus, and the principate generally, had done something on this score, and the Romans were not then so defenceless at sea as they had been during the Republic. The Nile, Danube and Rhine all had fleets; two were stationed in Italy, one on the west, the other on the east coast, and Britain also had a fleet, etc. Seen overall, however, this force was only adequate for purposes of maritime policing. Previously this had been enough to hold pirates at bay. But now the entire northern coast of the Black Sea was occupied by great seafaring nations. We are told, for example, that twenty years after the beginning of the war a Gothic fleet allegedly totalling 6,000 vessels manned by [MH.II, 275] 320,000 men set sail to devastate the coasts of the Roman Empire.[697] Others give the number of vessels at 2,000.[698] However many there were in fact, both figures may well be greatly exaggerated. It is also certain, as is clear from the ratio of crews to vessels, that the latter were quite small, probably no larger than barges. It is clear, nonetheless, that these were no ordinary freebooters. The defence against these enemies crumbled. We do not learn of a single sea battle, but only of more or less successful attempts at coastal defence.

Whenever the Goths invaded, it was always in association with the Carpi,[699] who resided between the Prut, the Danube and the coast. In 295 Diocletian relocated them to Roman territory in Moesia, and from that time on the Goths shared a border with Roman territory. Zosimus reports a Gothic fleet mustering in the river Tyras (Dniester).[700]

Given these circumstances it is understandable that the Romans sought to come to an arrangement with these bothersome neighbours. Since it was impossible to fend off their piracy, the Romans appear to have resolved to [MH.II, 276] pay them tribute. Ammianus[701] has the reference already mentioned to 2,000 ships which had penetrated the Bosporus and advanced as far as the Aegean islands. The successful dating of a fragment of Priscus[702] is important for reconstructing the chronology. The date of Julius Menophilus, a governor of Moesia under Gordian has been established from coins of the period,[703] confirming the chronology.

The fighting was savage from the very outset. The Goths destroyed a number of coastal towns, for example Istropolis south of the mouth of the Danube. The barbarians did not wage organized warfare, instead appearing and disappearing, plundering and pillaging incessantly without (for the time being) any premeditated, planned operations. Marcianopolis, an inland town, was destroyed in 244 under Philip. We then hear of a Roman success, a *victoria Carpica*.[704]

There then ensued, however, the terrible catastrophe under Trajanus Decius, who was otherwise an outstanding general and one of the finest Emperors. Initially he managed to restore peace to the much-troubled Danube [MH.II, 277] lands, but not for long. Cniva, king of the Goths, overran all of Moesia as far as Philippopolis in alliance with 3,000 Carpi, advancing both by sea and on land, but predominantly by land. Having sated themselves with pillage, they then turned back and returned home by land. This was a feat of immense audacity. They crossed the Haemus Mountains (Balkans) in 250. Decius took up positions against them between the Haemus and the Danube, barring their way. The annihilation of the Goths failed because of the betrayal of Decius by Gallus, his general, so that the fierce battle at Abrittus ended in total defeat for the Roman army; Decius himself fell.[705] Gallus, his successor, concluded an ignominious peace and paid the Goths tribute.[706] Nonetheless, the forays did not cease.

This catastrophe occurred at the same time as a fearful outbreak of plague, which began in 252 and ravaged the Empire for fifteen years. The angels of the

Apocalypse always appear together, and they did so here, too, where the fall of the Empire was to be rehearsed. The ensuing period was filled with a spate of pirate raids across the entire eastern seas. It is not our [MH.II, 278] intention to offer a list of names here, only to mention a few illustrative incidents. Pityus and Dioscurias, for example, the last remaining eastern fortifications on the eastern coast of the Black Sea, were destroyed. Trebizond, Chalcedon and Ephesus with its famous temple of Diana all fell, as did Athens, Argos and Sparta – proof that the enemy no longer restricted their activities to the coastline. No substantial opposition was offered anywhere. Salonica fell in 262. It was the Goths who were predominantly responsible for these campaigns of devastation. Besides them, others plundered inland. Although we have few written accounts of Roman losses, the monuments tell their story clearly. It is possible to give the exact date, for example, when Dacia was lost. In 254, four years after the catastrophe of Decius, the coins suddenly cease. Similarly, the last monuments from Viminacium near Belgrade on the right bank of the Danube date from 255; nowhere in these lands can we find monuments beyond [MH.II, 279] the first years of Valerian, i.e. beyond 254 and 255. This permits us to assert with certainty that these territories became barbarian in this period. The period from 250 to 269 marks the epoch of the first provisional destruction of Roman rule on the Danube. A mere handful of towns defended themselves on their own initiative. Byzantium, for example, managed to fend off a Herulian invasion with 500 ships; likewise Athens in 267 under Dexippus,[707] whom we have already had occasion to mention as a writer. This was the same period in which Verona was provided with new walls to repel assaults by Alamanni.

Events took a turn for the better again following the death of Gallienus in 268, although it is not certain whether this was due to Claudius Gothicus or Aurelian. The historiography here is probably coloured somewhat in favour of Diocletian as a result of sycophancy, since Claudius was regarded as his ancestor (by adoption).[708] Ammianus[709] attributes the principal decision to Aurelian, not Claudius; it is probably fairest to ascribe the beginning of the improvement in the situation to Claudius and its continuation [MH.II, 280] after Claudius's death to Aurelian.

It is difficult to ascertain which of the two was of more decisive moment, the arrogance of the invaders or the vigour of the defence. A huge Gothic invasion took place in 269, that already mentioned above, comprising 6,000 vessels, or 2,000 according to other accounts. Such a horde had never before overrun the Roman frontier. Marcianopolis warded off the invasion on the initiative of its own citizens; Tomi and Cyzicus were destroyed. The Germans landed on the coast of Macedonia. Having sated themselves with plundering, they then planned to set off on the return journey over land. This was an unspeakably audacious move and brought havoc upon them. At Naissus (Nish) on the southern Morava the Romans won a great victory, in which 50,000 Goths are said to have fallen. The Goths then moved on through the Haemus Mountains, where Aurelian succeeded in wresting another decisive victory. This catastrophe had major consequences, restoring Roman ascendancy against the Goths, as against the Alamanni, and for more than a fleeting moment.

The victory brought enduring results in its wake. Aurelian and Probus reorganized the frontier lands, albeit with [MH.II, 281] a substantial reduction in territory, as was also the case on the Rhine. Aurelian abandoned Dacia, where many Romans were undoubtedly still resident, and relocated the wretched remnants of the Dacians, in so far as they still wished to remain under Roman rule, to Dardania on the right bank of the Danube.[710] With the surrender of territories on the far side of it, the Danube, like the Rhine, was therefore recognized as the frontier. The victory itself must, therefore, be considered to some extent an admission of the Romans' defeat. From this time on, under Aurelian, Probus, Diocletian and Constantine, firm-handed military rule inside new, narrower frontiers was restored.

The Carpi were wedged between the Romans and the Goths, thus preventing them from being immediate neighbours. Aurelian left them in their homelands, but Probus brought the Bastarnae, a related German tribal group who resided close to the Carpi, across to the right bank of the Danube, where he settled them.[711] Both these peoples had probably already been influenced by Romanization, or at least touched by Roman culture. In 295 Diocletian brought the Carpi to Moesia.[712] This was a double-edged enterprise: while it effectively rid the Romans of both these peoples [MH.II, 282] as bothersome neighbours, from then on the left bank of the Danube was completely Gothic.

The Emperors took the fortification of the new Danube line most seriously; there was extensive construction work. Pest (*Contra Aquincum*, opposite Aquincum) was established as a bridgehead on the left bank, and this process was continued in the same way along the entire line. Diocletian and his co-regents built these great lines of entrenchment along the Rhine and Danube. There must have been frequent combat there. The complete series of Diocletian's victory titles survives, dating from 301: from this time on he bore the appellation *Sarmaticus maximus quater, Carpicus maximus, Germanicus maximus sexies, Britannicus maximus*, twice victor over the Persians, once over the Armenians and once over Adiabene.[713] The title *Carpicus* refers to the various battles fought from 289 to 301, *Germanicus* probably mostly also to battles fought against the Danube Germans, against the Marcomanni and the Goths. We can see from this that the principal battles still took place on the Danube. The honour and superiority of Rome was thus restored in the period 269–170. It is quite understandable that the Goths should come to the fore as direct neighbours under Constantine.

[MH.II, 283] Then, in the fourth century, came the battles of eastern Rome against the Goths, which fall outside the scope of our account. In 378 Valens lost the battle of Adrianople – one of the most terrible defeats the Romans ever suffered (see MH.III, 215ff.). The effects of Diocletian's victories had persisted for approximately a century.

Let us now glance at the effect of the events we have recounted on culture in the West. Within the diocese of Gaul – to use the terminology current at that time – Latin domination had probably already been overwhelmed by Germans: Frankish, Alamannic, Suevic and Vandal states were being formed. Nevertheless, these states bore no more than a semi-Germanic character; these people more or less adopted Roman civilization. It was from them that what we now call the 'Latin race' evolved.

The situation on the Danube, however, was substantially different. Here, Latin was obliterated, not assimilated. These lands became Germanic, or at least anti-Roman. When seeking the reasons for this, it would be difficult to sum them up in a nutshell. The vigour of the assault, the feebleness of the defence and the energy of the invading nations all played a part. [MH.II, 284] In Narbonensis, Spain and Africa Romanization had struck far deeper roots than in Pannonia and Dacia. However, it should be borne in mind that the view occasionally expressed, that the persistence of remnants of Romance civilization in these territories is the result of later, medieval immigration, is foolish.[714] Survivals of this kind found today in the Tyrol, Dacia or eastern Switzerland are undoubtedly ancient. Medieval sources, indeed, have placed it beyond doubt that these remnants of Roman culture in the Grisons and beyond once extended far further, as far as Salzburg and into Styria.[715] Dacia and Noricum were centres of Romance culture – Dacia because the original population had been exterminated, Noricum because it had been Romanized very early on and its urban centres were far more significant than those in Pannonia and Moesia.

Furthermore, immigration into the western Gallic lands should be envisaged on a much smaller scale. It was, like the invasions of the Northmen, the movement of an army, rather than of a whole people. It was from them that the nobility, the ruling class, of these territories traced their descent, but they were not sufficiently numerous to alter the national character as a whole. Legislation, for example, was promulgated in the language of the subjects, i.e. Latin. In contrast, the Baiuvarians [MH.II, 285] (the modern Bavarians) appeared in Raetia and Noricum in far larger numbers.

The diversity of national characteristics constitutes an additional factor here. Had Africa remained occupied by the Vandals, there would probably have evolved conditions like those we see in Spain. The Byzantine conquest of Africa under Justinian in fact paved the way for the Arabs. But the Arabs never accommodated themselves to Roman civilization in any of the places they reached, but obliterated it. The Romans and Germans share a greater congeniality, so that wherever they encountered one another the result was a mixed civilization with a strong Roman element. Along the Danube, however, Slavs, Scythian tribes and Sarmatians were also penetrating in huge numbers, and it was these who eradicated Roman culture in the Danube lands.

5

WARS IN THE EAST

It still remains for us to deal with the great theatre of war in the East.[716] The East is not of the same vital interest to us as the Rhine and Danube lands and the events which took place there. This derives from the geographical situation itself: in the West, Italy was always the immediate target and objective of invasion and whenever [MH.II, 286] events took a serious turn, there was an immediate threat to the ruling country and the ruling nation.

Nor is the question of the spread of Roman nationality and civilization an issue here. In the Orient, nationality, language and civilization were all Greek. So although coins with Roman inscriptions are also to be found in the East, for example, this is invariably a purely superficial phenomenon that occurs in those towns with a Roman municipal constitution. But even towns such as these, for example Alexandria Troas,[717] were also Greek-speaking apart from the official Latin required for municipal business. We can hardly speak of Latin-speaking enclaves in the East, therefore.[718]

Furthermore, the driving force of aggression was far more active in the case of the Germanic and other northern nations. In the East the aggressor and principal adversary was the Parthian state, and up to the third century this state was vacillating, enfeebled, and probably at times impeded from any form of vigorous action by internal rifts and the partition of its Empire. Although of oriental origin, the Parthian Empire was semi-Hellenized [MH.II, 287] and hence formed a midway, mixed state of sorts.

The Empire did not take a firm stand again until after the Sasanids had effected a national revival. In the fourth century Persian attacks[719] then became more energetic; at the same time, the shift of the Roman capital from Rome to Constantinople moved the Empire's most vulnerable point much closer to the Persians: the Sasanids remained a very serious threat for Constantine and Justinian; but this lies outside the scope of our account.

335

A) CONFLICTS WITH THE PARTHIANS

After the Median-Parthian War, Nero had established the order which we have already discussed earlier, through Corbulo.[720] In strategic and other respects, this was essentially a matter of regulating the position of Armenia,[721] which swung to and fro between its two great neighbours, invariably without a policy in its own right. Sometimes Roman influence predominated, sometimes Parthian. Nero abolished the dependent relationship between Armenia and Rome, with the result that it became a kind of inheritance received for the second son of the Parthian monarch. [MH.II, 288] A younger prince of the Parthian ruling house ascended the Armenian throne; formal confirmation, however, still lay with Rome, so that even then Rome did not relinquish her claim to Armenia's dependence on her. It would even appear from recent discoveries that Corbulo retained a garrison at Harput in Armenia.[722]

From that time on, however, the friendliest possible relations obtained between the Parthians and Armenians, and it is highly remarkable that when the Parthian king Vologaeses sent an embassy to Rome shortly after Nero's death, one of its tasks was to request the Senate to honour the memory of Nero (which, as we know, had been condemned). Similarly, the false Neros, of whom several appeared, invariably turned to the Parthians for support;[723] that was assuredly a relic of this war, and at all events proof that the memory of Nero was held in high esteem among the Parthians. It cannot be denied, after all, that his decision to relinquish Armenia had been reasonable. The Greek element – which was all that the Romans could rely on in Armenia – was very weak; and Corbulo, who knew the country well, had approved the decisions that had been taken.

[MH.II, 289] Relations with the Parthians remained good under Vespasian.[724] An interesting episode occurred when, during the reign of Vespasian, Vologaeses requested assistance from the Romans to repel an incursion by the Alani, whose homelands were located on the Tanais (Don) on the Sea of Azov.[725] The main invasion was undoubtedly made by sea, from the Caspian. The reasons which motivated the Alani to undertake this expedition are somewhat obscure. They were probably Scythians, related to the Huns; this is the first time that Huns, i.e. Turks,[726] beat on the gates of the East. Against these, the most barbaric of barbarians, the Parthians, themselves half-Greek – Seleucia on the Tigris, for example, was a Greek city with 500,000 inhabitants – and a civilized country, called on the assistance of that other great civilized country and protector of the Greeks *par excellence*. Vologaeses requested that Vespasian send one of his princes, Titus or Domitian, to lead the troops. The Emperor refused such assistance, but took some measures of his own. An inscription in the *Corpus Inscriptionum*[727] states [MH.II, 290] that Vespasian established a fort and a garrison opposite Tibilisi, and this measure may well have been connected with the invasion of the Alani. The

Caucusus was, in any case, the Roman buffer against the barbarians. Whether the Alani settled on the Caspian Sea is questionable. Although there are many later references to 'Caucasian Alani', it is quite possible that there is a confusion here with the Caucasian Albani. Relations between the Parthians and Vespasian remained good, perhaps on account of this serious attempt at frontier defence. Vespasian knew what he was about. He had not commanded a force against Jerusalem for nothing, and had certainly acquainted himself thoroughly with the situation.

There were no actual wars in the East during Vespasian's reign, but a great deal of administrative reorganization. Jerusalem of course was destroyed, thereby tearing the heart out of this persistently recalcitrant nation.[728] Judaea, which had hitherto been governed by a procurator, was transformed into the province [MH.II, 291] of Syria Palaestina, equipped with a garrison of one legion commanded by a legate. The primary purpose of this command was to keep the Jews themselves suppressed.

Commagene had hitherto been a client-state, a halfway measure that now came to an end. Vespasian incorporated the state in 72.[729] It became a province with a one-legion garrison, stationed at Samosata (Samsat) on the Euphrates. This measure was important on account of the border with Armenia and as a guarantee of security there. Cilicia acquired a legate but no garrison. On the southern coast of Asia Minor, Lycia and Pamphylia were so-called free cities, formally organized in leagues. This act of magnanimity was now also brought to an end.[730] Here, too, provinces were created, each with a legate and no garrison. Cappadocia had long since been incorporated, but without a garrison, so that there were no troops stationed along the frontier, except in Syria. Vespasian installed a legate and some legions there, one [MH.II, 292] with fixed quarters at Melitene (Malatya) on the Euphrates,[731] the other Satala on the north-western border of Armenia.[732]

Fighting forces in the East were thus considerably increased. The force in Palaestina was provided by Syria; that in Commagene and the two Cappadocian legions were newly formed. Since there was a reduction of the forces on the Rhine at this time, the army as a whole became no larger. A long period of peace ensued. Although we learn of tension between Artabanus of Parthia and Titus,[733] this did not amount to much.

A remarkable letter of Pliny[734] was written in the time of Trajan in 111 or 112, immediately prior to the outbreak of the Parthian War. According to this, there were contacts between Decebalus and the Parthians. This was unpleasant for Rome. Pacorus made accusations against Trajan which also fall within this period. Pacorus died in 111.[735] Ultimately, however, these did not amount to real threats; disagreeable matters often arise in the relations between great powers that do not [MH.II, 293] have to lead straight to war. The Parthian War that broke out shortly thereafter was clearly brought on by an offensive initiated by Rome, and was purely a war of conquest. Trajan was the most military Emperor Rome ever had. He was aroused by the memory of Alexander[736] and the fairy-tale-like attraction of the distant East. He wanted war, and when someone wants war, he will find a reason to make war.[737]

The succession to the Armenian throne was again the bone of contention. King Exedares had been deposed by the Parthian king, Chosroes, who without seeking Roman confirmation had installed Parthamasiris, the son of Pacorus and his own nephew. In response, Trajan immediately declared war; he had found the pretext he sought and was formally in the right. In 114 Chosroes dispatched an embassy to Trajan in Athens in an effort to avert war. Parthamasiris,[738] the new king, was willing to seek confirmation. Trajan responded with a rude rebuff, asserting that the time for negotiation was over. Before Trajan had even entered Armenia, Parthamasiris appeared at his camp, took the diadem from his head and threw [MH.II, 294] it down at the Emperor's feet, expecting that the latter would replace it on his head so that he would receive his crown back from Roman hands. But Trajan did no such thing. While he allowed the former king to leave unharmed, he declared Armenia a Roman province and demanded that the king's retinue remain in the camp with their new master.[739]

Initially, Armenia seemed to offer no resistance to being subjugated. The designated legate of Armenia marched in without bloodshed at the beginning of 115. The Parthians too remained quiet at first. Trajan went on to incorporate further territories as Roman provinces, thereby making direct inroads into the Parthian sphere of influence. The Parthian king was, after all, 'king of kings' and counted Mesopotamia, including Edessa (Urfa) and Osrhoene, those first affected by incorporation, among his special vassal states. Abgar, the king of these territories, submitted and was treated with clemency, reputedly on account of his son, an attractive youth who found favour with Trajan.[740] Mesopotamia became a province, ruled by a legate. [MH.II, 295] Then, at the end of 115, Trajan advanced to the province of Adiabene on the upper Tigris, continuing his campaign in 116. It became clear that in his boundless lust for conquest his aim was to bring not only the Euphrates, but also the entire Tigris region under his sway. The Romans advanced downstream towards Parthia proper.

It is difficult to tell the various campaigns apart, especially since operations were never halted in these parts, even in winter. There was hardly any serious fighting. Although our extant accounts are scant, they are not so scant that major incidents can have been omitted. It is at all events evident that Trajan had to contend with deployment and transport difficulties. He did not encounter serious resistance from the enemy; they did not offer battle. In keeping with their tried-and-tested tactics, the Parthians refrained from attacking and remained on the defensive, constantly retreating. Trajan did not betake himself into the interior, keeping largely to the courses of the great rivers. [MH.II, 296] Even the large cities captured by the Romans, such as Seleucia and Ctesiphon, were defended not by regular Parthian troops, but by their own valiant citizens. Trajan plundered the famous golden throne of the Parthian king and took the latter's daughter prisoner.[741]

He carried out his resolve to incorporate Parthia into the Roman Empire, and consequently established two new provinces: aside from Mesopotamia, already incorporated earlier, there were now Adiabene and Assyria.[742] It is not quite clear exactly how we should envisage Assyria; the middle course of the Tigris was certainly included in this province, but we do not know whether it also included the southern course and, given the ephemeral character of all these conquests, it does not matter a great deal. Trajan had his men march as far as the mouth of the Tigris and the city of Mesene located there.[743] The entire daring campaign, which followed in the footsteps of Alexander the Great, and his self-confessed wish 'to be as young as Alexander',[744] give us a glimpse into what motivated Trajan.

[MH.II, 297] His treatment of the Parthians was as harsh as could be: he deposed King Chosroes and installed a ruler of his own choice, Parthamaspates; his coins, which bear the inscription *REX PARTHIS DATUS*,[745] are ample proof of his intention to relegate the Parthian state to the group of client kingdoms dependent on Rome. Parthamaspates received the kingdom from Trajan as a fiefdom. These were great successes, but they proved all too delusive.

This moment, when Trajan seemed to have achieved all he had set out to do and stood at the peak of his power, was now seized on by all the recently subjugated nations to throw off their allegiance. Seleucia, the entire region of the Euphrates and Tigris, even Edessa (Urfa), so close to the old frontier with Rome, now rose in revolt. These weak peoples, accustomed to compliance, would not have risen up had they not regarded Trajan's position as desperate. Trajan did not march against them himself, but sent troops under the command of Maximus, who himself fell, although the uprising was successfully quelled. Trajan himself was held up on his return [MH.II, 298] by fighting over the well-fortified small Arab town of Hatra, west of Seleucia. The attempt to conquer it failed; Trajan himself came within an inch of his life and was compelled to depart with the matter unresolved.[746]

What the accounts fail to tell us, with their court bias, is what happened to the three new provinces. This is in itself a reflection of the rootlessness, superficiality and purely nominal nature of the entire enterprise. Had the Romans truly intended to retain possession of the Parthian Empire and to shift their frontiers so far east, then they would have had to establish camps along the entire line of defence and relocate legions not merely to the Euphrates, but to the Tigris. In fact they did none of this; of course Trajan soon died, leaving his plans cut off in mid-execution. Nevertheless, they cannot be accorded much chance of survival; they was a great deal of vainglory in them,[747] and the entire enterprise is not to be taken seriously.

The events recounted here fall in the year [MH.II, 299] 116, perhaps also the winter of 116–17. Trajan planned to set off for the East again in the spring of 117, but fell ill, was obliged to return and died at Selinus in Cilicia, in August 117. Fate pre-empted an answer to the question as to how far Trajan might have been able to carry out his objectives.

His successor Hadrian introduced an entirely different policy, as was called for by both reason and necessity. It was not appropriate to abandon King Parthamaspates entirely – he was compensated with a small kingdom. Hadrian did, however, relinquish all the conquered provinces,[748] restored total independence to the Parthians and thereby also good relations with both them and their reinstalled king Chosroes.

By and large, Hadrian was not a pleasant character; he possessed a repellent manner and a venomous, envious and malicious nature which cruelly avenged itself on him. His immediate decision to retreat from the path laid out by Trajan in the East was promptly interpreted as envy of his predecessor,[749] but unjustly so. All he was doing here was what the situation clearly required. The Roman state lacked the necessary power, the whole basis for the enterprise was lacking, and above all what was lacking was [MH.II, 300] Greek nationality, which was the only element the Romans could rely on in the Orient. Hadrian honoured the memory of Trajan in every respect, even granting him a triumph after his death and deification; for this reason Trajan was the only Emperor with the title *Divus Parthicus*, because he was already dead when he celebrated his triumph.[750]

At first there were no more wars in the East for a time: the situation was resolved cheaply and favourably. Two curious documents survive from this period by Flavius Arrianus, governor of Cappadocia from 131 to 137. One is a report in Greek of a tour of inspection through his province from the Black Sea to the Caspian.[751] This was not the formal report he was obliged to compile in his capacity as governor —this would undoubtedly have been written in Latin. The other was intended for the public and published in book form. It provides some interesting information, particularly concerning garrisons.[752] The same author also wrote a description of an order of battle against the Alani, likewise a semi-literary work.[753] At that time there was a prospect of war with them (i.e. the Massagetae or Scythians, as Dio[754] explains). Vologaeses again requested support from Rome. Rome prepared for combat [MH.II, 301], but again did not involve itself actively in the fighting, but instead made use of a Caucasian–Iberian state whose king was called Pharasmanes.

A profound peace reigned under Pius. Nonetheless, severe storms were brewing that were later to break out under Marcus and Lucius, or under Commodus. Pius was excessively peace-loving.[755] His much-acclaimed motto 'Better to save the life of one citizen than kill a thousand enemies'[756] is all well and good, but was scarcely politic for the ruler of an Empire such as Rome's. The Parthians, up to their old tricks, made feints to occupy Armenia. Pius wrote a threatening letter – he would have done better to move up his troops. War was looming on the horizon when Pius died.

The reign of Marcus Aurelius witnessed an explicitly aggressive war by the orientals.[757] Essentially this was brought on by the weakness of Pius, although internal factors exacerbated the situation. The Parthian Empire had been consolidating itself and had sloughed off its former weakness. This was the first occasion on which there was aggression against Rome in this area and initially there were heavy defeats on both the northern and southern fronts, in Cappadocia and in Syria. The complete colourlessness and lack of substance in the narrative of these events is the fault of our sources, whose scantiness [MH.II, 302] it is difficult to fill out.

Severianus, governor of Cappadocia, was attacked and his forces destroyed. War flared up for Armenia. Vologaeses removed the Armenian king and installed Pacorus. Hardly had Severianus set foot on Armenian soil before he was annihilated at Elegia (near Theodosiopolis, now Erzurum). Soon events in Syria took much the same course. Attidius Cornelianus was defeated within the province itself, at Europos on the Euphrates;[758] even the feeble Syrians were thinking of secession!

Rome was compelled to make great efforts. Not only did the legions have to be brought up to strength, but extensive new forces had to be levied as well. Pius had died in 161 and by 162 Marcus sent Lucius, his co-regent, to lead the army. But he remained at Antioch, where he continued to indulge in the contemptible revelling that had been his wont in Rome. It was left to the, fortunately, distinguished junior commanders, Statius Priscus, Martius Verus and Avidius Cassius, to restore the honour of the Roman name.[759]

We are obliged to use imperial titles in order to reconstruct a scant historical outline. They suggest a three-pronged war. [MH.II, 303] In Armenia, Roman superiority was rapidly restored; as early as 163 Lucius Verus was acclaimed as *Armeniacus*.[760] Artaxata was conquered by Priscus.[761] Martius Verus succeeded him as governor of Cappadocia. At the same time, Avidius Cassius launched an energetic offensive against the Parthians.[762] Either at the end of 164 or during 165 the Emperor assumed the name *Parthicus Maximus*,[763] which leads us to infer some decisive victories. Although the Parthians at first seized the offensive, the Romans soon mastered them. There is a reference that Vologaeses was abandoned by his allies. This probably means that his vassals, with their reinforcements, failed to join him, since there can be no question of any other allies. The major cities were conquered. Some 30,000 souls are reputed to have perished during the capture of Seleucia. Even Ctesiphon, close by the Roman frontier,[764] was captured.

The Romans were not content with these successes; the final phase of the war is called 'against Media', although it is not clear what this means. Media was the Parthian heartland. On the other hand, [MH.II, 304] we learn that Cassius was obliged to beat a rapid retreat after his major successes, and that he had to overcome great difficulties on this retreat. This cannot have occurred after the capture of Seleucia and Ctesiphon: these are too close to the Roman frontier to make a withdrawal difficult. Probably, therefore, he advanced into Media, and the campaign will have gone well enough to justify the imperial appellation Medicus, but little more than this. Hence also, presumably, the modest silence with regard to the details.

We can see from this that the serious Parthian offensive was repelled, but without being exploited for any further territorial or other adjustments. This was prudent. Pacorus, the Armenian king installed by the Parthians, died a prisoner in Rome, and the throne was passed by Rome to the Arsacid, Sohaemus.[765] Otherwise all conquered territory was returned. Experience gained from the Marcomannic War will have played a major role, as did the plague, a legacy of the Parthian War. The Parthian catastrophe of Seleucia is reputed to have deposited its contagion [MH.II, 305] in this plague, which spread from there across the Roman Empire. Peace prevailed in the East during the latter part of Marcus's reign and under Commodus.

Severus marks an important turning point in the history of the East.[766] What was the motive behind his great and momentous wars? All the sources tell us it was his ambition and, up to a point, we must concur with this assessment. There were sufficient objective reasons for the second war, but his exploitation of his successes, the pointless and futile extension of the frontier undertaken by Severus, must be attributed to personal ambition.[767]

Internal Roman entanglements were the trigger for these events.[768] The East had raised Niger to the throne, and the vassal states, including Armenia, the king of Edessa and up to a point of the Parthians, followed the vote of the eastern legions. For a time Niger was the recognized Emperor in the eastern part of the Roman Empire. Severus marched against him and swiftly defeated him with his own electorate, the Illyrian legions, thereby restoring unity in the Empire. [MH.II, 306] This provided occasion for war with the Parthians – or not, according to choice. There was a certain contradiction in the title he assumed in the aftermath of the war: Severus refused the appellation *Parthicus*, yet styled himself *Arabicus* and *Adiabenicus*, or in fact, even more oddly, *Parthicus Arabicus* and *Parthicus Adiabenicus*.[769] This leads us to conclude that he sought neither a direct break with the Parthians nor a direct war against them, but rather war against their dependent states.[770] By 'Arabs' we should understand the inhabitants of southern Mesopotamia.

342

All in all, the war was very brief: Pescennius Niger was defeated in 194, the Euphrates crossed in 195.[771] The Parthians refrained from direct involvement in these acts, while Severus acted as the consummate shrewd statesman that he was in refraining from drawing them into the affair.

More important and richer in repercussions than the war itself, and more hostile to the Parthians, were the organic [sic] arrangements implemented in these territories: Mesopotamia was made into a new province. In a certain sense, the Emperor was resorting to Trajan's objectives here, but without also imitating the total superficiality of the latter's measures. Instead of promulgating merely nominal [MH.II, 307] decrees, he demonstrated through further measures his serious intention to retain the northern districts in particular, which were capable of sustaining civilization. First, he undertook to increase substantially the size of the army by establishing three new legions; by naming them the 'Parthian' legions he was sending a clear message to his neighbours. The *Secunda Parthica*, however, was sent to Italy, which was equipped with a garrison from this time onwards; but the first and third legions were stationed in Mesopotamia – on the Tigris, no longer on the Euphrates, as previously.[772]

These military measures were bolstered by crucial civil ones: he bestowed Roman municipal constitutions on numerous towns – Nisibis, in particular, was his own creation, on which he bestowed colonial rights and undoubtedly a great deal more besides.[773] He appears to have brought a substantial number of western colonists there, and for a long time this large and important city was more effective than the legions in defending the interests of Rome from attack by its eastern neighbours.[774] Similarly, he bestowed municipal rights on numerous other towns, while others became locations for camps.

Severus likewise avidly cultivated and deepened Roman ties with the city of Edessa (Urfa) and with the territory of Osrhoene, which had long had the character of a client-state. [MH.II, 308] Its long previous existence is attested to by coins bearing Greek[775] legends dating from the time of Marcus.[776] Now, King Abgar of Edessa was afforded an extraordinarily magnificent and ostentatious reception at Rome.[777] His kingdom was to form a buffer for the Romans. Naturally the new province was provided with a military commander and on this point we can observe the first sign of a restriction of senatorial government. The commander was a *praefectus Mesopotamiae*, not a *legatus*, which means that, like the *praefectus Aegypti*, he was recruited from the equestrian class,[778] and not from the men of senatorial rank. The man chosen for this post was a particularly close confidant of the Emperor.

We can detect a totally transformed policy here: the former neutral zone consisting of semi-dependent intermediaries such as Armenia and Mesopotamia was abandoned, and Mesopotamia became the most fiercely defended Roman province. From now on the two great powers marched side by side. The consequences of this soon became clear: from now on the threatened Parthians responded with incessant incursions.

[MH.II, 309] Severus knew what he was doing, and having recognized the reasons for his aims, we cannot deny the consistency, energy and well-thought-out nature of his means. This notwithstanding, the ailing condition of Rome, and in particular its unsatisfactory military circumstances, rendered this entire enterprise a most perilous one. Dio, who wrote thirty years after Severus and could judge not only as a contemporary, but also as an unbiased and sensible one, bitterly criticized the incorporation of Mesopotamia, most particularly from the financial standpoint, asserting that the province cost more than it yielded.[779] This in itself need not be so bad, since there are other, more important viewpoints than merely the financial one; nonetheless, this step merits censure for more fundamental reasons: Rome was too weak and unfit for the task.

Soon the great Parthian War broke out: Severus had been called away from the East to deal with Clodius Albinus, and his absence was immediately exploited by the Parthians to launch an attack. Nisibis had to withstand the first of many sieges for the sake of Rome. The war in Gaul was brought to an unexpectedly swift conclusion, and Severus reappeared in the East in 198 and resumed [MH.II, 310] the war against the Parthians. Both the invasion and the defence were necessary. For Rome, this was a war of self-defence, not of ambition. Rome and Parthia had moved too close to each other to be able to live in peace.

The Parthians resorted to their time-honoured tactics: as long as Rome appeared weak they attacked, but as soon as the Romans took to the battlefield in full force they retreated, only to make a renewed unexpected advance. Severus crossed the river and from then on the war proceeded exactly as that of Trajan had done: Seleucia and Ctesiphon were reconquered and razed to the ground and there was even a re-enactment of the unsuccessful siege of Hatra, lasting for twenty days.[780]

Initially Rome's position appeared more powerful than ever. The peace concluded was peculiar: although Severus retained all his other conquests he ceded part of Armenia to the Parthians. This was no great sacrifice on his part – it was a matter of complete indifference to Rome who ruled in this remote, strategically insignificant corner – so it was probably intended as a political ploy, a salve for wounded Parthian pride and a concession for the conquest of Mesopotamia. [MH.II, 311] If this was the case, however, it failed to accomplish its purpose: the grievance festered in the Parthian heart.

The true reasons for Rome's subsequent misfortunes are to be sought in the decline of military discipline. As we have seen, conscription became an increasingly localized affair and the eastern conscription areas contained predominantly non-warlike peoples who could not be compared with the Illyrians and Germans. This was exacerbated by the morally enervating quarters and the debilitating climate. The nature of the adversary to be fought likewise exerted an influence: combat against Germans was far better training for troops than combat against the Parthians, with their long-distance tactics. Lastly, there were the evil effects of incessant military insurrections. How is a state to thrive when it changes its rulers by force every five years on average?

The demoralized state of discipline is apparent from individual episodes, accounts of which happen to have survived: we are told, for example, that when Severus issued the command to storm Hatra during its siege, the European troops refused to obey; the Syrians did obey, but were repulsed.[781] This is related by the way [MH.II, 312] and no explicit conclusions are drawn. What a turn of events, however, and what a light it throws on conditions in the army! Were the historical tradition not so meagre, we should undoubtedly also know of countless other symptoms, for such an event cannot have been an isolated occurrence.

At first, the structure erected by Severus remained secure, despite the misrule of his successor, Antoninus, generally known as Caracalla. The latter was a small-minded, worthless individual who succeeded in making himself as ridiculous as he was contemptible. In 216 he travelled east in search of a war. Historiography has not spared him: he was universally hated. Even the most favourably disposed account, however, could scarcely extenuate his conduct in the East. He oppressed all the dependent kings and meddled in their family affairs. He had King Abgar of Osrhoene imprisoned[782] and interned the mother of the king of Armenia. His demented craving for glory fostered in him the ambition to become king of the Parthians and he thought [MH.II, 313] he could obtain that throne through a marriage alliance. He requested the hand of the daughter of King Artabanus[783] so that he would have a claim to succeed to the Parthian throne as the king's son-in-law. Artabanus thanked him for the honour and declined. At this, Caracalla marched into Parthia, plundering and destroying as he went; he desecrated the royal graves and carried off the remains contained there, entirely without reason or purpose. Elsewhere, the Romans were given a beating: Theocritus, a former actor and general of Caracalla, was defeated in Armenia.[784] The entire expedition was as ridiculous as it was contemptible. And yet the ascendancy of Rome managed to weather even these ignominies. In 217 Caracalla was – fortunately, we are entitled to say – assassinated near Edessa.[785] Astonishingly, the Emperor enjoyed the favour of his men, who mourned him sincerely.[786]

The Parthians immediately continued their aggression against his successor, Macrinus. Their demands are significant: withdrawal from Mesopotamia, restoration of the desecrated royal graves and the destroyed fortresses;[787] in other words, an attack on both the predominance and the honour of Rome [MH.II, 314] and a natural response to the wanton attack by Caracalla on the predominance and honour of the Parthians. This would have been an ignominious disgrace; Macrinus refused to meet Artabanus's demands and resumed the war. He suffered a severe defeat at Nisibis, however, and was obliged to conclude a peace. The conditions are somewhat puzzling: the Romans paid 500 million *denarii* as reparations for the war – an enormous sum. On the other hand, they retained Mesopotamia and it would appear from this that the Parthians contented themselves with monetary compensation alone. It is not quite clear whether Armenia remained Roman. King Tiridates probably recognized Roman sovereignty. We can see that these are merely the *disiecta membra*[788] of a narrative which does not go beyond externals.

B) CONFLICTS WITH THE SASANIDS AND PALMYRANS

Some far-reaching internal transformation must have taken place within the Parthian state around this time.[789] All we have is the Roman account. According to this the ruling house of the Arsacids was ousted from the throne by the Sasanids. The state had probably already been divided for some time, the lowland territories [MH.II, 315] separated from the Iranian plateau and the Parthians thereby internally weakened. The Arcasids had always remained half-Greek – this much is clear from their coins, their culture and everything we know of them. This was, so to speak, the last Macedonian successor state, the last remnant of the system of monarchies that had emerged from the Empires of Alexander. Now they were replaced by nationally mixed regions under their ruler Ardashir, known to the Greeks as Artaxerxes.

There[790] ensued a nationalist reaction, during which the Persians revived their ancient religion and their national rights. There was heavy internal fighting – the Arsacid house had struck deep roots. From now on, we speak again of Persians, not of Parthians. This new movement manifested itself chiefly in the military sphere and in their brusqueness towards the Romans, behind which lay the fundamental idea of completely ejecting the Romans from their country: 'Asia for the Asians' was their slogan.[791] Nonetheless, Roman rule was too securely anchored, particularly in the neighbouring provinces, for this attempt not to encounter the stiffest possible resistance. It may be asserted that the later decline of Roman rule occurred more as a result of the Romans' own weakness than as a consequence of unfavourable circumstances.

[MH.II, 316] First, under Alexander Severus, there ensued a bitter war against the orientals, beginning with an attack by the latter on Cappadocia and ending with the complete subjugation of Mesopotamia and the land up to the far shore of the Euphrates.[792] There was war again between 231 and 233, the conclusion of which is little known to us on account of the dearth of reliable sources. Both those accounts favourable to and those hostile to the Romans are probably exaggerated. The war appears to have ended in a stalemate. Alexander Severus probably divided his army into three parts, the first of which attacked Armenia, the second Ctesiphon, while the third, commanded by the Emperor, took up a central position. The latter, however, was never brought into play. The first two divisions initially scored some successes, but then suffered some severe setbacks, particularly the Armenian corps. Ultimately, the Romans probably did no more than maintain the previous frontier, without making any gains.

There then followed the ill-fated years on the Danube, which brought setbacks. It may be asserted that in 237 civil war amongst its members brought the state to the brink of total collapse. [MH.II, 317] We have a report of the conquest of Mesopotamia by the Persians dating to this year.[793] This should scarcely surprise us, since Rome was in such a profound state of corruption as to be incapable of offering any serious resistance. Still during the reign of Artaxerxes, indeed, the Persians are reputed to have advanced as far as Syria and Antioch. When Artaxerxes died, around 240, he was succeeded by his fierce, barbaric, but energetic son Sapor, who proved an exceptionally suitable leader for his people, and appears to have made an even greater mark than his father. The Persian people were now thoroughly consolidated and an extraordinary threat to the Romans. Not until Mesopotamia had fallen under Persian rule, however, and the same fate threatened Syria, did the Romans feel compelled to take to the field against their adversary.

In this period the throne came to a mere boy, Gordian III, a grandson of the proconsul of Africa of the same name. He assumed this awesome [MH.II, 318] task with some measure of success.[794] Furius Timesitheus, Gordian's uncle, led the government on his behalf.[795] The first campaign of 244 was crowned with great success: there are accounts of a conflict in the wake of which Mesopotamia was once again wrested from the Persians. Nevertheless, these successes were erased as a result of discord among the officers. Timesitheus died or was assassinated, and was replaced by Marcus Julius Philippus,[796] who became Emperor after the assassination of Gordian.

Philip conceded far too favourable a peace to the Persians,[797] although his withdrawal from Armenia is not authenticated. At all events the war ended without defeat and the Romans remained lords of the lands on the Euphrates.

The year 251 witnessed the terrible catastrophe in the Danube lands that ended with their loss to the Romans (see MH.II, 276f.). Poor Rome was visited with every conceivable misfortune in this period. Internal wars especially ravaged the Empire, and it was during these that the Emperor Decius met his death, probably at the hands of his successor [MH.II, 319] Gallus.[798] The latter remained only briefly at the helm before the Illyrians replaced him with Aemilianus.[799] He, too, did not survive for long, before being succeeded by Publius Licinius Valerianus.

This period witnessed the disintegration of the East. Reliable sources report that Armenia fell into the hands of the Persians. Then in 252 the plague[800] broke out, first in Ethiopia, then Egypt, whence it spread across the entire East, and from there to the West. We are told little about the Emperor Valerian, who presided over the state during this harrowing period. He was of good family and yet – typically for the period – had worked his way up through the ranks in the army. Although some witnesses ascribe the best of intentions to him with regard to restoring order, he was no match for his task, which was of such vast dimensions that only quite an exceptional personality could have fulfilled it. Circumstances recommended that he appoint his son Gallienus as co-regent,[801] since the times required him to have a [MH.II, 320] reliable person at his side and an able military man to lead his soldiers. There were wars to be fought in all kinds of places, which necessitated a plurality of supreme commanders. No Emperor could rely on any general any more. His son, born around 218 and thus sufficiently mature, had to some degree qualified himself for this office in successful fighting against the Germans. Gallienus now went west, and the Emperor himself east.

The East was in desperate straits. Sapor and his Persians were overrunning all of Syria and laying siege to Edessa.[802] Meanwhile, from the opposite flank, the provinces of Asia Minor were under threat of assault by the Goths. The towns of Trebizond, Nicomedia and Nicaea were captured by them in 259, the latter two even burnt to the ground.[803] Given these circumstances, Valerian felt compelled to travel to the theatre of war in person, since no-one else seemed to him sufficiently trustworthy.

There followed the catastrophe of Edessa around which a whole body of legend has grown up. The citizenry defended themselves valiantly against the Persians. Valerian marched to relieve them and a battle ensued before the city gates; the Romans lost. Valerian himself fell into [MH.II, 321] enemy hands. How this occurred is not clear; it would appear that Valerian hoped to be able to bribe Sapor. Treacherously, however, Sapor had him taken prisoner; the exact course of events is uncertain.[804] The capture of the Emperor broke the resistance of Rome; Mesopotamia, Cilicia, Cappadocia, even Syria, were all conquered, and passed without resistance into the hands of the enemy. Asia seemed to be lost to Rome. At this point, however, events took an unexpected turn; just as under Postumus the Gauls had launched an independent defence against the Franks when imperial defence had been broken on the Rhine, so now the inhabitants of Palmyra came forwards as defenders of the Empire.

Palmyra[805] lies in the desert between Mesopotamia and Syria, in a palm-shaded oasis from which it probably also derives its name. Its location lent it great importance as a centre for caravan traffic. This is the sole oasis capable of sustaining civilization along the roads running east from Damascus and Emesa in Syria; it is also necessary to travel via Palmyra to reach the Persian Gulf and the cities on the Euphrates.

The town must have been incorporated into the Roman Empire very early on, and it was always its policy to maintain favourable trading relations with both the Romans and the Parthians. Support for this interpretation can be found in the frequent occurrence of bilingual inscriptions in Palmyra, such as, for example, a recently found trading tariff dating from the time of Hadrian,[806] from which we can also see that the Palmyrans enjoyed the rare [MH.II, 322] privilege of being permitted to continue using Aramaic in addition to Greek. Roman rule in Palmyra goes back to the incorporation of Syria as a Roman province, but the Romans did not enjoy *de facto* control of the town until the time of Hadrian. The latter appears to have done everything in his power to bolster the Roman position in Palmyra and to Romanize its inhabitants. He bestowed Italian rights[807] on the city, for which reason it is also known as 'Hadriana Palmyra'.[808] Nonetheless, Latin never became the language of commerce there.

Severus reinforced these ties even further. When Mesopotamia was made a Roman province, Palmyra became an imperial city. It was thus from Palmyra that reorganization along Roman lines now emanated and, later, from where the attempt was launched to establish a separate government, independent of Rome.

Although Palmyra's location was very important for commerce, it was not a felicitous one from which to play a leading historical role in the world. The power of Rome was broken, and now it was every man for himself. The task was rendered easier by the fact that the Persian attack was merely a superficial one, since they had already conquered too much territory to be able to occupy it all with any energy. The Roman garrison offered vigorous resistance in Samosata, the capital of Commagene. In Palmyra it was the town council who distinguished themselves in the defence, and chief among them Septimius Odaenathus,[809] who came from a notable family of councillors, which, as was frequently the case with indigenous notables, was repeatedly appointed to office by the Romans. Odaenathus attacked [MH.II, 323] the Persians with surprising success; the Palmyran army, reinforced with the remnants of the Roman garrison, advanced on Mesopotamia, even as far as Ctesiphon, lifting the sieges laid by the Persians to major towns. In this way the Romans managed to retain a presence of a kind in these lands.

Remarkably, Odaenathus did not have himself proclaimed Emperor, as so often happened in that period, an era which is, albeit unjustly, known as that of the 'thirty tyrants'.[810] Odaenathus maintained his ties with the Romans, who in turn recognized his status with the official title of *dux Orientis* or *strategos tes heoas*.[811] This is confirmed by coins minted during the reign of his son and bearing the title *dux Romanorum*;[812] this should probably be interpreted to mean that the Romans had invested him with exclusive and extraordinary powers over the East, so that resistance might proceed in an authorized manner. Odaenathus was certainly not recognized as co-Emperor, although the title might seem to make this conceivable. The circumstances here were quite similar to those in the West under Postumus, except that here a separation from the Empire actually took place. In this way the fall of the Empire was deferred for a time.

In 267 Odaenathus was murdered by his nephew Maeonius.[813] His wife, Zenobia, has also unjustly been held responsible for the death of her husband. Nonetheless, the work begun by him was not [MH.II, 324] destroyed, despite the fact that his children were not yet of age, for Septimia Zenobia herself succeeded him. It is difficult to piece together an objective portrait of her, since ancient writers, as in later times in the case of the Maid of Orleans, have heaped on her head every conceivable virtue and positive attribute. We can assert only this much: that she bore all the marks of an oriental beauty, was a formidable horsewoman and a fine connoisseuse of Greek authors, particularly Homer and Plato. This is borne out by the fact that her principal adviser was the Neoplatonist philosopher Cassius Longinus, who acquired a leading position among the philosophers of his day.[814] All else in the tradition about Zenobia, however, is stereotyped and does not permit us to draw any conclusions about her politics. For all that, we must recognize her achievements as being of great significance. She resolutely pursued the idea of uniting the East under a single government.

This decision emerges in a particularly interesting manner in what she did for Egypt. For actually it was from Egypt that, through Timagenes, who was probably the Roman prefect there, she received the request to occupy the country. She responded by sending an army of 70,000 [MH.II, 325] men, led by Zabdas. They encountered heavy resistance, led by one Probus,[815] who held command at sea against the pirates. Probus was defeated in Syria, and Egypt came under the sway of the Palmyrans. By 270 all of eastern Egypt and the greater part of the Near East was under Palmyran rule. This is manifested in a remarkable manner by some coins issued in the names of Vaballathus or Athenodorus,[816] the son of Zenobia. From the fact that the coins' legends refer to Aurelian as Emperor, we may deduce that Roman sovereignty was still recognized. Zenobia is not mentioned at all on the coins, while Athenodorus appears first with the epithet *vir consularis*,[817] i.e. as Roman subject, then with the title *rex*, which relates to his local status, and finally as *dux Romanorum*, which should probably be supplemented by *partium Orientis*. In Egypt too there are a number of epigraphical documents in which Zenobia and Athenodorus are designated as *regina* and *rex*.[818] Here, therefore, there is a parallel with the period of Theoderic, when the western Empire also became independent of Byzantium, but still nominally acknowledged its sovereignty. In the present case, however, this process was a much more ephemeral one.[819]

By this time, Rome had managed to master her most pressing [MH.II, 326] misfortunes. In 271, as soon as the incursion of the Goths had been repelled, Aurelian set about putting an end to the rule of Zenobia, which had by now effectively severed itself from Rome. Setting off with a mighty army, he subjugated Asia Minor immediately, since these states abandoned Zenobia as soon as the Romans approached. After Zenobia fled to Syria and refused to capitulate to Aurelian, the latter set out in pursuit, conquering Antioch *en route*. Zenobia was forced to evade him, but soon the decisive battle took place at Emesa (Homs); the superior western Illyrian troops decisively defeated the queen. Aurelian besieged and conquered Palmyra. Zenobia was seized and taken prisoner by the Emperor's cavalrymen in an attempt to flee to the Persians. In this manner the war was concluded without undue resistance and the former order soon restored.[820]

However, there was an epilogue to this war.[821] No sooner had Aurelian's army withdrawn than Palmyra ceded from Roman rule a second time, probably under the leadership of Odaenathus's family. With his characteristic swiftness, Aurelian turned back, captured Palmyra and razed it to the ground; a sentence that was as regrettable for the avengers as it was for its object, since the city was never restored to its former glory. The last sacrificial offering of Palmyra dates from August 272.[822]

[MH.II, 327] Another remarkable circumstance merits mention here; Aurelian introduced an[823] oriental cult to Rome. The Emperor is reputed to have seen in a dream a vision of the god Heliogabalus, who recommended to him a good battle plan.[824] In gratitude for this he erected a temple to him on the Quirinal Hill in Rome.[825] This god was a very special one, who even had his own *pontifices* (priests), and the two boards of *pontifices* date from this period; from now on they became *pontifices Vestae et Solis* (priests of Vesta and of the Sun), effectively of the West and of the East.[826] The Emperor Elagabalus had already attempted this. Aurelian styled himself *deus et dominus*, god and lord.[827]

Aurelian's victory not only made good the catastrophe of Zenobia, but also restored the supremacy of Rome in the East for another hundred years. Since there are few subsequent reports about the situation in the East, it can reasonably be assumed that Roman rule remained largely secure there. The sole exception is a campaign against the Persians during the reign of the Emperor Carus, but we know nothing of the reasons behind this.[828] At first the campaign was successful: the Persians were chastened and Roman rule in the area reinforced. This victory could not be pursued beyond the capture of Ctesiphon, however; some accounts have it that the Emperor was struck by lightning after [MH.II, 328] the main battle, others that he was assassinated by his prefect.[829]

There was a new crisis under Diocletian: yet again, there was fighting with the eastern neighbours, the origin of which is shrouded in obscurity. The Roman government demanded that the orientals again recognize the Tigris frontier; their response to this was armed resistance. The Egyptian uprising of 295–6 may also have played a part in the onset of this war,[830] since Diocletian was obliged to march on the Egyptians to chasten them, and the Persians may have seized this opportunity to capture Armenia. At first, the Caesar Galerius was defeated by the Persians in 296; then, however, he made an energetic advance. Diocletian marched out to his aid from Egypt, and together they won a glorious victory and an opportunity to capture the retinue and harem of the Persian king. As was often the case, the circumstance that the harem had been captured was decisive. The Persians capitulated unconditionally and the sultan, Narses, bought back his wives at the price of all his kingdom.[831] The result was a peace that was extremely favourable to Rome: the five provinces of the area from the Tigris as far as Lake Van were ceded back to Rome and southern Armenia was incorporated into the Empire.[832] Thus peace was restored again in 297, to endure for another forty years. There was no further unrest until the end of the reign of the Constantine, [MH.II, 329] but that falls outside the scope of our inquiry here. This now concludes our history of Roman foreign policy in the three main theatres of war.

To summarize this period, we may assert that by the end of it the Romans had everywhere re-established their supremacy; at the same time, however, the shortcomings of their defences are glaringly apparent. These consisted of a chain of fairly small garrisons stretching across all the conquered territories. In the event of a heavy assault on any one point, therefore, they were naturally incapable of withstanding it. Here, too, Diocletian[833] brought about a regeneration. The army he raised was strengthened by a new element in the form of the so-called *exercitus praesentalis*. This consisted of freshly conscripted, massive military forces which, instead of having permanent quarters, accompanied the Emperor wherever he travelled. The Emperor had no permanent residence. Accordingly the *magistri militum* (Masters of the Soldiers) were also further divided into those *in praesentia* and those *in provinciis*. The army was increased to three times its former size. This gave Rome a mighty, combat-effective army at its disposal, which could be deployed anywhere at any time. Nevertheless, this reform was not merely quantitative, but also qualitative, as it introduced many more barbarians into the standing army. They came to constitute [MH.II, 330] its main element. Conscripted foreigners, including Franks, even began to work their way up to the highest ranks.

6

DOMESTIC POLITICS II

We can now let biographical accounts of individual Emperors recede into the background, partly because they are relatively unimportant in terms of the historical process, and partly because such accounts are readily available. In every respect the period we are looking at was a poor and insignificant one, but particularly so with regard to the Emperors. Only an exceptionally small number of important men can be recorded in the era from Vespasian to Diocletian, with the possible exception of Hadrian[834] and Aurelian, although we know very little about the latter.[835] Otherwise all the Emperors were ineffectual and dreadfully mediocre, exerting the barest modicum of personal influence on the course of history. If we were to exchange the infamies of a man such as Commodus with those of Caracalla, we would still conclude that the historical process would have been exactly the same. It is most regrettable that in both ancient and modern times many historians have seen it as their scholarly duty to perch like bluebottles on such unwholesome matter. At best, the sole exceptions to this assessment would be Trajan[836] and Pius,[837] of whom the former was very courageous and the latter very good. Since, however, they were no more than very courageous [MH.II, 331] and very good, they too failed to make any lasting mark on the course of events.

In contrast, the domestic political scene in this period in particular is of immense interest, since virtually all the institutions established by Augustus underwent significant changes during this time.

A) THE EMPEROR AND THE COURT

It is unhelpful to see the Roman principate as a straightforward monarchy. On the contrary, in its best sense the *princeps* is no more than an administrative official, albeit in the most senior position and with a monopoly of power.[838] The tenure of the principate by a person not yet of age was hence something unheard of: the *princeps* had to be capable of administering and ruling, or at least, in the very worst event, of fighting at the head of his troops. This notwithstanding, Augustus had already stamped the principate with the mark of predetermined succession. Already during his own lifetime the *princeps* generally designated his successor, in whom proconsular and tribunician authority were then united. We shall now examine how the concept of successor evolved during the period in question.

Under Augustus there had been no specific expression to denote the rank of successor, apart from tribunician and proconsular authority; this is particularly apparent in the case of Tiberius, [MH.II, 332] who attended to virtually all business of government in the latter part of Augustus's reign and yet still remained a simple, private citizen.

This was changed by Hadrian, who invested his successor with the formal title of 'Caesar'. Under Augustus all male members of the *princeps*'s family had been called 'Caesar' and when Caesar's lineage died out with Gaius[839] the Flavians adopted the name. Only Vitellius refused the name of 'Caesar'.[840] Here, therefore, the title of 'Caesar' might be defined as 'prince of the blood'.

As has already been stated, this was changed by Hadrian. Since he was himself childless, he adopted Lucius Aelius Verus[841] and Marcus.[842] Hadrian bestowed the name of 'Caesar' on Lucius, while refusing it to Lucius's son, his adoptive grandson. When Aelius died soon after this and Hadrian adopted Titus Antoninus Pius[843] in his stead, Pius was also given the title 'Caesar'. It was, nonetheless, not granted to Aelius's son, Lucius Verus, whom Pius had adopted in his turn.[844]

When Antoninus Pius became Emperor, the title 'Caesar' was given to Hadrian's[845] second adoptive son Marcus, who was henceforth known as Marcus Aelius Aurelius Verus Caesar. It emerges from this, therefore, that from Hadrian onwards the title of 'Caesar' may be defined as heir-apparent, or crown prince. Where more than one person bore the title of 'Caesar' simultaneously, this indicates that they were intended to succeed one another. The fact that a crown prince was appointed from the time of Hadrian onwards [MH.II, 333] is a clear indication of how deeply ingrained the dynastic principle had become.

A further innovation followed under Marcus, namely a plurality of *principes*. This is not quite as nonsensical as might at first appear. The *duo consules* of the earlier period evince a comparable arrangement of two supreme rulers of equal status. Here too they will have cancelled each other out when their decisions were at odds over any given issue. Augustus may already have considered this option; at any rate he seems to have treated his two adoptive sons Gaius and Lucius equally. But the situation did not arise at that juncture, which proved positive for the development of Rome. The collegial principle did not come into effect until Marcus,[846] who made his brother Lucius Verus co-Emperor with fully equal powers,[847] although we do not know why. Perhaps he saw his brother as a military complement to himself – a conviction that was beneficial neither to himself nor the Empire.

Generally speaking the role of co-ruler was of little importance, since the junior partner was usually chosen so as to be incapable of ruling independently. Where he turned out to be capable of this after all, it still had no major consequences. This became apparent in the case of Caracalla and Geta after the death of the Emperor Septimius Severus.[848] When Maximinus died in 238 the Senate, remarkably, elected two Emperors, [MH.II, 334] Pupienus and Balbinus, probably in an attempt to evoke the consulship of former times. Although this joint rule lasted only a few months it did, from the juristic standpoint, prompt the interesting question of the relationship between two such Augusti. All we know is that formally they had completely equal rights.

The first question which interests us is the extent to which the Caesar was called on to carry out the business of government. Prior to Hadrian, this question relates to the 'princes of the blood' and after him to his heirs-apparent. Generally speaking the Roman system did not allow for this, although the Caesar was invested with both proconsular and tribunician authority. However, there is the important proviso that the Augustus was at liberty to permit the Caesar the right to be involved in the business of government. Although they sometimes bore other titles over and above that of 'Caesar', for example 'imperator', this seems to have had no constitutional significance. Frequently the Caesars played a not insignificant role, although in each case it was bestowed on them by the Augustus, as we know, for example, of Germanicus.[849] Titus similarly held an influential position as heir-apparent. An heir-apparent was never put in command of the Guard, however.[850] To sum up, therefore, the office of Caesar in this period may be defined as follows: the Caesar had the constitutional right to hold extraordinary offices which had been assigned to him. In this respect there seems to have been no change.

After this digression, we now return to the institution of the principate and inquire how this altered as time went on. The change occurred as a result of there being several *principes* side by side, whose spheres of authority were therefore necessarily curtailed. This occurred for the first time [MH.II, 335] with Valerian and his son Gallienus. Here we have a *de facto* division of power, as with Carus and Carinus. This division later brought about a split in the Empire itself, with one ruler of the West and another of the East, an arrangement that was constitutionally and permanently instituted by Diocletian. From then on there was no longer an *imperium Romanum*, but only *partes occidentales et orientales*, western and eastern parts, which, although they shared legislation and the consulship, had *de facto* become two distinct halves with separate destinies. So although the two empires were reunited on more than one occasion, for example under Theodosius and under Justinian,[851] the reunification was superficial and impermanent. In reality, the Empire was in a state of dissolution. A prelude to the division of the Empire by Diocletian was the debate in the Senate following the death of Severus,[852] when the Senate too was to be divided into a western and an eastern half. The mother of the co-Emperors prevented this. This is why it is proper to consider the institution of the principate at this point.

After Diocletian's division of the Empire, the institution of the Caesars acquired a different meaning.[853] They became co-rulers who also had a *de iure* say – vice-Emperors, so to speak. Up to the time of Diocletian the law was oblivious of the existence of the Caesars, but thereafter mention is made of them in the opening preambles. By that time they were already co-rulers, therefore, and in many cases played a crucial role. Indeed they often even forced the old Emperor to abdicate in order to seize power for themselves. Nonetheless, this institution never achieved far-reaching significance and we seldom find Caesars of major importance.[854]

Major innovations can be registered in the imperial civil service. The *princeps* was the only official whose competence encompassed the entire Empire; all other officials had only partial competence. The *princeps* commanded the entire army. Under him there were [MH.II, 336] several sub-imperators. The same applies to the administrative and judicial spheres: the Emperor wielded sole supreme administrative authority, including that over the legal system. Although the appointment of extraordinary officials did sometimes occur, this was rare and only for particular sections of the Empire. From time to time these sections were merged, and officials with special competence appointed over them. Never, however, did such competence extend over the entire Empire.

The position of officials in the capital, for example the consuls, might appear to refute these remarks, but these institutions were a relic from a bygone age[855] and in fact the consuls were imperial officials. However, this applies only to their titles and to the running of the Senate. The involvement of the consuls either in government business or in military institutions was never entertained; any influence over military affairs in particular was denied them. The magistrates of the city of Rome wielded somewhat greater influence over the judiciary and administration. This is evident principally from the fact that the *aerarium populi Romani* (the national treasury),[856] remained under the administration of the capital's magistrates as a kind of Roman 'Juliusturm'.[857]

The praetors too were officials for the whole Empire, not merely urban magistrates. It is interesting to note the Emperors' opposition to the relics of Republican institutions. The establishment of the praefecture did away with the anomaly in the administration of the treasury. Although the competence of the innocuous *praetor urbanus* spanned the entire Empire, it was restricted to *fideicommissa*.[858] In the *Notitia Dignitatum*, the [MH.II, 337] register of late Roman officials, we find no trace of consuls, praetors or magistrates of the city of Rome. Only the urban prefects are listed, although these were imperial administrative officials. The Emperors thus looked on them as the city magistrates – magistrates who had been granted a privileged rank.

When we compare the situation of imperial officials during this period with that in the fourth century, we find in the latter case a fully developed class of officials,[859] and it is interesting to trace the growth of this institution. There is invariably an element of self-delusion in any form of personal rule such as the Roman. Under the principate, the private staff of *servi* and *liberti*, the *familia Caesaris*, took over the business of government. By the fourth century, however, we find fully developed government by civil servants, characterized by a separation of military and civil administration.

As far as non-military officials were concerned, the Emperor initially had assistants for keeping accounts and attending to correspondence, as did all prominent Romans. Exactly the same applies to the fiscal administration.[860] In this case centralization was vital for both aspects of finance: the *patrimonium* or the *res privata*, and the *fiscus*. On the one hand the Emperor, like every prominent Roman, possessed a fortune of his own inherited from his forebears. This, however, needed to be distinguished from income which accrued to the Emperor as such and which was not his private possession in any other sense. Thus a proportion of the taxes paid by the population flowed into his coffers, out of which he then had to cover the cost of military administration and the provision of corn for the city. [MH.II, 338] The central administration of the taxes of the entire Roman people came to have an official, bureaucratic character. The imperial procurators raised taxes in the provinces; an imperial slave, the *a rationibus*, led the central administration.[861] Administrative departments were not markedly autonomous and were obliged to send their so-called general accounts – *summae rationes* – to the central administration, the head auditing office, as it were. There was no actual treasury connected with this head office; only the accounts were sent there. Money transfers were then made by means of cheques, so that we find no cashiers, *arcarii*[862] or *dispensatores*.

In the early period financial affairs were in the hands of subordinate freedmen from among the emperor's servants, who thus frequently intervened in affairs when the Emperor was weak. But they cannot be regarded as officials at all. In this respect there was again no change until the time of Hadrian, the great reformer.[863]

A similar situation pertained with regard to correspondence. On no account should we imagine that the so-called officials *ab epistulis* wielded particularly great influence: they are not at all comparable with modern cabinet secretaries. Private correspondence was dealt with either by the Emperor himself or by persons who held no office, for example Horace.[864] Scribes were entrusted with [MH.II, 339] the drafting and verbal composition of documents, so that we find notable philologists and stylists among them. After a similar attempt had already been made by Vitellius,[865] Hadrian took these posts away from freedmen and created official posts; this institution endured.[866]

A reorganization ensued in the fourth century with the *comes sacrarum largitionum* and the *comes rei privatae*, i.e. the two ministers of finance, and the *magistri scriniorum*, who conducted correspondence.[867] The high-status ministers of finance and palace affairs thus developed out of simple cashiers. The same applied to the four cabinet ministers,[868] who also occupied prominent positions, if not quite so high as the former. Equestrians were appointed to these posts because they served as officers to the Emperor anyway, and were rivals of the Senate. These changes were quite natural, since as soon as these positions were transferred from freedmen to equestrians, they had to be given a wider sphere of influence. The posts were transformed from servile into official ones.

A similar evolution took place with the Council of State.[869] Here too we do not find that its members were particularly impressive at first. Sometimes the Emperor summoned a narrower *consilium*, as happened under Augustus,[870] Tiberius[871] and Alexander Severus.[872] In general, of course, the Council of State comprised the entire Senate, and the Emperor normally negotiated with the Senate as a body. When the Emperor was too decrepit with age to consult with the entire Senate, he would summon a smaller number of senators. Whenever such a narrower Council of State was formed, we may assume that the Senate wielded greater influence, [MH.II, 340] since confidential discussion with the Senate as a body was prohibited by both the numbers and quality of the senators. Its very size rendered it powerless, whereas a committee of twenty to thirty persons would have had great influence.

Initially this Council of State – *consilium* or *sacrum consistorium Caesaris* – was concerned with the administration of justice. Each individual judge of course surrounded himself with a similar council, and we have already seen how the Emperor also had a duty to attend to civil law. Therefore the Emperors too would consult with *consiliarii* conversant with the law while administering justice; they initially had an entirely unregulated status and were only summoned to deal with specific cases. The precise date when this changed is not known, although it probably happened under Hadrian, who created a judicial council whose members had a permanent position and a salary of 60,000 to 100,000 sesterces. There were six of these officials – *a consiliis sacris* – appointed by the Emperor personally and thus holding positions of trust. The appointment by the Emperor of equal numbers of senators and equestrians to this body was an early development, however. Domitian had already mixed senators with equestrians. We soon also find that particular persons become permanent members of the Council of State, such as princes related to the Emperor, for example Titus under Vespasian.[873] Others included court officials, particularly Praetorian Prefects, who never seem to have been omitted.

In the third century the prefects were [MH.II, 341] appointed from among the most highly regarded jurists, since the members of the Council of State had to have great expertise in the law.[874] So we see the same process at work here too.

Initially the administration of justice by the Emperor was direct and personal; the council had no more than an advisory role. Ultimately, however, decisions concerning legal questions were taken by the *consiliarii* quite alone, and this marks a substantial step towards the creation of a regime of civil servants. In the third century the *consistorium sacrum* acquired immense legal and political importance.

B) THE ARMY AND THE SENATE

As in the civil, so in the military sphere, the Emperor exercised his supreme command in person, and had subordinate officials solely in order to carry out his orders. There were no subordinate military commanders as such,[875] e.g. no commander for Italy. For reasons already gone into earlier, military officers in Italy and Egypt could be neither Senators nor plebeians and had, therefore, to be equestrians. The fleet[876] and the *vigiles*[877] likewise had equestrian officers.

The supreme command of the Praetorian Guard developed in an unusual way.[878] Under Augustus there was initially no commander of the Guard, or rather the Emperor himself was commander of the Praetorian cohorts. In the middle of Augustus's reign, in 2 BC, a double command was instituted in the form of two *praefecti praetorio* (*praefectus* means representative of the Emperor), although in fact this was not an autonomous post, [MH.II, 342] since the Emperor always remained the supreme military commander.[879]

[MH.II, 349] Everything to do with the army – the entire supreme command, the appointment and promotion of officers – was the personal privilege of the Emperor. Nonetheless, this did not apply to one particular group: Augustus operated on the principle of not excluding the ruling class, but of appointing men of noble birth to senior military posts. Legates were invariably drawn from among the senators,[880] and the *tribuni militum* too were almost invariably[881] drawn from the Senate; indeed even the *praefecti alae* were originally men of senatorial rank.[882] Later, when these proved insufficient in numbers, equestrians were resorted to.

One group of military posts was reserved not for senatorial, but for equestrian *tribuni militum*, namely posts in Italy and Egypt. We have already had frequent occasion to mention the unique status of Egypt as a special imperial domain. Great as Rome's predisposition towards the aristocracy was, naturally not just any Roman could become an officer there, only men from the ancient *ordo*. It should be borne in mind, however, that the drawing up of the equestrian list was the business of the Emperor, so that if he wished to appoint someone to such a position, he could quite easily place him *ad hoc* on the equestrian roll. The equestrian's horse did not pass automatically to a son when his father died, but had to be specially bestowed on him, although this regularly happened in fact.[883] The composition of the equestrian class thus lay largely in the hands of the Emperor.

[MH.II, 350] How, then, did the Emperor treat this officer class? He was fully aware of the danger which might arise. The principle behind the principate was a highly personal style of government which could not allow any other person to grow too powerful. Initially, therefore, we see efforts to divide command in all spheres – in the Guard, in the city,[884] in the fleet and in Egypt – and not to concentrate too much power in any one person's hands.[885] An exception, which has only recently become known through an as yet unpublished inscription,[886] were the two Egyptian legions, which were under a single commander. Nonetheless, this is the sole exception and Egypt was a long way from from Rome.

Augustus knew full well that the principal danger lay in the Guard, and he appointed no senior Guards officers in the first half of his reign. Indeed the Guard was not even stationed in Rome, but outside the city in a camp; the duty of guarding the Emperor at the palace rotated among individual cohorts under tribunes. Not until the second half of his reign did he appoint one, or rather two, *praefecti praetorio*,[887] and very soon the distinction between servant and master became blurred. It was no longer possible to distinguish between the two. The *praefectus praetorio* was in command of all cohorts, but not of the centurions. Whenever one of these was accused of misconduct, judgement was reserved for the Emperor himself. Only here in the case of the Guard did Augustus uphold the principle of collegial command which had already been abandoned in all other spheres.

Under the Republic the legion had been under the orders of six tribunes;[888] Augustus added a legate as commander-in-chief;[889] but the Guard was commanded [MH.II, 351] collegially,[890] just as the Republic had replaced a single king with two consuls in order to reduce the danger of this powerful office, thereby playing one devil off against the other. The danger from Guard commanders lay in the unclear nature of the emperor's orders. The Emperor was supposed to issue every single order personally, but in practice this was impossible. Naturally it was equally impossible to tell whether an order issued by the imperial palace came from the Emperor himself or from an officer, civilian or perhaps even slave. Maecenas and Seneca governed in this manner, without ever holding any actual office. The *praefectus praetorio* regularly found himself in the immediate presence of the Emperor; it was he, therefore, who received orders from the Emperor to be transmitted to the outside world. A centurion, for example, is ordered to carry out an execution – was it on the Emperor's orders? How could anyone outside know? There was thus a tendency for the office of *praefectus praetorio* to become not only comparable with that of a modern prime minister, but indeed to develop directly into that of a deputy Emperor. Whenever the Emperor was indisposed or chose not to attend to business for a time, the *praefectus praetorio* stood in for him. His position was thus both irresponsible and impossible to monitor, which is how such an anomaly as that of Sejanus[891] could arise. Weary of governing, Tiberius went into self-imposed exile, and the result was the autocracy of the Prefect of the Guard, who was furthermore unfettered by a colleague.

Despite its inherent dangers, however, this post was not abolished and perhaps could not be abolished. Vespasian attempted [MH.II, 352] to promote his successor Titus to the office of Praetorian Prefect[892] and thereby take the sting out of its tail, but this attempt failed to set a precedent. In the third century the competence of the Praetorian Prefect was defined in such a way that in reality it became a deputy emperorship. He was not given supreme command of the army; that role, with command in the provinces and the appointment'of officers, was retained by the Emperor personally. In contrast, however, military provisioning[893] was centralized under the Praetorian Prefect – a crucial sphere involving a mass of detail which the Emperor could not possibly handle alone. He was similarly given supreme command of the troops in the capital, and thus over Italy and Rome. Then he was appointed to supervise the *basileioi*, the servants, slaves and freed slaves of the Emperor. Acts of injustice must have been a frequent occurrence among these people: it was a vast household which also embraced the taxation system, as well as the entire staff of the procurators. Precisely under the better Emperors, such as Marcus and Septimius Severus, the office of Praetorian Prefect became particularly crucial in this regard, since it exercised particularly firm control over staff and service departments.

Over and above this, the Praetorian Prefects also took part in the imperial administration of justice, as well as in legislation. They were obliged to intervene in this sphere since it was for the most part impossible for the Emperor to be effectively involved in it, [MH.II, 353] because very few Emperors, such as Severus, were either jurists themselves or trained in the law. The administration of justice hence passed to the *consilium principis*, the Emperor's council, of which the Praetorian Prefect was in charge. There is a most interesting surviving record of its proceedings dating from the time of Caracalla, actually an extract from the records of a lawsuit pertaining to the return of a deportee.[894] The persons present are enumerated: first the two Praetorian Prefects, who are mentioned by name, then the 'friends of the Emperor', the departmental secretaries (*principia officiorum*),[895] and lastly senators and equestrians (*utriusque ordinis viri*). This was the composition of the college. It was thus by virtue of their appointment as Praetorian Prefects that Papinian, Ulpian and Paulus, for example, became experts on the law. By the same token, however, this is a clear indication of the general decline in the armed forces which is clearly documented by this development.

De iure, legislation was a matter of senatorial decree; however, jurisdiction on administrative and taxation matters devolved on the Emperor and hence on the Praetorian Prefect, which underlines the latter's role as vice-Emperor. Quite early on, therefore, we find both promulgations issued by the Prefect, and the organization of a special body of officials for this purpose. In the case of all other officials, such as legates and proconsuls, who had only servants and slaves to attend to more menial work, there were no subordinate officials at all. The legate, for example, had an *a commentariis*, a chief clerk, but he was a common soldier.[896] Early on we find the Praetorian Prefect having a similar assistant, titled slightly differently [MH.II, 354] as a *commentariensis*[897] (a diary-keeper). And, just as the Emperor had his *consilium*, so the Praetorian Prefect also had his, made up of high-ranking members.[898]

In the fourth century, the period of Diocletian and Constantine, the institution of the Praetorian Prefect underwent both expansion and modification: civilian and military authority were separated, and at the same time the office became geographically defined.[899] As we have seen, in the course of time the Praetorian Prefecture, originally a military office, gradually became associated with more important civilian duties. Diocletian now completely stripped this office of its military functions and reorganized the Guard under a *magister officiorum*.[900] The Praetorian Prefect retained control of jurisdiction and administrative affairs, apart from the army. In addition, with the division of the Empire into two halves, two Praetorian Prefects were installed in each of the two halves and their spheres of activity distinguished geographically, but not professionally, so that in the western half one was given jurisdiction over half the Empire in Gaul, Spain and Britain and his counterpart acquired jurisdiction over Italy, Africa and Illyricum. We can thus discern a development here from personal rule by the Emperor to an administrative and constitutional state. Previously the Emperors often handled matters badly, but they did at least handle them. Later Emperors, such as Arcadius and Honorius, were completely unable to do this and officials had to step in for them.

[MH.II, 355] In the division of power between the Senate and the *princeps*[901] the lion's share had initially fallen to the Emperor, especially anything to do with the army. At first, however, the Senate had shared in government; this power was gradually eroded, although one cannot always put one's finger on detailed instances of when this occurred. The Senate had a direct and positive involvement in government as long as a number of judiciary appointments were reserved for senators. The fact that the Emperor was restricted to the senatorial circle when appointing legates and governors represented an appreciable curb on his power and considerable influence for the Senate.

The status of the Senate was high in terms of legislature and jurisdiction. The Augustan constitution was tantamount to what we would understand by a constitutional monarchy. This notwithstanding, there was a great deal of pomp and circumstance about laws themselves and subsequent developments imperceptibly eroded this high status. The wheels simply stopped turning and came to a standstill.

Legislation,[902] both civil and criminal, had found its way into senatorial hands largely at the behest of Tiberius. In the third century, however, senatorial decrees

362

ceased,[903] to be replaced (perhaps from the time of Severus) exclusively by imperial decrees which, when they were statutory, were passed on to the Senate and promulgated through this channel, and when they were administrative did not require this ratification. After the division of the Empire, of course, there was both a Roman and a Constantinopolitan Senate to which each respective Emperor had recourse.

[MH.II, 356] The Senate was ostensibly in control of the central state treasury, the *aerarium populi Romani*. As we have seen, however,[904] the importance of this treasury was firstly diminished by the establishment of other treasuries, and then from Nero onwards the remainder came under imperial administration. Although this did not directly bypass the senatorial approval of expenditure from the *aerarium populi Romani*, it did, however, leave it a shadow of its former self. By the third century it persisted in name only and Diocletian's constitution was silent on the subject.

With respect to civil and criminal law the highest authorities were equally the Emperor and the Senate, a dual authority that had been unknown under the Republic. Nor was it ever abolished: the Emperor Tacitus was still familiar with the authority of the Senate as a court of appeal, and even impressed this fact on it.[905] In practice, however, this power was exercised by the Emperor alone. In the later Empire the Senate continued to exercise it in the criminal sphere only; it was expedient for the political regime to be able to foist the odium for judicial murder on to the Senate. The ignominious death penalties passed by the Senate were, if anything, even more numerous than those passed by the Emperors. As late as the fourth century we find the Senate convicting people of high treason – for example, the tumultuous and chaotic trumped-up court martial of Gildo, who had rebelled against Honorius in Africa,[906] which scarcely merits being called a trial.

The Senate likewise operated as a kind of supreme [MH.II, 357] privy council: earlier the Emperor had been the principal Senator and as long as he remained in the Senate he was no more than the first among equals, the first senator. Augustus spoke a great deal in the Senate[907] and Trajan still made frequent appearances there,[908] but later the practice was dropped, although it was never formally abolished. By the third century appearances by the Emperor in the Senate were rare, and by the fourth century they had ceased altogether.[909]

Aside from the imperial office itself, the Senate made no official appointments. Originally the Emperor was elected either by the Senate or by the people, i.e. the army. Later this practice was modified, but not discernibly changed. In the early period, in the event of election by the army, the Senate at least recognized the army's choice. Under Gaius the day on which he had been proclaimed Emperor by the Senate was celebrated,[910] and even Vespasian was recognized by the Senate, although the celebration related to the day of his election by the army.[911] By the third century, however, we observe recognition by the Senate being dispensed with,[912] and only on one further occasion do we find an exceptional instance of the army calling on the Senate to elect an Emperor, resulting in the appointment of Tacitus.[913] Otherwise it was the army who appointed Emperors, and this practice persisted.

Not inconsiderable influence accrued to the Senate initially in connection with the composition of a major, indeed the most important, group of officials, since the Emperor did not hand-pick the proconsuls, governors and a major proportion of administrative officials, but instead drew them by lot from among those who had already held the offices of consul and praetor. [MH.II, 358] After Tiberius consuls and praetors were elected by the Senate,[914] thus placing the election of officials directly in their hands. The procedure was a somewhat complex one, combining elements of lottery and seniority. This was already restricted by Severus Alexander: Dio[915] states that the senatorial link with the offices of consul and praetor remained, but that consideration of seniority ceased. The Emperor selected two candidates and had them draw lots for the provinces of Asia and Africa. He likewise appointed candidates for the praetorian provinces, who then drew lots for them.

This practice was retained in Diocletian's reorganization,[916] but the division of provinces between the Emperor and the Senate changed: probably as early as under Hadrian senatorial provinces requiring an army presence became imperial provinces, such as Bithynia and Pontus, which needed garrisons, despite being frontier provinces. The same applies to Sardinia, which was treated quite anomalously in this respect: at first it was an imperial province, then it was transferred to the Senate,[917] the sole senatorial province with a garrison, albeit only two cohorts strong.[918] Soon, however, it was taken back from the Senate by Severus[919] and made into a proconsular province. Others remained under senatorial administration for longer, but gradually [MH.II, 359] Baetica, Narbonensis, Macedonia, Sicily, Thrace and Crete were all taken from the Senate. Under Diocletian's constitution it retained only Achaea, Asia and Africa.[920]

Elections to consulships and praetorships were transferred by Tiberius from the *populus Romanus* to the Senate. Diocletian also extended this power; up to his time the imperial right of commendation had been in effect, i.e. the Emperor compiled a list of those *personae* who were *gratae* and from among whom appointments were to be made. From Diocletian onwards the Senates in Rome and Constantinople held free elections, but only after all offices had lost every trace of political importance and were no more than urban appointments. Only the *consules ordinarii* were imperial officials with Empire-wide authority,[921] because the years were dated after them. From then on, however, the Emperor was no longer obliged to find posts for erstwhile consuls and praetors. All in all, however, we can discern a huge difference between the Senate of Augustus and that of Diocletian: the former was an integral part of government, whereas the latter was a figurehead.

It cannot be emphasized too often or too much that the crux of co-rule lay in the obligation of the Emperor to elect certain persons. Initially there was a clear distinction between the Emperor's household and imperial officials of senatorial rank. Even the Praetorian Prefect, the [MH.II, 360] principal and most distinguished court official, was not a senator until the time of Alexander Severus. It may have been Severus and Caracalla who eradicated this distinction, since in their regimes we find Praetorian Prefects who were senators. All Alexander did was to stipulate the already organic fact that every Praetorian Prefect had to be a senator *eo ipso*. However, this should be construed as an enhancement not of senatorial status, but of the rank of Captain of the Guard.

The Emperor himself was originally a senator and in the better days of the principate hailed from the most distinguished families. Until the third century we cannot find a single Emperor who was not born into a senatorial family. Pertinax was the first, since although he was a senator when he ascended the throne, he had been born an equestrian, and his comparatively lowly origin[922] was soon to lead to catastrophe. The first Emperor of the equestrian class was Macrinus,[923] but he had the status of a *vir clarissimus* even as Praetorian Prefect. From then on there was a marked increase in the number of Emperors from the lower orders, which resulted in a general decline in the preferential treatment of the privileged classes. The government became plebeian and brutalized. What else can one expect, when an Emperor sits on the throne who was once a junior officer!

After Severus Alexander the *tribuni militum* vanished from the army. The military tribunate had been the elementary schooling of senatorial youths in the army; from there a young man moved on to a career as a magistrate. This ceased with [MH.II, 361] the last dynasty on the throne of imperial Rome – with Severus. From then on parvenus became the order, or rather disorder, of the day. Gallienus is attributed with having forbidden military service to senators,[924] but in doing so he was simply setting the legislative seal on an already 20-year-old practice.

Each legion and every province was presided over by an official of senatorial rank, a *legatus*, something akin to a modern adjutant.[925] This ceased from the second half of the third century onwards. As late as around 260 we find an inscription erected by a legate of senatorial rank in Britain;[926] the latest known mention of such a legate is in an inscription from Hispania Citerior and refers to Valentinian, a senator and *vir clarissimus* under Carinus.[927] There were masses of others besides these, as was inevitable if Gallienus indeed banned senators from military service.

The legions had the remarkable and relatively time-honoured institution of the *praefecti castrorum* or *legionis*.[928] In a manner of speaking this officer was a supplement to the legionary commander, who had to be a senator, and hence may not have been familiar with the details of military service. The *praefectus castrorum* was thus appointed as his second in command, a man who had worked his way up through the ranks and understood everything that the former did not. There is already mention in an early inscription from Britain of a *praefectus legionis* beside the *legatus legionis*. Later the legate [MH.II, 362] was dispensed with, thereby striking at the higher orders and their involvement in army command. From then on legionary commanders, like the Emperors, were drawn from among junior officers. Although these may have been more competent than their earlier noble counterparts, the army *esprit de corps* degenerated into ever greater brutalization.

Extant documentation about this period is extraordinarily scant on this score: much has been lost, and the official lists were forged. If we look to them for information we will be on very uncertain ground. One particularly baffling aspect is the use of the word *praeses* for provincial governor, regardless of whether the person in question was of senatorial rank or not.[929] We can generally assume, however, that this titulature was largely accorded to non-senatorial officials; the sole reliable criterion is the title of *vir clarissimus* for a senator,[930] and wherever this is not given the person in question was probably not a senator. Legates, who had to be of senatorial rank, were thus followed by the *praesides*, for whom this was not essential. Change occurred not by statute, but gradually, as personal or other circumstances required it; in Pannonia, for example, it occurred a full twenty years earlier than in Spain. When senators were excluded from the camps under Gallienus,[931] no systematic alternative arrangements were made; we can only speak of a general trend.

This notwithstanding, wherever a senator-governor still happened to be at the helm, he was deprived of his military command, thus bringing about that separation of military from civil service which was the hallmark of Diocletian's reorganization and which had been unknown in either the Republic or the early imperial period. A most interesting surviving [MH.II, 363] inscription from Pannonia[932] states that command was given to a prefect acting on behalf of a legate (*praefectus (legionis) agens vices legati*), and the context leads us to supplement this with *legionis*, not *provinciae*. It would have been possible simply to put *perfectissimus* or *egregius* beside *legatus*, but this was avoided in that the substitute was assumed to be *agens vices legati* or *praesidis*. The military authority of the legate was thus eroded by dividing the office between himself and a nominal substitute. In time both appointments were given to men of non-senatorial rank,[933] which was an outrageous act.

It should be added that purely civilian posts were left to senators; it was bad enough that they were excluded from all military command and most senior posts in civil administration. This reform had much the same effect as if the nobility today were declared unfit to hold comparable office in the state. Indeed, there was even an extension of senatorial competence in this regard, since from that time onwards Italy was also treated as a province and placed, like the *civitates liberae*, under *correctores* who, devoid of all military authority, were drawn from the senatorial class.[934]

This reform, in which civilian posts were essentially filled with senators and military posts with non-senators – in short, the separation of the military and civilian spheres – was organized under Diocletian, the great innovator. Soon, therefore, a separation occurred between the [MH.II, 364] military and civil spheres, which had up to that point completely corresponded. So-called 'duchies' were introduced for the purposes of military command. *Dux* (leader) had been a current word even earlier, but had had no meaning in terms of the military hierarchy. When speaking of a *dux* one had no particular rank in mind – it could equally well be the Emperor or a senior centurion, and corresponded approximately to the German word *Feldherr* (general, strategist), or *Führer* (leader). Such *ducatus militum*, akin to generalships, were now established on all frontiers. By and large, however, the former divisions remained intact. The Danube frontier or *limes Danubiensis*, to offer a specfic example, obtained eight *duces*, four of whom belonged to eastern, and four to western Rome. The eastern ones coincided with the provinces, but the western ones did not.[935] *Duces* were never drawn from the senatorial class; Ammianus[936] expressly states that even Constantius never appointed a *dux* who was a *clarissimus vir*. This was the realm of the common soldier and the man who had worked his way up.

The presidial or civil governorships were made a separate category, and the general rule here was that the most prestigious posts were filled by senators. Later a change of name occurred, in so far as a *praeses* who was an ex-consul was known not as *praeses consularis*, but simply as *consularis*. These offices were, all the same, presidial or civil governorships.

[MH.II, 365] Two further remarks concerning subsequent developments would be appropriate at this juncture. First, the old order had been unfamiliar with the concept of intermediate authorities as introduced by Diocletian – the proconsul had been directly responsible to the highest authority in the Empire. Diocletian introduced the diocese,[937] a sizeable administrative region comprising several provinces, a measure which probably related to the increased duties of the Praetorian Prefects. These auxiliary regions were subordinate to vicars, representatives of the Prefects, who already existed earlier. The huge scope of their business, therefore, was subdivided because it had to be. This marked the beginning of the dioceses. Twelve large regions were initially created, each headed by a vicar who was solely a civilian official and was not at all involved with the duties of his ducal counterpart. Diocletian appears not to have created similar intermediate authorities for the military. Later, under Constantine, but perhaps not until the time of Constantius II, local Masters of the Soldiers[938] were installed to whom the *duces* were subordinate, as the *praesides* were to the vicars.

A separation of civilian and military activities was also set in motion for the most senior post below the Emperor, that of Praetorian Prefect. Unfortunately our knowledge of this area is scant, but it would appear that circumstances continued unchanged until the time of Constantine,[939] under whom two Praetorian Prefects governed the entire Empire, [MH.II, 366] united under him. The vicars were called *vicarii praefectorum praetorio*, i.e. representatives of these two.[940] The division of the Empire probably manifested itself in a division of competences and of duties. Like the Praetorian Prefects, the Caesars were appointed for the whole Empire.

The combined civilian and military post of Praetorian Prefect probably persisted until the time of Constantine. The disbanding of the Praetorian Guard set in motion by Diocletian was completed by Constantine,[941] and probably went hand in hand with the loss of his military duties by the Praetorian Prefect and the introduction of the Master of the Soldiers. This probably occurred in the latter part of Constantine's reign and is documented by Zosimus.[942] The Praetorian Prefect retained the most senior civilian post, as it were the premiership, but not his military command. Later there was a further division of the Praetorian Prefect's competence. Three great imperial territories were created: a western one, comprising Spain, Gaul and Britain; a central one, comprising Italy, Africa and the Danube lands; and the entire East. This undoubtedly went hand in hand with a division of hierarchical authorities and competences.

The picture which has unfolded before you in these lectures is not a pleasant one; not one of the actors has really been able to arouse any lasting interest and it is, indeed, appropriate to ask [MH.II, 367] whether it is even a good idea to set one's shovel to such rubble. History, however, is not a toy, but a serious matter, and the history of that period, in particular, is of the greatest importance for the immediate present.

All history, however, should be considered in terms of how it relates to the present, so that even knowledge of that dreadful heap of rubble will not be entirely useless, for without it the history of the early Middle Ages in particular would be quite incomprehensible. Moreover, these ruins gave rise to fresh shoots of life and, ultimately, our own life.[943]

A HISTORY OF ROME UNDER THE EMPERORS III FROM DIOCLETIAN TO ALARIC

Winter Semester 1885/6 and Summer Semester 1886 [MH.III]

From the fair copy of lecture notes by Sebastian Hensel

1

GENERAL INTRODUCTION

[MH.III, 1] The era of Diocletian bears the mark of decline, and does not attract our sympathy. The significance of this era, however, is all the greater because of this very decline and the paucity of intellectual resources at its disposal. The dominate of Diocletian and Constantine differs more sharply from the principate than the latter does from the Republic. The oriental ruler provides the model for the dominate. Whereas the unity of the Empire prevailed under the principate, the division of the Empire prevailed under the dominate. The nationalities divided into a Greek and a Latin half. Whereas the principate had been Latin-Greek, the dominate was Greek-Latin. There is a different capital city; Italy loses its privileged status, and there is a complete reform of the administration. The military machine turns into an effective and mobile one; the principate had had only frontier garrison troops. Foreigners now join the army, above all Germans. An effective administration of finance also develops and Constantine reintroduces a universally current gold coin, the *solidus*. A new religion emerges which, although not exactly Christian, nevertheless still differs from that of the principate.

[MH.III, 2] The historiography of events is also an improvement on that under the principate.[1] Eunapius and his like are not of high calibre, but Ammianus Marcellinus of Antioch, an imperial *protector*, is better. Although actually a Greek, he writes in Latin, since Latin was regarded as the language of the educated. He has an honest and upright nature. His geographical and antiquarian digressions are of little merit, but the historical content as such is excellent. The period from 353 to 378 survives. We are worse off for the following period, since the better works have been lost. A good school of history nevertheless continues in Byzantium, including Priscus and others. One can raise some objections against Procopius, for example of his contradictory assessments of Justinian in his published writings and in the *Secret History*. He is, nonetheless, a very important author.[2]

State registers and collections of decrees have survived: the *Notitia Dignitatum*[3] and the *Codex Theodosianus*,[4] although the former contains later insertions and corrections. The section on Britain in the *Notitia* gives an account of conditions in the previous century. Generally it records the conditions at the time of Stilicho (died 408). Seeck estimates the date of authorship [MH.III, 3] at 413–16. The *Codex Theodosianus* is likewise unique: earlier collections of decrees, the *Codex Gregorianus* and the *Codex Hermogenianus*, contain judgments passed by the Emperor's court. The *Theodosianus* is a collection of laws published under Theodosius II in 438 and extending from the time of Constantine up to Theodosius II. Almost all of it has survived, apart from some gaps in the first five books.

Religious polemics comprise a major source, albeit one far removed from real political life. It only takes account of it in passing. Perhaps the sole exception to this is Lactantius's *De mortibus persecutorum*, written in 313.[5] Julian's writings are important from a different perspective.

Modern accounts of the period begin with Tillemont; his is the real seminal work. Tillemont was first and foremost a Church historian, fanatically Catholic, but a fine collator of material. Gibbon still represents the most important work ever to be written on Roman history, offering a fine résumé and telling characterizations. The scholarship is overestimated, and it is also partisan, a counterbalance to Tillemont, since Gibbon is an atheist. Hertzberg is bad. Jacob Burckhardt's *Constantine* is brilliant and stimulating, although perhaps not right in its interpretation. H. Richter's *Geschichte des weströmischen Reichs*, which in fact deals only with the period from 375 to 388, has a good introduction. [MH.III, 4] There is nothing really good to read on administration and the constitution. Excellent as an introduction is Bethmann Hollweg's *Civilprocess*.[6]

2

GOVERNMENT AND SOCIETY

[MH.III, 5] The Constantinian monarchy transformed the principles of government.[7] The principate and the Republic had concurred in their fundamentals: administration was in the hands of a man capable of governing, and power in the hands of the aristocracy. Italy dominated the provinces.

The principle of hereditary succession asserts itself in every monarchy, but never was it as insignificant as under the principate, and that did nobody any harm, as those who came to power through inheritance demonstrate: Gaius, Domitian and Commodus. The standard mode of succession is the selection of a successor by his predecessor, known as adoption. Natural children were frequently passed over in the process.[8] Dynastic proclivities are in evidence among the Julians and the successors of Septimius Severus, in the former instance sanctioned by the people, in the latter by the *soldatesca*. Aside from the first half of Nero's reign, we can discern no signs of ministerial government: the actions of the government are represented as the actions of the Emperor.

The ancient aristocracy survived up to the Flavians, who ushered in government by the middle classes, the 'municipals'. However, even this second regime was that of a privileged class. This is expressed through co-rule by the Senate, which should not be construed as something akin to a parliament. It is based on the principle that all high-ranking administrative and military offices were the preserve of the highest social circles, corresponding to a career ladder which involved a rigid sequence of offices. Parvenus were effectively excluded, as in England. During the third century, however, this system broke down. The group which elected the *princeps* was changing. Theoretically, the principle was that election was by the Senate or the soldiers – the latter point is of great importance. We should not envisage here some kind of formal military constitution. Whether an election was deemed high treason or not depended on whether or not it was successful. This was already apparent in 68–9, the Year of Four Emperors. In the third century, however, the principle of election by the soldiers became established and marked the [MH.III, 6] end of the aristocracy's power. It was once even explicitly stated[9] that a senator was incapable of being a soldier. Thus the soldiers also elected men from their own ranks.

Italy's dominance over the provinces came to an end in the period of the principate. Once the Emperors had been Italians, and even Trajan's family had moved to Rome. There were no Italians among the soldier-Emperors: most of them were Illyrians.

In the new age the monarchy became dynastic. In terms of their origins Diocletian and Maximian were still Emperors of the old school, but Diocletian laid the foundations for a new world: a monarchy with a succession, a true monarchy. This began not with Diocletian himself, however, but with his co-ruler Constantius I. A fictive genealogy is indicative of this: the lineage of Constantius is traced back to the Emperor Claudius II, for example in the *Panegyricus* addressed to Constantine in 310. His son and grandson were the first to style themselves in this way in the inscriptions, inconsistently and incorrectly. The fiction itself indicates that it was needed.[10]

Diocletian and Maximian were called *Aurelius* and *Valerius*; although these names were transferred to the Caesars, they were dropped. The crucial name is that of the *Flavii*. The new system was introduced in the guise of a *gens Flavia*; we also find *Julius* and later *Claudius*. The dropping of the *praenomen* is noteworthy: the last Emperor to use it was Maxentius.[11] This too is not without significance: the Greek name outweighs the Latin form – Maxentius represented the reaction of the *urbs Roma*. The family name had become so unspecific that it had ceased to have any importance: the important name was the *cognomen*.

The dynastic idea soon gained huge potency; Constantine was accepted as ruler by hereditary right. [MH.III, 7] The catastrophe which occurred after his death in 337 bears this out: the officers demanded of the three sons of Constantine that they be ruled by no one else.[12] Recourse was thus made to the princes. The dynasty of Valentinian lasted for a further century, albeit only if we include Theodosius.[13]

An era of utter confusion set in after the mid-fifth century. Only the dynasty of Augustus can be compared with it in Roman history. The Emperors were in fact incapable of governing, and yet enjoyed undisputed power. Not even then, however, was there a succession in our understanding of the term – a developed system of monarchy. In fact the earlier principle of the Empire being passed on by the Senate or the soldiery still prevailed. Appointments were now invariably made by the soldiery; all the Senate did was register their choice. It was possible to avoid this by installing a co-regent; the sons of Constantine, who were Caesars, did not become Augusti *eo ipso*. There were periods of vacancy: for six months the Empire was ruled in the name of the deceased Constantine. Then the soldiers appointed the three sons of Constantine as Augusti.[14] In general, appointments were now made in a more orderly fashion, with the Emperor emerging after consultation with the officers of the main army.[15] Even in the case of hereditary succession confirmation was given in the same way: there had been no change under constitutional law.

What was the key idea behind the monarchy in this period?[16] The contrast between princeps and Senate ran through the entire principate. From the earliest time the *princeps* was viewed as legitimate and dominant; the office of *princeps* is, after all, a blend of familiar features from the Republic – *pontifex maximus*, *tribunis plebis*, *proconsul*, etc. The old titulature was not discarded; it survived [MH.III, 8] in the city of Rome in particular, the last known instance perhaps being on the Ponte Cestio, in 369.[17] It seldom occurred in the West and hardly at all in the East. On coins it disappeared.

There was increased emphasis on the title *Augustus*, since the old tripartite title[18] highlighted the magisterial nature of the Emperor's position. The title *Pius felix* made an early appearance[19] and was already imbued with supernatural overtones. Later there was frequent use of the titles *perpetuus Augustus* and *semper Augustus* (forever Augustus). The word *dominus*, which initially denoted slave-owners, became a new title for the Emperor, as well as for a god.[20] Throughout the entire principate this title vied with the legitimate one; even the earlier Emperors had difficulty fending off adulation of this kind.[21] Gradually the dominate prevailed. Domitian was already a key figure in this process.[22] In the third century this way of addressing the Emperor began to gain ground, but there was still reluctance about introducing it as a formal title. The coins are an expression of official power: in the reign of Aurelian the title *dominus* first appeared on coins, combined with *deus*: *domino et deo nato* – born to be lord and god.[23] We might supplement this with: *servi nati cives Romani* – Roman citizens born to be slaves. From then onwards it appeared more frequently on coins, especially in the case of other Emperors, but still the Emperor did not style himself as such until the era of the sons of Constantine. This marks another victory for the Greek element:[24] among the Greeks the deification of the living is as ancient as monarchy itself. The ceremony of adoration was a practical application of this; people shook hands with the earlier Emperors, or kissed them, like other distinguished persons. Diocletian introduced genuflection.[25] This, too, represented a move closer to the oriental idea.[26] It aroused opposition in Rome. The idea of the Emperor as a deity could not be reconciled with Christianity: the idea of the god on earth was abandoned, the lord on earth remained.

There was a marked increase in symbolic insignia, pomp and circumstance.[27] Previously the Emperor had been essentially indistinguishable from a magistrate. The royal purple was then no more than the red cloak of the general, worn by the Emperor as sole holder of that office. Diocletian adopted the use of [MH.III, 9] gold embroidery on imperial robes, and Constantine introduced the diadem, which had earlier been worn only by women and deities.[28]

To what extent may we still speak of the unity of the Empire? The starting point of the entire transformation was division – the introduction of localized, separate spheres of competence. Those elements of imperial unity that still remained lent the Empire the appearance of a unified state. This was expressed in the titulature. Technically, reference was made to the *partes Orientes* and *partes Occidentes*.[29] There was complete parity in administration, though promotion occurred only within one of the sectors of the Empire.[30] Unity continued to manifest itself in three areas: outwardly in matters of war and peace, and internally in legislation and the consulships. All acts of government were carried out in the name of both Emperors, in order of seniority. The manner in which legislation was enacted also marked a break with the past: the *princeps* did not really have the power to legislate, since laws were enacted by the Senate. *De facto*, although not formally, the boundaries between *edictum* and *lex* became highly fluid. Edicts addressed to private individuals gradually ceased, although the right to approach the Emperor was not actually banned until Justinian. In contrast, the Emperor now assumed the right to legislate. It is certainly no coincidence that the *Codex Theodosianus* begins in the year 312.[31] Lawmaking devolved on the Augusti, not on the Caesars. Where the latter are named in the texts of laws,[32] therefore, this is purely out of deference. How did the Emperors conduct themselves, now that there were two supreme sources of legislation? The *status quo ante* seems to have prevailed for another century. In 429 a decree was passed stipulating that a law to be promulgated in one Emperor's part of the Empire first had to be sent to his counterpart, and only came into force when it had also been promulgated in the other part of the Empire.[33] These regulations applied to the *Codex Theodosianus* itself, as well as to the Novels[34] of the Theodosian Code. It would appear that, following the fall of the western Roman Empire, the laws of eastern Rome were formally also promulgated [MH.III, 10] for the West.

The consulate no longer had any direct political significance. Even its presidency of the Senate may have lapsed in this period. The honour consisted solely in that the first pair of consuls gave their names to the year[35] and this system of dating remained valid for the entire Empire. The right to appoint consuls lay with the Emperor; during the tetrarchy it seems to have been reserved for Diocletian.[36]

The formal division of the Empire occurred in 364.[37] An agreement seems to have been reached that each ruler would propose one of the consuls and both be promulgated simultaneously. The dating *post consulatum*, which first occurred in 307, indicates confusion.[38] This was a frequent occurrence, since the procedure resulted in delays. There was a change in 399.[39] The eunuch Eutropius had been designated consul for this year, but the court at Ravenna and Stilicho objected.[40] This evidently led to a break with the old system: joint promulgation was temporarily abandoned in favour of a new practice of first nominating the consul for one's own part of the Empire.

It is remarkable how this was handled in the barbarian states after the fall of the western Empire.[41] Both the Vandals and the Visigoths at first continued to date years in the manner customary in the Empire. The western consul, of course, had precedence. Some inconsistency can be discerned among the Franks: for the most part dating followed the years of government, although the ancient custom tended to prevail in regions which had previously been Burgundian. From 501 there was evidently a joint system agreed between Theoderic and the eastern Empire; from then on the western consul reappears. According to Procopius, the eastern Empire wished to appoint him too. Cassiodorus states that Theoderic appointed the western consul.[42] Probably the king or his Senate had the right to make a proposal, but the appointment was confirmed by the Emperor. In the kingdom of Theoderic years were dated by the western consul only. This ceased with the outbreak of the Gothic War. *Post consulatum Paulini* (i.e. 534) *anno NN*[43] then became the official Gothic date during this war.

[MH.III, 11] The new administration differed from the earlier one in three respects. There was government by civil servants, with the Emperor withdrawing to the position of a true monarch. There was a hierarchy of officials with a chain of authority. The concept of a sphere of competence was not applicable to the princeps,[44] since all offices merged in him. This persisted, but administration became diffused on the basis of locality and specific branches of administration. Although the separation of administration from the judiciary was still unknown, there was, nevertheless, a sharp distinction between the civilian and military spheres.

The division of spheres of competence was along geographical lines. The consequences of Diocletian's division of the Empire into two, with four subdivisions, are still with us. The foundations of this are of global historical importance and date back to a much earlier period. The Republic and the principate alike had tried to paper over the gulf between East and West. But an external separation was already apparent in the Augustan organization of the army, in the distinction it made between western and eastern legions, as manifested in changes in their encampments. What initially applied to the military sphere alone later came to regulate the entire Empire.

Marcus Aurelius appointed his brother Lucius Verus to rule beside him;[45] up to this time there had only ever been one Augustus. Even now, however, they ruled without a separation of spheres of authority, just as the consuls had done before them. Diocletian thus introduced something new, and of his own volition. A tetrarchy soon arose, with two rulers subordinate to the first two: in 292 the Augusti added two Caesars with a certain authority, but a subordinate one.[46] This tetrarchy essentially persisted; later it developed into the four districts of the Praetorian Prefects.

The principal region of the Empire was always *Oriens et Aegyptus*,[47] by now a specific geographical term. Dependent on it as its Caesarian region were Greece, Macedonia, Thrace and eastern Illyricum. The linguistic boundary was always

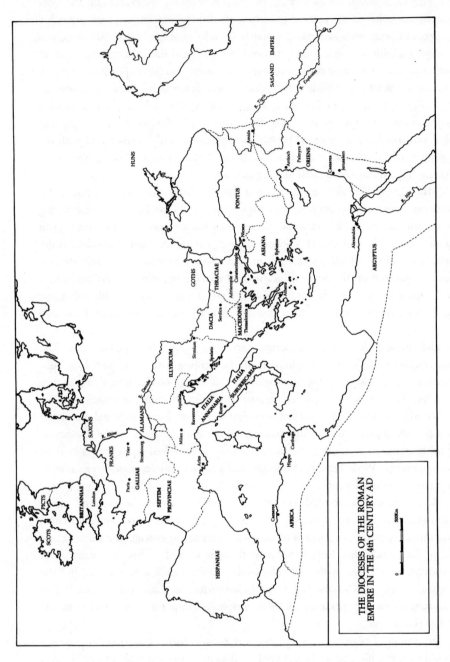

Map 3 The dioceses of the Roman Empire in the fourth century AD

taken as a basis.[48] The region of the western Augustus consisted of Italy and Africa, including western Illyricum (Pannonia). Gaul, Spain and Britain formed the Caesarian portion of the West. During this period Illyricum was to some extent the centre of the Empire; it was divided up. But this division was primarily associated with the person of the Emperor: it was not intended that these four parts should always remain the same. [MH.III, 12] In a certain sense, therefore, we cannot speak of a division of the Empire until later.

Constantine ascended the imperial throne after the ensuing confusion. Even so, the former division was again used to demarcate governmental regions: the four Praetorian Prefects were ministers with a certain authority. Subsequently two such Praetorian Prefects were appointed as subordinates to every Augustus.

In addition to this division of the supreme offices there were also second and third tiers which now manifested a threefold, and effectively fourfold, chain of authority. Supreme authority was, of course, still in the hands of the Emperor, whose personal intervention was not precluded in exceptional circumstances. But the first point of decision lay with the representative of the province, then that of the diocese, then the Praetorian Prefect.

Diocletian divided the Empire into thirteen dioceses[49] – this is a Greek word; Cicero[50] had already been familiar with dioceses as judicial districts in Asia. The same term is also encountered in a different context, primarily denoting Africa and Tarraconensis, which were subdivided into administrative districts. But in the new order the provinces were grouped into dioceses. With respect to the Praetorian Prefect they were either governed by a Praetorian prefect directly, or by a *vicarius praefectorum praetorio*. The vicars too were officials of the Emperor, not of the Prefects. Complaints relating to them passed directly to the Emperor. The dioceses comprised: *Oriens et Aegyptus* (i.e. Syria and Egypt), Pontus (from the lower Danube onwards) and Moesia, Pannonia (on the central and upper Danube), *Urbs Roma*, including southern Italy (the *vicarius in urbe Roma*), *Italia* (i.e. northern Italy, Gallia Cisalpina and Picenum), Viennensis (southern Gaul, or *quinque* or *septem provinciae*), northern Gaul, Spain, Africa and Britain. Later *Aegyptus* was also separated from Syria.

Each diocese was made up of provinces, and a glance at these shows that the proposition that the provinces were broken up is correct. Italy was now drawn into the ranks of the provinces. The *vicarius in urbe* governed seven provinces, including the three islands,[51] plus Bruttia, Calabria, Campania and Tuscum. *Oriens et Aegyptus* united five previous provinces; *Aegyptus* had previously comprised Egypt and Cyrenaica, but now it was broken up into Upper, Central and Lower Egypt. Gallia consisted of five provinces: Germania [MH.III, 13] Inferior and Superior, Belgica, Lugdunensis, Alpes Graiae and Cottiae; the diocese was now subdivided into seven departments: Germania I and II, Belgica I and II (Alpes Graie and Cottiae remained as they were) and Lugdunensis I and II. There was thus an attempt to create equivalent entities. We have no Latin technical term for the highest administrative level, the region of the Praetorian Prefect. The two capitals, Rome and Constantinople, governed by Urban Prefects, were exempt from provincial administration, as were the proconsulships.[52]

Italy had previously governed itself autonomously under senatorial supervision. This privilege was now reserved for Rome alone, albeit under a chief of police, the Urban Prefect.[53] The new Rome, Byzantium, was administered in the same manner. In terms of rank and absolute power the Urban Prefects were equal to the Praetorian Prefects. The proconsular regions comprised what was left of the senatorial provinces. Appointments other than those made by the Emperor were abolished: proconsuls were now appointed by the Emperor. Those who remained, however, were directly responsible to the Emperor, not to the Praetorian Prefects; Africa was by now little more than Carthage and the surrounding area, and Asia comprised Ephesus and its immediate surroundings.

The official was perceived as a thoroughly military figure. Imperial governors were all officers. In the case of the procurators this was not originally the case, but now the idea was implemented here, too. The sole exceptions were the Urban Prefect, who still wore the toga, and the proconsuls. The *cingulum* (belt) marked out other officials as military. Even civilian officials were regarded as military: people spoke of *militia militaris* or *armata* and *militia palatina* ('military' military service, or 'armed' or 'court' military service). The old system of junior officers [MH.III, 14] set its stamp on junior *officiales*. The principle of heredity gained a certain sway over the civil service philosophy; that originated from the military sphere, where heredity played a crucial role in military service. Camp children were regarded as born to the obligations of a soldier's life. The same applies to the low-status *officialis*. The hereditary principle became a widespread phenomenon applying to every service to the state, *functio*. Promotion was awarded according to years of service. The term of the subaltern career was twenty to twenty-five years. Regular periods of service were natural in the military sphere: it is the state within the fully developed military-bureaucratic state.

Relative ranks acquired a significance they had certainly not had previously.[54] The principate inherited from the earlier Republic the distinction between senators and non-senators, as well as a hereditary nobility. Non-senatorial officials were regarded as domestic officials and were paid; this distinguished them from senatorial magistrates. In the case of the imperial offices the salaried classes became social ranks. A new hierarchy arose through the conflation of these two career structures. But social rank was always a personal matter. A personal aristocracy of office arose. Heredity persisted in the case of senatorial rank, i.e. for the *clarissimi*, the penultimate of the four ranked classes. There is, however, also a nobility not based on office-holding, the patriciate, which was always bestowed by the Emperors. Little use seems to have been made of this prior to Constantine, when it was made into the highest rank, but was not hereditary.[55]

The hierarchy of ranks in the latter period probably goes back to an act passed by Valentinian and Valens in 372.[56] It is based on the three status groups, with the senatorial *clarissimi* being added. The highest-ranking officials, responsible directly to the Emperor, were the *viri illustres*: essentially the Praetorian Prefects, Masters of the Soldiers and Urban Prefects. [MH.III, 15] On the second level were the *viri spectabiles*, i.e. the vicars of the Praetorian prefects, the proconsuls and later also the *duces*. The third level comprised the *viri clarissimi*, i.e. the ex-consuls. The fourth level were the *perfectissimi*, a title which already appears in the third century; previously it had belonged to the second class in the procuratorial career. The rank of *egregius* was evidently eliminated after Constantine. These were now governors in general.[57]

The first, second and fourth ranks developed out of the procuratorial career structure, the third out of the senatorial. This was still hereditary, and was often connected with the rank of the *illustres*. In terms of personal ranking the consuls belonged to the *illustres*, among whom they held the senior position during their period of office; then came the patricians, and only then the Praetorian Prefects. When listing his titles, a senator would ususally describe himself as *vir clarissimus*. Besides the patriciate there was an aristocracy not based on office, created by the grant of an honorary office through *honorii codicilli*.

With respect to the periods of office, the old system for the most part continued. The principate had appointed its officials for an arbitrary length of time. Under the new monarchy too there was no instance of anyone being appointed for life. Every appointment was made until the functionary was recalled, generally after three to four years, although people were frequently reappointed to the same office.

A reorganization of the army had become imperative.[58] It was required by threats to the frontiers, peasant unrest, the Bagaudic movement and the uprising in Egypt. A similar situation prevailed in Asia Minor, which was wracked by banditry and incessant blockades against the Isaurians. The army was quadrupled in size (see MH.III, 16). A clear distinction was made between the army proper and the *intra palatium* troops, who included *domestici, protectores* and *scholae*. There were also *comitatenses* and *palatini* in the army proper, though these were field forces.[59] The cavalry and infantry were kept completely separate through all the ranks up to the supreme command.[60] In the cavalry, the units had the titles *vexillatio, cuneus equitum* and *ala*, which probably denotes simply a difference of rank. The *vexillatio* was the most distinguished designation, probably for the old legionary cavalry, often used as a separate detachment. Nothing can be said [MH.III, 16] about its numerical strength, although the old system of divisions of 1,000 or 500 men may well have been retained.

The infantry was more important. Here, too, the old system of divisions was probably retained. The legion comprised 5,500 men, as before, as well as (auxiliary) cohorts. Now, however, these were joined by a third component, the *auxilia*, not to be confused with the old auxiliary cohorts. As far as the numerical strength of the army in general is concerned, it was long believed that the size of specific legions was reduced, but it should be stated that normally they still numbered 5,000–6,000 men. All later authors quote this figure.[61] The frontier armies corresponded to those of the earlier period. We have exact details about Pontus, for example in Arrian;[62] the same two legions, cohorts and *alae* were still stationed there. The situation on the Danube and Euphrates was left as it was, which is a strong indication of the stability of the body of legionaries. Arrian provides a reliable enumeration of all the legions in particular;[63] for this reason there is a widespread assumption that (in the fourth century) there were 132 legions. This figure, however, applies to the field army only; it does not include the frontier army.[64] If this is included we arrive at a figure of around 100 legions for the East and some seventy for the West. Besides these there were also cavalry and *auxilia*. The figure for the legions, then, is 800,000 men and, when all the rest are added, some 1,200,000 men. This figure should come as no surprise. We have two other sources of information: Lactantius[65] criticizes Diocletian for quadrupling the size of the army. This, of course, should be taken with a pinch of salt, although it does concur with our results if Lactantius is thinking of the usual strength of the army in the better imperial era: 400,000 men. We can also find traces of the increases of the fourth century in the *Notitia Dignitatum*. Lactantius's assertion of a quadrupling may, therefore, be an exaggeration. The second source is Agathias.[66] He states that the normal size of the army was 645,000 men, but that at that time, under Justinian, it was not nearly so large and comprised only 150,000 men. Bearing in mind that these figures pertain to the East only, this brings us back to our previous [MH.III, 17] figure. This number of troops is of great importance, both for historical and political reasons. This seems to be a remarkable achievement, but the other side of the coin was the invisible discrepancy between effective numbers and numbers on paper. Under Justinian only a quarter of the forces on paper were actually in service. The situation must have been desperate earlier too, however, when seven legions and an armed force of citizens within a city numbered just 20,000, even if this was in the dark days of the Persian Wars.[67]

The common soldier increasingly hailed from the very lowest orders of the population. Augustus had wanted to bring the educated classes into the army, but the extent to which this had changed is indicated by Henzen no. 6686, which dates from the third century.[68] The task of enlisting troops, which devolved mainly on landowners, was thus for the most part carried out using *coloni*, many of whom were settled barbarians. This latter element should not, however, be over-estimated, or the distinction between the legions and the *auxilia* would have disappeared. Educated men could be found among the officer ranks.[69] It was unheard of for a man from a respectable background to enter the army as a private. Heredity was a crucial factor: frontier troops were permitted to marry. The cohorts disappeared at this point because few new ones were formed; they were found only among the frontier troops, like the *alae*, since the frontier troops constituted the old army.

The new element in this age were the *auxilia*; in the *Notitia Dignitatum* this designation applies to foot soldiers only. They were held in higher esteem than the legions and dated back to the time of Diocletian. It is possible to ascertain their numbers. There were more *auxilia* in the West and the *Notitia* gives their number as 102 overall. It is not known how many men there were in specific units, but these were probably based on the numerical strength of the old cohorts and thus under no circumstances amounted to more than 100,000 men in total. The *auxilia* consituted the purely barbaric elements – the Germanic ones, we might say. Even this primacy of Germanic soldiers was not quite new, if we remember the Batavian *equites singulares*. The names of virtually all *auxilia* in the *Notitia* are those of Germanic tribes, apart from the Scottish [MH.III, 18] Attacotti and some auxiliary levies. The Batavians and Salians were part of the Empire, but most of the other tribes were not. Ammianus Marcellinus[70] reports that opposition to Constantius arose out of his breach of an agreement with the Gaulish-Germanic *auxilia*, whom he summoned to the East from their service in Gaul, in contra-vention of their contract. This shows that most of them were foreign volunteers. There were Frankish officers at court later, too,[71] but they were no longer the dominant element they had been earlier. The ethnic origins of the later Byzantine Emperors themselves can already be sensed – they were Armenians and Isaurians.[72] The principle remained the same, to inject fresh blood by using barbarians; the next step was the dissolution of the Empire into barbarian king-ships.[73] The *foederati* were evidently *auxilia* who had accepted a treaty, a *foedus*, on entering service.

A semi-military institution, also known from the *Notitia*, as the *laeti et gentiles*. Were these soldiers or farmers? Their settlements, which are found only in Italy and Gaul,[74] were partly German, partly Sarmatian. They were administered as *praefecturae*; each settlement was presided over by a prefect, which is a military designation. *Gentiles* is a term that requires no clarification: they were barbarians. *Laeti* is a word that has no equivalent in Latin; it is simply Germanic and must be identified with the *liti* of Salian law and other Germanic law codes. They were the dependent local *Leute*, 'people' (like the Roman *laeti*) but not subject to a private individual, but in a subject relationship with the state as *coloni*. Thus the same people were not necessarily *laeti* in their own homelands. Ammianus[75] expresses this succinctly when he says that Julian wanted to send to Constantius 'Some *laeti*, a tribe of Germans from this side of the Rhine, or those who have come over to our side'. This also answers the question of where all the *auxilia* came from. These prefectures were intended to be their training schools. The *praefecturae* should not be ascribed an immediate military significance; conditions here were similar to those on the military frontier.

The troops stationed at court were under the command of the *comites domesticorum*[76] and the *magister* [MH.III, 19] *officiorum*.[77] Known as *scholae*, these troops were divided into two divisions, each under separate command. The *schola* was a waiting area, particularly for subaltern officials, who needed it as a place of assembly. The Latin word *statio* is equivalent to the Greek *scholé* (bureau). It was, after all, the nature of court troops that they were deployed at specific points in the palace. There was a special corps of veterans and cadets (*protectores domestici*)[78] and the *scholae* in the stricter sense of the term. The latter, the palace troops proper, were the flower of the barbarian militia. These were divided into the *scutarii*, *armaturae* and *gentiles*, the latter title being a clear indication of their origins. The barbarian origins of the entire corps is documented.[79] Procopius[80] states that previously, by which he means the time of Leo (457–74), they were levied from among Armenians. Indigenous inhabitants of the Empire were not accepted into the corps. Agathias[81] discusses their high pay and magnificent appearance. We learn of their numbers from Procopius: at that time they totalled 3,500 men. Their division evidently comprised[82] 500 men, equivalent to the smaller cohort. Among the *scutarii* we find a cavalry troop; the *armaturae* must likewise have served on horseback. Nonetheless, the majority of the *scholares* were foot soldiers. In Ammianus[83] the *scutarii* are described as *gentiles scutarii*, which provides another indication of their origins.

The Guards unit was under the command of the Master of Offices, or majordomo.[84] In earlier times this duty had belonged to the Praetorian Prefects, who were stripped of their military offices in the Constantinian period[85] and their command was transferred to the Master of Offices. In the Theodosian Code[86] this office is referred to as 'Tribune and Master of the Offices'. The legionary tribunate disappeared, although the cohort tribune in the frontier army remained. Previously every Praetorian cohort had had a tribune. This was adopted for the individual *scholae*, whose commanders were among the most distinguished officers in the whole army.

However, the imperial court employed another set of officials holding officer rank who were hence also called *tribunus*, [MH.III, 20] for example the *tribunus stabulorum*.[87] There is frequent mention of *tribuni et notarii*,[88] where 'tribune' is again merely a rank. The same applies to the 'Tribune and Master of the Offices' of which the second half of the title on its own remained the customary form. This officer had the *officia*, i.e. the bureaux, under his command, the so-called *scrinia*.[89]

We can distinguish between four departments (*scrinia*) in the imperial chancellery under *magistri*: *memoriae*, *epistolarum*, *dispositionum* and *libellorum*. The Master of the Offices was in charge of *admissiones*, i.e. audiences. Under his supervision were the *curiosi omnium provinciarum* (the police) and the *agentes in rebus* (the subordinate police), as well as the *interpretes omnium gentium* (interpreters of barbarians). We can see even from the earliest of these arrangements that the Master of the Offices received petitions from all over the Empire. He had the title *vir illustris*.

The nature of the new era was nowhere more clearly discernible than in the *protectores domestici* (see MH.III, 19). Already in the previous era it was not unknown for private soldiers who had served in the ranks to work their way up to an officer's post, but only rarely. This also applied in the Guard, but the Emperors became ever more suspicious of them, so that soon individual tried-and-tested soldiers who had already run their term of service were appointed as 'Protectors of the Emperor's Person'; initially they did not form a corps, but were individually appointed to the imperial staff, where they constituted a kind of officers' training school cum veteran corps. Probably from the time of Constantine, these *protectores* were joined by the *domestici*, who were young men of ancient lineage who wanted to become officers, i.e. cadets.[90] This represented a reinstatement of the nobility. Since both groups were would-be officers, they were united in a single corps, the *protectores domestici*, which included both cavalry and infantry. These, too, were designated *scholae*, but did not form part of the Guard proper, since they were only used on individual duty. All of them began with service in the palace. Later on they came under the command of a *comes domesticorum* (*equitum* and *peditum*), presumably therefore under the Master of the Offices.[91]

In general we may distinguish between two groups: the old frontier army and the new field army. The fighting men of the frontier army, made up of *legiones* and *vexillationes*, were called *riparienses* or *ripenses*, *castriciani* or *pseudocomitatenses*.[92] Officer ranks are listed in the *minor laterculus*.[93] The other army, also made [MH.III, 21] up of *legiones* and *vexillationes*, consisted of *comitatenses*; for the frontier army was in fact tied to the *castra* (fortresses), which were located almost exclusively on *ripae*, the frontier rivers of the Empire. The field army comprised those in the Emperor's entourage *qui sunt in comitatu imperatoris*.[94] The designation *palatini* is more recent. In inscription *CIL* III, 5565,[95] dated 310, we already find a reference to a troop of Dalmatian cavalry, *equites Dalmatae*, as *comitatenses*, which means that this institution must predate Constantine. The bulk of the frontier army was made up of legions, with additional *alae*, *cohortes*, etc. *Auxiliares* are not the same as *auxilia* but local militias in Illyria. They lacked the more distinguished troop categories of the *auxilia* and *vexillationes*. The commander was called the *dux limitis*; we are dealing here only with the frontier army. These were responsible for the frontiers of the Empire, with the exception of Isauria, where there were forces under a *comes* to deal with bandits,[96] as in the case of the *comes litoris Saxonici per Britanniam*[97] on both sides of the Channel, and the *dux tractus Armoricani et Nervicani*,[98] to deal with Saxon pirate raids. Regions of this kind can be found virtually right across the Empire; each one was fairly large and their commanders were called *duces limitis*.[99] This *dux* was the equivalent of the old provincial legate. We know that the old governorships did not cease until the third century, like the old legions. As a result of this we often find *duces* appointed as extraordinary commanders with no specific duties.[100] Later *dux* became the standard title of a military commander. Inscription *CIL* III, 5565, dated 310, records conditions under Diocletian. Probably older still is *CIL* III, 764,[101] which refers to a *dux limitis provinciae Scythiae*; later he was generally known simply as *dux*, as in Zosimus.[102] On this basis we can assume that when Constantine introduced the office of Masters of the Soldiers the post of *ducatus* was already in existence.

The crucial feature here was total separation of the military and civilian spheres.[103] The *dux* wielded only military authority. Hence the increasing prevalence of military trials, which from Honorius on even applied to civil actions brought against soldiers.[104] The sole exception to this rule was in certain districts where the civilian governor was called *dux* and *praeses*, but this was in districts of extreme barbarity and insecurity, in Sardinia, Isauria, Arabia and Mauretania. The *duces* and frontier troops were directly responsible to the Emperor. Only when an accusation was brought against a *dux* did it go before the [MH.III, 22] Master of the Soldiers, since the Emperor increasingly avoided real intervention. It was a mark of Stilicho's encroachment in this regard that the *duces* were made subordinate to the Master of the Soldiers.[105] The word came to be used as a title replacing the name of the office held; the more distinguished *duces* were given this title.

The field army[106] marked the real innovation of this age and was the brainchild of Diocletian. It comprised the seventy legions of the East and the sixty-one legions of the West. It was invariably commanded by officers of the highest rank. The legionary and vexillation commanders were directly under the Master of the Soldiers. Evidently the original idea was that the Augusti and Caesars should be in supreme command, and alongside them the Praetorian prefects.

The great expedition against Carausius was led by the Praetorian Prefect Asclepiodotus.[107] We do not know whether there were four or two Praetorian Prefects at that time, but at that stage they were still predominantly administrative officials. Here, too, Constantine effected a separation by introducing the Masters of the Soldiers.[108] This was something entirely new. The intention was to give new life to the old office of Praetorian Prefect in this way; the Masters of the Soldiers were constantly in the Emperor's presence, hence they were called *praesenti* or *praesentales*. Nonetheless, they were only so named later in order to distinguish them.[109] Their numbers correspond. Exceptions are indicative here;

there is a separation of spheres, in normal times into cavalry and infantry, but sometimes the offices of *magister equitum* and *magister peditum* were united. The division was only meaningful at court: when the *magister* was sent to a specific diocese he became *magister equitum et peditum*.[110] Command of the Guard was taken from him: that lesson had been learned.

Later the civilian and military spheres were separated here, too; the Praetorian Prefect was given the civilian sphere, as supreme state official. The expansion of this institution probably occurred during the reign of Constantius. The original intention had been to have one imperial army for the East and another for the West. At first there were no local competences for different parts of the Empire. However, now other Masters of the Soldiers, within designated areas and with local competences, were appointed beside those at court: Masters of the Soldiers for the East, i.e. essentially Syria on the Euphrates; for Illyricum, on account of the Danube Wars; and for Gaul for the Rhine.[111] Under Theodosius we find a Master of the Soldiers for Thrace.[112]

After the creation of the new Masters of the Soldiers the *riparienses et comitatenses* were joined by [MH.III, 23] *scholae palatinae*, which was the name given to the troops of the distinguished Masters of the Soldiers in the imperial presence. This brought into the Emperor's proximity generals who had hundreds of thousands of men at their command – something that had previously been avoided. This organization in no way suggests lack of trust. This strong command structure contributed a great deal towards a successful army reform.

The title of *amicus* for the Emperors' friends had already been important under Augustus.[113] The designations *comes primae, secundae, tertiae admissionis*[114] derived from the morning visits, the *levée*. This arrangement did not acquire any great importance under the principate. Now, however, anyone 'who adored the purple' is of a very high rank. Out of the *amici* grew the *comites*, companions of the Emperor. The Emperor would take a voluntary selection of people (*cohors amicorum*) with him on his travels. They would receive public reimbursements, as did the *amici* of high-ranking governors,[115] and were made use of for a variety of business.

Even in the Augustan era *comes* had been expressed as a formal title, but the institution lapsed after Constantine, probably because the Emperors delegated more and more of their personal power to others. Constantine appears to have abolished it outright, i.e. the *comites* receive indefinite spheres of competence. Any financial official, any *dux*, could be a *comes*. Like the modern 'privy councillor', this was a discretionary title bestowed in accordance with rank. Titles in general mushroomed; previously the *comites*[116] had been distinguished according to rank, in so far as senators and equestrians were separate. Now there were three levels: *comites ordinis primi, secundi, tertii*, perhaps imitating the three ranks of the former *amici. C.Th.* VI, p. 27,8 names *cubicularii* (chamberlains) as 'counts of the second rank'. The network of counts covered the entire country. The tribune was treated similarly, although this office had previously had a real official function. The rank was now bestowed as a title, with gradations. Even prior to this, a clear distinction had been made between tribunes of the Praetorian cohorts and others. Distinguished tribunes were thought of as being on the same level as the *tribuni scholarum*.

There was little change to administration in the financial sphere.[117] The fundamental idea was to distinguish, on the one hand, between *rationes (patrimonium)*, i.e. state revenues – in so far as these flowed into the imperial coffers and were kept, used and audited by the minister of finance – and, on the other hand, the property of the Emperor, and in particular his landed possessions. The distinction between *aerarium* and *fiscus* ceased to exist: there was no longer an *aerarium* of the Empire. The finances of the state and the private administration of the Emperor had, after all, always overlapped. The imperial provinces were viewed as belonging to the Emperor. The succession, of course, was not regulated by private law. The Emperor managed his finances like other people, but very early on [MH.III, 24] this ceased to be the work of slaves and was entrusted to a procurator. The cashiers themselves were always slaves, however. The chief of finance, the minister, was the *procurator a rationibus*. *Rationes summae* refers not (as Hirschfeld[118] asserts) to the Emperor's administration, but to the civil service as a whole. Here there was a two-tier gradation, with a 'procurator of all accounts' and below him *procuratores summarum* (of particular accounts), since in the provinces these constituted the principal administrative bureaux. The *procurator a rationibus* was later known as the *procurator summae rei* or *summarum rationum* (of all accounts), then *rationalis*; the latter designation was already widely current by the second century, but did not become an official title until the post-Diocletianic era. This official was also frequently referred to as *rationalis summarum*. Under Constantius and later he became known as *comes* (what else?) *sacrarum largitionum* Count of the Sacred Largesses,[119] a name which refers to only a portion of his duties.

The financial and administrative divisions of the Empire were not entirely identical, but were generally analogous: the same model was used for both. In the East too the principal financial adbuicrators were also known as *comites sacrarum largitionum*, but in the West they were known as *rationales*. The Praetorian Prefects were also responsible for collecting taxes. The treasuries consist of six sections: three for gold and three for silver and copper. These were headed by the *obryzum*, ('pure gold') followed by the *aurum ad responsum* for imperial medallions, jewellery, etc. used for donatives; then came the *vestiarum sanctum* (sacred wardrobe), since a lot of gold was used for ornamentation. Silver was needed for silver ingots and for *miliarenses* (minted silver coin). *Pecunia* was the copper coin, the Emperor's treasury, which was augmented from the *thesauri* in the individual provinces.[120] The minister of finance also had jurisdiction over frontier customs dues (*commercia*), because of the customs treasury. Lastly, all the Emperor's manufactures[121] were under his administration.

The monetary system had declined greatly; centralization of coinage was abandoned. There were now mints in the provinces.[122] Clothing fabrics were frequently also manufactured within the imperial establishment: linen was woven in the *linythia*, wool in the *gynaecea*, purple-dying was carried out in the *baphia* and brocades were produced by the *barbaricarii*.[123] It is not clear whether they were intended for imperial consumption only; probably they were, for this consumption was very significant. The Emperor's wardrobe was large and clothes quite a customary gift. The manufacture of purple dye remained an imperial monopoly,[124] which meant that whatever reached the marketplace had to come from these manufactures.

Administration of the imperial domains is in theory far simpler to grasp. [MH.III, 25] The Emperor's landed property was immense. The *praefectus a rationibus* was probably never empowered to administer the imperial domains. Under Septimius Severus the separation was completed. *Procurator Augusti a patrimonio* was the title in earlier times, then *magister rei privatae*, then, under Constantius, *comes rerum privatarum*.[125] Here too administration was divided up along provincial lines, although far more arbitrarily. Subordinate to this official were *rationales rei privatae*, in some cases for provinces, in others for dioceses.

Transport was of great importance to late antique administration, constituting as it did a major burden for the provinces. *Bastagae* were the men responsible for supervising transport. There were also stud farms subordinate to ministers of the imperial estates, with *praepositi gregum et stabulorum*.[126] Under Anastasius the *comes sancti* also appears,[127] probably because of the great increase in imperial estates.

The taxation system itself is more important. Diocletian introduced universal imperial taxation throughout the Empire, which was necessary, given that the army had increased fourfold.[128] This was a new system of raising taxes based on a new land register. The bases for the institution of land tax were not new, they were simply increased. The valuation of land occurred very early on. But account was also taken of the size of the workforce. The new tax was called *iugatio* or *capitatio*. In general, however – we must set aside Egypt – this was not a poll tax. We know the procedure from the Syro-Roman lawbook.[129] Valuation was carried out by taking a tax unit as a basis (later expressed as 1,000 gold pieces), for which *caput* or *iugum* was the technical term. Vineyards and arable land were divided into three classes. One *iugum* amounted to 3 acres of vineyard, or, depending on the landed property, 20, 40 or 60 acres of arable land.

It can be inferred from the fragments of the land register that first of all the name of both the owner and the parcel of land were registered, then the type and class, after this the slaves and cattle, and lastly the *coloni*. All *capita* ('heads') were included in the total, master and slaves alike. The term *capitatio* is thus correct, but not comprehensive. Perhaps this inclusion of the labour force was precisely what was new. Children under 14 and old men over 65 were not counted, and women infrequently.[130] A panegyric in praise of Constantine[131] reckons the municipality of the Aedui at 32,000 *capita*.[132] Cattle tax and land tax were thus linked [MH.III, 26] to it. A poll tax as such was quite unknown to the Romans;[133] *capitatio* always means the taxes described here. The 'human and animal poll tax' in the Theodosian Code only differs from this in its exemption of senators and imperial officials.[134] It is clear from the act registered in the Code of Justinian XI, 55,1[135] that the institution as it later existed dates back to Diocletian; the *annona* is given here as its object. As a universal imperial tax, therefore, it derives from Diocletian. However, one passage in the *Digest*[136] indicates that this had already existed earlier, for example in Syria. This can be traced back as far as the municipal charter of Genetiva.[137] Diocletian's tax reform was accompanied by the abolition of inheritance tax, in one sense the only tax of the earlier period. This is an important point; during his lifetime the Roman citizen was free of tax liabilities, but he paid for this after his death. It says something for the Emperor's sense of justice that the old tax was abandoned when the new one came in. However, we can trace the continued existence of the *vicesima hereditatis*, the 5 per cent inheritance tax, as far as the third century.

The second point concerns the throne: it had already been the Republican practice, and remained so under the principate, for the provinces to be taxed for the benefit of Rome. This fiscally privileged status – now applying to both Romes – persisted even after Diocletian. Northern Italy was taxed to maintain the imperial household. In contrast, the taxes paid by the *provinciae urbicariae* in central and southern Italy[138] flowed into the treasury of the capital for the benefit of the urban plebs. Constantinople now obtained the Egyptian supplies and Rome obtained wood and charcoal. Other supplies were collected as a contribution from individuals, as the *frumentum* (grain) had once been.

It is difficult to tell how oppressive these taxes were. Lactantius[139] complains bitterly about the excessive tax burden under Diocletian; a generation later Victor[140] asserted that the tax burden then was intolerable compared to what it had been in the days of Diocletian. We do, perhaps, have one instance where we can calculate this: the 32,000 *capita* of the Autun area (see MH.III, 25). Having ascertained the territory of the *civitas Aeduorum* (the later bishoprics of Autun, Châlons and Mâcon) [MH.III, 27] one can then divide the total and arrive at an estimate for the size of each unit. According to Ammianus the individual *iugum* paid 25 *solidi* before the arrival of Julian, and 7 *solidi* after his departure.[141] This is another indication of how shoddy the administration was before Julian. In what form was the tax paid? It is not specified. We move back, so to speak, into the realm of payment in kind. Money could be taxed, though presumably only silver and gold, not debased copper. Sometimes, therefore, gold was required, generally corn; this was what was most important. Payment in gold was required for the *auri lustralis collatio*.[142] Nonetheless, we can find payment being made in all manner of forms: cattle, *tirones* (recruits), bacon or wood.

This explains another institution of the period, the *indictio*. On 1 September what was required for the year was announced. This was further augmented in many years by the *superindictio* (additional requisition). The first year of the process is said to have been 312.[143] (This reference may be to a new census, a revision of the land register.) Earlier the urban records already seem to have been revised every fifteen years. In the later period this fifteen-year interval became regular, hence *indictio prima*, *secunda*, etc. for specific years. The institution of reckoning time according to tax years originated in Egypt, where we already find this in the fourth century. The practice did not become current in other regions until the sixth century.

In the case of army pay and official salaries, payment in kind was introduced. Payment was calculated according to *annona* and *capitum*; the *stipendium annuum* (annual allowance) now became the *annona*; *capitum* indicated the sum required to keep a horse for a year. As officials were promoted, they acquired several *annonae* and *capita*. Obviously this was not the manner of payment, but the change in the value of money explains this development; the *pecunia*, coin, was no longer a measure of value. Instead of money people sometimes liked to use weighed gold. This could not be used for soldiers' pay, however. We can see from a list of fees from Numidia that even [MH.III, 28] *sportulae* (fees) were calculated in corn. But they could be paid in gold, based on the price of a bushel of corn at the Roman cornmarket.[144] This was obviously extremely inconvenient. Soon, therefore, the system of *adaeratio*[145] appeared, whereby the *annona* was converted into money, once the currency had recovered and even reached a high degree of stability again. From about the time of Valentinian onwards the term *annona* is obsolete. The fiscal significance of the *indictio* lay in the elastic nature of the tax. This was probably the sole direct form of taxation there was in the Empire.

It is striking that cities largely remained exempt from taxes.[146] This is documented by *C.Th.* XIII, 10.2 from the early part of Constantine's reign. It must also be borne in mind that the capital assets of city-dwellers were far more tied up in landed property in those days than in the nineteenth century. Now, as a result of the disappearance of the companies of tax farmers, the shift in the wholesale trade and the impoverishment of the guilds, there were far fewer fortunes aside from those in land. Side by side with the land tax, Constantine instituted a *collatio auri lustralis* or *chrysargyron*, which was a tax on commercial activity (see MH.III, 27). Merchants, therefore, were taxed in gold (and silver). This tax probably developed out of the donatives given to the Emperor by subordinate

391

officials. This was already an old practice. It is said of Alexander Severus that he remitted the *aurum coronarium et negotiatorum*.[147] The *quinquennalia* were very frequently celebrated at the beginning of the fifth year of an Emperor's reign, and it is easy to associate these donatives with this. Anyone *qui pecuniam habet in conversatione*[148] was eligible for this tax. The only aspect of the tax which is uncertain was the scale; there does not seem to have been one. Presumably the *indictio* was reckoned as the basis. We hear of terrible complaints about totally unreasonable assessments. Anastasius [MH.III, 29] did away with this tax and replaced it with others.[149] Farmers, of course, were exempt from this tax, since they paid land tax.

Senators were liable to a special tax, the *gleba senatoria*[150] or *follis* (bag for copper money). This was simply the usual land tax, applied to senators. The fact that it was regarded as a special tax is due to the way the Empire was administered. The capital cities were not under the Praetorian Prefect, who therefore could not raise taxes in them. Although the Urban Prefect was in charge, taxation was the special concern of the *magister census*.[151] The minimum rate for senators was 7 *solidi*.

An improvement seems to be in evidence in the sphere of indirect taxation. It appears that internal customs dues were abandoned, leaving only frontier customs dues, *commercia*. There is little reference to other indirect taxes, for example of the continued existence of the taxation on auctions. In fact, however, taxes were of secondary importance; the state was supposed to make ends meet with its available funds, as was the private citizen. Imperial estates etc. constituted a substantial part of the national economy. Aside from many parcels of land the government also owned all mines,[152] although this was not a royal prerequisite.

For the Romans, administration and justice always went together. Although Rome had to some extent ceased to be the capital, it was always regarded as the centre of the Empire. The Senate remained in Rome; the city was [MH.III, 30] exempt from administration by the Praetorian Prefect. Rome merely ceased to be the Emperor's residence, which for a long time was not fixed. Diocletian was by no means hostile to the status of Rome, as is shown by the thermal baths he erected[153] and the Vicennalia he celebrated there.[154] The defence of Italy's northern frontier was once again a matter of survival, and the government moved to Milan, since it needed to be closer to the frontier. The *vicarius in urbe Roma* had his seat in Rome.[155] The troops were also kept mainly in the north, where they would be needed. This is clear from the history of Maximian. In 403 the residence was moved from Milan to Ravenna,[156] since Milan was vulnerable to incursions by the Goths, whereas the new residence was very secure.

The establishment of Constantinople, *Nova Roma*, as the opposite number to ancient Rome, naturally meant a decline in Rome's status. It set the seal on the division of the Empire. The constitution of Constantinople was essentially a poor imitation of the Roman. The Urban Prefect there was not installed until 359,[157] until which time the new city was without a municipal constitution. The Senate did not have municipal jurisdiction. It had a right of consultation on imperial matters, but in matters concerning the city it had less of a say than the Senate of the smallest town. The specific branches of administration in the city were subordinate to representatives of the Emperor, for example the *annona*, and harbour and river management. The *praefectura urbis*, the policing of the capital, was another such institution. This *praefectus*, instituted by Augustus,[158] played an [MH.III, 31] increasingly important role, ultimately also being given formal control of all the particular branches of administration. His sphere of competence was almost as diverse as the Emperor's. It basically originated in his power of jurisdiction.[159]

[MH.III, 33] The right to a criminal trial was actually a privilege of the upper classes; it did not exist for the lower classes, and the slave was as utterly devoid of rights as a dog or a dangerous animal.[160] Foreigners were subject to an arbitrary authority, or at least police control. Only the *civis* enjoyed the protection of the law, and perhaps at a push the *foederati*: the foreigner was utterly devoid of rights.

A contributory factor was the massive development of the urban economy, which attracted riff-raff in their droves, hence calling for virtually unlimited police powers. We gain some idea of the primitiveness of Roman civil law from the fact, for example, that a person who had been robbed could only file a private lawsuit for damages against the thief; no action was taken by the state.[161] In the age of the Emperors cases of theft were brought before the Urban Prefect, since it is normally the lower classes who steal and in practice a civil lawsuit is inappropriate. An additional factor was the decline in the *quaestiones* procedure of trial before criminal jury-courts; the Urban Prefect inherited their powers too. But he also came to control civil jurisdiction. However, he did not retain the extent of his jurisdiction to the hundredth milestone[162] that he had had earlier in the principate. Instead his jurisdiction was limited to Rome. He was permitted, however, to banish criminals from the [MH.III, 34] city and its environs as far as the hundredth milestone and in this way look after the security of this wide area.[163]

The Urban Prefect was the normal court of first instance for senators.[164] Senators were obliged to reside at Rome, where they thus had their legal domicile.[165] The Senate was also the court of first instance for the guildsmen, *corporati*, among whom the *suarii* (pig-dealers), for example, were very important and influential, and for all people permanently resident in Rome. Appeals against its judgments could only be made to the Emperor. However, it was also court of appeal for all lesser courts in the capital;[166] the last remnants of the praetorian sphere of competence, the guardianship and manumission courts, were still in existence. The prefects of the corn supply and of the watch were also empowered to judge criminal cases in certain instances, and appeals from them likewise passed to the Urban Prefect.

The struggle between the two principles of senatorial authority and military force under the Emperors found expression in the struggle between the Urban Prefect and the Praetorian Prefect. According to the first principle all appeals passed to the former, according to the other to the latter. In the fourth century a compromise was reached. Appeals generally passed to the Praetorian Prefect,[167] but some were assigned to the Urban Prefect,[168] for example those from specific parts of Italy and Africa; these, therefore, were assigned to him, although originating from outside his primary sphere of competence. [MH.III, 35] When we examine his military status, he was *de iure* and *de facto* in the same position as owls in Iceland: he didn't have any;[169] in origin the Urban Prefect was the sole toga-wearing official, and he was intended to regard himself entirely as a civilian official. In fact, however, things were very different, and what still remained of military authority in Rome fell to him;[170] an urban commander appointed beside him would have completely annulled his office.

In earlier times there was a threefold garrison in Rome: the Praetorians, the urban cohorts, whose numbers were later added to the nine cohorts of the Praetorians to make the tenth, eleventh and twelfth cohorts,[171] and the *vigiles* (watch).[172] The two latter groups were in real terms subordinate to the Urban Prefect, who used them to implement his administration. To these was generally added a legion stationed in the vicinity.[173]

The abolition of the Guard was the inevitable consequence of Rome no longer being the Emperor's residence. This occurred without being instigated by any particular act on the part of Rome, partly for reasons of economy and partly on account of the double danger of troops being in the city without the Emperor on the one hand, and the Emperor being without troops on the other. Even so, there was long hesitation over this. Diocletian was still unable to draw the necessary conclusion from this change of the residence, and even his abdication may be connected with this situation. Lactantius[174] states that not until Galerius did an Emperor want to move the Praetorian Guard elsewhere. The revolution of Maxentius [MH.III, 36] was in fact nothing else than the urban Guard's rejection of the new regime. Constantine finally made a clean sweep and disbanded both the Praetorian Guard and all other troops stationed in Rome.[175] The Guard was moved elsewhere and initially had no permanent base, like the Emperor himself, until of course it finally came to Constantinople and Milan. We do not know exactly how matters lay in the West later. One source has it that the Praetorians and the *in armis vulgus* were disbanded.[176] This probably refers to the *vigiles*, the sole corps in which freedmen were permitted to serve as freedmen – a police troop created from and intended for the lowest social orders. They no longer existed in the fourth century;[177] in contrast the urban cohorts remained, as a later inscription of the Constantinian period[178] shows, but instead of four there were now only three, the tenth, eleventh and twelfth; the thirteenth had disappeared. These cohorts were under the command of the Urban Prefect; their fixed quarters were at the *forum suarium*, the pig market, and their special commander was the *praefectus foro suario*. Constantinople had no troops equivalent to the urban cohorts; their duties were performed by the Guard.

As previously, the *praefectus annonae*,[179] who was under the Urban Prefect, oversaw the entire system of provisioning, of which southern Italy was now the source, as Sicily and Africa had been before. If the [MH.III, 37] *mensores*[180] gave short measure the matter came before the *praefectus annonae*, whose special area of jurisdiction similarly included the civilian aspects of provisioning, as well as related criminal matters. The *praefectus vigilum*,[181] a kind of deputy police commissioner, had under him the fire brigades and the night-time police.

Responsibility for building activities,[182] and chiefly for the great magazines which lay below the Aventine Hill, was detached from the department of the *praefectus annonae* and transferred to the *curator horreorum Galbanorum*. Aqueducts were the responsibility of the *curatores aquarum*; a *comes formarum* was responsible for the maintenance of their structures and a *consularis* for water allocation. Special officials were in charge of riverside buildings, the sewage system and wine supply respectively.

This brings us to the office of *praefectus praetorii*,[183] as he is known to distinguish him from the earlier, grammatically more correct *praefectus praetorio*.[184] That office changed considerably. The magistrate was intended to administer, rule and judge personally, which had always been a fiction in one sense. Such a degree of self-sufficiency in an extensive department is as inconceivable as the idea that there should always be a monarch who rules personally. Vice-regency had existed from the very outset and the influential Praetorian Prefects of the earlier principate detracted as little from the glory of their monarchs as Colbert, Richelieu and Mazarin did from the great French kings under [MH.III, 38] whom they held their influential sway. For public consumption the fiction of personal rule by the Emperor was always strictly upheld; the public was supposed to believe that the Emperor did everything himself; his assistants were kept behind the scenes. Under the first Emperor Augustus, especially, the real co-regents were entirely anonymous, and even without formal office. There is a characteristic belief that Maecenas,[185] the most influential of Augustus's assistants, was the first Praetorian Prefect. In formal terms this is quite definitely incorrect, but by the same token it is correct in terms of substance; Maecenas did indeed occupy a position equivalent to the concept of Praetorian Prefect.[186]

There was a natural preference for appointing officers of the Guard to this post. The Emperor lived in Rome and front-line troops were located on the frontiers, so that high-ranking officers of the army proper were not available; officers of the

Guard, however, who did not rank high in the military hierarchy, were available and constantly in the Emperor's presence. The Guard naturally came to assume a privileged position. They were not there to fight, but to be responsible for the person of the Emperor and the capital generally, which was not in fact real soldiers' work.[187] They were given preferential treatment through the manner of conscription: only [MH.III, 39] Italians[188] of good birth were accepted in the Guard, in stark contrast to the legions, where there was a steady decline in service by Italians in the lower ranks. Initially not even all Italians were accepted, but primarily Latins. The Guard had a relatively short term of service;[189] admittedly they were not eligible for civilian provisions, but discharged men were comfortably provided for with good posts in the civil administration. Officers moved on almost without exception to careers in higher administration; the actual military career was different.

These officers had an unusual position *vis à vis* the Senate. They were not senators; on the contrary, if a Praetorian Prefect was dismissed, he subsequently became a senator. Some have ascribed this to the Emperor's distrust of the Senate; this is only partially true, even though such distrust was beyond doubt and entirely justified. But there was certainly no lack of loyal senators who could have been appointed to such positions of trust without reservations. The main reason lay in the in some sense parallel position of the Senate as co-regent alongside the Emperor, which meant that its members were not eligible to serve the Emperor personally, just as a procurator of the Emperor's property was not drawn from among the Senate. Indeed, some Praetorian Prefects had a low-ranking military career background, and had previously been senior centurions working their way [MH.III, 40] up from private soldier to centurion.[190] We know that Burrus, the all-powerful Praetorian Prefect under Nero (see MH.I, 187f.), had first been a Guards officer, then *procurator Augusti* in Livia's household, in other words in the private fiscal department of the imperial household,[191] and hence not a true state official, but in a position of trust of the most personal kind. If in the third century we find leading jurists as Praetorian Prefects,[192] this is simply a consequence of the fact that the position had been a non-military one even earlier. The post of Praetorian Prefect was a double-edged sword because of the ever-present danger of abuse of trust and the suspicion of planning a usurpation. This is probably why there were two Praetorian Prefects; dual command would have been nonsensical if it had been a military post.

Formally, the Praetorian Prefect was no different from any other state official. There was no fixed term of office, though in practice there were important differences. Elsewhere the term of office was usually three, four or five years; but Dio[193] asserts, in the well-known speech by Maecenas (probably merely a figment of the imagination of a high-ranking Greek about the best form of the state) that he advised Augustus to appoint all officials for brief terms, but the Praetorian

Prefects for life. We can prove that many men died while holding this post, and even if such direct evidence were lacking, it is natural to assume that such influential posts, based so strongly on personal trust, should not be filled for brief terms.

If we inquire after the influence exercised by the Praetorian Prefect, the answer is: sometimes good, sometimes bad, depending on the person, as it was with every senior official, [MH.III, 41] and indeed with the Emperor himself. Some of the finest acts of government demonstrably stemmed from prefects. Although Tacitus[194] portrays Sejanus in the darkest colours, and lays them on thick at that, even he is forced to admit that the best measures passed by the model government of Tiberius can be traced back to him.[195] The same applies to Burrus under Nero. Both Sejanus and Burrus were sole Praetorian Prefects with no colleagues. Although, we can find even three of them from time to time,[196] it was natural when the post came to be equivalent to a premiership for there to be only one.

How did the public view this post? It was not regarded as a misfortune when the Praetorian Prefect controlled affairs, any more than Bismarck's position is viewed as being injurious to the prestige of the Crown nowadays – rather the contrary. In Hadrian's day, when real decline was still a long way off, the relationship between the Emperor and the Prefect was likened to the earlier one between the Dictator and his Master of the Horse.[197]

It is in fact meaningless to define the field of competence of the Praetorian Prefect. It was precisely as extensive as the Emperor's. Whatever the Emperor could do, whatever matter he could take up, the Praetorian Prefect could do as well. In the military sphere, recruitment, passwords and suchlike were responsibilities which devolved specifically on him, but this of course was not the real source of the importance of his office, which depended entirely on individuals and was not constitutionally defined. The importance of this position, as we have already seen, [MH.III, 42] did not lie primarily in the military sphere. Although we do have instances, such as during the Dacian and Marcomannic Wars, of Praetorian Prefects joining in campaigns and even dying on the battlefield,[198] these remained exceptions.

Not immediately under Diocletian, but under Constantine, the Praetorian Prefect lost his military status entirely; already under Diocletian he was deprived of command of the Guard. The Praetorians themselves were disbanded and the new guard troops placed under a Tribune and a Master of the Offices.[199] The Praetorian Prefect had previously been responsible for making appointments, much the same function as the modern German military cabinet – but now this too ceased. He had never had anything to do with fiscal matters.[200] He retained his administrative jurisdiction.

The far-reaching reform of the administration can be ascribed to Diocletian, who divided the Empire into dioceses. The former provincial divisions were broken up into smaller administrative regions, which were then in turn made up into larger ones, which did not correspond to the former provinces. In this way the thirteen administrative units mentioned earlier were formed. In the East these were: *Aegyptus, Pontus, Asiana, Thracia, Dacia (Moesia)*. In the West: Britain, Viennensis and Septem Provinciae (the two Gauls), two Italies (Italia, Urbs Roma), Illyricum (western and eastern, or Pannonia and Moesia) and Africa.[201]

These provinces were overseen partly by Praetorian Prefects and partly by their vicars, *vicarii praefectorum praetorio*; the latter should be thought of more as an equivalent, rather than a subordinate office. For the thirteen dioceses there were a corresponding thirteen officials, of whom four [MH.III, 43] were Praetorian Prefects and nine vicars. We also find other names for the diocesan rulers, e.g. the one for Egypt was called not vicar, but Prefect of Egypt,[202] even though he was a vicar. Syria was under a *comes Orientis*;[203] both the Illyrias (West and East) were under Praetorian Prefects, since they were crucial heartlands of the Empires. The third diocese under a Praetorian Prefect was northern Gaul with its capital, Trier, the fourth probably *Oriens*, although this is still debatable. Soon two were dropped: *Oriens* came under a *comes Orientis* and Gaul under the vicar of the *Septem Provinciae*. This restored purity and simplicity to the nature of the Praetorian Prefects. The intermediate rank between the supreme and subordinate authorities was dropped. Equality in the functions of the Prefect and the vicar is strikingly revealed in the fact that appeals from the vicar went not to the Prefect, but directly to the Emperor. Similarly the vicar was called not 'Vicar of the Prefect', but 'Vicar of the Praetorian Prefects'.

The job of the Praetorian Prefect was overall administration, not the administration of individual regions. The right to propose people for governorships, and hence *de facto* appointment to such offices, resided not with the vicar in his diocese, but with the prefect, as did supervision of the treasuries[204] and payment of the frontier troops (these were the *acta praefectorum praetorio*). Complaints about governors came to him and he was empowered to dismiss them. He was supervisor of the Emperor's civilian officials, with power over appointments, payment of salaries, discipline and dismissal. His appeal jurisdiction [MH.III, 44] was limited and only applied in territories he administered directly, where there was no vicar.

Some involvement in the raising of taxes also devolved on him, chiefly in terms of his responsibility for recording and assessing public needs. He did not control expenditure; he simply managed the overall tax screw. But there is also evidence that he had a role in the collection of taxes, which was a highly complex operation devolving in the first instance on the *praesides*, then lower down the scale on the municipalities, who collected the taxes directly from those who were liable. The *praefectiani* and *palatini* were chief tax collectors sent from the central office out into the provinces to oversee tax affairs, and probably in exceptional cases also to take action themselves. Allocations were probably imposed as uniformly as possible, so that the Emperor probably saw to an equitable tax distribution between the Praetorian Prefects at the highest level.

The Praetorian Prefect was also the postmaster general. The *cursus publicus* was under his management, for the simple reason that the postal service naturally extended right across the Empire without provincial barriers.[205]

Lastly, he also had a share in legislative power; his decrees, which were normative regulations for his prefecture, carried equal weight with those of the Emperor and were promulgated alongside them. But all important matters were dealt with by the Emperor, even though there was no clear boundary indicating where the competence of the Praetorian Prefect ended and that of the Emperor began.

[MH.III, 45] Taking a further look at the change which took place in the position of Praetorian Prefect from Diocletian onwards, we can see that it fitted more closely into the administrative hierarchy than in the earlier state. The deputy-Emperorship, with its entirely undefined competence, was abolished. Whereas the Praetorian Prefect had previously often remained in office until his death, this privileged position now ceased. He was appointed just as the *praeses* was, and brief terms of office were not rare. This was underlined by the geographical restriction of his sphere of competence, aside from the division of the Empire into eastern and western Rome. Within half the Empire, his intervention was more limited, both in geographical terms and in terms of competence. In the East his prefecture extended almost as far as the imperial frontier, whereas the Illyrian prefect had only the Greek peninsula and northern Illyricum, which made the two colleagues unequal. In the West the two halves were geographically fairly balanced.

It is not quite clear when these changes came about. It is not possible to document geographical demarcation before 359; it can certainly be traced back to before Constantius II, to Constantine, perhaps even to Diocletian. The Prefect lost his military competence under Constantine, but the system of vicars existed prior to this and does not make sense without separate regions. The demarcation of competences is the crucial factor constitutionally. After Constantine there were four Praetorian Prefects;[206] Diocletian and Maximian probably appointed two each. No appointment of Urban Prefects is known [MH.III, 46] to have been made by the Caesars. Here too, the real innovative idea as a whole was probably the brainchild of Diocletian, this remarkable man. A new Praetorian Prefect thus came into being with restricted competence, partly geographical, partly in substance. The disappearance of personal rule by the Emperor at the end of the principate was accompanied by the disappearance of his shadow, the omnipotent and undefined Praetorian Prefect.

Strictly speaking, the vicars were not subordinate officials, but they did rank lower than the Praetorian Prefects. The highest overall rank was held by the *consul ordinarius*, although he had no significance within the state aside from this, and merely enjoyed the privilege of being able to spend his good money providing games for the mob, and perhaps from time to time presiding over the Senate. The patricians were likewise superior in rank to the Praetorian Prefect; this peculiar personal aristocracy of Constantine's[207] was ranked according to seniority. It is not possible to ascertain whether a patrician was given the rank of *clarissimus* or *perfectissimus*. Constantine turned this hereditary nobility into a personal nobility. Aside from these two cases, however, the Praetorian Prefects were the most senior officials, the foremost among the *illustres*, whereas the vicars were foremost among the *spectabiles*. Similarly, the *comes Orientis* did not rise above the rank of *spectabilis*.[208]

Appeals went in the first instance to the vicars: the vicar judged in second place, i.e. instead of the Emperor, *vice sacra iudicans*, since all appeals were regarded as [MH.III, 47] addressed to the Emperor. From the Praetorian Prefect there was no appeal to the Emperor, any more than there could conceivably be an appeal from the Emperor to the Emperor; this represents another vestige of the old idea that the Praetorian Prefect was a deputy Emperor. The line of appeal was thus some-times twofold, sometimes threefold, passing either from the governor of the province to the vicar and then to the Emperor, or from the provincial governor to the Praetorian Prefect.

Comites provinciarum only existed in the last years of Constantine's reign, between 327 and 336. In every diocese there must have been a vicar and a *comes* besides. We do not know how their competences were defined – perhaps not at all. It seems to have been a purely competitive institution, born of mistrust, which soon disappeared. By the time of Constantine it was already a thing of the past. In the East an echo of it survived in the titling of the vicar there as *comes Orientis*.[209]

All that now remains is to define the immediate activities of the Emperor himself. The earlier principate had been based completely on the idea of personal rule, on the assumption that the Emperor knew everything and gave all the orders in his own person. The less visible the activity of others, the more perfectly he fulfilled his role.

Now all tasks were systematically distributed among senior officials; where the need arose they could, and sometimes even did, manage without the Emperor. Previously the Emperor had to rule, whether he was [MH.III, 48] good or bad. Now, it was possible to rule without him, whether he was good or bad. I say 'possible', because we still should not think of the imperial system of Diocletian that followed as a structure similar to the modern constitutional state. There was only the constitutional possibility of a *roi fainéant*; the Emperor could still intervene, and did so often enough, but he no longer needed to do so. He could judge, administer, command armies, but if he did not intervene there were other wheels in the machine to carry out his role. Perhaps with a single exception:

legislation still devolved on the Emperor and was enacted by means of decrees to the Senate or the people.[210]

Then there was a special machinery for expediting his legislative activity: the *quaestor sacri palatii*,[211] of mysterious origin. We do not know the origins of this office. Some think it derived from the *quaestores Augusti*, who were assigned to the Emperor in his capacity as proconsul, making them cabinet secretaries of sorts. This is one possibility; at all events the office is worlds apart from the earlier *quaestor* and the analogy is purely nominal. In substance it was something quite different: most importantly there were several *quaestores Augusti*, but now we have only one *quaestor sacri palatii*, who was far higher-ranking than the former. The idea of renewing ancient titles by means of institutions reminiscent of the Republic, however distantly, [MH.III, 49] was far too powerful, so this derivation is not very likely. On the other hand, in an inscription[212] of Caelius Saturninus we encounter the office of *vicarius a consiliis sacris* (vice-president of the privy council). This is precisely the task of the *quaestor sacri palatii*. The privy council probably had no president and the Emperor himself presided, hence the title *vicarius*.

In order to assess the work of the *quaestor sacri palatii* it is first necessary to examine the institution of the *consilium sacrum*. During this period the name was changed and it became the *consistorium*,[213] which was originally the name of the place where the consilium assembled. At first the *consilium* was neither permanent nor tied to any particular place of assembly, since the Emperor convened and assembled it whenever and wherever he wished. Later the privy council was allocated a special room where it had to wait until the Emperor needed it, and this room in the palace was the *consistorium*.

Let us examine the privy council first from the point of view of form, then of substance. Its membership comprised the highest dignitaries: the *comites ordinis primi 'a consistorio'*, then *ex officio* the *quaestor sacri palatii*, the Master of the Offices and the two ministers of finance.[214] As regards who presided over the privy council, we can see clearly here the decline in the Emperor's personal influence. As late as Diocletian's time there was still a *vicarius* of the *praeses consistorii*, which means that the Emperor himself still presided. Now the *quaestor sacri* [MH.III, 50] *palatii* presided, which means the Emperor no longer had control. We have the minutes of a session attended by the Emperor Julian in the year 362;[215] like modern minutes today, they begin with a list of those present, which comprised the officials just mentioned. All senior officials were probably entitled to attend, but not privy councillors by descent. Perhaps it was simply understood that a highly distinguished person was permitted to attend sessions of the privy council.

The privy council included stenographers (*notarii*); we know that the Romans were as advanced in this skill as we are. The chief of these stenographers, who were not bureau officials as such, was the *primicerius notariorum*, who was not the 'boss' in the sense that we interpret the word today, but simply the seniormost stenographer. These *notarii* might merely hold positions of honour; then they were called *tribuni et notarii* and had an officer's commission and the rank of colonel. In Orelli[216] we have an inscription referring to the poet Claudian, who was a *tribunus et notarius* and well-paid as such. Another inscription in Orelli gives the entire biography of a young Roman prominent at that time:[217] his father had been Praetorian Prefect and consul. He himself was principal candidate for the office of urban praetor, who was responsible for organizing the games; then he was *tribunus et notarius Praetorianus*, i.e. on the council of the Praetorian Prefect, who had his 'auditorium', just as the Emperor had the privy council. He achieved all this honours *in primo aetatis flore* – as a very young man. He then became Urban Prefect and regular consul. This was the career of a young man of the finest pedigree. Stenography was an [MH.III, 51] essential skill for an educated young man.

How did the Emperor's personal intervention fit into the organization business? It should first be borne in mind that the privy council was more of ornamental value than a wheel of any real practical importance in the machinery of state; by and large other considerations influenced the decision-making process. We have some information about the organization of business. First, the highest administrative authorities dealt with matters that were intended to be passed on to the Emperor for a decision. If, therefore, a city or individual had a petition to file, this was almost invariably done through embassies which arrived in person and delivered their *preces* to the Emperor by means of ambassadors.[218] The Praetorian Prefect's task was to submit an opinion on the matter, but he had explicit orders not to decide it; he was only supposed to offer his own opinion and vote; then the matter passed to the *scrinia*, the most important authority, which we shall be discussing directly. Only then was the matter passed to the *consistorium*, which was presented with a draft reply after the Praetorian Prefect and the *scrinia* had given their opinions; the only function for the *consistorium*, therefore, was to conclude the matter formally.

The *scrinia*, the Emperor's secretariat, derived from ancient institutions which can be traced back as far as the Republican era and which have their model in an institution of the well-to-do private household, the private secretariat. The Dictator Caesar gave a high-born Gaul the *cura epistolarum et anuli*.[219] The job of secretary was made into an official post under Hadrian; up to that time it had been performed [MH.III, 52] predominantly by freedmen. Hadrian transformed what had previously been a purely domestic position into an official one listed in the state calendar.[220]

There were three departments: *scrinia memoriae, epistolarum et libellorum*,[221] of which the first was the most important, being directly involved with the Emperor, drafting replies, collecting the Emperor's memoranda and receiving instructions added to them in the margins (*adnotationes omnes*). For this reason the officials in charge frequently had to deal with the appointment of officers and military matters in conjunction with the *quaestor sacri palatii*. The frontier troops were an exception (see MH.III, 53f.).

The two other *scrinia* – *epistolarum* and *libellorum* – recorded incoming petitions, and their division of labour revealed the incipient separation between administration and judiciary. The *scrinium epistolarum* dealt with administrative matters; the embassies and the *consultationes*, i.e. questions addressed to officials. Within this *scrinium* there was a special department, which received petitions from Greek-speaking areas (around 400 Latin was still the sole official language). In exceptional cases[222] requests could be written in Greek, and either replied to directly in Greek, or the Latin reply would be translated. The *scrinium libellorum* dealt with matters related to trials and also had limited jurisdiction over cases which were not tried by lay judges.

In so far as there was personal intervention by the Emperor, therefore, it took place through these *scrinia*. So what was there [MH.III, 53] for the *consistorium* to do then? The highest-ranking official, the Praetorian Prefect, had pronounced judgement, or the Emperor had pronounced judgement. All that really remained was to promulgate it. Direct intervention by the Emperor did still occur with respect to legislation, which was formally reserved to him and could consequently only originate from him. The institution at his disposal for this purpose was the *quaestor sacri palatii*, whose task it was to draft laws. These were then read out in the *consistorium* (*recitata in consistorio*) and signed, i.e. sanctioned, by the Emperor before being sent to the appropriate Senate and published, i.e. promulgated. No one was bound to observe a law that had not been promulgated. Even here there was little room for manoeuvre for the *consistorium*; perhaps the matter was sometimes debated, but as a rule it was an open and shut case. Only a few judicial procedures may have taken place before the *consistorium*, prepared by the *magister libellorum*; in this case personal intervention by the Emperor receded into the background.

The position of the *consistorium vis à vis* military matters was such that although consistorial competence was generally as extensive as the Emperor's, it stopped short of military matters, which were decided solely by the Masters of the Soldiers and the Emperor without the privy council. An exception to this were [MH.III, 54] the frontier troops, who were not under the Master of the Soldiers and whose affairs were passed to the *consistorium*. A listing of the units of frontier troops was submitted to it annually; they had no one to represent them at court.

To see the Emperor receding more and more into the background is interesting, if not gratifying. The appeals system had previously called for comprehensive and emphatic action by the Emperor. Theodosius II, the Emperor who had a passion for calligraphy, but greatly disliked ruling, and was perhaps the most slothful ruler who ever lived,[223] abolished the practice of appeal to the Emperor and delegated it to a committee consisting of the Praetorian Prefect and the *praepositus sacri palatii*, i.e. a court of appeal.[224]

An equally ungratifying innovation was the encroachment of what were purely court appointments into the official sphere. Previously these two spheres had been kept as separate as possible and the whole army of personal servants had no business outside the private apartments and domestic life of the Emperor. In this late period things went downhill to such an extent that the chamberlain, *cubicularius*, i.e. keeper of the 'sacred bed', *cubiculi sacri*, ranked among the highest officials, the *illustres*, and even ahead of the Master of the Offices, the marshall.[225] Furthermore, these court servants were now usually eunuchs;[226] the *primicerius cubiculi* was the highest-ranking in the second class.[227] These people had no roles as civil servants, [MH.III, 55] apart from the *comes domorum in Cappadocia*, who performed judicial functions.[228] The *castrensis sacri palatii* had the *cura palatii*,[229] responsibility for the palace building, supervision of the slaves, domestic servants and children. There was a *paedagogium* for educating the children of female slaves.[230]

Let us take a final look at Roman barristers; we find them in all spheres, so we may add them here, rather arbitrarily. The former distinction between jurist and barrister – *iuris consultus* and *causidicus* – had been erased. Usually the barrister (like the surveyor) was known as *togatus*, evidently because the toga was by now only worn as the official garb by these two (and by the Urban Prefect). Previously barristers had not been officials; their work had been an unpaid profession of honour. Now it was an official state post with a lucrative scale of fees, albeit paid by the public, not the state. A fixed number of barristers was employed by all authorities, enabling the client to choose. The figures are interesting: at an ordinary subordinate level 30, at a middle-tier level (e.g. that of the Prefect of Egypt) 50, at the highest level (Urban Prefect) 80, and at that of the Praetorian Prefect 150.[231] *Corpus* VI, 100[232] gives us the early career of an *advocatus*: starting with the vicar of Africa as *causidicus non ignobilis*, then *in consistorio principis*, [MH.III, 56] then in the three *scriniis*, from where he moved into the administration.

If the choice of barristers at each level of authority indicates the importance of the respective tribunals, we can likewise clearly discern from these figures the decline of the Empire in the last decades before its final collapse. In 442, instead of the thirty permitted entry into subordinate capacities there were only sixteen, and these were reduced to four by 451. Following the conquest of Carthage by the Vandals, the barristers there naturally had no means of subsistence and out of pity they were permitted to work elsewhere, but not in the supreme court.[233]

Terms of office and competence were applied to the post of barrister, as to all other categories of officials; they were ranked according to seniority, which was also associated with a title of distinction. Their training, for which they had to produce a diploma, was obtained at law schools, which were organized along exactly the same lines as modern university faculties; it might perhaps be said that no institution of the Roman Empire has been passed down to us in such continuous, uninterrupted form as the university.[234] Aside from the Byzantine law schools there was undoubtedly also one in Ravenna, from which the school which appears at Bologna in the eleventh century derives. As has already been indicated, however, it only becomes visible at that time; these schools were unquestionably there throughout [MH.III, 57] the intervening centuries, even though we have no direct evidence of the fact. The entire manner in which law is taught as a subject for instruction at universities corresponds precisely to the way it was done then. The method of textual interpretation is identical, and it has to be said that the Code of Justinian never entirely fell into disuse. The very name of Ravenna as a law school speaks eloquently enough; this was the seat of the Emperor of western Rome, the centre of the Latin-speaking Empire. Ravenna undoubtedly had a Latin law school. We see here in reality what has been asserted, and denied, about the Italian municipal institutions:[235] that there was a direct continuity from that era up to our own.[236]

3

A HISTORY OF EVENTS

The more abundantly the sources flow for the administration, the scarcer they are for history. And this should come as no surprise: history is made in the Cabinet and information about what goes on there does not pass to the contemporary as it really happens. Those accounts we do possess stem from outsiders who in fact know nothing. Generally speaking, we are not much better informed about the earlier Emperors either, but the rapport with the Senate did allow certain information to filter through to the public, even though the Senate did not have much of a say in government, [MH.III, 58] particularly on crucial matters. Now this was no longer the case; there was no further need to justify decisions in the eyes of the public. The fragile remnants of something reminiscent of the public opinion which had still existed in the early principate had long since evaporated, and the Emperor was as little accountable to the people as the master of a house feels it necessary to keep his servants informed about his activities. The relationship was identical.

Even more crucial than this is the unfortunate coincidence that it is precisely wherever we would most wish to be informed about a period or individual that the veil is all the more closely drawn over them. History too is 'mysterious in broad daylight'.[237] This is the mystery that almost always hangs over new, innovative thinkers; ultimately we are as perplexed about Caesar and Augustus as we are about Diocletian and Constantine. We are better informed about the period when Constantius, the great formalist, reigned, or when Julian made the attempt to set back the world clock and help the dying old religion back to power; but the developmental process, the construction out of the old material, is a mystery to us.

At no time had the government sunk to greater depths than from 254 to 258 under Valerian and Gallienus; under no other regime did everything go so [MH.III, 59] thoroughly off the rails. This was clearly the beginning of the end. Invasions by external enemies were occurring on all sides and on all frontiers of the Empire; the Alamanni were invading Italy and the Franks (a collective name) the West. They crossed the Rhine and went on to Spain and Africa.[238] The entire West trembled before their hordes – and their ships, since these were largely seafaring pirates. Greece suffered from the piracy of the Goths and in the East the Persian Empire, newly strengthened by the Sasanids, went on the offensive. 'Enemies all around'[239] was the slogan of the day. This was matched by the complete disarray and inner disintegration of the Empire.

It has to be admitted that no individual was perhaps ever faced with such a daunting task as Gallienus. Earlier he was reputedly quite an able officer, but he could not cope with the task of commander-in-chief. He let matters slide in an apathetic, womanish manner. It proved to be his undoing that while Zenobia, a heroic female, was manfully defending Palmyra against invasion from the east, Gallienus was glorifying himself in female attire as *Galliena Augusta*[240] on his coins – this was the ultimate ignominy. The various parts of the Empire were obliged to fend for themselves. It is a surprising, and yet amusing spectacle to see how Palmyra, a desert city of caravan traders, became militant and its queen was acknowledged as a kind of co-regent.[241] The East and West were going their separate ways. The government had no answer to this and stood idly by.

[MH.III, 60] But external enemies were not the only scourges of the Gallienic regime: a plague that had been raging for fifteen years was decimating the population. This was exacerbated by confusion in the coinage and a complete breakdown in the concept of money, which is based on state credit, so that on his accession to the throne Diocletian could rightly assert: 'Money no longer exists; the bushel of corn is everything.'[242] Some maintain that death could not be long in coming, with such death throes, but the life of states is tenacious; often in history, and even today, we see that the disintegration of even the most decrepit state edifice is protracted.[243]

But there were signs of improvement. First of all, the accounts we have of the situation at that time are like those of bad novelists who cannot describe the villain in horrific enough terms. Things were not as desperate as all that. The wars were, after all, only wars against barbarians. The Goths and Franks were no more than pirates who destroyed, took prisoners, murdered and pillaged, but who had no understanding of the state, no idea of the new Empires they were to found. Founders of states, such as Theoderic and Genseric,[244] had yet to make their appearance; the present trouble-makers had no inkling of what a state is. We should imagine them, on an incomparably larger scale, in terms of the Indian raids in America in the period when they were still of some significance. [MH.III, 61] These hordes were unable to build and, devoid of political purpose, their deeds were also without political results; once they had pillaged enough they did not remain, but turned back and withdrew of their own accord, just as a flame goes out when it no longer finds anything to burn.

One further point: we have already frequently referred to the position of Illyricum as heartland of the monarchy, and this region was relatively free from invasion by barbarians. Dacia was overrun,[245] but the Danube frontier held. The warlike tribes who resided there defended themselves and lived in relative peace, and this nurtured the seeds of recovery.

Elsewhere too things were happening: Palmyra and other cities revealed that strength was still there and that only harmony across the far-flung Empire was lacking. In this particular respect Gallienus exerted a healing influence; it was clear to Italians and provincials alike that all was lost without unity. The system whereby each part of the army proclaimed as monarch the man popular among them had outlived its usefulness. Hearts everywhere were filled with a yearning for unity whatever the cost. The election of Tacitus as Emperor is indicative.[246] The armies, waiving their right – and it undoubtedly was their right to elect an Emperor – urged the Senate to select an Emperor for them. Even officer circles were deeply imbued with the idea that there was only one way out, namely [MH.III, 62] 'to stick together'.

Aurelius Victor[247] rightly reproaches the Senate that it did not know what to do with its position: instead of electing the man the Empire needed, it had elected an old, rich, very good senator, who was however weak. And yet improvement did become visible immediately after Gallienus, since although Tacitus himself was followed by soldier-Emperors (the senatorial election did not work), the four next Emperors, Claudius, Aurelian, Probus and Carus, were able men and dragged the Empire back out of the quagmire. Admittedly, the last of these Emperors also fell victim to army conspiracies and reigned only for brief periods. But Aurelian in particular was an organizing type and set about dealing with the scourge of monetary confusion,[248] albeit without success.

And yet another point of infinite importance: religion. The early principate had suffered from indifference. From Augustus until now there had been no official religion: the machinery of the old religion was completely worn out. The masses had long felt a need for a real religion, and these new Emperors were not members of the old Roman aristocracy, but men of obscure origin who had worked their way up from among the common people. We thus find in almost all of them a strong, fatalistic faith. Face to face with the members of a conspiracy that had come to light, Aurelian said: 'Do not think that the Emperor is in your hands. [MH.III, 63] He is sustained by faith in his star, the mighty one.'[249] Diocletian likewise possessed a highly developed religious sense; his god was the Sun god, the cult of Mithras.[250] Then came the Christians. Herein lay the seeds of regeneration: indifference on the part of the sovereign is a bad thing; nothing can be accomplished by this.

We know even less about Diocletian's predecessor, Marcus Aurelius Carus (282–3), than we do about Carus's predecessors, Probus and Aurelian. Carus was an able soldier and led a campaign against the Persians. He met a mysterious death at Ctesiphon, probably by assassination, although another widespread version was that he had been struck by lightning.[251] He left two sons, Carinus and Numerian.[252]

The former, the elder, had remained in the West; the younger was with the army. He was proclaimed Emperor, but the campaign was interrupted. Numerian was a notable poet[253] and an educated man, but he remained too much his father's son, and the officers may have felt that no good could come of such leadership in war. Perhaps it was also the shrewder option: they therefore retreated and, once at Chalcedon, the rumour spread that the Emperor was dead. We do not know how he lost his life – probably by a criminal act – but the fact was that the throne was empty again. Aper, the Praetorian prefect, was regarded as the culprit, but made no [MH.III, 64] attempt to seize the empty throne. The officers summoned a council of war and debated whether or not to give their allegiance to Carinus, still in the West. They decided in favour of Diocletian.

A) DIOCLETIAN (284–305)

The situation shows remarkable similarity to the one at the time of Vespasian's election (see MH.I, 216ff.). This was undoubtedly an act of rebellion: the army had shown allegiance to Carinus, the elder brother, whose title was in no way affected by the death of the younger Numerian. But the course of events from 17 December 284[254] does differ from others of its kind. It represented a decision by the highest state officials and officers to replace a bad ruler with a better one, and this is where the parallel lies with the proclamation of Vespasian against Vitellius. It is also quite beyond doubt that Diocletian himself did not seek the purple for himself, but the only alternatives for anyone proposed in such a way were either to take his chance or choose death. This was a perilous move by the officers, and yet it was not actually unlawful, at least not in wider historical terms. It was consonant with Diocletian's character that he had no personal desire for power. All the same, a question mark hangs over the whole course of events. It was made possible and prepared for by the murder of two Emperors. If the question is posed: to whose benefit?, the answer could well point to Diocletian, but there is no evidence that he was either involved in, or the author of this crime – not even on the part of his bitterest enemies, the Christians. And in any case people did not otherwise hold back from expressing such suspicions.

[MH.III, 65] The official handling of the matter, of course, was repulsive: when Diocletian, in accordance with custom, presented himself before the soldiers to address them following his election, Aper, the Praetorian Prefect, who was openly accused as the one directly responsible for the murder, was standing beside him. Diocletian swore by Sol that he was innocent and had not sought the throne – and cut Aper down.[255] We would undoubtedly call that murder, but Rome did not call it so, and could not. At any rate it was swift justice; it lay entirely within the authority of the Emperor, who was not bound by any formal procedure if he was convinced of the culpability of an offender. Vespasian had also had a senator summarily cut down in like manner.[256] But it is suspicious: had there been any evidence against Aper that did not compromise anyone else one supposes that it would have been made public.

Be that as it may, the fact remains that this course of events removed a bad Emperor and replaced him with an infinitely better one. We know little of Carinus; naturally in the Diocletianic era he was painted as black as possible and depicted as a mass of blemishes. As a soldier he seems to have been not unable,[257] but coarse, brutal and lecherous,[258] quite on the model of Vitellius, and a danger to the honour of the Empire.

The eastern legions, then, had declared their allegiance and the East and West were up in arms against each other, just as during the conflict between Vitellius and Vespasian. Diocletian's victory came almost by chance. Carinus had military superiority, since in East–West [MH.III, 66] conflicts the West always had greater military strength; moreover he also had the able Aristobulus at his side as Praetorian Prefect. The latter and Carinus seem to have taken the matter very lightly at first; they did not march against Diocletian immediately, but first against Julianus, who had rebelled in Italy[259] – another quite harmless revolt, since Italy was unarmed and of no military importance at all. Even so, it cost some delay, enabling Diocletian to cross to Europe unhindered. The moment of decision came in Moesia at the confluence of the Morava and the Danube.[260] In fact the easterners had drawn the shorter straw, but matters took a different turn with the death of Carinus. He too was undoubtedly assassinated, and again the assassin cannot be identified. Aristobulus may have played a part in it. In any case the consular list for 284 and 285 hides a political secret: war broke out in autumn 284; everything that happened – the mobilization, the diversion to Italy, the march to Moesia – undoubtedly called for so much time that we have to date the final confrontation to spring 285. At the beginning of that year Carinus was consul, but the consular list for the following year names Diocletian and Aristobulus![261] It is highly likely that this important man also turned his back on Carinus too, and helped Diocletian to turn military defeat into political victory.

[MH.III, 67] Diocletian is one of the most remarkable individuals in history. Again the gaps in the tradition are most irritating, in permitting us little more than guesswork around this interesting problem. Originally he was called not Aurelius, but Gaius Valerius. He died in 313 at 68 years old; this brings us to 245 as the year of his birth, which means that he ascended the throne at a very mature age.[262] His origins are obscure; it is certain that he was a Dalmatian. He certainly did not come from the town of Dioclea; this was the ridiculous idea of a later Byzantine playing with the suggestiveness of words,[263] and made all the more ridiculous by the fact that the same person simultaneously derives Diocletian's name from that of his mother. His enemies called him Diocles,[264] which suggests that he was a freedman[265] and originally bore this Greek name, which he later Latinized. He may well also have been illegitimate, as is suggested of him. A freed slave is necessarily born outside wedlock; his mother is named, his father is not.

Of Diocletian's career, we know that he was commander (*dux*) of Moesia and a graduate of Probus's school. This was militarily a recommendation, as was the fact that Carus, Constantius and Aristobulus numbered among his friends. He then entered the Guard; later authors[266] refer to him as 'commandant of the mounted *domestici*', which were probably in fact the *protectores*, as the imperial bodyguard was then known after the disbanding of the Praetorians. Immediately prior to his election as Emperor he took part in the Persian campaign under Carus.

His nature and character are difficult to make out from the tradition. He was by all accounts a genius as a statesman. The way he reshaped the derailed Empire [MH.III, 68] speaks clearly enough. He was is called *magnus vir*,[267] 'great man', and revered like a god by all his fellow-Emperors. Witnesses who were at one and the same time near to him and yet objective speak of him as being outstandingly talented. His inclination was more towards statesmanship than the military sphere. He is said – by his enemies – to have been a coward, but this is absurd. It is refuted by his entire career, which came from his status as an honourable soldier. Lactantius,[268] a Christian and his enemy, makes this accusation, but all it means is that Diocletian used the army as an executive instrument and that, with that remarkable clear thinking about himself that was typical of him, he recognized that he was no military genius and therefore declined to take on major military tasks. This clarity about the limitations of what he could and could not accomplish is revealed in all the major wars of his reign, which he always waged through others. This should be counted as one of his merits, not one of his faults. His nature was one of remarkable sobriety and realism about the nature of things, and no one like him has perhaps ever appeared again since. He represents, for example, virtually the only instance of a man not born to be Emperor who appointed men who were not related to him to his side, a man who never even attempted to found a dynasty – always the prime aspiration of the parvenu. Of course he had no children, but passing over all those in his immediate vicinity he selected his comrades from good army material, and also made Maximian, after Maxentius was born, adopt a son who was older than he was himself.

He exerted a huge influence over his own followers, particularly those closest to him. References to his veneration like a god have a serious aspect. The man who replaced [MH.III, 69] the administrative union of the Empire with a unity based on loyalty to himself, separated the East from the West, and installed two Emperors, each with his own sphere of competence, was presumably aware that this would prompt the dissolution of the Empire. He said that his greatest accomplishment had been to preserve the unity of the Empire. But he was aware

411

that it could not last. Maximian obeyed him without reservation for twenty years, but when one of the Caesars was no longer prepared to acquiesce,[269] Diocletian abdicated and retired to his home country, the land of his childhood, and to private life. Once this single individual had let go of the rudder, the Empire went completely off the rails.

Diocletian was inclined to clemency, and disinclined to all abruptness and ruthlessness. Never was a conflict ended less bloodily than that between him and Carinus. No executions followed on the victory that had been won. Carinus had certainly been a lawful ruler, but the unlawful victor does not generally inquire after such things. The ruthlessness and cruelty of Maximian had always been repugnant to him. Diocletian preferred to let others carry out his sterner judgements, since he knew only too well that reforms such as he sought could not be embarked on wearing kid gloves. As with the military campaigns, he left the unavoidable acts of severity to others.

True statesman that he was, he always had an eye for the fiscal side of government. He practised prudent economy. His opponents called it greed, but this was King Frederick's sense of economy, which seeks to reshape an Empire and needs must have the means to do it. In order to achieve this the tax system had to be reorganized and tightened up; but he declared [MH.III, 70] war on all useless and frivolous expenditure (for example, the games, which devoured vast sums throughout the Empire). The basic principles of his character were liberty, ingenuity and cleverness. He reflected on the position and duties of the Emperor and was thoroughly objective. His voluntary abdication is unparalleled, but only possible for such an objective spirit. It might also be mentioned that he was taciturn and a man of few words.

The trend towards monotheism was at that time becoming universal, among the lower orders and the loftiest philosophical circles alike. Polytheism had become outmoded. In military circles the great god Mithras was greatly revered; this was Sol, who surpassed all the rest in might and power. Diocletian, whose own origins were among these circles, shared their religious views. It should be emphasized, however, that he was devoid of religious fanaticism, and the persecution of Christians attributed to him did not originate with him (see MH.III, 104).

He has been accused of love of pomp,[270] and one particular set of malicious critics have charged him with plain vanity. At all events he replaced military dress with the gold-embroidered toga and shoes adorned with precious stones – the attire of the triumphant victor; similiarly the practice of adoration during audiences also became customary during his reign. With Diocletian, however, this was more than a simple desire to wear particularly flamboyant clothing. Rather it was related to his religious fatalism. He aimed high, and sought generally to place the Emperorship on a higher plane. These accoutrements were the visible

expression of the Emperor's exalted [MH.III, 71] position in the eyes of the public. Previously the Emperor had ranked as an officer among other officers, distinguished only by his red military cloak. Now, all this was to change, and new wine
calls for new bottles.

Diocletian was a genius with a passion for building[271] – a quality he shares with
most great statesmen – with Caesar, Augustus and Trajan. But he set a trend
towards utility in his buildings, and the thermal baths of Diocletian in Rome still
stand as testimony to his creative genius. If the question is posed as to whether
baths or a luxury building are of greater utility, then – depending upon one's
answer to the question – one might wish modern policy[272] to be directed towards
the utilitarian or the luxurious. Diocletian's principal building works were
walls.[273] He rebuilt the walls of most of the major cities of the East and West
– Milan, Carthage and thousands of others – which had fallen into disrepair over
the centuries. In this period of barbarian invasions this was highly necessary
building work, and it was far more important for a city to have walls then than it
is now. Once it had successfully escaped the initial onslaught of a barbarian horde,
it was generally saved, since a real siege was of no interest to pirates.

Who can say what went on in Diocletian's mind, or what the inner man
was like? Since nothing written by him has survived, we are obliged to judge him
by his deeds. He was open to family feeling, although he did not allow it to
dominate his policy; that would have been too costly. Through his marriage
alliances he sought to bolster the weak spot in his brainchild, [MH.III, 72]
replacing administrative unity with unity centred on his own person. He adopted
Maximian as his brother – in fact 'adoption' is the wrong term here, since no such
form of fraternal adoption existed. But the *princeps* is exempt from the constraints
of private law. In short, he declared Maximian to be his brother and from then on
the two of them bore the clan name Aurelius Valerius.[274] Appointment of the two
Caesars was added later, both adoption and marriage relationships were utilized
to secure firmer family bonds: Constantius became Maximian's adoptive son
and at the same time married Maximian's stepdaughter Theodora.[275] Galerius,
Diocletian's adoptive son, took his daughter Valeria in marriage.[276] The creation
of such family bonds was not disdained even by the very greatest rulers, although
their political weight should not be exaggerated. But they made Diocletian's later
years miserable, as he sought in vain to rescue Valeria from the oriental confusion
in which she had become deeply embroiled. And, just as his creation of such
family bonds shows that Diocletian had a feeling for the domestic side of life, so
too the manner in which he created them shows that he regarded and made use
of his daughter as a political tool.

Maximian, originally called Marcus Aurelius, was but a few years younger than
Diocletian; 250 may be assumed to be the year of his birth. The fact that we have

no inscription referring to Maximian as Caesar suggests that Diocletian was consciously working towards a division of the Empire. Diocletian reigned from 284 on and Maximian must have been appointed Caesar in 285. [MH.III, 73] On 1 April 286 he became Augustus;[277] there is only a difference of one year between his accession and Diocletian's.

Maximian's personality is straightforward and not in the least puzzling. He too was an Illyrian, had worked his way up the same military ladder, and he might be called the Hercules of the new Empire. His was to some degree a plebeian nature.[278] It should not be forgotten that Diocletian called himself Jovius, not Jupiter. Maximian was in many respects reminiscent of Mark Antony – a hopeless politician, very able as a second in command, but lost as soon as he was given first place with no one above him. Maximian had a marshall's temperament that fitted him more than any other to assist Diocletian. Crude, wild, barbaric and cruel, moreover prodigal in the excess of his energy, his attributes often set him at odds with Diocletian, and he also aroused the animosity of the public. His soldier's capacity for prompt action and his unconditional loyalty, on the other hand, were invaluable. Although legally equal in rank he was de facto subordinate and abdicated when Diocletian did. His subsequent attempt to return to public life and a political career without Diocletian exposed his total lack of political will and acumen. This absence of a will of his own was exactly what Diocletian looked for in his co-ruler.

The two Caesars, Constantius and Galerius, appeared later on 1 March 295.[279] The immediate reason for their appointment was probably the military turmoil in Britain and the West; the Empire was too vast even for two Emperors. Constantius and Galerius likewise wielded supreme authority, but only as Caesars. Caesar, at first simply a name, later became the title of the successor, but had no sphere of competence of its own. The term was [MH.III, 74] roughly synonymous with what we would call crown prince. The two Diocletianic Caesars, however, had quite a different status; they had their own spheres of competence and the authority of Emperors, though not with regard to legislation. On the other hand they did possess the tribunician potestas, and their succession was automatic. Constantius must have been older than is generally believed; the year of his birth can be set at 250 at the latest, which means he was at least as old as Maximian and that the imitatio naturalis[280] was set aside for this adoption. The primary aim was in any case not to secure the succession, for which a much younger man would have had to be chosen, but to meet the need for immediate assistance. The adopted men were expected to work.

Galerius was probably somewhat younger, but since his daughter married in 305 and was therefore probably born in 285, the year of her father's birth probably cannot be far off 255, which means he also came to power in his forties.

Constantius continued the regime and won the hearts of the public. Lactantius does not include him among the *persecutores*, those who persecuted the Christians, while painting Galerius as black as possible. It can probably be asserted that in general Christian writers paid their persecutors back with interest. Objective individuals refer to Galerius as sensible and militarily experienced.[281] He was a heavy eater, corpulent, with a stately appearance. The restrained regime of Diocletian had not been [MH.III, 75] to his taste and he dissociated himself from it. He has been accused of wanting to replace the Roman Empire with a Dacian one.[282] Put in these terms this is absurd, although there is a grain of truth in it: we have already seen frequently that Illyria was the heartland of the Empire, and Galerius was a native-born son. He is reputed to have been a cowherd in his youth and this is quite possible,[283] for soldiers were taken from the plough and the herd and Galerius too had had a soldier's career. The fact that he now sought to shift the Empire's centre of gravity to the land of his birth, which was at the same time the most robust in the Empire, is explicable both from the personal and political standpoint.

Constantius was also an Illyrian. His subsequently recreated family tree is a fake,[284] but it probably is true that he came from a superior family; he had forbears.[285] He was *protector*, then *tribunus*, then *praeses* (governor) of Dalmatia. He was interested in education and concerned about the welfare of subjects, seeking to eliminate the tax burden as far as possible. In contrast to Diocletian's great price edict, which fixed the prices for anything and everything and which could not be exceeded when trading (revealing a serious failure and misunderstanding of economics), Constantius, who protected trade interests wherever possible, had a golden saying which many a politician could make do with today: money was better kept in the pockets of the citizens than in the state treasury, and hoarding was stupid.[286] He was incidentally an able soldier and reconquered Britain, which Maximian had failed to do.

The chronology of this period is badly confused, making it virtually impossible to reconstruct a coherent narrative around its [MH.III, 76] central point. Considering what the Roman world still means even today, it is best to deal with its history territory by territory.

Gaul had been of crucial importance to the Empire from the very outset; its conquest by Caesar amounted to a refounding of Rome and this country was as inexhaustible in the resources it provided them as it is today. But no territory was so severely afflicted in its time. Internal decline culminated in the revolt of the Bacaudae.[287] This is a Celtic,[288] not a Roman word (which means that the vernacular was by no means yet dead). All explanations of the etymology of the word are apocryphal, and all that is clear (and this is important) is that it originated from the Celtic group. It was in fact a peasant war, a jacquerie. The word Bacaudae is also used quite generally to mean 'conspiracy'. These were poor folk, driven to despair by the tax burden and misrule. It is probably closest in

415

meaning to the English word 'outlaws'. Instead of paying up, the peasants took up their pikes and mounted their horses, assuming they still had any. In this way bands of robbers formed who then made war on the peaceable population. In a truly civilized country such a phenomenon would have been impossible, but in that country, at that time – a partly devastated land where wasteland, forests and marshes offered suitable hiding places – it became a chronic condition that dragged on for centuries. We find the same phenomenon later in Spain – *Bacaudae Tarraconenses*[289], [MH.III, 77] providing the best evidence that the name did not refer just to a particular area.

When Diocletian ascended the throne his commitments in the East, as we have already seen, compelled him to install special Emperors for the West; but these events must date from much earlier. In one Latin panegyrist we find an event under the Emperor Claudius Gothicus which may belong to this context: Bibracte (Augustodunum), a leading Gallic city, was attacked by a *Batavica rebellio* and besieged for seven months. It requested help from Claudius in vain. What was the *Batavica rebellio*? Evidently a precursor of the Bacaudae. It must already have been a significant insurrection to be able to attack one of the foremost cities and besiege, seize and plunder it so thoroughly that it was still lying in ruins twenty years later. It is also feasible that the location of these events was in the northern, less civilized part of the country, another factor being the renowned fighting spirit of the Batavians, who supplied the core of Roman troops in those parts.[290]

At the beginning of Diocletian's reign Aelianus and Amandus are named as leaders of the Bacaudae.[291] This is significant in as much as they are Roman names. This means that Romanized Celts were involved in the movement – in a word, all people oppressed by taxation. But they did not make Emperors of their leaders. Although there are some coins on which 'Aelianus' and 'Amandus' are described as Emperors, recent research has proved beyond doubt that these are forgeries.[292] Unfortunately this is no help, now that the mischief has been done and they are there wearing their crowns in all the modern picture-books.

Since there was now a serious attempt to deal with the Bacaudae the revolt was crushed, but not all their hiding places [MH.III, 78] were rooted out, nor could they be, given the nature of the land and the fact that the source of the trouble – the inordinate tax burden – had not been dealt with. From that time on this kind of peasant war remained a persistent malady. The name Bacaudae is restricted to the Celts, but this phenomenon occurs throughout the far-flung Empire. We shall find the same phenomenon in Egypt under the name *boukoloi* (herdsmen) (see MH.III, 92). The same causes, the same effects.

In Gaul this was exacerbated by external enemies, the Germans. The repercussions of the second half of the third century were never erased. In this period the East played first, the West second fiddle, so that in the East the frontier still tended to be pushed forward, whereas it was receding in the West. The right bank of the Rhine was now lost forever. From Gallienus on this was final and no more attempt was made to improve the situation. On the lower course of the river the right bank of the Rhine had never really been subjugated in the same way as on its upper course, in modern Swabia. All that was required was tight control and to prevent the emergence of a strong German power on the right bank. This much was indeed accomplished under the better Emperors. In the fourth century, however, we find substantial German confederations forming, partly as a result of fresh pressure behind them from peoples from the East, but primarily as a result of a strengthening of internal power among the frontier peoples, and without any serious preventive measures on the part of the Romans. The tribes mentioned are first and foremost the Alamanni and the Franks, then the Burgundians and Saxons and smaller tribes, such as the Heruli and Vandals. [MH.III, 79] We can pass over still others here.

The Saxons originally inhabited the Elbe estuary[293] and came into contact with the Romans mainly on the coasts through their piracy, which was aimed principally at the northern French and British coasts.[294] Initially there was no direct contact with the Romans. These were the beginnings and precursors of the raids of the Norsemen. But they did not yet venture far inland.

There is early mention of the Burgundians;[295] first we find them far to the east in the lands between the Oder and Vistula. Then, under Probus, they moved to the Danube with the Vandals, and from then on appear to the rear of the Alamanni, a nomadic people who should most probably be located near the sources of the river Main. Roman policy aimed at playing them off against the Burgundians.[296] Although conflicts between Germans and Romans are viewed as the most important, it should never be forgotten that side by side with, and indeed prior to, these there were also conflicts between Germans and Germans; Goths, for example, frequently faced Goths on the battlefield. The spectacle offered to us is one not of unified action, but of sometimes highly confused strife among these peoples.

The Alamanni appear early on in the sources.[297] Caracalla fought a Germanic war against the Chatti and the Alamanni, one an old and the other a new tribe. In reality the Alamanni comprised a people pressing forward out of the great wave of nations from the East who flooded into the devastated lands of modern Baden and Swabia. It will be recalled that Roman policy was to keep these lands [MH.III, 80] unpopulated and to make the true frontier secure by creating a wilderness in front of it. Here, therefore, the immigrating peoples had an easy time. The name 'Alamanni' suggests that they were a mixed people formed of fragments of diverse tribes.[298] They fought on horseback,[299] which was not customary among pure Germans. It proved the calamity of the third century, wreaking severe havoc in the period that followed, that the creation of a foreign state was tolerated in this vulnerable frontier area. Aurelian was compelled to act against the invasions in his time, but the response was inadequate. From now on, therefore, this people became the chief adversary.

Alongside them stood the Franks, whose name and its etymology remain unclear.[300] They were probably old tribes already known from Tacitus; conjecture on the subject may be correct or incorrect, but is immaterial. We first find mention of them on the map of the world dating from the time of the Emperor Alexander (222–235).[301] Under Postumus (259–268) they carried out such aggressive raids into the lower Rhineland provinces that the Emperor moved his residence to Cologne, from where he directed the defence of the frontier.[302] These people were Franks; it is irrelevant whether they are referred to as such or not. The Salians are first mentioned in the fourth century.[303] Their incursions were made simultaneously on land and from the sea, but all of them had predominantly the character of raids for plunder. For the time being it was on the right bank of the Rhine that the consolidation of the Germans into a state was slowly proceeding.

When Maximian inherited the West, peace reigned among the Alamanni and conflict among the Franks. There were not yet continuous invasions and a tribe often disappears [MH.III, 81] from view for a considerable time. Things were particularly bad at sea, and the fleet, which had been allowed to lapse into complete disarray, had to be rebuilt. Carausius, a Menapian skipper by profession, was chosen to reorganize the fleet. He rose from the lowliest rank to become *dux Armoricanus* on the Gaulish and *comes litoris* on the British coast.[304] He acquitted himself of his task brilliantly, but aroused mistrust concerning his further plans. He was accused of coming to terms with the pirates and it was rumoured that he was prepared to turn a blind eye in return for a share of their booty. Finding himself in an impossible position, Carausius was compelled to declare independence from the Empire, take command of the fleet, and secure Boulogne, then the key port on the Gaulish coast, offering the most convenient crossing-point, from where he crossed over to Britain. The legion stationed there joined him and he styled himself not a leader of insurgents, but Emperor. Carausius's ties with the Franks and Saxons made him a serious threat to the Empire; in particular he had Frankish troops at his disposal.

It is impossible to envisage a more difficult task for Rome. Compared to this the first conquest of Britain had been child's play. Then it had been a confrontation between the civilized world, with all its inexhaustible resources, and barbarians – something like the conquest of America by European discoverers. Now Britain had a Roman [MH.III, 82] commander at the head of disciplined troops. The Channel fleet, the bulwark for Gaul, was in the hands of the insurgents. Maximian was not even able to recapture Boulogne, and the Romans had to content themselves with concluding a peace with Carausius. This was a peculiar peace and its terms are obscure; it was evidently construed quite differently by Britain and the Empire. Maximian considered the external state of affairs as at peace, but not peace with a co-ruler. Carausius regarded himself as an Emperor, alongside, or at least under, Diocletian and Maximian. Later Carausius was termed *archipirata*[305] and treated as a *rebellis*. This dragged on until Carausius's death, when Constantius was appointed Caesar and there was a great change.

The chronology of this period is extremely complex; but if we are to have some hope of understanding history the most accurate possible knowledge of the sequence of events is of the utmost importance. Three or four strands of historical tradition run disjointedly side by side in the sources available to us, depending on the diverse locations of the various events: the wars and events in the East, those in the West, those on the Danube, and the wars in Africa. Although few and far between, the chroniclers of this era are at least reliable. We have definite data which are beyond doubt: the crossing of the Danube by the Alamanni in 285[306] and Galerius's victory over the Persians in 297.[307]

The situation with regard to the chronology of Gaul is as follows. [MH.III, 83] We must go by the data provided by the writers of panegyric for the events in question here, specifically *Panegyricus* IV and V. Poor as these show-pieces are, they are nevertheless the speeches of contemporaries at the centre of these events, who at least knew something of the background to them. *Panegyricus* V[308] gives the date of 1 March 296 and describes the reconquest of Britain as having immediately preceded it. Since this cannot have been a winter campaign, we must set the date of this event in 295. It gives the periods when the British tyrants were in power: three years for Allectus, seven years for his predecessor Carausius.[309] Working back from 295 this gives 293 as the date when Allectus came to power and 286 for Carausius.[310] Seen from a different angle this is somewhat too early: Maximian became Caesar in 285 and Emperor in 286; this leaves only some twelve years for the events of his first period of rule. It would perhaps be best, therefore, to date the rebellion of Carausius to the beginning of 287. At any rate he died in 293.

This was the year when Diocletian and Maximian were joined by the two Caesars. If we ask what prompted Diocletian to install them, we have the explanation for it right here in the events in Gaul. The Danube was quiet, and the unrest in Africa was too trifling to warrant such a measure, while profound peace still reigned on the Persian frontier. Here in Gaul, however, there lurked a great danger for the Empire.

[MH.III, 84] Maximian, able soldier that he was, had failed to bring about the reconquest of Britain and did not even succeed in wresting Boulogne from the enemy. The peace with Carausius was after all no more than tacit acceptance of an insurrection. Carausius himself was perhaps just about bearable, but something definitely had to be done about his successor Allectus.

Another chronological question concerns the period of Constantine's Alamannic War. This is mentioned in the panegyric of 1 March 296[311] (see MH.III, 83), which means it must have taken place before that date. Since it also refers to the thawing of the ice on the Rhine, we must date the war to the winter of 295/6. This means that Britain was reconquered in the summer of 295 and war waged against the Alamanni the following winter. This also agrees with Eutropius's view[312] that the two wars occurred simultaneously. We shall be looking later at the causal relationship between the two wars.

Let us return to the historical narrative! Carausius died, possibly assassinated,[313] along the lines of famous precedents, by Allectus, who was his Praetorian Prefect.[314] There was no other sea power in those waters aside from that in his own hands; this and his links with the Franks constituted a huge danger to Rome. This was also why the government had allowed so much to go by without intervening, but could not let this go by; they had to intervene here. The danger for Batavia and Gaul was too pressing. Whoever had command of the fleet also had command of the Channel and the North Sea, and Roman territory was also [MH.III, 85] open to land attacks by the Franks and Saxons. The war waged by Constantius was one of unparalleled audacity. The first objective was to recapture Boulogne. They had no ships and Allectus was able to assist the city from the sea unhindered. Using a great barricade Constantius blocked the entrance to the harbour, thereby rendering Allectus's fleet powerless, and forced the city to surrender. He then proceeded to build a fleet and, during the lengthy period required to accomplish this, suppressed the Franks. This made him master of modern Flanders and Brabant, which in those days was even more than today a region of half land, half water.

He then crossed to Britain. He divided his fleet and posted the smaller detachment, commanded by himself, off Boulogne, the other, stronger one off the Seine estuary near modern Rouen, commanded by Asclepiodotus. A murky, foggy day was chosen to venture the crossing and they succeeded in evading the watchful eye of the enemy fleet, anchored off the island. The landing was successful and Asclepiodotus burned all his ships – partly to prevent them falling into enemy hands and partly to impress on the minds of his troops the imperative necessity of either being victorious or dying. Allectus does not appear to have found any real support among the Roman Britons; he could only rely on the *cunei* (the wedge-formations) of his Franks.[315] He died in a cavalry encounter, after which a second battle seems to have taken place [MH.III, 86] in the vicinity of London. The remnant of his defeated army plundered the city, but fell into the hands of Constantius, who had successfully managed the crossing with the other section of the fleet. The great gamble had paid off.[316]

Roman civilization seems to have struck far deeper roots in Britain than in Gaul at that time. This is indicated by the fact that Constantius took British building artisans back with him to Gaul to rebuild the city of Augustodunum (Autun), which was still in ruins after the peasant revolt.[317]

The riskiest aspect of this war was the fact that it necessitated completely denuding Gaul of troops; and it is easy to understand what the flattery of the panegyrist is really referring to when we read that Maximian went to the Rhine and held Germany at bay with his mere name. He simply had no troops. The Alamannic War now followed logically on from this, once the subjugation of Britain was complete and troops were available once again. Fortunately the Germans had remained peaceful during the summer, but during the following winter they reappeared on the scene, albeit too late.

The Alamanni pressed forward in great hordes – 60,000 are mentioned – into the territory of the Lingones and besieged Langres, their city. Constantius [MH.III, 87] arrived from the north just in time, and two battles are said to have been fought in one day. First Constantius suffered a defeat, but this was erased by a glorious victory. He is reputed to have been wounded and his army driven into the city in a complete rout; the gates had been closed and the commanders locked out, so that he had to be hauled up the wall on a rope.[318] Then, however, events took a more fortunate turn. We do not know to what extent these details are correct. There was a further battle at Vindonissa; finally the thawing of the ice on the Rhine cut the Alamanni off from their homeland and condemned them to destruction. The panegyrist[319] states that the land was subjugated from the Rhine bridge as far as the Danube crossing. Where was this Rhine bridge? Not at Mainz, which is too far downstream; we should undoubtedly look for it some-where between Strasburg and Lake Constance, perhaps at Basle. The Danube crossing may have been at Günzburg,[320] somewhere near Ulm. In any case the area is poorly specified in this passage. The victory was conclusive. After 295/6 order prevailed in Gaul, until war broke out again after Diocletian's abdication. With spirited eloquence the panegyrist describes the devastation and regenera-tion, as well as the triumph that these once feared enemies now worked the fields and tended flocks – which indicates the settlement of relocated barbarians [MH.III, 88] – and that they had to provide military service. This helped to alleviate the depopulation. Constantius reduced the taxes in this war-ravaged country, thereby laying the foundations for his popularity, which carried over to his son after his death.

Constantius died in York in 306.[321] His last accomplishment was a war against the Picts and the restoration of the Wall.[322] It is indicative that in Britain, aside from smaller garrisons and of course the guards on the northern Wall, the over-whelming majority of the army were concentrated at a single point: in Dover (Dubris).[323] This simply indicates the importance of links with the mainland, which were maintained at all times. Only in this way could the Channel be secured and piracy be held in check.

This concludes what we know, or think we know, about conditions in Gaul during this period. Military work was followed by peacetime work. The river crossings on frontier rivers were fortified,[324] and more was done in this respect in the fourth century than in the three previous ones together. This marked a complete change in the system. Previously the frontiers had been secured either by taking possession of the foreshore on the far side of the rivers, or by leaving it as wasteland. Now secure bridgeheads were built. We have direct evidence of this in the case of the Euphrates and the Danube: across the river from Aquincum (Buda), on the left bank, Contra-Aquincum (Pest) was built in 294;[325] and the same will have been done with all the frontiers. This was a consequence of the Diocletianic reorganization as surely as [MH.III, 89] night follows day. The tradition does not provide us with direct information about the Rhine,[326] but where the literature is silent the stones speak: recently very important excavation work has been carried out at the castrum at Deutz, which tells the story of this 'Contra-Agrippina', as it might be called, by analogy with Contra-Aquincum. Foolish people have dated this foundation to the first three centuries: at that time Cologne was an open city and certainly had no Rhine bridge. Moreover all the tiles that have been discovered date from the Diocletianic and Constantinian eras. The potential for reorganizing the severely damaged territory of Gaul depended on this securing of the frontiers, along with the resolute abandonment of the land beyond.

The events of this period in the Danube lands are less well known to us, nor are they as important as those in Gaul. The scourge of the third century was the pirate raids of the Goths, which originated around the Black Sea, specifically the Crimea, which had never been within the Roman sphere of influence. Now, quite suddenly, these pirate raids ceased; the reason for this abrupt curtailment is to be sought in the fact that Diocletian promoted Nicomedia to the status of a capital city, thereby acquiring direct control of the Dardanelle straits from their immediate vicinity. The Dardanelles are much more easily blocked than the Channel, and as soon as a strong power was established there the pirates inevitably disappeared.

In contrast we find numerous wars on land; the roles of the Alamanni and Franks were played here by the Sarmatians and the Carpi. The name of the Sarmatians is as much a collective one as that of the Alamanni; they consisted of substantial masses of agglomerated individual tribes, for the most part Iazyges. The enormous mistake the Romans had made in not subjugating the Hungarian plains proper when they had occupied Pannonia [MH.III, 90] and Dacia as far as Buda and Pest, and then Transylvania beyond, now took its toll. These plains were not a desirable possession; there were no gold mines there, either in the literal or the figurative sense, as there were in Dacia; but it was military nonsense to leave the territory in between unoccupied, a wedge between two parts of the Empire. Now the penalty for this mistake was paid; it was from here that the Sarmatian incursions occurred. Perhaps these were the first Slavs to be seen by the Romans.[327] There was also political dissension among the Iazyges, particularly in later times. They seem to have been a two-tier population, made up of a master nation and vassals. This gave rise to civil wars,[328] resulting in a less resolute opposition to the Romans.

Aside from the Germans, Diocletian most frequently had occasion to fight wars against the Sarmatians: *Germanicus maximus VI, Sarmaticus maximus IV* were his titles in 301;[329] this presupposes four great victories against the Sarmatians. The theatre of war began at the river Tisza, and the war was in any case linked with the Alamannic one. The entire land from Swabia to Hungary was in turmoil. Raetia had to be reconquered; there is another mention of the Quadi here, after which they disappear.[330] Thereafter all the territory is described as Sarmatian. Victory was exploited in the same way here as on the Rhine; here too the resettlement system was employed. [MH.III, 91] The Sarmatians were mainly moved to devastated regions of Italy. We have accounts of this from Constantine's period,[331] but his measures were certainly only a continuation of Diocletian's reorganization.

We have already mentioned the securing of the Danube line; in better times inner Hungary from Pest as far as Lake Balaton was encircled by Roman garrisons, but entirely uncultivated. Galerius's main accomplishment had been his civilizing work here, and it was not for nothing that the province of *Valeria* was named after Diocletian's daughter, Galerius's wife.[332] The paucity and disjointedness of the sources make a reasonably orderly historical narrative impossible here.

The same applies to Africa, where conditions had remained the same since the very outset, and indeed have done so to this day. The task of the army here was always that of defending the civilized, relatively narrow coastal strip from the nomadic tribes. Maximian felt compelled to cross to Africa. The frontier war, basically a task for a semi-organized police force, called for the intervention of the Emperor, a case which had never arisen before. There could not conceivably be more striking proof of the pitiful state of the government. *Quinquegentiani* was the etymologically obscure name given to the rebellious frontier tribes; likewise in the inscriptions, with an equally corrupt morphology: *Quinquegentanei*.[333] This war is documented as having lasted for over thirty years. During the terrible period after 260, when everything in the Empire was going off the rails, larger cities were already being besieged by them and were obliged [MH.III, 92] to defend themselves. By that time, of course, the African garrison was far too weak. Even in the period of the best Emperors it had not numbered more than 20,000 men for the entire protracted territory from Morocco to Egypt; here was the clearest shortcoming of the Augustan system.

Things were worst in Mauretania, better in Carthage. Inscriptions show that the frontier between Numidia and Mauretania, where the *Transtagnenses*,[334] i.e. 'those from the other side of the swamps' (the Shetts) operated, was the main location of the incursions. Oran and Morocco–Tangiers were Roman territory. The territory between, the land of the Rif brigands,[335] was never Roman.

Frontier defence was now energetically reinforced and the peace thereby created endured for the entire imperial period. The Vandals, who put an end to Roman rule, came from another quarter, from the sea;[336] it was not the Moors who brought down the Empire in Africa. The Moorish invasion was not directed at the centre of Roman rule; if it had been, the denigrators, of whom there were certainly enough, would have told us so.

Egypt had little to contend with in the way of external enemies, but suffered a great deal from oppressive taxation. The 'herdsmen' (*boukoloi*) already mentioned earlier resided in the immediate vicinity of Alexandria.[337] In good times they were herdsmen, in bad times robbers. They already appeared under Marcus.[338] This was exacerbated by the terrible consequences of Palmyran rule.[339] When Aurelian marched against the Palmyrans they drew support from their Nabataean[340] frontier neighbours – barbarian tribes among whom human sacrifice and cannibalism were [MH.III, 93] prevalent, perhaps the worst of all barbarians, but able, trained to fight and extremely dangerous.[341] Summoned away to the West, Aurelian was unable to complete his work, and Egypt remained for the most part in barbarian hands. Things improved somewhat under Probus, but were still far from satisfactory.

The quarrel between the Palmyrans and the Romans, i.e. in fact between the East and the West, brought about a rift among the higher social strata. Alexandria was divided, and conducted a bitter civil war with the obduracy typical of the Egyptian character.[342] The Egyptians preferred to be cut down to the last man rather than give an inch. This seed was not eradicated; but we know few specific details.

During Diocletian's reign a pretender was active in Alexandria whom the commentators call Achilleus and who may be identical with the Lucius Domitius Domitianus of the coins.[343] Alexandria was besieged, Busiris and Koptos[344] razed to the ground, and Diocletian himself appeared in the theatre of war. We gain some idea of the obduracy of the rebels from the fact that Alexandria, a city of half a million inhabitants, only fell after eight months of siege. The military task was not in fact too onerous, but the political one was all the more so. The garrison was greatly reinforced, from one legion to six or eight with numerous cavalry, both to keep the *fellahin* in order, and to defend the frontiers. The southernmost part of Egypt was abandoned and the frontier set at Syrene (Aswan) at [MH.III, 94] the cataracts, but that frontier was then maintained. Egypt, (later) the source of corn supplies for Constantinople, absolutely had to be secured.

The Persian War is the part of this story best known to us, perhaps by chance, and also because the anecdote hunters found what they wanted here. For politically and militarily it was not as important as the Egyptian rebellion, which had far greater repercussions for the future of the Empire, leaving aside the situation in Britain.

We have frequently had occasion to emphasize that Diocletian's policy was cautious and prevaricating, perhaps on occasion even cowardly. No attempt was made to restore the former frontiers, or recapture the land beyond, and thereby – this cannot be denied – steer a course back to the bolder and more aggressive policy of earlier times. The position chosen by Diocletian, behind the great rivers with their fortified bridgeheads, does have something of the besieged fortress mentality about it. Earlier policy had been more expansionist, but Diocletian's was more appropriate to an ageing Empire. The tolerance shown towards Carausius in fact came close to excising Britain from the body of the Empire, and it was then the personal initiative of Constantius and imperial interests in Gaul that led to the concerted effort here and to the great reversal described earlier.

What the Romans achieved on the frontier with Persia[345] was essentially a defensive war;[346] the Persians were unquestionably the belligerent party. The catastrophe under Gallienus[347] had far-reaching [MH.III, 95] effects. It will have been the campaign of Carus that restored the situation, at least in as much as lost territory as far as the Euphrates was recaptured. Whatever lay on the far side of this river was abandoned. The historical tradition is poor and piecemeal, but it seems certain that the Romans succeeded in resubjugating Armenia and Mesopotamia, despite the assassination of Carus.

Complete peace reigned when Diocletian ascended the throne, and Armenia and Mesopotamia were, if not Roman provinces, then at least within the Roman sphere of influence. A glance at the map suffices to convince us that if Armenia was Roman then Mesopotamia was bound to be so too, although Eutropius and Victor do not expressly state as much about Mesopotamia. It was probably a dependency, and the ruler of Edessa a vassal prince. In any case this is irrelevant, since such vassal princes were no more than hereditary provincial governors. The Romans, then, had nothing more to gain on this frontier, and this alone makes an offensive war by the Romans unthinkable. *Panegyricus* III of 289,[348] our most important source for this period, explicitly states that all was well in the East. Moreover civil war was also raging among various Persian pretenders, which made Roman peace seem assured.

When, however, internal dissension was brought to an end by the accession of Narses, the Persians launched an invasion into Armenia and Mesopotamia.[349] We can date the outbreak of war to 296. There was probably an internal [MH.III, 96] connection with the Egyptian rebellion. There are demonstrable links in the Palmyran period which make a causal relationship between the two wars highly likely. The sources are silent on this point.

Diocletian turned his attention to Egypt, and the conduct of the Persian War fell to the Caesar Galerius. He has already been described earlier; he was a reckless, young, daring officer, and these qualities ill became him in the beginning. His lack of circumspection brought about a severe defeat. Great numbers were not involved here; it is plain that Diocletian's army reforms were not put into effect until after this period, otherwise the numbers of troops used in combat would be incomprehensible. They amounted to no more than a collection of fortress garrisons, since before the army reorganization the Romans had no more at their disposal. The battle took place at Carrhae, in the same region where Crassus's catastrophe had occurred in 53 BC. The Romans were forced to retreat, but Galerius's talent as a commander[350] proved itself here. The Persians did not exploit their victory and the lost battle was not militarily decisive.

The winter of 296/7 was spent rearming. Alexandria had meanwhile fallen and Diocletian turned against Mesopotamia, while Galerius mustered the core troops of Illyria, thereby of course denuding everything of troops for vast distances around, ultimately to appear with only 25,000 men on the battlefield – further proof that the increase in army size with its reorganization had not yet taken place. Once again battle was given. This time Galerius had marched on the offensive into Armenia, avoiding the ill-fated region where the war had been fought in the previous [MH.III, 97] year. He was victorious, and fortune smiled on him in a special way. A happy chance brought the entire harem of the Persian king into his power, including all his wives, the princesses and his entire retinue. This exerted a more decisive effect than a political or military factor could perhaps have done. King Narses, who was more successful as a husband than as a ruler, concluded peace at any price in order to regain his harem. Roman witnesses report that there was a possibility of considerably expanding the frontiers, and that it was Galerius's wish to follow in the footsteps of Trajan and found a new Roman province on the far side of the Tigris. But Diocletian only gave in to his wishes to a limited extent. The words attributed to the Persian negotiators are typical: the Romans should bear in mind what the destruction of the Persian Empire would mean – it would put out one of the two eyes of the world on which civilization rested.[351] There is some truth in this: instead of the Persian Empire, which might well be called of equally noble birth as Rome, barbarian rule would have ensued, which which have proved irksome for Rome as well.

Diocletian contented himself with moderate territorial concessions on the upper course of the Tigris and took territorial possession of only a few areas in the region where this river has its source beyond the former Roman frontier. Like the rest of the frontier, this land was brought into the best state of defensive preparedness and Diocletian certainly secured Roman rule for a long time in these parts. The forty years of [MH.III, 98] uninterrupted peace which followed were long unmatched, either before or since. The Roman sphere of influence extended as far as the Caucasus, for Iberians[352] are named among the peoples subject to Rome. Nisibis became an entrepôt for the highly significant Persian–Roman trade.

The essential features of domestic history have already been dealt with in the first section. Here we might add a few words about Diocletian's coinage reform.[353] It was long assumed that the reformer of the confused coinage was Constantine, and that Diocletian had only improved small coins. It was left to the Viennese scholar Missong[354] to shed an entirely new light on this situation in his painstakingly detailed research and to allow Diocletian to be recognized as the mastermind behind the reform of the gold currency.

When a coin is short-weighted this is nothing other than the incurring of an unadmitted debt. Diocletian clearly recognized this truth. At that time this applied to all money, and such a coin was no longer a coin; gold bracelets or cups might just as well have been taken in payment. The gold pieces of Carus and Probus varied in weight from 3.91 to 5.11 to 5.20 to 6.50 grammes. You may call this anything you like, but not a coin. Although they were still minted, they were essentially a New Year's donative, because that was what the Emperor needed them for. Their monetary value was purely fictitious. [MH.III, 99] Alloying, and the poor quality this brought about, did not occur in the case of gold money, but the lack of full weight was appalling. In contrast, huge amounts of putative silver coin made of a poor copper and tin alloy were in circulation, and these were then given the same kind of value as poor paper money, whose value is also based on the credit of the state. Writing 'This is worth 1,000 Marks' on a piece of paper, or putting the stamp of a coin on inferior metal amounts to precisely the same thing. Furthermore, the state itself spent this money to pay the troops' and officials' salaries, but would not accept it for the payment of taxes, demanding instead either goods or payment by weight. Aurelian attempted to regulate copper coin, but this only led to dangerous street rioting, particularly by the mint employees, of whom there were thousands, all evidently deeply involved in the fraud.[355] All that Aurelian managed to achieve was a slight improvement of the poor mint quality. Otherwise he left everything as it was.

Diocletian established the principle that the state minted silver and gold, but that the value of the money was according to weight only, and no-one was obliged to assume otherwise. This put an end to the defraudation in one fell swoop, since it removed all basis for it. He established a fixed unified weight for gold.[356] The erroneous earlier assumption that this reform was carried out not by Diocletian, but by Constantine, derives from the fact that Diocletian fixed the minting standard twice. He did not succeed with his first attempt, so it was [MH.III, 100] assumed that he had not resolved the confusion at all. We shall be discussing later the very debatable contribution of Constantine to the solution to this problem.

Diocletian's earlier gold coins bear the mark '70', later ones '60', the latter beginning with the year 290. This means that at first there were 70, then 60 to the pound. From then on each coin weighed 5.45 grammes, which makes it simply the restored *aureus* of the era of the better Emperors, such as the Antonines. This reform of the coinage thus perfectly follows on from the entire work of his reign, and should be seen as part of this era. This is the gist of Missong's studies.

In contrast, it had long been known that Diocletian was the reformer of the silver coinage.[357] His *argentei* are marked with '96', i.e. there were 96 pieces to the pound of silver, and the *argenteus* was exactly equal in value to the Neronian *denarius*, with the same weight and of the same purity.

The reform of copper coin culminated in the incorporation of Egypt. The earlier coinage system had operated with two separate zones; apart from the imperial coins, there was also provincial silver and copper coin in circulation in Asia, Syria, Cappadocia and Egypt (for example the *Cistophorus* in Asia,[358] the tetradrachm in Asia, etc.). These provincial coins had a fixed value *vis-à-vis* the imperial denarius, the latter's value always being somewhat higher. Gold, on the other hand, existed only as imperial coin. Moreover, provincial silver coin was only minted by governors, i.e. as an internal prerogative, not by individual cities, which could, on the other hand, mint provincial copper coin. This institution of provincial currency, incidentally, only existed in the East; the West had only imperial currency in general.

[MH.III, 101] Diocletian now cleared away these provincial coins. Most of them will probably already have been swept away in the great tumults of the pre-Diocletianic era; the last of this small coinage had been retained in Egypt, and these Diocletian now withdrew. This necessitated the establishment of local imperial mints, which had previously been restricted to Rome, and were now set up in all the more important provincial cities. Whereas the previous Egyptian provincial currency had consisted of a worthless alloy, Diocletian now bestowed a certain value on it. He had the pieces minted larger and more carefully. The lead was removed from the alloy and silver added. This was a wholesome monetary policy. Under Constantine good copper coin declined again.

The minting of coins at 60 to the pound persisted until 312, the threshold of the Constantinian era. In 315 the new Constantinian system[359] began, with the mark 'OB', over which there has been so much racking of brains: we now know that these are Greek numerals: 72.[360] Seventy-two (and this is exactly accurate) *aurei* were minted to the pound. This means, therefore, that Constantine began with the principle of minting 60 *aurei* to the pound, revising it to 72, and thereby brought about a disgraceful repudiation of the state's debts, as has occurred so often both before and after him. For it is a pure and simple repudiation of the state's debts when one gives the same name to a lighter coin, thereby permitting debts entered into to be met with money of inferior value. We can see, therefore, that the true reform was the work of Diocletian; what Constantine [MH.III, 102] added was a decidedly retrograde step, and a deterioration.

Let us cast a glance at the famous price edict, the *edictum de pretiis rerum venalium*.[361] This is of inestimable value for our understanding of a great many details around the year 301 since, according to Diocletian's titles,[362] it must have been promulgated in that year. Regrettably, it has so far proved impossible to resolve the question as to which coinage the prices are expressed in. It was the *denarius*, but we do not know what this *denarius* means. It cannot be the one minted at 96 pieces to the pound. This was initially called the *argenteus*, but internal details show it to be impossible, for that assumption would result in non-sensical prices. Later we also know of another *denarius* which counted as the smallest unit of calculation and 6,000 of which made up one *solidus*. It cannot have been this *denarius* either, for then the prices given would have been far too low. A pound of pork reputedly cost 12 *denarii*, but this price determination does not get us much further. Unfortunately the price of corn is not given in any of the copies of the Edict extant so far.[363] The Edict does tell us that this was used to denote medium prices, but this still leaves everything very mysterious for us.

In contrast, the political significance of this law was great: it shows us what false ideas about the power of the state and the Emperor as a god on earth could be nurtured by even such a clear-headed man as Diocletian, in other respects a man of such sober judgement. This craving to determine the indeterminable – the price of things – shows that Diocletian [MH.III, 103] was not free of the humbug of sovereignty.

His colleagues did not share it: the Edict was valid exclusively in the East, in the territory of Diocletian and his Caesar Galerius. Neither Constantius, nor even the loyal Maximian published it. We are quite certain of this; for, since countless copies of it could have been pinned up in every town and village, some trace of it would, after all, have been found in the West, but this is not the case; we find it only in the East.[364]

The price edict proved impossible to implement, like everything that goes against the nature of things. First and foremost it became the cause of lawsuits on a mass scale. Since in consequence of the appalling judicial system all cases of this kind were capital offences, this led to the imposition of death sentences[365] and gave rise to dangerous local intrigues. Then it was thrown on the scrapheap; it was already stillborn. Constantius, realizing what a rod it would become for the backs of rulers and ruled alike, spared the West.

Diocletian has been accused, probably rightly, of a penchant for hoarding. The amassing of vast sums in order to be armed for any eventuality is in accordance with his character. His building programmes prove that his national treasury was well-filled. Nicomedia (Ismie) was entirely his creation, but he also built a great deal in the rest of the Empire, for example in Rome, despite his aversion to the city. The thermal baths which still bear his name were in fact built by Maximian, but on the orders of Diocletian.[366]

Moving on to the question of religion, we must first take a look at the sources. Lactantius's *De mortibus persecutorum* (*On the Deaths of the Persecutors*) is a biased work[367] and naturally so, for it dates from the period of the struggle between

Christianity [MH.III, 104] and the old religion, or perhaps it would be better to say between religion and the state. Lactantius lived in the midst of this struggle and was completely and utterly on the side of religion, but despite this he is as objective as he possibly can be. In such matters a contemporary cannot be completely objective. Lactantius had every opportunity to become closely acquainted with the conditions on both sides: he lived in Nicomedia, held a high position, and had acquaintances among both Christians and pagans, for he taught literature at a university.[368] Reasonable and honest, he is the most agreeable figure in Christian literature at that time, which did not have many agreeable figures. However, he was not a man of genius, like Augustine.

People frequently refer to the struggle between Christianity and paganism; expressed more correctly, it is a struggle between the ancient educational culture and the new faith. Lactantius himself once said as much, and to some extent admits the justification behind the feeling that a good deal of the railing of non-Christians against Christians lay in the fact that the Bible and Christian literature were generally so poorly written. It was in fact a plebeian religion and so, too, therefore, was its style. But Lactantius always wanted to tell the truth honestly. Of course he is unfair to the bitterest enemies of the Christians, but he is much more fair to the peace-loving nature of Diocletian than modern critics in their over-sophistication will often admit. Looking for deep connections, they dig around, leaving the green meadow[369] untouched.

Let us investigate the causes of the persecution of Christians.[370] [MH.III, 105] The stimulus was trifling, as it is always is wherever great contradictory principles clash; it would be equally false to look for the cause of the recent Franco-Prussian War in the Spanish marriage of the Hohenzollern prince. Lactantius was unable to see these great causes, as a contemporary is very often unable to do. However, Burckhardt was even less able to see it.[371]

The principle behind the Roman state religion can be summed up in one word: toleration. Foreign gods were at first tolerated in accordance with whether the public wanted them. Whenever their veneration became quite widespread, they were granted citizenship of the Roman Olympus, just as people of other tribes were in the Roman state after a certain time. The salient feature is not that these deities were venerated alongside Jupiter, Minerva and Juno, but that this was a system of absolute toleration, thereby representing first and foremost the starkest possible contrast with Judaism, where there was no place whatsoever for any god besides Jehovah. In contrast, the Roman disposition was towards lax, thoughtless toleration: it was not asked whether a god or faith was good or bad; its very 'existence' gave it the right to exist.

In one sense we even find the idea that foreign deities were more powerful than indigenous ones. The clear-headed Roman mind had originally recognized nothing incomprehensible higher than itself, but in contrast – whether it be the Phrygian mother, Isis and Serapis, or Mithras – in these they saw something mysterious. The Romans penetrated further and further east, ultimately finding the sun god in distant Persia. Mithras[372] seemed all the more powerful because he was foreign; the Persian dress and mysterious environment were impressive, but in the end he became a Roman god. His birthday was the day of the winter solstice, 25 December, [MH.III, 106] which is the origin of Christmas.[373] The mighty power of the sun impressed the Romans. The sun cult was originally not Roman, but it was early Republican and, when the Persian sun god made his appearance in Rome, a home had already been prepared for him. After Aurelian had then built him magnificent temples[374] there were two priestly colleges of the sun in Rome, and the traditional Jupiter put up with his new colleague.[375]

In some places the foreign cults also evoked opposition. There is no trace of the cult of Mithras on coins before the time of Gallienus, although this cult had already made its appearance in Rome a hundred years earlier. The privilege formally to introduce the Mithras cult was reserved for this weak and awful regime, not however under the name of Mithras, but as Sol. This was constitutionally permissible, for the Sol cult had long been accepted. It thus represented a compromise between the demand for a new faith and the old religion. As the most mighty, invincible *deus invictus*,[376] Sol did not usurp his colleagues in the wonderfully constituted world of Olympus. He tolerated them and they tolerated him.[377]

But it was a different matter with the Jews and the Christians. They claimed their own territory for themselves, tolerated no god besides their own and were not amenable to bargains; the idea that Dionysus, Bacchus, has something in common with the Jewish cult is an old, but nevertheless false, assumption. This negative, strictly isolationist position of the Jews and Christians was the great politico-religious problem. If one wants to consider the matter historically, one must first and foremost set aside denominational prejudices: there were thoroughly honest and convinced people on both sides, as there were also swindlers, hypocrites and frauds. Viewed historically, the negation of the heathen gods [MH.III, 107] is a thoroughly revolutionary element. Jews and Christians refused to recognize the gods or to make sacrifices to them. No other faith known in antiquity forbade this. The believer in Mithras could sacrifice to Jupiter and vice versa.

Then there was a second factor. The old cult had grown hollow and empty, but all ancient education was linked to it. Christianity directed its barbs as much against all education as against Mithras and Jupiter; hence the heathen believer was indeed fighting for a principle and, as has already been stated, first and foremost against the intolerance of the Christians. And another thing: the proselytism of Christianity was new and odious to the heathen. While believers in Mithras undoubtedly also practised proselytism, it was not necessary to renounce all old, familiar, venerated faiths in order to acquire the Mithraic faith. Belief in Mithras went hand in hand with the cults of other deities, with something new added. When we examine the inscriptions of distinguished Romans of this period, we are struck by the manysidedness of their religious veneration.[378] We have the impression that they adhered to the principle: Better play safe. The *pater patrum*[379] and all the gods without distinction have a role to play. Anyone who was a Christian had done with all heathen gods, and antagonized equally all those who believed in the heathen cults.

Finally, however, the Christian hierarchy introduced a principle that threatened the state, subversive to the utmost degree, and one that was quite new. We do not know whether the worship of Mithras was associated with some kind of organization, such as an association of Mithraic priests of the same province, but it is highly unlikely. The Christian episcopate, on the other hand, is about as old as Christianity itself, and already constituted, at least in the fifth century, an immense power. The bishops in Rome, Alexandria and Antioch practised a kind of alternative government. The Christian community was a state within a state, albeit [MH.III, 108] initially without a monarchical head. The association of bishops, the council,[380] already existed however, and was completely independent of the state. This represents a far-reaching distinction between Christianity and Judaism.

Bearing all these factors in mind, one might almost be tempted to say that the persecutions of the Christians were excusable. The state had to defend itself against proselytism, against hierarchy, against all the principles of Christianity. It is a highly remarkable fact that it was the weakest of all the Emperors who gave Christianity the greatest leeway. Gallienus, that most pitiful of rulers, was the most lax towards the Christians. Thereafter no steps were taken against them for thirty years and the reason lies in the weak, ephemeral governments of that period. The only Emperor with plans to intervene against the Christians in this period was Aurelian, who had an iron nature, but was the most far-sighted Emperor.

Diocletian's thoughts on such matters may be deduced from some of the decrees contained in the Gregorian Codex, whose preambles, with their long-windedness and indifference to the facts, full of empty phrases, are after all typical of Diocletian's way of thinking. Diocletian assumed that anything regulated by law would also be faithfully and religiously abided by, including for example, the decrees against incest.[381] Marriage between, for example, uncle and niece was to be treated as such. He revived this juristic monstrosity in all its contrived and barbaric severity, for no-one bothered any longer about this legal category of incest. Just as Diocletian revived the old *aureus*, so he did the same with this. And similarly in all spheres, of which numerous examples might be cited.

[MH.III, 109] At first Diocletian was tolerant both towards Christians and generally, with one sole exception: the decree against the Manicheans.[382] This came under the umbrella of politics, not religion. The Manicheans were a pagan

sect permeated by Christian elements, rather than a Christian sect. First and foremost they were Persians; the edict against the Manicheans was issued during the
Persian War and its explanation lies in that fact. In other respects Diocletian was
a thoroughly peaceable man, allowing things to continue as they had already
done for a long time. His prevarication, his fear of decisions is also in evidence
here. The fight had to be fought, this much was as clear as day, but Diocletian
did not want to fight it, and procrastinated for twenty years. When the change in
policy finally came, it was necessary to distinguish between root causes and the
immediate trigger, which was of a more trivial nature.

Diocletian was a deeply religious man, a true believer in miracles and oracles.
The world generally had lost that indifference which treats religion purely as a
matter of form, such as we already find in Cicero. Religious faith now spread
through all sections of society, even if it was a charcoal-burners' faith. But this
faith has adherents not only among charcoal-burners, but also among counts and
barons, and this was the case here, too. Distinguished senators 'believed' in the
same way as the simple soldier Diocletian 'believed' too, whether we see him
as an Emperor, or as a simple old soldier. Miracles and signs, oracles and the
reading of entrails were not treated, as they previously had been, as traditional,
obligatory acts, but as an inner necessity; they were believed in.

According to Lactantius's account,[383] Diocletian ordered such rituals to be
observed by the palace priests. The palace was teeming with Christians, who lived
there with complete impunity as a result of Diocletian's toleration. The oracle
produced no result and the Emperor was annoyed. The Christians [MH.III, 110]
were blamed for having made the sacrifice illusory by making the sign of the
Cross. It is uncertain to what extent the priests deluded themselves and to what
extent they deluded others; the fact is beyond doubt. The Emperor was adamant,
he removed the Christians and ordered that they leave the palace precincts.
He was not prepared to have the oracle disrupted. Naturally great dissatisfaction
arose among the dismissed Christians, but at the same time Galerius and the more
energetic among Diocletian's statesmen were dissatisfied with Diocletian's weakness and this half-measure. Galerius appeared at court and demanded harsher
intervention. A series of fires then occurred in the palace. Who started these, and
whether they were started at all, or whether it was merely coincidence, has not
been clarified. The Christians blamed Galerius, and Galerius blamed the
Christians. From then on things became more serious. The Emperor stepped up
his measures, but was still very cautious. First he summoned the privy council;
a majority decided that it was too dangerous to let them go. Diocletian refused
to take more drastic action, asserting that it was just as dangerous to begin a
persecution with no prospect of bringing it to an end. The gods were consulted
again, and counselled intervention. Diocletian hesitated for a long time and, when
he finally relented, at least demanded that no blood be shed and the Christians

only deprived of their status under civil law. The Christian faith should not become a capital offence.

A ban on Christianity was declared on 24 February 303.[384] The churches were to be pulled down, Christian scriptures burned and Christians deprived of their legal status. Their outlawing was carried out only in piecemeal fashion. [MH.III, 111] There was harsh intervention in the East, where Galerius had more influence than the old Emperor. There was also drastic action in Italy and Africa under Maximian,[385] but in Gaul, under Constantius, there was restraint.[386] The order to deprive all Christians of their rights could be promulgated as law, but it was practically impossible to implement, since Christianity was already too strong.

Diocletian's departure was as remarkable and unique as his entire reign; we have no other comparable example in the whole history of Rome under the Emperors. After the events in Nicomedia described earlier, associated with the edict on the persecution of Christians, Diocletian travelled to Rome for the first time since becoming Emperor.[387] The purpose was to celebrate twenty years of rule in glorious, magnificent style. A good deal of superstition and mystery cult was involved, in which the twenty-year period played a key role; at the same time, however, the festival was also intended to be a celebration encompassing all the Emperor's victories and offering them as a spectacle for the ancient capital in a single, magnificent procession. The harem and entourage of Narses played a part in this – naturally not in person, but in effigy.[388]

This was the first triumph to be celebrated within Roman walls for a long time, and was to be the last ever.[389] And yet this festival was a deception on both sides. The Roman public, unable to forgive him for removing the capital from Rome and shifting the centre of gravity to the East, was ill-disposed towards Diocletian. The magnificent buildings which Diocletian had erected in the old capital were seen as a poor consolation for this injury. Diocletian, for his part, was dissatisfied with the conduct of the public. Accustomed to Nicomedia, a smaller town which he himself had founded, he was offended by the licence, lack of restraint and barbed words of the Parisian-like mob of the capital, [MH.III, 112] against whom the police were powerless. The whole character of Rome disagreed with his controlled, moderate and formal mores. His thriftiness will also have been wounded. His decree to refrain from all superfluous pomp contrasted oddly with the exaggerated, grand airs of Rome, making him feel more like a censor than a triumphant Emperor. Even the 'huge triumphal donatives' mentioned by his eulogists[390] did not amount to much by the standards of the period. Carus had given every Roman 500 denarii; Diocletian gave only three times that amount in twenty years. The natural consequence of this ill-feeling on both sides, then, was that Diocletian did not tarry for long in Rome, instead leaving the city as soon as possible – already on 20 December 303. He was appointed consul for the following year (304) and the public expected a celebratory procession to mark the occasion. But they were to be disappointed. Diocletian could not stand all the city bustle and withdrew, initially to tranquil Ravenna.[391] From then on the disappointments and resentments mounted up which gradually led to his decision to abdicate.[392]

Among the reasons for this step, one of the most important was a severe year-long illness of Diocletian's. For nine months he made no public appearances at all; Nicomedia even believed that he was dead, and that his death was merely being kept a secret because of Galerius's absence. Age alone cannot have been the reason for his retirement, for he was not yet 60 years old. But when he did show himself again people saw a worn-out old man. Although he did recover physically later in peace and quiet, his troubled relationship with Galerius was a crucial factor. The latter's penchant for more draconian measures, and the belligerent, violent facet of his character, [MH.III, 113] were distasteful to Diocletian. Galerius did not spare him the accusation that he was enfeebled by age, and the accusation was not unfounded. Galerius was unquestionably pressing for his retirement. At first Diocletian resisted: he pointed to the personal danger to which he would expose himself were he to retire. He offered to make Galerius Augustus, fully equal in rank to himself and Maximian. But Galerius now refused this office, recollecting Diocletian's own example. Harmony was, and had to be, the basis for multiple rule and someone had to be the leader, otherwise multiple rule would deteriorate into anarchy. Once the rulers were at loggerheads, the basis of the whole artificial edifice was removed. Galerius demanded that they adhere to the existence of two *maiores* and two *minores*, two Augusti and two Caesars.[393] Religious factors, portents of disaster, must also have affected Diocletian's decision.

Ultimately, therefore, he acknowledged that if the unity of the Empire was to be secured, there had to be one *de facto* ruler. The formal abdication of Diocletian and Maximian took place on 1 May 305.[394] Maximian evidently did this reluctantly. This is proved by subsequent events; harsh inducements must have been employed to bring him to do so. Galerius threatened civil war and the danger of this was at all events imminent. Disturbances threatened in various parts of the Empire. On the Euphrates and in Antioch, persecutions of Christians had led to uprisings, which were significant even though they were suppressed. If Maximian refused to abdicate, then conflict would be inevitable. And the lifelong loyalty he had shown Diocletian also played a part. They had been through thick and thin together this far and they went through it again now.

All the officers were assembled and the two Augusti laid down the purple. Diocletian retired to his home country, Dalmatia,[395] [MH.III, 114] where he built himself the magnificent palace whose remains are still admired by the world today and within whose confines the town of Spalatum (Split) named after it was to find room. Galerius now had a free hand, and he proceeded according to Diocletian's model by making appointments that would ensure that he retained a free hand, or at least could do so if he wanted to. Two *maiores* and two *minores* were installed, the previous *minores* now moving up into first place.[396] Constantius became first Augustus, which was necessary in so far as Gaul would otherwise inevitably have seceded from the Empire. There were new appointees to the posts of Caesar. Constantius had an illegitimate son, Constantine.[397] But we cannot apply the usual concept of illegitimacy here. The Emperor can acknowledge whomever he will, and Constantine was never regarded as an interloper in antiquity. Maximian like-wise had a son, Maxentius, probably born in 280, who was around 20–30 years of age when the abdication took place. Constantine had an appointment as Tribune in the Guard at Constantinople.[398] Galerius would dearly have liked to place men of his own choice in the Caesarian posts, who would have stood by him as Maximian had stood by Diocletian. Instead of Constantine, he wanted to appoint Severus to the post of Caesar, a useful officer, but of rustic education, whereas Constantine had had the finest education his age could provide. Galerius would probably also have preferred to make a different appointment to the post of second Augustus. Constantius was ill and evidently close to death; Galerius thus accommodated himself to the necessity of appointing him Augustus,[399] intending to move Licinius, an able officer, into his place after his death.[400]

B) CONSTANTINE (306–337)

Constantius accepted the appointment. Constantine, however, left Constantinople without leave,[401] as if fleeing – an act of open insubordination which may none-theless have been necessary, since it is not unlikely that [MH.III, 115] his life was in danger.[402] A demotion of the kind he had undergone was as good as a death sentence. He travelled to the headquarters of his father, who at that time was in northern Britain, at war with the Picts. His father died shortly thereafter in York on 25 July 306.[403] The Gaulish officers did not want the Caesar who had been imposed on them. It has already been pointed out how profoundly different Constantius's handling of all affairs of state, taxes and religious confusion in Gaul was from that in the East, and naturally the Gauls wished to go on being ruled along these lines. They declared Constantine Augustus. Galerius met them half way. Certainly no Diocletian, he was far less of a statesman and recognized Constantine as Caesar, but not as Augustus, appointing Severus to that post instead; there was no immediate place for Licinius now.

This paved the way for conflict. It did not come to an open break just yet, for a more pressing conflict, the secession of Italy, intervened. Maxentius, Maximian's son, had been passed over in the Augustan appointments and was now proclaimed Augustus in Rome.[404] Maxentius was undistinguished, with very little ambition and a dissolute character. He was also no leader, merely a tool. Italy had been demoted in favour of the East; it had lost its leading role and its exemption from taxation; the Italian Guard, the Praetorians, were half-discharged and there was no-one there to make an impression on the existing remnant. This was the character of the war: 'Italy versus the East'.

At first Gaul conducted itself as a passive bystander. Old Maximian now acted in a manner that seemed calculated to confuse everyone.[405] First he refused to involve himself and demanded that the old *seniores* – Diocletian and himself – reassume the positions of Augusti. But he met with no support from Diocletian, who [MH.III, 116] replied with a resolute no. At this, Maximian made a stand solely on behalf of and beside his son, which, given Maximian's immense popularity, resulted in the North Italian troops, who formed the core of those available, joining Maxentius. This gave rise to a revolution within a revolution. Africa seceded and constituted a separate realm under Lucius Domitius Alexander, which was however rapidly defeated.[406]

Galerius had Severus put an end to this Italian rebellion; he went to Italy in the winter of 306/7. However, the attempt to gain mastery over Maxentius and Maximian misfired lamentably. Severus's men deserted and went over to Maximian. Severus took refuge in fortified Ravenna, capitulating when promised that his life would be spared, a promise that was at first kept, but in 307 he was murdered.[407] Now Galerius went to Italy, but with virtually the same results, although without the same conclusion. Galerius was forced to retreat and avoided a hopeless battle.[408] Maximian first restored control over Italy and Africa for his son to rule.

Galerius now attempted to draw Constantine on to his side against Maxentius. The most remarkable 'conference' of Carnuntum took place in this period, in 307. We have a surviving memorial of it, on which the blessing of the god Mithras is implored.[409] Diocletian also attended this conference. Galerius made Licinius co-Emperor[410] and recognized Maxentius and Constantine as Caesars, thereby not recognizing Constantine as the Augustus which the army had already years earlier proclaimed him to be.

The Conference at Carnuntum exposed the overall weakness and fundamental failings of the Diocletianic system. Politicians of genius very often judge everything from the personal point of view that a powerful individual [MH.III, 117] can bring everything into submission. The whole thing worked quite well as long as Diocletian was at the helm; now that Galerius wanted to continue Diocletian's work, it became clear how much the system had been tailored to suit his personality. This power over colleagues who nominally had a free hand failed lamentably in Galerius's hands, and yet he was not in fact incompetent. He was an able man and a good soldier, but not blessed with the gift of statesmanship, as will become patently clear when we come to deal with the religious issue.

At the Carnuntum conference of *Iovii et Herculii*, Galerius sought through his installation of Licinius as co-Emperor[411] (replacing Severus) to recreate what Diocletian had had in Maximian — an absolutely devoted commander of the same age — but unfortunately Galerius was no Diocletian, nor was Licinius a Maximian. The arrangement worked out badly on all fronts. Licinius did not dare to take up the first task given him, which was to take action against Maxentius in Italy. He was certainly unequal to the task militarily, since the best military forces were near Rome, and Africa was also loyal to Maxentius. Constantine, with the Gallic army, at first held back and left the others to fight out their differences. Licinius, who regarded the task as hopeless, was glad that Maxentius did not attack him. But both Caesars, and thus also Constantine, were deeply offended and it was, so to speak, a constitutional injustice which had been done to them through the preferment given to Licinius.[412] The idea behind the Diocletianic constitution had been that the two Caesars would move up in the event of a vacancy in the position of Augustus. Constantine could not accept his secondary role, and moved closer to Maxentius.

[MH.III, 118] A middle course was suggested by Galerius, whereby the two Caesars would be named *filii Augustorum* (sons of the Augusti),[413] thereby at least giving them the legal prospect of inheriting the position of Augustus. This naturally proved ineffective. In 308 he was obliged to make them Augusti, of whom there were now four, plus Maxentius in Italy. Galerius thereby in a sense gave up. Maximinus Daia ruled the East, Licinius Illyricum and Galerius, although he had his residence in Bithynia and Thrace, in fact ruled nothing, since his colleagues had control of the troops; he was, so to speak, a titular Emperor.[414]

Reconciliation with Maxentius was impossible. Constantine's conduct is difficult to make out, and that of the old Maximian even more so. Constantine acted very shrewdly in allowing matters to proceed without compromising himself by committing himself one way or the other. By claiming the title of Augustus he was courted by both sides. Maximian even went to Gaul to pave the way for a reconciliation through a marital alliance. The marriage between his daughter Fausta, i.e. the sister of Maxentius, and Constantine is as significant as the later marriage between Licinius and Constantine's sister Constantia.[415] It can only mean that Constantine favoured Maxentius's party up to a point. But only up to a point, for neither of them wanted to give recognition to the other. All the same it was the beginning of an agreement. Then old Maximian returned to Rome, and from that time on his actions become ever more incomprehensible. A conflict arose between father and son, Maximian and Maxentius. The old man himself wanted to be *imperator* again, but the Praetorian Guard resolutely declared its support for his son, and the old man fled back to his new son-in-law.[416] What he wanted with him is again unclear. Perhaps [MH.III, 119] the entire dispute between father and son was no more than a ruse and the old man had plans to compromise Constantine. At all events he soon began to intrigue against the latter, and open quarrelling and blows followed. Maximian fled to Massilia, where he was besieged, defeated and executed by Constantine, having long since lost and outlived his power and prestige.[417]

How the relationship between Constantine and Maxentius developed immediately after these events is obscure. Elsewhere the attention of the world focused on the death of Galerius. He died of cancer after terrible suffering in 311; Christians naturally saw the hand of God in this.[418] Several weeks before his death, on 30 April 311, he passed the remarkable Edict of Toleration,[419] a recantation of the persecutions of the Christians which had lasted for eight years. Galerius realized that persecution had been a mistake and that Christianity could not be crushed by police and criminal justice. Christian writers have exaggerated the direct influence of Christianity on this decision. The rulers were neither for nor against. The conviction had gradually gained ground that oppression was no use. Galerius said, quite in Diocletian's vein, that he had wanted to order religious matters according to ancient Roman custom; he had not sought to persecute Christians as such, but they had been too divided among themselves. This was not, of course, the reason for the persecution, but it does give an indication of the level which denominational strife and discord had already reached at that time. The Edict, therefore, was revoked and Christians were permitted to return to their meeting-places. It has been said that Galerius instructed Christians to pray for his recovery. This is not what is recorded; he said they should pray to God for both the Emperor's welfare and their own, which is a more general formulation. Nevertheless, Galerius made sure there was no shortage of prayers to the gods; apart from his physicians he constantly consulted miracle-workers and priests, and so perhaps he did not forget to ask for intercession from the God of the Christians either.

[MH.III, 120] This was the last attempt[420] to suppress the Christians. They could no longer be eradicated, but the fact that Galerius still felt the need to say so is nevertheless itself remarkable. He died a few weeks later. At first it was of no importance that his place was vacant, since in fact he had had nothing to rule over. Licinius and Maximinus Daia divided his domain (see MH.III, 120). But continuing disputes among them about precedent flared up immediately.

Throughout all this Maxentius conducted himself completely passively, which was a great mistake. He was simply a weak personality; he consulted an oracle for advice as to what he should do and is reputed to have been counselled not to step beyond the wall that ringed Rome, or he would be destroyed.[421] Anyone who allows his plans to be guided in this way is heading for disaster. The break with Constantine originated with him, but even then he did not take the offensive, but was the object of offensive action.[422] Why he declared war only to remain idle thereafter is a mystery. His father's murder will have played a part, since although he had been on hostile terms with him, he did not forgive Constantine for the murder. This would support the theory that there was a tacit understanding between the two which we mentioned earlier. Constantine put an end to it and took the offensive.

At the same time a crisis developed in the East. Maximinus Daia and Licinius were heading for a confrontation over the boundaries of their domains.[423] Before it came to combat in 311, however, they reached an agreement that the sea, i.e. the Hellespont, should form the boundary. Constantine sought an agreement with the rulers of the East which was complicated by the fact that Licinius had been elevated there expressly to eliminate Constantine. To set the seal on the agreement Licinius was betrothed to Constantia (see MH.III, 118). In response Maxentius made overtures towards Maximinus Daia, but this did not come to much.[424] The decision was made too swiftly and the combination of Constantine plus Licinius against Maxentius plus Maximinus was never put into effect.

Our accounts of Constantine's war in Italy are poor and contradictory. Some assert that Constantine initially suffered severe [MH.III, 121] defeats,[425] others that he celebrated an uninterrupted series of triumphs.[426] There are unmistakable parallels between his campaign and that of Bonaparte in northern Italy. With weaker forces he fought his way to consummate results through the strength of his offensive and the deficiency of his adversary. Crossing the Mont Génèvre, then the major route across the Alps, he found the passes undefended and launched his campaign in the spring of 312. Constantine is reputed to have had 25,000 men, according to other sources 100,000 men, Maxentius 170,000 foot soldiers and 80,000 cavalry, and thus by any standard a huge superiority of numbers. The first major confrontation took place near Turin and was celebrated in all the colours available to orators depicting battle scenes – how the cavalry of Maxentius, weighed down with metal, had to be struck down with clubs because they were impregnable to swords. It is questionable whether this confrontation was of great strategic importance. All major cities capitulated, such as Brescia (Brixia), Mutina (Modena), etc.; the greatest battle was fought near Verona. Constantine concentrated all his forces, whereas Maxentius fragmented his; Maxentius's commander, Pompeianus, was a good soldier. The crossing of the river Adige was likewise forced by Constantine, and once Verona had been captured the whole of northern Italy was conquered and he could march unresisted into Rome, where Maxentius had so far stood idly by as an observer.

On 28 October 312 the famous battle of the Milvian Bridge (the Ponte Molle, near Rome on the Flaminian Way from Rome to Rimini) was fought, immortalized by Raphael.[427] The position taken up by Maxentius on the Etruscan side, with the river to his rear, is baffling. There was no pontoon bridge there, only the Milvian Bridge should it be necessary to retreat. But perhaps Maxentius was not thinking of this: between Verona and the Milvian Bridge the eulogists (see MH.III, 120f.) are silent about Constantine's deeds, but Lactantius[428] speaks of defeats which cannot possibly have taken place in northern Italy. Seen in this light, the march on Rome seems to have been a show of desperation, and this would make it partly conceivable for them not to have considered the possibility of retreat in the face of a less [MH.III, 122] powerful, severely battered enemy. Maxentius, however, was utterly defeated. The Christian version is well known; although it probably has some basis in truth, events certainly did not proceed as it suggests. No defection of Christian troops to Constantine took place. But we do indeed know about conflicts between the Roman citizenry and the troops – of street riots in which 6,000 citizens were killed.[429] This may have damaged the morale of the army. The Praetorians were cut down to a man; the others put up less resistance and the conflict between the Praetorians and the citizens probably had an effect here. At all events it was a battle of annihilation. The bridge was either occupied through an outflanking manoeuvre by Constantine, or it collapsed (it seems to have been a wooden bridge). Maxentius himself drowned.

This catastrophe had significant political repercussions. It is a painful sight to see the pitiful manner in which the great figure of Roma concluded her role. For this revolt by Maxentius was the last occasion for a long time on which Rome intervened in the political destiny of the world; and this was a revolt against the new imperial order, whose representative was a totally incompetent, cowardly creature. It has to be said that Constantine exploited his victory with admirable restraint. Of course Rome had to be rendered politically harmless and the repetition of similar occurrences preempted. Thus the Praetorian Guard was completely and definitively disbanded and not replaced with anything.[430] Their *castra* was not completely pulled down, but opened up on the city side; the ruins of the three other sides of the wall still stand today. The *vigiles* were also disbanded[431] and the urban cohorts reduced. The city could not be left at the mercy of the common people, entirely without custodians of law and order, but their 3,000 men were restricted to local [MH.III, 123] functions, and this small force was certainly in no position to pose a political threat. It was the Praetorians who had been the dangerous element. While they should by no means be thought to be Romans – like all the army they consisted of non-Italians – nevertheless the troops stationed in Rome inevitably identified with the interests of the capital. For Rome did in a certain sense remain a capital, even after Maxentius's catastrophe. Rome was demilitarized, if the term may be permitted, rather than degraded from its position as the capital. The imperial residence had already been moved by Diocletian, but the founding of Constantinople by Constantine, which then really did deal the death blow to Rome, occurred later and was not connected with the catastrophe of Maxentius. The Senate was left untouched, but of course it was viewed as a mere ornamental emblem. Nor was there a great deal of bloodshed after the battle, the victor conducting himself with all clemency. The failure of the majority of the enemy troops contributed to this; only the Praetorians had fought tenaciously for their survival.

The imperial regime now had a different face; the situation had been substantially clarified. Constantine, Licinius and Maximinus Daia now headed the state in mutual recognition. It is significant that the Senate accorded Constantine first place among the three Augusti.[432] The first period of Constantine's rule, up to Maxentius's catastrophe, is strikingly reminiscent of the peculiar status of Postumus in Gaul.[433] This now came to an end.

Constantine's position *vis-à-vis* Licinius is strange; unfortunately here again the sources are very poor. Licinius had not joined in the struggle. He was restrained by his betrothal to Constantia (see MH.III, 118) and compelled at least to passive non-intervention, although we should never forget that he had been the alternative candidate [MH.III, 124] to Constantine from the outset. Because of Licinius's neutrality the war booty – Italy and Africa – also fell to the victor. Here Constantine became the sole ruler.

Obviously of still greater importance was the relationship between Licinius and Maximinus Daia. They went to war,[434] which perhaps was the other half of Maxentius's war, and this may help to explain Licinius's non-intervention. These two wars only occurred consecutively because events in the West came to a head so quickly. Maximinus Daia was the aggressor. He crossed the Hellespont, and the decisive battle took place at Adrianople. Maximinus Daia was defeated and returned across the Hellespont. Since he wanted to go on fighting, he sacrificed Asia Minor and retreated to Cappadocia and Syria. Here he died; we do not know whether from illness or poison.[435] The East capitulated to Licinius. Here everything fell to him, just as in the West it had fallen to Constantine. In 313 we have the old dyarchy, just as before, with the same boundaries. The two Emperors met again at Milan – everything was just as it had been in the early Diocletianic period. Here the marriage between Licinius and Constantia (see MH.III, 120) took place and was celebrated, in order to give the public a clear sign of the unity of its rulers.[436]

Important religious decrees also date from this period, for example Licinius's famous Edict of Toleration at Nicomedia, dated 13 June 313.[437] We know of Licinius's Edict, and Constantine will have passed one that was essentially the same, although the situation in the West differed somewhat and was less highly charged. Christians take this Edict to mark the end of a decade of persecution. In fact it had only lasted for eight years, but understandably the Christians did not want to give their bitterest mortal enemy, Galerius, the credit for having ended the persecution.

[MH.III, 125] Licinius's war with Maximinus Daia was probably also one of the reasons behind the Edict of Toleration. Licinius was by no means a Christian Emperor, any more than Maximinus Daia was a persecutor of Christians, but the latter did nevertheless have decidedly pagan sympathies.[438] The Edict gives Christians the *libera potestas* (free right) to practise their religion. It takes a position, not in terms of the Christian religion, but high above it, in terms of an omnipotent, unifying deity embracing both Christians and pagans. Licinius went considerably further than Galerius. He returned to the Christians their confiscated property and forfeited burial places, stipulating that wherever property had passed into the hands of private owners the state would undertake to pay compensation. The question of landed property generally plays an enormous role in these religious conflicts. The sullen tone of the Galerian edict had disappeared and to this extent Licinius may be said to have furthered the Christian interest.

This state of harmony lasted for just a year and ended in a remarkable war which has no apparent political explanation. At the root of these disputes between Constantine and Licinius was probably always the fact that the agreement between them was forced and unconsecrated by friendship or loyalty. These old adversaries had been united by chance against a common enemy, but we have already seen how each of them acted alone. The foundations on which this alliance was constructed were shaky, making it inevitable that they would turn against each other. The immediate trigger came with the arrangements for the succession. Constantine's proposal was not accepted by Licinius and it came to war, short but bloody. The battle, in which Licinius was defeated, took place on 8 October 314 on the middle Danube near Cibalae.[439] [MH.III, 126] He retreated. Constantine took up quarters at Philippi, Licinius at Adrianople. Further combat took place on Thracian soil in between these two places, and Licinius was defeated again.

This was followed by a strange tactical relocation of armies. Constantine marched towards Constantinople (or rather Byzantium, as it was then), but Licinius did not want to be forced towards the East, probably aware that this would set the seal on his definitive defeat. With great skill that speaks for his ability as a commander, he took evasive action, taking up a strong position in Constantine's rear in Illyricum. An agreement was concluded in which Licinius forfeited part of his territory and remained confined entirely to the East, retaining only the Thracian diocese in the West. Illyricum was ceded to Constantine.[440]

Some time after this the succession was arranged, but here too Constantine's superiority was revealed. A son whom Constantia had born to Licinius in 315 was designated as his successor. Constantine had two sons and both were earmarked to become Caesars.[441] However this was something quite different from Diocletian's Caesars. At that time the Caesars had been mature men who participated in government, but now they were mere children. This was done purely to regulate the succession. But here too Constantine's position was superior, in that he at least had one son who was capable of ruling – Crispus, who was already growing up. The other, later Constantine II, was a child.

This revised relationship did not endure, either. The reasons for the previous break were the old ones, and they could not be eradicated: the harmony of the Diocletianic monarchy was missing. The pretext was trivial. Along the lower course of the Danube, where the frontier may well have been blurred, Constantine had violated Licinius's territory in order to eject the same Goths.[442] Whether he wanted to provoke Licinius is uncertain; at all events this would have been no reason for a break [MH.III, 127] between colleagues who were in harmony. It also appears that Christian hands were involved, although there seems to have been a great deal of exaggeration in this, for Licinius always abided by the Edict of Toleration.

In this war Licinius was stronger at sea and Constantine on land. Constantine took the offensive, attacking Licinius at Adrianople. The latter then retreated to Byzantium, where he had a more favourable position, since the sea was his. The straits were an escape route from which as an able general, he derived great advantage, despite his inferior forces. Then Constantine, through his 23- or 24-year-old son Crispus, won a naval victory with a rapidly formed fleet. Licinius retreated to Asia Minor, and this largely decided the outcome of the war. Then, on 18 September 324, the decisive battle occurred at Chalcedon and Licinius handed himself over to the mercy of his brother-in-law, who had him executed a few months later. The idea that his soldiers forced him to do this is patently untrue and a fabrication intended to gloss over the breach of loyalty which casts a dark shadow over Constantine's character.[443]

There was thus once again a single monarchy and a single monarch. Julian asserts that if the name of Constantine appeared beside those of Caesar, Augustus and Trajan among the candidates in Olympus for the title 'Great' (since he too bore the name *maximus*, even though this accolade was denied to Diocletian), then this was incomprehensible and purely fortuitous.[444] The great deeds of Constantine which impressed posterity were his development of Constantinople[445] and the creation of a state religion.[446] But the repercussions of both deeds were beyond his estimation – beyond all estimation. And the Emperor Julian, albeit not a particularly sound judge, is closer to the truth than the eulogizing panegyrists when he says that Constantine's victories against the barbarians were paltry and laughable. In any case this era, aside from the civil wars, was a predominantly peaceful one, interrupted only by relatively unimportant frontier wars. Constantine had already dealt energetically with frontier defence [MH.III, 128] at the time of his separate rule of Gaul, at least according to the panegyric accounts, which tell of numerous victories over the Alamanni, and he had given the army excellent training during these wars.[447] Later incursions by the Franks were fended off by Crispus[448] and the river frontier held firm.

On the Danube something more than this happened. The Sarmatians on the middle Danube were repelled. Two events are particularly worth noting. It has already been pointed out that the Sarmatians were split into a master and a vassal people, the former probably conquerors, the latter enslaved previous inhabitants. The Sarmatian masters were expelled and were accommodated – allegedly

300,000 of them – by the Empire. They were settled in Thrace, Macedonia, Illyricum, even in Italy.[449] This was merely a continuation of the Diocletianic system. We likewise hear of a Gothic War again for the first time after a long interval.[450] The Goths had been inactive since the bad times of Gallienus and Aurelian. There must have been a great deal of turmoil on the left bank of the Danube. The Goths were evidently being pressed by the peoples behind. Some time around 330 Constantine's son Constantine (later II) ordered the Goths back. After the civil wars Constantine I no longer took command on the battlefield. No blame would attach to this, on the contrary the highest and most praiseworthy acclaim, if, soon after the confusion connected with Diocletian's abdication, an era of peace had set in and, despite the weakening of the Empire through the civil wars, external enemies were given no chance to penetrate the frontiers. But it seems that Julian[451] was right: there was a purchased peace and this is the worst, and in the long run most damaging, kind of peace.

Absolute calm reigned on the Euphrates, presumably because the Persian king Sapor, who was born after his father's death and was therefore king even before he was born,[452] had not yet reached an age when he would be capable of ruling, [MH.III, 129] and consequently a protectorate government was at the helm which was either unwilling or unable to undertake external ventures. Once he did come of age Sapor gave the Romans plenty to keep them busy. Constantine I died just as the Persian declaration of war arrived and he prepared to go to battle once again, on the march at Chalcedon.[453]

It is a difficult and thankless task to portray Constantine's character. However closely or critically one observes Diocletian, he remains a magnificent, personable man who achieved great things through deliberate strength of mind, not by chance. Compared with him, Constantine acquitted himself at best as Augustus did compared to Caesar; all the fruitful ideas are Diocletian's and the age should be called the age of Diocletian, not of Constantine. But history is unjust and only when successes are palpably visible to people's eyes do they notice them and acclaim the ruler they see at the helm just then. On the other hand, Constantine's misfortune also had to be overshadowed by the unbearable flattery of Christian eulogists, dripping with cant and falsity,[454] which fails to reveal precisely what was great in his approach, and on the other hand by the hate-filled exaggeration of Julian, which goes to the opposite extreme and blurs his characteristics beyond recognition. But what one does discern is not pleasant.

He is said to have been a fine figure of a man, which is confirmed even by the poor contemporary accounts: of powerful build, a good officer; his command in battle against his co-rulers was a first-class [MH.III, 130] achievement. But a noticeable thread of inconsistency runs through his actions, or rather a gradual deterioration. Outstanding, mediocre, poor, might be called the three successive periods of his thirty-year reign,[455] and they coincide with the Gallic period, with the Emperorship, or more properly with the move from the West to the East and residence at Byzantium.

He was born in 275,[456] the first ruler born and educated for the throne. He grew up as a crown prince born to the purple, and this has to be taken into account when assessing him in comparison with other personalities of his time. According to the standards of the day his private life was above reproach, since although all his children were the children of concubines – he had none by his wife[457] – there was nothing illegitimate about this in Roman eyes. Concubinage was not forbidden.[458] No one ever accused him of gross excesses. But he succumbed to the luxuries of the table and hairdressing; Julian[459] calls him the chief imperial hairdresser and table-layer. Pedantic order, precise regulation of affairs, court etiquette and the hierarchy of rank – everything we call Byzantinism – were his milieu. The patriciate, a rank with no internal substance,[460] was very properly his creation.

Constantine was treacherous and fickle. Diocletian's honourable nature would have had qualms about conduct such as Constantine's towards Licinius. But this at least still had some political basis and motivation, which was entirely lacking in the case of the dreadful domestic tragedy to be mentioned later. This was his despotic temperament, alongside which there was an uncontrolled system of favourites. Courtiers were [MH.III, 131] promoted and demoted at the vicious and unpredictable whim of their master, ending in the harsh, draconian measures of unrestrained tyranny. By and large Constantine was greedy, obtaining vast sums by blackmail, e.g. for the founding of his city of Constantinople, while his favourites on the other hand were extravagant. But all this applies only to his latter years. We shall be dealing with his relationship with Christianity later in the proper context.

There is little to be said about Constantine's political innovations. It has already been stated that his coinage reform was in fact a deterioration. One exception is the creation of the Masters of the Soldiers, and yet even this is more a new name than a new thing.[461] Diocletian's system had been based on the creation of two, in practice four great regions into which the Empire, too vast for a single ruler, was divided up. Constantine returned to a unified monarchy, so that the role of the Caesars had be replaced by the seniormost officials. Previously there had been Maximian's individual section of the Empire, now there was a corresponding military sphere for the Master of the Soldiers, and a civilian one for the Praetorian Prefect; this represents a system in which the division of the Empire is associated with a unified monarchy. Constantine is accused of having given away the highest officer posts to barbarians.[462] This did not occur under Diocletian; we find it for the first time from Constantine onwards.[463] His policy is understandable if one recalls that he was the former ruler of Gaul, where the Germanic soldier had played the leading role. And not only did he allow settlers on Roman soil to rise to the highest political positions, but servants too. [MH.III, 132] This was the other aspect of the policy of buying off barbarians by paying them tribute.

Let us examine the founding of Constantinople. The idea was not a new one; Diocletian had not lived without a residence either and it was unthinkable for an Emperor to wander around with his armies and live in field camps like a general. He was no mere general, but a god on earth ruling an entire Empire. Diocletian had selected Nicomedia as his residence; Constantine founded Constantinople in 326 and completed it in 330 on the site of the ancient, medium-sized trading centre of Byzantium.[464] Under Diocletian the city would not have been called Constantinopolis, with a Greek ending – this was entirely Constantine's idea. But the choice of location was a great coup of statesmanship: many places had been considered – Salonica, Chalcedon, Serdica, Troy.[465] The establishment of Ilion would have been quite characteristic for this age of portents, pregnant with dreams of destiny. A glance at the map suffices to show that today, just as 1,500 years ago, Constantinople, the final choice, is the only international location. The East could not rule the West: the military superiority of the West over the intellect-oriented East was too great; this would have been the mistake in any residence located on the Asian side. Byzantium, however, was situated on the European side, close to the heartland of Illyricum. No spot in the world would have been so oriental and at the same time so occidental as this, and this was even more crucial for the two-part Empire then than it is today.

Another factor [MH.III, 133] is that Constantine evidently did not build in the same way as Diocletian, who contented himself in Nicomedia with erecting the unavoidably necessary palaces and government buildings. Constantine wanted to create a cosmopolitan capital, albeit using oriental means, conjuring them up out of nowhere, depopulating other cities for the purpose and transferring their inhabitants to it. Contemporary witnesses[466] complain that he ruined the Empire by depopulating it for the sake of this one city. But the success for the city was spectacular. Constantinople rapidly became the trading centre of the Empire. You cannot put new wine in old bottles. If a Graeco-Christian state was to emerge in place of the pagan Roman one, something like the foundation of Constantinople was essential. But what we have come to call Byzantinism is not a pleasant development. It came into being together with the new religion and the new learning. Perhaps Constantine failed to foresee all the consequences that would inevitably follow on from the founding of his city. Not everyone in the act of making world history has that ability; but that is only a criticism of the person, not the deed.

Constantine's family politics is a particularly sorry affair; it represents a black page in his history. It has already been mentioned that his proceedings against Licinius fall into the wider political sphere, not the domestic. But the execution of his son Crispus and his wife Fausta,[467] such dreadful acts as the incarceration of Crispus at Pola, have never been explained. Fausta was Maximian's daughter, had remained faithful to Constantine throughout twenty [MH.III, 134] years of marriage, and had informed him about the intrigues of his father-in-law. Now, she had to die. But why? We know nothing, except for negatives: neither of the two executions was politically motivated. Crispus had never sought after the life and throne of his father; he had faithfully and successfully fought all his wars for him. He would in any case have had to have adherents and accomplices, but nothing of that kind was ever discovered, nor did anyone suffer with him, aside from Fausta.[468] It was an utterly personal act – one is almost tempted to think there was an illicit relationship between the two of them. The Emperor is said to have had pangs of remorse about this act of tyranny later.[469]

Deviating from Diocletian's system, Constantine ruled entirely alone. Having removed Licinius he did not consider the participation of his sons: this went against his tyrannical nature. What he later provided for in his will is most peculiar.

To return again to Constantine's relationship to Diocletian: historical perception has not been entirely wide of the mark in attaching the new institutions to the name of Constantine. The public focuses on and inquires after the harvest, not the seed. The result of Constantinople's founding was the end of a national basis for the Empire, created by Augustus as a Graeco-Roman Empire with the emphasis on the 'Roman'. Along with *Nova Roma*, it now emerged as a Graeco-oriental Empire. The old capital lived on in a state of widowhood – sulky, resentful and critical. [MH.III, 135] This is strikingly apparent in the sphere of literature. In the first three centuries Greek intellectual culture had notoriously been predominant and had contributed to the creation of a national identity. Art had been Greek from Homer to Diocletian. Now, political events compounded matters in these spheres, and literature became associated with the court. Milan and Ravenna had been unable to compete with Rome, although they were court residences, but *Nova Roma* could. Aristocratic Roman circles railed against this, creating from now on that wonderful, magical position for Virgil that he was to enjoy throughout the entire Middle Ages.[470]

Barbarism set in: we see this principally in the work of legislation, invariably *ad hoc* constructs. Here everything was influenced by the Orient. The juristic sources are less imperfect than the historical ones. In these spheres we encounter a revival in the East – admittedly an autumn flowering, but a second flowering produces roses too. All this was a consequence of Constantine. And yet, aside from the period of construction, he resided in Constantinople for only seven years.[471] They were enough to set his stamp on the city and on its future.

Turning to religion,[472] the work he did here was significant by any standards. It was not a great work of statesmanship, nor was he the genius that Burckhardt would like to make him out to be. Whether Constantine himself became a Christian[473] or not is quite immaterial: his private convictions are of minimal importance. Constantine started [MH.III, 136] where Diocletian had left off, with toleration, and a good two-thirds of his reign is characterized by that. His coins[474] show this clearly; unfortunately they are undated, but we have coins of the Caesars which help to fill this gap. Crispus became Caesar in 317 and was executed in 326; Constantine II became Caesar in 323. The inscriptions on the Crispus coins are unashamedly pagan, bearing the inscriptions 'to the unconquered Sun' (Mithras, of course) and dedications to Jupiter. These pagan inscriptions are absent on the coins of Constantine II, which means the change took place around 322.

Then, in the Codex of Justinian, we have a remarkable decree relating to the hallowing of Sunday.[475] Augustus had already recognized the seven-day week[476] according to the planets and their various influences on human destiny.[477] The day of the sun had always been a day of grace, holy even in the Republican period. Mars was inauspicious. We possess an inscription of a soldier to whom everything happened on a Monday.[478] This cult of the planets had always been a private affair. It was now decreed on 3 March 321 that all official business should cease on the 'Venerabe Day of the Sun' and all artisans have the day off, but that work would be permitted on farms, since the weather did not pay heed to such statutes – *tout comme chez nous*. This, then, had nothing whatever to do with Christianity: on the contrary it was directly related to the Sun, Mithras. All Christians did was to adopt it very adroitly, like so much else that is deeply rooted among the people.

Dating from the same year is a decree[479] whereby in the event of lightning striking [MH.III, 137] religious expiation was to be carried out by the owner of the land; this was repealed by Constantine in 321! Where the land and the estate on which the lightning struck was public, however, expiation was to be made by the Emperor. The *haruspex* was also to be called in by private citizens, but private domestic sacrifices were to be omitted. Probably for this reason Constantius II, a devout Christian, states that his father had banned sacrifices.[480] This was not the case, however, for public sacrifices were still permitted, and indeed necessary, if Mithras and Jupiter were still recognized.

Constantine did not give up all pagan connections, even later on. We have inscriptions documenting this: an Athenian, a very high priest, has made a journey to Egypt and thanks the gods that he may behold what Plato saw, concluding: 'Blessed be Plato'. This is quite a Christian idea, except that the name is different. He was a learned pagan theologian travelling on Constantine's business. So Constantine was on the one hand a Christian, on the other a venerator of Plato.[481]

The Emperor thus stood above both these religions, but at the same time also stood between the two. The account of Constantine's conversion is indicative: he is said to have felt great remorse over the execution of his wife and taken pains to atone for it. Lustrations of this kind were quite common. He is reputed to have been rejected by pagans, who declared his crimes to be inexpiable – which was certainly not true – whereas Christians had given him [MH.III, 138] to understand that Christ was powerful enough to expiate any crime. Although undoubtedly contrived to suit the Christian standpoint, the story is characteristic.[482]

When Constantinople was being founded, equality was likewise upheld with respect to temples. A temple to Castor and Pollux was built, and a temple to Tyche,[483] but two Christian churches beside them.[484] Although these temples may have been of earlier origin, they were at all events tolerated. There was no Christian consecration of the new city, but oracles were consulted. When the corn fleet failed to arrive from Egypt with supplies for Constantinople, Spater, a favourite Neoplatonist at the court of Constantine, was accused of having cast a spell on it, and was executed.[485] Although of doubtful origin and of highly questionable credibility, these stories do have some value in terms of gauging the mood.

It is beyond doubt that in his latter years Constantine inclined more and more to Christianity. We have two coins of his on which the famous Christogram appears to be hidden, but on closer examination is clearly discernible, in one case on the Labarum, in the other on the Emperor's helmet.[486] This thus represents a kind of crypto-Christianity, based on general toleration. It is certain that the Emperor's private faith was latterly Christian. He is reputed to have been baptized on his deathbed by Eusebius, [MH.III, 139] much to the distress of the orthodox, since Eusebius was a dreadful Arian heretic. Since, however, he was one of the most untruthful scribblers, we may be permitted to doubt whether the baptism really took place.[487] It is not improbable, but it would be entirely plausible that the pagan gods were also invoked.

Parallel to this personal position, there was also an attempt to bring about, aside from toleration, a unifying cult of all religions, a neutral ground for heathen and Christian belief alike, which was intended at the same time to be a positive religion. This was clearly an impossibility which was doomed to failure. The government had previously sought to achieve a state without an official religion, since there is no religion that suits everyone. This was the position adopted by the Licinian Edict of Toleration, which states that such toleration would be in accordance with the 'highest sublimity', in other words a supra-religious position, in a sense a Catholic Church to hold pagans and Christians equally dear. In this context Eusebius[488] has preserved a soldier's prayer in which that God is addressed who is acknowledged by all, without any specific indication of the special quality of the religion. Keeping Sunday holy is reconcilable with the idea of the stars affecting the destinies of human beings. And how did theologians cope with the idea of the Emperors being proclaimed divine, *divi*? Or with the tenure of the chief priesthood by the Emperors? The Emperor was still *Pontifex maximus*: Eusebius calls him *episkopos ton panton*, supreme bishop, i.e. overseer of the whole Empire, which is *Pontifex maximus* translated into Greek.[489] We also have a very remarkable festival calendar for [MH.III, 140] Campania[490] dated 387 (thus some fifty years after Constantine): on 13 May and 15 October the festivals of the roses

and the vintage, i.e. seasonal cults, are celebrated; on 1 May and 25 July purifi-
cation festivals, on 11 February the festival of the Genius of the Roman People,
and on 3 January votive prayers are said for the Emperor. These were all festivals
that could be celebrated by pagan and Christian alike. Roses, wine and the Genius
of the Roman People were common to all, but the origins of these festivals were
nonetheless, pagan.

Constantine took a great deal of trouble over the Christian Church, acting, so
to speak, as his own court preacher and being wont to give long sermons to his
palace officials. From the literary viewpoint, these speeches (one of which
has been preserved)[491] are frightful products, revealing his general proclivity for
moralizing, his pedantic nature and his penchant for regimentation.

The privileged position assumed by Christianity under his rule remained highly
remarkable. It was already apparent in the education of his sons, whom he
entrusted to devout Christians, thereby opening up the prospect of a future for
the Empire under Christian rulers. The persons chosen to be educators were
likewise noteworthy: Crispus's was Lactantius.[492] Equally striking is the fact that
this occurred at a time when Constantine had not yet publicly distanced himself
from pagan beliefs and was still having coins minted with the inscription *Iovi optimo
maximo*. As has already been mentioned, Lactantius was a highly educated man, an
outstanding author, and hence by any standards an agent of reconciliation between
learning and Christianity. He was also, moreover, loyal, unreservedly devoted to
the Emperor, and yet not loyal in the repugnant way of such men as the court
cleric, Eusebius.[493] The fact that Christianity could be united with the allegiance
of a subject, in the way it was with Lactantius, [MH.III, 141] presumably also
affected this choice.

Christianity enjoyed substantial privileges. Concurrently with the Edict of
Toleration another edict was promulgated granting priests exemption from
munera[494] – a great boon in those days, for the pecuniary and personal burdens of
the municipalities were crushing. This exemption led to a huge influx into the
priesthood of people both with and without vocations. The Church was likewise
granted the right to inherit, which other corporative bodies did not enjoy under
Roman law.[495] It had been conferred on individual temples, certainly, but the fact
that all churches were granted the same rights at a single stroke is the beginning
of a development towards a state Church. Christianity enjoyed privileges not
merely alongside, but in preference to pagan faiths. Finally the act of 320, which
abrogated the penalty for celibacy,[496] should be mentioned here. Although
celibacy had not yet acquired the significance in the Church that it was to have
later, the monastic lifestyle and the view of marriage as an unnecessary evil are
virtually as old as the Church itself[497] and were spreading more and more from
Egypt to elsewhere.

Looking for the reasons behind the unusually early development of the episcopate, we find its source in Judaism. The Jews in Egypt and Syria already constituted communities within the community and were able to resolve their disputes at a court of arbitration composed of elders. But the Jews in Antioch, for example, did not claim to represent the whole community. The Christians now took this a good step further; let us not forget that even Paul had already shown his strength beside Peter, in that the numbers of gentile Christians were growing apace [MH.III, 142] alongside those of Jewish Christians. So we can already see here the germs of an alternative government. The Christians were obliged to aspire to encompass the community as a whole; this was certainly no longer something that the Jews alone attempted. The bishop thus made quite different claims from those of the Jewish elders. The hierarchy both copied and transposed the political constitution, making the episcopate nothing less than the spiritual authority over every municipality. Provinces were already beginning to function as units, i.e. the dioceses of the bishop; and ultimately, e.g in the council, whole regions of the Empire functioned as units. At the ecumenical Council of Nicaea, the bishops of the whole Empire assembled. The episcopate, then, was already a power in its own right. This is most clearly discernible in the case of Carthage, seat of the proconsul and of a bishop who set up a fully-fledged counter-government.[498] The bishop's court, *episcopalis audientia*,[499] was something quite different from the Jewish court of arbitration: it was recognized by Constantine,[500] whereas the Jewish court of arbitration was merely tacitly tolerated. The name 'hierarchy' is equally indicative, meaning as it does 'spiritual rule'.

Charity, good works as a system, are institutions that were first created by Christians. The ancient state was non-interventionist as regards education and care for the poor: these did not concern it.[501] The beginnings evident in this sphere in the pre-Christian era had their roots in the needs of the state, for example the alimentary schemes,[502] which arose out of the army's need to recruit troops. The aspiration towards benevolence and goodwill, practical love of one's fellow human beings, is Christian: almshouses, hospitals, care for travellers and foreigners.[503] The opposition of the Emperor Julian[504] to these [MH.III, 143] Christian, non-governmental aspirations is indicative. He sought to transfer these activities to the state and beat the Christians at their own game. State recognition of such institutions is crucial, since they are by their very nature unable to flourish when hidden.

Now to orthodoxy. Differences over articles of faith are as old as the Church itself. Orthodoxy is a Christian invention: anyone who recognizes principles which deviate from generally held opinion is not a Christian. The conflict between Jewish and gentile Christians is revealed in the dispute over the reckoning of Easter.[505] It is no superficial matter whether the Passover is determined according to Jewish or more liberal precepts. Then there was the matter of how to deal with the lax, who had proved weak and malleable in the face of persecution, and the controversy as to whether they should be allowed to return to the community. These disputes began with the Valerianic persecutions and lasted into the fourth century.

Once Christianity had been recognized within the state, non-intervention in these questions was no longer possible. Constantine was overseer of the whole Empire and had to adopt a position. Thus in Africa, a dispute arose over the surrender of the sacred scriptures by *traditores*. Records of this have survived.[506] Each community dealt with this differently – some more leniently, some more strictly. The government had to be involved and Constantine had to intervene. Intrinsically he was faced with the task of creating a recognized Church denomination; anyone who rejected this would be persecuted. In this way orthodoxy was already demanded by an Emperor who was not even a Christian. Africa was quickly dealt with, but Egypt was more dogmatic. This was where the well-known dispute over the Trinity flared up between Arius and Athanasius, both of them in Alexandria, [MH.III, 144] about whether Christ and God had one single nature, or different natures. Homoousians opposed Homoiousians. At first the dispute raged among the clergy, but soon Constantine was obliged to step in. The general Council of Nicaea was convened in 325.[507] It was apparently intended that representatives from the whole Empire should attend, but the East greatly predominated. The very language difference prevented most westerners from attending. The dispute was decided in favour of Arius's interpretation, whereby Christ was subordinate to the Father. But Constantine simply rejected this.[508] He went on to decide in favour first of one thing, then of another – apparently depending on the influence of whoever happened to be the leading court cleric at the time; in 325 it was an Athanasian. At that stage all Constantine was deciding was a simple disagreement among experts. Here, therefore, the state had a dominant position over the Church. All but two bishops acquiesced.[509] When Constantine did choose to intervene, then he definitely upheld the supremacy of the state in this instance. In the end Constantine died an Arian; his son Constantius was even a devout believer in this doctrine.

In 335 Constantine decided on arrangements for his succession, which were to prove fatal.[510] It is a most remarkable plan, revealing a singularly erratic character. He stipulated that after his death the Empire should break up into four, or in fact five, regions. Constantine had three sons; the eldest (Constantine) was to have Gaul, Spain and Britain, the second (Constantius) the East and the third (Constans) the central part: Italy and Illyria. But this was not adhered to. All three were still [MH.III, 145] very young. We do not know when the eldest was born; the second was born in 316, the third in 320, which means the eldest could not have been much more than 20 when these arrangements were made. Constantine evidently met with opposition among government officials on account of the extreme youth of his successors. A fourth, Flavius Julius Dalmatius, Constantine's brother's son, who was older and showed promise, was therefore included in the succession. He was to have the lower Danube lands, i.e. the Illyrian heartland and the capital. His younger brother Hannibalianus became a king (he styles himself *rex* on the coins)[511] and was to have, probably in a subordinate position, the Bosporan region, the old monarchy of Mithridates, the southern shore of the Black Sea (Pontus) with Cappadocia. But the worst act of Constantine's reign was to break up the unified monarchy, his life's work, simply because he had three sons and a suitable nephew. He died on 22 May 337.[512] Shortly afterwards a palace revolution erupted (see MH.III, 146ff.) which we can reconstruct, despite the fact that the records are missing, and which we shall be examining in more detail shortly.

C) THE SONS OF CONSTANTINE (337–361)

It would be no exaggeration to say that Constantine's arrangements for the distribution of the Empire among his heirs necessitates the severest condemnation of his reign. A division of the vast Empire into an eastern and a western half, such as Diocletian had introduced, was feasible, perhaps even imperative. But this constant switch from dyarchy to unified monarchy and then return to dyarchy, then introducing triarchy, tetrarchy and pentarchy, [MH.III, 146] is not the behaviour of a statesman. History did, indeed, rectify this: it remained a completely ephemeral act. The sole motivation discernible behind it is the desire of a father to see all his children and nearest and dearest equally taken care of, but no politician acts in this way.

On the other hand, it emerges clearly from this act yet again that the issue is neither that of a simple hereditary monarchy, nor of absolute control of the succession by the Emperor, but that the soldiery, or in this case influential individuals, had a considerable say in the matter. Constantine had had one of the longest reigns of any Emperor and was widely acknowledged as the man who had restored the Empire, as a 'new Augustus'. He had controlled the Empire, and had proclaimed his three sons and nephew Dalmatius as Caesars, signifying the explicit institution of a crown prince. He had made specific arrangements concerning the parts of the Empire each was to have, and yet no straightforward succession occurred. The Caesars did not proceed simply to the rank of Augusti; instead, an odd situation arose, a four-month interregnum. Those with the authority to do so either could not, or would not, reach agreement, and Constantine continued to rule from the grave. In this period the Caesars styled themselves *principes*, not Augusti; it was not until 9 September 337 that Constantine's sons were proclaimed Augusti,[513] shortly after the palace revolution which we shall be referring to directly.[514]

The soldiery in Constantinople would only countenance a succession by Constantine's sons.[515] Dalmatius and Hannibalianus were therefore eliminated, and along with them all the male relations who could ever possibly be considered for the succession. Only two children were spared: the 11-year-old, sickly Gallus, who was not expected to live anyway, and the 6-year-old Julian.[516] Two brothers of the dead Constantine [MH.III, 147] and five of his nephews died in this slaughter of the princes. It was a strange kind of loyalty that was at work here. Admittedly Constantine himself had provided the model for the method of eliminating the offspring of a rival in order to render him harmless, as in the case of Licinius. But the elimination of princes of the blood is still a highly dubious means of securing legitimacy, simply in order to ensure that they cannot be proclaimed at some future date. This was a horrific inauguration of the seraglio regime that was to prevail in Constantinople from this time on. Several senior officers also fell victim, including Constantine's brother-in-law,[517] Flavius Optatus, and Ablabius, who had probably favoured Dalmatius.

The affair had still worse aspects, however. This was no spontaneous military insurrection, but one directed from within by persons of higher rank, and all the indications are that Constantius II himself was involved. We would not believe that a 21-year-old person could perpetrate such terrible deeds against his close relations, were there any possibility of doubt. But, aside from the fact that it is confirmed by objective witnesses, Constantius himself explicitly admitted it. Faced later with the prospect of his line dying out and longing for children in vain, he acknowledged God's punishment for an early act of bloodshed, which can only have referred to this one. Naturally he will have condoned rather than instigated it;[518] others will have manipulated him. The motive is also understandable, but certainly no exoneration: the division of the Empire arranged for by Constantine entailed a slighting of his sons. Dalmatius was the eldest and most experienced of the Caesars, a seasoned soldier. He would have had the upper hand. No sensibility was so developed in Constantius as his love of the principle of legitimacy pure and simple. He felt that a deep injustice was being [MH.III, 148] done to him in this regard.

Were we able to glance at the cards being shuffled at that time in the privacy of the palace, we would undoubtedly also find quarrels among officers, cliques and counter-cliques. In contrast, there is not so much as a shred of a statesmanlike idea. If there had been any opposition to the principle of tetrarchy, then we would have heard of it, but this was not the case, for acquiescence in triarchy is, after all, insufficient justification. The remarkable thing is that Constantius exercised restraint towards his brothers. Had he had them all killed, it would have been no better, certainly, but more understandable. It would have brought him sole rule. But this can probably be explained in the same terms, the principle of legitimacy, which was everything to him, whereas statesmanship meant nothing to him. The nephew had no just claim, whereas the brothers did, so that Constantine's sons were spared and a triarchy initiated.

No opposition was raised to this division. We do not know exactly who obtained the portion of Dalmatius. One source states that Constantius II was given Constantinople, but not Illyricum.[519] At all events there was another geographical division later, with Thrace and the lower Danube falling to Constantius. No agreement was reached about the division of the West.[520] Constantine II received Gaul, Spain and Britain, Constans Illyricum, but Italy and Africa were disputed. Relations between the brothers were not good.

The burden of the onerous Persian War rested on the East alone. Constans could have intervened with his crack Illyrian troops, but did not do so. The beginnings of the war go back to Constantine, his father, and Constantius II inherited it. The outbreak of war is generally attributed to an act of reprisal by the Persians, who were the aggressors once the long minority of Sapor was over. But the most reliable source, Ammianus,[521] albeit only in an incidental [MH.III, 149] reference (the main account has been lost), states that Constantine was the aggressor. If it is correct, and it would seem to be according to the detailed account of a later author[522] that appears to be based on Ammianus's original, then there has seldom been such a puerile cause for war. It relates how a traveller[523] from India and Asia brought Constantine curios and precious goods, claiming that even greater treasures had been stolen from him by the Persians. Constantine is said to have demanded the return of these undoubtedly non-existent treasures, and this led to war. It is beyond doubt that the religious situation also played a part. By this time one can describe the Roman Empire as Christian. There were many Christians among the Persians too, but they were persecuted[524] and will have had Roman sympathies, just as we have spoken earlier of the reverse situation of Persian sympathies among the Manicheans.[525]

Constantine died (337); Constantius II, whom he had sent out to the frontier, first returned, and the events we have just described unfolded. Then Constantius resumed the war. It is impossible to give any account, especially a chronological one, of this war. It was long, bloody and inconclusive. No great battles were fought; the Romans drew the shorter straw in everything, especially when the Emperor was present. He was a poor military commander – too cautious, restrained and anxious, particularly when faced with such an unpredictable enemy. On one occasion the Romans almost won a decisive victory, having taken and plundered the Persian camp, but the Persians regrouped and transformed the Roman victory into a terrible defeat.[526] And yet the Emperor persisted and did his duty: the defeats were not decisive routs and brought the Persians no strategic advantages. Mesopotamia must have been well defended. The Persians proved unable to hold on to their gains; the war was fought defensively, but not without skill by the [MH.III, 150] Romans, the Persians being repulsed again and again. Nisibis was besieged three times and under severe pressure, but the brave garrison and the inhabitants defended themselves successfully. For these Mesopotamian Christians, however, it was a matter of life and death. Edessa was not captured either. Ultimately, therefore, it was only a frontier war, of which it may be said that honour was lost, but no more. Constantius achieved more than is generally supposed. The Emperor, moreover, stood alone. He had not only this conflict to fight, but also to intervene in the situation in the West. But similar conditions obtained among the Persians too: they were being pressed from the East by the Scythians and other barbarians. Were this not the case, then this war, one huge campaign of pillage and plunder, would be incomprehensible. This was the golden age of the pillaging tribes of the desert, who were in clover. The latter phase of the war will be described in connection with Julian, when it was an unfortunate war against the Persians under an incompetent commander.

The West had two rulers, Constantine and Constans, who were at war with each other. The war was resolved to Constantine's disadvantage in 340 at Aquileia, where he fell. He is said to have been the aggressor and invaded Italy; another version has it that Constans lured his brother to Italy and treacherously kill him.[527] The inheritance passed undivided to Constans. Constantius, preoccupied with the Persians, did not hinder him. On the whole Constans seems to have had a peaceful time and to have held the frontier barbarians in check. In other respects reports of him are unfavourable; he was said to have been a slave to base lusts.[528] The population groaned under oppressive taxation, and corrupt officials ruled: there is general agreement on this. Constans fell victim to a military revolution, of which an account immediately follows.[529]

[MH.III, 151] In its way, the 25-year reign of Constantius is as important as those of Diocletian and Constantine the Great. The general upheaval, the great decline begins, and the heirs of Roman world dominion appear on the scene. But the seeds of what happened under Constantius were already present under Constantine; Constantius was merely his father's son. Under him, destiny worked out the consequences of Constantine's deeds. All his frontier enemies – the Persians and the Germans – were arming themselves. The war against the Persians was in fact never concluded, but merely interrupted by brief truces until the complete collapse of the Byzantine Empire, although this did not actually occur until a thousand years later.[530]

The elimination of Constans by Germanic officers in 350 is a highly remarkable historical fact, the cause of which can likewise be traced back to Constantine. It has already been mentioned in the relevant section of the account that in the natural course of events, as a result of his early rule in Gaul and having them as comrades-in-arms in all his wars, Constantine had come to show a strong preference for the Germanic element in the army, especially appointing Alamanni and Franks to senior officer posts.[531] The influence of the *auxilia palatina* thus grew to such an extent that they came to replace the disbanded Praetorians as Emperor-makers. They came to the conclusion that the government had recognized them as the best forces. Stilicho, Ricimer and Theoderic were the fruits of [MH.III, 152] seed sown by Constantine. Characteristically, these phenomena only occurred in the West, where the Germano-Gallic element in the army was far more preponderant than in the East. Their first trial run came after the death of Constans.[532] The choice of Magnentius as Emperor represented the usurpation of the throne by a soldier of fortune. The story goes[533] that at a banquet in Augustodunum (Autun), Marcellinus, a financial official in league with Magnentius, arranged for the latter suddenly to make an appearance before the officers dressed in the purple. Whatever the truth of this is, the accession of Magnentius represents the first attempt by the Germans to assert supremacy for themselves and not just for others.

Magnentius was the first foreigner, the first real barbarian on the throne, which could not but arouse the opposition of the Roman world, and which probably proved more his undoing than any of the other negative traits which have been, perhaps rather too heavy-handedly, ascribed to him – harsh, vicious, unconcerned about his subjects, he swelled the ranks of his army using the free Germans, and oppressed the indigenous population with severe taxation. He himself was a Frankish settler from a military colony.[534] He was proclaimed Emperor on 18 January 350[535] and his primary concern was to eliminate Constantine's son,[536] who was on a hunting trip in the Pyrenees. This was accomplished by German troops in Aquitaine.

The Roman armed forces refused to recognize Magnentius, and two other Augusti set out to oppose him: in Italy Nepotianus, a nephew of Constantine the Great, [MH.III, 153] was proclaimed Emperor by the mob.[537] Rome, however, was utterly defenceless: a few companies of gladiators was all that the Emperor could rely on. After a reign of only a month he was easily removed and Magnentius was recognized in Italy and Africa. But in Illyricum there was more serious opposition. This heartland looked on itself as Roman, and the Illyrian troops pressed the imperial crown on Vetranio.[538] Propelled into this position to some extent by chance, he was an old, mild-mannered man who had worked his way up through the ranks and was so uneducated that he was even reputed to have been unable to read.[539]

How did Constantius respond to these events in western Rome? He could have accepted them as a *fait accompli*. Up to that point his attitude towards the West had been somewhat lax and indifferent, since he was heavily committed by the Persian War, and prudence clearly recommended coming to an arrangement with Magnentius, who declared himself ready to do the same. But Constantius would have none of this, and set out on a crusade of legitimacy: the house of Constantine the Great was to reign. Constantius's keen sense of legitimacy was the sole magnanimous trait in this otherwise petty human being, and there is certainly no lack of parallels with him in the modern age. The means at Constantius's disposal were grossly inadequate. The danger on the Euphrates was not pressing at that moment, and Constantius ensured the succession by naming his eldest nephew, Gallus, as Caesar,[540] which he had thus far avoided doing, and by handing over to him command against the Persians.

He himself [MH.III, 154] turned his attention to the West. In order to face this imminent danger, Magnentius and Vetranio joined forces, thereby confronting Constantius with the seasoned troops of the German and Illyrian armies. First Constantius launched an attack on Vetranio. The latter had been made Augustus against his will and had no taste for combat. It was agreed that they would allow the soldiery, i.e. the officers, to come to a peaceful decision. A great council of officers from both sides was convened; almost all of them were veteran officers of Constantine the Great, and so powerful was the sense of legitimacy and allegiance to the son of their old commander that the vast majority decided in favour of Constantius. It has been said that the forcefulness of the latter's oratory worked superbly in his favour, but in fact his gift for oratory was so poorly developed that he set greater store by verse-writing, because he was more successful at it than at prose oratory.[541] Vetranio was obliged to lay down the purple, and this was a great moment and magnificent act in the paltry life of Constantius.[542] This victory of the idea of legitimacy over the sword shifted the balance of power quite significantly against Magnentius. The entire Vetranio episode had lasted from 1 March 350, when he had donned the purple,[543] until 25 December of the same year, when he retired unmolested to private life.[544]

Magnentius, on the other hand, had to be dealt with, and the two armies confronted each other in Illyricum. Magnentius had the advantage on the battle-field, secured by the military skill of his Frankish and Alamannic soldiers from across the Rhine. At last, on 28 September 351, the decisive battle came at Mursa.[545] Even before this, [MH.III, 155] opposition to the usurper had arisen among his own army and Silvanus, himself a Frank, left him, so that even here among the Germans the magical power of legitimacy made itself felt.[546] It was an extremely savage conflict, not only between the candidates for the throne, but also among the different peoples. Magnentius's supporters were massacred in droves and only the superior numbers of Constantius's cavalry decided the battle in his favour. This did not mark the end of the war, however: it was resumed in 352 in Italy. But Magnentius's strength had been sapped and in 353 he was defeated in Gaul, not by the military might of Constantius, but by dissension among the Germans. Magnentius drew his support from the Franks, while Constantius had been able to win over the Alamanni to his cause, with the result, as so often in history, that Germans fought and won against Germans. The cities too, e.g. Trier, abandoned Magnentius. Gaul had been milked dry and was glad to shake off the

459

heavy yoke. Realizing that all was lost, Magnentius first killed his mother, brothers and sisters near Lyon, then took his own life.[547] Legitimacy and German discord had won the day.

Constantius, petty, suspicious and cruel, villainously persecuted Magnentius's supporters after their military defeat, with the secondary object of filling his own coffers.[548] Gallus was also eliminated, perhaps not without reason. He was worthless. In Antioch he had wanted to have all the councillors executed for some trifle, and this had only been averted by the courageous refusal of Honoratus, Count of the Orient.[549] We have the most incredible, and yet authenticated, accounts of Gallus's conduct at Antioch:[550] militarily incompetent, he was not with the army on the Euphrates, but looked on [MH.III, 156] from Antioch, where he wallowed in his pleasures. Idle, cruel and naive, he was totally unfit to rule. Characteristically, however, his removal was left until after the overthrow of Magnentius. Constantius kept this miserable representative of the family in reserve until the dynasty had been established on a firm footing. The manner of his execution was also vile: it was a murder, not a death sentence. He was lured to court on a pretext by Constantius, who gradually took all his troops from him until, alone and harmless, he was executed at Pola.[551]

Let us pass on to examine the religious situation, the crucial aspect of this era. The world of ideas had been completely reduced to that of religion, and religious dissension fills the reign of Constantius. This was the harvest of what Constantine had sown. The way was paved for the great conflicts between state and Church. Constantius was the first Emperor to be born a Christian and he immediately initiated that struggle of the Church against state power that has hardly ever abated since. The long line of great religious leaders – Gregory, Luther, the spiritual apostles – begins with Athanasius.

The relationship with paganism, to take this aspect first, naturally assumed greater intensity during the reign of this first Emperor to be born and brought up as a Christian; Constantius was the first resolute opponent of paganism. The true son of his father, he himself helped build the edifice of theology. Of course, Christianity had yet to be proclaimed the sole state religion, so he contented himself with establishing a universal religious faith for pagans and Christians alike, and even for those who were neither.[552] It is quite [MH.III, 157] beyond doubt, for example, that the numerous senior officers from the barbarian lands, where Christianity had never been heard of, were pagans. They were not called on to make any particular profession of faith. Incidentally, as has already been indicated earlier, the paganism of that period amounted to more than a mere negative reaction against Christianity. It had been improved and was now devout and religious. Besides this there was also neutral ground, on which some of the finest people of the age stood (e.g. Ammianus),[553] with the educated disdain of men of the world both for the Christian God and for Mithras. What Christians were demanding was the removal of the outward signs of pagan worship, the closing of temples and a ban on sacrifice, but not political recognition of the Christian faith.

The year 341 witnessed the once-and-for-all ban on sacrifice by Constantius, which includes the misconstrued reference to a decree of his father, as we have already seen.[554] Indicatively, this ban on sacrifice was complied within the East, but not in the West. We have a remarkable work, *On the Error of Pagan Cults (De errore profanorum religionum)*, by Firmicus Maternus, dated 346/7, which calls for the energetic suppression of temple institutions and the removal of the silver and gold images of the gods. 'These should be melted down to make coins' – the financial motive, greed for temple land, played a part here, as in the Reformation.[555] But there was no change in the basic situation yet.

Concerning the situation within Christianity itself, unification and orthodoxy were definitely required, and the ruler was obliged to concern himself with these issues. The first step had been the Council [MH.III, 158] of Nicaea, where the clergy had attended in a purely advisory capacity and the Emperor had made the decisions. The dispute about the date of Easter, too, may seem purely a matter of externals to us, but it was more than that. If Easter was celebrated on the same day throughout all Christendom, this was catholicity, a clear expression of unity for the public at large. The year 325 was important for the later division between the western and eastern churches. Rome and Alexandria, the two main seats of Christendom, essentially reached agreement on the issue of the Trinity. The rejected interpretation is commonly known as Arianism. There has been much derision of the fuss made over such a minor point of detail. This is an erroneous and superficial view. The deepest nature of Christianity found expression in this question: the relationship of the Son to the Father and the Trinity. Orthodoxy assumed both to be equal, whereas Arius denied this. If the Son and the Father are equal, then we have a true religion, an expression of the ineffable. If the Son has only a human nature, being only comparable to God, as the Arian doctrine asserted, this does not provide that expression of the miraculous that the believing human soul seeks. This did not come into the world until it was brought there by Athanasius, and this faith rightly belonged to the future. In the true seats of faith, the Athanasian doctrine prevailed, while the more rational Arian belief flourished in those lands saturated by Greek influence. As has already been stated, the Emperor Constantine opted for Athanasius. The slogan *homoousios* had been uttered, but a really [MH.III, 159] clear distinction had not yet been made.

Constantius thus inherited the situation and the controversies which arose out of it. After the Council, Constantine had vacillated, switching sides to the Arian camp and thereby coming into personal conflict with Athanasius. This change was partly caused by differences of outlook, but probably even more so by political considerations. Athanasius had been Bishop of Alexandria since 328 and is reputed to have said that he was the true master of Egypt and that it was up to him whether the corn fleet would arrive in Constantinople or not.[556] It is by all accounts true that the Bishop of Alexandria wielded enormous influence in that religious wonderland. This was the first time that clerical power set itself up against secular power. Constantine removed Athanasius without actually deposing him, offering him an opportunity to reflect on the consequences of his presumption in exile on the Rhine.[557] Links with the West and the bishops there were significant: it was at the court of Constantine II that the influence of Alexandria on the West was established.

Constantine's three sons agreed in 338 that all exiled clergy be allowed to return home.[558] This was an act of clemency such as is common when a new government comes to power. Athanasius was among those who returned, and fresh conflicts flared up immediately. Constantius was and remained an Arian, while the two other sons were on friendly terms with Athanasius. On his return Athanasius was ruthless, removing his opponents from their positions. In many ways he [MH.III, 160] reminds us of Luther. It was neither his learning nor his dialectical power that made him a leader, but his firm conviction and the faith that can move mountains. It was through his fearlessness and unconcern for the world that he towered above all his contemporaries, and this was the secret of his success. A grim conflict arose between the government and the Church, such as would have been unheard of under Constantine I. Constantine had simply dismissed the bishops: he controlled the Council. At that time the state was omnipotent and virtually without opposition. Constantius summoned the bishops to Antioch. Athanasius was removed and sent into exile again, and Gregory of Cappadocia installed as his successor by force of arms.[559] The Emperor was once again victorious.

Athanasius sought refuge in the West, going to Constans and finding support among the western bishops. The issue came to a head: did the Emperor have the right to dismiss bishops? The Council had conceded such a right, but only under pressure from the Emperor. All this was exacerbated by the conflict between Constantius and Constans. The latter demanded a conclave of bishops and Constantius, weighed down with the Persian War, gave in in 343. The Council was convened at Serdica (Sofia) in Illyricum[560] and dissension arose immediately. The West demanded recognition of Athanasius as Bishop of Alexandria; the East refused, and the result was schism. The eastern bishops reassembled at Philippopolis. The Council of Serdica is important in being the first occasion on which the primacy of Rome was officially recognized. Liberius, [MH.III, 161] Bishop of Rome, presided and demanded that when a bishop was removed from office he be permitted to appeal to the Bishop of Rome. This effectively gave Rome supremacy over the episcopate. Athanasius, the most important eastern bishop, assented to this resolution. Constantius was obliged to acquiesce, and in 347 he gave way to Athanasius. This was the first time an Emperor ever did such a thing. The power of the Emperors was broken.

462

Magnentius was also a Christian,[561] but under him the pagans had enjoyed greater toleration. Nocturnal sacrifice, i.e. paganism in its most excessive form, had been permitted. Following Magnentius's downfall Constantius did away with this;[562] he closed the temples, and the pagan cult was also rigorously suppressed in the West. Had the pagan world had the same zeal for faith as the Christians in similar situations, this might well have had repercussions, but after some half-hearted resistance they acquiesced. Constantius sought to capitalize on his victory over Magnentius *vis-à-vis* the bishops, especially Athanasius.[563] In 353 a council was convened at Arles with the aim of desposing Athanasius. But the West proved to be intractable, as it did again at Milan in 355. Liberius, Bishop of Rome, was resolutely opposed. When the bishops demanded that a bishop be judged only by bishops, the Emperor reached for his sword. Finally they acquiesced. Athanasius was forcibly deposed, soldiers broke into the churches, blood flowed, and in 356 Athanasius went into exile [MH.III, 162] for a third time, this time to the anachorites of Thebes, where there was a monastery inhabited by robust, armed men, part Christians, part refugees from oppressive taxation. He lived in seclusion there for many years. Constantius had won the day yet again and in 359 a universal formulation of the doctrine of the Trinity was found after all, accepted even by Liberius himself.[564] This paved the way for an acceptable universal state Church. As with the Persian war, Constantius waged this struggle too with many setbacks, often on the verge of defeat, but ultimately upholding the supremacy of the state. Amid all this confusion, the crucial issue – more so than is generally supposed – was whether or not the Emperor was permitted to depose a bishop.

When we cast an eye on Constantius's personality[565] as we approach the end of his career, there is not much to be said in his favour. He was neither likeable nor a significant man, although it must be conceded that he has been much maligned and that in some cases condemnation of him has been unfair. An unbiased examination of both the governmental and religious spheres reveals evidence of substantial achievement on his part, and compels one to say that he was a better ruler than most in that bleak century. His private life was utterly above reproach. Not only did he restrain himself from lunatic excesses; he was moderate, and lived an orderly, austere life – a narrow, conventional man, but one of moral integrity. As a soldier [MH.III, 163] he was no cowardly rascal: an able horseman and a good shot, he was a better soldier than all the other Constantines. His educational accomplishments were not outstanding; he was a very mediocre orator, but an orthodox theologian, devout and dogmatic. None of this is particularly appealing, but he did, all the same, have a highly developed sense of duty. His one ruling idea was legitimacy, a tendency which was notably prevalent among all his family, even in his nephew and successor Julian, who in other respects was very unlike him. Julian too was quite in the thrall of the Constantinian sense of family.

But when Constantius, imagining that everything focused on his own person, went so far as to attribute all successes to himself, for example in the official reports of his battles on the Rhine, this was taking the autocratic idea to absurd lengths. This exaggerated sense of his own importance went hand in hand with a deeply rooted distrust of his agents, most especially of the princes. We have already seen the effects of this distrust in connection with Gallus, where, however, it was entirely deserved, but Constantius trusted Julian just as little. Grudgingly, he acknowledged him as his last remaining kin. Given Constantine's childlessness and the assassination of all his other kin, Julian was all that remained of the house of Constantine. Of course this did not help to imbue him with a more trusting attitude. His officers also suffered [MH.III, 164] from his suspicion of the ablest men, and from the fact that his ear was always ready to listen to any calumny. The network of informers flourished.

His public appearances were made with great dignity and decorum. He would have deemed turning his head or spitting to be an infringement of the deportment required of him.[566] This austerity of character made a positive impression, however, with the result that Constantius cuts a finer figure than his incomparably abler successor. It is defamatory to assert that Constantius was utterly indifferent to everything. His wife, the beautiful and clever Eusebia, had influence over him, but whenever dynastic sensibilities were involved all other considerations took a back seat.[567] It has to be conceded that, despite a series of major defeats, he managed to hold the Persians in check and, despite his strong religious convictions, kept the the hierarchy under control with a firm hand. The pagan sympathies of his successor did more to liberate the Church from the state than Constantius's Christianity had ever done. As we have seen, he reunited the whole Empire. This had less effect on the government as such than might be supposed; bureaucracy had already grown too powerful by that time. The figureheads changed, but the officials, the Praetorian Prefect, etc. remained.

The conflict with Magnentius over, Constantius went to Gaul, where he convened the Council of Arelate (Arles),[568] but he could not stay for long, for developments [MH.III, 165] on the Danube required his presence there. The war with Magnentius had demolished the entire framework of the Rhine defences. After Constantius's departure the Alamanni flooded into Gaul and wrought havoc. Although the towns were for the most part protected by their walls,[569] since the Alamanni would not and could not lay siege to them, they did nevertheless thoroughly pillage the countryside. A revival of the bands of Bacaudae exacerbated this situation.

Constantius sent Silvanus to Gaul as Master of the Soldiers,[570] where this able man succeeded in expelling the Alamanni. But Silvanus was ruined by palace intrigues. Although only a particular example, this incident is too characteristic of Constantius to overlook: he had no truer servant than Silvanus. We have already encountered him once. This was the Frank with the Roman name whose

464

desertion in 351 had saved the day for Constantius at Mursa (see MH.III, 155). Changes of name like that of Silvanus are frequent,[571] and reveal that even among senior officials with apparently Roman names there were still many Germans, and barbarians generally.[572] A heavy-handed plot was concocted against this man who had given many long years of service. The Emperor was presented with letters from which part of the original handwriting had been erased and replaced with treasonable remarks. He was resident at Milan at that time. Silvanus was charged with high treason, [MH.III, 166] although all the Frankish officers who knew him and were convinced of his innocence spoke up vociferously on his behalf. The Emperor sent Ursicinus, Silvanus's main rival, to call him to account, thereby compelling Silvanus to commit unwillingly the very crime with which he was charged. Having been dubbed a conspirator, he became one. He had himself declared Augustus by the troops, but was defeated and eliminated after a rule of only twenty-eight days.[573] Gaul, abandoned once again, had to endure another Alamannic invasion.[574]

D) JULIAN AND JOVIAN (355–364)

At this point the Emperor decided to bring the last prince of the house of Constantine, Gallus's brother Julian, out of the obscurity in which he had hitherto lived.[575] Born in 331, he was now 22 and had been brought up in semi-imprisonment until then. Julian had filled his time with the study of literature and the classics and had not yet publicly lapsed from the Christian faith which, although not required of every private citizen, was required of every prince of the house of Constantine. Summoned to Milan, he believed he was going to his death, a fate he would perhaps have already met long before, had the empress Eusebia not shown an interest in him. He was first sent to Athens, where he took up literary connections that were to prove important to him in later life.

After the fall of Silvanus, policy dictated the installation of a Caesar, and Julian was nominally made ruler [MH.III, 167] of the West; but Constantius's mistrust immediately undid what he had just done. Julian was given a paltry escort of 300 men[576] and Constantius also made sure through instructions to the commanding officers that they should hold the real power, and Julian not be allowed to run affairs. The young scholar and Greek philosopher was incidentally not seriously regarded as fit to rule.

Meanwhile the barbarians had captured Agrippinas (Cologne) and were threatening not to quit the land at all, but to make themselves at home there. It was beginning to look as though the West was set to become permanently German. Over the winter of 355/6 Julian and a handful of men were besieged by barbarians at Augustodunum (Autun).[577] They had all of Alsace-Lorraine in their hands.

We have two accounts of these events: a long, detailed one by Ammianus and a short one by Julian himself.[578] The latter's tones are modest, while Ammianus purports to recount the brilliant exploits of a hero. According to both accounts Julian fought valiantly, but it is probably true, as he himself states, that not much was achieved by it. His force was small, both materially and numerically, and he was hampered by the Emperor's instructions to the senior officers. Marcellus, the Master of the Soldiers, was totally hostile towards him.[579]

The following winter (356/7) Julian sojourned among the Senones, and in the summer after that things looked up.[580] Marcellus was replaced by Severus,[581] with whom some kind of understanding was reached. [MH.III, 168] On the other hand, there was the openly hostile attitude of the general Barbatio, operating out of Italy, who refrained from any helpful intervention in Julian's support.[582] In 357 Julian was thus obliged to fight the famous battle of Argentoratum (Strasburg) on his own with his handful of men, 13,000 against an infinitely superior force. This is perhaps the only battle of which we have a detailed description by a fighting soldier, which makes it highly instructive about German battle tactics. This account is provided by Ammianus.[583]

The Alamanni were the aggressors, their troops being transported across the Rhine for three days and three nights to take up positions with the river to the rear. Julian's headquarters were on a hilltop near Strasburg. The Alamannic commanders were Chnodomar and his nephew Serapio – another Roman name, and this time among the Alamanni, who fought among the enemy ranks, which at the same time also indicates that the cult of Serapis had spread among them.[584] Chnodomar fought with five kings and ten princes in his entourage, all fighting at his side. His army consisted of 35,000 men, a figure we can well believe. The Alamannic infantry demanded that the princes dismount and fight with them on foot. Evidently because of the danger of the river to the rear, they demanded that their commanders take their chances with the rest of them. The German left flank and the Roman right flank were made up of cavalry. On the Roman side stood heavy and fully armoured riders [MH.III, 169] and horses, while the Alamanni had light cavalry mingling with the foot soldiers, which was to prove critical for the unwieldy armoured horsemen. The German battle order was made up of *cunei*, massed columns, the Roman battle order of a phalanx-like shield formation. The cavalry combat went badly for the Romans, their cavalry retreating and being broken up, despite all Julian's efforts to bring them to a standstill again. Then the foot soldiers advanced into hand-to-hand combat, and it was on this that victory hinged. The core of the Batavians, under their indigenous chieftains, appeared on the battlefield; a troop of Alamanni and all their princes made another fresh advance, getting as far as the commanders' tent and the first legion, but it achieved nothing; they were obliged to retreat, and a rout began. The topography was crucial; no mercy was shown and those who did not fall to the sword were driven into the Rhine. Chnodomar has escaped, attempts to reach his encampment of ships, but his horse falls and he is surrounded. He and 203 men, mostly noblemen, are obliged to surrender.[585] Six thousand Alamanni lie dead on the battlefield,[586] not counting those who drowned. Roman losses were relatively light. This battle proved Julian's military prowess, and from then on supremacy was on the Roman side.

The following year he restored order on the lower Rhine. The river and its navigation were entirely under Frankish control; Florentius, governor of Gaul, had wanted to buy the navigation rights back, but Julian refused.[587] He defeated [MH.III, 170] the Franks,[588] with the result that Gaul could once again be properly supplied. Agriculture in Gaul was in ruins; the corn fleet had to come from Britain.[589]

Having seen to his supplies, Julian went on to make successful efforts towards reducing the crushing burden of taxation.[590] Intervention in this matter was undoubtedly outside his sphere of competence, since the Emperor's intention had been for Julian to act as figurehead, not to administer. Florentius, the Praetorian Prefect, complained about Julian's interference,[591] and in legal terms this dispute must be decided against Julian, even though his usurpation was effectively legitimated by flagrant abuses. Gaul suffered not so much from genuine overtaxation than from the perverse and irregular levying of taxes by the municipal councils, which distributed the taxes for which the municipalities as a whole were liable among the individual inhabitants, thereby creating gross inequities.

The municipal officials were even worse than the imperial ones. Municipal councillors were well-off, but saw to it that they themselves were not over-burdened when it came to distributing taxes, foisting them instead on to the less well-off, on whom the tax burden was both by nature and by experience the heaviest, even when distributions were made equitably. Julian stepped in with the authority he now commanded as the victor of Argentoratum; in Belgica Secunda he dismissed all the tax officials of the Count of the Largesses and took the levying of taxes into his own hands.[592] He acted with particular stringency against the arbitrary and supplementary surcharges which, being entirely unforeseen, of course most severely burdened and confused [MH.III, 171] the budgets of municipalities and individuals. These measures increasingly gave him the status of a true ruler.

In 358, partly with the cooperation of Constantius pushing forward from the Danube, the Alamanni found themselves caught between two fires.[593] Julian crossed the Rhine, advancing as far as the eastern border of Alamannic territory, severely humiliating them.[594] An event of huge importance in 359, although the historians do not tell us so, was the restoration of the former frontier defences, which also restored peace to the area for some time to come.

These accomplishments by Julian were bound to make him feel proud and the

467

Emperor jealous, creating a tense relationship between them that was inevitable, given the insufficient trust, or rather total distrust, that the Emperor felt towards Julian, besides the formal position of power that he was obliged to confer on him by the force of circumstances.[595] The Empire was not truly united. It had only been by sheer chance and by the fortunate turn of events in the war against Magnentius that Constantius had succeeded in reuniting two inwardly divided and already estranged halves of the Empire under his own person. The soldiers and people of the western half of the Empire wanted to have a separate ruler for the West again. The soldiery had wanted to proclaim Julian Augustus immediately after the battle of Argentoratum, and he had difficulty in restraining them from doing so;[596] such a development would have undoubtedly done him harm at that stage.

[MH.III, 172] Julian does not appear to have been responsible for the break with Constantius. It evolved out of conditions in the East. Astonishingly enough, the Persians had remained quiet during the conflict with Magnentius. A thorough and systematic attack undertaken at that time could have proved fatal for Constantius. In 358, however, Sapor was given a respite by those pressing against him from the East,[597] as mentioned earlier, and was able to turn his attention to the Romans with full force. Although peace had never been concluded, he made something akin to a fresh declaration of war, couched in very bombastic terms, referring to the old claims of Darius whereby all of Asia and the land as far as the river Strymon in Macedonia in fact belonged to him, but then, growing more moderate, Sapor declared that he would content himself with Armenia and Mesopotamia. Constantius's reply was, of course, negative.[598]

The beginning of the war went badly for the Romans. Amida (Diyarbakir) fell into Persian hands and the Romans suffered huge losses. Constantius had once again hampered the action of his military commanders because of his distrust of them.[599] In 360 the Persians scored some fresh successes. They attacked Nisibis and gained control of a series of towns. The Emperor was obliged to consider mustering all the imperial armed forces, including those of the West, and sent Julian an order to hand over his core troops. There was no formal reason to object to this order, but in real terms it was highly questionable, both for the West and for Julian personally. The division of the Empire had, after all, [MH.III, 173] necessitated a division of the army. The crack western troops were German volunteers, so-called *foederati* with specific contracts which for the most part only required them to serve in Gaul.[600] Constantius had taken into account neither the mood of the troops nor Julian when he made this demand. The troops considered the suggestion that they move east as a breach of their contracts and, as future events were to show, a state is lost that entrusts its defence to vassals and not to its own citizens. Although not exactly mutinous, the troops became difficult and resentful. Julian was fully justified in being suspicious of Constantius's order. It was entirely in keeping with the Emperor's character to see in it a means of disarming Julian as a rival. The number of troops demanded was not exactly large, but Julian's overall army was small and it was the core of seasoned professional soldiers which was being demanded.

We are told that Julian acted with the utmost loyalty. As evidence of this we have only his own account and those of authors well-disposed towards him,[601] but he invariably showed himself to be truthful, and his account fits the facts. At first he made alternative proposals, pointing out how dangerous it would be not to respect the contracts with the soldiers, and how it would put off all future volunteers. When this argument failed, he issued his soldiers with the command to carry out the Emperor's order and march. Julian spent the winter of 359/60 in Paris;[602] this is the first mention of the city.[603] Paris was the [MH.III, 174] seat of the military headquarters, chosen on account of its commanding and easily defensible position on the island between the arms of the Seine. Julian may be regarded as the creator of Paris as a capital city. The troops were supposed to pass through Paris on their march, but Julian issued a warning, pointing out the danger of a mutiny if the troops were now to glimpse the victor of the battle of Argentoratum face to face. The Emperor's representatives, however, failed to heed this warning, and what Julian had foreseen would happen did so: the soldiers proclaimed him Augustus and placed themselves under his command. The march to the East was abandoned.

Julian maintained that he had not sought this position. With remarkable faith in the effects of destiny, he consulted the gods and they are said to have concurred.[604] This is probably true in literal terms, but there was latent ambition in this remarkable man. Anyone who acts beyond his sphere of competence, as Julian did in Gaul, or organized the Persian campaign as he did, must be ambitious.

It was an irrevocable step. By refusing, Julian would manifestly have been signing his own death warrant, given Constantius's character. Julian offered the Emperor terms: co-rule, of course, i.e. the legalization of his position, since he was ruler of the West. But he also offered him major concessions: he did not demand absolute parity of status; Constantius was to appoint the supreme official, the Praetorian Prefect, Julian the rest.[605] Constitutionally this is notable as the only instance of [MH.III, 175] one Augustus having a right which the other did not have – unless we have a precedent in the relationship between Diocletian and Maximian, on the assumption that the latter's subordinate role was not entirely of his own volition. Julian declared his willingness to despatch reinforcements, albeit on a somewhat reduced scale.

The army was entirely on Julian's side,[606] but not so the civilian officials. Florentius, the Praetorian Prefect, remained loyal to the Emperor.[607] The religious question had also probably played a part: Julian ostensibly ruled Gaul as a Christian,[608] but even then it was widely known that he had pagan sympathies.

Here, too, there was disparity between West and East. The western troops were still mostly pagans, the eastern troops already Christianized. This exerted hidden pressure.

Once again, Constantius was faced with the same issue as at the time of Magnentius. On the verge of being obliged to fight a difficult Persian War, his attention was diverted by the necessity of deciding who was to rule the West. Here too, however, his austere, not easily ruffled character is revealed. He did not allow the West simply to go its own way, but set out to confront Julian, as he had done in 351. Julian was likewise determined to burn his bridges and preferred to be the aggressor rather than an object of aggression. Had it come to war, the outcome might have been quite uncertain. Italy at least resolutely backed Constantius's side, with Aquileia closing its gates to Julian.[609] At this point fate intervened. Just as he was about to depart for Constantinople, death caught up with Constantius in Cilicia on 3 November 361,[610] [MH.III, 176] just as he was about to depart for Constantinople. Reliable accounts state that on his deathbed he named Julian as his successor, which would also be in complete conformity with his views on legitimacy. It was the vocation of the house of Constantine to rule and, since only Julian was left, it had to be him. This brought resistance to an end. The East acquiesced immediately; only Aquileia continued to resist for some time.[611] On 11 December 361 Julian marched into Constantinople at the head of the western army.[612]

It is a difficult task to describe Julian's character, although there are few rulers about whom we have such detailed information as about him. We have pamphlets and letters by him in quantity,[613] both from the period when he was forced to play the loyal subject and Christian believer, and from the later period. We have the accounts of friends and foes, Christians and Ammianus. But Julian's is too unique a personality, and it is difficult to think one's way into the conflict between West and East, or between Christianity and paganism. It is not simply that he was inhabited by two souls, and the most widely disparate elements. First and foremost, his unhappy youth should never be forgotten. His first memory was of the great slaughter of the princes, in which he lost his father, brothers and all his relatives, he himself falling as an orphan into the power of their murderer. He then lived in constant fear of death, since it is scarcely more than pure coincidence that he himself did not come to a bloody end. He was prepared to meet it at any moment. These were the early years of this animated, sprightly man, which is why he retained this restlessness all his life long, like the slave who has broken his chains.

[MH.III, 177] The memories of lack of freedom in his childhood and youth haunted him for the rest of his life. This was reinforced by his disposition. His was a Greek nature, and he said of himself that he was the first Greek[614] to sit on the imperial throne. His religious observance, education and literary tastes were all intensified in him because he had only been able to develop himself under severe pressure. The spiritual pressure on him – his profession of Christianity, which he hated profoundly – must also be taken into account. Christian institutions and pagan education side by side, Christian by religious affiliation, pagan through and through, made for a disagreeable, unharmonious mixture.

We are very precisely informed as to the Emperor Julian's external appearance, both by Ammianus and himself.[615] He did not flatter himself and describes himself as uncommonly ugly. He seems also to have sought to do what he could to complete the harm nature had already inflicted on his appearance, further compounding the ugliness by allowing an enormous beard to grow. The powerful, soldierly gait he cultivated was ill-suited to his diminutive, puny figure. Lack of harmony was the hallmark both of his character and of his outward appearance. He was perhaps the only monarch who not only went about unwashed and unkempt, but even became renowned for it. Having once cultivated the vast forest of his beard, it was quite in the order of things for it to be inhabited by forest creatures – lice. He had no time to wash his hands; he had too much writing to do, so his fingers were invariably inkstained. It is still [MH.III, 178] rather odd that he should become renowned for this. And this is how it was with Julian in everything. Few rulers can compare with Julian in terms of humanity, courage, education or spirit, and yet the overall impression of him, in spite of all these noble traits, is a disagreeable one, because of his gross lack of deportment, tact and self-control, but above all of good looks and charm.

None was more diligent than he was; it is astonishing what he managed to accomplish in the two years of his rule: the reform of religion and of the civil service, the preparation and execution of the great Persian War, a prolific correspondence which, it would seem, was originally intended for publication, and the writing of a quantity of pamphlets. All this was only made possible by his lifestyle,[616] which was the most frugal imaginable; the pleasures of the table were unknown to him and he needed very little sleep; he would leave his hard couch and seat himself straight at his writing desk before sunrise. But all this lacked a sense of beauty and charm: even his chastity is hardly merited, for it stemmed from a complete indifference to female charms. A repellent bookishness, cranky disposition, spitefulness and the envy associated with a writer – all the negative traits of men of letters darken this portrait of the courageous soldier.

Julian's lack of political acumen and his efforts to wage a war of the pen is reminiscent of Napoleon I. Like the latter, he was no 'gentleman'. And thus, for these and other unharmonious and repugnant qualities, [MH.III, 179] he never grew into a well-rounded, great statesman or commander. Devoid of blessings and good fortune he swam against the tide in a lost cause which even he himself was bound to acknowledge as such. Hence his rancour against Christianity. However deeply he despised Christianity, and however acutely he was aware of its

471

shortcomings, he still knew he could not compete with it, that paganism was a thing of the past. This was why he attempted in his own way to transpose as many Christian ideas as possible into pagan institutions.[617] Obviously it could not work. But the saddest thing of all is the spectacle of the skirmishing man of letters side by side with the statesman and commander in him.

Having attained the throne without bloodshed, through a special blessing of fate, Julian set a religious, administrative and military revolution in motion. It was presumably necessary to make up for the tyrannical regime of Constantius and do away with the venal, slimy courtiers who bore much of the guilt for what had been perpetrated under him. But the investigating tribunal installed by Julian to oversee political events was nonetheless a questionable enterprise, already on account of its membership.[618] Through a perverse kind of impartiality, his choice fell in some cases on the worst tools of the previous regime. The idea that Julian himself took part in the arbitrations of the tribunal is a libel, although a good proportion of its decisions do deserve severe criticism. That it dealt severely with all those who had been involved in the execution [MH.III, 180] of Gallus, including Apodemius and Paul, was probably the result of its members' desire to please Gallus's brother Julian, but does not essentially deserve censure and may have been a matter of political exigency.

Court life had lapsed into a sorry state as a result of the strict etiquette of Constantius and the excessive luxury that had been a hallmark of the Emperors in all ages. The barbers and cooks who had assumed a pre-eminent position among court functionaries were dismissed *en masse*, and there was a return to simplicity. But Julian created a great deal of bad feeling here through his hasty and ruthless measures.[619] At any rate a great deal of money was saved, and if Julian became famous for having reduced expenditure throughout the Empire by a fifth,[620] the lion's share of this can probably be attributed to the cessation of needless extravagance at court.

Examining his conduct with respect to the religious question, it is clear that as Caesar in Gaul he had not yet resolutely and openly rejected Christianity.[621] Not until he had marched into Constantinople as Emperor[622] did he profess his adherence to paganism and proclaim complete toleration – nothing more.[623] But this toleration was directed against the Church, which had been shown ever greater favour under his two predecessors. These privileges, greatly enhanced under Constantius, disappeared in one fell swoop. The temples were restored, and their property, confiscated [MH.III, 181] for the benefit of the Christian churches, was to be returned. But complete toleration was also to be shown to all Christians; no one was to be forced to sacrifice, and all sects were to enjoy complete freedom. What Julian envisaged was the implementation of his plan, already mentioned, to create a state orthodoxy, a universal faith from the top down. Although the abstract idea of toleration was a factor, so too undoubtedly was the expectation that he could use no surer means towards ruining Christianity than by giving free play to dissension among its sects. This effectively did away with the united nature of Christianity, which was a danger to the state. It is very like Julian not only to look on with glee at the disputes among Christians, but also to intervene in the disputes between bishops of different denominations and, unable to make himself heard amid the clamour of squabbling voices, proclaim that they had better listen to him, whom even the Franks and Alamanni had heeded.[624] This may have been effective, but it was not decorous to talk to the bickering clergy in this way on their own level.

As a consequence of universal toleration Athanasius also returned to Alexandria, where he reclaimed his bishopric. Aware of Athanasius's subversiveness, however, Julian would not countenance this and forbad him to act in the capacity of bishop. Since a legitimate successor had been installed and Athanasius refused to acquiesce, Julian exiled him for a fourth time.[625] No Emperor could be on good terms with this priest.

[MH.III, 182] From the point of view of statesmanship, this policy towards Christianity was equally wrong. Once Christianity had acquired such importance that it could no longer be ignored, it was incumbent on the state to ensure that there was a recognized orthodoxy, otherwise the situation would be untenable and inevitably result in general disruption in the Empire, to the detriment of the general good.

In the teeth of what was theoretically universal toleration, Julian fostered pagans, not by completely excluding Christians from public office, but by preferring to appoint pagans.[626] It was simply impossible to remain strictly on neutral territory. One measure did go directly against Christianity – one of the utmost practical importance. Christians were no longer allowed to educate the public: rhetoric, grammar and philosophy could now be taught only by pagans.[627] All larger towns had places of learning similar to modern grammar schools and, if not universities, then at least particular faculties. This effectively precluded Christians from educating the upper classes and coming into contact with young people. Julian was fully mindful of where the principal danger for paganism lay: in Christianity's progression from a religion for the lower classes to one for all classes. We have a letter from him[628] in which he states with a certain naivety, but inner conviction, that Homer and Herodotus had believed [MH.III, 183] in Hermes and the Muses; whoever, therefore, wanted to expound Homer and Herodotus should not insult Hermes and the Muses for the sake of a few drachmas. As long as the pagan cult had been suppressed, it had been stalwart. Now the Christians could expound Matthew in their churches, but they would have to leave the ancients to those who still shared their faith. This was rubbing salt into the wound of the gulf between ancient education and the new faith. These measures roused fierce opposition, even among better pagans.[629] Julian was accused of intolerance.

Much to his chagrin, the Emperor was forced to concede that paganism was a thing of the past. The temples were open, but no-one entered them. Two trends may be discerned within paganism: spiritual-philosophical Neoplatonism, and paganism in its crude form, with the whole paraphernalia of soothsaying and sorcery. More intelligent people rejected these excesses. But Julian was absurdly addicted to the realm of dreams, oracles and sacrifices, and he has not unjustly been accused of having been no more than a sacrificial acolyte.[630] He thus fought in a futile struggle for the old, dead religion against the new, living one. Antioch incurred his fury for not being able to fill its temples. One elderly priest who sacrificed a goose comprised the entire gains made by the old gods in this [MH.III, 184] city, as Julian saw it.[631] Although perhaps merely an anecdote, it is illustrative. Even Julian had enough insight to realize that as often as not it was only toadying to himself which forced certain social elements, whom it was hardly desirable or flattering to control, into the arms of the religion he favoured. He was always keenly aware that his task was impossible. He also sought, therefore, to transpose the ethical content of Christianity into paganism.[632] This comprised good works, the organization of the priesthood along the lines of the Christian hierarchy, and the founding of poorhouses and hospitals, for which purpose he allotted substantial state funds. He recognized the head start that Christianity had in these spheres, and wanted to equip paganism with them as well. But all in vain: the vessel could not contain the contents.

He also planned a change in foreign policy. His central idea was to create a new world order: he wanted to set in motion in the East, against the Persians, the great deeds he had accomplished in the West against the Germans. Characteristically, in response to the question as to whether he wanted to act on the Danube against the Goths first, he answered that the Goths were too insignificant for him.[633] His life's dream was to subjugate the Persians; in his fervour he sought to resume, continue and complete the work of [MH.III, 185] Alexander the Great, thereby crowning the restoration of paganism in the political sphere. Politically, it was a correct idea to take radical action, rather than simply scoring up a series of minor defeats. Another factor was his desire to put his predecessors in the shade. His advent was to mark the dawn of a new age. In the second year of his reign (362) he set about carrying this out.

But he need not have made such massive preparations. He might have achieved his aims by peaceful means. Realizing that the Romans meant business, Sapor struck a more peaceful note. He would have been glad to avoid having to settle the issue by force of arms, but his overtures met with a brusque rebuttal. In 363 Julian set off from Antioch. We have a reliable account of his campaign;[634] we know more about Julian in general than about most people of that age. He mustered 100,000 men. But the initial plan of the campaign already contained the seeds of its failure. Mesopotamia and Armenia were completely loyal to the

Romans and King Arsaces utterly reliable. Alexander's route, through Upper Mesopotamia across the Tigris to the most sensitive spot in the Persian Empire, was thus open and without peril. An alternative route led [MH.III, 186] directly to an attack on the Persian capital, Ctesiphon, which lay near the border. Previously one or other of these two routes had always been chosen. Julian decided to go both ways, i.e. to divide his army.

The condition of the troops was far more crucial than their numbers. Since the division of the Empire the Persians had only ever had to deal with eastern armies; now Illyrians and Gauls, the crack western troops, who were intended to have won the crown for Julian, were being sent against them. The quality of Trajan's army cannot have been remotely as good. In this respect the campaign was very well planned. But – as so often has to be criticized in Julian – his impetuousity did a great deal of harm. The campaign was launched too late in the year; in March[635] Julian moved off from Antioch towards the Euphrates, where harvest time was already approaching and time for operations would run out. It is probably correct that preparations, particularly for the transport fleet of 1,100 ships[636] with 60 war galleys, took up a lot of time. But they might as well have waited another year, since there was no pressing reason to make a strike.

Julian pressed forward with the whole army between the Tigris and the Euphrates as far as Carrhae, on the northern edge of the Mesopotamian desert. This was where the fateful [MH.III, 187] division took place: we are told that 35,000 men,[637] under the command of Procopius and Sebastianus, and with the king of Armenia, crossed the Tigris together at Arbela, advancing along the old invasion route. With 65,000 men the Emperor himself turned back to the Euphrates, and then followed the river towards Ctesiphon. It is difficult to say what he hoped to achieve by this. Both routes were feasible, but it is a mystery why he chose to take both at the same time. The first army had no particular tactical objective and was bound ultimately to rejoin the main army, so why march separately when they would have to attack together? On the other hand, the commander and generals alike were competent and familiar with the conditions. There can be no question of unfamiliarity with the region. The Romans had been at war with the Persians for centuries. Hormisdas, a Persian prince, served in their ranks as a cavalry general.[638] We cannot assume, therefore, that there were no sound, convincing reasons leading them to take this step, which was to prove so much to their detriment. It was probably concern about supplies. The difficulty of supplying an army naturally increases with its size. This task was to be met through the 1,100 transport ships, since foraging was impracticable. The dangers [MH.III, 188] which might hamper the two armies from joining forces again were probably underestimated. We know very little about what happened to the smaller of the two armies. It appears that its leadership was inept, consisting of a prince and a general. Procopius had only his remote kinship to the family of Constantine to thank for his rank, being something akin to a prince.[639] Sebastianus was assigned to him as commander. There was probably dissension between them, since they do not seem to have got any further than the Tigris. But even if all had proceeded more smoothly, they would still have been camped some 20 to 30 days' march away.

Julian, then, returned to the Euphrates, from where the route passed downstream. The march was arduous, but not dangerous. His left flank, towards the desert, was covered by cavalry, while the fleet sailed on the right flank as far as Ctesiphon. Here combat was launched, with the besieging of advance fortifications. The Persians fought well, but the Romans were far superior to them. In this way they reached the narrow isthmus near Ctesiphon where the courses of the Euphrates and the Tigris run close together. Here Trajan's old ship canal was made navigable again and the fleet transferred through it to the Tigris. Seleucia on the right bank lay in ruins; Ctesiphon lay on the left [MH.III, 189] bank and the crossing of the river in face of the enemy was very difficult. The generals refused to take responsibility, but Julian ventured the attack despite this, at first with a few ships, which were immediately set alight by the Persians, using incendiary arrows. This was the agreed signal that the ships had arrived safely, Julian proclaimed; and the crossing was indeed successfully made in a night battle, the Persian forces occupying the bank being forced back by the Romans with incomparable bravery. Julian had vindicated himself against the caution of his generals.

Thus they found themselves before the walls, but what now? The Persians refused to surrender and Julian was not particularly interested in taking the city. This would not satisfy his ambition. His plans were loftier: he had visions of Alexander's career. What was one city compared to that? With this in mind he rebuffed the Persians' peace proposals, mediated by Hormisdas, even ordering that news of them be kept completely secret, so that it should not leak out among the army that negotiations had taken place. But a further advance into the heart of the Persian Empire would be immensely difficult. He had had the whole army at his command and might have been able to abandon communications with his base, just as Alexander had done, whose army had also been a world unto itself, with itself as its centre. Even so, an unconquered [MH.III, 190] Ctesiphon in their rear would still have been a great nuisance. But the army was not united and Sebastianus was still absent.

Julian therefore took the opposite route, retreating to Arbela. This might be construed as a change of mind when he realized the difficulties of penetrating inland. But this is probably incorrect, since it appears to have been his intention from the very outset and he only pretended otherwise because Sebastianus had not reached as far as had been hoped. As he found him only half-way there, matters now stood quite differently. The fleet, which had been of good service so far, was useless as soon as they wanted to leave the river as their base of operations. It was not feasible to sail up the Tigris: not for nothing is this river known as the 'arrow'. The fleet was only an encumbrance. Some of the ships were taken with them on carts, so as to be used as pontoons. The most sensible thing to do, however, would have been to turn back, which is what the army wanted to do. But Julian was loath to abandon his high-flown plans, and burned the fleet.[640] This has been criticized, probably unjustly. He is even reputed to have ordered the fires to be extinguished when it was already too late. If he did so, it was certainly only out of consideration for his men. The fleet was useless and it was not practicable to leave troops to guard it. The fleet would have become booty for the Persians.

[MH.III, 191] The march was now resumed on the left bank of the Tigris. At first it passed through pleasant, fertile countryside. But for the Persians this was a war of national liberation, and it was waged with all the ruthlessness of one. Everywhere they went the Romans found the land devastated; they began to run short of water and supplies, and this was exacerbated by the midsummer heat, to which Julian's Nordic soldiers were unaccustomed. Precisely as had happened on Mark Antony's homeward march,[641] incessant attacks by the Persians using cavalry and elephants prevented the Romans from sleeping at night and forced them into relentless combat and marching. This was all highly unpleasant, but all was still not lost: their objective could yet be accomplished.

Then came the fateful 26 June.[642] A battle not so different from many: light Roman troops against heavy Persian cavalry. Soldier that he was, not like a commander, Julian always stood at their head among the vanguard. He had discarded his armour because of the heat, and was hit in the side by an arrow. From a Persian bow? The Gallic army claimed it was a Roman arrow. Nothing definite was ever discovered, nor was any specific person ever accused. The situation was such that it could easily have been an enemy arrow. Anatolius and other distinguished officers also fell at Julian's side. The Emperor was carried off to headquarters, where he died composed and courageously. The Socratic speeches put into his mouth [MH.III, 192] and those of the philosophers standing around his deathbed are probably not authentic.[643] He had set out to do the impossible, and so perhaps his unexpected death on the battlefield was a good thing, or at least not to be grudged. For the state his death was ruinous, as it always was where so much hinged on personalities, as in the case of the imprisonment of Valerian (260) or later (378) with the death of Valens. Julian's death turned a dangerous march into a political catastrophe. The most horrendous aspect was the way the Christians reacted to his death.[644] He had never persecuted them: he had only deprived them of the dominant position they had recently achieved. But the Christians showed no consciousness whatever that the Empire faced an imminent defeat of a kind that could scarcely be more crushing or frightful. Consumed with personal hatred, they completely forgot that Christians were also Romans. Later, they did recognize his achievement, but only in contrast to the atheism with which they reproached him.[645] Roman hegemony in the East came to an end with Julian.

Like Alexander, Julian had not thought of a successor or made any decision about who should assume supreme command. It has been asserted that on his deathbed he appointed Procopius,[646] but this is probably untrue. Understandably enough, the generals demanded that the choice of a successor be postponed until they had rejoined the other half of the army, and suggested an interim arrangement.[647] An additional [MH.III, 193] factor, it would appear, was dissension between the officers of the East and West.[648] At last they managed to agree on the generally highly regarded Sallustius, who however refused on the grounds of his age, much to the Empire's detriment.[649] Suddenly the name of Jovian cropped up and was widely applauded, apparently because of a misunderstanding among those further away, who thought they heard the name Julian and assumed that the Emperor was not dead. But Jovian was agreed on,[650] since a minority choice would have been still worse.

Jovian is a colourless figure for us. He was probably only elected because he was the son of a widely respected man and a well-liked Guards officer.[651] Easygoing, objectionable to no one, cutting the right kind of military figure – this was the character of the man perhaps made Augustus of the Empire through a misunderstanding and entrusted with the virtually impossible task of leading the army home. It would not have been a completely impossible task – the situation was no worse than when Antony undertook his homeward march. But what the situation called for above all else was a real leader who could command the love and unreserved confidence of the troops. Julian had had the required qualities, and the glory of his earlier successes. He might well have managed it. But Jovian, unknown and irresolute, was lost before he even started.

The first move was to try to reach the Tigris, since their most pressing need was for water. Putting up some brilliant defensive fighting, in which Persian elephants were killed[652] and proof was given that the courage of the troops was not yet broken, they reached the river after some days. The troops supposed this to be the end of [MH.III, 194] all their troubles, and that support and friendly country were awaiting them on the opposite bank. They had no idea of the vast distances that still separated them from their homeland. They moved rapidly to cross the river, and despite the lack of military back-up a division of 500 Rhinelanders[653] did indeed succeed in reaching the other side and in driving off some Arabs, who were waiting on the heights, hungry for booty, in a night raid. But this did little to enable the still sizeable army to cross the wide and torrential river. They tried to build rafts out of skins, but this did not work. The situation was exacerbated by the complete lack of supplies: now that they had water, they increasingly felt the lack of food.

At this point Sapor appeared with overtures for peace,[654] and there was nothing cleverer he could have done. Even the complete annihilation of the enemy would have brought him only minimal political leverage. But to force peace on the Romans and obtain legal possession of disputed territory, this was true and, as it turned out, lasting success. Julian would probably have refused peace on the conditions offered. Jovian negotiated, and it has to be said he had little option. The conditions were not all that harsh. Briefly, they were the Euphrates line, lost to the Romans forty years earlier, plus Mesopotamia. But if they gave up Mesopotamia, there was of course no way they could keep Armenia. But the Romans did not pledge to withdraw from Armenia, nor could they do so, [MH.III, 195] since Armenia was nominally independent. All they did promise was not to interfere in Armenia's internal affairs, which effectively meant that Armenia, having been a Roman vassal principality, was now to be a Persian one.

It was the most ignominious peace the Romans had ever concluded. There was huge indignation across the Empire.[655] In Carrhae in the furthermost East and in Gaul in the furthermost West the messengers bringing the news were killed by the incensed people.[656]

Jovian now crossed the river unhindered, but the rest of the march still took its toll in heavy losses. The Arabs swarmed around them and the hardships of the desert march claimed many lives. They found the second army in northern Mesopotamia, where it had probably remained immobile. Thus they came to Nisibis. Sapor's envoys, who were escorting the army, demanded that it be handed back to them. It should not be forgotten that Nisibis had defended itself tenaciously and successfully from 337 to 350 and was a largely Christian city. Even now the inhabitants implored the Emperor not to refuse them the right to defend themselves. But this would have been a violation of the peace agreement, and Jovian did not succumb to this temptation. The Persian flag was raised on the battlements of the city[657] and the inhabitants left Nisibis. The same scenario was repeated in Carrhae. The way the Romans regarded this peace treaty as binding is remarkable. Valentinian and Valens did not undermine its conditions, nor was there any thought of revenge. Apart from brief interludes under Justinian and Heraclius, the Romans [MH.III, 196] resigned themselves to this loss of hegemony in the East.

The death of Julian resulted in general reversal. The dynasty of Constantine, whose members had, each in his own way, sought to preserve the supremacy of the state, came to an end. The Emperors who followed them did not. Then there was the collapse of paganism: Jovian was a pillar of the Christian faith.[658] It has even been asserted that he only agreed to accept the Emperorship on condition that the army pledge its allegiance to the Christian faith.[659] This is highly implausible, since his first act on being elected Emperor was to consult the *haruspices* concerning the march.[660] But Christianity was at all events given a free hand. Athanasius returned to Alexandria and from then on encountered no resistance, although Valentinian was of a different religious persuasion.[661] The demise of paganism went hand in hand with the demise of state supremacy over the Church.

E) VALENTINIAN AND VALENS (364–378)

On 17 February 364 Jovian was found dead in bed.[662] It is unlikely that he was murdered. The only purpose of his existence had been to take on himself the shame of the Persian peace treaty; we know nothing else about him. Once again the officers convened for an election. The claims of the house of Constantine, which had still given them pause for thought during the election that followed Julian's death, were now swept aside. Procopius, who was descended from that house, albeit only on the distaff side, was not elected. This led to an insurrection (see MH.III, 205). [MH.III, 197] The choice fell on Valentinian, who was absent.[663] He too was a well-liked Guards officer, in his prime, between 30 and 40, better known on account of his father, Gratianus, and another Illyrian. His election prolonged this people's hold on the imperial office by another 100 years.[664] Valentinian was quite sensible, although Ammianus is not entirely reliable and does not describe him quite as impartially as is his wont, being inclined to paint too rosy a picture. He particularly exaggerates Valentinian's military achievements;[665] credit for the best of them goes to Theodosius, his commander.[666]

The officers and state officials who were assembled at Nicaea demanded the immediate election of a colleague.[667] This was for two reasons: first, the danger inherent in the Emperorship resting on one person's shoulders was simply too great, and the election after Julian's death had in any case been a stopgap. Another reason, however, was the strong conviction among all of them of the impossibility of East and West being ruled by one man, and that what Diocletian had started, which had subsequently only been temporarily suspended a few times, ought now to be concluded, i.e. to separate the two halves of the Empire. The negotiations at Nicaea and thereafter at Constantinople[668] on Valentinian's accession to the throne demarcated the *partes Orientis* and *Occidentis* for the first time.[669] Although these were reunited again briefly under Theodosius[670] and Justinian, from 364 onwards the Empire was effectively made up of two parts. The most substantive mark of imperial unity was that when one of the rulers died the other appointed his successor, although this mainly occurred with respect to appointments to the [MH.III, 198] western throne. This indicates the dominance of the East. Even so, the perfect symmetry of the two Empires in all institutions is remarkable. The two Emperors divided the troops among themselves and there were two of all authorities and offices. This had already been intrinsic to the reforms of Diocletian, but now came their slavishly detailed implementation. The frontier demarcating the two Empires was also essentially that of Diocletian, i.e. according to nationality; the West was Latin, the East Greek.[671] The linguistic boundary thus gave Macedonia to the East and Africa to the West. Unfortunately we do not know any more about the precise details of these arrangements.

The balance of power between Rome and Persia was secure at first. Mesopotamia was not occupied by the Persians.[672] An unusual situation developed in Armenia. Although the Armenians preferred being Persian to being Roman, they would have preferred independence even more to being Persian. They sought to safeguard their national independence by observing a see-saw policy in the conflict between their two great neighbours, always inclining towards the one that was not in the ascendancy at the time. This means that in these lands it was less a question of a Roman and a Persian side, than of a national one drawing support alternately from the Romans and the Persians.

At first the Romans refrained from interfering in Armenia in any way. Sapor gained control of the loyal Roman ally, King Arsaces, blinded him and then had him executed.[673] But the Persians did not gain much by this act of violence. Arsaces's widow, Olympia, a daughter of Ablabius, who had been Praetorian Prefect under Constantine the Great and murdered in the slaughter that followed Constantine's death, [MH.III, 199] as well as their son, Paras,[674] put up resolute resistance and prevailed. Sapor sent an army against them, but its commanders defected to the Armenian side, at which point the Romans stepped in when Paras turned to them for support. Valens refused to undertake a direct occupation of Armenia. In the Caucasus the Persians had also removed the king, Sauromaces, and installed another. The pro-national side there immediately sought Roman support. The Romans sent Terentius and reinstated Paras in Armenia, although insisting that he not wear the crown too openly.

Sapor, infuriated by this Roman interference, in contravention of the peace treaty, resorted to stiffer measures. The Romans grew increasingly resolute in their support of Olympia and Paras and at last the transparent veil around the Persian–Roman conflict was cast aside. We have a speech dating to 373 from which the renewed political ascendancy of the Romans in the region is clear; it refers to three expeditions, against the Caucasians, Iberians and Armenians respectively.[675] The breach of the thirty-year peace thus occurred after only a few years. It was the Romans who violated the treaty; the Persians took the offensive, but without success. Vadomarius, king of the Alamanni, was the bulwark of Roman might, and pursued war energetically together with the Count Trajanus.[676] As a result, Paras, following the favourite see-saw strategy, immediately inclined towards the Persian side. The Romans resorted to a method by then already frequently used, of luring a disloyal [MH.III, 200] ally into the Roman camp on some pretext, treating him benignly at first, but then murdering him like bandits. This had gradually been elaborated into a system, both during Valentinian's

Alamannic wars, and in Valens's Persian wars.[677] Roman politics had never exactly been clean, but their adoption of bare-faced treachery and their flouting of even the most rudimentary decorum as normal tools of government shows just how Hellenized Roman civilization had become. Sapor reopened peace negotiations, demanding neutrality on both sides and offering in return the unhindered return of Roman troops who had been cut off.[678] Negotiations reached deadlock and Valens mobilized a great expedition against the Persians in alliance with the Scythians. All these plans were thwarted by the Gothic catastrophe.

In the West Julian's eastern expedition had opened up a sensitive spot by removing the crack troops, thereby giving the barbarians on the Rhine and Danube a free hand. We are better informed about this period than about many others and can take a glance at neighbouring areas, and hence also into the detailed workings of how such provinces were administered. The signs are the same everywhere: shortage of troops and the unhindered operation of barbarians, for example in Britain and Africa. This was exacerbated by misrule and a despotic officialdom even more deplorable than ever. Julian's attempt to rule everything single-handedly was wreaking heavy vengeance. The eye [MH.III, 201] of the monarch could not be everywhere, and arbitrary officialdom of the very worst kind was rife everywhere, with the result that the provinces suffered more at the hands of the governors and troops than they did from the barbarians. In Britain, for example, the Picts and Scots – all the border peoples, sometimes still practising cannibalism[679] – overran the country, and the inhabitants made common cause with them. In the south, the Saxons invaded and there was a rapid deterioration in the prosperity which even in Julian's day had enabled Britain to send supplies to Gaul.[680] Valentinian sent over the elder Theodosius, who energetically redressed the situation. Again and again we see the same process: as soon as an able general, and above all an honest man, intervenes, things sort themselves out. Theodosius even extended the Empire again in the north, establishing the province of 'Valentia' between the walls and naming it after the Emperor.[681] The pirates were also defeated, and an expedition was even launched against Frankish territory,[682] which was necessary in order to root out the pirates' retreat.

Next Theodosius went to Africa. The situation there was similar to what it is today. Whenever frontier defence fails, the land is exposed to raids by the desert tribes. Tripolitania was in the most serious state, where the coastal strip is quite narrow and the desert extends almost to the sea. Ammianus gives us a detailed account of the events in Tripolis, which is illustrative and instructive about the deplorable conditions there: impossible demands on the population had reduced them to despair, for example, the raising of 4,000 camels, a number which the whole of Tripolis did not even possess. Camels are [MH.III, 202] mentioned here for the first time.[683] Envoys were sent to the Emperor to bring charges against the

Count Romanus, the worst extortioner. The Emperor had the best of intentions, sending plenipotentiaries to make an investigation, headed by the cabinet secretary Palladius. But Romanus bribed him, and Palladius from then on made common cause with him. His report found against the complainants, who were then treated as guilty of having made false accusations and their envoys sentenced to particularly cruel deaths. This gives us a good glimpse of how the machinery worked: the Emperor's intervention only made matters worse. Widespread corruption made impartial reports impossible to obtain and the lamentable judicial system knew of no other penalty than the death sentence. How a state ruled in such a way managed to stay together at all is incomprehensible.

The wars waged against Firmus, the Moorish prince,[684] are vividly reminiscent of the the Jugurthine War. He took the purple, but ruled as king of Africa, not as Augustus. Theodosius was only able to muster 4,000 men for the war for this vital province. Firmus put up courageous resistance, but in the end was defeated by treachery. Although uninteresting in themselves, these events are typical.

Of greater importance were the events on the Rhine and Danube, where Valentinian intervened personally. The fact that he did not go to fight the Persians indicates the depths to which the West had sunk, and that [MH.III, 203] Valentinian saw the more important and difficult personal challenge to himself here, for his was a nature that willingly and self-sacrificingly took the heaviest burdens on to its own shoulders.

It is also necessary to modify the descriptions of the two brothers' characters, as handed down to us by contemporaries. Valentinian has often been likened to Trajan in his ability and the good fortune of his reign,[685] but it should not be forgotten that Valentinian founded a dynasty and that all those who founded dynasties (Augustus, Constantine, etc.), have acquired a certain aura that was not entirely deserved. Above all Valentinian tends to be emphasized at his brother's expense. Valens was unfortunate, and hence at fault in the eyes of the public; everything creditable he achieved was forgotten as a result of his final disaster (see MH.III, 217f.). The attitude of the two brothers towards Christianity also needs to be borne in mind. Both were Arians;[686] Valentinian is even reputed to have given up his career under Julian on account of his Christian faith.[687] Valentinian dealt with religious matters like a warrior. He declared to the bishops that they might meet and dispute over the mysteries as much as they pleased; dogmas did not concern him.[688] Valens, on the other hand, was a devout Arian and the founder of Arianism among the Goths, which was to have important repercussions.[689] Valens's approach was perhaps the more statesmanlike: neutrality and indifference in these areas were impossible for the state at that time. At all events [MH.III, 204] the Athanasians were most ill-disposed towards Valens on account of his Arian beliefs.

Generally speaking, they both ruled commendably. They were not exactly highly educated – in this they contrast starkly with Julian. Although not actually hostile to literature, their attitude towards it was one of indifference.[690] Valentinian was an officer through and through; Valens was not. The latter, therefore, was an organizer, which was perhaps more important in terms of frontier defence than a battle won or a defeat suffered here and there. He has been accused of personal cowardice,[691] which is to do him a great injustice, as his death shows. He died an honourable soldier's death, refusing, when all was lost, to save himself by flight – this was not cowardice. He was an excellent administrator: the East neverhad better fiscal administration.[692] Although this tends to win less acclaim than glorious feats of arms, it is ultimately virtually the most crucial thing of all. It may be said in praise of them both that they had the will to rule justly and wisely. In the case of Valentinian, justice was blended with a good measure of ruthlessness,[693] with the result that his justice led to appalling injustices, as in the case of the African incident mentioned earlier. One pleasant aspect was the complete harmony between the two brothers,[694] which rested on the subordination of the younger and more flexible of the two. When Valentinian died and Valens ruled alongside his nephew and the Frankish officers under his command, there was serious instability.

The consequences [MH.III, 205] of Julian's disaster were averted. Valentinian was particularly fortunate in his choice of senior officers; he was also well-versed in the art of trust, which experience shows is not easy for anyone on a throne.[695] The focal point of Valentinian's work was on the Rhine and the Danube. Trouble with the Alamanni flared up immediately after his accession. Throughout the fourth century the Germanic frontier peoples and the Empire had an arrangement very similar to tribute payment. Barbarian neighbours provided the Emperor with supplies and received 'gifts' which were scarcely distinguishable from indemnities. Julian will not have paid for his eastern campaign in this manner, and so the rift began on Valentinian's accession. The Alamanni sent envoys to the new Emperor, were dissatisfied with the gifts, i.e. were not paid the tribute they expected, and declared war.[696]

This coincided with an uprising in the East prompted by the proclamation of Procopius, last descendant of the house of Constantine.[697] The latter had links with the Goths, and Thrace had been under his rule for a time. Valens was on the point of capitulating to him. Valentinian may well have paused to consider whether it was his duty to stand by his brother, but he is nevertheless reported as saying that the task of securing the Rhine frontier against the barbarians was more pressing;[698] given the notoriously good relations with his brother, this denotes a magnificent subordination of family interests to those of the state. So Valens dealt with the crisis by himself.

[MH.III, 206] In 366 the war began with an offensive by the Alamanni, who crossed the Rhine and advanced, laying everything waste as far as Châlons. They were driven back by Jovinus.[699] It was no particular act of heroism to curb such expeditions, which were no more than pillaging raids. But what is illustrative of the weakness and undermined state of the Empire is that they were able to advance so far into imperial territory at all. In 367 Moguntiacum (Mainz) was plundered by the Alamanni. Vithicabius, son of Vadomarius and their king (if these bandit chieftains merit the title of king), was eliminated by being treacherously assassinated.[700] In 368 Valentinian at last scored some decisive victories, crossing the Rhine and Neckar and advancing as far as the Heidelberg region. When Ausonius asserts that he reached the source of the Danube, allegedly hitherto unknown to the Romans, this is extreme poetic licence, for this source had long been known to the Romans.[701] In 369 the frontier forts were restored and the frontier appropriately secured.[702]

In 370 trouble broke out in another quarter: the Saxons launched a raid and plundered the coasts. These were dealt with by first coming to terms, and then treacherously attacking them on their homeward march and cutting them down to a man.[703] Although this was a victory, it provides further proof of how honour had departed from Roman warfare. One hardly knows whether more to admire their naivety or their cheek in vaunting such victories.

[MH.III, 207] Conflict proved more long drawn out with the northern Alamanni, on the bank opposite Mainz, under their king Macrianus. The Romans hoped to eliminate them and, when they did not succeed, Valentinian in the end had to be content to make a pact with them; a parley was arranged between him and the Alamannic leader.[704] History is silent about what made the Alamanni retreat, but apparently they were bought off and paid tribute. There was peace with the Franks, with whom relations were good: there were many Frankish officers among the Romans.

But there was bad news from the lands of the middle Danube. The Quadi were on the move again in Moravia, naturally in alliance with other Germanic peoples. Here too the response was to establish forts on the non-Roman bank. In order to secure the main river crossings, Valentinian had permanent bridgeheads set up. From the Roman perspective this made military sense, but the Quadi's resistance to it is understandable. Murder and treachery also played a part here in eliminating the king of the Quadi, who was lured into the Roman camp. Outrage at this led to a great war in which the Quadi laid waste Pannonia and even threatened Illyria.[705] In 374 Valentinian went to Carnuntum, invading Quadian territory with two columns in 355 and achieving his aim of defeating them.[706] There, in his camp at Komorn (Brigetio), he suffered a stroke, allegedly as a result of his violent temper. He scolded a Quadian envoy, working himself into such a rage that it brought on his death.[707]

Valentinian's death proved critical for the Empire, because of the rule by minors that now came into effect. Long before his death he had appointed his 8-year-old

[MH.III, 208] son Gratian as his co-regent, but without any territorial division of the Empire.[708] This was nothing new; even a boy being made Augustus was not unprecedented. It did, however, go against the Diocletianic order, according to which any Augustus or Caesar should be fit to rule. In this case he was a titular Augustus; as long as his father was alive he was not called on to do any work. But even for this election[709] the consultation of officers was not neglected entirely, even though they were only permitted a formal say in the course of the election itself. The throne, therefore, was not available for disposal when Valentinian died, although events took a surprising course; it is difficult to say whether it was a palace or an officers' coup. At any rate the Emperor's widow, Justina, seems to have had a hand in matters. Gratian was far away from his father's deathbed, in Trier. There was a fear, or the feigned fear, that the officers would set about proclaiming a different Augustus – there were obvious grounds for such concern. In order to secure the succession whatever happened, Merobaudes the Frank,[710] who was devoted to the imperial house, had the army proclaim as Augustus Valentinian's young son by Justina, who was later to become Valentinian II.[711] He was to take the place of Gratian, who in turn was to step into the place of the dead Emperor. It did not come to a conflict between them, and Gratian resigned himself to co-rule, which was for the time being only [MH.III, 209] nominal. Gratian, or whoever ruled in his stead, controlled the entire, undivided West.

The elimination of the foremost generals was a monstrous act. Theodosius the Spaniard, saviour of Britain and Africa and conqueror of the Alamanni, was decapitated at Carthage.[712] Exactly why is not known; it was a shameless judicial murder – Theodosius was undoubtedly innocent. He was probably feared as a potential candidate for the throne. He was the sole Roman among the generals, and there was an inherent danger in this,[713] for the Empire had not yet sunk so low as to make a Frank Emperor. (Magnentius was the sole exception so far: Ricimer (d. 472), who long acted as a maker of Emperors, did not make himself one.) Sebastianus was dealt with in a similar way, being removed from the camp.[714] How did Valens respond to these changes? Basically, he was not consulted.[715]

This brings us to the brink of the great catastrophe that might well be called the end, since it shook the Empire [MH.III, 210] irrevocably to its very foundations, and the time has now come to take a look at the people that brought about this upheaval. It was they who destroyed the eastern Empire and inherited the western; although numerous fragments of it came into the hands of other rulers, the lion's share nevertheless went to the Goths.[716] A further factor is that among no other people were the beginnings of Christianity and semi-Roman education either so prevalent so early on or so important as among the Goths. The core of the Gothic people had been among those Germans who were known to the Romans soonest.[717] The remarkable journey of Pytheas[718] to the Baltic via the Atlantic took place before the German peoples had come into contact with the civilized world, and it would seem beyond doubt that it was Goths who at that time resided along the Baltic and were then driven to the Black Sea. How? We do not know. Then, in the third century, they played a part in the first great catastrophe. This was followed by a lull, during which time they inhabited the north-western coast of the Black Sea from the the Don estuary as far as the Danube. The reasons for the cessation of their invasions during this time have been examined earlier, chief among them being their involvement with other peoples (we invariably know the situation from one aspect only – their relations with the Romans, not those of the tribes with one another) and the great success of Diocletian's policy, the blocking of the Bosporus by moving the focal point of the Empire eastwards. This put an end to their piratical raids, and even on land neighbourly relations could be established.

[MH.III, 211] A knowledge of the internal organization of this people would be of great importance for us; but all we do know is indistinct and based on legend. All we know for certain is that they were divided into Ostrogoths and Visigoths (eastern and western Goths).[719] One question is whether these tribes were organized uniformly. One old, apparently sound tradition asserts that both had two kings. The Goths seem to have been monarchical in general,[720] i.e. having a more uniform organization than the western Germanic Franks and Alamanni, who were ruled by many petty chieftains.

At first it was the western Goths with whom the Roman Empire came into conflict, as early as under Constantine, who managed to fend off Gothic raids, although he was not able to gain a foothold on the left bank of the Danube.[721] These had been prompted by Licinius calling on the Goths for support in his war with Constantine.[722] When Procopius was later in command in Constantinople and Thrace, he renewed links with the Goths, again seeking their support. The *iudex* Athanaric (who had the title 'judge' not 'king')[723] sent him 3,000 Goths to aid him against Valens.[724] Valens took them prisoner when he defeated Procopius. Athanaric sent a message requesting their release, claiming to have been duped into thinking that Procopius, as a descendant of the house of Constantine, was the legitimate ruler and that he, Athanaric, had felt duty bound to provide him with the reinforcements he had requested. [MH.III, 212] This does not sound implausible. Valens, however, refused to return the prisoners and a war broke out in which Valens was the aggressor.[725] The victory won by the Romans has been greatly exaggerated. Valens crossed the Danube at Noviodunum, and peace negotiations soon ensued. Athanaric had taken an oath never to set foot on Roman soil, so Valens acceded to his demand to parley on the river itself; the result was essentially a restoration of the status quo ante.[726] The Danube marked the frontier as before. Here too the forts the Romans built were located on the right bank.

The final catastrophe was triggered largely by the religious situation, which we shall have to examine in rather more detail, particularly since the venerable name of Ulfilas appears. No Germanic tribe adopted Christianity so early as the Goths. In all probability it was first brought to them in the mid-third century by prisoners, who probably also included Ulfilas's forefathers, so that his ancestors had already been Goths for some generations, but were originally Romans.[727] As early as the reign of Constantine Gothic bishops were taking part in councils.[728] In 348 Ulfilas went to Constantinople and was consecrated as bishop of the Goths. A severe persecution of Christians then took place among the Goths,[729] with the same character as the persecution among the Persians. The more the Roman state identified with Christianity, [MH.III, 213] the more the nations who opposed Rome identified with paganism. In the Gothic case Athanaric's opposition was more anti-Christian than pro-pagan. Because of this persecution Ulfilas asked Constantius to provide him and the Christian community with asylum. These Gothic Christians were given domiciles in Nicopolis, where, as 'Gothi minores', they led a peaceful existence and where Ulfilas wrote his translation of the Bible,[730] a work of immense historical importance, being the first ever translation of the Bible, and what is more into German![731]

However, this Christian way of life also began to exert a political influence. Fritigern, another Gothic ruler, arose to challenge Athanaric and negotiated with Valens to provide him with missionaries.[732] This had repercussions, in that all Goths, including Ulfilas, were Arians, the Arian doctrine being the predominant religion in all the Roman East.[733]

The catastrophe we are about to relate has been called the beginning of the great migrations. This is inaccurate, for their beginnings lie much further back in the past. The Goths had already migrated to their homelands on the Black Sea. What we do have here, however, is the first historically visible outline of such a migration. The Mongolian peoples were exerting pressure on the eastern Goths. Ermaneric, their centenarian king, is a legendary figure,[734] but what is certain is that the eastern Goths were overpowered and, under Hunnish [MH.III, 214] hegemony, pushed forward against the western Goths. Athanaric tried to hold his own; he is said to have built a great wall from the Black Sea as far the Carpathians to stem the swelling tide of peoples. Remains of such a wall have recently been found.[735] The western Goths did not capitulate in face of the still unstemmed tide. Athanaric fled to the mountains of Transylvania.[736]

Fritigern, with the bulk of the Goths, was granted asylum by the Romans behind the protective frontier of the Danube.[737] Situations of this kind occurred frequently, on all frontiers; Ulfilas's resettlement was another example. Now, however, hitherto unheard of hordes were pressing to be let in. Although refugees, these people were undefeated, armed and warlike. The Emperor was resident at Antioch. There were lengthy negotiations, after which permission was at last granted. But the Goths were given a poor reception. The deplorable behaviour of Roman officials did a great deal of harm here. The Goths should have been well received, if they were received at all. They were abandoned, mistreated and milked dry. Hair-raising stories are told of horrendous extortion.[738] Lupicinus, the Roman commander, sought to seize Fritigern by treacherous means. Fritigern was invited to a banquet at Marcianopolis (south of modern Varna); there was friction between Fritigern's bodyguard and Roman soldiers. [MH.III, 215] Lupicinus ordered an attack on the bodyguard, with the intention of seizing their leader. But Fritigern mounted his horse and escaped. This failed murder attempt turned the docile immigrants into a hostile army. They mustered their scattered fellow tribespeople and allowed the Alani and Huns, resident on the opposite bank, to use the Danube crossing which they controlled, thereby dangerously swelling their ranks.[739]

Energetic measures were now taken by the Romans.[740] The eastern troops were mobilized, but first and foremost there were negotiations with western Rome about a common course of action, since the western Empire was clearly also at risk. In 377 Valens personally took to the field, while Gratian approached slowly – too slowly. At first they succeeded in containing the war and forcing Fritigern into the extreme corner of the right bank of the Danube, into the marshland at the estuary along the Black Sea. But soon the Romans were being forced to retreat. Marcianopolis and the Balkan passes were abandoned, and the Goths flooded through, almost to the very walls of Constantinople, mainly because western Rome did not have its forces in place. A great joint campaign was agreed on for 378.

Gratian's advance guard forced a heavy defeat on a Gothic division; the prisoners were taken to Italy.[741] Gratian himself was on the point of marching off to the theatre of war, [MH.III, 216] when an incident called for his presence on the Rhine. The Alamanni north of Lake Constance judged this moment as the right one to make a plundering raid, with the Roman frontier garrisons depleted in order to fight the Goths. They crossed Lake Constance and invaded Gaul. This provides another clear indication of the insufficiency of the army's effective strength, despite its vast numbers on paper. Any incident at one end of the Empire necessitated depleting all garrisons, so that it was only possible to plug one gap by opening up another. On receiving news of this, Gratian immediately turned back, and succeeded in defeating the Alamanni at Argentovaria.[742] It is uncertain whether Gratian himself decided the outcome of the battle by his own bravery, or whether this was just an embellishment of court rhetoric.[743] It does not seem impossible. Gratian crossed the Rhine in his turn. The campaign was a glorious one for the Emperor, but fatal for the Empire, for valuable months were lost in the war against the Goths. Although Gratian immediately marched east at the head of his victorious troops, it was already too late.

Valens had meanwhile gone to Illyricum and taken the offensive against the Goths, who had made poor use of his absence. Here again the chief deficiency of these barbarian peoples is revealed in their inability to conduct sieges.[744] Adrianople and Constantinople[745] constituted insuperable obstacles to them. Sebastianus, who had been deposed on Gratian's accession to the throne,[746] now commanded the armies of eastern Rome. It is not improbable that rancour against Gratian motivated Valens's [MH.III, 217] decision not to await the arrival of his nephew,[747] even though the latter had sent Ricimer on ahead with news of his impending arrival.[748] The eastern Roman troops were concentrated at Adrianople, and the council of war decided to launch an immediate attack to ensure victory. It has also been asserted that Valens was jealous of Gratian's laurels in the Alamannic campaign (see MH.III, 216). What is certain is that relations between uncle and nephew were frosty. Valens decided to attack.

The opening of the battle[749] was clumsily precipitate. The Goths were encamped behind their fortified barricade of wagons. It was a terribly hot day on 9 August 378.[750] The troops were weary after their long march, and many hours had been wasted after their hasty advance. Fritigern, by all accounts a most outstanding man, did not have his cavalry to hand and offered terms in order to gain time. When his horsemen returned from foraging the negotiations were suspended, and battle commenced late in the day. The Roman cavalry were scattered in all directions. The left flank was forced back upon the barricade of waggons, where it was surrounded, and a massacre began comparable only with that at Cannae.[751] Combat took place on a completely exposed battlefield, with neither cover nor escape route in sight, and Adrianople far away. So certain had the Romans been of victory that they had made no contingency plans for retreat. Sebastianus, Trajanus and Valens were among the fallen. According to one contemporary account Valens was burnt beyond recognition in a hut in which he had taken refuge; another version has it that [MH.III, 218] when he saw that all was lost he discarded the purple and took his own life.[752] At all events he died an honourable soldier's death. It was not possible to hold the field; Thrace was lost, apart from the cities. The booty taken by the Goths was paltry, since the Romans had left their baggage behind in Adrianople, and once again the Goths could do nothing against its walls.

F) FROM THEODOSIUS TO ALARIC (379–410)

Gratian stood idly by during the castastrophe of the eastern Empire. Although he might well have entered the fray with a prospect of success, he held back. This reveals that, although capable of leading a middle-ranking campaign such as that against the Alamanni, he was not equal to a major undertaking. A young, educated and well-liked man, his character nevertheless lacked sterner stuff. As a replacement for Valens he gave the East an Augustus, who was son and namesake of the

Theodosius who had been executed in Africa, and who had been sent back to his Spanish homeland.[753] Theodosius was the only surviving officer, and moreover a Roman, which weighed heavily in his favour. Even now the Romans still shrank from clothing a barbarian with the purple. Gratian completely disregarded family considerations. (Incidentally, he had no male relations, apart from a brother not yet of age.)[754]

Theodosius was faced with a terrible task. He could not possibly defy the Goths with the decimated armed forces of the East. Capitulation was inevitable. The interregnum following Valens's death had lasted for four months and he was installed on 19 January 379. Since there was no chance of wresting the conquered territory back from the Goths, a *modus vivendi* had to be worked out with them, [MH.III, 219] and Theodosius acquitted himself well in this task. It did, all the same, give permanent recognition to the catastrophe. The shortage of manpower is revealed by the fact that Egyptian troops were called up who had never before been needed in any previous engagement.[755] Some partial advantages over the Goths were even gained. After their great victory, a degree of division had set in among them. Fritigern was no longer ruler: once victory had been won, he lost the power conferred on him by the need of the moment. The hordes dispersed and scattered aimlessly. Some of them were even lured to the Roman side by Theodosius; others he defeated. Ultimately a contractual relationship was worked out, the conditions of which are only sketchily known to us, since Ammianus ceases to be available as a source at this point, and those sources we do have are not worth much. Fritigern disappeared, and we do not know what became of him.[756]

In contrast, Athanaric, the old enemy of the Romans who had sworn never to set foot on Roman territory, suddenly appears as *iudex regum*,[757] 'judge of kings', concluding a treaty with Theodosius, and dying in 381.[758] We can see that the Danube defences were essentially broken, and remained so. Thrace and Moesia were exposed to barbarians. The right bank of the Danube was ceded to the Goths, who were nominally subjects. This is indeed formally so, for they recognized the Emperor as their overlord. In other respects they were taxed[759] and faced conscription like subjects. These Goths lived as internal *foederati*; in fact they were allies on an equal footing, [MH.III, 220] who, although they provided levies, did so only in return for annual payment. The Empire was exposed to these federates on the right bank of the Danube. A few decades later they would be threatening Rome and Constantinople. To this extent, this marked the beginning of the end. It also made a deep impression on contemporaries: Synesius, bishop of Cyrene, writes quite correctly (and he was looking at things from a safe distance): 'Shame on us that foreigners do our fighting for us. We are women, the Goths are men. What a catastrophe when they summon all their compatriots, settled all over the place, to make common cause with them!'[760] Indeed, the entire Empire was already so overrun with Germans that it posed a huge threat. But how could it be otherwise? Theodosius's course of action was regrettable, but imperative and inevitable.

Valens's catastrophe also had major repercussions on the religious situation. Valens had been a devout Arian, whereas the West was loyal to the Athanasian doctrine. Valentinian had been so indifferent (although himself an Arian),[761] that he had allowed Gratian to be brought up in the Athanasian faith at Milan by Bishop Ambrose.[762] This created tension between uncle and nephew over this point too. Arianism fell with Valens. Theodosius was completely devoted to the Nicene Creed. He propounded it zealously in the East, as did Gratian in the West. Apart from the Goths,[763] Arianism was finished from then on. It should not be forgotten that the Arians and [MH.III, 221] Athanasians hated and persecuted one another as bitterly as Christians and pagans did. The death throes of paganism in Rome itself fell in the same period.[764] The statue of Victory, which Julian had set up again in the *curia*, was once again removed by Gratian,[765] and when the pontifical college requested, according to ancient custom, that he take up the office of *pontifex maximus*, Gratian, good Christian that he was, refused.[766] He thus sealed the death sentence of paganism.

With the loss of the Danube frontier, the die was cast for the Roman Empire, and it would be both distasteful and futile to follow the course of its death throes. The centre of events was now among the Germanic peoples. The spectacle of the Emperor Honorius in his marshy fortress at Ravenna, doing nothing apart from saying 'No', is all too pitiful. Things were not quite so bad in the eastern Empire. Constantinople, with its incomparable location, had the advantage of being an indestructible city, both an imperial residence and the centre of an Empire. There is a major difference from Italy, divided between Rome and Ravenna. Constantinople was still putting forth blossoms, winter blossoms of course, but the eternal plant of Greek art and poetry was impossible to eradicate. Rome no longer had anything like this. The respective intellectual portraits of East and West are utterly different, with every comparison favouring the East.

What is more, the East was suddenly proving more fortunate: the Persian Empire was keeping quiet. This was partly thanks to Theodosius, whose approach to the Persians, as with the Goths, was one of wise forbearance. But the chief reason [MH.III, 222] for Persian inactivity will have been the death of Sapor II, who died in 379, having been on the throne for nearly seventy years and having waged war against Constantine, Constantius II, Julian, Jovian and Valens. This outstanding ruler had been hostile to Rome all his life. After his death, foreign policy was crippled by disputes over the succession, that eternal curse of Persian history. In 384 a peace was concluded by Theodosius in return for concessions, but in 390 he voluntarily resigned himself to the division of Armenia and ceded the greater portion to the Persians.[767] This was a sensible sacrifice, to relinquish a relatively unimportant outpost at this point, when it was necessary to struggle for the most vital and pressing interests elsewhere. The peace between Persia and eastern Rome largely survived the whole fifth century on the basis established by Theodosius. Not until the sixth century did the wars flare up which were ultimately to lead to the collapse of eastern Rome.[768]

Theodosius was also fortunate in other ways. In the western Empire he revived unity – or at least the shadow of it that remained. In 383 Gratian fell victim to a military revolt which broke out in Britain with the proclamation of Maximus as Augustus.[769] Valentinian II recognized him, so that for a while there were three Augusti again: Maximus in Britain, Spain and Gaul; Valentinian II in Italy and the rest of the West; and Theodosius in the East. In 387 Maximus violated the agreement, and Valentinian fled to Theodosius in search of support.[770] The latter eliminated Maximus in 388 and restored Valentinian as Emperor of the entire West.[771] [MH.III, 223] Then a fresh crisis broke out: Arbogast, a high-ranking general, had Valentinian II killed in 392, not making himself Emperor, but having Eugenius proclaimed as such: the last pagan to sit on the Roman throne.[772] In 394 Theodosius marched across the Alps and defeated Eugenius at Aquileia.[773] In 395 he then divided the Empire, since the line of Valentinian had died out, between his own two sons, Arcadius, who was given the East, and Honorius, who was given the West.[774]

Theodosius's reign marked the calm before the storm, although the real death blow had already been dealt before that. With his death in 395[775] this calm came to an end. The kind of warfare of which Alaric is a typical example[776] everywhere had the same face and the same results: it was purely personal in nature. A courageous commander gains power for a brief period, but there is no trace of creating a state. Every government is inherently ephemeral. These peoples, these commanders, effected the execution of the Roman state, but created nothing enduring: they did not enter into the Roman inheritance. The Goths are called 'all the Gothic peoples', *universae gentes Gothorum*.[777] There is no mention of outstanding rulers, but of many princely families. As a result there was no foundation of a new Empire. They were at first settled in Thrace and Moesia, but it was not from these domiciles that subsequent history unfolded, but from individual commanders, who may reasonably be compared with the *condottieri* of the Middle Ages.

[MH.III, 224] Alaric, one of the most outstanding among them, was born on an island in the mouth of the Danube at a time when the Danube crossing was still blocked to the barbarians.[778] We first encounter him as a Roman officer in command of a group of Goths. It seems that he was only driven to pursue hostilities when he was refused a request for his command to be extended in 395 after Theodosius's death.[779] Alaric was an outstanding soldier, but we cannot really see him as making political history.[780] Such men may establish isolated pockets of power, but they do not build Empires. Orosius[781] says of Athaulf, Alaric's brother-in-law and successor, who was probably at least as important, that he had explicitly voiced a desire to make a *Gothia* out of *Romania*, to build a Gothic Empire out of the Roman. This, however, he judged impossible, for the Goths were neither amenable to discipline nor law-abiding. He had hence been unable to do anything except use Gothic forces to prop up the Roman Empire and incorporate the Goths in the Roman federation of states. Athaulf's entire force consisted of 10,000 men – sufficient to overthrow an enfeebled, decaying Empire, but not to found a nation state. We can similarly observe how the Goths – for example, in the administration of justice, or the levying of taxes – simply worked according to Roman models. They fell victim to the same fate as all uncivilized peoples who conquer civilized Empires, [MH.III, 225] and which to a certain extent the Romans themselves succumbed to in relation to the Greeks. The warm baths, the villas, the good food, luxury in general, as well as the poetry and rhetoric, the science and art, all affected them – they became Romanized. The national identity of the first generation collapsed in the second and third generations. This is most clearly apparent in the case of the Vandals, who settled in Africa in 429, furthest from their tribal homelands.[782] Naturally enough, there were relatively few women among those who migrated to the new domiciles, with the result that subsequent generations were increasingly racially mixed. The only people who succeeded in establishing a state in this period were the Franks.[783] But northern Gaul was already thoroughly populated by Franks in Roman times and the new homeland they gained was geographically very close to their old one. After all, moving from the left to the right bank of the Rhine is quite a different matter from moving from the Danube, Elbe and Vistula to Spain and North Africa. To sum up again, then, the Goths were the executioners, not the heirs of the Romans.

The relationship between Alaric,[784] Radagaisus, and other commanders is obscure, but even more obscure is how the Romans stood in relation to all of them, and specifically to Alaric. An intricate game of intrigue was set in motion between the courts of Arcadius and Honorius. Particularly enigmatic is the figure of Stilicho,[785] who was a kind of Wallenstein. What sources we do possess – poets and preachers[786] – make it impossible for us to get at [MH.III, 226] the historical truth.

In 395 Alaric opened the fighting, invading Epirus and Greece.[787] Athens and Sparta, big names with no resistance to offer, surrendered to him, and he plundered on a large scale. He was believed to have been goaded by Rufinus, the minister of Arcadius, into making these westward plundering raids. Stilicho, sprung from half-Vandal stock and given in marriage Serena, niece of Theodosius,[788] along with the safekeeping of the Empire, specifically the West[789] – Rufinus's great rival Stilicho, I mean – went to Greece in 395. He scored some successes against Alaric, but then allowed him to escape.[790] It appears that he did not want to crush him entirely, perhaps wanting to use him against Rufinus, just as Rufinus had used Alaric against Stilicho. We must always keep an eye on the political game behind the military events of this period. Alaric profited from this and now achieved his purpose. We suddenly find him in a senior military position as Master of the Soldiers of Illyricum.[791] He thus now had a position on the border between the two realms from which he could intervene and invade both. In 400 he went to Italy, to the secret satisfaction of the eastern Empire. There was warfare in northern Italy and Stilicho won a victory in Piedmont in 402.[792] But the repercussions of this victory were analogous to those of a defeat, for the Goths crossed the Po and threatened Rome. And once again there was plotting behind the scenes – Alaric withdrew; it appears he was bribed to do so.[793] [MH.III, 227] These comings and goings, incursions and withdrawals, are the affectations of a bandit chief, but not of a brilliant statesman. Radagaisus imitated Alaric, invading Italy with other hordes, but suffered a crushing defeat by Stilicho in 405.[794]

In the final act of the great drama in which the Roman Empire was dissolved by the Germans, one figure arouses greater sympathy through his importance in this deeply depraved age: Stilicho. Contemporaries showered him equally liberally with both love and hatred. Some[795] depict him as the Emperor's loyal subject, propping up the tottering edifice with his strong arm as long as there was still a breath in his body, while others[796] condemn him as a traitor to his country and a malefactor. Both interpretations are correct up to a point; there is some truth in both. Understandably, the East judged him more favourably than the West. The West bore the brunt of his deeds, and it was here that Stilicho died as a condemned criminal.[797] His statues were toppled, his name disgraced,[798] his memory stigmatized. These are events which influence the superficial judgement of the public. The East hence judged more objectively and favourably – more as history should.

The government of both parts of the Empire, and all of the western part, to all intents and purposes rested on Stilicho's shoulders.[799] He was a fine soldier of the Theodosian school and, as already mentioned, close to the royal household. On his deathbed, Theodosius may have conferred on him *de facto* custodianship of the two halves [MH.III, 228] of the Empire.[800] Stilicho's personal relations led him to be seen as a member of the royal household. In a sense he was brother-in-law to both Emperors, for Serena, Theodosius's niece, whom he had married, was as close as a daughter to Theodosius, taking the place of the one he had never had.[801] Stilicho was also father-in-law to Honorius, who married two of his daughters in succession.[802] Had these marriages produced offspring, Stilicho would have become the founder of an imperial dynasty. Not only, however, was he brother-in-law and father-in-law to the Emperors, but he had also earmarked his own son Eucherius as heir to the throne.[803] And indeed, since Honorius had no children, there was no-one closer to the throne or the succession. Not even his bitterest denouncers ever accused him of coveting the throne for himself. He remained utterly loyal to the pitiful Honorius. He ruled the Empire as a soldier, introducing one particularly telling reform in the military sphere: the concentration of supreme command in one person's hands.[804] This should in fact be the Emperor's role. Since the Emperor did not bother to concern himself with it, however, Stilicho in fact had little option but to eliminate the senior officers, Masters of the Soldiers, and to unite the authority of the *magister equitum et peditum in praesenti* in his own person, as *generalissimus*.[805] [MH.III, 229] This, of course, was unconstitutional, but had these senior military posts remained occupied, then unified command of the army would have been impossible, since the Emperor was ineffectual. In any case all political and state affairs passed into his hands.

Stilicho encountered strong ideological opposition among two groups, the patriots and the orthodox. The patriots accused him of being unRoman. His origins were obscure. His father was probably a Vandal,[806] his mother Roman. Since the Vandals were part of the great Gothic family, they also saw him as a Gothic destroyer of the Roman Empire, according to the conventional classification. Although he had entered the service of Theodosius early on, in the eyes of Roman patriots he always remained Germanic. Furthermore, Athaulf's view that the Goths could not stand alone and that an alliance of the two peoples was necessary was greeted with sympathy on the Roman side, and such an alliance was sought after. After all, Theodosius had already allowed himself to be led into his conciliatory policy by considerations of this kind.[807] It was quite apparent, of course, how dangerous such an infusion of new blood would inevitably be, but it was equally clear that there was no safe, easy, or risk-free cure for the ailing Roman Empire. It was either drastic treatment or certain death. [MH.III, 230] There was no third alternative.

Stilicho himself drew his support exclusively from foreigners: his immediate circle consisted of barbarians. His personal bodyguard was a troop of Huns whom he found loyal;[808] this was no longer the case among the Goths, who had already been corrupted by too much contact with the Romans. Stilicho had opponents among the Goths,[809] in whom real soldierly loyalty had died out, forcing him to resort to a more distant branch of barbarians. The Senate, soldiery and patriots were all outraged by this method of defending Rome by employing its worst enemies, all too akin to a capitulation.[810] And this is, indeed, what it was. The mind of the ordinary senator – if one may say so – was aware of how precarious the situation was, but the important question is, how could it have been managed better? There was no other way. Stilicho did what had to be done, and yet he was bitterly resented for it.

Then there were the orthodox. They called Stilicho a pagan,[811] an Arian. But these religious questions were not of central importance to him. Other things were more imperative; above all he sought to prop up and keep together the state, which was falling apart at the seams. As a leading statesman he viewed these questions from a different angle than the individual orthodox citizen. The Huns were still pagans; the [MH.III, 231] Goths, who were no longer pagans, were Arians. Stilicho drew his men where he could find them and as they could be of use, without inquiring too much after their religious denomination. He was hugely resented for this by the orthodox, which made his already difficult position even more difficult. His only support was the highly unreliable Honorius. The inordinate power that legitimate rule had at Rome is illustrated nowhere more clearly than in the varying fortunes of this, the pettiest of all rulers. The Empire was falling apart, and officers were cut down *en masse* by rebellious soldiers during the final downfall of Stilicho, but Honorius was sacred to them, not a hair on his head was harmed.[812] And Stilicho had to rely on this Emperor, Honorius, who betrayed his trust in the vilest possible manner in his final hour of need. But the very fact that Stilicho was able to hold his own for twenty-three years in such a hopeless struggle is a magnificent achievement.

Stilicho handed the land over to the Germans, and yet still remained loyal to the Emperor. He was on the same wavelength as Alaric, who was in essentially the same position as himself: also a Roman officer, also a pupil of Theodosius, both Germans in the service of Rome. It is quite understandable that Stilicho did not want to destroy Alaric, even though he could have done. Since Rome had need of Germans, Alaric was [MH.III, 232] at least in tune with Roman ideas, and better than a crude barbarian. Stilicho's indulgence of Alaric, which led to his being accused of treason, is quite understandable. He had already proved to Radagaisus in 405 that he knew the art not only of defeating, but also of wresting complete victory, as long as it was simply a question of a lawless bunch of barbarians.[813] During that time Alaric had lain low. It was through Alaric that Stilicho retained his hold on western Illyricum, on the border between eastern and western Rome, but ostensibly part of western Rome. Alaric exacted payment for this, and this led to Stilicho's downfall.

Before going on to examine this, we should not lose sight of another aspect. West Roman rule was overthrown in Britain by an unusual kind of military revolt. The legions deserted, largely out of antagonism to the Germans, who predominated here. The sense of humiliation at the way Honorius, or Stilicho, was dealing with Alaric was most acute in Britain. This was compounded by personal ambition and in 407 Constantine III took the purple.[814] The rebellion spread to Gaul, where the troops joined Constantine. This was a fully-fledged alternative Emperorship. It was impossible to crush this desertion with the Italian troops, so Stilicho resorted to the fatal step of giving up the Rhine, just as the [MH.III, 233] Danube had been given up earlier. On the last day of 406 the Germanic peoples – the Vandals, Alani and Suevi, all those who inhabited Pannonia – crossed the hitherto long-defended bulwark of this river and established themselves in Roman Gaul.[815] The question is, did this happen at Stilicho's instigation? He probably did not invite this invasion as such, but understandably he wanted it to happen. He realized that it was impossible to retain Gaul for Honorius; but he would rather cede it to the Germans than to Constantine.

This was a step which had consequences for all ages to come. All the peoples who later came to divide the West among themselves make their appearances here. Even the Franks, so far mentioned either as inhabiting this region or as unwelcome neighbours in Gaul, are now mentioned more specifically.[816] Indeed, we learn little of northern Gaul generally. But Saint Jerome[817] states that Reims and Tournai were occupied by the Franks shortly before 406. There are accounts of the Vandals suffering setbacks in battle against the Franks on crossing the river, which means it must already have been Frankish domain. Perhaps it had not yet openly seceded from Rome; but only a little later we find it independent. Now the Germanic armies overran southern France as well, crossing the Pyrenees in 409 and moving into Spain, which had thus far been [MH.III, 234] spared.[818] Later [in 429], the Vandals crossed to Africa. Stilicho probably has to take the responsibility for all this.

At the same time Alaric was claiming his reward, demanding the huge sum of 40 hundredweight of silver.[819] Stilicho recommended meeting this demand, but the Senate, which would otherwise not have had anything to say, suddenly spoke out in opposition. It must have been difficult to persuade them to agree, but at last consent was wrested from them. The decision was probably taken with a view to the situation in Gaul, and Stilicho wanted to make use of Alaric against the rebellious Gauls. This is borne out by Alaric's demand for land in Noricum (modern Bavaria and Upper Austria); Stilicho also supported this – it was his last official act. The army revolted in Pavia (Ticinum), where the headquarters were located. The Emperor was there, Stilicho was not. The officers were killed, the revolt being aimed at Stilicho and his officers, who were looked on as his minions.

The degrading truce maintained the pretence that the Emperor was in safe hands. Our sources are meagre concerning Stilicho's conduct, but are borne out by internal logic. According to these Stilicho decided to wait and see how the troops would behave towards the Emperor, and the latter towards himself. If the Emperor [MH.III, 235] was put at risk, he intended to crush the rebellion. If, however, the troops remained loyal to him, the Emperor would have to decide between Stilicho and the rebels. His conduct was thus utterly loyal, but based on the assumption that the Emperor was honourable. The second alternative occurred and Stilicho set out for Ravenna. He was met halfway by his own death sentence, extracted from the king [sic] by Stilicho's opponent, the corrupt eunuch, Olympius.[820] Stilicho surrendered. His Huns remained loyal and offered to rescue him. Rejecting their support, he was executed.[821]

Now the storm broke over the Empire. Alaric was not paid his sum of money, and had no option but to set his forces on the move and march on Rome. The city was defenceless. It did have walls, recently put in a good state of repair by Stilicho;[822] but the still enormous population was poorly supplied, and severing its link with Ostia would have been enough to force the city into a rapid surrender. Alaric thus had good reason to reply to a deputation from the city, which sought to kindle his compassion for the great mass of suffering inhabitants: 'The closer the stalks stand together, the easier they are to mow.'[823] Rome was captured in 410.[824] [MH.III, 236] Alaric would dearly have liked to inherit Stilicho's political position *vis-à-vis* the imperial throne, but his attempt to exert pressure on Honorius, secure in his residence at Ravenna and uninterested in what was happening in the rest of the Empire, backfired. Honorius left the city to its fate.[825]

Alaric's aspiration towards a Roman position in addition to that of king of the Goths is striking proof of just how strong the feeling was that only in conjunction with Rome could anything lasting be created. Honorius always said simply: 'No, the legitimate ruler cannot entertain such ideas.' Then Alaric made an unusual bid.[826] He proclaimed the urban prefect, Priscus Attalus, an ancient Roman aristocrat, Emperor by the grace of Alaric, appointing himself as his Master of the Soldiers and Athaulf as Count of the Household, with the aim of assuming Stilicho's coveted position under another Emperor. He incorporated his Gothic troops into the Roman army. But this bid was wrecked by opposition from the Romans. Attalus rebuffed his creator and was of course deposed.[827] Alaric turned to Honorius again, [MH.III, 237] who repeated his monotonous 'No'. Alaric's political plans backfired; there seemed no prospect of creating anything enduring. But even from the military point of view he was now unable to make any real headway. He made an attempt to conquer the desirable province of Africa, but this failed because of resistance by the African governor and the lack of seafaring skill on the part of the Goths. An attempt to cross over to Sicily to conquer this island likewise had to be abandoned, since even these narrow straits proved insurmountable to the Goths.[828] Then Alaric died at Cosentia in Calabria. There is a well-known story of how the Goths laid their hero to rest in a drained riverbed and then reflooded the burial site in order to preserve the remains of their great king from desecration by the Romans.[829]

Alaric was succeeded by Athaulf, already mentioned earlier,[830] who continued in Alaric's footsteps and was perhaps politically the more important of the two. There was then a sudden change of scene. Alaric died in autumn 410; 412 finds Italy abandoned by the Goths, who are now in southern Gaul. Athaulf had evidently given up the idea of creating a Gothic Empire in Italy. Italy was too Roman, and the Goths too few in number. They were after all an army on the march, not a migrating people. The same opposition that had proved Stilicho's downfall also wrecked the plans of Alaric and Athaulf in Italy. Athaulf ruled for only a few years, but they were extremely interesting and successful. Again, the tradition is very scant.

[MH.III, 238] Wars against the pretenders were raging in Gaul. Athaulf attempted to intervene, sometimes on the side of Honorius, sometimes on that of the pretender Jovinus.[831] All negotiations broke down under the intractable obstinacy of the primary legitimate monarch at Ravenna. Then Athaulf resorted to an unusual step. The most precious prize gained during the capture of Rome had been the princess Galla Placidia, daughter of Theodosius, who since then had been living as a prisoner in the Gothic camp. But she seems to have been politically more astute than her brothers. What Honorius stubbornly refused, an alliance with the Goths, she entered into with her own person, thereby giving it her political support. Her marriage to Athaulf took place in Narbonne in 414, in Roman costume and according to Roman custom,[832] in a bid for legitimacy. Of course this did nothing to mitigate the intractable obstinacy of the court at Ravenna. But the court had no objection to the Goths founding a kingdom in Gaul, where a vacuum had been left by the departure for Spain of the Vandals and other peoples around 409. Here Athaulf laid the foundations for the kingdom of Toulouse, which was to flourish so successfully later. Significantly, he named his son by Placidia after Theodosius; this points to the aspirations invested in the child. But he died even before his father, who himself fell victim to murder in 415.[833] But his plans did not die with him.

[MH.III, 239] In the final years of Honorius and under Wallia, Athaulf's successor, the way was paved for improved relations which were to endure for another hundred years. Placidia was sent back to the court at Ravenna.[834] In return the Goths were granted permanent homelands in southern Gaul, in Aquitania Secunda, a land outstanding for both its wealth and its learning, more prosperous than Italy, with the major cities of Tolosa (Toulouse) and Burdigala (Bordeaux). The Goths received these as hereditary possessions, to some extent as Roman subjects, since they had an obligation to serve in the army. The reconquest of Spain, for example, was their work, and the Goths sent the chieftains they captured to Ravenna. Part allies, part vassals, in constant opposition and yet under contract, this relationship endured for a century, and their kingdom provided the model for all the Germanic kingdoms later to be built on the ruins of the western Roman Empire. The kingdom of Burgundy was established in this way; the Vandal kingdom in Africa was initially a usurpation, but then there was a similar treaty, something like the relationship the Numidian kings had had with the Roman Republic, or the sovereignty of the German Kaiser over the individual dynasties.

This marked the beginning of assimilation. With the Vandals the Germans also acquired maritime supremacy, [MH.III, 240] and German fleets sailed the Mediterranean. On closer examination, the German element lost out in the mixing process. Roman education and rhetoric made their appearance, their princes enjoyed the education of prominent young Romans, and the language was Latin, not German.[835] Salic law is a case in point: the Franks had the most liberal and autonomous law of all these kingdoms, and yet it was codified in Latin.[836] Sidonius Apollinaris[837] calls Syagrius the Solon of the Burgundians. All these Germans automatically adopted the Roman cultural milieu. Their aspiration, therefore, was not to detach themselves from Rome, but rather to associate themselves with it as closely as possible. In this way the homogeneity of Roman education brought about that remarkable hybrid culture based on a Germanic foundation which was the final outcome of Roman civilization.

Eastern Rome had a different fate. Greek nationality held its own for longer, but at last, arid and defeated, it too disintegrated. The Arabs and Turks who made an end of the eastern Roman Empire allowed Greek civilization, or rather what was left of it, no room for movement. Greek civilization was thus destroyed. [MH.III, 241] Although Roman civilization was defeated, new life sprang up out of its ruins. The Latin peoples appeared: Roman elements were permeated with Germanic. Transmuted and diluted, Roman civilization thus lived on, fresh blossoms bursting forth on the same branch in happier times. But this process of world history was begun by Alaric and Athaulf, and the political visions of Stilicho, Alaric and Athaulf took on a life of their own which continued long after their originators were no longer alive, and indeed they continue to be powerfully alive to this day.

Explicit liber feliciter

NOTES

INTRODUCTION

1 This introduction is based substantially on my article in *Gymnasium* 93 (1986).
2 Winston Churchill, who received the Nobel Prize for Literature for his *History of the English-speaking Peoples*, and Stanley Engerman, who received the Nobel Prize for Economics in 1993 for his work on the economic history of nineteenth-century America, might be considered exceptions.
3 1816–94, a National-Liberal German novelist.
4 The same publishers who had prompted Jakob Grimm in 1838 to undertake their *German Dictionary*.
5 Hartmann 1908, pp. 58f.
6 Adolf Stohr writes in the same vein in the introduction to his translation of Suetonius, published by Langenscheidt (around 1857).
7 Wickert III 1969, p. 416.
8 Wucher 1968, p. 202.
9 Wickert IV 1980, p. 18.
10 'Der letzte Kampf der römischen Republik', in *Ges. Schr.* IV, pp. 333ff.; 'Trimalchios Heimath und Grabschrift', in *Ges. Schr.* VII, pp. 191ff. Both in *Hermes* 13 (1877/8).
11 Revised ed., I 1827, p. 333; Mommsen's leaflet was reprinted in 1927 and 1954. Wickert III 1969, p. 674.
12 Wickert III 1969, p. 674; see below.
13 Schwartz 1935, p. 164.
14 Wucher 1956, p. 136.
15 Wucher 1923, no. 32.
16 Ibid., no. 33.
17 Goldammer 1967, p. 136. Storm (1817–88) had been a fellow student of Mommsen's at Kiel; Keller (1819–90) was a Swiss writer.
18 Teitge 1966, p. 125.
19 Malitz 1983, pp. 132f.
20 The date given in Schwartz no. 179 is corrected by Bammel 1969, pp. 225f.
21 Schwartz 1935, p. 218.
22 Schwartz 1935, pp. 190f.
23 Norden 1933/66, p. 654.
24 Bammel 1969, p. 224.
25 *Prix Nobel 1902*, pp. 34ff.
26 Kornemann 1938/9; Heuss 1960.
27 Bleicken 1978.
28 Bengston 1967 (to AD 284); Christ 1988 (to AD 337); Demandt 1988 (from AD 284).
29 Wickert 1954, p. 11.

30 *The American Commonwealth* I–III, 1888.

31 Fisher II 1927, p. 225.

32 Rink and Witte 1983, p. 272.

33 Schmidt-Ott 1952, p. 38.

34 Mommsen, 3 April 1876 to Degenkolb; Wucher 1968, p. 127.

35 Wucher 1953, p. 415.

36 Wucher 1968, p. 132. F. Sartori considered this to be the decisive reason for the non-appearance of volume IV.

37 Butler 1939, p. 125.

38 Malitz 1983, pp. 126f.

39 Schwartz 1935, p. 164.

40 'I no longer have the courage of youth to make mistakes': Bolognini 1904, p. 259.

41 Wucher 1953, pp. 423, 428f.; 1968, pp. 41ff.

42 Max Weber, *Jugendbriefe* (1963), no. 165, of 16 June 1885.

43 Hirschfeld 1904/13, p. 947; Momigliano 1955, p. 156.

44 Hartmann 1908, p. 80.

45 Ibid., p. 141.

46 Wickert III 1969, p. 670; Heuss 1956, pp. 253ff.; Sartori 1963, p. 86.

47 Mommsen, *RA*, p. 352; Malitz 1983, p. 133.

48 Wilamowitz 1918/72, pp. 35ff.; Wucher 1968, p. 134.

49 Hartmann 1908, p. 81. On Mommsen's relationship to Christianity see below.

50 Teitge 1966, p. 32.

51 Zahn-Harnack 1950; Croke 1985, p. 279. Cf. already Bolognini 1904, p. 258.

52 Adolf von Harnack (1851–1930) was a patristics scholar and liberal theologian. Appointed Professor of Protestant Theology at Berlin by Bismarck in 1888, he saw the Christian faith as developing through time within particular historical contexts.

53 *Verhandlungen*, 1901, pp. 142, 147f.

54 A reference to Aurelius Victor (5,2): 'quinquennium tamen tantus fuit [sc. Nero], augenda urbe maxime, uti merito Traianus saepius testaretur procul differre cunctos principes Neronis quinquennio.' The doubling is a lapse of memory on the part of Mommsen.

55 'That almost classic question: why did Mommsen not write the history of the Empire?' Momigliano 1955, p. 155.

56 Neumann 1904, p. 226.

57 Hirschfeld 1904/13, pp. 946ff.

58 Hartmann 1908, p. 62.

59 Fowler 1909/20, p. 260.

60 Norden 1933/66, p. 655.

61 Weber 1937, p. 334.

62 Bengtson 1955, p. 94.

63 Wilamowitz 1918, pp. 29ff.; 1927/59, pp. 70f.; 1928, p. 180.

64 Meyer 1922, p. 327.

65 Wucher 1953, pp. 424f.; 1968, p. 128.

66 Klement 1954, p. 41.

67 Instinsky 1954, pp. 443f.

68 Yavetz 1983, p. 26.

69 Timpe 1984, p. 56.

70 Wickert III 1969, p. 422.

71 Wickert 1954, p. 12.

72 Momigliano 1955, pp. 155f.

73 Fueter 1911, p. 553.

74 Heuss 1956, p. 98. Cf. (without evaluation) Bringmann 1991, p. 76.

75 Toynbee 1934/48, pp. 3f.

76 Collingwood 1946/67, p. 127.

77 Calder III 1983, p. 59.
78 Grant 1954, p. 85.
79 Bammel 1969, p. 229.
80 Instinsky 1954, p. 444.
81 Srbik 1951/64, p. 131.
82 Wucher 1953, p. 427; 1968, p. 135.
83 Gollwitzer 1952, p. 61.
84 Christ 1976, p. 50.
85 Mommsen, *RA*, p. 109.
86 Hartmann 1908, p. 255; Schöne 1923, p. 17: 'straightforwardly monarchical sentiment'; Weber 1929, p. 26.
87 Highet 1949/67, p. 476.
88 Lasky 1950, p. 67.
89 Mommsen, *RA*, pp. 104ff.
90 Mashkin 1949, p. 6.
91 Irmscher 1990, p. 234. Mashkin is not mentioned.
92 Kuczynski 1978, pp. 113ff.
93 Oncken 1922.
94 Demandt 1979, pp. 77ff.
95 Croke 1985, p. 285.
96 Mommsen, *RA*, p. 176.
97 Wickert IV 1980, p. 227.
98 Wickert IV 1980, p. 231.
99 Sc. the conflict between Rome and Christianity.
100 Wickert III 1969, p. 670.
101 Bardt 1903, p. 36.
102 Bolognini 1904, p. 258.
103 Neumann 1904, p. 229.
104 Gooch 1913, p. 467.
105 Instinsky 1954, p. 444.
106 Dilthey 1923, no. 37.
107 Schwartz 1935, XIV; pp. 166f.; pp. 137, 152, 160, 189, 479ff.
108 Malitz 1985, pp. 41, 53.
109 Wilamowitz 1918/72, pp. 37ff.
110 Ibid., p. 30.
111 Calder and Schlesier 1985, pp. 161ff.
112 Weber 1937, p. 334.
113 Weber 1929, pp. 16, 19.
114 Wucher 1953, pp. 427ff.: 1968, p. 137.
115 Heuss 1986, p. 613.
116 Wickert 1954, p. 18.
117 Wucher 1968, p. 127.
118 Neumann 1904, pp. 228f.
119 Hirschfeld 1913, p. 947. A major fragment, regarded by Hirschfeld as preparatory work for volume IV, is published in Mommsen, *Ges. Schr.* V, pp. 589ff.; see MH.II, 105.
120 Ehrenberg 1960/65; Wickert IV 1980, p. 341; see p. 538 n. 268.
121 The story of this discovery was described (with occasional dramatizations) by Jürgen Busche in 1982.
122 Wilamowitz 1918/72, p. 36.
123 Demandt 1986, pp. 507, 511.
124 C. Lowenthal-Hensel 1986; also in W. Hensel 1981, pp. 12ff.
125 This should be: two winter and two summer semesters, i.e. winter 1882/3, summer 1883, winter 1885/6 and summer 1886; cf. lecture notes 9, 12 and 13; see p. 21.

126 This refers to the banker Gottlieb Adelbert Delbrück (1822–90), a co-founder of the Kaiserhof Hotel. Adelbert was the brother of Berthold, father of the later historian Hans Delbrück.

127 This is contradicted by the lecture notes taken by Sebastian Hensel himself; see below.

128 S. Hensel 1903/4, pp. 416ff.

129 Rickert 1930.

130 Schwartz 1935, p. 81.

131 The letters from Hensel to Mommsen published here are housed in the manuscripts section of the German State Library in East Berlin, as part of the Mommsen papers. I am grateful to the Chief Librarian, Dr H.-E. Teitge, for permission to publish these.

132 Glockner 1972, pp. 58f.

133 According to her own account, it had once been looked at by Gerhard Wirth, who was a friend of Fanny Kistner, née Hensel during his time in Erlangen. Like Wilamowitz before him, however (see above), he had not thought it to be of any particular importance.

134 A lively description of Paul Hensel is available in Curtius, 1950/58, pp. 226f.

135 In later editions of RG.I, pp. 872f., Mommsen cites Plutarch, Cato the Elder 20,7.

136 S. Hensel 1903/4, pp. 142f.

137 Leo 1960, XVII.

138 B. Schemann, 'Aus Ludwig Schemanns Leben und Schaffen', in F. Kerber (ed.) Volkstum und Reich. Ein Buch vom Oberrhein (1938), pp. 173–80, 176f.

139 The title on the spine of Hensel's notebook, 'From Diocletian to Honorius', does not derive from Mommsen, who regarded Alaric as marking the end of an epoch: MH.III, 223ff.

140 On this event, Mommsen wrote: 'Infelicissimo casu accidit ut funesto incendio, quod proximo anno accidit paucis diebus post absolutam textus impressionem, una cum domo mea quattuor illi libri toti et cum his maiore ex parte Vindobonensis n. 203 interirent' (MGH.AA.VI, 1882, p. LXXI). On the house fire, see Wilamowitz to Usener, 15 July 1880; in his preceding letter of 14 July 1880 to Wilamowitz, Usener refers to a detailed report by the Kölner Zeitung. Cf. also Schöne (1840–1922) Schöne 1923, pp. 30f.; and Adelheid Mommsen, Mein Vater, 1936/92, pp. 82ff. The Mommsens stayed with the Schöne family while their house was being repaired.

141 Klement 1954, p. 41 (Fama); Glockner 1972, p. 58.

142 Demandt 1986.

143 I am grateful to Dr Knobloch and Dr Clauss for permission to publish.

144 For the general view of the age of the emperors in Mommsen's period, see A. Heuss, ANRW II 1, (1974) pp. 66ff.; Bringmann 1991.

145 Christ 1982, pp. 66ff.; for Kornemann's 'four eyes' metaphor: MH.I, 168; III, 163; 197.

146 See Hartmann 1908, p. 148; Croke 1990 ('Mommsen and Gibbon').

147 Schwartz 1935, pp. 160, 189.

148 Wickert III, p. 633.

149 The English text of Mommsen's letter is available in Croke 1990 ('Mommsen and Gibbon'), p. 56.

150 Wilamowitz 1928, p. 160.

151 Bolognini 1904, p. 259.

152 Curtius 1950, p. 333.

153 MH.II, 365f.; RE Suppl. XII 1970, 561f., 576.

154 Wickert IV 1980, pp. 180ff. On Christianity elsewhere, see Mommsen, Strafrecht, pp. 595ff.; Ges. Schr. III, pp. 389ff, 423ff., 431ff.; VI, pp. 540ff., 546ff., 570ff.

155 Demandt 1984, pp. 403ff.

156 Wickert IV 1980, p. 342; MH.II, 315. For a different view, however, MH.II, 140.

157 Mommsen, RA, p. 107.

158 Mommsen, Ges. Schr. V, p. 492.

159 Mommsen, RA, p. 106.

160 Wucher 1951, p. 263. Max Weber (Jugendbriefe 1963, p. 346) on 18 April 1892 writes of the 'almost childish hatred of Bismarck among men such as Mommsen, escalating and being expressed in truly depressing forms'.

161 Wucher 1968, p. 136.
162 Mommsen, *RA*, p. 69.
163 Mommsen, *RA*, p. 69.
164 Bammel 1969, p. 240.
165 Calder and Schlesier 1985, p. 162.
166 A.J. Toynbee, *Experiences* (1969), pp. 109f.
167 Hirschfeld 1904/13, p. 947.
168 P. Ganz (ed.), *Jacob Burckhardt, Über das Studium der Geschichte* (1982), p. 13.
169 'He had ordered the poem to be destroyed in the swift flames': E. Diehl (ed.), *Die 'Vitae Vergilianae'* (1911), p. 18 (Donatus/ Suetonius 38)
170 See Hensels own comment at MH.II, 342ff.

THE BERLIN ACADEMY FRAGMENT

1 The reference is to Petronius's *Satyricon*.
2 Gennaro Riccio, *Le monete delle antiche famiglie di Roma*.
3 should read: 43.29.
4 should read 'left', cf *Bell. Hisp*. 31.5.

A HISTORY OF ROME UNDER THE EMPERORS I

1 On the following: Syme 1939; Christ 1979, pp. 424ff.; id. 1988.
2 Mommsen characterized the imperial age in more detail in his lectures of 1872/3, according to notes taken by L. Schemann, extracts from which are quoted in Wickert IV 1980, pp. 341ff:

> The history of the imperial age unfolded, like that of the Republican age, as an uninterrupted, discrete process, undisturbed either by the intervention of foreign nations or by the appearance of over-mighty individuals. In recent times this can only be said of North America. Roman history is, nevertheless, somewhat colourless and lifeless, bearing the character of being universally valid. The only exception is the all-powerful Caesar, at the turning point between the two eras: the imperial age produced as few first-rate men as the Republic had done. The imperial age of Rome shows us the Roman people moving into advanced old age, until their final disintegration: it was not the barbarians who overthrew Rome. In the imperial age we see the Romans without aspiration, without hope, without real political ambition. Efforts were restricted to preserving frontiers. The joyous period of growth was over, all problems had evaporated. Previously, statesmen had at least had ideals, albeit reprehensible ones: now, however, they no longer had any. However lengthy this epoch, it remained one of status quo. For all that, the history of the Roman Emperors remains an interesting field, and the fact that it has recently been the subject of study, not without success, is to be welcomed. The imperial age is also important in as much as our own culture is largely based on it: the course of classical studies in schools stems from the schools of the imperial age. The laws of absolutism were first legislatively formulated in that period. The vast disparities between the German and Latin characters, which still shape our world today, likewise first took shape in the imperial age, where the roots of this immense problem are to be found.

3 Pompey escaped to Egypt, where he was murdered.
4 6 April 46 BC. Mommsen concluded volume III of his *History of Rome* with this event.
5 Bassus's insurrection in Syria, 46 BC: App. *Civ*. III, 77; IV, 58f.. See Berlin Academy Fragment, p. 9 left.

6 Caesar's murder on 15 March 44 BC: App. *Civ.* II, 117ff.; Plut. Caes., 60ff.; Puet. *Caes.* 81ff. Mommsen spoke in detail about the assassination in 1868 (MK, pp. 7ff.).

7 Livy II, 1, 9.

8 App. *Civ.* III, 34.

9 In the text below Hensel (like MK) uses the names 'Caesar junior', 'Caesar minor' and 'Octavian' without distinction or system. To avoid confusion, we use 'Octavian', although Mommsen generally spoke, sometimes (MH.I, 23) confusingly, of 'Caesar'. R. Syme 'Imperator Caesar. A Study in Nomenclature', *Historia* 7 (1958), 172–88 = Roman Papers I (1979), 361–77.

10 App. *Civ.* III, 25.

11 I.e. Caesar's assassins.

12 App. *Civ.* III, 30.

13 Actually the son of Caesar's niece.

14 App. *Civ.* III, 45.

15 In fact the fifth, *hoc bellum* (*sc. Mutinense*) *quintum civile geritur*: Cic. *Phil.* VIII, 3.8.

16 App. *Civ.* III, 49.

17 Hensel writes 'Plancus'.

18 App. *Civ.* III, 50.

19 App. *Civ.* III, 70f.

20 App. *Civ.* III, 72.

21 App. *Civ.* III, 83.

22 Governor of Hispania Citerior and Gallia Narbonensis.

23 App. *Civ.* III, 88f.

24 App. *Civ.* III, 94, on 19 August 43: *ILS* 108.

25 App. *Civ.* III, 95.

26 43 BC: App. *Civ.* IV, 2. The date is provided by the *Fasti Colotiani*: *Inscriptiones Italiae* XIII 1, 274. It is 27 November.

27 W. Kolbe, 'Der zweite Triumvirat', in Schmitthenner 1969, pp. 12ff.

28 In 1868/9 Mommsen mentioned further laws of Antony's:

> Caesar's grand design had been to free Rome from mob rule, meaning (among other things) the transferral of jurisdiction into the hands of the higher ranks. Since this decree appeared reactionary, Antony abrogated it, introducing a democracy blended with militarism that splendidly revealed the crudeness of his political nature.
>
> (MK, p. 13)

29 App. *Civ.* III, 44, 48.

30 App. *Civ.* IV, 5f.; Plut. *Cic.* 46.

31 The proscriptions of Sulla against the *populares* under Marius and Cinna, 81 BC: App. *Civ.* I, 95; Plut. *Sulla*, 30ff.

32 In 1868/9 Mommsen said:

> As far as the proscriptions are concerned, however, these were not so much a political as a financial measure, since a great deal of money needed to be raised immediately. Similarly, these measures seldom affected men of standing – Cicero was an exception.
>
> (MK, p. 26)

33 App. *Civ.* IV, 2.

34 Hensel has 'Caesar', but here, as elsewhere, probably means Octavian.

35 App. *Civ.* IV, 6, 19f.; Plut. *Cic.* 47ff.

36 App. *Civ.* IV, 65ff.

37 App. *Civ.* IV, 76ff.; Plut. *Brut.* 30ff.; Dio XLVII, 33f.

38 App. *Civ.* IV, 84f.; Cic. *Phil.* XIII, 12; Vell. II, 73.

39 App. *Civ.* IV, 87; Dio XLVII, 35ff.

40 App. *Civ.* IV, 115f.; Plut. *Brut.* 47,1; Dio XLVII, 47.4.

41 Plut. *Brut.* 38ff.; *Ant.* 22; App. *Civ.* IV, 88ff.; Suet. *Aug.* 13.
42 In 1868/9 Mommsen had added:

> The victory of Brutus and Cassius might also have led to absolutism – given that Brutus
> had his likeness stamped on coins. What, therefore, was in hand was not a decisive battle
> for one or other constitution, but for one or other person.
>
> (MK, p. 21)

43 App. *Civ.* V, 2.
44 App. *Civ.* V, 3.
45 Hensel adds here '(Legion)', although the Praetorian guard was not organized as a legion, but in nine cohorts; Mommsen: *Ges. Schr.* VI, pp. 6ff.
46 Dio. XLVIII, 12.5.
47 Suet. *Aug.* 13.3; App. *Civ.* V, 12f. L. Keppie, *Colonisation and Veteran Settlement in Italy 47–14 BC* (1983).
48 App. *Civ.* V, 15; 18; Dio XLVIII, 18.1.
49 Dio XLVIII, 24.4ff.
50 App. *Civ.* V, 3. This policy was Caesar's, loc.cit.
51 Lucius Antonius; Publius Servilius Isauricus was the second consul.
52 App. *Civ.* V, 12; Suet. *Aug.* 13.3.
53 Horace *Ep.* II, 2,50f.; Virg. *Ecl.*, 1,4; 9,28; *Georg.* II, 198; Servius, *Vita Virg.* 7; Tibullus I, 1.19; Prop. IV, 1.127f.
54 *Mon. Anc.* V, 25; Dio XLVII, 12.3.
55 Menas/Menodorus, Menecrates, Demochares, Apollophanes; see Vell. II, 73.1.
56 App. *Civ.* V, 14.
57 App. *Civ.* V, 8; Plut. *Ant.* 25ff.
58 App. *Civ.* V, 14ff.
59 App. *Civ.* V, 23.
60 App. *Civ.* V, 33ff.; Suet. *Aug.* 14f.
61 App. *Civ.* V, 48.
62 App. *Civ.* V, 66.
63 App. *Civ.* V., 51.
64 App. *Civ.* V, 65; Plut. *Ant.* 33f.; Festus, *Brev.* 18.
65 App. *Civ.* V, 55.
66 Plut. *Ant.* 35; App. *Civ.* V, 56.
67 In fact it is: App. *Civ.* V, 59.
68 See note 83.
69 App. *Civ.* V, 64. Maecenas had already fought at Mutina. Credit for the Peace of Brundisium goes, according to App. *Civ.* V, 60ff., to Lucius Cocceius Nerva.
70 App. *Civ.* V, 64.
71 According to AW.,p. 17; in fact, Pollio was a Republican.
72 App. *Civ.* V, 64f.; Plut. *Ant.* 30f.
73 *CIL.* I, p. 1, second ed. p. 180; *Mon. Anc.* 4; App. *Civ.* V, 66.
74 Virg. *Ecl.* IV, 5: 'The great sequence of the ages is born anew.'
75 In 1868/9 Mommsen said of the peace of 40 BC:

> There thus also came about a marital alliance between the two monarchs, through the
> marriage of Octavian's sister Octavia to Antony. Virgil henceforth speaks specifically of
> the forthcoming birth of a child who is to mark the advent of a golden age following the
> iron one, and in speaking of this child he undoubtedly means the child expected by
> Octavia. The view held by earlier commentators, that he was referring to the child
> expected by Pollio, is entirely without foundation. This information from the poet is
> particularly noteworthy, in that it provides us with the sole chronological clue enabling
> us to place the treaty of Brindisi at the beginning of the year 714.
>
> (MK, p. 33)

76 Plut. *Ant.* 32.
77 App. *Civ.* V, 53.
78 Vell. II, 73.2; the full title appears on coins: *CRR*.II, 560ff.
79 According to Dio XLVIII, 45.5; App. *Civ.* V, 78ff., gives the name 'Menodorus'.
80 Winter 39/8 BC in Athens: App. *Civ.* V, 76; Plut. *Ant.* 33.
81 App. *Civ.* V, 81ff.
82 Dio XLVII, 26.5.
83 Mommsen uses the Latin *imperator Parthicus* (as above, note 68). He was captured in Cilicia in 39 BC: Dio XLVIII, 40.6; Plut. *Ant.* 33.4.
84 App. *Civ.* V, 93ff.
85 App. *Civ.* V, 109ff.
86 Suet. *Aug.* 16; App. *Civ.* V, 118ff.; the two warring sides agreed on a date for the battle.
87 Dio XLIX, 12.
88 App. *Civ.* V, 123ff.
89 On Antony's Parthian War see Dio XLIX, 25ff.; Plut. *Ant.* 37ff.; E. G. Huzar, *Mark Antony* (1986), ch. 11, pp. 169–84.
90 Plut. *Ant.* 36f.; Dio XLIX, 34.
91 Plut. *Ant.* 57.3.
92 It is not clear here whether Mommsen means the father or the son.
93 Dio XLIX, 25.
94 App. *Civ.* V, 138.
95 Plut. *Ant.* 37.
96 *CRR* II, 525, no.179. 'Matri' before 'filiorum' would mean 'to Cleopatra . . . mother of royal sons'.
97 Dio XLIX, 40.3f.; Plut. *Ant.* 50.4.
98 Dio XLIX, 41.
99 Dio L, 4.4f.
100 Plut. *Ant.* 57.
101 Appian concludes (*Civ.* V, 144) with the death of Sextus Pompey in 35 BC at Miletus and a brief survey of Octavian's Illyrian War.
102 For a different view, see Syme 1939, pp. 270f.
103 Dio XLIX, 36.
104 Dio XLIX, 44.1f.; Plut. *Ant.* 53.6.
105 Dio L, 2.2; Suet. *Aug.* 17.
106 Dio L, 2.6. There must have been over 300 of them: Syme 1939, p. 278.
107 What follows is based largely on Dio L.
108 Hensel writes 'war', which does not make sense here.
109 According to Plutarch (*Ant.* 58), they had already changed sides in 32 BC, betraying Antony's last will to Octavian.
110 There is no documentary evidence suggesting that Sosius changed sides. He was captured at Actium and pardoned: Dio L, 14.2.; LI, 2.4.
111 Dio L, 33.
112 Plut. *Ant.* 71ff.
113 In 1868/9 Mommsen said:

> Antony had a sensual, physically over-lusty nature, which made him a valiant soldier without ever cherishing a single political conviction. A turbulent youth, in which he grew into a man during the many battles of his day, shaped this character. Although gifted, this coarse nature was not liberally formed, making Antony an outstanding, practical military man, especially as a cavalry officer. His growth into a notable politician was thwarted by his lack of noble national sentiment, which arose out of his huge political indifference. He was a Caesar, although motivated not by an ideal, democratic way of thinking, but by his vanity and lust for power. It particularly flattered his pride to picture himself as

an oriental-style monarch. At the root of this, however, lay not so much ambition as the raw sensuality and voluptuousness that were inherent to his nature. This inordinate fondness that Antony had for the life of an oriental monarch, as well as his relationship with Cleopatra, awakened in him the desire to move the seat of his government to Alexandria. It was thus his desire to dissolve the unity of the Empire. Had he succeeded, this decisive political event would have occurred 300 years sooner than it did.

(MK, p. 11)

114 Plut. *Ant.* 63ff., 71.

115 In Mommsen's lectures of 1872/3, according to L. Schemann's notes, we find:

Cleopatra (born in 68, thus dying at the age of 39), is a monstrous, demonic phenomenon. On the one hand a siren that no man, not even the dictator Caesar, was able to resist, on the other a woman who epitomizes, in all its horrifying historical reality, every evil attributed to such phenomena by mythology.

(Wickert IV 1980, p. 344)

116 *ILS* 108. Mommsen, *Ges. Schr.* IV, pp. 259ff. (from 1882).

117 Suet. *Aug.* 4.1.

118 What follows is drawn largely from Suetonius.

119 According to AW, 28.

120 Suet. *Aug.* 62f., 69, 71, *contra*.

121 Also known as the *Monumentum Ancyranum*; Mommsen, *Ges. Schr.* IV, 247ff.

122 Mommsen gives a more detailed description of Augustus in the lecture notes taken by Ludwig Schemann in 1872/3, published in Wickert IV 1980, pp. 342ff.:

Caesar Augustus had a compact, attractive figure, well-built, but not sturdy. Pale, blond, with shining eyes. Oblivious to his external appearance. Poor health, was said to suffer from a chest complaint. Severe illness, even in his crucial phase, did not impede him. Sensitive to cold and sun, he was afraid of thunderstorms. Not actually a great man. Augustus had partaken of a Greek education, but not to the same degree as others. When he had to speak Greek he composed it in Latin. He loved and cultivated literature, twice writing his own commentaries. He made attempts to write verse: like a tragic poet, he treated his successes with a touch of irony. The outstanding feature of the speeches, and in Augustus's style generally, is accuracy, rather than brilliance. Archaisms were as scrupulously avoided as neologisms (in contrast, for example, with the oriental bombast of Antony). Augustus avoided speaking *ex tempore*, always carefully composing what he had to say. He preferred correspondence to personal communication, and even with his wife Livia often dealt with important matters by letter.

In everyday life Augustus appears to have been amiable and comfort-loving. Mindful that the ruling house should set an example for all family life, he set great store by family mores. He enjoyed playing, especially with children. He delighted in physical exertion and was a passionate angler. Although equally genial as host and guest, he set no example in tippling.

Augustus effected a certain restoration of existing theology and scrupulously avoided patronizing the free-thinking spirit; in religion he was somewhat narrow.

Augustus was of an intelligent and benevolent (altogether mild and conciliatory), but not of a brilliant or magnificent, nature.

In politics, we find him adhering to the traditional, rather than the innovatory. Waiving his right to govern autocratically, he relied on political nobles. He was never entirely self-reliant: initially he depended on the Caesarian dictatorship, then on his alliance with Antony, then on Agrippa, later Tiberius, and indeed in many respects on his wife Livia. The dictator had not been like this: mighty thoughts had stirred in him of which he never spoke to those around him. Despite such proclivities, however, Augustus never succumbed to a system of advisers as such, as we observe occurring in such a repugnant manner in the later imperial age <Schemann had originally written 'later in the imperial age', which is the correct version>. Nor did he ever fail to uphold the obligations of good faith. He maintained a constant interest in all those persons, such as Agrippa, the friend of his youth, with whom he always had a close, confidential relationship. Naturally, he also at the same time possessed a strong sense of his own status as monarch. He took no nonsense from these men, in themselves his friends, and even Livia was only permitted access to confidential matters under the proviso of absolute discretion.

Of the dictator Caesar it may be said that if anyone at that time was to rule at all, then it was he. This is not at all the case with Augustus. Among those around him, he was not, for example, the one best suited to become ruler. He was, certainly, a ruler by birth; but had he not been the grandson, and later the adoptive son, of Caesar, and not taken on his name and all the tradition which accrued to it, then he would have been hard pressed to attain the monarchy. His sense of dynastic destiny was largely inherited.

He was as circumspect in his military policy as he was conservative in his governmental policy. Whereas Caesar had seriously entertained the idea of expanding the Empire, nothing could have been further from the mind of Augustus. He only extended the northern frontier out of caution, since in fact Italy at that time had no northern frontier. Conquests occurred under Augustus purely by chance, and were by no means made in accordance with a fixed plan.

Augustus has been accused of cruelty, duplicity and deceit. Certainly deeds may be found in his life which suggest such traits, but they are to be found in any ruler in his position. More significant is the accusation of a certain half-heartedness, which was particularly apparent in the military context. Augustus did, indeed, curb the military to an extent that endangered the state. The Varus disaster was the direct consequence of this, and just reproof for Augustus's ineffective military policy.

Unlike his great father, Augustus did not formally institute a monarchy. He sought to reconcile the irreconcilable: seriously to restore the old Republic and seriously to found the new monarchy. He inherently lacked all initiative, even at the outset of his policy, which ultimately degenerated more and more into petulance and quietism. The calm and stagnation of the final years of Augustus's reign, interrupted only by the storm of the Varus disaster, became the foundation for a global conflagration, a final catastrophe. The achievement of Augustus is not dissimilar to the federal constitution of Count Metternich. When, on his deathbed, he called on the public to applaud him for the role he had played for 60 years, he was right to do so; but it was just that – a role he had played. Augustus was by nature a crown prince, but ought to have done his duty in that role.

123 Dio LIII, 3ff.

124 Dio LIII, 16.6; *Mon. Anc.* 34; Suet. *Aug.* 7.2.

125 On the nature of the principate see Mommsen, *RA*, pp. 104ff.; id., *Staatsrecht* II, 2, pp. 745ff.; summary pp. 148ff.

126 In 1868 Mommsen declared of Octavian: 'With immense calculated shrewdness he created the hybrid of a state that fused the old Republic with an absolute military monarchy' (MK.202).

127 K.W. Nitzsch, *Geschichte der römischen Republik*, I (1884: published posthumously), p. 65.

128 Mommsen, *Strafrecht*, pp. 151ff.

129 R. J. A. Talbert, *The Senate of Imperial Rome* (1984), ch. 16.

130 In *Staatsrecht* III, p. 346 Mommsen refers to further assembly laws of AD 19, 23 and 24.

131 'Quorum extra ordinem ratio habebitur.' Cf. 'Lex de imperio Vespasiani' (*ILS* 244): 'quibusque extra ordinem ratio habeatur'.

132 Tac. *Ann.* I, 15.

133 Dio LIII, 17f.; J. A. Crook, *Cambridge Ancient History* X (2nd ed. 1996) ch. 3; W. Liebeschuetz 'The Settlement of 27 BC' in: C. Deroux (ed.) *Studies in Latin Literature and Roman History* IV (1986), pp. 345–65.

134 In 1868 Mommsen described the Emperor as the 'principal state official' in the 'highest office in the official career structure' (MK, p. 202): Mommsen, *Staatsrecht* II, pp. 749ff.

135 Aur. Vict. 36.1.

136 This is incorrect: Claudius's death, on the morning of 13 October 54, could only be kept secret for a few hours: Tac. *Ann.* XII, 69. Following the death of Claudius Gothicus his brother Quintillus ruled after him. Mommsen may have had in mind the two days prior to the reign of Claudius: *Suet.*, 11.

137 According to Mommsen's theory in *Staatsrecht* (I, pp. 116f.; II, pp. 74ff.), the *imperium* rather implies a magistracy (dictatorship, consulate or praetorship), and indicates its official authority over life and death.

138 Mommsen uses the word 'Schilderhebung' appropriate to the proclamation of Germanic kings.

139 Plut. *Otho* 25 states 'not more than twenty-three soldiers'.

140 Hensel continues, 'There is no gap here!! Oscar Schwartz in remorse!!' He leaves half a page blank. He evidently brought the preceding account up to date using the lecture notes of the above-mentioned fellow student. A comparison with the Wickert notes reveals that there is nothing substantial missing from the Hensel version.

141 Mommsen, *Staatsrecht* II, pp. 755ff.

142 'A princeps is exempted from the laws.' This formula was devised by Ulpian (*Dig.* I, 31.3) for the Emperors of the principate, whose will had the force of law (*Dig.* I, 4.1). Dio (LIII, 18.1) asserts this even for Augustus.

143 *ILS* 244, the 'law concerning the *imperium* of Augustus'. Cf. MK, p. 56: this law points the way 'to absolute monarchy'.

144 Syme, 'Imperator Caesar'. Cf. note 9 p. 507.

145 Dio LV, 9.9; Tac. *Ann.* I, 3; Mommsen, *Staatsrecht* II, pp. 1141f.

146 Dio LIII, 17f.

147 Extending the *pomerium* presupposes expanding the Empire: Tac. *Ann.* XII, 23f.; *ILS* 213, 244.15; Mommsen, 'Der Begriff des Pomerium', *RF* II, pp. 23ff.

148 *ILS* 1998: *censor perpetuus*; Dio LXVII, 4.3.

149 Syme, 'Imperator Caesar' Cf. note 9.

150 Dio LIII, 32.5f.

151 Dio LIII, 32.3ff.

152 Mommsen, *Staatsrecht* II, pp. 869ff.; MK., p. 67: these assert that every monarchy seeks to legitimate itself through divine grace and the will of the people, and that Augustus reconciled the two brilliantly by means of the sacrosanct *tribunicia potestas*. H. Last, 'Über die *tribunicia potestas* des Augustus' (1951), in: Schmitthenner 1969, pp. 241ff.; in English in the *Rendiconti del Istituto Lombarbo* 84 (1953), pp. 93–110.

153 *ILS* 244; the relevant passage is now lost, but seems to have immediately preceded the extant text: *foedusve cum quibus volet facere liceat*: Mommsen, *Staatsrecht* II, pp. 954ff.

154 Mommsen, *Staatsrecht* II, pp. 958ff.

155 *Dig.* XLIX, 1.

156 It is not clear how Mommsen is able to reconcile this with the allegedly constitutional character of the principate (MH.I, 32, 119; MH.II, 355).

157 Dio LIII, 21.7.

158 Foreign policy also fell within the sphere of competence of the *princeps*: 'It is a principle of inordinate importance to an absolute monarchy that the people's representatives have no right of consultation at all in foreign affairs —as it is today, so it was also true for Roman absolutism' (MK, p. 61).

159 L. Wickert, 'Princeps', *RE* XXII (1954), 1998ff.

160 Mommsen, *Staatsrecht* II, p. 846f.

161 Only a plebeian could become *tribunus plebis*. Emperors were patricians by virtue of their office: Dio LIII, 17.10.

162 *Princeps* is the Latin word for 'monarch' (MK, p. 69).

163 Syme, 'Imperator Caesar'.

164 On 16 January 27 BC: Dio LIII, 16.6ff.; Suet. *Aug.* 7.2.

165 Dio LIV, 27.2; Suet. *Aug.* 31.1.

166 Suet. *Aug.* 94.12.

167 Augustus called himself *Imperator Caesar Divi Filius Augustus*: Suet. *Aug.* 7; *ILS* 83ff.

168 Mommsen, *Staatsrecht* II, pp. 821ff.

169 Mommsen, *Strafrecht*, pp. 538ff.

170 Instead of 'tribunate'.

171 A. Alföldi, *Die monarchische Repräsentation im römischen Kaiserreiche* (1970; 1st edn 1934).

172 The best-known coins of this type show Quinctilius Varus as *proconsul Africae*: Mommsen, *Ges. Schr.* IV, pp. 183ff.; *Staatsrecht* II, pp. 261f.; M. Grant, *From Imperium to Auctoritas* (1946), p. 230 and plate VII, pp. 30f.

173 On later organization, see MH.I, 51f.

174 On the Senate under the Emperors see Mommsen, *Staatsrecht* II, pp. 894ff., 937ff.; III, pp. 1252ff.; id. *Abriss*, pp. 270ff.

175 Dio LIV, 13f.; Suet. *Aug.* 37; Mommsen, *Staatsrecht* II, p. 946.

176 The Republican censor had had the right to strike unworthy Senators from the *album senatorium*: Plut. *Cato maior*, 16ff.

177 Dio LIV, 13.4.

178 Mommsen, *Staatsrecht* III, pp. 905ff.

179 Mommsen, *Abriss*, pp. 281ff.

180 Dio LIII, *passim*.

181 Mommsen, *Staatsrecht* II, pp. 997ff.

182 After Nero these were the *praefecti aerarii*: *ILS* 1001.

183 Strabo XVII, 1.12.

184 For example the plundering of Sicily by Verres: Mommsen, *RG* III, pp. 97, 542.

185 Mommsen, *Staatsrecht* II, pp. 1025ff.

186 A. Bay, 'The Letters SC on Augustan *Aes* Coinage', *JRS* 62 (1972), pp. 111ff.

187 Quinctilius Varus as *quaestor Augusti* in 21 BC: cf. *ILS* 8812.

188 According to MK. 71f., Mommsen described 'the spurious seesaw policy' between the hereditary and moneyed elites, i.e. between the senators and equestrians whose dissension had led to the revolution, as the cornerstone of the Roman monarchy.

189 Mommsen, *Abriss*, pp. 204ff.

190 Mommsen is probably thinking here of Musicus Scurranus: *ILS* 1514; see MH.II, 180.

191 Mommsen, *Staatsrecht* II, pp. 82ff.

192 Tac. *Ann.* II, 59.2; Suet. *Tib.* 52.2; Dio LIII, 13.

193 Dio LIII, 15.2ff.; Mommsen, *Staatsrecht* III, pp. 552ff.

194 Suet. *Caes.*, 33; *Tib.*, p. 59; Mommsen, *Staatsrecht* III, pp. 499f. Hensel mistakenly writes '400,000 *denarii*, approx. 100,000 gold marks'.

195 J. B. Campbell, *The Emperor and the Roman Army 31 BC–AD 235* (1984).

196 Mommsen, *Staatsrecht* III, pp. 240ff.

197 Dio LVII, 6.5.

198 Mommsen, *Ges. Schr.* VI, pp. 20ff.

199 For the list, see Tac. *Ann.* IV, 5.

200 Not quite, since both the Flavians and Emperors of the second century established new legions: see MH.II, 56ff.

201 Dio LIII, 25.

202 Tac. *Ann.* IV, 5 given them two legions each.

203 An additional three in Spain, making a total of twenty-five: Tac. *Ann* IV, 5.

204 Dio LIV, 22; Horace *Odes* IV, 4.14.

205 Missing in MH.

206 Mommsen, *Ges. Schr.* VI, pp. 1ff.

207 Mommsen 1866 (AG, p. 2): 'Guards are essential instruments of absolutism.'

208 With the addition of auxiliary troops.

209 Tac. *Ann.* IV, 2; Suet. *Tib.* 37.

210 Mommsen, *Staatsrecht* II, p. 1055.

211 Livy I, 59,12; Tac. *Ann.* VI, 11; Mommsen, *Staatsrecht* II, pp. 1059ff.

212 Hensel writes 'Pyrrhic'.

213 Suet. *Aug.* 49; Tac. *Ann.* IV, 5.

214 H. Bellen, *Die germanische Leibwache der römischen Kaiser des julisch-claudischen Hauses* (1981).

215 Aur. Vict. 33.3; Zos. I, 71.2.

216 According to the *Lex Ursonensis: ILS* 6087,103.

217 Suet. *Aug.* 29.1.

218 *Mon. Anc.* 20.

219 O. Hirschfeld, 'Die römischen Meilensteine', in: id. *Kl. Schr.* (1913), pp. 703ff.; T. Pekary, *Untersuchungen zu den römischen Reichsstrassen* (1968).

220 Dio LIII, 22.1.

221 The main source is Frontinus, *De aquaeductibus urbis Romae*; Mommsen, *Staatsrecht* II, pp. 1044ff.

222 *ILS* 5926.

223 Mommsen, *Staatsrecht* II, pp. 1037ff.

224 Cic. *Att.* IV, 1.7; Dio XXXIX, 9; LIV, 1.3.

225 Dio LIV, 1.

226 Mommsen, *Ges. Schr.* IV, pp. 193ff.

227 From 320,000: Suet. *Caes.* 41.

228 Dio LV, 10; Suet. *Aug.* 40ff.; *Mon. Anc.* 15.

229 Juvenal X, 81.

230 W. Schmitthenner, *Oktavian und das Testament Cäsars* (2nd edn 1973).

231 Suet. *Caes.* 38.

232 *Mon. Anc.* 15; Suet. *Aug.* 41.

233 I.e. senators and equestrians.

234 L. Friedländer, *Darstellungen aus der Sittengeschichte Roms* (10th edn, 1921/3) II, pp. 1ff.

235 Mommsen is in error: chariot races have also been documented elsewhere: Tac. *Ann.* XV, p. 23; Pollack, 'Circus', *RE* III 2 (1899), pp. 2583ff.

236 Ovid *Amor.* III, 2,78; Plin. *NH* VII, 186; *ILS* 5277ff.; Pollack, 'Factiones', *RE* VI 2 (1909), 1954ff; A. Cameron, *Circus Factions* (1976).

237 Tac. *Ann.* XIV, 17.

238 It was considered dishonourable: *ILS* 6085, line 123. During the famine of AD 6 the *lanistarum familiae*, amongst others, were expelled from Rome (Suet. *Aug.* 42.3; Dio LV, 26.1), so they were not illegal in principle.

239 This one-sided assessment by Mommsen contradicts what he himself says about specific authors, such as Petronius, Marcus Aurelius and Ammianus, as well as overlooking the legacy of the imperial age in terms of specialist literature, particularly in the field of jurisprudence.

240 Mommsen's assessment is different in MH.II, 116f.

241 There is no documentary proof that this occurred under Augustus.

242 Dio LIII, 25; L. A. Curchin, *Roman Spain: Conquest and Assimilation* (1991).

243 Juba had antiquarian interests and wrote historical works which are quoted by Plutarch in the *Lives* of Romulus and Numa.

244 (Caes.) *Bell.Afr.* 25.

245 Strabo XVII, 1.54ff.; Dio LIV, 5.4; Pliny NH VI, 181.

246 Strabo XVI, 4.22ff.; Josephus, *Ant. Iud* XV, 9.3; Dio LIII, 29.3ff.

247 Dio LIII, 26.3.

248 Dio LIII, 25.1; LIV, 24.4ff.

249 E. Yarshater (ed.), *Cambridge History of Iran*, vol. 3.2: *The Seleucid, Parthian and Sasanian Periods* (1983).

250 *Mon. Anc.* 29; Vell. II, 91.1; Dio LIV, 8.2.

251 *RIC.*I, p. 63; the inscriptions read: *SIGNIS RECEPTIS* and *SIGNIS PARTHICIS RECEPTIS*. The scene is depicted on the breastplate of Augustus's statue from Primaporta in the Vatican.

252 Dio LV, 9.

253 Dio LV, 10, 17ff.; Vell. II, 101; *Mon. Anc.* 33.

254 Dio LV, 10a; Strabo XI, 14.6.

255 Dio XLIX, 36.

256 Dio XLVIII, 2,3; Strabo IV, 3,4; Tac. *Germ.* 28.

257 O. Doppelfeld, *ANRW* II 4 (1975), pp. 715ff.

258 Dio LI, 23ff.

259 Tibullus I, 7,1ff; II, 1,33f.

260 Lollius's disaster: cf. Dio LIV 20.4ff.; Vell. II, 97. On the general policy of Augustus towards the Germans, see Mommsen, *RA*, pp. 316ff.

261 Suet. *Claud.*, 1.

262 Mommsen is thinking here of the crown prince era of the liberal Friedrich III (Queen Victoria's anglophile son-in-law).

263 Horace *Odes* IV, 4 and 14; Dio LIV, 22; Vell.II, 95.2; Strabo VII, 1,5. Mommsen *RG* V, pp. 15ff.; F. Staehlin, *Die Schweiz in römischer Zeit* (1948), pp. 107ff.

264 Dio LIV, 19–25.

265 Dio LIV, 28.1.

266 Dio LIV, 28.3.

267 Dio LIV, 31.1; Vell.II, 96.2.

268 Dio LIV, 34.4.

269 Dio LIV, 34.3f.; Suet. *Tib.* 9.

270 *ANRW* II 6 (1977), pp. 183ff.

271 Dio LIV, 32.

272 Tac. *Germ.* 29; *Hist.* IV, 12.17.

273 Dio LIV, 32; Vell. II, 97; Florus IV, 12; Tac. *Ann.* IV, 72.1; id. *Germ.* 34.

274 This was not achieved until 9 BC; see MH.I, 85.

275 Dio LIV, 33; Livy. *Per.* 140; Tac. *Ann.* I, 56.1.

276 Vell. II, 120.4. Dio LIV, 33.4 spells it 'Elison'.

277 Vell. II, 108.1; Oros. VI, 21.15.

278 Dio LV, 1.2f. Drusus was allegedly confronted by a superhumanly large woman, who demanded that he retreat.

279 Dio LV, 6.5.

280 Here the second of Paul Hensel's notebooks begins: MH.Ib.

281 Tiberius went to Rhodes in 6 BC: Suet. *Tib.* 10f.; Vell. II, 99.4; Dio LV, 9.

282 *neque . . . vitrico (sc. Augusto) deseri se etiam in senatu conquerenti veniam dedit (sc. Tiberius),* Suet. *Tib.* 10.2.

283 Dio LV, 10a.

284 Dio LV, 13.

285 Vell. II, 108.

286 Dio LV, 28; Vell. II, 109.5.

287 Dio LV, 29; Mommsen, *RG* V, pp. 35ff.

288 Dio LV, 32ff; Vell. II, 112ff.

289 Mommsen, *RG* V, pp. 39ff.; id. *Ges. Schr.* IV, pp. 200ff. C. Wells, *The German Policy of Augustus* (1972), ch. 4, pp. 59ff.

290 Tac. *Ann.* I, 60.

291 Dio LVI, 18.5.

292 A mistake: see MH.I, 90.

293 On the basis of coin finds Mommsen established the location (*RG* V, p. 43; *Ges. Schr.* IV, pp. 200ff.) of the battlefield not in the (modern) forest of Teutoburg, but in the Wiehen mountains north of Osnabrück at Barenaue. Recent finds by W. Schlüter near the Kalkrieser mountain at Bramsche have brilliantly corroborated this thesis. Cf. Wells (n. 289 above) on p. 240.

294 Dio LVI, 19.

295 In *RG* V, p. 41 Mommsen estimates the casualties at slightly above 20,000.

296 Claudia Pulchra, a granddaughter of Octavia, sister of Augustus: Tac. *Ann*. IV, 52.66.

297 Suet. *Aug*. 23.2: *Quintili Vare, legiones redde!*

298 Vell. II, 119.4.

299 Vell. II, 119.5.

300 Dio LVI, 22.

301 According to Velleius (II, 120.3) Asprenas led the two legions down *ad inferiora hiberna*; they were probably stationed somewhere upstream on the Rhine, not at Minden: Groag, *RE* XVII (1936), pp. 868f.

302 Vell. II, 120; Dio LVI, 24.6; 25.2f.

303 Tac. *Ann*. II, 7 states otherwise; see MH.I, 127.

304 Ranke, *Weltgeschichte* III 2 (1886), p. 275.

305 Florus II, 30.29ff.

306 Dio LVI, 18ff.

307 Vell. II, 117ff.

308 Tac. *Ann*. I, 55ff.

309 The exact date of the triumph has not been established; possible dates are 23 October AD 12 and 16 January AD 13: Suet. *Tib*. 20; Vell. II, 121.3; *CIL* I 2nd ed., p. 231 (*Fasti Praenestini*).

310 Tac. *Ann*. IV, 5.

311 Metaphorically the 'dregs' of the people, as in Cic. *Cat*. II, 7; *Fam*. IX, 15.3.

312 Tac. *Ann*. I, 9,11.

313 Suet. *Cal*. I, 1; Tac. *Ann*. I, 31.

314 On the whole issue, see Mommsen, 'Die germanische Politik des Augustus', (1871), in ibid: *RA*, pp. 316ff.

315 In 28 BC Augustus became consul for the sixth time, Agrippa for the second time, and both became censors. In 27 BC they were both consuls again, but not censors.

316 In 23 BC Agrippa obtained the seal ring of the sick Augustus: Dio LIII, 30.2.

317 In 40 BC: App. *Civ*. V, 64.

318 Plut. *Marcellus*, 30; Suet. *Gramm*. 21.

319 Dio LIII, 30.2.

320 Dio LI, 15.7; Plut. *Ant*. 54.

321 H. Willrich, *Livia* (1911).

322 Mommsen is presumably alluding here to Suet. *Ant*., 71: *ad vitiandas virgines promptior, quae sibi undique ab uxore conquirerentur.*

323 Tac. *Ann*. I, 3.4; 5.1; 6.3; Dio LV, 10a. 10.

324 He died in September 23 BC in Baiae of disease: Dio LIII, 30.6; Prop. III, 18. *Perniciosa febris* is malaria.

325 Suet. *Aug*. 100.

326 Dio LVII, 12.3 expresses a different view. In 1868 Mommsen called Livia a 'thoroughly political woman'. (MK, p. 140; compare pp. 99f.)

327 Suet. *Aug*. 69; *Tib*., 4.3.

328 Suet. *Tib*. 50; Tac. *Ann*. I, 14; IV, 57.

329 Suet. *Aug*. 63ff.

330 see MH.I, 100.

331 The star of Caesar: Suet. *Caes*. 88.

332 MH has 'daughter'.

333 MH has 'strike' in English. On this, see Dio LIII, 28ff; Vell. II, 93.2; Jos. *Ant*. XV, 10.2.

334 Dio LIII, 30.5.

335 Suet. *Aug*. 64.1; Dio LIV, 18.1.

336 Tac. *Ann*. I, 3; Sen. *Benef*. III, 32.4.

337 Dio LIV, 28.

338 Suet. *Tib*. 7.2; Dio LV, 9,7; P. Sattler, 'Julia und Tiberius', in Schmitthenner 1969, pp. 486ff. F. Millar and E. Segal (eds), *Augustus Caesar: Seven Aspects* (1984), ch. 6.

339 After the death of a baby son: Suet. *Tib*. VII, 3.

340 Suet. *Tib.* 10f.; Dio LV, 9; Vell. II, 99.4.

341 Tac. *Ann.* I, 53; Dio LV, 10.14.

342 Sen. *Benef.* VI, 32.

343 Ovid *Trist. passim*; Jerome, *Chron.* on AD 17.

344 'Plans for patricide': Plin. *NH.* VII 46/149.

345 Dio LV, 10; Sen. *Brev.* IV, 6; Tac. *Ann.* IV, 44.

346 The freedwoman Phoebe: Suet. *Aug.* 65.2.

347 Aside from his *adulteria* documented in Suet. *Aug.*, 69 and Martial XI, 20.

348 Suet. *Tib.* 12.1.

349 Macrobius II, 5.9.

350 Dio LV, 10. 19.

351 Suet. *Tib.* 12; Tac. *Ann.* III, 48.2. He had suffered a defeat against the Sugambrians in 16 BC.

352 Suet. *Tib.* 15.1; Dio LV, 10a. 10.

353 Gaius died in AD 4, Lucius in AD 2. Within eighteen months: Suet. *Aug.* 65.1; *intra trennium*: Suet. *Tib.* 15.2; Dio LV, 10a. 9.

354 Augustus once called him in a letter *meus asellus iucundissimus*: Gellius XV, 7.

355 Suet. *Tib.* 15.2; Dio LV, 13.1f.

356 'For the sake of the state': Suet. *Tib.* 21.3.

357 Tac. *Ann.* I, 3.4. Agrippa was sent to Planasia near Elba.

358 *ILS* 6354ff.

359 For example Corinth and Berytus (Beirut). See also B. Levick, *Roman Colonies in Southern Asia Minor* (1967).

360 Suet. *Aug.* 49.3; S. Mitchell, 'Requisitioned Transport in the Roman Empire', *JRS* 66 (1976), 106ff.

361 Caes. *Civ.* III, 101,3; *Hisp.* 2.

362 Herodotus VIII, 98; Xenophon, *Cyropaedia* VIII, 6.17.

363 Mommsen, *Strafrecht*, pp. 691ff.; A. Wallace-Hadrill, 'Family and Inheritance in the Augustan Marriage Laws', *Proceedings of the Cambridge Philological Society* 207 (1981), pp. 58–80; S. Treggiari, *Roman Marriage* (1991), pp. 60ff.

364 18 BC. The law commands the *ordines*, i.e. Senators and equestrians, to marry: Suet. *Aug.* 34.

365 In AD 9: Dio LVI, 10.3.

366 Suet. *Aug.* 40.3; Gaius I, 13 (*FIRA* II, p. 11).

367 Suet. *Aug.* 31.1.

368 In 17 BC: *Mon. Anc.* 22; Mommsen, *Ges. Schr.* VIII, pp. 567ff.

369 Suet. *Aug.* 31,5; SHA, *Sev. Al.*, 28.6; P. Zanker, *Forum Augustum* (1969).

370 A correct account is given at MH.I, 233ff.

371 Suet. *Aug.* 86.

372 Mommsen, *Ges. Schr.* VII, pp. 269ff.

373 G. Williams in: K. A. Raaflaub and M. Toher (eds), *Between Republic and Empire* (1990), ch. 12, pp. 258–5.

374 Tac. *Dial.* 18.2.

375 Quintil. X, 1.113.

376 Melissus was a freedman of Maecenas, hence the name: Ovid *Pont.*IV, 16.3; Suet. *Gramm.*, 21. The *trabeata (fabula)* is named after equestrian attire (*trabea*).

377 Verg. *Aen.* I, 254ff.; VI 789ff.; VIII, 626ff.

378 E. Diehl (ed.) *Die Vitae Virgilianae* (1911), pp. 18 (Donatus/Suetonius 38) and 20: *obtrectatores Virgilio numquam defuerunt*.

379 Thus Hensel. Mommsen will have said, or meant, 'Trojans'.

380 Rather, those heroes who had made Rome great: Suet. *Aug.* 31.5. Imitation of the kings is suggested only by his choice of a burial place: App. *Civ.* I, 106.

381 *Amata* was the salutation of the vestal by the Pontifex Maximus (Gell. I, 12) as well as the name of Latinus's wife.

382 Mommsen, *RA*, pp. 168ff.; 351ff.

383 Meaning access to female slaves.

384 'Cleverest': Sen. *NQ* III, 27.13.

385 In 1868 Mommsen said of Ovid 'that the least moral of his works were the best' (MK. p. 116).

386 More precisely 'poetastery': rhyme is a post-antique phenomenon.

387 Actually a tragedy.

388 Suet. *Aug.* 29.3; *Gramm.*, 20; Plut. *Marcellus*, 30.

389 'On making pictures and statues publicly available'. Hensel has *omnibus* for *signisque*. Cf. Pliny *NH* XXXV, 26.

390 Hensel writes, probably mistakenly, *Forum Romanum*. P. Zanker, *Forum Augustum*, (1969?).

391 What follows is located here in the correct place, in Hensel in the wrong place, in notebook Ib, at the top of p. 123. Hensel started taking notes on a wrong page, and, realizing his mistake, put the text as far as 'stunning work' in square brackets.

392 Dio LIII, 27; F.W. Shipley, *Agrippa's Building Activities in Rome* (1933).

393 The building which survives today – notwithstanding the inscription (*ILS* 129) – was erected by Hadrian: SHA, *Hadr.* 19.10.

394 A biography of Tiberius in the spirit of Mommsen was written by his student Ernst Kornemann and published posthumously in 1960 by Hermann Bengtson. According to Bengtson (p. 5), Kornemann had attended Mommsen's lectures on the history of imperial Rome. English biographies of Tiberius: R. Seager (1972); B. Levick (1976).

395 The *vetus et insita Claudiae familiae superbia* is ascribed to the new Emperor by Tacitus (*Ann.*I, 4.3; cf. Livy II, 56; Suet. *Tib.*) Mommsen, *RF* I, pp. 285ff.

396 Suet. *Tib.* 68.

397 Suet. *Tib.* 18.

398 Dio LVII, 1.

399 Suet. *Tib.* 61ff.; Tac. *Ann.* VI, 1.

400 This play on his name, attested by Suetonius (Tib., 42), is an allusion to the prince's predilection for mulled wine.

401 Suet. *Tib.* 26f.; Taeger 1959, pp. 262ff.

402 Tac. *Ann.* VI, 21f.; Suet. *Tib.* 14.4; 62.3; Dio LVII, 15.7ff.

403 On the following, see Suet. *Tib.* 70f.

404 Poet at the court of Antiochus III. Only fragments have survived. In addition to Euphorion, Suetonius also mentions Rhianus and Parthenius.

405 Suet. *Tib.* 21.

406 On 19 August 14; Tac. *Ann.* I, 5; Suet. *Aug.* 97ff.; *Tib.*, 22.

407 'What a monster ruling is': Suet. *Tib.* 24.

408 Tac. *Ann.* I, 12; Dio LVII, 2. Cf. W. Liebeschuetz, 'The Settlement of 27 BC', in Deroux, *Studies in Latin Literature and Roman History*, pp. 345–65.

409 A similar description is offered by Mommsen in MK, pp. 147f. and in the lecture notes taken by Ludwig Schemann in 1872/3, published by Wickert IV 1980, pp. 344ff.:

> In the case of Tiberius we must be extremely circumspect in our evaluation. He was one of the most important men ever to head a state. The portrayal of his character has changed through history, distorted by hatred and partisan feeling. The sullen grimace he displayed in his lattermost period has sometimes become an overall appraisal.
>
> Tiberius was sturdy and robust, a thoroughly military figure. His education was unusually profound for his time (nor was it impervious to literature: he had a particular penchant for Alexandrian erotic poetry). He was not unfeeling, as is especially clear from his first marriage. Tragically, all those circumstances of his that were based on warm relationships went awry, and it is to this that Tiberius's bitterness of heart must be traced.
>
> 'Break with his mother Livia'. In the end, Tiberius was left without a single unblemished human relationship. . . . All his love, now perverted into hatred, invaded the very roots of Tiberius's nature to create that shadow image which we now have of him (even

in Tacitus). Fate drastically reshaped Tiberius, but hardened, rather than softened him. Tiberius was one of those people who never had a childhood to open up their hearts in a joyful, unconstrained way. His environment, saturated with disdain and derision, filled him with a contempt for mankind, which he nevertheless combined with a rigorous sense of duty (not *oderint, dum metuant* (Let them hate me, so long as they fear me), but *oderint, dum probent* (Let them hate me, so long as they approve). His affected indifference to the public was a grave political error: no one goes unpunished for disdaining the affection of his people.

In keeping with the times, Tiberius was of course without religious faith as such, a thoroughly rational man. And yet he was completely ruled by a fatalism that frequently directed his political actions. Tiberius had a tendency towards the abstruse: in Rhodes especially, unusual proclivities gained the upper hand in his nature. Similarly, the refinement of his excesses, blended with a disagreeable erudition, emerged chiefly after his sojourn on Rhodes. In his lattermost period this was augmented by the moroseness which made Tiberius into such a spectre of horror.

As a statesman, he was arguably among Rome's greatest. . . .

If we want to assess the fiscal achievements of Tiberius, we need only think of Augustus's incessant shortages of money.

Tiberius had an earnest desire to rule in accordance with the constitution . . . he scorned anything that did not indicate the Roman state to be a free state governed by a head of state chosen for life.

The reform of elections was of crucial importance – an extension of the Augustan constitution. Tiberius deprived the assemblies of election privileges and granted them to the Senate. The Augustan state had already made the transition from democratic to aristocratic state, elections by the Assemblies were but the final echo of former democracy. From now on, this *populus Romanus* was a mere governmental title, not a governmental entity. Senatorial elections represent a progression from preliminary to direct elections. The resolutions of the Senate are at the same time those of the *populus Romanus*.

Notwithstanding his great achievements for the state, the consequences of Tiberius's propitious rule were completely dwarfed by his dissolute, joyless and loveless disposition. The relationship between the people and their ruler was a tarnished one; in this, too, Tiberius was a tragic figure. . . .

Germanicus, on the other hand, was decidedly Republican-minded, the leader of the liberals. His position *vis-à-vis* Tiberius was, of course, a thoroughly disagreeable one, because it was one of opposition: Germanicus, the crown prince, the most popular, Tiberius, Emperor, the most unpopular man in the state. Bearing in mind the awkwardness of this situation, we are bound to acknowledge Germanicus's loyalty, on the one hand, and Tiberius's conduct on the other; despite the mortifying events on the Rhine, he continued for years to leave him in command.

Tiberius drew monarchy to its logical conclusion in every respect: where Augustus had often remained mild and circumspect, Tiberius displayed the necessary ruthlessness. His was one of those unfortunate natures that can abide neither servility nor candour. Tiberius lacked the talent for grasping that some things are minor and insignificant. He took everything uncompromisingly and seriously on a grand scale.

Tiberius saw to it that all the nobility invested at least two-thirds of their fortunes in Italian real estate. The capital had to be called in; in order to avert a crisis, Tiberius assisted out of state funds. This idea was one of his most brilliant. The aristocracy should not be composed of bankers, since this would set the seal on social decay. The lax governments that followed failed to pursue this idea any further.

Inquiring, finally, after the arts and sciences, we are nevertheless faced with a joyless, dreary epoch. Velleius and Valerius Maximus, otherwise disparate in every respect, concur solely in their slavish adulation. Otherwise, only the elder Seneca is worthy of note. The intellectual pressure of the times made itself felt throughout the literary sphere. Admittedly, Tiberius did not instigate literary censorship, but it did first become significantly widespread under his rule. Good, straightforward Latin was on the decline, incidentally: instead of using words, writers misused them (one need only compare the speeches of Livy with the rhetorical exercises of Seneca). The Emperor's own clumsy style may have exerted an effect on the entire epoch.

Overestimation of Tiberius is now as prevalent as previous condemnation of him. For all his more enlightened aspects, we cannot permit ourselves to hide his shadowy aspects. In general, that which is asserted about Prussia is equally true of the Roman monarchy: its three first rulers (Gaius Julius Caesar, Augustus, Tiberius) laid its firm foundations, albeit on nothing less than entirely natural principles.

Parallels drawn between Tiberius and Frederick the Great are in many respects pertinent. Excellent general, still better administrator. Domestic and similar misfortune, bitter experiences, lapse into melancholy – only surmounted by their indefatigable sense of duty. On the other hand, the toying with arts and sciences of the dilettante. The moroseness of the final years, but endurance to the very end in affairs of state.

It is with regret that we depart from this earlier epoch to turn to another, about which one knows not whether it is more childish or evil, and is unable to understand how the very pillars of the state failed to collapse under its strain.

410 Suet. *Tib.* 26f.; Dio LVII, 8; Tac. *Ann.* IV, 37f.; Kornemann, pp. 108f.

411 *ILS* III, 262.

412 Hensel notes in the margin: 'Pliny VII, pp. 149/50 *Hist.Nat.* misconstrued by Schiller'. Plin. *NH* VII, 46/149 gives an account of the misfortunes in the life of Augustus. Hermann Schiller dedicated his *Geschichte des römischen Kaiserreichs unter der Regierung des Nero* (1872) to Mommsen.

413 Tac. *Ann.* I, 6; Suet. *Tib.* 22, 25.1; Dio LVII, 3.5f.

414 Tac. *Ann.* II, 39f.; Dio LVII, 16.3f.

415 Tac. *Ann.* I, 16ff.; Dio LVII, 4ff.; Vell.II, 125.

416 In the Republican legion the *triarii* (in the third line) were the most tried and tested fighters.

417 Here follows the section on Augustan building policy moved to MH.I, 144, enclosed in square brackets by Hensel.

418 Tac. *Ann.* I, 31ff.

419 Tac. *Ann.* I, 50ff.; Mommsen, *RG* V, pp. 46ff.

420 Tac. *Ann.* I, 55ff.

421 Including auxiliary troops.

422 Tac. *Ann.* II, 7.

423 The Saalburg was not built until later, in AD 83: L. Jacobi, *Das Römerkastell Saalburg* (1897); D. Baatz and F. R. Herrmann, *Die Römer in Hessen* (1982), pp. 469ff. Generally see H. Schönberger, 'The Roman Frontier in Germany: An Archaeological Survey', *JRS* 59 (1969), 144ff.

424 Strabo VII, 1,4; Tac. *Ann.* I, 57.

425 Mommsen later again idiosyncratically describes the Germans under Arminius as 'Saxons' (MH.I, 128).

426 Tac. *Ann.* I, 60ff. Germanicus visited the battlefield in the Teutoburg Forest.

427 Paternal uncle of Arminius.

428 Tac. *Ann.* I, 69.

429 Tac. *Ann.* II, 5ff.

430 Tac. *Ann.* II, 9.

431 Tac. *Ann.* II, 16.

432 On the Angrivarian dyke: Tac. *Ann.* II, 19ff.

433 The *titulus*, according to Tac. *Ann.* II, 22, reads: *Debellatis inter Rhenum Albimque nationibus exercitus Tiberii Caesaris monimenta Marti et Iovi et Augusto sacravit* ('Having conquered the peoples

between Rhine and Elbe, the army of Tiberius Caesar dedicated monuments to Mars, Jupiter and Augustus').

434 Tac. *Ann.* II, 23ff.
435 MH.I, 132: 'severe beating'; Elder Seneca *Suas.* I, 14 reports the lament of a shipwrecked man, probably from this campaign.
436 Tac. *Ann.* II, 26.
437 MH.I, 130f. are blank.
438 Celebrated on 26 May, AD 17: Tac. *Ann.* II, 41.
439 Tac. *Ann.* II, 26.3.
440 Tac. *Ann.* II, 44.4.
441 Tac. *Ann.* II, 44ff.
442 Tac. *Ann.* II, 62f.
443 Tac. *Ann.* II, 88.
444 Tacitus, *ibid.*, calls him *liberator haud dubie Germaniae.* 'undoubtedly the liberator of Germany'.
445 'The barbaric peoples sing his praises to this day'.
446 'Shortage of pay and recruits' on the part of Rome.
447 Tac. *Ann.* II, 41ff., 53ff.
448 Tac. *Ann.* II, 3f.
449 This was the war against Tacfarinas, as described by Tacitus in the first books of the *Annals.* Mommsen, *RG* V, pp. 633ff.; A. Gutsfeld, *Römische Herrschaft und einheimischer Widerstand in Nordafrika* (1989).
450 Mommsen, *RG* V., pp. 375ff.
451 Tac. *Ann.* II, 3f.; Dio LV, 10a.4ff.; Strabo XI, 13.1; *Mon. Anc.* 27.
452 Tac. *Ann.* II, 56.
453 Dio LVII, 17; Tac. *Ann.* II, 42, 56.
454 Tac. *Ann.* II, 43, 55ff.
455 Tac. *Ann.* II, 59ff.; Jos. *Contra App.* II, 5/63.
456 *RIC* I, p. 104, no. 8f.
457 Tac. *Ann.* II, 69ff.
458 Tac. *Ann.* III, 12ff.
459 Tac. *Ann.* II, 69ff.; Suet. *Cal.*, 3.3.
460 *Inferiae Germanico* are recorded for 10 October in the *Fasti Antiates: CIL* I, 1, 2nd ed., p. 249.
461 Tac. *Ann.* II, 80.
462 Book containing his military orders: Tac. *Ann.* III, 7ff.
463 'Implicated in the trial'.
464 Tac. *Ann.* III, 10ff.
465 Tac. *Ann.* III, 15.
466 Tac. *Ann.* IV, 1: (Tiberius) *Germanici mortem inter prospera ducebat.*
467 Tac. *Ann.* VI, 31ff.; Dio LVIII, 26.
468 Tac. *Ann.* IV, 6; Dio LVII, 7ff.
469 Tac. *Ann.* I, 15.
470 In 1868 Mommsen made an exception, describing the participation of the Senate in the election of magistrates as [MK, p. 122]:

> an extension of that influence of representation which tempers monarchy, entails a furthering of constitutionalism, so that in general we are bound to designate Tiberius the most constitutional ruler of Rome.

471 *Romae ruere in servitium consules, patres, eques:* Tac. *Ann.* I, 7.
472 Tac. *Ann.* III, 11.
473 Tac. *Ann.* III, 56.
474 Tac. *Ann.* II, 85. MK, p. 134 asserts that Tiberius freed Rome and Italy from 'clerical scum' (*Pfaffengeschmeiss*).
475 Suet. *Tib.* 32; Dio LVII, 10; Tac. *Ann.* IV, 15; Pliny *NH* XIX, 110.

476 Tac. *Ann.* III, 38, 66ff.; IV, 3,36.

477 Likewise Macedonia; Tac. *Ann.* I, 76.

478 Tac. *Ann.* I, 80; F. B. Marsh, *The Reign of Tiberius* (1931), p. 159.

479 Tac. *Ann.* IV, 2; Suet. *Aug.* 49; Dio LVII, 19.

480 Tac. *Ann.* II, 47; IV, 13.

481 Tac. *Ann.* VI, 16f.; Suet. *Tib.* 48.1; Dio LVIII, 21.4f.

482 MH.I, 147 is left blank.

483 Mommsen, *Strafrecht*, pp. 537ff.

484 *Ibid.*, pp. 504ff.

485 'Injuring the greatness of the Roman people'.

486 Anyone who had cause to fear the death penalty could evade it by voluntary exile.

487 Tac. *Ann.* I, 72; IV, 21.

488 Lat. *delatores*, often translated as 'informers'.

489 Tac. *Ann.* II, 27ff.

490 In 1868 Mommsen deplores the 'servile crawling' of the Senate to Tiberius, adding: 'We see here, too, as always, that not only the tyrant is guilty of tyranny, but also those who tolerate it.' (MK)

491 'The laws must be enforced', Suet. *Tib.* 58.

492 Tac. *Ann.* IV, 1.

493 Tac. *Ann.* I, 24.

494 Maecenas and Sallustius Crispus, great nephew and adoptive son of the historian, both had great but extra-constitutional power as Augustus's advisers. Sallustius ordered the murder of Agrippa Postumus: see MH.I, 121.

495 Tac. *Ann.* III, 29.

496 Tac. *Ann.* IV, 59. The incident occurred in Sperlonga (*Sperlunca*); Suet. *Tib.* 39. A. F. Stewart, 'Sperlonga, Laokoon, and Tiberius at the Dinner Table', *JRS* 67 (1977), pp. 76ff.

497 In 1868 (MK, p. 137) Mommsen's assessment of Sejanus was much more negative: 'Here there emerged in the history of Rome a man to whom all that was unwholesome in the imperial Roman period can be attributed. He was the ruin of the Julio-Claudian house.'

498 Tac. *Ann.* IV, 3ff.

499 Here the second notebook of Paul Hensel ends and the third begins (MH.Ic), dated 22 January 1883.

500 Mommsen refers to Livilla (as she is called in Suetonius, as well as in MK) by her official name 'Livia', which, however, leads to confusion with the mother of Tiberius.

501 Dio LVIII, 3, 8ff.; Tac. *Ann.* IV, 7ff.

502 Tac. *Ann.* IV, 8.

503 Livia obtained this name through the will of Augustus: Tac. *Ann.* I, 8; Mommsen, *Staatsrecht* II, pp. 764, 794f.

504 Suet. *Tib.* 50f.

505 Suet. *Tib.* 53.

506 In 1868 Mommsen stressed that Tiberius was only unpopular 'with the mob of the capital', who were nevertheless 'authoritative in a much more far-reaching manner than is the case today in France' (MK, p. 133).

507 Suet. *Tib.* 59, 66.

508 Dio LVIII, 1; Suet. *Tib.* 39; Tac. *Ann.* IV, 57ff.

509 Suet. *Tib.* 53.

510 Dio LVIII, 2. Hensel: 'eighty-two years'.

511 Suet. *Tib.* 65.

512 Suet. *Tib.* 65; Tac. *Ann.* VI, 8; Dio LVIII, 4.3.

513 Dio LVIII, 3.9.

514 Suet. *Tib.* 65; Tac. *Ann.* V, 8; VI, 47; Jos. *Ant.* XVIII, 6/181ff.

515 Suet. *Tib.* 65.

516 'the disgraceful election meeting on the Aventine', *ILS* 6044; Mommsen, *Staatsrecht* III, p. 348.

517 Jos. *Ant.* XVIII, 6/181ff.
518 This was the successor to Tiberius, known by his nickname Caligula: Dio LVIII, 8.
519 Dio LVIII, 9.
520 Tac. *Ann.* IV, 3; Dio LVIII, 9ff.
521 Suet. *Tib.* 54; Tac. *Ann.* VI, 23; Dio LVIII, 22.4.
522 Tac. *Ann.* VI, 44f.
523 Tac. *Ann.* VI, 50. In 1868 Mommsen had believed in a violent death: MK, p. 145.
524 Suet. *Tib.* 7.
525 In 1868 Mommsen expanded on this comparison: MK, pp. 147f.
526 Suet. *Cal.* 53,2. The quotation refers to the style of the younger Seneca, the philosopher.
527 A.A. Barrett, *Caligula: The Corruption of Power* (1990).
528 *Bis . . . Romam redire conatus*: Suet. *Tib.* 72.1.
529 Tac. *Ann.* VI, 50; Suet. *Tib.* 74.
530 Dio LVIII, 9.2.
531 Dio LIX, 1 asserts otherwise.
532 'He was in doubt as to whom to pass his rule on to'; Tac. *Ann.* VI, 46.
533 Suet. *Tib.* 73.
534 Suet. *Tib.* 73.1; Dio LIX, 1.
535 Suet. *Cal.* 15. The urns of Drusus and Agrippina were placed in Augustus's mausoleum: Dio LIX, 7.1.
536 Suet. *Cal.* 24; Dio LIX, 11.
537 Dio LIX, 9; 20.4.
538 A half per cent auction tax (Suet. *Cal.* 16).
539 Dio LIX, 8.2; 12.2; 24.1; LX, 8.
540 Suet. *Cal.* 16.
541 Suet. *Cal.* 12.2; 26.1; Dio LIX, 10.6.
542 Suet. *Cal.* 23.1.
543 Suet. *Cal.* 35.1. The Torquati were so named after a torque which Manlius Torquatus had taken from a defeated Gallic warrior in 361 BC.
544 Suet. *Cal.* 34.
545 Suet. *Cal.* 19.
546 Dio LIX, 8.1. Tiberius is reputed to have wanted the death of Caligula.
547 Suet. *Cal.* 26; Dio LIX, 10.
548 Suet. *Cal.* 24; Dio LIX, 22.
549 Suet. *Cal.* 40.
550 Dio LIX, 16.8ff.
551 Suet. *Cal.* 39; Dio LIX, 21ff.
552 Under Tiberius, Germanicus had made Cappadocia a province in AD 18: Suet. *Cal.* 1,2. A key client kingdom was Commagene, under Gaius Julius Antiochus IV Philocaesar: Dio LIX, 8.2.
553 Dio LIX, 25.1.
554 Dio LIX, 20.7; Tac. *Hist.* IV, 48; Mommsen, *RG* V, 626f.
555 Suet. *Cal.* 9; *caliga* is a soldier's boot.
556 Dio LIX, 25.2f. The shells served as booty for the triumph over the ocean.
557 Dio LIX, 29; Suet. *Cal.* 56ff.; Jos. *Ant.* XIX, 1.
558 At this point Hensel gives the date: 29 January 1883.
559 According to Dio LIX, 30 and Jos. *Ant.* XIX, 1,20, Valerius Asiaticus made this statement in the Forum.
560 Suet. *Cal.* 58.
561 Dio LX, 1.
562 Suet. *Claud.* 10; Jos. *Ant.* XIX, 2,1; Dio *ibid.*; B. Levick, *Claudius* (1990). For Josephus's account, see T. P. Wiseman, *Death of an Emperor* (1991).
563 According to Suet. *Claud.* 2 he was initially called Tiberius Claudius Drusus. From 9 BC he was

known as Tiberius Claudius Germanicus (Dio LV, 2,3), from AD 4 as Tiberius Claudius Nero, asserts Groag (*RE* III, (1899), p. 2782), contradicting Mommsen, *Staatsrecht* III, p. 213.

564 In AD 37: Suet. *Claud.* 7.

565 *CIL* I, 1,2, 2nd ed., 308; Suet. *Cal.* 59; Jos. *Ant.* XIX, 4.

566 Suet. *Claud.* 10.3.

567 Jos. *Ant.* XIX, 4.

568 Suet. *Claud.* 13.2; 35.2.

569 Annius Vinicianus: Dio LX, 15.1.

570 Suet. *Claud.* 11,1; Dio LX, 3.4.

571 This should surely read 'Gaius'.

572 *ILS* III, 265.

573 Suet. *Claud.* 30.

574 Suet. *Claud.* 3.

575 Suet. *Claud.* 5.

576 Suet. *Claud.* 41f.

577 *FIRA* I, p. 43; Tac. *Ann.* XI, 23f.

578 *FIRA* I, p. 71; *ILS* 206; Mommsen, *Ges. Schr.* IV, 291ff.

579 Suet. *Claud.* 41; the new letters are documented in inscriptions: *ILS* III, 839. The third letter designated the vowel 'y'.

580 Suet. *Claud.* 28; Dio LX, 14ff.

581 This amounted to 400 million sesterces according to Dio LXI, 34.4.

582 Dio LXI, 34.5.

583 Twenty-seven times: *ILS* 218, 1986, 5504.

584 Tac. *Ann.* XI 8ff.; XII, 44ff.; Mommsen *RG* V, pp. 379f.

585 Dio LX, 8.7, 30.4ff.; Suet. *Claud.* 24.3.

586 Dio LX, 8f.

587 Hensel gives the date: 1 February 1883.

588 Mommsen *RG* V, pp. 158ff.; P. Salway, *Roman Britain* (1981), pp. 65ff.

589 Dio LX, 19ff.; Tac. *Agr.* 13,5f.; Suet. *Claud.* 17; *ILS* 216.

590 Mommsen prefers the less well-documented form of *Camalodunum*: Hübner, *RE* III (1899), pp. 1448f. Colchester is actually 60 miles north-east of London.

591 Ptol. II, 3,11.

592 *CIL* VII, 1201f.

593 Tac. *Ann.* XII, 31ff.

594 Suet. *Claud.* 17.2.

595 Sees *in partibus infidelium* are bishoprics in territories which no longer have any Christians, but are still nominally claimed by the Catholic Church – analogously to the 'province' of Britannia, which was only nominally Roman.

596 Pliny *NH* XXX, 4/13 states otherwise.

597 Suet. *Claud.* 25.5; Strabo IV, 4.4f.

598 Strabo IV, 5.2.

599 The second, ninth and twentieth: Salway, *Roman Britain*, pp. 94ff.

600 MH.I, 174 asserts otherwise.

601 Mommsen, *Staatsrecht* III, pp. 346, 1238.

602 Groag, *RE* III (1899), pp. 2827f.

603 Mommsen, *Staatsrecht* II, pp. 103f.

604 Suet. *Claud.* p. 25.2.

605 *FIRA* I, pp. 288ff.

606 Suet. *Claud.* 24.2; Tac. *Ann.* XIII, 29.

607 Suet. *Claud.* 16.1; *Vitellius*, 2.4. This was the father of the Emperor of the same name.

608 Suet. *Claud.* 25.3.

609 Tac. *Ann.* XI, 23ff.; *FIRA* I, p. 43.

610 Tac. *Ann.* XI, 25; *ILS* 946; Suet. *Otho*, 1.

NOTES

611 Aulus Gell. XIII, 14.7; Tac. *Ann.* XII, 23f. What is meant here is the sacred city boundary, the *pomerium*.
612 Tac. *Ann.* XI, 15.
613 The Isis Temple in the Field of Mars was erected some time before 68: Dio LXV, 24; Suet. *Dom.* 1,2.
614 Suet. *Claud.* 25.5; see MH.I, 176.
615 Suet. *Claud.* 14.
616 Sen. *Apoc.*, 7; Pliny *Ep.* VII, 21: court recess.
617 Suet. *Claud.* 20; Groag, *RE* III (1899), 2830ff.
618 Front. *Aqu.* 13.
619 Suet. *Claud.* 20.3; Proc. *Bell. Goth.* I, 26.7ff. This was the port of Portus Augusti to the north of Ostia.
620 Suet. *Claud.* 20.
621 Messalina as Augusta: Dio LX, 12.5. Agrippina received the title in AD 50: Tac. *Ann.* XII, 26.
622 Suet. *Claud.* 29.1.
623 Dio LX, 8.5.
624 Dio LX, 22.4f.
625 Tac. *Ann.* XI, 1ff.
626 Dio LX, 14.4; Suet. *Claud.* 29.1; 37.2.
627 Dio LX, 30.6; Suet. *Claud.* 28.
628 Suet. *Claud.* 26.2; Dio LX, 31.4f.
629 There were exceptions, such as Anicetus, who rose from freedman to prefect of the fleet: Tac. *Ann.* XIV, 3. For earlier instances see Livy, *Per.* 74; App. *Civ.* I, 49.
630 Tac. *Ann.* XII, 5–7; Suet. *Claud.* 39.
631 The text reads: 'Sejanus'.
632 *RIC* I Claudius, p. 127, no. 54. Coins showing the head of Livia under Tiberius, in contrast, do so only by way of representing *Salus* or *Iustitia*.
633 Dio LX, 33.5.
634 Tac. *Ann.* XII, 25; *ILS* 229.
635 Claudius had Agrippina adopted into another family: Dio LX, 33.
636 Tac. *Ann.* XII, 41; XIII, 21.
637 Tac. *Ann.* XII, 42.
638 Tac. *Ann.* XII, 8.
639 Suet. *Claud.* 44; Dio LX, 34; Tac. *Ann.* XII, 66ff. Tacitus bases his account on contemporaries of the events: *illorum temporum scriptores*.
640 Biographies of Nero include M. T. Griffin, *Nero: The End of a Dynasty* (1984) and B. H. Warmington, *Nero* (1969).
641 *ILS* 225; 227f.
642 Tac. *Ann.* XIII, 1.
643 Tac. *Ann.* XIII, 2f.
644 Aur. Vict. 5.2; Tac. *Ann.* XIII, 2.
645 Tac. *Ann.* XII, 42; XIII, 2; 6; Isidore *Etym.* I, 27,4: *pro Burro dicimus Pyrrhum*.
646 Suet. *Nero*, 28; Dio LXI, 7.
647 Pallas lost the *arbitrium regni* (power over the kingdom) in 55 (Tac. *Ann.* XIII, 14) and died in 62 (Tac. *Ann.* XIV, 65).
648 Tac. *Ann.* XIII, 19ff. reports this following the murder of Britannicus.
649 Dio LXI, 7,4; Tac. *Ann.* XIII, 14ff.
650 Hensel writes 'Cassius'.
651 Tac. *Ann.* XIII, 8; Mommsen, *RG* V, pp. 382ff.
652 Tac. *Ann.* XIII, 35.
653 Tac. *Ann.* XIII, 37ff.
654 Plin.NH.II, 72/180; Tac. *Ann.* XIV, 12. The eclipse occurred on 30 April 59: Boll, 'Finsternisse', *RE* VI (1909), p. 2360.

655 Tac. *Ann*. XIV, 23f.

656 Tac. *Ann*. XV, 6.

657 Dio LXII, 21.

658 Tac. *Ann*. XV, 10.

659 Suet. *Nero*, 13; Dio LXIII, 1; Tac. *Ann*. XVI, 23f.

660 Corbulo was in fact a brother-in-law of Caligula: Pliny *NH* VII, 4/39. Mommsen corrected this error in *RG* V, p. 382.

661 The last was Amm. XV, 2.5; XXIX, 5.4.

662 Dio LXIII, 17.6.

663 Tac. *Ann*. 29f.; Mommsen, *RG* V, pp. 162ff.

664 A reference to the 'Ephesian Vespers' in 88 BC, when Mithridates VI had tens of thousands of Romans and Italians killed in Asia Minor: App. *Mithr*. 22f.; Plut. *Sulla*, 24; Tac. *Ann*. IV, 14.

665 Suet. *Nero*, 18; 40.2.

666 Tac. *Agr*. 16.

667 Griffin, *Nero*, pp. 197ff.

668 *RIC* I (1984), 137ff.

669 Dio LXIII, 11.1.

670 Suet. *Nero*, 26.

671 Suet. *Nero*, 37.3; *negavit quemquam principum scisse quid sibi liceret*.

672 Mommsen gives a similar description in the lectures of 1872/3, in the notes taken by Ludwig Schemann published by Wickert IV, pp. 347f.:

> Nero was a thoroughly ineffectual person, with a head as small as his heart was cold. In a certain sense this was good for the state: unlike Claudius, Nero took no part in political affairs. This is even more glaringly apparent in the military sphere. Never, either before or after Nero, were such major wars waged in the entire imperial age. Nero himself, however, showed no inclination whatever to share, even formally, in the laurels. This, however, was related to his utter cowardliness. His fondness for gutter scandal displays a blend of knavery and childish malice. His vanity regarding his artistic attributes (*qualis artifex pereo!*) is fatuous; he was not even remotely vain about his position as Roman Emperor, master of a world that was magnificent in its very deformity. His being lacked the stature for such a feeling.
>
> 'The Parthian War of Nero': Nero completely outside the real running of affairs. This passivity is the sole positive trait that can be ascribed to Nero. A low and base nature, a malicious adolescent, a contemptible creature. Of the long line of Roman Emperors only Gaius, at a stretch, could be compared with him, but even here the latter's madness defies parallels. Nero lacked even the brilliance that one otherwise finds in extremely depraved individuals. Inclined to baseness in all his proclivities, Nero possessed not so much as a drop of military blood. He studied philosophy and rhetoric for a time, but practised verse-writing more. He wrote a good deal of love poetry. (A third-rate lyric poet – this was his sole strong point!)
>
> The epoch we have just been examining was one of unremitting intellectual dreariness and indifference. The Augustan epoch had been rich in notable statesmen and generals. In Nero's epoch, too, there are a handful of able men, such as Corbulo and Burrus, but what a gulf separates these men from those of Augustus – Maecenas and Agrippa!

673 Suet. *Nero*, 19.2.

674 Tac. *Ann*. XIV, 1–13.

675 Tac. *Ann*. XIV, 59f.

676 Tac. *Ann*. XIV, 4f.

677 Tac. *Ann*. XIV, 8.

678 Tac. *Ann*. XIV, 51.

679 Ventotene to the west of Ischia; Tac. *Ann*. XIV, 60.

680 Tac. *Ann*. XIV, 60.

681 Tac. *Ann.* XV, 23.

682 Tac. *Ann.* XV, 61 asserts otherwise.

683 Tac. *Ann.* XIV, 48.

684 Tac. *Ann.* XV, 38ff; *ILS* 4914.

685 Pliny *NH* XVII, 1/5.

686 For the *Domus Aurea*: Suet. *Nero*, 31.1.

687 Tac. *Ann.* XV, 44.

688 Flavius Josephus reports no persecution of Jews in Rome under Nero.

689 MK, pp. 184f. has more on this:

> Christianity was a radical element in the development of the Roman state during this period. Its genesis and development away from Judaism did not affect Rome, but it did make its presence felt through the Apostle Paul. His Epistle to the Romans dates from AD 50; under the Emperor Nero this brilliant man entered the decayed Roman world and awakened a new spirit, a higher feeling, in that age consumed by its own baseness. Christianity sounded the death knell of the ancient world. However, not only was the Roman state overwhelmed by Christianity, but equally the decayed Roman state found a lone point of reference in this new revival of the human spirit. The concurrence of a process of growth with a process of destruction always poses immense problems for narratives. In this case they are compounded by the fact that the treatment of each aspect falls within a different discipline: historical research and theology. It is possible to give an approximate account of the beginnings of Christianity. The consciousness in individual minds of the futility of the prevailing state of affairs took control, but so, too, did a fantastic premonition of a future life after the imminent Last Judgement, which would bring reward and retribution. We find this latter trend in the *Apocalypse* of John. However, the idea of divine justice and omnipotence developed in a more definite way; this seed was brought by Paul to Rome, where many must have been captivated by a doctrine that confronted the dominant, shameful, but already dying trend. Christianity transcended the frontiers of nations, as it was said, but all the violence was done by the Roman state.

Further, from L. Schemann's notes of Mommsen's 1872/3 lectures:

> In the Neronian epoch Christianity came to the West – that Christianity which taught the human self-sacrifice and poverty of spirit. The *Apocalypse* of John was written at this time – those bleak visions of another world. Christianity began to gain ground for the first time, and had to be persecuted by the state.
>
> (Wickert IV 1980, p. 348)

690 Great-great-grandson (by adoption through Tiberius's son Drusus; he was also a lineal descendant of Augustus's sister Scribonia).

691 Tac. *Ann.* XIV, 22.

692 Tac. *Ann.* XIII, 47.

693 Dio LXII, 14.1; Tac. *Ann.* XIV, 57ff.

694 Tac. *Ann.* XV, 48ff.

695 Tac. *Ann.* XVI, 21ff.

696 Dio LXIII, 17.6.

697 Livy I, 49ff.

698 Hensel has 'national property' (*Nationaleigentum*). On Lugdunum: Mommsen, *RG* V, pp. 74ff.

699 Tac. *Ann.* III, 44. J. Deininger, *Die Provinziallandtage der römischen Kaiserzeit* (1965), pp. 99ff.

700 There is still documentary evidence of the Gallic language in the fifth century: Demandt 1989, p. 308.

701 Tac. *Ann.* III, 40–7.

702 *Resumendae libertati tempus*, 'Time to take up freedom again'; Tac. *Ann.* III, 40.

703 On the following see Dio LXIII, 22ff.; Plut. *Galba*, 4ff.; Suet. *Nero*, 40ff.; *Galba*, 2. Mommsen, *Ges. Schr.* IV, pp. 333ff. (= *RG* IV, pp. 9ff.).

704 They were Gauls by origin, as Mommsen himself suggests at MH.II, 167.

705 Tac. *Hist.* IV, 13.

706 Suet. *Nero*, 40ff.; Dio LXIII, 27ff.

707 Suet. *Nero*, 49.1. His last words were: *qualis artifex pereo*.

707 Suet. *Galba* 11; Dio LXIV, 1ff.; Plut. *Galba*, 7ff.

708 Suet. *Galba* 14.

709 Plut. *Galba*, 10; Suet. *Vit.*, 7.1; Tac. *Hist.* I, 9; Dio LXIV, 3.

710 Suet. *Galba* 15.2.

711 Ibid., 15,1.

712 Ibid., 16.

713 Plut. *Galba*, 22; Dio LXIII, 4; Suet. *Galba,* 16.

714 Tac. *Hist.* I, 12.

715 Plut. *Galba*, 22; Dio LXIII, 4; Suet. *Vit.* 8. In 1868 Mommsen called him an 'Emperor of the battlefield and camp' (MK, p. 188).

716 Tac. *Hist.* II, 87 numbers the Rhine army at 60,000 men.

717 Tac. *Hist.* I, 56f.

718 Tac. *Hist.* I, 12ff.; Plut. *Galba*, 23.

719 I.e. the Roman troops on the Rhine.

720 Nero had stolen Poppaea from Otho and had him removed to Spain: Tac. *Ann.* XIII, 45f.; Suet. *Otho*, 3.

721 Suet. *Galba* 17ff.; Dio LXIII, 6ff.; Plut. *Galba*, 26ff.; Tac. *Hist.* I, 23ff.

722 Galba had him killed: see MH.I, 207.

723 Tac. *Hist.* I, 58 reports only the death of a centurion in expiation for that of Capito.

724 Plut. *Otho*, 4.

725 The text has 'May'.

726 Tac. *Hist.* II, 20ff.

727 Tac. *Hist.* II, 49; Plut. *Otho*, 5ff.; Dio LXIV, 10ff. Mommsen, 'Die zwei Schlachten von Betriacum im Jahre 69 n.Chr., *Ges. Schr.* IV, pp. 354ff.

728 Tac. *Hist.* II, 69.

729 Suet. *Vit.*, 8.2; Tac. *Hist.* II, 62; 90.

730 This is ironic: *Germanicus* was the appellation indicating victory over the Germans. The soldiers gave Vitellius this appellation: Tac. *Hist.* I, 62; Plut. *Galba*, 22.

731 Tac. *Hist.* I, 58.

732 Suet. *Vit.* 13.

733 Tac. *Hist.* II, 64.

734 Tac. *Hist.* I, 88. The first marriage of Dolabella's wife had been to Vitellius: Tac. *Hist.* II, 64.

735 Tac. *Hist.* II, 59.

736 The sack of Cremona took place after the second battle of Betriacum on 24 October 69: Dio LXV, 15; Tac. *Hist.* III, 30ff.; see MH.I, 220f.

737 Tac. *Hist.* II, 87ff.; Suet. *Vit.* 11.1.

738 Tac. *Hist.* II, 94.

739 The text reads 'Italy'.

740 In fact Constantine abolished the Guard (see MH.III, 35, 122).

741 *ILS* 242.

742 In the third century too the consulship was held by two persons.

743 There were consuls regularly until 541.

744 Plut. *Otho*, 18.4.

745 Tac. *Hist.* II, 67.

746 Suet. *Vesp.* 4,5; Jos. *Bell. Jud.* III, 1,2.

747 Hensel writes 'Cappadocia'.

748 Mommsen deduces this from Tac. *Hist.* II, 77.

749 He hailed from Reate in Sabine country: Suet. *Vesp.* 2.

750 Suet. *Vesp.* 1,3.

751 Suet. *Vesp.* 6.3.

752 Tac. *Hist.* II, 77.

753 Tac. *Hist.* II, 79; Suet. *Vesp.* 6.3.

754 Tac. *Hist.* II, 83.

755 Jos. *Bell. Jud.* IV, 11.1 and 5; Tac. *Hist.* II, 82; III, 48; IV, 81; Suet. *Vesp.* 7.

756 Tac. *Hist.* III, 6.

757 'Through crime'. Antonius Primus had been sentenced in 61 under Nero for falsifying a will: Tac. *Ann.* XIV, 40.

758 Tac. *Hist.* II, 100.

759 Tac. *Hist.* II, 100f.; III, 12.

760 Tac. *Hist.* II, 93ff.

761 Tac. *Hist.* II, 99.

762 Tac. *Hist.* III, 13.

763 Tac. *Hist.* III, 14.

764 Tac. *Hist.* III, 15ff.

765 Tac. *Hist.* III, 22–35.

766 Tac. *Hist.* III, 31.

767 Tac. *Hist.* III, 63.

768 This did not occur until after the death of Vitellius: Dio LXV, 22; Tac. *Hist.* III, 84.4; IV, 2f.

769 Tac. *Hist.* III, 68; Suet. *Vit.*, 15.

770 Suet. *Vit.*, 15.3; Tac. *Hist.* III, 71f.; Domitian escaped disguised as a priest of Isis: Suet. *Dom.*, 1.2.

771 Tac. *Hist.* III, 74.

772 Tac. *Hist.* IV, 54.

773 Suet. *Vit.*, 17.2; Tac. *Hist.* III, 85; Dio LXV, 20; Jos. *Bell. Jud.* IV, 11.4.

774 From here on the text follows Wickert's *Anonymous* (AW), pp. 164ff; Hensel's fourth note-book is missing. The numbering is so arranged that AW, 164 becomes MH.I, 221 in order to achieve consecutive page numbering.

775 Tac. *Hist.* IV, 12ff.; Jos. *Bell. Jud.* VII, 4.2. A detailed account of the ensuing Batavian revolt is given by *RG*.V, book 8, ch. 4.

776 MK, p. 200: 'It was an entirely nationalist uprising.'

777 Tac. *Hist.* IV, 61.

778 Tac. *Hist.* IV, 60f.

779 Tac. *Hist.* IV, 59.

780 Tac. *Hist.* IV, 61, 70.

781 Tac. *Hist.* IV, 68.

782 Tac. *Hist.* IV, 76.

783 Tac. *Hist.* IV, 72ff.; V, 14ff.

784 Tac. *Hist.* V, 14ff.

785 Tac. *Hist.* V, 22.

786 Mommsen *RG* V, book 8, ch. 11. E. Schürer, *The History of the Jewish People in the Age of Jesus Christ* I (1973), pp. 484ff; M. Goodman, *The Ruling Class of Judaea* (1987).

787 Flavius Josephus, *De bello Judaico*; id. *Vita*, 4ff.; Tac. *Hist.* V, 1–13; Suet. *Vesp.* 4–8; id. *Tit.*, 4f.; Dio LXVI, 4–7.

788 Suet. *Vesp.* 5.6; Jos. *Bell. Jud.* III, 8; IV, 10.7; id. *Vita*, 414ff.

789 Jos. *Bell. Jud.* II, 14.5.

790 Jos. *Bell. Jud.* II, 15.2.

791 Jos. *Bell. Jud.* II, 19.

792 Jos. *Bell. Jud.* III, 1; Suet. *Vesp.* 4.5; 5.6.

793 Jos. *Bell. Jud.* III, 23ff.

794 Tac. *Hist.* V, 1ff.; Dio LXVI, 4.1.

795 Jos. *Bell. Jud.* V, 6.1.

796 This statement is evidently based on a gross misunderstanding – probably not of Mommsen's,

but of Wickert's Anonymous: Josephus (*Bell. Jud.*VI, 5.2) reports 6,000 killed without the knowledge of Titus after the city fell.

797 Sulp. Sev.*Chron.* II, 30.6; Jos. *Bell. Jud.* VI, 4.3.

798 Suet. *Titus*, 6.1; Jos. *Bell. Jud.* VII, 5.3ff.; *ILS* 265. The triumph is depicted on the inner panel of the arch of Titus in the Forum.

799 Jos. *Bell. Jud.* VII, 6.6. 'Such wars had to be fought out in order to smooth the path for the state apparatus of the later and better Roman imperial age' (MK, p. 205).

800 According to Irenaeus V, 30.3, the Apocalypse was not written until the end of Domitian's reign. Apoc. 11, 1f. refers to the Temple fire.

801 Tac. *Hist.* I, 2; II, 8f.

802 There is earlier documentary evidence for the Messianic idea: Genesis 49, 10f.; Deut. 24, 17f. Isaiah 7, 14ff.; 45,1ff. and elsewhere.

803 Jos. *Bell. Jud.* II, 8.14.

804 This book purports to have been written under Nebuchadnezzar (who died in 562 BC), but in fact dates from the Maccabean revolt in 164 BC.

805 Acts 9,11.

806 Matthew 22, 21; Romans 13,7.

807 Romans, 13.

808 Mommsen is probably thinking here of the apocryphal correspondence between Seneca and Paul: E. Hennecke and W. Schneemelcher, *Neutestamentliche Apokryphen* II (1964), pp. 84ff.

809 *Lucanus . . . videtur historiam composuisse, non poema*: Servius on Virgil, *Aen.* I, 382.

810 'Umpire of taste': Tac. *Ann.* XVI, 18.2.

811 On this topic we have Mommsen's critique of literature from the 1872/3 lecture notes taken down by L. Schemann and published in Wickert IV 1980, p. 348:

> Literature, particularly poetry, was becoming ever more aristocratic. Virtually all poets were born into the noblest aristocracy. The achievements of these poets with the *latus clavus* bears no comparison with superior ancient literature. Silius Italicus set the histories of Livy to verse pompously and without poetic feeling; the poetry of Lucan is even less readable. In his tragedies, Seneca, a brilliant man, likewise evinces a dismal, devitalized dreariness and emptiness. Persius tries to conceal this ubiquitous dreariness, common to all, in obscurity and mystery. Scholarship offers a welcome relief from the indigence of the poetry. . . .
>
> In his so-called satires, Petronius, confidant and *maître de plaisir* of Nero, who met his downfall in the Pisonian conspiracy, offers us the most interesting literary work of the entire epoch. Here, for the first time, we have a novel in its purest form, an exact and brilliant portrayal of everyday life devoid of all poetic mediation. We have to look to Dickens and others to find its equivalent. We can also find in Petronius metrical and stylistic merits of a significant kind. He likewise affords observations of the utmost brilliance, often of trenchant veracity. Petronius shows us people living in an epoch in which they knew that the life around them no longer had any value. Only remnants survive of this work; we have no notion of its overall plan. It is, however, possible to discern an absolute lack of form, i.e. the exact opposite of earlier compositions, in which the greatest store was set by a rigid, closed form. Petronius's comic novel reveals a truly horrendous depravity and lack of morality: the atmosphere in which it is enacted is nothing less than that of the brothel. We are thus obliged to show more deference to the genius of Petronius than to his character.

812 On Vespasian, see the forthcoming biography by B. Levick.

813 In 1868 Mommsen saw in Vespasian the transition between the Julian–Claudian epilogue to the Republic and the prologue to the Diocletianic–Constantinian monarchy, saying that Vespasian had instituted 'pure militarism' (MK, pp. 200ff.).

814 Tac. *Hist.* IV, 40ff.; 80.

815 Suet. *Dom.* 1.3.

816 Jos. *Bell. Jud.* VII, 4.
817 Orosius VII, 19.4.
818 *ILS* 245ff.
819 Apart from AD 73 and 78.
820 Suet. *Titus*, 6.1.
821 Suet. *Vesp.* 4.6.
822 Suet. *Vesp.* 16.
823 Suet. *Vesp.* 23.3; Dio LXVI, 14.5.
824 An internal customs duty of 2½ per cent.
825 Suet. *Vesp.* 9.1.
826 'He made the best use of ill-gotten gains': Suet. *Vesp.* 16.3.
827 Suet. *Vesp.* 9.1.
828 Suet. *Vesp.* 8.5; Tac. *Hist.* IV, 53.
829 Suet. *Vesp.* 10.
830 Suet. *Vesp.* 11.
831 Dio LXVI, 11.2; 13.1.
832 Dio LXVI, 12.1a; Suet. *Vesp.* 18.
833 Mommsen, *Staatsrecht* II, pp. 857f. The title of this official was later *corrector civitatis*.
834 Suet. *Vesp.* 8.4.
835 Tac. *Hist.* IV, 51.
836 Suet. *Vesp.* 8.4.
837 Suet. *Vesp.* 15; Dio LXVI, 12.1.
838 Tac. *Ann.* III, 55.
839 Suet. *Vesp.* 8.1; id. *Titus*, 6.1; *ILS* 256.
840 'Ordo uterque': senators and equestrians.
841 This was to change later.
842 Suet. *Vesp.* 1f.
843 Suet. *Vesp.* 4.4.
844 Jos. *Vita*, 342.

A HISTORY OF ROME UNDER THE EMPERORS II

1   'Writers of the Augustan History', a series of biographies of second- and third-century Emperors, purporting to be by six different authors writing in the early fourth century, but actually by one author *c.* AD 400. For one interpretation of the *Historia Augusta*, see R. Syme, *Emperors and Biography* (1971).
2   'Bread and circuses', 'Utilities', 'Dead head'.
3   What follows corresponds to MP.1ff.
4   'Edessa' Hensel: 'Chosren'(?)
5   Dio LX, 17.4.
6   *Ab epistulis Latinis/Graecis*: ND. Or.XIX, 8.10.
7   This was Cyrus the Egyptian, who was removed from office as urban and imperial prefect in Constantinople in 441: John Lydus, *Mag.* II, 12; III, 42.
8   Scholia: marginal notes with comments on ancient texts.
9   Examples indicating the opposite are the Greek poetry of Hadrian and the prose writings of Marcus Aurelius and Julian.
10 This contains epigrams by, *inter alia*, Marcus Argentarius, Cerealius, Commodus, Cornelius Longinus, Fronto, Germanicus, Hadrian, Tiberius and Trajan.
11 Compare MP.7.
12 J. B. de Rossi, *Inscriptiones Christianae Urbis Romae* I (1857), II (1888).
13 J. B. Frey, *Corpus of Jewish Inscriptions* I (1975) gives 534 Jewish inscriptions, 76 per cent Greek, 23 per cent Latin, with three inscriptions in Hebrew.

14 Greek elements in Latin inscriptions: *ILS* III, 852ff.

15 Horace *Sat.* I, 10.30: 'Canusini more bilinguis'.

16 *Utraque lingua doctus*: Horace *Odes* III, 8.5.

17 Strabo VI, 1,2. See K. Lomas, *Rome and the Western Greeks 350 BC–AD 200* (1193), chs. 8–10.

18 *CIL*.X, 1481. In AD 81 (Hensel writes 71), while he was gymnasiarch of Naples, Titus had buildings renovated that had suffered earthquake damage during an eruption of Vesuvius.

19 Strabo V, 4.7; Tac. *Ann.* XV, 33.2; cf. MP. 10.

20 Suet. *Aug.* 98.5; Dio LV, 10.9; LVI, 29; Vell. II, 123; *ILS* 5082.

21 Diod.XIII, 35.3; XVI, 70.6.

22 *Mon. Anc.* 28.

23 *CIL* X, p. 772.

24 San Marco on Sicily; *CIL* X, p. 770.

25 In Isid. *Orig.* XV, 1.63. Cf. MP.11.

26 Caes. *BC* II, 22.

27 Tac. *Agr.* 4.3; Agricola was shielded from the tempting sins of youth by his character and by Massilia, his place of study: *Massilia, locum Graeca comitate et provinciali parsimonia mixtum et bene compositum.*

28 Strabo IV, 1.9.

29 T. Mommsen, *Die unteritalischen Dialekte* (1850).

30 *CRR* II, pp. 326ff.nos.17ff.

31 H. Nissen, *Italische Landeskunde* I (1883), p. 523.

32 This refers to Dolly Pentreath, who died in 1777 in Mousehole, Cornwall.

33 On the contrary, Strabo (V, 3.1) stresses that the Sabine–Samnite way of life persisted into his own day, even though their towns had declined into villages (V, 4.11).

34 Varro, *De lingua Latina* V, 32.142; VII, 3.29.

35 C. de Simone, 'Die messapischen Inschriften', in H. Krahe (ed.), *Die Sprache der Illyrier* II (1964).

36 C. Pauli, *Corpus Inscriptionum Etruscarum* 1893–1902; H.L. Stoltenberg, *Die wichtigsten etruskischen Inschriften* (1956). Cf. MP.13f.

37 Livy XL, 42.13. Cumae was a *civitas sine suffragio* from 338 BC: Livy VIII, 14.11.

38 This is not entirely true. Testaments written in Celtic, Punic or any other vernacular were legally valid: *Dig.* XXXII, 11 pr.; see MH.II, 174ff.

39 The *Notitia Dignitatum* (Or. XI, 52) lists the 'interpreter of various languages' as part of the office of the *magister officiorum*; cf. Occ. IX, 46.

40 Cf. MP.15.

41 *CRR* II, pp. 348ff.; Mommsen, *Münzwesen*, pp. 667ff.

42 *CRR* II, pp. 566ff.; Mommsen, *Münzwesen*, pp. 671ff.

43 A. Beltran, *Las monedas de Tingi; Numario hispanico* I (1952), pp. 89ff.

44 Mommsen, *Staatsrecht* III, pp. 709ff.; 759ff.

45 Mommsen has no inhibitions about referring to the dependent status of Prussia's supposed partners in the second German Reich.

46 Juba's Fragments: *FGrH* no. 275.

47 Hensel erroneously wrote 'Pompey', but the father of Cleopatra Selene was Mark Antony. In 20 BC Augustus married her to King Juba (II); Dio LI, 15.6.

48 A currency law of 9 July 1873 had reformed and standardized the coinage of the German state.

49 E. Muret and A. Chabouillet, *Catalogue des monnaies gauloises de la Bibliothèque nationale* (1889).

50 Caes. *BG* 29,1.

51 Cf. MP.16ff.

52 Mommsen, *Münzwesen*, pp. 739ff.

53 This refers to a donation by Q. Veratius Philagros for the gymnasium of Cibyra in AD 71: Mommsen, *Münzwesen*, p. 28.

54 Mommsen, *Münzwesen*, pp. 400ff.; *CRR* I, pp. liiff: gold coins from 217 BC onwards.

55 Mommsen, *Münzwesen*, p. 699; *BMC*, Pontus, etc. (1899) pp. xxxiiff.; A.N. Zograf, *Antitshnye Monety* (Moscow 1951).

56 R. Göbl, *Sasanidische Numismatik* (1968), pp. 28f.; J. Curtis *Ancient Persia* (1989); F. Paruck, *Sasanian Coins* (1924), pp. 31ff.

57 'The king of the Persians may mint silver at will, but may not place his head on a gold coin, nor may any other barbarian king': Proc.*Bella* VII, 33.6.

58 From the time of Theudebert in 539: E. Zöllner, *Geschichte der Franken* (1970), pp. 172f. On the Franks, I. Wood, *The Merovingian Kingdoms* (1994); E. James, *The Franks* (1988).

59 Silver money from Osca in Tarraconensis: Livy XXXIV, 10,4; 46,2.

60 Mommsen, *Münzwesen*, pp. 760ff.

61 In June 23 BC: *Mon. Anc.* 10,1; Dio LIII, 32.5f.

62 On this see Mommsen, *Münzwesen*, pp. 744f.; 760. K. Kraft, 'S(enatus) C(onsulto)', *Jahrbuch für Numismatik* 12 (1963), pp. 77ff., however, asserts that all administration of coinage was centralized under the Emperor. A. Bay, 'The Letters SC on Augustan *Aes* Coinage', *JRS* 62 (1972), pp. 111ff.

63 Statius, *Silvae* IV, 7.13ff.; Florus II, 25 (IV, 12.10ff.).

64 Cf. MP.19.

65 *RIC* I (1984), pp. 133ff.

66 *CRR* II, p. 527.

67 Aur. Vict. 35.6.

68 M. Crawford, *ANRW* II 2 (1975), pp. 560ff.

69 This refers to the 'Marble of Thorigny', published by H.G. Pflaum, *Le Marbre de Thorigny* (1948); cf. A. Stein, 'Le Marbre de Thorigny', *Eunomia* I (1957), pp. 1–7.

70 *Strenae*, Ovid *Fasti* I, 192, 221; Martial VIII, 33,12; Lydus *Mens.* IV, 5. A. Müller, 'Die Neujahrsfeier im römischen Kaiserreiche', *Philologus* 68 (1909), p. 464; silver is not mentioned.

71 Isid. *Etym.* XVI, 18.11.

72 Alexander Missong, 'Zur Münzreform unter den römischen Kaisern Aurelian und Diocletian', *Numismatische Zeitschrift* I (1869), pp. 105ff.

73 Cf. MP.27ff.

74 The state treasury. Cf. *FIRA.* II, pp. 86f. (Gaius II, 206f.). Riccobono, pp. 192ff.

75 I.e. the complex mechanism of the *comitiae* (Assemblies).

76 Riccobono, pp. 166ff.

77 *Ibid.*, pp. 219ff.

78 Mommsen, *Staatsrecht* III, pp. 1124ff.

79 Dio LV, 25.5.

80 Suet. *Cal.* 40

81 Suet. *Vesp.* 23; Dio LXVI, 14.

82 See MH.I, 237.

83 Dio LXXVII, 9.4f.; *FIRA*. I, 445ff. (*Constitutio Antoniniana*).

84 Mommsen, *Staatsrecht* II, p. 1094; III, pp. 731ff.

85 Tac. *Hist.* I, 8.

86 Marquardt II, pp. 77ff.

87 Suet. *Vesp.* 16.

88 *quasi quaedam praedia populi Romani sunt vectigalia nostra*, Cic. *Verr.* II, 7; *Agr.* III, 15.

89 Marquardt II, pp. 77ff.

90 Mommsen, *Staatsrecht* III, pp. 631f.

91 *Digest* L, 8.5 and 7; Mommsen, *Staatsrecht* III, p. 684.

92 Cf. MP.28.

93 *Vectigal est ad modum ubertatis per singula iugera constitutum: Gromatici veteres*, ed. C. Lachmann I (1848), p. 205.

94 Judaea became a province in AD 6; Publius Sulpicius Quirinius was in office from AD 6 to 7 (Jos. *Ant.* XVIII, 2,1); Herod, during whose reign Jesus is said to have been born, died in 4 BC (Jos. *Ant.* XVII, 8,1).

95 Suet. *Tib.* 33.2.

96 Dio LIX, 8; Mommsen, *Staatsrecht* II, p. 1015.
97 See MH.III, 27.
98 App. *Syr.* 50 states this figure at 1% of capital per annum.
99 See MH.III, 25ff.
100 See MH.III, 170.
101 Marquardt II, pp. 269ff.
102 Marquardt II, pp. 271ff.
103 Strabo (IV, 5.3) writes: 'The tributes were absorbed by the costs of the occupation and necessitated a reduction in customs duties.' Cf. Cic. *Att.* IV, 17.7.
104 According to Pliny (*NH* XII, 41/84) the Romans imported pearls for this amount; customs duty is not mentioned.
105 Text: J. B. Chabot, *Choix d'inscriptions de Palmyre* (1922), pp. 23ff.; commentary: J. G. Février, *Essai sur l'histoire politique et économique de Palmyre* (1931), pp. 29ff.
106 *CIL* VII, 4508 in Lambaesis. S. J. De Laet, *Portorium* (1949), p. 264.
107 The *octroi* was a customs tax in French municipalities which was not abolished until 1948.
108 Marquardt II, pp. 309ff.
109 Cf. MP.33.
110 Marquardt II, p. 295.
111 Gellius V, 6; Livy XXXVIII, 37.4.
112 Payable on the anniversaries of a reign.
113 Suet. *Aug.* 101; Mommsen follows Marquardt II, p. 294.
114 *manubiae*: Marquardt II, pp. 282ff.
115 *multae, bona damnatorum*: Marquardt II, p. 287.
116 Sc. *hereditas*: property with no heir fell to the state.
117 See MH.II, 38.
118 *C.Th.* VII, 16.1; 17.3f.
119 W. Waldstein, 'bona damnatorum', *RE* Suppl.X (1965), pp. 96ff. Cf. MP.35.
120 Marquardt II, p. 159; pp. 280ff. refer to the salt monopoly.
121 Pliny *NH* XXXIII, 118; *minium*.
122 Exception: Suet. *Nero*, 32.3.
123 *C.Th.* X, 19.
124 Cf. MP.36.
125 See MH.II, 97.
126 Amida lies on the upper Tigris in Armenia and was not involved in the Parthian Wars. Perhaps Mommsen was thinking of Nisibis, *orientis firmissimum claustrum*, Amm. XXV, 8,14, or of Proc. *Bell.Pers.* I, 7.4.
127 *Lex Ursonensis*, 103, *FIRA.* II, pp. 190f.
128 Tac. *Ann.* IV, 5; SHA, Hadr. 15.13; Marquardt II, pp. 443ff. B. Campbell, *The Emperor and the Roman Army 31 BC–AD 235* (1984); Y. Le Bohec, *The Imperial Roman Army* (English translation 1994).
129 Plin. *NH* III, 30.
130 Cf. MP.38. Marquardt II, pp. 462ff.; D.B. Saddington, *ANRW* II 3 (1975), pp. 176ff.
131 Tac. *Germ.* 29; *id. Hist.* IV, 12.
132 Tac. *Ann.* IV, 5.
133 Marquardt II, pp. 475ff.
134 Marquardt II, pp. 495ff.; C.G. Starr, *The Roman Imperial Navy 21 BC–AD 324* (3rd edn 1960).
135 Suet. *Aug.* 49; Tac. *Ann.* IV, 5; Vegetius IV, 31.
136 Suet. *Dom.* 7,12; Zon. XI, 19; Marquardt II, p. 96.
137 Cf. MP.39.
138 Vegetius II, 20; Marquardt II, p. 562f.
139 Marquardt II, pp. 515ff.
140 *donativa*: Marquardt II, p. 140f.
141 Plut. *Caes.* 68; Dio XLV, 6f.; XLVI, 46.5.

142 Tac. *Ann*. I, 8.

143 Suet. *Claud*. 10.4; Jos. *Ant*. XIX, 2.

144 Dio LXV, 22; Suet. *Vesp*. 8.2.

145 SHA, *Marcus* 7,9: 20,000 sesterces.

146 Dio LV, 23.1; Tac. *Ann*. I, 17, 78; *Dig*. XXVII, 1,8,2; *Cod. Just*. VII, 64.9 (Diocletian).

147 MP.42: 'The state is accused of having allowed itself to be ruled by the soldiery. This is quite erroneous.'

148 Mommsen on *CIL* III, 6194; Servius *ad Aen*.II, 157: *qui habent plenam, militiam, nam viginti et quinque annis tenentur*. This is contradicted by the above-mentioned documentation of a twenty-year period of service still in effect under Justinian.

149 Marquardt II, pp. 542f.

150 Tac. *Ann*. I, 17.

151 Marquardt I, pp. 118f.

152 Tac. *Ann*. XIV, 27.

153 *ILS* 2460.

154 Colonia Ulpia Traiana Poetovio (Pettau): A. Mocsy, *Pannonia and Upper Moesia* (1974), index s.v. Poetovio.

155 *praemia militiae*: Marquardt II, p. 564.

156 Cf. MP.43.

157 *Cod. Just*. V, 16.2; VI, 46.3.

158 Septimius Severus had already legalized the marriages of soldiers: Herod. III, 8.5.

159 'Camp soldier' according to *C. Th*. VII, 15.2 from AD 423. A critical commentary on this in H. Nesselhauf, 'Das Bürgerrecht der Soldatenkinder', *Historia* 8 (1959), pp. 434ff.

160 Marquardt II, pp. 104f.

161 Cf. MP.44.

162 *ILS* 1486 (discovered 1880/1) with the parallels mentioned there. Mommsen, 'Observationes epigraphicae', *Ephemeris epigraphica* V (1884), p. 108.

163 The equestrian career began with the *tres militiae*: 1. as *praefectus cohortis* (with command of over 500 men), 2. as *tribunus legionis* (field officer), 3. as *praefectus alae* (500 cavalry), and could then lead to the rank of procurator.

164 Marcus Antonius Pallas was a freedman of Antonia the younger who held various high offices under Claudius and Nero and was killed by the latter for his wealth in 62: Tac. *Ann*. XIV, 65; Dio LXII, 14.3.

165 Cf. MP.45.

166 Sebastian Hensel adds: 'What do you think, Paul?', just as he elsewhere also draws attention to the gaps in research mentioned by Mommsen; cf. MH.II, 90.

167 Mommsen, *Staatsrecht*, II, p. 1076.

168 The valley of ancient Bagradas.

169 Ancient Theveste in Algeria.

170 Suet. *Aug*. 49.3. O. Seeck, 'cursus publicus', *RE* IV (1901), 1846ff. See Mitchell (Part I, n. 360), p. 138.

171 The costs were shifted from the state on to the municipalities: *ILS* 214.

172 *RIC* II, p. 229, no.39. The Nerva sestertius bears the inscription: *VEHICULATIONE ITALIAE REMISSA*.

173 Septimius Severus devolved it once again on to the *fiscus*: SHA, *Severus* 14.2.

174 *ILS* 5743.

175 *ILS* 298.

176 Marquardt II, p. 90.

177 Cf. MP.48.

178 App. *Civ*. I, 21; Cic. *Tusc*. III, 48; Liv. *Epit*. 60.

179 The senatorial and equestrian classes.

180 Suet. *Caes*. 41 speaks of a reduction in recipients from 320,000 to 170,000.

181 In his *Res gestae* (18) Augustus mentions 100,000 'or more'.

182 Dio LXVIII, 5.4. On alimentary foundations, see Mommsen, *Staatsrecht* II, pp. 949f.; 1079f.

183 Cf. MP.49.

184 Dio LIV, 2; Mommsen, *Staatsrecht* II, pp. 236f.

185 This view is contradicted by the numerous hippodromes in Greek cities (Alexandria, Antioch: Dio LXVII, 25.5; Edessa: Proc.II, 12, 18f.; Athens, Caesarea, Delos, Delphi, Ephesus, Corinth, Nemea, Sparta, Thebes, etc.). In Italy there were hippodromes at Aquileia, Asisium, Bovillae, etc. See J. H. Humphrey, *Roman Circuses* (1986).

186 Viz. the dedication of the Colosseum: Suet. *Titus*, p. 7.3, or the Millennium celebrations in AD 247: Aur. Vict. 28.1.

187 'Urban plebs in receipt of public grain'. As in AW. 216, Mommsen refers here to Marquardt II, p. 134, i.e. Joachim Marquardt, *Römische Staatsverwaltung* II (2nd edn 1884), pp. 130f.

188 This presumably refers to those coins whose reverses celebrate the *liberalitas* of the Emperor; specific sums are not mentioned.

189 This is the chronicle of Emperors from the Filocalus calendar of 354: *Chron. Min.* I, 145ff.; cf. Suet. *Nero*, 37.

190 The *congiaria* are specified in the *Fasti Ostienses*: A. Degrassi, *Inscriptiones Italiae* XIII I (1947), pp. 173ff.; H. Kloft, *Liberalitas Principis* (1970), p. 91.

191 MP.50 refers to 'ruinous' administration of finances.

192 Hensel: 'Nero'.

193 These calculations are based on Marquardt II, pp. 71ff.

194 *ILS* 6675.

195 Marquardt II, pp. 302ff.; Mommsen, *Staatsrecht* II, pp. 131ff.; 545ff.; 1005ff.

196 Mommsen, *Staatsrecht* II, pp. 998ff.; H. Bellen, ANRW II.1 (1974), pp. 91ff.

197 Dio LV, 25.

198 *ILS* 5598.

199 Estates without legitimate heirs; see MH.II, 38;53.

200 'Today they are claimed by the *fiscus*.' The jurist Salvius Julianus died around AD 170. Mommsen was presumably thinking of a saying of Marcellus: *Dig.* XXVIII, 4,3.

201 See MH.II, 49.

202 Cf. MP.53.

203 Dio LV, 25.2f. for the year AD 6.

204 Tac. *Ann.* II, 42.4 for the year AD 17.

205 H. Nesselhauf, 'Patrimonium und Res Privata des römischen Kaisers', *Antiquitas* Series IV, vol. 2 (1964), pp. 73ff.

206 Gaius II, 21 (*FIRA.* II, 51): *Stipendaria sunt ea, quae in his provinciis sunt, quae propriae populi Romani esse intelliguntur; tributaria sunt ea, quae in his provinciis sunt, quae Caesaris esse creduntur.* ('Stipendiary are properties in the provinces that are considered as belonging to the Roman people, tributary those in the provinces that are held to belong to the Emperor').

207 On the *longi temporis praescriptio*, see A. Borkowski, *Textbook on Roman Law* (1994), p. 195.

208 Suet. *Cal.* 14.1; Dio LIX, 1.

209 And his son: Dio LXXIII, 7.3.

210 Suetonius (*Aug.*, 101) reports that the freedmen Polybius and Hilarion assisted the Emperor in the drafting of these papers; Tac. *Ann.* I, 11.4.

211 Cf. MP.56.

212 *ND*, Or.XIII; *ND*, Occ.XI.

213 In late antiquity the title was *rationalis* (or *praefectus*) *summae rei*: PLRE.I, p. 1064.

214 Hirschfeld 1876/1905.

215 R. His, *Die Domänen der römischen Kaiserzeit* (1896); D. Flach, *Römische Agrargeschichte* (1990), pp. 82ff.

216 This was already true of Augustus.

217 Tac. *Hist.* I, 11; *Ann.* II, 59; Marquardt I, p. 441.

218 *OGIS* 188f.; 669; 38f.; 41; 44.

219 'The Emperor's fields were few': Tac. *Ann.* IV, 6.4.

220 Cf. MP.57.

221 Mommsen is thinking here of the legionary brickworks and those of the city of Rome. Margareta Steinby (*RE* Suppl. XV (1978), 1519) lists 181 private brickworks.

222 Suet. *Nero*, 31.3.

223 The inscription of *Saepinum* (Altilia): *CIL* IX, 2438 with Mommsen's commentary (1883). Cf. C. R. Whittaker (ed.), *Pastoral Economies in Classical Antiquity* (1988).

224 D. P. Kehoe, *The Economies of Agriculture on Roman Imperial Estates in North Africa* (1988).

225 Pliny *NH* XVIII, 7.35 relates that six landowners owned half of Africa when Nero executed them.

226 Mommsen, 'Decret des Commodus für den saltus Burunitanus', *Hermes* 15 (1880), pp. 385ff.; 478ff. (cf. *Ges. Schr.* III, pp. 153ff.). The inscription dates from the period AD 180–3, *FIRA*. I, no.103; *ILS* 6870.

227 SHA, *Sept.Sev.* 12.

228 Nesselhauf, see n. 205.

229 *ND*, Or.XIV; *ND*, Occ.XII.

230 Tac. *Ann.* IV, 6; *si quando cum privatis disceptaret* (sc. Tiberius) *forum et ius*. Cf. II, 34; III, 76; IV, 21.

231 Suet. *Claud.* 15.1; Tac. *Ann.* XII, 60.1;4.

232 This is contradicted by the fact that Nerva created an office of *praetor fiscalis* to oversee the jury courts drawn by lot which administered justice between the *fiscus* and private law: *Dig*.I, 2.2.32; Pliny *Pan.* 36; Mommsen, *Staatsrecht* II, pp. 203, 226.

233 Hensel writes in the margin: 'Regarding owls in Iceland: 'There are no owls in Iceland'.

234 Pliny *Ep.* X., 23f.

235 Sebastian Hensel adds in brackets: *Avis au lecteur* – another challenge to Paul to apply himself to research into ancient history; see MH.II, 68.

236 *ILS* 6354ff.; H. Geist, *Pompeianische Wandinschriften* (1960).

237 Hensel erroneously writes *tribunatus*. On this subject see Mommsen, *Staatsrecht* III, pp. 227ff. Cf. MP.63.

238 Pliny *Ep.* X, 54f.

239 The survey of Neapolitan estates in H. Philipp, *RE* XVI 2 (1935), p. 2119 contains no reference to territory on Crete. Mommsen is probably thinking of Capua, to which the territory of Cnossos belonged: Dio XLIX, 14.5.

240 Cic. *Fam.* XIII, 7.1.

241 This was Lucius Caecilius Jucundus, whose wax tablets were published by C. Zangemeister: *CIL* IV Suppl.1 (1898); Mommsen, *Ges. Schr.* III, pp. 221ff.; J. Andreau, *Les Affaires de monsieur Jucundus* (1974).

242 On this see J. Oehler, 'Calendarium', *RE* X 2 (1919), 1565ff.

243 Pliny *Ep.* X, 54f. The 'members of the Senate' are the decuriones; Trajan quoted the *iustitia nostrorum temporum* as in the letter about the Christians, X, 97.

244 Mommsen is in error: the sources for communal customs duties are provided in Jones 1964 III, pp. 231ff., notes 45, 46 and 49.

245 *CIL* VIII, 10327f.; *ILS* 5874.

246 *ILS* 38 from Termessos in Pisidia.

247 *Lex Ursonensis*, 98; *ILS* 6087 II, p. 509.

248 Hensel: *iugerum*.

249 *Lex Ursonensis*, 92 (*ILS* 6087 II, p. 507); Pliny *Ep.* X, 43f.; *Cod. Just.* X, 65; *Dig.* L, 7.

250 Mommsen presumably refers here to the *praefectus arcendis latrociniis* of Nyon (*Noviodunum*), *ILS* 7007; cf. Mommsen, *Die Schweiz in römischer Zeit*, ed. G. Walser 1969, p. 34.

251 A long list of civic obligations is given by the jurist Charisius: *Dig*.L, 4,18.

252 For a critical commentary on this, see H. Horstkotte, *Die Theoriec vom spätrömischen 'Zwangsstaat' und das Problem der Steuerhaftung* (1984/8).

253 *Lex Ursonensis*, 65ff.; 128 (*ILS* 6087).

254 *ILS* 5450.

255 Juvenal X, 81.

256 In accordance with Mommsen's erroneous belief that there was chariot-racing only at Rome: *ILS* III 2, p. 916 s.v. *ludi circenses*.

257 *Lex Ursonensis*, 71 (*ILS* 6087). The sum is given as 1,000 sesterces.

258 Joh. Chrys. *de educandis liberis*, 4ff.

259 *ILS* III 2, p. 918 s.v. *pro ludis*.

260 Documentary evidence in *ILS* III 2, pp. 701ff.

261 'Priest of Augustus freely installed': *ILS* 6313; 6566; 6984.

262 Livy's fable about the schoolmaster of Falerii (V, 27) is hardly historical.

263 Suet.*Vesp.* 18; *Dig.* XXVII, 1,6,1 and CIC.III, p. 802 state otherwise. According to MP. 67, Mommsen said that the state paid teachers of rhetoric. Cf. MH.I, 238 and Mommsen, 'Zur Rechtsstellung der athenischen Professoren in der römischen Kaiserzeit', *Ges. Schr.* II, pp. 50ff.

264 Plut. *Cato maior*, 20f.

265 *ILS* 1119.

266 Pliny *Ep.* X, 47f.

267 Mommsen, *Staatsrecht* II, p. 858; 1086. Cf. MP. 69.

268 It would be appropriate here to insert a reference to Mommsen's article, 'Boden- und Geldwirtschaft in der römischen Kaiserzeit', *Ges. Schr.* V, pp. 589–617, which, according to Otto Hirschfeld, *inter alia*, was 'apparently intended for [inclusion in] Volume four of the *History of Rome*'.

269 On the following see Mommsen, *RG* V, chapter 5. Cf. MP.69ff., *ANRW* II 3 (1975), pp. 284ff. S. Frere, *Britannia* (2nd edn 1978); P. Salway, *Roman Britain* (1991); M. Millett, *The Romanization of Britain* (1990).

270 A history of the legions arranged numerically is provided by E. Ritterling, *RE* XII (1925), 1376ff.

271 Tac. *Agr.* 35.

272 Hensel's text refers to Mons Graupius.

273 Hensel's text has 'Diocletian'.

274 This is uncertain: Ritterling, op. cit. (n. 270), 1668f.; see MH.II, 113.

275 Tac. *Hist.* II, 66.

276 AW writes: 'in the time of Domitian', which Mommsen undoubtedly did not say.

277 Suet. *Vesp.* 4.1.

278 In 70: Tac. *Agr.* 7.3.

279 Tac. *Agr.* 18; Pliny *NH* II, 77/187; Tac. *Ann.* XIV, 29.3; 30.1.

280 The misunderstanding about the location of the Clyde and the Forth is likely to have been Hensel's.

281 Tac. *Agr.* 39f.

282 Tac. *Agr.* 29ff.

283 Tac. *Agr.* 24.3.

284 Fronto, 217 (Naber); Mommsen, *RG* V, p. 171.

285 H. Nesselhauf (BJ.167, 1967) demonstrates that the ninth legion was not annihilated, but reposted to Germania: A. Birley, *Septimius Severus* (1971), p. 245.

286 SHA, *Pius* 5.4.

287 SHA, *Hadr.* 11.2; *CIL* VII, pp. 99f.

288 This was originally a wall: J. Collingwood-Bruce, *Handbook to the Roman Wall* (1978), pp. 14ff. D. J. Breeze and L. B. Dobson, *Hadrian's Wall* (rev. edn 1978). The German mile was 7420.438 metres long.

289 SHA, *Pius* 5.4; *CIL* VII, 191ff.

290 According to MH.II, 114; AW writes: 'Prussia'.

291 SHA, *Pius* 5.4; *ILS* 340 indicates that the year was 142.

292 On this, see Mommsen, 'Das römische Militärwesen seit Diocletian', in: *ibid. Ges. Schr.* VI, pp. 206ff., 225ff.; and E. Kornemann, 'Die unsichtbaren Grenzen des römischen Kaiserreiches', in id., *Gestalten und Reiche* (1943), pp. 323ff.

293 K. Miller, *Itineraria Romana* (1916), p. 14; id., *Der Peutingersche Tafel* (1962), pp. 4f.; 17.

294 Mommsen refers to the *Notitia Dignitatum* (Occ. XL).

295 Dio LXXII, 8.22f.

296 Mommsen is thinking of the era of the principate. This repeatedly happened after Diocletian: see MH.II, 118.

297 MH reads 'German', but the next sentence shows that this is an error. Cf. Dio LXXIV, 13ff.

298 Dio LXXIV, 14,3 states they had three each.

299 Dio LXXV, 6.

300 SHA, Sept., 18.2; Aur. Vict. 20.18; Eusebius–Jerome *Chron.* on 207 gives the number of miles as 132. It was, in fact, Hadrian's Wall: Birley, *Septimius Severus*, p. 263. Mommsen *RG* V, p. 170, however, disagrees.

301 Dio LXXVI, 13. Mommsen, *RG* V, p. 172 n. 2 states otherwise.

302 Dio LXXVI, 13.

303 Dio LXXVI, 15.

304 In MH.I, 72 Mommsen described the conquest of Britain as 'detrimental'.

305 Dio LXXVII, 1.1.

306 *ILS* 432f.

307 *ILS* 452; 454.

308 Hensel writes 'Normannen', normally used for the Normans.

309 Main sources on the 'separate British Empire': *Panegyrici Latini* VI; VIII; X *passim*; Aur. Vict. 39.20ff; Eutrop. IX, 21f. Allectus's end came in 296; cf.MH.III, 82ff. N. Shiel, *The Episode of Carausius and Allectus* (1977); P. J. Casey, *Carausius and Allectus* (1994).

310 Stilicho fell in 408; in 407 Constantine III had rebelled and crossed over to Gaul, and was abandoned by his general Gerontius in 409, PLRE.II *sub nominibus*.

311 Zos. VI, 5.2f.; 10.2.

312 Tac. *Agr.* 19 (tax relief), 21 (Romanization).

313 App. *Rom.* prooem. 5.

314 Hensel writes 'Agrippa'.

315 *CIL* VII, (ed. by E. Hübner, 1873). The standard edition is now *Roman Inscriptions of Britain* (vol. I, 1965; vol. II, 1991 on). The CIL volumes covering Gaul appeared in 1888 (vol. XII) and 1898ff. (vol. XIII).

316 Julian, 279D; Zos. III, 5.2.

317 Mommsen, *RG* V, chs. 3 and 4. Cf. MP. 80ff.; M.-T. and G. Raepsaert, 'Gallia Belgica et Germania Inferior', *ANRW* II 4 (1975), pp. 3ff.

318 Still a *desideratum*, even today.

319 Ptol. *Geogr.* II, 9.17.

320 According to AW. 239. Hensel writes 'in the vicinity of Wesel, Coblentz'.

321 Ptol. *Geogr.* II, 9.18.

322 A transfer of the *legio* VIII from Argentoratum to Moguntiacum cannot be substantiated and is unlikely: E. Ritterling, op. cit. (n. 270), 1655.

323 Helmuth von Moltke (1800–91), who planned the Prussian victories of 1864, 1866 and 1870; not to be confused with the World War I general, who was his nephew.

324 *Der deutsch-französische Krieg 1870/71*, ed. by the military history department of the *Grosser Generalstab* I 1 (1874), pp. 132ff.: 'Das Grosse Hauptquartier in Mainz'.

325 Cf. MP. 82.

326 Ptol. *Geogr.* II, 9.14.

327 Two border stones of the Upper and Lower German legions prove that the Vinxt (Fins) brook, which flows into the Rhine at Rheinbrohl, was the boundary river (previously the boundary between the Ubii and the Treveri, subsequently between the dioceses of Cologne and Trier).

328 Tac. *Hist.* IV, 61; 65; V, 22; 24; *Germ.* 8; Statius *Silvae* I, 4.90.

329 Tac. *Germ.* 28.2.

330 The Agri Decumates: Tac. *Germ.* 29.

331 Frontinus merely reports that after his victory (*Strat.* I, 1.8) Domitian adopted the appellation 'Germanicus' (II, 11,7). Suetonius, *Dom.* 13.3, documents the triumph.

332 The 1885 Teubner edition of Frontinus by A. Dederich gives *in finibus Cattorum* at *Strat.* II, 11.7. Mommsen, *RG* V, p. 136 likewise takes this to be *Cubii*, a reading likewise preferred in the editions of McElvain (Loeb, 1925) and Bendz (*Schriften und Quellen*, Berlin, 1963).

333 Frontin. *Strat.* I, 3.10.

334 MP.84ff. confirms that in 1883 Mommsen did not consider the *limes* to be a fortification. Mommsen modified this view in 1885, impressed by the *limes* work of Colonel A. von Cohausen. Mommsen, *Ges. Schr.* V, pp. 444ff.; *RG* V, p. 136; cf. pp. 111f. On the story of how Mommsen established his control over *limes*-scholarship in Germany, see Rainer Braun, *Die Anfänge der Erforschung des rätischen Limes* (1984).

335 Vell. II, 120.2.

336 Tac.·*Ann.* II, 7.

337 E. Hübner, 'Der römische Grenzwall in Deutschland', *Jahrbücher des Vereins von Alterthumsfreunden im Rheinlande* 63 (1878), pp. 17ff. Id., 'Zum römischen Grenzwall in Deutschland', ibid., 66 (1879), pp. 13ff.

338 Hensel has 'abdisidirt'.

339 Here Mommsen contradicts what he elaborates below. He was later a supporter of *limes* research: Mommsen, *RA*, pp. 344ff.; E. Fabricius, *Der obergermanisch-rätische Limes des Römerreiches* A I (1936), pp. 111ff.

340 The existence of such a camp can only be assumed on the basis of tombstone finds: H. Schoppa, *Aquae Mattiacae* (1974), pp. 17ff.

341 Pliny *NH* XXXI, 17: *Sunt et Mattiaci in Germania fontes calidi trans Renum* ('There are also hot springs at Mattiacum in Germany across the Rhine').

342 Tac. *Germ.* 29: *ultraque veteres terminos imperii*.

343 Frontin. *Strat.* I, 3.10.

344 Tac. *Germ.* 29.

345 Likewise MP.85.

346 Should read: 'at Eining'.

347 AW writes 'Aquileia' (*Aquilegia* is a Latin form for Aalen). Should read: 'to Lorch'.

348 Should read: 'the north–south arm of the German *limes*'.

349 AW. 243 and MP. 86 provide sketches, presumably drawn by Mommsen on the blackboard. A fair copy is given here.

350 A. Duncker, *Beiträge zur Erforschung und Geschichte des Pfahlgrabens* (Kassel 1879).

351 *CIL* XIII, 6449ff.

352 *Tab. Peut.* IV, 1.

353 *ILS* 282ff.

354 Hensel writes *Canninephaten*, adding in a footnote '*Canninephates* according to Kiepert'. This is followed in brackets by a note addressed to his son:

> That's what I finally thought the word must have been; at first I thought they were *Kaminfeger* [chimneysweeps]. It's the devil's own job to understand Mommsen when he's on to names. It is undoubtedly wrong; if it interests you, you can look it up in Tacitus, but it makes no difference, in any case, what these ancient Mynheer van Streefs and Mynheer van de Jongher were called.

355 Mommsen is thinking of the *ala Parthorum*; *Ges. Schr.* VI, p. 247.

356 AW. 244 refers to 'CIL III'; presumably Mommsen is referring to the military diploma *CIL* III 2, p. 852, 881, etc. for Canninefates.

357 Dio LXVIII, 3.4.

358 Eutr. VIII, 2.

359 The inscriptions of Sumelocenna-Rottenburg do not carry the appellation *CIL* XIII, 6358ff.

360 Mommsen probably means the Civitas Ulpia Sveborum Nicretum: *CIL* XIII, 6414ff.

361 Civitas Aurelia Aquensis, or simply 'Aquae'; *ILS* 5848; *CIL* XIII. 6288ff.

362 Amm. XVII, 1,11; *Munimentum quod in Alamannorum solo conditum Traianus suo nomine voluit appellari*, without reference to the precise location.

363 Sidonius, *Carmen* VII, 114f.; Hensel writes 'Suetonius'.

364 SHA, *Hadr.* 10.2: *pacis cupidus.*

365 SHA, *Hadr.* 12.7.

366 SHA, *Pius* 5.4.

367 SHA, *Marcus*, 8.8: an invasion of Germania and Raetia by the Chatti; Aufidius Victorinus was sent to fight against them.

368 *Leuga una habet mille quingentos passus, Laterculus Veronensis* XV, in: O. Seeck, *Notitia Dignitatum* (1876), p. 253. On the Gallic mile, see Isid. *Etym.* XV, 15.3.

369 Cf. MP.91.

370 Cf. MP.91.

371 The minutes of the Arval Brethren: *ILS* 451.

372 Dio LXXVII, 13.4f.

373 Fragment handed down by the Greek Agathias (I, 6.3); there is no evidence to suggest that Asinius Quadratus himself wrote in Greek.

374 The Chatti were either largely or completely absorbed into the Franks: K. E. Demandt, *Geschichte des Landes Hessen* (1972), pp. 93ff. On the ancient tribes which later constituted the Alamanni, see L. Schmidt, *Die Westgermanen* II (1940), pp. 3ff.

375 SHA, *Probus* 14; Amm. XVIII, 2.13.

376 Mommsen is probably thinking of the victory of Chlodwig at Zülpich. The *rex* (*Alamannorum*) mentioned in Gregory of Tours (*Hist. Franc.* II, 30) was not necessarily the king of the Alamanni; he may also have been *one* of their kings. Cf. Cass. *Var.* II, 41.

377 Gregory of Tours, *Hist. Franc.* II, 9. Hensel writes 'Ligosius'.

378 According to AW Mommsen suspected 'prompting by a personality such as Arminius' behind the emergence of the Alamannic alliance.

379 Aur. Vict. 24; SHA, *Alex.* 49ff.

380 SHA, *Max.* 12.

381 *RIC* V 1, pp. 69f., nos. 17f.

382 The advance on Tarraco and Africa is related in Aur. Vict. 33.3; Orosius VII, 41,2 speaks of twelve years, but this is considered an exaggeration: E. Zöllner, *Geschichte der Franken* (1970), p. 8.

383 Eutr. IX, 7; Zos. I, 37.

384 *ILS* 544.

385 *ILS* 569.

386 In fact the right bank of the Rhine.

387 In O. Seeck, *Notitia Dignitatum* (1876), p. 253. Mommsen, *Ges. Schr.* V, pp. 561ff.

388 Hensel mistakenly writes 'Montiacense'.

389 This would suggest that the list was compiled in, or after, the time of Diocletian; in the opinion of Jones, 1964 III, p. 381, around 313. To this extent, therefore, the information is not 'incorrect'.

390 As in the *Scriptores Historiae Augustae*, drawing an analogy with the oligarchic regime in Athens in 404 BC.

391 Cf. MP.97. J. F. Drinkwater, *The Gallic Empire* (1987).

392 SHA, *Trig. Tyr.* III, 8.

393 See MH.II, 319f.

394 Zos. I, 38.2; Zon. XII, 24.

395 Mommsen is referring to the 'separate Gallic Empire' under the generals Aegidus, Paulus and Syagrius, who was defeated by Chlodwig in 486: Greg. Tur. *HF* II, p. 27. K. F. Stroheker, *Der senatorische Adel im spätantiken Gallien* (1948), no. 370; Demandt, *RE* Suppl.XII (1970), 691ff.

396 Britain: *ILS* 560; Spain: *ILS* 562.

397 *RIC* V 1, nos. 343; 350; J. Lafaurie, *ANRW* II 2 (1975), pp. 853ff.

398 Eutr. IX, 9.

399 Cf. n. 395.

400 The coins of Postumus: *RIC* V 1, nos. 310–68; inscriptions: PLRE.I, p. 720. I. König, *Die gallischen Usurpatoren von Postumus bis Tetricus* (1981).

401 *ILS* 560ff.

402 From 259 to 268.

403 Aur. Vict. 33.8f.

404 Cf. MP.98.

405 Aur. Vict. 35.2; Zos. I, 49.1; SHA, *Aur.* 21.1.

406 Aur. Vict. 35.7; Zos. I, 49.2.

407 The Aurelian Wall was built of brick: J. Richmond, *The City Wall of Imperial Rome* (1930); Coarelli 1974, pp. 23ff.

408 Dexippos: *FGrH* 100,6 (Exc.*de leg.*, pp. 380ff. de Boor). Cf. F. Millar, 'P. Herennius Dexippus', *JRS* 59 (1969), pp. 12ff.

409 Aur. Vict. 21.2.

410 The first line of Schiller's, *The Bride of Messina*: 'Der Not gehorchend, nicht den eignem Triebe'.

411 Eutr. IX, 13; Aur. Vict. 35.4f.

412 Zos. I, 62; Aur. Vict. 35.8.

413 SHA, *Prob.* 13.6.

414 And not, for example, the Elbe, SHA, *Prob.* p. 13,7; Zos. I, 67f. J. Straub, *Regeneratio Imperii* (1972), pp. 418ff.

415 SHA, *Prob.* 13.8: *contra urbes Romanas castra in solo barbarico posuit ac illic milites collocavit.*

416 Tac. *Germ.* 41.1: *Hermunduronum civitas fida Romanis.*

417 This sentence, contained in AW 251, is historically inaccurate: the Huns did not make their appearance until a century later.

418 Cf. MP.102ff. E. James, *The Franks* (1988), introduction.

419 Joh. Lyd. *Mag.* I, 150.

420 Wenskus 1961, pp. 512ff.

421 *Tab. Peut.* II, 2.

422 Greg.Tur. *Hist. Franc.* II, 9.

423 Amm. XX, 10,2: *(Franci) quos Atthuarios vocant.*

424 For example, Claudian and Sidonius.

425 Caes. *Bell. Gall.*VI, 9f.; Dio XLVIII, 49; Strabo IV, 3.4.

426 In narrative sources: SHA, Gall., 7.1.

427 Aur. Vict. 33.3; Eutr. IX, 8.2.

428 SHA, *Prob.* 18.2; Zos. I, 71.2.

429 Eutr. IX, 21; see MH.II, 118 and MH.III, 82ff.

430 Oros. VII, 25.3.

431 *Paneg.* VI (VII), 5.3. Since AW. 253 also has *ipsos*, Mommsen must have said this, although the text gives *ipsas (gentes)*. Baehrens (Teubner edn, 1874) reads *Romana* and takes *ipsas* with *nationes.*

432 Amm. XVII, 8.5 (Cod. Vat., Clark) gives *Toxiandria.*

433 Amm., loc.cit.; see MH.III, 167ff.

434 Cf. MP.105.

435 Ptol. *Geogr.* II, 2.8; 11.7.

436 Eutr. IX, 21.

437 Hensel writes: 'Schauten ['madmen'] (I cannot vouch for the correctness of this name, dear Paul, and I should be most sorry if the ancient Hanoverians turned out to be such madmen)'. He adds a gloss: 'Chauci, according to Kiepert'.

438 Zos. III, 6.1; see Mendelssohn's note.

439 Hensel again writes 'Schauten'.

440 Hensel adds: 'I quite agree.'

441 W. Lammers (ed.), *Entstehung und Verfassung des Sachsenstammes* (1967).

442 J. F. Drinkwater, *Roman Gaul 58 BC–AD 260* (1983); A. King, *Roman Gaul and Germany* (1990).

443 Mommsen, *RG* V, ch. 3; *ANRW* II 3 (1975), pp. 686ff.

444 AW reads: 'the civilized land proper'.

445 MP. 106 reads 'closely related'.

446 Aherbelste, Edelas, Leherenn, Herauscorritseha, Ilixo, etc.: E. Desjardins, *Geographie de la Gaule romaine* (1878).

447 Through Cn. Domitius Ahenobarbus in 118 BC: Vell.II, 10.2.

448 Herodotus V, 9.3; Solinus II, 52.

449 Strabo IV, 1.12.

450 Pliny *NH* III, 5/31.

451 Southern French Provençal and northern French, distinguished by the word for 'yes': 'oc' or 'oui'.

452 Tac. *Ann.* XI, 24; *FIRA.* I, pp. 281ff.; *ILS* 212.

453 Mart.VII, 88 mentions only Vienne.

454 R. Mowat, *Remarques sur les inscriptions de Paris* (1883).

455 Tac. *Ann.* III, 43.

456 Caesar (BG.VI, 14.3) states that Druids had to learn a 'large number' of verses by heart and sometimes studied for twenty years.

457 Cf. MP.110.

458 Suet. *Claud.* 25.5.

459 Pliny *NH* XXX, 4/13.

460 Suet. *Claud.* 25.5.

461 Tac. *Hist.* IV, 5.54.

462 SHA, *Sev.Alex.* 60.6; referring to a female Druid.

463 SHA, *Carus* 14,2ff.

464 See MH.II, 109ff.

465 *ILS* 4613.

466 *ILS* 2536; 2610; 9060; 9141f.

467 *CIL* XIII, 8655. E. Wightman, *Roman Trier and the Treveri* (1970).

468 *ILS* 1992; 1998.

469 *ILS* 2579; 2587; 3381.

470 AW. 258 gives: '(formed) of Belgians in Brittany.'

471 See MH.II, 57, following Tac. *Germ.* 29 and *Hist.* IV, 12.

472 According to Tac. *Ann.* XII, 27 Claudius exalted Cologne to the status of a *colonia* (Plin.*NH* IV, 31/106), but granted merely *ius Italicum*: Dig.L, 15,8,2. Mommsen, *Ges. Schr.* IV, pp. 277f.

473 Tac. *Ann.* XI, 24; *FIRA.* I, pp. 281ff.; *ILS* 212.

474 Tac. *Ann.* XI, 23.4.

475 Mommsen, 'Schweizer Nachstudien', *Hermes* 16 (1881), pp. 445ff. = *Ges. Schr.* V., pp. 390ff.

476 W. Drack and R. Fellmann, *Die Römer in der Schweiz* (1988).

477 Avenches is in fact some distance from Lake Neuchâtel.

478 *ILS* 7008.

479 *FIRA.* I, pp. 445ff.; Dio LXXVII, 9.4.

480 See n. 368 above.

481 Hensel's text has 'for reasons of Empire' for 'legally' (*Reichs/Rechtes*).

482 Jerome, PL, 26, 382. Cf. MP.114f.

483 *Dig.* XXXII, 11 pr. (MH and AW. 260: XXXII, pp. 1.11). See MH.II, 19.

484 These are not mentioned in loc.cit.

485 From the time of Severus, wills written in Greek were legally valid: *P.Oxy.* 907 (with commentary by Grenfell and Hunt); 990.

486 Jord. *Get.* 237f.; Sidon. *Ep.* III, 9. Demandt 1989, p. 174.

487 On Strabo, see MH.II, 160.

488 See MH.II, 15ff.

489 M. Lejeune (ed.), *Recueil des inscriptions gauloises* I (1985).

490 In Latin.

491 Should read: 'wrote'.

492 Cf. MP.117f.

493 Reprinted without footnotes in O. Hirschfeld, *Kl. Schr.* I (1913), pp. 133ff.

494 Tac. *Hist.* I, 65.

495 Mommsen is probably again thinking of *ILS* 1514 (see MH..I, 54, n. 190; and MH.II, 338, n. 861), the epitaph of Musicus Scurranus, Tiberius's 'dispensator ad fiscum Gallicum provinciae Lugdunensis', to whom his 'underslaves' erected a monument when he died in Rome. This mentions a business agent, an accountant, three assistants, a physician, two slaves in charge of silver and one in charge of the wardrobe, two chamberlains, two footmen, two cooks and a woman whose role is unspecified.

496 J. Deininger, *Die Provinziallandtage der römischen Kaiserzeit* (1965), pp. 99ff; D. Fishwick, 'The Temple of the Three Gauls', *JRS* 62 (1972), pp. 46ff.

497 Tac. *Ann.* I, 39; 57.

498 Pliny *Ep.* IX, 11.2.

499 On Mommsen's hypothesis that there was an essential affinity between the Romans and Germans, see Introduction pp. 29f.

500 Caes. *BG.* VI, 11ff.

501 The *corporis custodes*: G. Wissowa, *RE* VI (1901), pp. 1900ff.; Mommsen, *Ges. Schr.* VI, pp. 17ff.; H. Bellen, *Die germanische Leibwache der römischen Kaiser des iulisch-claudischen Hauses* (1981).

502 Tac. *Germ.* 28.5.

503 Poem written by Max Schneckenberger (1819–49) in 1840; it was set to music in 1854 by the later Kaiser Wilhelm I and effectively became the German national anthem during the 1870–1 war.

504 *CIL* XIII, nos. 6661ff.

505 G. Rupprecht (ed.), *Die Mainzer Römerschiffe* (1984).

506 Here AW. 265 reads: 'On Mainz, see *Westdeutsche Zeitschrift*, vol.I by Berg', referring to T. Bergk, 'Die Verfassung von Mainz in römischer Zeit', *Westdeutsche Zeitschrift für Geschichte und Kunst* I (1882), pp. 498ff.; the author refutes Mommsen's view of the genesis of Roman camp towns.

507 Strabo IV, 3.4; Dio XLVIII, 49.

508 Tac. *Ann.* I, 39; 57.

509 Tac. *Ann.* XII, 27.

510 Loc.cit.; cf. MH.II, 169.

511 In AD 14 the first and twentieth legions were stationed at Cologne; towards the end of Tiberius's reign they were transferred to Neuss and Bonn respectively: Tac. *Ann.* I, 37,39; Hist.IV, 25; *CIL* XIII, 8553ff.

512 B. and H. Galsterer, *Die römischen Steininschriften aus Köln* (1975).

513 H. Heinen, *Trier und das Trevererland in römischer Zeit* (1985); Wightman, *Roman Trier*. Cf. MP.122.

514 Tac. *Hist.* IV, 62.

515 *pergere ad Treviros et externae fidei comitti*: 'They [Agrippina, the wife of Germanicus, and her entourage] make for the Treveri [fleeing from the mutinous legionaries] and commend themselves into the protection of foreigners': Tac. *Ann.* I, 41.

516 Paul Hensel comments on this: 'just as whether or not the Chinese have molar teeth'. The Porta Nigra probably dates from the late second century AD: E. Gose et al., *Die Porta Nigra in Trier* (1968), p. 58.

517 Zos. III, 7.2.

518 F. Hettner, 'Die Neumagener Monumente', *Rheinisches Museum* 36, (1881), pp. 435ff.

519 On the following, see Mommsen, *RG* V, ch. II, pp. 57ff.; MP. 124ff.; *ANRW* II 3 (1975), pp. 428ff.

520 *Mon. Anc.*; Hor. *Ep.* I, 18.55; Suet. *Aug.* 20; 85,1; Dio LIII, 22; 25.

521 Tac. *Hist.* IV, 68: *Sexta ex Hispania accitae*. E. Ritterling, 'legio', *RE* XII (1925), p. 1680, takes a different view on the *Decima Gemina*.

522 Tac. *Hist.* II, 11; III, 22; Dio LV, 24.2.

523 The dual name is ancient: Zon. IX, 8 (from Dio).

524 H. Kiepert, *Lehrbuch der Alten Geographie* (1878), p. 483. Mommsen does not comment on Celtic civilization in Spain in *RG* V.

525 German 'Castell' (e.g. Bernkastel) from Latin *castellum*, a fort.

526 Carthago Nova was founded in 221 BC by Hasdrubal: Diodorus XXV, 12; Polybius II, 13.1.

527 Shekels from Carthago Nova bearing the portrait of Hannibal displayed the head of Scipio after 209: E.S.G. Robinson, 'Punic Coins . . . ', in: *Essays in Roman Coinage, presented to Harold Mattingly* (1956), pp. 34ff. Mommsen was probably thinking of the pieces from the Berlin collection, published by Dressel.

528 Strabo III, 15.

529 Pliny *NH* III, 3ff.

530 J. M. Roldan-Hervas, *Hispania y el ejercito romano* (1974).

531 Cic. *pro Archia*, 26.

532 *L. Annaeus Seneca Cordubensis*: Jerome *Chron.* on AD 66; see MH.I, 187ff.

533 Jerome *Chron.* on AD 63: *M.Annaeus Lucanus Cordubensis poeta*.

534 From Tingenterae: Mela II, 96.

535 Jerome *Chron.* on AD 88: *Quintilianus ex Hispania Calagurritanus primus Romae publicam scholam et salarium e fisco accepit et claruit.*

536 Jerome *Chron.* on AD 68.

537 The native towns of Horace and Virgil.

538 Aur.Vict., 13.1.

539 Gellius *NA* XVI, 13.4.

540 On the following see Mommsen, *RG* V, ch. XIII, pp. 620ff.; MP. 132ff.; ANRW II, 10.2 (1982).

541 Dio LIII, 26.2.

542 Cleopatra Selene: Dio LI, 15.6.

543 Plut. *Ant.* 87; Suet. *Aug.* 17.

544 Dio LIX, 25.1.

545 As governor of Algeria between 1840 and 1847, Bugeaud (1784–1849) imposed French control over the Atlas mountains. During Mommsen's short stay in Paris in September 1844, he was particularly impressed by a triumphal procession celebrating Bugeaud's victory.

546 Tac. *Ann.* II, 52; III, 20f.; IV, 13, 23ff. A. Gutsfeld, *Römische Herrschaft und einheimischer Widerstand in Nordafrika* (1989).

547 *ILS* 2487; see Mommsen's commentary in *CIL* VIII, p. XXI, note 4. The passage *quod nostra memoria bis non tantum mutastis castra sed et nova fecistis* probably means: 'since in my memory you have changed camp twice, and even established a new one'. S. Gsell, *Inscriptions latins de l'Algérie* I (1922); II (1957).

548 Should presumably read 'Afri'.

549 The *corpora* are listed by W. Huss, *Geschichte der Karthager* (1985), p. 554.

550 Augustine *Ep.* 17.2; 66.2; 108.5; Jerome *PL* 26.382.

551 SHA, Sept., 15.7.

552 Augustine (*Ep.*, 17.2; 108.5) documents the existence of Punic books, presumably translations of the Psalms. The language is later mentioned by Proc, *Bell. Vand.* II, 10.20.

553 *ILS* III, p. 698 s.v. 'Sufetes' (= Hebrew *Shofetim*, 'judges') were the equivalent of *duumviri* ('mayors').

554 J. Geffcken, *Der Ausgang des griechisch–römischen Heidentums* (1929), pp. 184f.

555 P. Rancillac, 'L'Insuccès du mithraicisme en Afrique', *Bulletin Trimestriel des Antiquités . . . d'Oran* 52 (1931), pp. 221ff.

556 Fronto, *epistulae ad amicos* I, 3.5.

557 Apuleius was born in Madaura and brought up in Carthage: Apul. *Flor.* 18/86; 20/97f.; *Apol.* 24; *Metam.* XI, 27.9; Augustine *Ep.* 102.32.

558 Recent research has concluded from quotations of the Bible in Tertullian and Cyprian that the earliest translations of biblical texts into Latin did in fact originate in North Africa; see MH.II, 216ff.

559 Mommsen, *Ges. Schr.* VIII, pp. 395ff.

560 These have not yet been compiled into a single corpus: see A.G. Woodhead, *The Study of Greek Inscriptions* (1967), p. 98.

561 H. von Soden, *Das lateinische Neues Testament in Afrika zur Zeit Cyprians* (1909); D. de Bruyne, 'Saint Augustin reviseur de la Bible', *Miscell. Agost.* 2 (1931), pp. 521ff.

562 This should be *Caecilius Natalis.* The priority dispute between Tertullian's *Apologeticum* and Minucius's *Octavius* has been resolved in favour of the former: B. Axelson, *Das Prioritätsproblem Tertullian/Minucius Felix* (1941).

563 Sc. Latin writer. Minucius Felix was a layman, Tertullian a priest.

564 See MH.III, 3.

565 MP.146f. has the note: 'Augustine an African through and through', which differs from Mommsen, *RG* V, p. 659.

566 On the following, see Mommsen, *RG* V, ch. VI, pp. 178ff. Cf. MP. 147ff. Pernice gives the date as 1 July 1883. *ANRW* II 6, (1977); A. Mocsy, *Pannonia and Upper Moesia* (Eng. trans. 1974); J. Wilkes, *The Illyrians* (1992).

567 The Seduni inhabited the area of the upper Rhône valley; the Eburodunum Mommsen refers to here (there are several places of this name) is Yverdon on Lake Neuchâtel.

568 Livy V, 33; Justin's *Epitome of Trogus*, XX, 5,9. H. Nissen, *Italische Landeskunde* I (1883), pp. 483ff.

569 For example in the Val Camonica: R. Heuberger, *Rätien* (1932).

570 *ILS* 6708 names a *pontifex sacrorum Raeticorum.*

571 Mommsen is probably thinking of Ladino, spoken in the Dolomites, and Furlanic in Friauli.

572 Vell. II, 109 describes Carnuntum as situated in *Noricum regnum.* See G. Alföldy, *Noricum* (1974), p. 57.

573 Tac. *Ann.* I, 46f., 52; XV, 25f.

574 The name suggests that it belonged to the Indo-European group of languages. See R. Katicic in G. Neumann and J. Untermann (eds), *Die Sprachen im römischen Reich der Kaiserzeit* (1974/80), pp. 103ff.

575 Pliny *NH.* III, 146.

576 M. Todd, *The Early Germans* (1992); P. Heather, *Goths and Romans 332–489* (1991).

577 Boiohaemum (in German *Böheim*, later *Böhmen* – 'home of the Boii'): Vell. II, 109. Mommsen, *RG* V, pp. 34ff.

578 Catualda was a Marcoman who had taken refuge with the *Gotones*: Tac. *Ann.* II, 62f. Schmidt 1938, p. 157.

579 Tac. *Ann.* XII, 29f.

580 Dio LXVII, 7.1ff.; *ILS* 9200 from Baalbek.

581 *Mon. Anc.* 30.

582 *CIL* III, 3831ff. from Colonia Iulia Emona.

583 *CIL* III, 4712ff.

584 Flavia Solva: *ILS* 2734.

585 H. Stiglitz et al., *ANRW* II 6 (1977), pp. 583ff.

586 Vell. II, 109.5.

587 O. Hirschfeld, *Archäol.-epigr. Mitteilungen aus Österreich* 5 (1881), pp. 208ff. Cf. *Kleine Schriften* pp. 968ff.

588 Hensel's text reads 'Vespasian'.

589 Suet. *Dom.* 6.1. B. W. Jones, *The Emperor Domitian* (1992), ch. 6.

590 *ANRW* II 6 (1977), pp. 849ff.

591 Hensel continues: 'whose name, however, Mommsen mumbled so indistinctly that the

gentleman unfortunately remained unknown to me throughout all the lectures'. Mommsen was probably referring to Diegis (Dio LXVII, 7.3) or Vezinas (10.2).

592 Mommsen, *RG* V, p. 201.

593 Should read: Dio LXVII, 10. This victory fell into the period around AD 89. The passage in the *Histories* has been lost.

594 Dio LXVII, 7.3.

595 Ibid., 7.4.

596 *CIL* III, 1699, p. 269 = *ILS* 5863 on the Iron Gate. Trajan mentions work to remove rocks and fill gullies; cf. *AE* 1973, pp. 474f.

597 Dio LXVIII, 8ff.; Mommsen, *RG* V, pp. 202ff.

598 Dio LXVIII, 14.

599 *CIL* III, 1260ff.

600 He took his own life: Dio LXVIII, 14.3. M. Speidel, 'The Captor of Decebalus', *JRS* 60 (1970), pp. 142ff.

601 Representations of the spiral relief in Coarelli 1974, pp. 118ff.; L. Rossi, *Trajan's Column and the Dacian Wars* (1971); C. Cichorius, *Die Reliefs der Trajanssäule* III (1900). Y. Le Bohac, *The Imperial Roman Army* (Engl. trans. 1994), fig.14.

602 Eutrop. VIII, 6.

603 This is obscure. There is no known city by the name of Metropolis in Dacia. Mommsen already knew in 1873 (*CIL* III, pp. 160 and 228ff.) that the capital was Sarmizegethusa. (However, see MH.II, 239, where Mommsen refers to Trajan calling Sarmizegethusa 'Metropolis'.)

604 Cf. MP. 161. For evidence that there is no continuity between modern Romanian and the Latin spoken in Dacia (a view unacceptable to any Romanian regime), see A. Du Noy (pseud.), *The Early History of the Rumanian Language* (1977).

605 O. Fiebiger and L. Schmidt, *Inschriften zur Geschichte der Ostgermanen* (1917), nos. 1 and 3.

606 SHA, *Pius* 9.9.

607 K. Golenko, 'Pontus und Paphlagonien', *Chiron* 3 (1973), pp. 467ff.

608 Paus. X. 34.5.

609 The expression on the faces of the dying.

610 *CIL* III, 1627.

611 Pliny *NH* IV, 25.

612 Ptol. *Geogr.* III, 8.9; VIII, 11.4; *ILS*. III, p. 647, see below. W. Schindler, 'Et caput eius pertulisset ei Ranisstoro. Zur Königsstadt der Daker – eine Vermutung', *Klio* 63 (1981), pp. 551ff.

613 AW.286 has: 'in the region of Galt'. Hensel writes: 'somewhere else (where? says the intelligence bureau, – I didn't understand)'.

614 Potaissa (Kluj, Klausenburg) is not in fact on the Marisus (Mariçus).

615 Schmidt 1938, pp. 162ff.; Mommsen, *RG* V, p. 209; MP. 166; *Ges. Schr.* IV, pp. 487ff. Mommsen writes *Markomanen* (i.e. with one 'n' instead of the customary two).

616 This may be deduced from Dio LXXI, 34.5 and 33.4.

617 SHA, *Marcus* 7.5f.; Eutr. VIII, 9.

618 MP.167 states that this collective rule was a 'most imprudent step'.

619 Mommsen means the extant *Meditations* (*De rebus suis, Eis heauton*) of Marcus Aurelius.

620 SHA, *Marcus* 14; *Verus* 9.7; Verus went to the East in 162.

621 Verus was regarded as dissipated: SHA, *Verus*, 9.7. The Emperors left Rome in 166.

622 The text reads 'dual division'.

623 On this (alleged) financial crisis see T. Pekary, 'Die Staatsfinanzen unter M. Aurelius and Commodus', *Historia* 8 (1958), pp. 448ff.

624 SHA, *Marcus* 17.4f.; *Epitome de Caesaribus*, 16,9.

625 SHA, *Marcus* 13.3.

626 SHA, *Marcus* 14; Eutr. VIII, 12f.; Dio LXXI, 3.

627 SHA, *Marcus* 14.1.

628 Dio LXXI, 3, 1a.

629 *ILS* 281.

630 Amm. XXIX, 6.1.

631 SHA, *Marcus* 14.5; Dio LXXI, 3.5.

632 Probably an error on the part of Hensel. Mommsen was speaking of the inscription *ILS*. 1098.

633 Aur.Vict. 16.9; P. von Rohden, *RE* I (1894), 2296f.

634 'Rex Quadis datus': *RIC* III, p. 110, no. 620; p. 155, no. 1059.

635 Dio LXXI, 13.

636 Dio LXXI, 11.2. The Quadi promised to return a further 50,000.

637 Like the Silingians, one of the tribes who made up the Vandals.

638 Later Emperor: SHA, *Pert*. 2.6.

639 Cf. MP.169.

640 *RIC* 3, 172, p. 231 nos. 236–40.

641 Dio LXXI, 13.3f.

642 Dio LXXI, 10.4.

643 Mommsen (cf. *Ges. Schr*. IV, pp. 498ff.) is referring to the rain miracle (Dio LXXI, 8ff.; Tertullian, *Apol*. 5.6) depicted on the Column of Marcus. C. Caprino et al., *La colonna di Marco Aurelio* (1955).

644 SHA, *Marcus* 24.5f.

645 'Unconnected pieces'.

646 Dio LXXI, 15 states 38 stadia (5 miles).

647 Dio LXXI, 16.2.

648 Dio LXXI, 18.

649 SHA, *Avidius Cassius* 7; Dio LXXI, 17; 22ff.

650 Hensel writes: '27 September', AW: '23 December'. According to SHA, *Comm*. 2,4, Commodus was made co-Emperor on 27 November 176, probably at Marcus Aurelius's triumph. On 23 December 176 Commodus celebrated a triumph (SHA, *Comm*. 12,5), probably without Marcus Aurelius. The inscription *ILS*. 374, which derives from the triumphal arch of Commodus, specifies the *tribunicia potestas XXX*, which corresponds to the period from 10 December 175 to 9 December 176.

651 MP.171: the Marcomanni were 'knocking on the door of the succession'.

652 Dio LXXI, 33.4; (Aur. Vict.) *Epitome* 16.12.

653 Dio, loc. cit.; Aur. Vict. 16.14.

654 Herod. I, 6; SHA, *Comm*. 3; Dio LXXII, 1ff.

655 SHA, *Comm*. 13.5.

656 MP.181; Mommsen, *RG* V, p. 228.

657 *ILS* III, p. 466.

658 SHA, *Marcus* 21.6ff.

659 The ordinary masses.

660 Dio LXXI, 19.

661 Aur. Vict. 16.12.

662 SHA, *Marcus* 21.7: 'He made robbers from Dalmatia and Dardania into soldiers.'

663 Ibid.: 'he also purchased German auxiliary troops against the Germans'.

664 Marcus took on 8,000 horsemen: Dio LXXI, 16.2.

665 *ILS* 22ff.

666 Book I of the *Meditations* ends with the sentence: 'among the Quadi on the Gran'.

667 This may be a reference to the undated dedication to Sabazios, *ILS* 4088.

668 W. Goffart, *Caput and Colonate* (1974).

669 Dio LXXI, 21.

670 Legionaries were not permitted to marry until Septimius Severus: Herod. III, 8.5.

671 Cf. MP.184.

672 Dio LIV; Herod. II; SHA, *Pert*; Aur. Vict. 18ff.

673 See n. 138 on MH.I. 36.

674 This is followed in brackets by Hensel's comment '(hint! hint!)'; he took this to be a veiled reference to militarism in contemporary Prussia.

675 SHA, *Sept.* 1.1.

676 SHA, *Max.* 1.5; *Epitome*, 25.

677 Gordian III died in February or March 244; Zos. I, 19.1.

678 Aur. Vict. 27.8; SHA, *Gord.* 30.9.

679 Zos. I, 20f.

680 Zos. I, 21.

681 MP.186: 'The Emperor was, at best, a junior officer setting himself up as a general.'

682 Dio LXXXVI, 16.1.

683 Aur. Vict. 39.26.

684 As Mommsen calls the *Notitia Dignitatum* of the fourth and fifth centuries. Mommsen may have assumed that there was a third-century predecessor.

685 Aur. Vict. 33.34.

686 The purple stripes on the tunic of senators.

687 Cf. MP. 188.

688 *Diplomata militaria: CIL* XVI.

689 This should rather read: 'immediate reason', since elsewhere Mommsen emphasizes inner causes: cf. Wickert IV 1980, p. 342; Demandt 1984, pp. 403ff.

690 *Gotones* are first mentioned by Tacitus in *Germ.*, 43.6; *Ann.*II, 62; *Guttones* by Pliny in *NH* IV, 28/99; XXXVII, 11.1/35 (following Pytheas). Schmidt 1941, pp. 4ff.; 195ff.; Wolfram 1988, pp. 32ff.; Heather, *Goths and Romans.*

691 SHA, *Geta* 6.6.

692 Gaibomarus: Dio LXXVIII, 20.3.

693 Herod. VII, 3.4ff.

694 Herod. VIII, 8.7.

695 *FGrH.* 100,20; cf. F. Millar, 'P. Herennius Dexippus', *JRS* 59 (1969), pp. 12 ff.; SHA, *Balb.* 16,3.

696 Should read: 'the Heruli'; see MH.II, 279.

697 Zos. I, 42.

698 Amm. XXXI, 5,15; Mommsen, *RG* V, p. 221, Note 1.

699 Amm. XXVIII, 1.5.

700 Zos. I, 42.

701 Amm. XXXI, 5.15.

702 AW.299 says the same. However, this should be Peter the Patrician in Constantine Porphyrogenitus, *Excerpta de legationibus*, FHG.IV, p. 186,8.

703 *BMC* 1877 (ed. R. S. Poole), Thrace, p. 40; A. Stein, *Die Legaten von Moesien* (1940), pp. 98ff. The *gentilicium* should be *Julius.*

704 *RIC* IV 3, 61f. on AD 247.

705 Decius fell in 251: Aur. Vict. 29; Lact. *MP* 4; Zos. I, 23. Cf. MP., p. 192.

706 Zos. I, 24; Jordanes, *Get.* 106.

707 SHA, *Gall.* 13.8; Zos. I, 39; John Syncellus 717. Cf. MP. 195.

708 It is not clear where Mommsen gets this from. After 310, Constantine claimed Claudius Gothicus as a true progenitor, not an adoptive one: *Panegyrici Latini* VI, 2.1f.

709 Amm. XXXI, 5.

710 SHA, *Aur.* 39.7.

711 Zos. I, 71.1; SHA, *Prob.* 18.1.

712 Amm. XXVIII, 1.5 claims they were brought to Pannonia.

713 This is the titulature given in the *Edictum de pretiis*: *ILS* 642, where the sequence differs, however.

714 See MH.II, 235.

715 H. D. Kahl, 'Zwischen Aquileja und Salzburg' etc., in H. Wolfram and F. Daim (eds), *Die Völker an der mittleren und unteren Donau im 5. und 6. Jahrhundert* (1980), pp. 33ff.

716 For what follows see Mommsen, *RG* V, pp. 382ff.; MP. 200ff.

717 *ILS* 1018; 2718; 7192.

718 An exception being Berytus (Beirut), 'Colonia Augusta Julia Felix'.

719 Hensel writes 'Parthians' on both occasions, but Mommsen would have said 'Persians': *RG* V, p. 419.

720 See MH.I, 191ff.

721 M.L. Chaumont, *ANRW* II 9 (1976), pp. 71ff.

722 *CIL* III, 6741 (= *ILS* 232), 6742 from the fort of Ziata castle = Harput (Amm. XIX, 6.1). Mommsen, *RG* V, pp. 393ff.

723 Dio LXVI, 19.3.

724 Tac. *Hist.* IV, 51.

725 Suet. *Dom.* 2.2. Hensel adds 'beyond the Caspian Sea', clearly a misunderstanding.

726 This ethnic classification is incorrect; the Alani were related to the Persians.

727 From Harmozika near Tibilisi: Mommsen, *RG* V., p. 395. *ILS*. 394 from Armenia Maior dates from the time of Commodus.

728 Jos. *Bell. Jud.* ; Mommsen, *RG* V., pp. 487ff.

729 Suet. *Vesp.* 8.4.

730 Ibid.

731 *ND*, Or., 38.14; Jos. *Bell. Jud.* VII, 1.

732 *ND*, Or., 38.13.

733 Dio LXVI, 19.3 (= Zon. XI, 18) refers to the recogniton given to a false Nero by Artabanus IV; see MH.II, 288 and n. 723.

734 Pliny *Ep.* X, 74. In fact this letter does not prove any military co-operation between the two monarchies.

735 Mommsen, *RG* V, p. 397, note 2: 'It is not possible to establish satisfactorily the period in which this Parthian king reigned.' R. Frye, *The History of Iran* (1984), p. 360 estimates the date of his death at around AD 105.

736 Dio LXVIII, 29.1.

737 Mommsen revised this assessment in *RG* V (1885), 397ff.:

> Trajan had war against the Parthians forced upon him, he did not seek it; it was Chosroes, not he, who violated the agreement on Armenia. [It would be] unjust to [Trajan] to attribute his conduct in the East to blind lust for conquest.

738 In *RG* V, p. 397 Mommsen used the forms 'Axidares' and 'Parthomasiris'.

739 Dio LXVIII, 17ff.

740 Dio LXVIII, 21.

741 Neither SHA, *Hadr.* 13.8 nor SHA, *Ant. Pius* 9.7 assert that the throne was golden.

742 According to Dio LXVIII, 26 Adiabene was that part of Assyria which lay to the east of the Tigris. Festus *Brev.* 14 lists the new provinces as *Armenia, Mesopotamia, Assyria et Arabia*. So too Mommsen *RG* V., pp. 400; 480.

743 Dio LXVIII, 28.

744 Dio LXVIII, 29.1; cf. 30.1.

745 *RIC* II, p. 239.

746 Dio LXVIII, 31; Amm. XXV, 8.5.

747 MP.207 refers to the *Scheinglorie* (vainglory) of Trajan. Mommsen was also critical of Trajan in previous lectures: Mazzarino I 1974, p. 25, but positive in *RG* V, pp. 397ff.

748 SHA, *Hadr.* 5,3f. (here the king is called *Parthamasiris*); 9,1; Festus *Brev.*, 20. Mommsen, *RG* V., pp. 403ff.

749 Festus, *Brev.*, 20.

750 SHA, *Hadr.* 6,3.

751 John Lydus *De mag.* III, 53.

752 Arrian's *Periplus* has survived in Greek.

753 Arrian's work on the Alani is largely lost. There are Teubners of both texts edited by Roos, *Arrian* II (1968), pp. 103ff. and 129ff.

754 Dio LXIX, 15.

755 Likewise MP. 209.

756 According to SHA, *Pius*, 9.10 this was allegedly a saying of Scipio.

757 Dio LXXI, 2.1; SHA, *Marc.*, 8,6; SHA, *Ver.*, 6.9; Oros. VII, 15,2. Cf. A. Birley, *Marcus Aurelius* (2nd edn 1987), pp. 121ff.

758 SHA, *Marcus* 8.6.

759 SHA, *Verus* 7.1; Festus *Brev.* 21.

760 *ILS* 361; 5864; 6965.

761 SHA, *Marcus* 9.1; SHA, *Verus* 7.1.

762 Dio LXXI, 2.3; Amm. XXIII, 6.24.

763 *ILS* 366; 368; 4052.

764 Actually some 500 kilometres as the crow flies.

765 Dio LXXI, 3.1.

766 Mommsen, *RG* V., p. 409ff.; Birley, *Septimius Severus*, pp. 181ff.

767 Dio LXXV, 2,4.

768 Dio LXXV, 7f.

769 *ILS* III, 286; Festus *Brev* 21.

770 *excusavit et Parthicum nomen ne Parthos lacesseret*: SHA, *Sept.*, 9.11.

771 Dio LXXV, 2.1f.

772 Dio LV, 24.4.

773 Dio LXXV, 3.2.

774 *Orientis firmissimum claustrum*: Amm. XXV, 8.14.

775 AW.312 says 'Latin' legends. On Edessan coinage, cf. F. Millar, *The Roman Near East* (1994), pp. 112f., and generally pp. 471ff.

776 'The Roman coinage does not begin before the time of Macrinus': G. F. Hill, *BMC* 28 (1922), p. cviii.

777 Dio LXXX, 16.2; SHA, Sev., 18,1.

778 Dio LXXV, 3.2 (= Xiph., 304).

779 Dio LXXV, 3.2.

780 Dio LXXV, 9ff.

781 Dio LXXV, 12.3.

782 Dio LXXVII, 12; *ILS*. 857.

783 Dio LXXVIII, 1.1.

784 Dio LXXVII, 21.

785 SHA, *Car.* 7.1.

786 SHA, *Max.* 4.4.

787 Dio LXXVIII, 26.3.

788 'Scattered limbs': cf. Horace, *Satires* I, 4.62.

789 Mommsen, *RG* V, 412ff.; E. Yarshater (ed.), *The Cambridge History of Iran*, 3.2, *The Seleucid, Parthian and Sasanian Periods* (1983).

790 Hensel's preceding remark 'According to the information of our fellow attender' indicated that he was absent from the following lectures (up to MH.II, 342). The 'fellow attender' was Kurt Hensel: MH.II, 327. Kurt Hensel (1861–1941) was Paul's younger brother, later a mathematics professor at Marburg.

791 Dio LXXX, 3; Herod. VI, 2.

792 Herod.VI, 3ff.

793 Hensel continues to write 'Parthians', although the authentic version undoubtedly has 'Persians', as in AW.317 and elsewhere.

794 SHA, *Max.* 14ff.; Aur. Vict. 26f.

795 SHA, *Gord.* 23ff.; Zos. I, 17.2; *ILS* 1330.

796 'Philip the Arab': cf. J. M. York, *Historia* 21 (1972) pp. 321–32.

797 Zos. I, 19.1.

798 According to Zos. I, 23 Gallus betrayed him at the battle of Abrittus against the Goths; cf. Jord. *Get.* 103.

799 Zos. I, 28; Aur. Vict. 31.

800 Jord. *Get.* 104; Jerome. *Chron.* on AD 253.

801 Aur. Vict. 32.3; Zos. I, 30.1.

802 Jerome *Chron.* on AD 259.

803 Zos. I, 33ff.

804 Aur. Vict. 32.5; Zos. I, 36.2; Lact. *De mort.* 5. Cf. MP.225.

805 Cf. Mommsen, *RG* V, pp. 422ff.; MP. 226ff.

806 See MH.II, 50.

807 *Dig.* L, 15.1.

808 Stephanus, p. 498 (ed. Meineke).

809 SHA, *Val.* 4; SHA, *Gall.* 10.1; SHA, *tyr.* 15; *ILS* 8924.

810 As, for example, the title of SHA, *tyr.*

811 Zon. XII, 23.

812 The coins bear the legend *VABALATHVS VCRIMDR*, which Sallet interprets as: *Vir consularis, Romanorum imperator, dux Romanorum*: *RIC* V i, p. 260. See MH.II, 325.

813 Zos. I, 39.2; SHA, *Gall.* 13.1; SHA, *tyr.* 15.5 (name of the murderer); *ILS* 8807.

814 Longinus was previously head of the Academy in Athens: Eus. *Praep. ev.*X, 3,1; SHA, *Aur.*, 30,3. R. Stoneman, *Palmyra and its Empire* (1992).

815 Hensel adds: 'Prox? (without guarantee; recipient to check)'.

816 Hensel invariably writes 'Apollodorus', but the correct reading is in AW.320.

817 On the coins, see *RIC* V, p. 260. Sallet, op. cit., interprets the abbreviation *VC* as *vir clarissimus*, not as *vir consularis*.

818 *OGIS* 647.

819 And reversed: this time the Emperor was in the West.

820 Zos. I, 50ff.; Jerome *Chron.* on AD 274; Eutr. IX, 13; SHA, *Aur.* 22ff.

821 SHA, *Aur.* 31; Zos. I, 60f.

822 J. B. Chabot, *Choix d'inscriptions de Palmyre* (1922), p. 13 dates the last inscription to 271.

823 Hensel writes: 'the'.

824 Here Sebastian Hensel writes: 'Kurt is unsure on this last point.' See note 791.

825 Aur. Vict. 35.7; SHA, *Aur.*, 35.3; Zos. I, 61. In Mommsen's time the Temple of Serapis on the Quirinal hill was mistakenly taken to be Aurelian's Temple of the Sun, which was in fact located below San Silvestro: Coarelli 1974, pp. 220, 233.

826 SHA, *Aur.* 35,3; *ILS* 1243; 1259.

827 On coins: *RIC* V 1, pp. 258f.

828 Hensel comments: 'probably impudent legations, *whatever that may be*' (with the words in italics in English).

829 In addition to reports of death by lightning (Eutr. IX, 18; Aur. Vict. 38; Jerome *Chron.* on AD 284), there is also a tradition that he died from illness (SHA, *Car.*, 8,5ff.). It was Aurelian's son, Numerianus, who was murdered by the prefect (Eutr., Aur. Vict. locc. citt.).

830 Jerome *Chron.* on AD 293 and 298; Eutr. IX, 22f.; Oros. VII, 25,4; 8. Cf. MP.234ff.

831 Mommsen uses the language of oriental fairy-tale (there is no need to correct Hensel's 'all').

832 Jerome *Chron.* on 301/2.; Aur. Vict. 39.35; Eutr. IX, 22ff.

833 The reform of the army was carried out by Diocletian and Constantine: Demandt 1989, p. 255. See MH.III, 21; 131. See R. Tomlin, 'The Army of the Late Empire', in J. S. Wacher (ed.), *The Roman World* (1987).

834 MH.II, 299 refers to him unfavourably.

835 Mommsen is forgetting Septimius Severus here, whom he declares at MH.II, 116f. to have been perhaps one of the most outstanding Emperors; likewise Marcus Aurelius, to whom he pays respect in MH.II, 255; MP. 237ff.

836 MH.II, 295ff. is negative about Trajan.

837 MH.II, 301 is negative about him.

838 Cf. MP.238.

839 Actually Nero.

840 Vitellius was not a Flavian and ruled before them. Galba had also initially made the mistake of refusing to associate himself with the house of the Caesars.

841 SHA, *Hadr*. 23.11.

842 In fact, Hadrian adopted Antoninus on condition that the latter adopt Marcus: Birley, *Marcus Aurelius*, pp. 46ff.

843 SHA, *Hadr*. 24.1.

844 Pius simultaneously adopted Marcus Aurelius: SHA, *Hadr*., 24,1.

845 To be precise, the son he adopted at Hadrian's bidding (SHA, *Pius* 4.5).

846 On the dual principate, cf. MP. 240ff; Kornemann 1930.

847 See MH.II, 242f.; Amm. XXVII, 6.16.

848 Caracalla killed Geta before they entered upon joint rule: Dio LXXVII, 2.3.

849 Germanicus commanded the Rhine army; see MH.I, 93.

850 Except for Titus: Suet. *Titus* 6.1.

851 See MH.III, 10.

852 Herod. IV, 3.5. Caracalla was to obtain the West and Geta the East.

853 Cf. MP.245.

854 Mommsen is thinking of Galerius in relation to Diocletian.

855 Cf.MP.247.

856 See MH.I, 49ff.

857 The 'Juliusturm' was the keep of Spandau castle, which served as imperial Germany's state treasury.

858 On *fideicommissa* (trusts), see A. Borkowski, *Roman Law* (1994), pp. 236–40.

859 Cf. MP.248.

860 See MH.I, 50ff.; II, pp. 76ff.

861 Mommsen may here again be thinking of Musicus Scurranus: *ILS*. 1514; see MH.I, 54; MH.II, 180. Otherwise the *(procuratores) a rationibus* were freedmen: G. Boulvert, *Esclaves et affranchis impériaux* (1970), p. 101; F. Millar, *The Emperor in the Roman World* (1977), ch. 3.

862 Hensel writes '*arcani*'.

863 Hirschfeld 1905, pp. 476ff.

864 According to Suetonius's *Life of Horace*, Augustus offered Horace the *officium epistularum*, but he declined.

865 Tac. *Hist*. I, 58.

866 Hirschfeld 1905, pp. 318ff.; pp. 476ff.

867 See MH.III, 24f.

868 Mommsen probably refers here to the *procuratores ab epistulis, a libellis, a rationibus* and *a cognitionibus*.

869 Mommsen, *Staatsrecht* II, pp. 988ff.; Hirschfeld 1905, pp. 339ff.; J. Crook, *Consilium principis* (1955).

870 Suet. *Aug*. 35; Dio LIII, 21.3ff.

871 Suet. *Tib*. 55.

872 Herod.VI, 1,2; Dio LXXX, 1.

873 Suet. *Titus* 6.1.

874 See MH.I, 61; and MH.II, 353.

875 According to this thesis, the *legati Augusti* and commander-princes, such as Drusus, Tiberius and Germanicus, were not subordinate commanders 'as such'.

876 See MH.II, 58.

877 See MH.II, 58, 62.

878 Cf. MP. 255ff.; Mommsen, *Staatsrecht* II, pp. 848ff.

879 Here Hensel names his source:

> Up to here according to the notes of our fellow attender of the lectures [his second son, Kurt; he continues:]. Digression into the modern situation. In Stieler's *Handatlas*, on the map covering an obscure corner of the interior of Africa, we frequently find written, so

as to fill up a space: 'The valley plains of Basongoland, where sugar cane, bananas, etc. are cultivated, is subject, like Egypt, to annual flooding, when the water rises to a height of sixty feet'; or 'great herds of elephants, rhinoceroses, buffalo, etc'.

I should like to follow this precedent and, on these few empty pages, left over as a consequence of the lecture notes of our fellow attender being somewhat sparser than I had anticipated (in the main he has done his job very well, dear Paul, and deputized for me admirably), add a few notes which, strictly speaking, are not the story of the Roman Empire, but which may yet prove not entirely uninteresting and which will demonstrate, in particular, the colossal progress which civilization has made since that era. I shall give an account of how it came about that I had to be substituted for:

Just as great herds of elephants, rhinoceroses and buffalo rove about in the valley plain of Basongoland, so, too, am I [MH.II, 343] blessed with many children. Two of my daughters, the eldest and the youngest, were staying in Frankenhausen (*Domus Francorum*) at Kyffhäuser (*Kyffidomus*) – one because she needed to recuperate, the other because she wished to improve herself. In the time of the Roman Emperors this region appears to all intents and purposes to have been the domicile of wild boar in the forests; now the tamed pigs there have had houses built for them, where they live in peace and allow the people to do the same.

One day I was seized by a longing to see my daughters and resolved to visit them. In the days of Augustus I should have equipped myself with an imperial postal voucher for the *vehiculatio* and would have travelled to *Domus Francorum* (see above, sheet III on the postal service) from one town to another. Now, in accordance with our advanced civilization, I accomplish this matter far more simply: I went to the local railway station and requested a ticket to *Domus Francorum*: 'That's not on the railway line – never heard of it'. To Rossla (*Equulus*), then: 'Never heard of that either'. To Sangerhausen (*Domus cantorum*, then: 'Never heard of it either'. To Halle, then: 'Yes, we can manage that.' In Halle I obtained a ticket to Sangerhausen, where I arrived at one o'clock in the morning. I desired – since I had a four-hour wait there – to pass the night in a spacious waiting-room, constructed for the comfort of travellers. But, [MH.II, 344] with the wondrous punctuality with which everything on these railways manages to fall into place, it so happened that at the very moment the train pulled in and this building, erected at great expense for the comfort of travellers, was about to be used by such, it was closed, despite much begging and pleading from the travel-weary *viatores*. We were informed that the station at Sangerhausen offered no overnight services, despite the fact that a train arrived there at one o'clock in the morning and another departed at five o'clock in the morning. The intervening period was intended for sleep – by the railway employees. The *viatores* would be so kind as to walk into town; where there were, we were told, excellent guest houses.

And so we spent the night in town and in the morning were given a drink with which our barbaric distant forebears were quite unfamiliar. The name was introduced from Arabia, but it is brewed from some blue-flowered, wayside weed and tastes – of nothing at all. The biscuits provided with it, on the other hand, were undoubtedly left over from the victuals supplied to troops who had fought at the battle of the Teutoburg Forest.

Then, in the bracing morning chill, we set off cheerfully for the station; after all those hours of sitting around we could at least stretch our legs on a jolly stroll. [MH.II, 345] Now, at last, I obtained a ticket to Rossla, where I indeed travelled, being the sole *viator* on the train. After Rossla the route passes across the Kyffhäuser, with the castles, where the Emperor Barbarossa sleeps, waiting to rise again. A few years ago he rubbed his eyes, but fell asleep again.

His loyal Rossla subjects have followed his example and were still all asleep, and there was no *vehiculatio* there. How harmoniously everything works together nowadays on journeys. Two hours later, however, a span, as the *currus* is known in those parts, appeared and wheeled me in less than four hours to *Domus Francorum*.

Well, my daughters were pleased to see me and I was also pleased and took the air with them and ate three times with them in the 'Moor'. Then, however, the Moor had done his work and I could not only walk, but also run [sc. to the lavatory], and I ran all night and the following day and then I departed.

I had grown so used to running, however, that when I arrived at Westend (*Finis occidentalis*) I was still running, but by then had developed a heavy fever, and my beloved *Uxor* [wife] had her work cut out for her to put me back on my feet again. Still, I had the feeling of having been a *viator* of the Middle Ages, a sack of pepper, and the giants of Kyffhäuser had stepped on to me [two pages covered with drawing; MH.II, 348] and pummelled me all over. And so Kurtius was obliged to step into the breach in my stead and described his experiences at the first lecture as follows: in a letter to *Domus Francorum*:

Dear Papa,

And thus I sit in the seat that has so often rejoiced under your weight and am thinking of you and pleased that I have come so early as to be sure of not missing any disturbance made by anyone, even the very tiniest student.

To keep you in the running (if only the dear boy had known how little I needed it!) I will inform you briefly of the main events since your departure: nothing at all has happened to the human race, aside from the fact that we had rissoles and carrots yesterday. In nature, on the other hand, all manner of events have occurred. First thing this morning the thermometer registered 14° 2' 6.23" and the barometer 16 Prussian feet 8" 2'". There were signs of light cirrus cloud in the sky coming from the west. The clock, however, moved forward only a minimum as I arose, since it showed 6.15 a.m. Leaving my bed, a great wave of cold swept over me, making me shudder, but I dressed all the same. The water in my washbasin was billowing gently, the water level standing at about a quarter of a foot, but it was sufficient for superficial washing –. [In the margin: 'end of digression'.]

The door is just opening, the students applauded, but I, horrified, cried: 'Casimir! Casimir!', for Mommsen had transformed himself into Wagner and was lecturing not on Roman Emperors, but a brief outline of public finance!

And why didn't you tell me that Mommsen doesn't lecture in the barracks auditorium? I abandoned my hat and coat, rushed in my natural state out of the door and just caught Mommsen as he began with: 'Gentlemen!' – End of digression: *attacca dal segno*.

880 With consular or praetorian rank, rarely quaestorian: Suet. *Otho* 3.2.
881 Military tribunes in the imperial age had to be demonstrably of equestrian rank. Only *tribuni laticlavii* were senators: A. von Domaszewski, *Die Rangordnung des römischen Heeres*, (1908/67), p. 172.
882 The *praefecti alae* of the imperial period were equestrians: Domaszewski, *Rangordnung*, p. 130; 152.
883 *ILS* 6936: a military tribune called himself *equo publico per Traianum*; cf. *ILS* 2759 dedicated to an *equo publico ornato ab imperatore Commodo*.
884 The urban prefecture was a single appointment: Tac. *Ann.* VI, 11; *Dig.* I, 12. In late antiquity the *vicarius urbis* had a certain monitoring function *vis-à-vis* the *praefectus Urbi*: Amm. XXVII, 1,5ff.
885 There was always only a single *praefectus Aegypti*: *Dig*.I, 17; Tac. *Hist.* I, 11; Strabo XVII, 1.12.
886 *ILS* 2696.
887 See MH.I, 61; MH.II, 341.
888 Who were subordinate to the (pro-)consul.
889 He represented the (pro-)consul, as was already the case under Caesar: *BG.* I, 20f.
890 Dio LV, 10.10.
891 See MH.I, 151ff.
892 He also accomplished this: Suet. *Titus* 6.1.

893 The *annona*: *C.Th.* I, 5.6f.; XI, 1.3 and 15.

894 *CJ* IX, 51.1.

895 The *principes officiorum* were the head officials: SHA, *Marcus* 8.10.

896 *ILS* 2381ff.

897 *ILS* 1360; 1452; 9490.

898 *ILS* 1422.

899 See MH.III, 11.

900 'Master of the Offices'. The first documentary evidence of this office is under Constantine in 320: *C. Th.* XVI, 10,1.

901 On dyarchy see also MP. 261f.; see MH.I, 46ff.; 239; II, 79.

902 Sc. for people of senatorial rank.

903 The *senatus consulta* in *FIRA*. I, pp. 237–300 end in the year AD 178.

904 See MH.I, 49f.; MH.II, 76ff.

905 SHA, *Tac.* 18.5; 19.2.

906 In 397. *ILS* 795; Zos. V, 11. On the trial by the Senate: Symm. *Ep.* IV, 5.

907 Suet. *Aug.* 54; cf. 35.

908 Pliny *Paneg.* 23.1; 62; 64; 76.

909 Exceptions are the imperial visits of Constantius II, Theodosius, Honorius, etc.

910 *CIL* VI, 2028c (Arval documents for 18 March AD 38).

911 Tac. *Hist.* IV, 3; cf.I, 47. Vespasian was chosen as *imperator* by the army on 1 July 69: Tac. *Hist.* II, 79.

912 The Senate granted recognition without being asked to do so: Aur. Vict. 25.2; 31.3.

913 In AD 275: Aur. Vict. 35.9; 36,1; SHA, *Tac.* 4. In AD 238 Pupienus and Balbinus were also elected as Emperors by the Senate: Herod. VII, 10, 3ff.

914 Tac. *Ann.* I, 15. In practice this 'election' was no more than a ratification of candidates proposed by the Emperor: *Laus Pisonis*; Pliny *Paneg.* 51, 1f.; SHA, *Hadr.* 8,4; Tac. *Ann.* I, 14; Vell.II, 124.3; Dio LII, 20; *Dig.* XLII, 1.57. G. Wesenberg, 'praetor', *RE* XXII (1954), 1600f.

915 Dio LIII, 14.

916 Cf. MP.272ff.

917 In fact vice versa: Sardinia became a senatorial province in 27 BC (Dio LIII, 12.4) and an imperial one in AD 6 (LV, 28.1).

918 On the garrison, see Tac. *Ann.* II, 85.4. The anomaly is North Africa: Africa Proconsularis had a whole legion, but was still administered by the Senate. Cf. Y. Le Bohec, *La Troisième Legion Auguste* (1989).

919 In fact it was given back to the Senate: Birley, *Septimius Severus*, p. 86.

920 *ND*, Or., 20, 21; Occ., 18.

921 The Emperor appointed them: *Dig.* XLVIII, 14.

922 His father was a freedman: SHA, *Pert.* 1.1; Marcus Aurelius promoted him to senator: ibid., 2.5.

923 Dio LXXVIII, 11; Herod. IV, 14.2; Aur. Vict. 22.

924 Aur. Vict. 33, 34.

925 See also AW.339 and MH. At all events the legate in the army where the Emperor was currently present may be termed an adjutant.

926 *ILS* 2548; a further example is in *AE* 1930, p. 144. A.R. Birley, *The Fasti of Roman Britain* (1981), pp. 200f.

927 *ILS* 599; *CIL* II, 4102f.

928 'Camp' or 'legionary prefects'. According to AW.339 Mommsen was referring here to 'Willmann's vol.I, p. 101, *Ephemeris epigraphica über die praefecti*, i.e. G. Wilmans, 'De praefecto castrorum et praefecto legionis', *Ephemeris's epigraphica* (1877) pp. 81–105.

929 *ILS* III, 394f.

930 O. Hirschfeld, *Kleine Schriften* II (1913), pp. 646ff.

931 Aur. Vict. 33,34.

932 *CIL* III, 3434 = *ILS* 545.

933 See also *CIL* III, 4289 = *ILS* 3656.

934 After Diocletian: *ILS* 614 (*corrector Italiae*); Laterculus Veronensis in Seeck, *ND*, pp. 247ff.

935 *ND*, Or.I, 51–6; Occ.I, 40–3 with the lemmata.

936 Amm. XXI, 16,2.

937 See MH.III, 12; 42.

938 See MH.III, 22.

939 See MH.III, 11.

940 *ILS* 619; 1347; 2159.

941 John Lydus *De mag.* II, 10.

942 Zos. II, 33.3.

943 MP.275 concludes with the words:

> This epoch is not a pleasant sight. There is scarcely a single great moment in it. Is it worth studying at all . . . ? And yet it is an epoch of immense importance for the . . . historian. Roman history is inextricably linked with the . . . present. And this link with modern history lies in this period of decline before Diocletian. For that it is necessary to deal with the second and third centuries.

A HISTORY OF ROME UNDER THE EMPERORS III

1 A survey of our sources for this period can be found in A. Cameron, *The Later Roman Empire* (1993), ch. 2.

2 Procopius only edited the war histories (*bella*) and the work on Justinian's public works (*aedificia*) in his lifetime, not the *Historia Arcana* (*anecdota*), which is a satire on Justinian and Theodora. See A. Cameron, *Procopius and the Sixth Century* (1985).

3 Ed. by O. Seeck (1876).

4 Ed. by P. Krüger, P. Meyer and T. Mommsen (1904/5). On this, see also Mommsen, *Ges. Schr.* II, pp. 371ff. English translation C. Pharr, *The Theodosian Code* (1952).

5 Persuaded by S. Brandt, Mommsen later disputed the authorship of this work: *Ges. Schr.* VI, pp. 325ff. (in 1897); 559 (in 1893).

6 Mommsen is referring to the following works: L. S. de Tillemont, *Histoire des empereurs* (1690–); E. Gibbon, *History of the Decline and Fall of the Roman Empire* (1776–); G. F. Hertzberg, 'Geschichte des römischen Kaiserreiches', in: W. Oncken (ed.), *Allgemeine Geschichte in Einzeldarstellungen* (1880); J. Burckhardt, *Die Zeit Constantins des Grossen* (1853/80); H. Richter, *Das weströmische Reich, besonders unter den Kaisern Gratian, Valentinian II und Maximus (375–88)* (1865); M. A. von Bethmann Hollweg, *Der germanisch-romanische Civilprozess*, I: *Vom 5–8 Jh. Die Staaten der Völkerwanderung* (1868).

7 Mommsen already regarded Diocletian's state as the true turning point: 'Everything therein is, so to speak, new' (*Abriss*, p. 351).

8 Mommsen is presumably thinking of the adoption of Nero by Claudius to the detriment of Britannicus.

9 Aur. Vict. 33.34; cf. 37.5ff.

10 *Paneg. Lat.* VI (VII), 2.2.

11 *ILS* 669ff.: *Marcus Aurelius Valerius Maxentius*. One later exception was *Gaius Julius Crispus Caesar*: *ILS* 713.

12 Zos. II, 40.3.

13 As a result of his second marriage, to Galla, he became son-in-law of the deceased Valentinian.

14 Constantine died on 22 May 337 and the proclamation of the sons was made on 9 September (*Chron. Min.* I, 235f.).

15 Mommsen is thinking of the proclamation of Jovian and Valentinian: Amm. XXV, 5.3f.; XXVI, 1.

16 In 1866 Mommsen wrote of the dominate (AG, p. 1):

> Although there was no innovation in theory, it did occur in practice. Under the old constitution the Emperor was simply an official, but later, with the advent of state ministers, this changed. (AG, p. 2): Crude military acclamation by the mass of soldiers was replaced by a council of war.

17 Either Hensel or Mommsen is in error here: this should read 'Ponte Sisto'; it refers to inscription *ILS* 771.

18 *Imperator–Caesar–Augustus.*

19 Commodus: *ILS* 397.

20 K. J. Neumann, 'dominus', *RE* V (1903), 1305ff.

21 E. G. Suet. *Aug.* 53,1; id. *Tib.* 27.

22 *Sacratissimus imperator: ILS* 6105; *dominus et deus*: Suet. *Dom.*, 13.

23 *RIC* V i, 299; cf. *ILS* 585; 5687; Aur. Vict. 39.4.

24 *Epitome de Caesaribus*, 39,1: *Graium nomen in Romanum morem convertit.*

25 Aur. Vict. 39.4; John Lydus *De mag.* I, 4.

26 Eutr. IX, 26; Amm. XV, 5.18; Jerome *Chron.* on AD 296.

27 A. Alföldi, *Die monarchische Repräsentation im römischen Kaiserreiche* (1934/70); J. Matthews, *The Roman Empire of Ammianus* (1989), ch. 11.

28 *Epitome de Caesaribus*, 41.14; *Chron. Min.* I, 234.

29 *ND*, Or.I, 1; Occ.I, 1.

30 This was chiefly true of the fifth century.

31 The earliest laws in this collection date from this year; according to O. Seeck, *Die Regesten der Kaiser und Päpste* (1919), p. 159, *C.Th.* XIII, 10.2 dates to AD 311.

32 E.g. *C.Th.* IX, 42.2f.

33 *C.Th.* I, 1.5.

34 I.e. the supplementary laws.

35 Dio XLIII, 46.6.

36 Mommsen, *Ges. Schr.* VI, pp. 324ff.

37 Between Valentinian and Valens: Amm. XXVI, 5.

38 W. Liebenam, *Fasti consulares Imperii Romani* (1909), p. 33.

39 Ibid. p. 40.

40 Claudian XVIIIff. (*In Eutropium*).

41 Mommsen, *Ges. Schr.* VI, pp. 343ff.; 362ff.

42 Cass. *Var.* II, 2f.; VI, 1; IX, 22f.

43 E.g. *secundo*, i.e. in the second year following the consulate of Paulinus.

44 This title of the Emperor was still customary even in late antiquity.

45 Amm. XXVII, 6.16; Eutr. VIII, 9.

46 Lact. *MP* 18.5.

47 As it is designated in the *Notitia Dignitatum.*

48 On the linguistic boundary, see Gerov, in: G. Neumann and J. Untermann (eds), *Die Sprachen im römischen Reich der Kaiserzeit* (1974/80), pp. 147ff.

49 The *Laterculus Veronensis* of approximately 313 names twelve dioceses (but contains thirteen sections). Hensel's list here omits Asia and is very confused about what Pontus consisted of (the list given at MH III.42 is no great improvement). See map 3 on p. 378.

50 Cic. *Fam.* III, 8.4.

51 Sicily, Sardinia and Corsica.

52 Africa, Achaea and Asia.

53 Chastagnol 1960; id., *Les Fastes de la préfecture de Rome au Bas-Empire* (1962).

54 Cf. AG, p. 15: 'These empty titulatures were chiefly used in Byzantine government, as is also the case in our country with its orders, privy councillors, etc.'

55 W. Heil, *Der konstantinische Patriziat* (1966). AG, p. 4: 'The old aristocracy of lineage now became an aristocracy by epistle.'

56 This was the act of 5 July 372 which has come down to us in exerpts: *C.Th.* VI, 7.1; 9.1; 11.1; 14.1 and 22.4 (dated 2 June).

57 O. Hirschfeld, 'Der Rangtitel der römischen Kaiserzeit', in *Kleine Schriften* (1913), pp. 646–81.

58 Mommsen, *Ges. Schr.* VI, pp. 206ff.; R. Grosse, *Römische Militärgeschichte* (1920); Jones 1964, pp. 607ff.; Demandt 1989, pp. 255ff.

59 D. Hoffmann, *Das spätrömische Bewegungsheer*, I (1969), II (1970). R. Tomlin, 'The Army of the Late Empire', in J. S. Wacher (ed..), *The Roman World*, I (1987), pp. 107ff.

60 *Magistri equitum* as against *magistri peditum*: Zos. II, 33.3; John Lydus *Mag.* II, 10.

61 In 1889 Mommsen (*Ges. Schr.* VI, pp. 260ff.) also estimated the 'new legion' of late antiquity at 1,000 men. Grosse, *Römische Militärgeschichte*, pp. 30f.

62 Arrian, *Scripta Minora* (ed. G. Wirth, 1968).

63 The list of legions actually appears in Dio LV, 23.

64 Hensel is clearly confused. The figure of 132 legions is derived from the *Notitia Dignitatum*.

65 Lact. *MP* 7.2.

66 Agath. V, 13.7.

67 Amm. XIX, 2.14.

68 I. C. Orelli, *Inscriptionum Latinarum selectarum amplissima collectio* III (ed. W. Henzen, 1856), no.6686 = *CIL* V, no. 923, = *ILS* 2671. The Praetorians are praised for being *non barbaricae legionis*.

69 Mommsen is probably thinking of Ammianus or Ellebichus, but there were also illiterate men with the rank of general, such as Vetranio: PLRE.I *sub nominibus*.

70 Amm. XX, 4.

71 Merobaudes, Arbogast, Bauto.

72 Zeno was an Isaurian; there were no Armenians on the imperial throne in late antiquity. The majority of Emperors originated from the Danube lands.

73 Ricimer, Gundobad, Odovacar.

74 *ND*, Occ.XLII, 46–70. The peoples involved were Sarmatians and Taifali.

75 Amm. XX, 8,13. *laetos quosdam cis Rhenum editam Germanorum* (should read: *barbarorum*) *progeniem vel* (missing word: *certe*) *ex dediticiis, qui ad nostra desciverunt* (should read: *desciscunt*).

76 'Counts of the household (servants)': *ND*, Or.XV; Occ.XIII.

77 'Master of the Offices': *ND*, Or.XI; Occ.IX.

78 Grosse, *Römische Militärgeschichte*, pp. 138ff.; H.J. Diesner, *RE* Suppl. XI (1968), 1113ff.

79 Amm. XX, 8.13.

80 Proc. *Hist. Arc.* 24.16.

81 Agath. V, 15.2.

82 The reference that follows here ('N.d., 7') must refer to the list of troops in *ND*, Occ.VII, although this neither mentions numerical quotas nor deals with *scholae*.

83 Amm. XX, 2.5.

84 M. Clauss, *Der magister officiorum in der Spätantike* (1981).

85 John Lydus *De mag.* II, 10.

86 *C.Th.* XVI, 10, 1 of AD 321.

87 'Tribune of the Stables': PLRE.I, 1115; Amm. XX, 4.3; XXVIII, 2.10.

88 'Tribunes and Notaries': Amm. XXVII, 5.15; XXVI, 6.1; XXVIII, 6.12.

89 *ND*, Or.XI, 13ff.; Occ.IX, 10ff.

90 The best-known example is Ammianus Marcellinus: PLRE.I, s.n.

91 *ND*, Or.XV; *ND*, Occ.XIII. The *comites domesticorum* here ranked below the *magistri officiorum*, but were not under their orders.

92 *C.Th.*VII, 1.18. *Ripa* = riverbank, *castra* = fortress, *comitatense* = field army. The later designation (after 363: *C.Th.* XII, 1.56) was *limitanei*: *ND*, Occ.XXVI, 12. A.R. Neumann, *RE* Suppl.XII (1968), 876ff.

93 CF. Jones, 1964, pp. 575f.; 641.

94 See MH.III, 2.

95 *ILS* 664.

96 *ND*, Or.XXIX.

97 *ND*, Occ.XXVII.

98 *ND*, Occ.XXXVII.

99 *ND*, Or.XXVIIIff.; Occ.XXXff.

100 The following addendum by Hensel ('Sallet Palmyra. Beginning of Mommsen') refers to Mommsen's contribution to A. von Sallet, *Die Fürsten von Palmyra* (1866), which is retracted by Mommsen in *RG* V, p. 437, note 2.

101 *ILS* 4103.

102 Zos. II, 33.

103 AG, p. 10: 'Civil administration was completely separated from military authority by Aurelian, the founder of this new order.'

104 On the contrary: in 397 Arcadius and Honorius ordered the deportation of anyone who brought a civil action before a military judge: *C.Th.* II, 1.9.

105 In the *Notitia Dignitatum* the provincial *duces* rank behind the generals, but not below them. This indicates that they were subordinate in rank, but not that they were under their orders.

106 Hoffmann, *Das spätrömische Bewegungsheer*. Cf. R. Tomlin, n. 59 above.

107 Aur. Vict. 39,42.

108 Mommsen, *Ges. Schr.* IV, pp. 545ff.; VI, pp. 206ff.; A. Demandt, *RE* Suppl. XII (1970), 553ff.

109 Around 420, according to *ND*.

110 Or *magister utriusque militiae*, first in 370: *ILS* 774.

111 The installing of regional generals in fact can be traced back to Constantius II: A. Demandt, 'magister militum', *RE* Suppl. XII (1970), 569ff.

112 Mommsen presumably means Saturnius (PLRE.I, s.n.), but this office was not secured until 412 onwards: *C.Th.* VII, 17.1; Demandt, *RE* Suppl. XII (1970), pp. 719f.

113 *Dig.* IL, 1.13.

114 SHA, *Alex.* 20 gives only two ranks; comp. SHA, *Hadr.* 18.1; *Pius* 6.11.

115 We may assume from Hensel's following reference to the 'poems of Catullus', that Mommsen spoke at this point of how Catullus travelled to Bithynia in 57 BC as part of the entourage of the propraetor Gaius Memmius.

116 Hensel's text reads '*consules*'.

117 R. Delmaire, *Largesses sacrées et res privata* (1989).

118 O. Hirschfeld (1876/1905), pp. 32ff.

119 Literally 'Privy Councillor for Supreme Expenditure'.

120 *ND*, Or.XIII, 10; Occ.XI, 21ff.; XII, 2.

121 The *fabricae*: Jones 1964, pp. 834ff.

122 London, Trier, Carthage, Rome, Aquileia, Ticinum (Pavia), Siscia, Sardica, Salonica, Heracleia (in Thrace), Cyzicus, Nicomedia, Antioch, Alexandria.

123 Demandt 1989, pp. 341f.

124 *CJ*. IV, 40.1.

125 Holders of this office are listed in PLRE.I, p. 1062.

126 *ND*, Or.XIV, 6.

127 John Lydus, *De mag.* II, 27 and C.J.I, 34 mention a *comes sacri patrimonii*, which is what Mommsen is presumably referring to here. On the *comites* and *curatores* of the administration of the imperial household, cf. Jones 1964 III, pp. 103ff.

128 This assumption, based on Lact. *MP* 7.2, is erroneous; see MH.III, 16f.

129 Mommsen, 'Syrisches Provincialmass und römische Reichskataster', *Hermes* 3 (1869), pp. 429ff. A Latin translation of the codex is available in *FIRA* II, pp. 751ff. (*Leges saeculares*).

130 *C.Th.* XIII, 11.2.

131 *Paneg. Lat.* V/VIII, 11.

132 Hensel's entry which follows here, 'Sidonius *Carm*: XIII 19 capita tu mihi tolle tria', refers to an interpretation of this difficult passage by Mommsen that we can no longer reconstruct.

Sidonius called on the Emperor Majorian to repeal a tax increase, just as Hercules struck off the 'heads' of various monsters.

133 Mommsen is referring to the *cives Romani*. The provincials paid *tributum capitis*; Ulpian, *Dig*. L, 15.3.

134 As were also the landless *plebs urbana*: *C.Th*. XIII, 10.2; see MH.III, 28.

135 The *plebs rustica* provided the *annona* in accordance with the *capitatio*, not draught-cattle.

136 *Dig*. L, 15.3.

137 From Genetiva in the province of Baetica (Spain) derives the *lex coloniae Ursonensis*, a late Republican urban law often quoted by Mommsen: *CIL* II, 5439; *ILS* 6087; *FIRA* I no. 21. Mommsen, *Ges. Schr*. I, pp. 240f.

138 For a definition of their boundaries, cf. Mommsen, *Ges. Schr*. V, pp. 187ff.; Chastagnol 1960, pp. 39f.

139 Lact. *MP* 7.

140 Aur. Vict. 39.32.

141 Amm. XVI, 5.14.

142 Gold originally presented to the Emperor for every five years of his reign (see MH.III, 28): Jones 1964, pp. 431ff.; 871f.

143 Ibid., pp. 61f.

144 Mommsen is presumably alluding to the 13th *Novella* of Valentinian II of 445, from which it emerges that the *annona* of a soldier in Numidia and Mauretania was estimated at 4 gold pieces.

145 K. L. Noethlichs, 'Spätantike Wirtschaftspolitik und Adaeratio', *Historia* 34 (1985), pp. 102ff.; W. Goffart, *Caput and Colonate* (1974), pp. 83ff.

146 A rumour that Rome was to be taxed led to the revolt of Maxentius in 306: Lact. *MP* 26,2f.; the tax imposed on Antioch in 387 led to the outbreak of a major rebellion: G. Downey, *Ancient Antioch* (1963), pp. 187ff.

147 SHA, *Al.Sev*. 32.

148 *C.Th*. XII, 1.72: 'with money he had invested in business'.

149 The Emperor fell back on the crown lands: Zon. XIV, 3.11ff.; Joshua Styl. 31.

150 Jones 1964, pp. 431f.

151 *ND*, Occ.V, 8.

152 *Dig*. L, 16.17; *ND*, Or.XIII, 11; C.J.XI, 7; O. Davis, *Roman Mines in Europe* (1935). These also include the marble quarries (*metalla*).

153 *ILS* 646; *Chron. Min*. I, 148; Jerome *Chron*. on AD 302.

154 AD 303; *Paneg. Lat*. VII, 8.7f.

155 *ND*, Occ.XIX.

156 *C.Th*. VII, 13.15; the first law from Ravenna is dated 6 December 402.

157 *Chron. Min*.I, 239; cf. 234.

158 Suet. *Aug*. 37.

159 Hensel continues:

> Thus far from the notebook of Ludo Hartmann, from whom I learned quite by chance that Mommsen was lecturing. From here onwards my own transcript. It was really nice, though, to go to the lectures in the bracing morning air through the delightful avenue of chestnuts behind the university, and to see the old man walking along with his notes under his arm.

(MH.III, 32 then shows the picture of Mommsen in the chestnut grove.)

160 Mommsen, *Strafrecht*, pp. 65ff.; 80ff.

161 Mommsen, *Strafrecht*, pp. 733ff.

162 Dio LII, 22; *FIRA* II, 577f.; *Dig*. I, 12, 1.4.

163 Chastagnol 1960, pp. 84ff.

164 Senators were not subject to gubernatorial courts in the provinces either: C.J. XII, 1.14.

165 This applies to the principate. In late antiquity an increasing number of senators resided in the

provinces. Up to the time of Theodosius II, however, they required permission from the Emperor to do so: C.J.XII, 1.15 (? AD 434/5).

166 Chastagnol 1960, pp. 93f.

167 *C.Th.* I, 16,1; C.J.VII, 62,32. W. Ensslin, *RE* XXII (1954), 2469.

168 *C.Th.* I, 6,2f.

169 For Mommsen's use of this joke, see p. 537, n. 233.

170 Chastagnol 1960, pp. 225f.

171 *ILS* 722 (dating to between 317 and 337).

172 *ND*, Occ.IV, 4; Chastagnol 1960, pp. 262ff. The urban cohorts made no further appearance in the fourth century.

173 The *legio II Parthica* stationed at Alba disappeared from Italy in 312 (?) (Kubitschek, *RE* XII (1925), 1482) and appeared again in the East after 360: Amm. XX, 7.1; *ND*, Or.XXXVI, 30.

174 Lact. *MP* 26.3.

175 John Lydus *De mag.* II, 10.

176 Aurel.Vict., 39.47.

177 There were *praefecti vigilum* in Rome until well into the late fourth century: *ILS* 765; *CIL* VI, 1157.

178 *ILS* 772.

179 'Prefect of the corn supply': *ND*, Occ.IV, 3; Cass.*Var*.VI, 18.4. On the corn supply see B. Sirks, *Food for Rome* (1991).

180 The officials who 'measured' the grain.

181 *ND*, Occ.IV, 4; *C.Th.* I, 18.

182 *ND*, Occ.IV, 5ff. Chastagnol 1960, pp. 43ff.

183 This form was by no means generally current, as is already evident from the abbreviation PPO used in the *Codex Theodosianus*.

184 W. Ensslin (*RE* XXII), 1954, 2426ff.

185 Tac. *Ann.* VI, 11.2: *Augustus bellis civilibus Cilnium Maecenatem equestris ordinis cunctis apud Romam atque Italiam praeposuit.* Vell. II, 88.2; Dio IL, 16.2; Sen. *Ep.* 114.6.

186 Mommsen wrote in 1866 on the later Roman PPO (AG, p. 15): 'He was not as autonomous or powerful as the good philologists think he was.'

187 AG, p. 2: 'Guards are necessary tools of absolute rule.'

188 In his *Römische Geschichte* Mommsen prefers the less usual German forms *Italiker* ('Italic'), instead of *Italiener* ('Italian') and *italisch*, instead of *italienisch*.

189 After 13 BC the Praetorians served for twelve years, after AD 5–6 for sixteen years; legionaries served four years longer.

190 *ILS* 1321.

191 Dio LII, 24.1; LV, 10.10.

192 E.g. Papinian and Ulpian.

193 Dio LII, 23f.

194 Tac. *Ann.* IV, 1.

195 A positive description of him is in Vell.II, 127f.

196 PLRE.I, 1046 on the years 276, 303 (?) and 310–12.

197 Charisius cites *quosdam scriptores* in these terms: *Dig.* I, 11.

198 SHA, *Marcus* 14.5; Dio LXXI, 3.5; Eutr. VII, 23.4.

199 *ND*, Or.XI, 4ff.; Occ.IX, 4ff.

200 Although he did with the *annona*; see MH.III, 43 and n. 204.

201 Hensel's list here is as confusing as at MH.III. 12; this time Spain is omitted. See map 3.

202 The correct form is: *praefectus Augustalis*; *ND*, Or.XXIII.

203 *ND*, Or.XXII.

204 This refers to the *annona*.

205 Jones 1964, pp. 830ff.

206 Zos. II, 33; the passage is disputed: A. Chastagnol, 'Les Préfets du prétoire de Constantin', *Revue des Etudes Anciennes*, 70 (1968), pp. 321ff.

207 Zos. II, 40.2; W. Heil, *Der konstantinische Patriziat* (1966).

208 Hensel adds in brackets: 'which must have been very sad for the poor man, for I think the *comes* was ambitious'.

209 *ND*, Or.XXII; the *comes Aegypti* (*ND*, Or.XXVIII) and the *comes Isauriae* (*ND*, Or.XXIX) were officers, like the *comites domesticorum*.

210 The majority of decrees pertained to officials.

211 Zos. V, 32.4 ascribes this office to Constantine.

212 *ILS* 1214; on this, cf. T. Mommsen, 'De C. Caeli Saturni titulo', *Nuove Memorie dell'Instituto* 2 (1865), pp. 299ff.

213 P. B. Weiss, *Consistorium und comites consistoriani* (1975).

214 The *comes sacrarum largitionum* and the *comes rerum privatarum*.

215 *C.Th.* XI, 39.5.

216 *ILS* 2949; Johann Caspar Orelli (1787–1849).

217 Rufius Praetextatus Postumianus, consul in 448: *ILS* 1285.

218 Amm. XXVIII, 1.24; *C.Th.* XII, 12; J. Matthews, RAC.X (1978), 653ff; J. Matthews, *The Roman Empire of Ammianus* (1989), ch. 15.

219 This was the father of Pompeius Trogus, a Vocontian. Justin (XLIII, 5.11f.) relates of him: *Trogus ait maiores suos a Vocontiis originem ducere . . . patrem quoque sub Caesare militasse, epistularumque et legationum, simul et anuli curam habuisse.* J. Malitz, 'Die Kanzlei Cäsars', *Historia* 36 (1987), pp. 51ff., on the *cura epistolarum*.

220 Hirschfeld 1905, pp. 321f.

221 *C.Th.* VI, 26; *ND*, (Or.XI, 13ff.; Occ.IX, 10ff.) additionally mention a *scrinium dispositionum*.

222 The provincial and municipal administration in the East used predominantly Greek. The *Notitia Dignitatum* records the presence at court of a *magister epistolarum Graecorum*, adding: *eas epistolas, quae Graece solent emitti aut ipse dictat aut Latine dictatus transfert in Graecum* (*ND*, Or.XIX, 12f.).

223 Seeck VI, 70f.

224 C.J.VII, 62.32.

225 *ND*, Or.Xf.

226 P. Guyot, *Eunuchen als Sklaven und Freigelassene in der griechisch-römischen Antike* (1980); K. Hopkins, *Conquerors and Slaves* (1974), ch. 4.

227 *ND*, Or.XVI; Occ.XIV.

228 *C.Th.* VI, 30.2.

229 *ND*, Or.XVII; Occ.XV.

230 The *paedagogiani* (*C.Th.* VIII, 7.5; Amm. XXVI, 6.15; XXIX, 3.3) were not slaves of the Emperor; Mommsen was presumably thinking of the *paedagogium Palatini* of Domitian's palace: *ILS* 1825ff.

231 Jones 1964, pp. 507ff.

232 Mommsen was evidently thinking of *CIL* VI, 510 = *ILS* 4152, with the career of '*Sextilius Agesilaus vir clarissimus, causarum non ignobilis Africani tribunalis orator et in consistorio principum, item magister libellorum et cognitionum sacrarum, magister epistularum, magister memoriae, vicarius praefectorum per Hispanias vice sacra cognoscens,* etc.' The inscription dates from 13 August 376; on this man, see also Amm. XV, 5.4. Cf. PLRE Aedesius 7.

233 *C.Th.* Novella 2.3 of Valentinian III, AD 443.

234 On the question of continuity in institutions of higher learning, cf. Demandt 1989, p. 373. The institution with the highest degree of continuity is of course the Church.

235 Mommsen is referring to Karl Hegel, *Geschichte der Städteverfassung in Italien*, II (1847).

236 Sebastian Hensel adds the following comment for his son: 'There is still no exhaustive study of this topic so far, which is touched on in a great number of sources. What do you think, Paul?'

237 Hensel writes 'next day', but Mommsen was presumably quoting *Faust* (I, 672) correctly.

238 Aur. Vict. 33.3; Oros.VII, 41.2.

239 Marching song by K.G. Cramer, 1792.

240 *RIC* V 1, pp. 136f.; 141; 162.

241 See MH.II, 321ff.

242 Mommsen was probably thinking of the fact that the *Edictum de pretiis* opened with the price of corn.

243 The Ottoman Empire had been artificially preserved by the Great Powers at the Treaty of Berlin in 1878, although losing Bulgaria, Cyprus and Bosnia; Thessaly was lost to Greece in 1881.

244 This is the older form of 'Geiserich': *C.Th.* 9. Amendment of Valentinian III.

245 Eutr. IX, 15; SHA, *Aur.* 39.7.

246 SHA, *Tac.* 1ff.

247 Aur. Vict. 37.5ff.

248 Aur. Vict. 35.6; *RIC* V, 1248ff.

249 Peter the Patrician, 10.6 = *FHG* IV, 197.

250 The title *Iovius* and the Jupiter temple opposite the mausoleum of Diocletian suggest the contrary.

251 Aur. Vict. 38.3.

252 Aur. Vict. 38.1.

253 SHA, *Num.*, 11.2.

254 Diocletians's *dies imperii* was actually 20 November: Kolb, 1987, p. 10. For a seminal account of Diocletian's chronology, cf. Mommsen, *Ges. Schr.* II, 195ff.

255 Aur. Vict. 39.13.

256 Helvidius Priscus. Cf Suet. *Vesp.* 15; Dio LXV, 12; J. Malitz, 'Helvidius Priscus und Vespasian', *Hermes* 113 (1985), pp. 231ff.

257 This is borne out by his victories over Julianus and Diocletian (see MH.III, 66).

258 *libidine impatiens militarium mulierculas* (Damsté) *affectabat*: Aur. Vict. 39.11.

259 Aur. Vict. 39.9f.

260 *Chron. Min.* I, 229; 445.

261 Mommsen, *Ges. Schr.* II, 267ff. These difficulties are reduced by the redating of the uprising (see MH.III, 64 and n. 254).

262 Diocletian's dates are unclear: T.D. Barnes, *The New Empire of Diocletian and Constantine* (1982), p. 30.

263 *Epitome* 39.1.

264 Lact. *MP* 9.11; 19.5; 52.3; *Epitome* 39.1.

265 Eutr. IX, 19; *Epitome* 39.1.

266 Aur. Vict. 39.1.

267 Ibid.

268 E.g. *MP* 9.7.

269 Mommsen is referring to Galerius.

270 Eutr. IX, 26; Aur. Vict. 39.2ff.; *Chron.* of Jerome on 296; Amm. XV, 5.18.

271 Lactantius (*MP* 7.8) refers to Diocletian's *infinita cupiditas aedificandi*: *Chron. Min.* I, 148.

272 Hensel writes *Polizei*: 'police'.

273 *Paneg. Lat.* IX (IV), 18.4.

274 *ILS* III, 303f.

275 Aur. Vict. 39.25. According to *Anon. Val.*2 and Philostorg. II 16, Theodora was one of Maximian's natural daughters; the marriage may have taken place as early as 289: Barnes, *New Empire* 33; 126.

276 Jerome *Chron.* on 292.

277 *Chron. Min.* I, 229: 1 April 286. The date is uncertain. Kolb (1987, 28ff.) argues in favour of 13 December 285.

278 Aur. Vict. 39.17 (*Diocletianus*) *Maximianum fidum amicitia quamquam semiagrestem, militiae tamen atque ingenio bonum imperatorem iubet*.

279 *Chron. Min.* I, 230.

280 *Institutes* 11.4: *adoptio naturam imitatur*, meaning it was only possible to adopt someone younger.

281 Aur. Vict. (39.26) calls the tetrarchs *satis optimi rei publicae*.

282 Lact. *MP* 30.5.

283 *Epitome* 40.15.

284 He claimed descent from Claudius Gothicus: *Paneg. Lat.* VI (VII), 2.2.

285 According to SHA, *Claud.*, 13.2 they were called Eutropius and Claudia, but these are part of the fictive line of descent tracing back to Claudius Gothicus which Mommsen also refutes.

286 Eutr. X, 1.2; Eus. *VC* I, 14.

287 *Chron. Min.*I, 445; J. F. Drinkwater, 'The Bacaudae of fifth-century Gaul', in: J. Drinkwater and H. Elton (eds), *Fifth-Century Gaul: A Crisis of Identity?* (1992)

288 Salvian (*Gub. Dei* V, 24) translates it as *rebelles*.

289 *Chron. Min.*II, 27.

290 The panegyric Mommsen quotes from (IX [IV] 4.1) gives no dates; cf. however *Paneg. Lat.*V (VIII), 4.2.

291 Eutr. IX, 20; Aur. Vict. 39.17.

292 Only the coins bearing the name Aelianus are questionable, not those bearing that of Amandus: *RIC* V 2, p. 595.

293 Ptol. II, 11.7 and 9; Wenskus 1961, pp. 541ff.; see MH.II, 156.

294 Julian 34D; Amm. XXVII, 8.5; XXVIII, 5.1ff.; *ND*, Occ. XXVIII.

295 Pliny *NH* IV 14/99.

296 Amm. XXVIII, 5.9ff.

297 Dio LXXVIII, 13.4ff.; H. Steuer, 'Alemannen', in: J. Hoops (ed.), *Reallexikon der germanischen Altertumskunde* I, (2nd edn 1973), pp. 137ff.

298 Agath. I, 6.3.

299 Aur. Vict. 21.2: *gens populosa ex equo mirifice pugnans*.

300 Wenskus 1961, p. 513.

301 If Mommsen is referring here to the 'Tabula Peutingeriana', this refers to the land on the right bank of the lower Rhine as 'Francia', although most of this map dates from the late fourth century. The first definite mention of the Franks is regarded as being Aurelius Victor, 33.3, which refers to an invasion led by Gallienus.

302 Mommsen *RG* V, 149ff.; Stein, *RE* III (1899), 1656ff.

303 Jul. 280B.

304 Official rankings derive from commission and are therefore unclear: PLRE I, s.v.

305 'Archpirate': *Paneg. Lat.* VIII (V), 12.2.

306 Hensel writes 'Chatti 295', but this is unsubstantiated: L. Schmidt, *Die Westgermanen*, 2nd edn II 1, (1940), pp. 139f. Diocletian's 285 victory title 'Germanicus maximus' (*ILS* 615) could refer to a victory over Alamanni on the Danube: Schmidt, loc. cit., p. 24; cf. Mommsen, *Ges. Schr.* II, p. 267.

307 *Chron. Min.* I, 230.

308 *Paneg. Lat.* VIII (V) 3.1. The speech was given in 296.

309 Eutr. IX, 22.

310 As also in *Chron. Min.* I, 445. See P. J. Casey, *Carausius and Allectus* (1994), ch. 3.

311 *Paneg. Lat.* VIII (V), 2.1.

312 Eutr. IX, 22f.

313 Aur. Vict. 39.40.

314 This is doubtful: according to Aur. Vict. 39.41 he administered the *summa res*, i.e. Carausius's finances.

315 *Paneg. Lat.* VIII (V), 12.1.

316 *Paneg. Lat.* VIII (V), 11ff. Aur. Vict. 39.40ff.; Eutr. IX, 22.

317 *Paneg. Lat.* VIII (V), 21.2.

318 Eutr. IX, 23. Jerome *Chron.* on 300 AD.

319 *Paneg. Lat.* VIII (V), 2.1 (dated 296).

320 Mommsen infers this from the reference to a *Danubii transitus Guntiensis*: loc.cit.

321 See MH.III, 115.

322 *Paneg. Lat.* VI (VII), 7.2; *Anon. Vales.* 4.

323 Rutupia (Richborough), where tens of thousands of coins dating from the period around 400 have recently come to light, was more important: A.S. Edmonde Cleary, *The Ending of Roman Britain* (1989), 143. On troop deployments: *ND, Occ.* XXVII.

324 *Paneg. Lat.* IX (IV), 18.4.

325 *Chron. Min.* I, 230.

326 On the Rhine bridge at Deutz and the bank fortifications see: *Paneg. Lat.* VI (VII), 11ff.; 18.1; Lact. *MP* 29.3; *ILS* 8937.

327 The Sarmatians are nowadays thought to have been nomads of Iranian origin, like the Alani and Roxolani.

328 Euseb. *Vita Constantini* IV, 6; Amm. XVII, 12f.

329 In the preamble to the Great Price Edict: *ILS* 642.

330 *Paneg. Lat.* VIII (V), 10.4. The Quadi reappeared frequently in later sources, e.g. in Ammianus Marcellinus, Jerome and Paul the Deacon.

331 Eus. *VC; ND, Occ.* XLII, 46ff.

332 Amm. XIX, 11.4.

333 The morphology varies: '*Quinquegentiani*' in Eutr. IX, 22; '*Quinquegentanei*' in *CIL* VIII, 8924. Mommsen appears to reject the translation of this as a 'confederation of five tribes'.

334 *ILS* 628 celebrates the victory of Aurelius Litua, around 292, over the *Barbari Transtagnenses* (from *stagnum*, 'swamp').

335 Presumably the Kabyle of the Rif Mountains in Algeria.

336 Victor of Vita I, 2; Procopius I, 5.18.

337 Strabo XVII, 1.19.

338 Dio LXXI, 4; SHA, *Marc.* 21.1; SHA, *Cass.* 6.7. Instead of 'already', as in MH, read 'still'.

339 Hensel adds: 'as described in Volume V of Mommsen's *History* (Chapter 9)'.

340 Hensel's text reads 'Numidian'.

341 The sacrificing of children had been banned by Hadrian (Porphyrius, *de Abstinentia* II, 5.6; Tertullian, *Apol.*, 9.2). There is no evidence of cannibalism among either Numidians or Nabataeans.

342 Amm. XXII, 16.23.

343 Aurelius Achilleus, known from papyri (F. Preisigke, *Sammelbuch Griechischer Urkunden aus Ägypten*, VI (1958), no. 9167), Eutr. (IX, 22f.) and Jerome (*Chron.* on 298), should not be confused with Domitius Domitianus. Coins: *RIC* VI, 645ff.; F. Kolb, *EOS* 76 (1989), pp. 325ff.

344 Jerome *Chron.* on 293. J. Schwartz, *L. Domitius Domitianus* (1975).

345 Hensel begins this paragraph with the words: 'Conditions in Persia are dealt with in detail in Volume V of Mommsen's *History of Rome* (Chapter 9).'

346 Festus 25; R.C. Blockley, *East Roman Foreign Policy* (1992); T. Barnes, 'Imperial Campaigns A.D. 285–311', *Phoenix* 30, 1976, pp. 174ff., 182ff.

347 Valerian was defeated and taken prisoner in 259: Lact. *MP* 5; Aur. Vict. 32.5; Zos. I., 36.2.

348 *Paneg. Lat.* X (II) of 289 and XI (III) of 291 deal among other matters with the situation in the East.

349 Amm. XXIII, 5.11.

350 Festus 25; Aur. Vict. 39.34; Eutr. IX, 24.

351 Aur. Vict. 39.35f.; Eutr. IX, 24f.

352 Caucasian Iberians.

353 The monetary system of late antiquity is disputed in numerous respects: K.T. Erim (et al.), 'Diocletian's Currency Reform', *JRS* 61 (1971), pp. 171ff.; M. Hendy, 'Mint and Fiscal Administration under Diocletian, his Colleagues and his Successors, AD 305 – 24', *JRS* 62 (1972), pp. 75ff.

354 Hensel writes: 'Dissong'. A. Missong, *Numismatische Zeitschrift* I (1869), pp. 5ff.

355 Aur. Vict. 35.6.

356 M. Bernhart, *Handbuch zur Münzkunde der römischen Kaiserzeit* (1926), pp. 19f., states otherwise,

asserting that Diocletian experimented until 303 and that the coin weight established at that time was minted by Maxentius until 312 and by Lucinius until 324.

357 Ibid., p. 22.

358 Hensel writes: 'Christophorus'; *cistophori* are tetradrachmas of Asia Minor, minted from about 170 BC, bearing the image of a *cista mystica* and snakes from the cult of Dionysus. Cf. MH.II 26.

359 The new gold piece of Constantine began in 312: Bernhart, loc. cit., p. 70.

360 *OB* is also understood as an abbreviation for *obryziacum* – pure gold: Bernhart, loc. cit. This abbreviation begins in the time of Valentinian I: loc. cit.

361 For the best commentary on this, see: H. Blümner and T. Mommsen, *Der Maximaltarif des Diocletian* (1893); best bibliography: S. Lauffer, *Diokletians Preisedikt* (1971); best text: M. Giacchero, *Edictum Diocletiani* (1974). On prevailing circumstances: T.D. Barnes, *Constantine and Eusebius* (1981), pp. 10f; M.H. Crawford and J. Reynolds, *JRS* 65 (1975), pp. 160ff.: S. Williams, *Diocletian and the Roman Recovery* (1985), ch. 10. Cf. Mommsen, *Ges. Schr.* II, pp. 292ff.

362 *ILS* 642; *Chron. Min.* I, 230 on 302: *vilitatem iusserunt inperatores esse.*

363 M. Giacchero, in her edition of the *Edictum Diocletiani* (I, 1974), gives the subsequently discovered price of a camp shekel of corn as 100 'reckoning *denarii*' (*ED* I, 1).

364 In the East it was published on stone inscriptions, in the West on bronze tablets.

365 Lact. *MP* 7.7.

366 Nicomedia: Lact. *MP* 7.11f.; *ILS* 613; thermal baths: *ILS* 646.

367 The same applies to Mommsen's second apparently unesteemed source, Eusebius's *History of the Church* (*HE* VIII).

368 Jerome *vir.ill.*, 80.

369 Goethe, *Faust* I (1833).

370 Lact. *MP* 11f.; Eusebius *HE*. VIII; Jerome *Chron.* on AD 301; *Chron. Min.* I, 231 on AD 303; Oros. VII, 25.13ff. Mommsen, *Ges. Schr.* III, 389ff.; VI, 540ff.

371 This assertion is directed against Burckhardt 1853/1880, pp. 287ff.

372 R. Merkelbach, *Mithras* (1984); R.L. Gordon, 'Authority, Salvation and Mystery', in J. Huskinson et al. (eds), *The Mysteries of Mithraism* (1988).

373 *CIL* I, 2nd edn p. 278 on 25 December: *n(atalis) Invicti*. The term used for 25 December in Polemius Silvius's calendar of 448/9 AD is *natalis domini corporalis* (loc. cit., p. 279).

374 Eutr. IX, 15; SHA, *Aur.* 1.3.

375 Hensel adds the comment:, '24 June Lili's birthday. *Quod felix, faustum, fortunatumque sit!*' This refers to Paul's sister, Sebastian Hensel's daughter Lili, known as Pi, born in 1864 (information kindly given by her niece, Dr Cécile Lowenthal-Hensel, Berlin).

376 *ILS* 1615; III, p. 545.

377 *ILS* 2299.

378 *ILS* 1259f.

379 *ILS* III, p. 577.

380 Mommsen is referring here to provincial synods (Elvira around 306, *Arelate* in 314, etc.). Imperial councils had been a matter for the Emperor from the very outset, since the Council of Nicaea in 325.

381 *FIRA* II, pp. 558ff.

382 *FIRA* II, p. 580f.

383 Lact. *MP* 10.

384 Lact. *MP* 12.1: *Terminalia, quae sunt ante diem septimum Kalendas Martias*: 23 February.

385 Hensel writes: 'Maxentius'.

386 Eus.*HE*. VIII, 13.12f.

387 *Paneg. Lat.* VII (VI), 8.7f.; *Chron. Min.* I, 148.

388 *Zonaras* XII, 32.

389 The last triumph was celebrated by Maxentius over Africa in 311: Zos. II, 14.4.

390 *Paneg. Lat.* VII (VI), 8.8; Lact. *MP* 12.

391 Hensel adds: 'Diocletian, you were so right!'
392 Seeck I, pp. 1ff. Barnes, *Constantine and Eusebius*, 26; S. Williams, *Diocletian and the Roman Recovery* (1985), Ch. 15.
393 Lact. *MP* 18.5.
394 Lact. *MP* 19.1.; Zon. XII, 32. Regarding the date, cf. *ILS* 4145 compared to the erroneous *Chron. Min.* I, 231: 1 April.
395 Lact. *MP* 19; Zon. XII, 32. Maximian went to Lucania.
396 The succession traces back to Diocletian himself. Severus became Caesar in the West, and Maximinus Daia in the East: Lact. *MP* 19; *Chron. Min.* I, 231; *Anon. Val.* 5.
397 Constantine's mother was Helena, a Bithynian stable girl: Ambros. *De Obitu Theod.* 42; Oros. VII, 25.16.
398 In fact it was Nicomedia.
399 I.e. recognizing him as such.
400 This did not occur until 308 at the Emperors' conference of Carnuntum: *Chron. Min.* I, 231; Lact. *MP* 29.2; 32.1; see MH.III, 116.
401 In fact Nicomedia.
402 Accounts vary: Lact. *MP* 24; Eus. *VC* I, 20; *Anon. Val.* 2ff.; Zos. II, 8.2.
403 See MH.III, 88.
404 Maxentius declared himself *imperator* on 28 October 306: Lact. *MP* 26.1; 44.4; *Anon. Val.*, 6. At first he only titled himself *princeps*, adding the title of Augustus after 307: *RIC* VI, pp. 367ff.; *ILS* 669ff.
405 Lact. *MP* 26.7ff.
406 Zos. II, 12; Aur. Vict. 40.17ff.
407 *Anon. Val.*, 9f.; Lact. *MP* 26.5ff.
408 *Anon. Val.*, 10; Lact. *MP* 27.
409 This Emperors' conference is nowadays dated at 308: *Chron. Min.* I, 231. Inscription: *ILS* 659.
410 *Oros.* VII, 28.11; *Chron. Min.* I, 231; Zon. XII, 34.
411 *Zosimos* II, 11.1; Lact. *MP* 32.1; Eutr. X., 4.
412 Licinius became Augustus without having been Caesar first.
413 Lact. *MP* 32.5
414 Hensel uses the phrase *imperator in partibus*; for Mommsen's references to titular bishops; see n. 59, p. 524/5.
415 *Anon. Val.*, Ps. Aur. Vict. Epitome 41.4; Lact. *MP* 43.2; 45.1
416 Lact. *MP* 28.3f.; Eutr. X, 3; Oros. VII, 28.9.
417 Lact. *MP* 30 refers to suicide. The year 310: *Chron. Min.* I, 231.
418 Lact. *MP* 35; *Eus.HE.* IX. 1014f.; *Chron. Min.* I, 148; 231.
419 Lact. *MP* 34 gives an incomplete version of the Latin text; a complete Greek translation is given in Eus. *HE* VIII, 17.
420 It was followed by the interdicts of Maximinus Daia: Lact. *MP* 46.
421 Lact. *MP* 44.1.
422 Lact. *MP* 43.4.
423 There was a dispute between them over the territory of Galerius, which now stood between them, without a ruler: Lact. *MP* 36.1. Cf. MH.III, 124.
424 Lact. *MP* 43.3f.
425 Lact. *MP* 44.3.
426 *Paneg. Lat* IV (X), 19ff.; XII (IX), 5ff.; Eus. *VC* I, 26ff.; *Anon. Val.*, 12; Aur. Vict. 41.20ff.
427 The fresco in the Sala di Costantino in the Vatican, 5 by 11 metres, conceived by Raphael (died 1520) and executed by his pupil Guilio Romano from 1520–4.
428 Lact. *MP* 44.3.
429 *Chron. Min.* I, 148.
430 Cf. MH.III, 35f.
431 Error: cf. MH.III, 36.
432 Lact. *MP* 44.11.

433 Cf. MH.III, 144ff.

434 Lact. *MP* 36.1; cf. MH.III, 120.

435 Lact. *MP* 46f.

436 Lact. *MP* 45.1; Eus. *VC* I, 50.

437 Lact. *MP* 48.

438 Eus. *HE* IX. H. Castritius, *Studien zu Maximinus Daia* (1969).

439 Eus. *HE* X, 8; Eutr. X, 5; Zos. II, 18. The battle can probably be dated 316: T. D. Barnes, 'Lactantius and Constantine', *JRS*, 63 (1973), pp. 29ff., 36. Cf. Aur. Vict. 41.2.

440 Zos. II, 20.1; *Anon. Val.* 18.

441 *Chron. Min.* I, 232; *Anon. Val.*, 19.

442 *Anon. Val.*, 21.

443 *Anon. Val.*, 20ff.; Jordanes *Get.* 111; *Chron. Min.* 232; Eutr. X., 6: *(Licinius) contra religionem sacramenti Thessalonicae privatus occisus est.*

444 Julian *Caesares* 315ff.

445 Cf. MH.III, 133.

446 Cf. MH.III, 135.

447 On the Germanic wars: Schmidt 1940, pp. 28f.

448 Optat. *Porf.* V, 30; X, 24; XVIII, 8.

449 Eus. *VC* IV, 5f.; *Anon. Val.* 31; *Chron. Min.* I, 234.

450 *Anon. Val.*, 31; *Chron. Min.* I, 234; Wolfram 1980, pp. 64f.

451 Jul. 329A.

452 Agathias IV, 25.4.

453 Eus. *VC* IV, 56ff.; *Anon. Val.*, 35.

454 Mommsen is thinking ahead to Eusebius of Caesarea.

455 Eutr. X, 7 on Constantine: *Vir primo imperii tempore optimis princibus, ultimo mediis comparandus.*

456 The year of Constantine's birth is highly uncertain: PLRE. I, 223 estimates it at 272. According to the *Anonymus Valesianus* (3) he was *iuvenis* in 306.

457 Only Crispus was born to a concubine, Minervina; all other children were legitimate, including Constantine II; Demandt 1989, p. 70.

458 Concubinage was permissible instead of, but not as well as marriage: S. Treggiari, 'Concubinae', *Papers of the British School at Rome* 49 (1981), pp. 59ff.

459 Jul. 335B.

460 Heil, *Der konstantinische Patriziat.*

461 Zos. II, 33.3; Mommsen, *Ges. Schr.* IV, pp. 545ff.; VI, pp. 266ff.; A. Demandt, *RE* Suppl. XII (1970), 556ff.

462 Julian in *Amm.* XXI, 10.8; Aur. Vict. 41.20f.

463 The first German general (*dux*) is documented under Diocletian: *CIL* III, 10981.

464 *Anon. Val.*, 30; Jul. 6B; *Chron. Min.* I, 233; Zos. II, 30ff.; Eutr. X, 8.

465 Zos. II, 30; Sozom. II, 3.

466 Jerome *Chron.* on 330: *dedicatur Constantinopolis omnium paene urbium nuditate.*

467 *Epit.* 41.11; Aur. Vict. 41.11; Zos. II, 29; Amm. XIV, 11.20.

468 Eutr. X, 6.3 reports that many of Crispus's friends were killed after him.

469 Zos. II, 29.

470 Mommsen is thinking here of the *Saturnalia* of Macrobius, which came about in Roman senatorial circles at the beginning of the fifth century.

471 330–7.

472 Lact. *inst.*I 1.13ff.; Eus. *VC, passim, HE.* X; *Anon. Val.*, 33; Zos. II, 29.3f. See Barnes, *Constantine and Eusebius*; R. MacMullen, *Constantine* (1970).

473 Burckhardt 1853/80 disputes this.

474 P. M. Bruun, *RIC* VII (1966), 61: 'The coins give no positive evidence of any conversion, but only of a gradually changing attitude towards the old gods.'

475 C.J. III, 12.2. Earlier version given in *C.Th.* II, 8.1 on 3 July 321.

476 Dio XXXVII, 18f.; Jos. *c.Ap.* II, 39.

477 Suet. *Aug.* 94.12.

478 Mommsen is probably referring to the inscription of Vitalanius Felix of Lyon (*CIL* XIII, 1906), to whom everything happened on a Tuesday (!): birth, call-up, discharge and death.

479 *C.Th.* XVI, 10.1.

480 *C.Th.* XVI, 10.2 on 341.

481 This concerns Nicagoras, son of Minucianus (*PLRE* I, s.v.), an Eleusinian 'torchbearer' whose inscription was found in the Valley of the Kings: *OGIS*, 720f.

482 Related by the pagan Zosimus II (29), who may have taken it from the pagan Eunapius.

483 *Scriptores originum Constantinopolitanarum* (ed. T. Preger, 1901/7), pp. 6f.; Zos. II, 31.1. It is not stated that these shrines were first built by Constantine.

484 Of St Irene and the Apostles respectively.

485 Eun. *VS* 462f.

486 K. Kraft, 'Das Silbermedaillon Constantins des Grossen mit dem Christogramm auf dem Helm', *Jahrbuch für Numismatik* 5/6 (1954/5), pp. 151ff.

487 Constantine was baptized by Eusebius of Nicomedia, an Arian (Jerome *Chron.* on 337); the 'untruthful scribbler' is the Church historian Eusebius of Caesarea, who also refers to the baptism (*VC* IV, 62).

488 Eus. *VC* IV, 20.

489 Eus. *VC* I, 44. *Pontifex Maximus* was never so translated: H. J. Mason, *Greek Terms for Roman Institutions* (1974), p. 115.

490 'Feriale Campanum', edited by T. Mommsen, *Ges. Schr.* VIII, 15ff.; *ILS* 4918.

491 Eus. *VC* V, *passim*; H. Dörries, *Das Selbstzeugnis Kaiser Konstantins* (1954).

492 Jerome *Chron.* on 318: *Crispum Lactantius Latinis litteris erudivit.*

493 Mommsen is not taking into consideration here the obsequious addresses to the Emperor contained in Lactantius's *Divinae Institutiones*, particularly I, 1.13ff. and VII 26.11ff.

494 *C.Th.* XVI, 2.2 of 319.

495 *C.Th.* XVI, 2.4 of 321.

496 *Codex Justinianus* VIII, 57.1.

497 Cf. the apostle Paul in I Corinthians 7.

498 W. Marschall, *Karthago und Rome* (1971).

499 On this term, cf. *CTh.* XVI, 2.47 of 425.

500 *C.Th.* 27.1 of 318 (Seeck 1919, p. 166); *C.Th.* Sirm. I of 333.

501 The material is discussed by H. Bolkestein, *Wohltätigkeit und Armenpflege im vorchristlichen Altertum* (1939) and A.R. Hands, *Charities and Social Aid in Greece and Rome* (1968).

502 *Epitome* 12.4 (on Nerva); Dio LXVIII, 5.4 (on Trajan). Mommsen, *Staatsrecht* II, pp. 1079f.

503 O. Hiltbrunner, 'xenodocheion', *RE* IX A (1967), 1487ff.

504 Jul. 289A–291D.

505 It begins around 155 AD with the dispute between Polycarpus of Smyrna and Bishop Anicetus of Rome: Eus. *HE* V, 24.

506 Optatus of Mileve gives these in connection with his treatise against Parmenianus (ed. C. Ziwsa, 1893).

507 Eus. *VC* III, 6–22; J. Ortiz de Urbina, *Nizäa und Konstantinopel* (1964).

508 The Arians were never in the majority at the Council of Nicaea; Mommsen overestimates the Emperor's influence.

509 These were Theonas of Marmarica and Secundus of Ptolemais, who were exiled: Philostorg. *HE* I, 9c (p. 11 ed. Bidez).

510 *Epit.* 41.20; *Chron. Min.* I, 235.

511 *RIC* VII, p. 584; 589.

512 *Chron. Min.* I, 235f.

513 *Chron. Min.* I, 235.

514 MH has 'above-mentioned'.

515 Zos. II, 40.3; Jerome *Chron.* on 338.

516 These were the sons of Constantine's half-brother, Julius Constantius.

517 The relationship is unsubstantiated; Optatus was Constantine's first *patricius*: Zos. II, 40.2. Ablabius was Praetorian Prefect: *PLRE*. I, s.v.

518 Eutr. X, 9.

519 According to Zos. II, 89.2, Illyricum and the West were ceded to Constantine II and Constans.

520 *Epit.*, 41.21; Zos. II, 41.1.

521 Amm. XXV, 4.23.

522 Cedrenus 295A.

523 Metrodorus the travelling philosopher: Jerome *Chron.* on 330.

524 For the *Acts of the Persian Martyrs*, see J. P. Asmussen, 'Christians in Iran', *Cambridge History of Iran* 3(2), pp. 924–48. Cf. T. D. Barnes, 'Constantine and the Christians of Persia', *JRS* 75 (1985), pp. 126ff.

525 *Coll. Mos.* 15.3.

526 Festus 27. W. Portmann, 'Die 59. Reder des Libanios und das Datum der Schlacht von Singara', *Byzantin. Zeitschr.* 82 (1989), pp. 1ff.; AD 344.

527 *Chron. Min.* I, 452; *Epit.*, 41.21; Zos. II, 41.

528 Aur. Vict. (41.24) refers to his fondness for boys.

529 Hensel continues: 'This marks the end of the lecture course, and Mommsen has a way [MH.III, 151] of not picking up the threads from the end of a previous lecture course at the beginning of a new one, so the lecture of 8 July (1886) opened as follows:'.

530 Mommsen specifies Persians, Arabs and Turks: cf. MH.III, 222, but gives a different and correct interpretation at MH.III, 240.

531 Eus. *VC* IV, 7; Zos. II, 15.1. Although Julian criticised this policy, he himself continued it (Amm. XXI, 10.8; Jul. 285B). Constantine had a tribute-paying king of the Alamanni to thank for his appointment as Emperor (*Epit.* 41.3). Specific names of German officers under Constantine have not been verified, but Bonitus the Frank may have been among them (Amm. XV., 5.33), and perhaps also Flavius Ursus, Master of the Soldiers: *Cos.* 338 (*PLRE* I s.v.).

532 Constans was not killed until after the proclamation.

533 Zos. II, 42; Aur. Vict. 41.23.

534 *Epit.*, 42.6f.

535 *Chron. Min.* I, 237.

536 *Epitome*, 41.22f.; *Chron. Min.* I, 454.

537 Aur.Vict., 42.6; Zos. II, 43.2.

538 Aur.Vict., 41.26; Oros. VII, 29.9f.

539 Aur. Vict. 41.26; Eutr. X, 10.

540 Aur. Vict. 42.9; Jerome *Chron.* on 351; Amm. XIV, 11.

541 Amm. XXI, 15.4.

542 Jul. 31Aff.; 76Cff.; Amm. XV, 1.2.

543 *Chron. Min.* I, 237.

544 *Chron. Min.* I, 238. Hensel mistakenly writes 'September'. Vetranio lived for another six years in Prusa: *Zon.* XIII, 7.

545 *Chron. Min.* I, 237; 454.

546 Amm. XV, 5.33; Aur. Vict. 42.15.

547 Eutr. X., 12.2; Zos. II, 53.3.

548 Amm. XIV, 5.

549 Amm. XIV, 7.2.

550 Amm. XIV, 1; 7; 11.

551 Amm. XIV, 11; Aur. Vict. 42.12.

552 It is not clear what Mommsen has in mind here: perhaps a cult of the Emperor, perhaps Licinius's army prayer: Lact. *MP* 46.6.

553 Amm. XV, 7.7f.; XXII, 11.4ff.; XXVII, 3.11ff. A. Demandt, *Zeitkritik und Geschichtsbild im Werk Ammians* (1965), pp. 69ff.; J. Matthews, *The Roman Empire of Ammianus* (1989), pp. 424ff.

554 MH.III, 137; *C.Th.* XVI, 10.2.

555 Ibid. 20.7ff.; *Anonymus de Rebus Bellicis* (ed. E. A. Thompson, 1952), 2.1; *Anthol. Graeca* IX, 528.

556 Athan. *apol. contra Arianos* 9; 87.

557 He was exiled to Trier (actually on the Moselle, not the Rhine) in 335.

558 Emperors' conference at Viminacium: *C.Th.* X, 10.4; *Julian* 19A; Athan. loc.cit.; Seeck IV, 397.

559 Seeck IV, 54ff.

560 Theodoret *HE* II, 7f.; Seeck IV, 74ff.

561 This is simulated by christogrammes on the reverse of coins: *RIC* VIII, p. 216f.

562 *C.Th.* XVI, 10.5.

563 Athanasius had sought support from Magnentius: Athan.*apol. ad Const.*, 11.

564 At the double synod of Ariminium and Seleucia: Seeck IV, p. 161ff.

565 The following according to Aur. Vict. 42.19ff. and Amm. XXI, 16.

566 Amm. XVI, 10.10.

567 Eusebia supported him in this: Amm. XV, 2.8; 8.3.

568 Amm. XIV, 5.1; 10.1; Sulp. Sev. *Chron.* II, 39.2.

569 According to Jul. (279A) they conquered forty-five towns, according to Zos. (III, 1.1) forty; cf. Lib. *Or.* XVIII, 33f. Mommsen himself notes the conquest of sixty Gallic *civitates* during the time of Probus: MH.II, 150, according to SHA, *Prob.*, 13.6.

570 Aur. Vict. 42.15; Amm. XV, 5.2; Jul. 98C.

571 There is no evidence that Silvanus changed his name, and only one such instance is known, that of Agenaric in Serapion; Amm. XVI, 12.25. Roman–German double names: Petrus-Valvomeres (Walamer); Amm. XV, 7.4.

572 M. Waas, *Germanen im römischen Dienst im 4. Jahrhundert n.Chr.* (1971).

573 Aur. Vict. 42.16; Amm. XV, 5.

574 Amm. XV, 8.1.

575 Amm. XV, 8; Jul. 274f.; English biographies of Julian include R. Browning (1975) and G. W. Bowersock (1978).

576 Jul. (277D) mentions 360 soldiers.

577 Julian broke the siege of Autun laid by the Alamanni at the end of June 356 from Vienne, where he had spent the winter: Amm. XVI, 1f.

578 Amm. XVIf.; Jul. 268ff.

579 Marcellus was successor to Ursicinus: Zos. III, 2.2; Amm. XVI, 2.8; 4.3; Jul. 278B.

580 Amm. XVI, 3.3.

581 Amm. XVI, 10.21.

582 Barbatio was successor to Silvanus: Amm. XVI, 11.2; 11.6ff.

583 Amm. XVI, 12. There is no evidence that he participated in the battle.

584 This is confirmed by Amm. XVI, 12.25.

585 Amm. XVI, 12.60.

586 Amm. XVI, 12.63.

587 Jul. 280. Florentius was Praetorian Prefect in Gaul: see MH.III, 170.

588 Amm. XVII, 2.

589 Jul. 279D.

590 Amm. XVII, 3.

591 Jul. 282 C.

592 Hensel, probably mistakenly, writes: 'Baetica II': Mommsen cites Amm. XVII, 3.6, according to which Julian took the taxation of Belgica II away from the Praetorian Prefect and levied it himself.

593 Constantius drove the Sarmatians out of Sirmium in 358 (Amm. XVII, 12f.) and sent his Master of Soldiers, Barbatio, to deal with the Alamannic Juthungi in Raetia (Amm. XVII, 6).

594 Amm. XVII, 10.

595 Amm. XVII, 11.

596 Amm. XVI, 12.64.

597 See MH.III, 150.

598 Amm. XVII, 5.

599 Amm. XIX.

600 Amm. XX, 4.

601 Zos. III, 9; Amm. XX, 4; Lib *Or.* XVIII, 90.

602 Amm. XX, 1.1; 8.2; Jul. 340D.

603 This refers to the name 'Parisii': *Lutetia Parisiorum* (Paris) is first mentioned in Caes. *BG* VI, 3.4.

604 Jul. 284C.

605 Amm. XX, 8.14.

606 Amm. XX, 9.6f.

607 Amm. XX, 8.20f.; Jul. 282C.

608 Amm. XXI, 2.

609 Amm. XXI, 10f.

610 *Chron. Min.* I, 240.

611 Amm. XXII, 8.49.

612 Amm. XXII, 2.4.

613 Edited and translated into English by W. C. Wright, I–III, 1913–. (Loeb). Numbering follows the 1696 Spanheim edition.

614 Jul. 367C.

615 Amm. XXV, 4.22; Jul. 339B.

616 Amm. XVI, 1; XXV, 4.

617 Jul. 288ff.

618 Amm. XXII, 3.11.

619 Amm. XXII, 4.

620 According to Ammianus (XVI, 5.14), Julian reduced expenditure in Gaul *pro capitulis singulis* from 25 to 7 gold pieces.

621 Julian (*Ep.* 47; 434D) dated his inner rejection of Christianity to 350.

622 On 11 December 361: *Chron. Min.* I, 240.

623 Promulgated on 4 February in Alexandria: *Hist. Aceph.* 9; cf. Jul. *Ep.* 29.

624 Amm. XXII, 5.4.

625 Jul. 398Cff. (*Ep.*24); 435B (*Ep.* 47); Theodoret *HE* III, 9.

626 Jul. 376C = *Ep.* 37.

627 Amm. XXII, 10.7; *C.Th.* XIII, 3.5 of 17 June 362.

628 Jul. 422ff.; *Ep.* 36.

629 Amm. XXV, 4.20.

630 *victimarius*: Amm. XXII, 14.3.

631 Jul. 362B.

632 Jul. 288ff.

633 Amm. XXII, 7.8.

634 Ammianus (XXIII, 2–XXV, 3) took part; other accounts come down to us from Zosimus (III; see also the commentary by Paschoud, 1971 and 1979).

635 Amm. XXIII, 2.6.

636 Amm. XXIII, 3.9.

637 Ammianus (XXIII, 3.5) gives 30,000, Zosimus (III, 12.5) 18,000 men.

638 Amm. XXIV, 1.2; *PLRE*.I, s.v.

639 Amm. XXIII, 3.2: Julian's *propinquus*.

640 Amm. XXIV, 7.4.

641 See MH.I, 23.

642 Amm. XXV, 5.1.

643 Amm. XXV, 3.15ff.

644 Socr.*HE*. III, 21; *Malalas*, 333f.; Ephrem the Syrian, *Against Julian* Theodoret *HE* III, 25; Greg.Naz. *Or.* IVf.

645 Oros. VII, 30.2; Prudentius *Apoth.* 450f.

646 Zos. IV, 4.2.

647 Amm. XXV, 5.3.

648 Amm. XXV, 5.2.

649 Zosimus (III, 36.1), who shifts the offer of the throne to the vacancy following Jovian's death, calls him *Salustios*; in fact, however, he was Praetorian Prefect of the East, Saturninus Secundus Salutius: Amm. XXV, 5.3; *PLRE* I, s.v.

650 Amm. XXV, 5.4ff.

651 Amm. XXV, 5.4.

652 Amm. XXV, 7.1; Zos. III, 30.3.

653 *mixti cum arctois Germanis Galli*: Amm. XXV, 6.13.

654 Amm. XXV, 7.

655 Amm. XXV, 7.10ff.; 9.7ff.; Festus 29; Lib. *Or.* XVIII, 278ff.; Zos. III, 32 (with Paschoud).

656 Zos. III, 34.2.

657 Amm. XXV, 9.1.

658 *christianissimus Iovanus Augustus*: *Chron. Min.* I, 240.

659 Theodoret *HE* IV, 1.

660 *hostiis pro Ioviano caesis extisque inspectis*: Amm. XXV, 6.1.

661 Valens then exiled him again: *Hist. Aceph.* 15ff.

662 Amm. XXV, 10.12; *Chron. Min.* I, 240.

663 Amm. XXVI, 1.

664 Constantine's family were also from Illyricum: Jul. 348D; Jovian likewise: *Epit.* 44.1.

665 Seeck V, 12 shares this judgement.

666 On the elder Theodosius see Demandt, *Hermes* 100 (1972), pp. 81ff.; *Historia* 18 (1969), pp. 598ff.

667 Amm. XXVI, 4.

668 In Constantinople Valentinian proclaimed his brother: Amm. XXVI, 4.3.

669 The division occurred at Mediana near Naissus: Amm. XXVI, 5.1; *C.Th.* VI, 24.3 of 19 August 364 from Mediana (not Mediolanum). *Partes Orientis et Occidentis*: *ND*, Or. I, 1; Occ. I, 1.

670 From the death of Maximus in 388 until the proclamation of Eugenius in 392, and from his demise in 394 until the death of Theodosius in 395.

671 An exception to this were the Danube lands, which belonged to the East, but were a military region in which Latin was spoken. As a consequence Latin remained the mother tongue of the eastern Emperors until the time of Justinian.

672 Although Nisibis probably was, as well as the provinces from which Jovian withdrew: see MH.III, 195.

673 Amm. XXVII, 12.

674 Various Ammianus manuscripts oscillate between the forms 'Para' and 'Papa', although Armenian sources confirm the latter. Papa's mother was another wife of Arsaces: Pharandzem, *PLRE* I, s.v.

675 Themistius XI, 149b (Dindorf, 177). The date could also be 374.

676 Amm. XXIX, 1.2; cf. XXI, 4.3ff.

677 Amm. XXX, 7.7; XXX, 1.18ff. Even Vadomar himself was arrested by Julian while eating: Amm. XXI, 4.

678 Amm. XXX, 2.

679 This cannot be substantiated.

680 Amm. XVIII, 2.3; Jul. 279D; Eunap. Fr., 18 (Blockley).

681 Amm. XXVIII, 3.

682 Amm. XXIV, 4.5; *Paneg. Lat.* II (XII), 5.2.

683 Amm. XXVIII, 6. Camels had been common draught animals even before Herodotus (I, 80.2); in North Africa they were known in Salllust's time: *Histories* 3.29 (McGushin). Diocletian's price edict, edited by Mommsen in 1893, refers to pack saddles for camels (XI,6). On Romanus, see A. Demandt, *Byzantion* 38 (1968), pp. 333ff.

684 Amm. XXIX, 5.

685 Amm. XXX, 9.1.

686 Theodoret (*HE* IV, 8) reports that both Emperors were orthodox, but that Valens later inclined towards Arianism (IV, 12). This is not reputed to be the case with Valentinian, who was Catholic.

687 Theodoret *HE* IV, 6.

688 Amm. XXX, 9.5; *C.Th.* IX, 16.9.

689 Mommsen is presumably thinking of the missionaries Valens sent to Fritigern (see MH.III, 213).

690 This is contradicted by Amm. XXX, 9.4 in the case of Valentinian, and by Eutr. (*Praef.*) and Festus (10.30) in that of Valens.

691 *cessator et piger*: Amm. XXXI, 14.7.

692 Amm. XXXI, 14.2.

693 Amm. XXIX, 3: to some extent legendary.

694 *concordissimi principes*: Amm. XXVI, 5.1.

695 The *Epitome* (45.6) comments: 'Valentinian would have been an excellent Emperor if he had been less trusting of his poor advisers.'

696 Amm. XXVI, 5.7.

697 Amm. XXVI, 6ff.; Zos. IV, 4–8; *Epitome* 46.4.

698 Amm. XXVI, 5.13.

699 Amm. XXVII, 2.

700 Amm. XXVII, 10.1ff.

701 Amm. XXVII, 10; Aus. XIX, 31.

702 Amm. XXVIII, 2.

703 Amm. XXVIII, 5.

704 Amm. XXIX, 4.

705 Amm. XXIX, 6.

706 Amm. XXX, 5.

707 Amm. XXX, 6.

708 Amm. XXVII, 6.4 on 24 August 367: *Chron. Min.* I, 241.

709 On 17 November 375: *Chron. Min.* I, 242.

710 Hensel has 'Herobaudus' and adds: 'I don't know if this is really the gentleman's name; Mommsen spoke so indistinctly today.'

711 Amm. XXX, 10.

712 Jerome *Chron.* on 376.

713 Demandt, 'Der Tod des älteren Theodosius', *Historia* 18 (1969), pp. 598ff.

714 Amm. XXX, 9.3.

715 Hensel continues: '23 July '86. That's what comes of working through a lecture course to the bitter end! Without answering this question posed at the conclusion of the previous lecture (about which I shall now probably be in the dark forever, since none of my other acquaintances knows how Valens conducted himself at all, let alone on this issue), Mommsen continued this morning as follows:'.

716 On the Goths in general: Wolfram 1988; Heather 1991.

717 Tac *Ann.* II, 62; *Germ.* 43.6.

718 Whether the *Guiones/Gutones/Guttones* in Pytheas (*Pliny NH* XXXVII, 11/35) can be identified with the Goths is controversial. Pytheas' voyage to the land of amber falls in the period around 320 BC.

719 Jordanes *Getica* 82; see Heather 1991. 'Ostrogothi' actually means 'glorious Goths', 'Visigoths' means 'good Goths': Schmidt 1941, p. 203.

720 At the time of Tacitus (*Germ.*, 46.3) the Goths had kings; after the division the royal family of the Amal remained with the eastern Goths (*Jord.Get.*, 79ff.), while the *reges* of the western Goths (Amm. XXVI, 10.3) are taken to be an aristocracy; but see Heather 1991.

721 After 315 Constantine bore the victor's title 'Gothicus maximus': *ILS* 696; 705.

722 Rausimodus the Gothic prince was defeated by Constantine in 322 while plundering the territories of Licinius (*Anon. Val*, 21; Zos.II, 21.3). In 324 Licinius found support with the Gothic prince Alica (*Anon. Val.*, 27).

723 *iudex*: Amm. XXVII, 5.6; XXXI, 3.4; *rex*: Jerome *Chron.* on 369; *Chron. Min.* I, 243; 458; Oros.VII, 34.6.

724 Amm. XXVI, 10.3; XXXI, 3.4; Zos.IV, 7.2 gives 10,000.

725 U. Wanke, *Die Gotenkriege des Valens* (1990), pp. 73ff.

726 Amm. XXVII, 5.6ff.

727 Philostorg. *HE* II, 5. Contrary to this remark by Mommsen, research now assumes Ulfilas to have been half-Roman, half-Gothic in origin.

728 Socr. *HE* II, 41.

729 Jerome *Chron.* on 369; Oros. VII, 32.9.

730 Philostorg. *HE* II, 15.

731 The Syriac, Latin and Coptic translations of the Bible are of earlier date. The mistake will have been due to Hensel's enthusiasm rather than Mommsen's.

732 Oros. VII, 33.19.

733 This is not the case. On Arianism see R. C. Gregory (ed.), *Arianism: Historical and Theological Reassessments* (9th International Conference on Patristic Studies, Oxford 1983; 1985); R. Williams, *Arius: Heresy and Tradition* (1987); C. Luibheid, *Eusebius of Caesarea and the Arian Crisis* (1981); R. P. C. Hansen, *The Search for the Christian Doctrine of God: the Arian Controversy 318–381* (1988); M. R. Barnes and D. H. Williams (eds), *Arianism after Arius* (1993).

734 Amm. XXXI, 3.1f.; Jord. *Get.* 79; 116ff.

735 Amm. XXXI, 3.5 (*Greutungorum vallum*); 3.7 (wall from the Prut to the Danube). R. Vulpe, *Le Vallum de la Moldavie inférieure et le mur d'Athanaric* (1957).

736 Amm. XXXI, 4.13.

737 Amm. XXXI, 4.

738 Amm. XXXI, 5.

739 Amm. XXXI, 6; 8.4.

740 Amm. XXXI, 7.

741 According to Ammianus (XXXI, 7.15) the Romans fought an indecisive battle with the Germans in 377 at Salices (*aequo Marte*), but were victorious at Beroea (XXXI, 9).

742 Horburg in Upper Alsace: Amm. XXXI, 10.8; *Epitome* 47.2; Jerome *Chron.* on 377; in each case 'Argentaria'.

743 Eulogists exaggerated the number of Alamanni fallen: Amm. XXXI, 10.5.

744 Examples to the contrary at MH.III, 165, and n. 569.

745 Amm. XXXI, 12.1.

746 This does not follow from Amm. XXX, 9.3.

747 Amm. XXXI, 12.1.

748 Amm. XXXI, 12.4.

749 The chief source for the battle of Adrianople is *Ammianus* XXXI, 13; see also Zos. IV, 24.1f; Oros. VII, 33.16ff; Wolfram 1988, pp. 117–39; Heather 1991, ch. 4.

750 On the date: Amm. XXXI, 12.10; *Chron. Min.* I, 243.

751 This comparison is drawn by Amm. XXXI, 13.9.

752 Both versions have come down to us: Amm. XXXI, 13ff.

753 Zos. IV, 24.4; *Chron. Min.* I 243: on 19 January 379.

754 Valentinian II, who was Augustus from 375, was seven years old: see MH.III, 208.

755 I.e. Troops stationed in Egypt of whom only a fraction were Egyptians: *ND, Or.* XXVIII; Zos. IV, 30f.

756 Fritigern may have been the Gothic king who submitted to Rome in 382: *Chron. Min.* I, 243; Ammianus (XXXI, 5.4; 6.5; 12.9) repeatedly refers to Fritigern as *rex*. On the sources for Gothic history see Heather 1991.

757 There is no evidence to support the idea that Athanaric had such a title.

758 In Constantinople: *Chron. Min.* I, 243.

759 Their tax liability is unsubstantiated. The decisive treaty came in 382: *Them*. XVI.

760 Synes. *De regno* 21ff.

761 This is not true: see MH.III, 203.

762 Gratian's teacher was Ausonius, a half-hearted Christian, in Trier (*Aus*. XX), although Ambrose did send Gratian a treatise in 380 entitled *De fide ad Gratianum*, which criticised Arianism.

763 As well as the Vandals, Burgundians and Lombards.

764 R. MacMullen, *Christianizing the Roman Empire* (1984).

765 Symm. *Rel.*, 3; Ambros *Epitome*, 17f. See B. Croke and J. Harries, *Religious Conflict in Fourth-Century Rome* (1982).

766 Zos. IV, 36.

767 Negotiations with Armenia began in 384 (*Chron. Min*. I, 244; II, 61) and apparently concluded in 387 (Lib. *Or*. XIX, 62; XX, 47).

768 Mommsen again specifies Persians, Arabs and Turks: cf. MH.III, 151 and different version at 240.

769 Zos. IV, 35.

770 Zos. IV, 43.1; Socr. *HE* IV, 11.11.

771 *Chron. Min*. I, 298; Zos. IV, 46.2f.

772 According to the most reliable sources (Seeck V, pp. 242f.) Valentinian II took his own life in desperation. Eugenius was a Christian (cf. Ambr. *Ep*. 57 in contrast to Philostorg. *HE* XI, 2), but was tolerant of pagans.

773 Zos. IV, 58; Philostorg., *HE* XI, 2.

774 Oros. VII, 36.1; *Chron. Min*. II, 64.

775 *Chron. Min*. II, 64.

776 Schmidt 1941, pp. 424 ff.; *PLRE* II, pp. 43ff.

777 'cunctam Gothorum gentem': Oros. VII, 38.2.

778 *Claudian* XXVIII, 105; on Peuce. Wolfram 1980, pp. 160ff.

779 Zos. V, 5.4.

780 Nevertheless he did begin a succession of western Gothic kings: '*Halaricus creatus est rex*': Jord. *Get*. 146f. Mommsen, *Ges. Schr*. pp. 516f.

781 Oros. VII, 43.5f.

782 *Chron. Min*. I, 472; 658; Victor of Vita, I, 2; Proc.I, 5.18; L. Schmidt, *Geschichte der Vandalen* (1942), pp. 27ff.

783 I. Wood, *The Merovingian Kingdoms 450–751* (1994).

784 He too was *rex Gothorum*: *Chron. Min*. I, 652f.; Augustine *CD* V, 23.

785 S. Mazzarino, *Stilicone* (1942).

786 Poets: Claudian, Rutilius and Prudentius; preachers: Augustine, Orosius and Philostorgius.

787 Zos. V, 5f.; Philostorg. *HE* XII, 2; *Claud*. XXVI, 164ff.; *Chron. Min*. II, 64.

788 Claudian XXIX, 178ff.; Zos. IV, 57.2.

789 Claudian VII, 142ff.; Oros. VII, 37.1.

790 Zos. V, 7.2f.

791 Claudian XX, 214ff.; XXVI, 535ff.

792 Claudian XXVI; *Chron. Min*. I, 465. The battle was fought at Pollentia.

793 Zos. V, 29.

794 Oros. VII, 37; *Chron. Min*. I, 465; 652ff.; Zos. V, 26.3f.

795 He was extolled by Claudian in his lifetime, and by Olympiodorus (in Zos. V, 34.6f.), after his death. A. Cameron, *Claudian* (1970); on Gainas, id., *Barbarians and Politics at the Court of Arcadius* (1993).

796 Eunapius, in Zos. V, 1.11ff.; 12.1f.; Eun. Fr. 62; Oros. VII, 38.

797 On 22 August 408: *Chron. Min*. I, 300; on 23 August 408: Zos. V, 34.

798 *ILS* 799; 1277f.; *C.Th*. VII, 16.1.

799 Mommsen (AG.5) adds: 'In the West the imperial commander-in-chief was actually the Emperor, which is why there was resistance to introducing this institution in the East.'

800 Oros. VII, 37.1; Ambros. *de obitu Theod.* 5. That there was custodianship of Arcadius as well is based solely on the doubtful testimony of Claudian (VII, 142f.).

801 Zos. IV, 57.2; Claudian XXI, 69ff.

802 Zos. V, 4; 28.

803 Zos. V, 32; Oros. VII, 38.1 and Philostorg. *HE* XI, 3; XII, 2 all mention this as an accusation.

804 Zos. V, 4.2; On this process see J. M. O'Flynn, *Generalissimos of the Western Empire* (1983).

805 This is not so. The posts were retained, although apart from Stilicho their incumbents were of no significance.

806 Oros. VII, 38.1.

807 *Jord.Get.*, 146.

808 Zos. V, 34.1.

809 Sarus: Zos. 34.1.

810 Zos. V, 29.9.

811 Oros. VII, 38.

812 Zos. V, 32.

813 See MH.III, 227.

814 Oros. VII, 40.4; Zos. V, 27.2.

815 *Chron. Min.* I, 299; Zos. VI, 3.1.

816 Oros. VII, 40.3.

817 Jerome *Ep.* 123.15.

818 *Chron. Min.* I, 630.

819 Zosimos V gives 4,000 pounds of gold; Alaric claimed the money in repayment for levying Illyrian troops ready for action.

820 It is not the case that Olympius was a eunuch.

821 Zos. V, 34.

822 *ILS* 797.

823 Zos. V, 40.3.

824 *Chron. Min.* I, 466; Philostorg. *HE* XII, 3f.; Seeck V, pp. 599f.

825 At this point Hensel inserts: 'Last lecture 30 July. A crowd of previously unseen faces appears and will obtain confirmation that they have conscientiously scived their way through the course.' The official end of the semester was 15 August.

826 Zos. VI, 7; Philostorg. *HE* XII, 3.

827 Olymp.Fr. 13 (Müller).

828 Olymp.Fr. 15.

829 Jord. *Get.*, 158.

830 *PLRE.* II, s.v.

831 Olymp.Fr. 19.

832 Olymp.Fr. 24; Oros. VII, 40.2; Philostorg. *HE* XII, 4.

833 Olymp.Fr. 26.

834 Philostorg. *HE* XII, 4f.; *Chron. Min.* I, 468.

835 Proc. *Bell. Got.* I, 2.6ff. on Athalaric.

836 K. A. Eckhardt (ed.), *Die Gesetze des Karolingerreiches 714–911*, I *Lex Salica* (1953).

837 Sidon. *Ep.* V, 5.3.

INDEX

This index covers names and subjects which occur in Hensel's lecture notes and (occasionally) the associated footnotes, not those in the Introduction and in the Berlin Academy fragment. The page numbers are not those of this book, but those of Hensel's manuscripts, indicated in the text in square brackets. Thus the reference 'MH.I: 105' (for example) is to page 105 in the first of Hensel's notebooks, on p. 122 of this book.

621